AFRICAN HISTORICAL DICTIONARIES
Edited by Jon Woronoff

1. *Cameroon,* by Victor T. LeVine and Roger P. Nye. 1974. Out of print. See No. 48.
2. *The Congo,* 2nd ed., by Virginia Thompson and Richard Adloff. 1984
3. *Swaziland,* by John J. Grotpeter. 1975
4. *The Gambia,* 2nd ed., by Harry A. Gailey. 1987
5. *Botswana,* by Richard P. Stevens. 1975. Out of print. See No. 44.
6. *Somalia,* by Margaret F. Castagno. 1975
7. *Benin [Dahomey],* 2nd ed., by Samuel Decalo. 1987
8. *Burundi, by Warren Weinstein. 1976*
9. *Togo,* 2nd ed., by Samuel Decalo. 1987
10. *Lesotho,* by Gordon Haliburton. 1977
11. *Mali,* 2nd ed., by Pascal James Imperato. 1986
12. *Sierra Leone,* by Cyril Patrick Foray. 1977
13. *Chad,* 2nd ed., by Samuel Decalo. 1987
14. *Upper Volta,* by Daniel Miles McFarland. 1978
15. *Tanzania,* by Laura S. Kurtz. 1978
16. *Guinea,* 2nd ed., by Thomas O'Toole. 1987
17. *Sudan,* by John Voll. 1978. Out of print. See No. 53.
18. *Rhodesia/Zimbabwe,* by R. Kent Rasmussen. 1979. Out of print. See No. 46.
19. *Zambia,* by John J. Grotpeter. 1979
20. *Niger,* 2nd ed., by Samuel Decalo. 1989
21. *Equatorial Guinea,* 2nd ed., by Max Liniger-Goumaz. 1988
22. *Guinea-Bissau,* 2nd ed., by Richard Lobban and Joshua Forrest. 1988
23. *Senegal,* by Lucie G. Colvin. 1981
24. *Morocco,* by William Spencer. 1980
25. *Malawi,* by Cynthia A. Crosby. 1980. Out of print. See No. 54.
26. *Angola,* by Phyllis Martin. 1980. Out of print. See No. 52.
27. *The Central African Republic,* by Pierre Kalck. 1980. Out of print. See No. 51.
28. *Algeria,* by Alf Andrew Heggoy. 1981
29. *Kenya,* by Bethwell A. Ogot. 1981
30. *Gabon,* by David E. Gardinier. 1981
31. *Mauritania,* by Alfred G. Gerteiny. 1981

Historical Dictionary of
WESTERN SAHARA
Second Edition

by
ANTHONY G. PAZZANITA
and
TONY HODGES

African Historical Dictionaries, No. 55

The Scarecrow Press, Inc.
Metuchen, N.J., & London
1994

British Cataloguing-in-Publication data available

Library of Congress Cataloging-in-Publication Data

Pazzanita, Anthony G., 1959–
    Historical dictionary of Western Sahara / by Anthony G. Pazzanita and
Tony Hodges. —2nd ed.
        p.   cm. — (African historical dictionaries ; no. 55)
    Rev. ed. of : Historical dictionary of Western Sahara / by Tony
Hodges. 1982.
    Bibliography: p.
    ISBN 0-8108-2661-5 (alk. paper)
    1. Western Sahara—History—Dictionaries.   I. Hodges, Tony.   II.
Hodges, Tony. Historical dictionary of Western Sahara.   III. Title. IV. Series.
DT346.S7P39 1994
964.8′003—dc20   93-48064

CONTENTS

EDITOR'S FOREWORD

Few volumes in this series have been path-breakers to quite the same extent as the *Historical Dictionary of Western Sahara.* Relatively little had been known about what was going on within the territory, and even knowledge of the broader diplomatic dimensions was lacking. There were numerous articles in the press and some monographs, but nowhere could one find assembled the basis for a serious analysis. This gap was finally filled when the first edition of the present work appeared in 1982.

Since then, the situation has evolved notably, although scarcely as much as had been generally hoped. Western Sahara is still in limbo, and the struggle to decide its ultimate fate continues. No amount of diplomatic activity and no quantity of United Nations resolutions have been able to determine whether Western Sahara will be held by Morocco or become an independent state. Although the prospects are somewhat better now than previously, it could hardly be claimed that great progress has been made. Still, it is indispensable to know exactly what has been done over recent years, and that is clearly presented in this second edition.

The book wisely preserves most of the old material, part of it reaching much further back than the present conflict. It provides the historical background on which today's events can be better understood. The additions, quite numerous and extremely useful, bring the story up-to-date. That is very important, because the Western Sahara drama may be with us for some time to come.

The original material was gathered by Tony Hodges in an exceptional research effort, which took him to Western Sahara, Morocco, and Algeria and enabled him to personally interview many of the leading actors. The work was supported by an exhaustive study of the existing documentation. This has now been supplemented and updated by Anthony G. Pazzanita, who also shows an intense interest in Western Sahara and has written extensively on it, with articles appearing in scholarly journals and books.

Jon Woronoff
Series Editor

PREFACE TO THE SECOND EDITION

Since the publication of the first edition of this dictionary, in 1982, many additional events have transpired and much more material has become available on the Western Sahara conflict. The space needed to describe and analyze the events since late 1981 was to dictate the often-difficult elimination from the second edition of those entries that were of only comparatively minor or antiquarian interest, as well as—to some degree—the detailed descriptions of Saharawi tribal and lineage systems. However, some background information on most of the omitted entries has been retained in the sections that have been brought forward, and the complete chart of Saharawi tribes and their subdivisions appears in these pages as well. Readers wishing more in-depth data on all these subjects are referred to the first edition, where their explorations will no doubt be rewarded.

In order to provide a comprehensible summary of the historical events in Western Sahara, the Chronology and Introduction have been left intact regarding the pre-1981 period, with new material commencing from that point onward. The Bibliography has lost a few minor items, but many additional sources of more recent vintage, most of them in English, have been added.

At the end of this long process, I would like to thank Tony Hodges for allowing me the opportunity to prepare the second edition, and in the process hopefully illuminate some of the less-known aspects of this important region of the developing world.

Anthony G. Pazzanita
December 1993

USER'S NOTES

Western Saharans (and Mauritanians) are entered in this dictionary under their first names rather than family names. This is because Saharawi names are usually of the form "A son of B" of "M daughter of N," where B and N are male parents. The terms *ould* and *mint* denote son and daughter, respectively. Thus Khatri Ould Said Ould Joumani (Khatri Son of Said Son of Joumani) is entered under "K."

Titles, such as Sidi and Moulay, are not considered part of a person's name. Thus, Sidi Ahmed Mohammed Mahmoud is entered under "A" as Ahmed Mohammed Mahmoud, Sidi.

Every attempt has been made to enter names and terms under their most widely accepted spellings and forms. This is no easy task, for spellings often vary greatly. There is no universally accepted set of rules for the transliteration of Arabic. Much of the literature on Western Sahara is in Spanish, and Spanish transliterations of Arabic can sometimes be extremely confusing to an English speaker. The Spanish pronunciation of "j" and "y," for example, is very different from that in English. Much of the non-Spanish, non-Arabic literature is in French (published either in France itself or in Morocco, Algeria, or Mauritania) and, in general, French transliterations are more comprehensible to English speakers than their Spanish equivalents. Thus, the French rendering, Khatri Ould Said Ould Joumani, makes more sense than its Spanish version, Jairi Uld Said Uld Yumani. This is, however, not to deny that French transliterations can be misleading to the English speaker, as in the use of "ch" for the English sound "sh" (e.g., *cheikh* instead of *shaykh*). We felt that it would be most practical, on the whole, to adopt the most common French transliterations, though some general terms have been Anglicized.

In some cases, alternative spellings have been listed and cross-referenced to the spelling under which the entry appears.

Thus, though the spelling El-Ayoun is adopted for the capital, three common variant spellings—El-Aaiún (the standard Spanish spelling), El-Aïoun (the spelling used by *Le Monde*), and Laâyoune (the standard Moroccan spelling)—are also listed with instructions to refer to El-Ayoun.

Definite articles that form part of a name are taken into account in the alphabetical ordering. Thus, El-Ayoun is listed under "E" rather than "A," *La Realidad* under "L" rather than "R." Terms such as "de," however, do not influence the ordering—hence, Areilza, José María de.

All entries are alphabetized by the word-by-word method, not letter by letter, as in the sequence:

La Guera
La Realidad
Laaroussi Mahfoud

Note, however, that the Arabic definite article, variously *el* or *al*, has been hyphenated, as in "El-Ayoun," and that hyphenated words are counted as one; hence the sequence:

Al-Chirah
Algiers Agreement (August 5, 1979)
Al-Hizb Al-Mouslim

In order to facilitate the location of information, extensive cross-references have been included. Names and terms of relevance to the entries in which they appear are followed by "q.v." (plural, qq.v.).

ABBREVIATIONS AND ACRONYMS

AOE	Africa Occidental Española
AOSARIO	Association des Originaires du Sahara Anciennement sous Domination Espagnole
BPL	bone phosphate lime
c.	*circa* (about)
CCR	Council for the Command of the Revolution (of the SADR)
CMRN	Comité Militaire de Redressement National
CMSN	Comité Militaire de Salut National
CMV	Commandos de la Marche Verte
Dh	Moroccan dirham
DIR	Détachement d'Intervention Rapide
ENMINSA	Empresa Nacional Minera del Sahara, SA
FAR	Forces Armées Royales
FLN	Front de Libération Nationale
FLRSM	Front de Libération et du Rattachement du Sahara à la Mauritanie
FLS	Frente de Liberación del Sahara (bajo Dominación Española)
FLU	Front de Libération et de l'Unité
Fosbucraa	Fosfatos de Bu-Craa, SA
ICJ	International Court of Justice
INI	Instituto Nacional de Industria
MINURSO	United Nations Mission for the Referendum in Western Sahara
MLS	Harakat Tahrir Saguia el-Hamra wa Oued ed-Dahab (Movement for the Liberation of Saguia el-Hamra and Oued ed-Dahab)
MND	Mouvement National Démocratique
MOREHOB	Mouvement de Résistance ''les Hommes Bleus''

MPAIAC	Movimiento para la Autodeterminación e Independencia del Archipiélago Canario
OAU	Organization of African Unity
OCP	Office Chérifien de Phosphates
P	Spanish peseta
PCE	Partido Comunista de España
PCM	Parti Communiste Marocain
PKM	Parti des Kadihines de Mauritanie
pl.	plural
PLO	Palestine Liberation Organization
PLS	Parti de Libération et du Socialisme
Polisario Front	Frente Popular para la Liberación de Saguia el-Hamra y Río de Oro
PPM	Parti du Peuple Mauritanien
PPS	Parti du Progrès et du Socialisme
PRP	Partido Revolucionario Progresivo
PSOE	Partido Socialista Obrero Español
PUNS	Partido de la Unión Nacional Saharaui
q.v.	*quod vide* (which see)
RNI	Rassemblement National des Indépendants
SA	Sociedad anónima
SADR	Saharan Arab Democratic Republic
sing.	singular
SPLA	Saharawi Popular Liberation Army
UCD	Unión de Centro Democrático
Ugesario	Unión General de los Estudiantes de Saguia el-Hamra y Río de Oro
UMT	Union Marocaine du Travail
UN	United Nations
UNFP	Union Nationale des Forces Populaires
UNHCR	United Nations High Commissioner for Refugees
UNMS	Unión Nacional de Mujeres Saharauis
USFP	Union Socialiste des Forces Populaires

CHRONOLOGY

Headings of relevant dictionary entries are printed in all-capital letters here. Within each chronological period, the least precisely dated entries are given first.

c. 5000 B.C.	Beginning of Neolithic period
c. 2500 B.C.	Savannah begins to give way to desert
c. 1000 B.C.	Beginning of SANHAJA Berber migrations into Western Sahara from the north and beginning of iron culture
c. A.D. 50	Arrival of the camel from the east
c. 100–400	Introduction of the camel on large scale ensures Sanhaja dominance in the increasingly arid desert
c. 700–900	Zenata Berbers assume control of the northwestern fringes of the Sahara (DRAA and Tafilalet)
early 9th century	Sanhaja takes control of Aoudaghost under Tiloutan
c. 990	Sanhaja lose control of Aoudaghost to the Soninke
c. 1039	Abdallah Ibn Yacin arrives among the Gadala
c. 1041–42	Abdallah Ibn Yacin assembles nucleus of ALMORAVIDS at a *ribat* (retreat)

1042	Yahya Ibn Omar appointed commander of the Almoravid army
1054	Almoravids seize Aoudaghost from the Soninke and Sijilmassa from the Zenata, establishing Sanhaja supremacy over Saharan trade routes
1056	Yahya Ibn Omar killed in battle. Command of the Almoravid forces passes to Abu Bakr Ibn Omar, who, with Abdallah Ibn Yacin, starts Almoravid invasion of Morocco
1059	Abdallah Ibn Yacin killed in battle
1061	Tribal conflicts in the Sahara force Abu Bakr Ibn Omar to leave Morocco after giving command of the Almoravid forces there to Yusuf Ibn Tashfin
1062–76	Abu Bakr Ibn Omar leads reunited Sanhaja in war against Soninke kingdom of Ghana
1069	Yusuf Ibn Tashfin captures Fez
1076	Abu Bakr Ibn Omar decisively defeats Ghana
1082	Yusuf Ibn Tashfin captures Algiers
1086	Yusuf Ibn Tashfin lands in Spain and decimates Castilian army near Badajoz (October 23)
1087	Abu Bakr Ibn Omar killed in battle in Tagant
1106	Death of Yusuf Ibn Tashfin
1110	All of Muslim Spain is by now reunited under Almoravids

c. 1218   BENI HASSAN reach the Draa and the Atlantic after migrating along fringes of the desert from the east

c. 1280   Beni Hassan start migrating southward into Western Sahara and Mauritania, slowly subduing or fusing with Sanhaja over following three centuries

1346   Jaime Ferrer sails past BOUJDOUR but never returns

15th century   Hannin, alias Tidrarin, flourished; Sufi movements begin to influence Western Sahara

1405   European raids on coast begin—Jean de Bethencourt lands at Boujdour and attacks a TEKNA caravan

1434–35   Gil Eannes is first European seaman to succeed in returning from south of Boujdour

1436   Saharan coast explored by Afonso Goncalves Baldaia

1445   Joáo Fernandes is first European to travel extensively in Western Saharan interior

1449   Juan II of Castile gives Saharan coast opposite the Canaries to Juan de Guzman, the Duke of Medina Sidonia

1468   Enrique IV of Castile gives Saharan coast to Diego García de Herrera (April 6)

1476   Diego García de Herrera founds SANTA CRUZ DE MAR PEQUENA

1479	Castilian-Portuguese Treaty of Alcacovas gives African coast south of Boujdour to Portugal (September 4)
1480	Portuguese rights to coast south of Boujdour confirmed by Treaty of Toledo (May 6)
1485	Death of Diego García de Herrera; Santa Cruz de Mar Pequeña abandoned
1494	Portuguese-Castilian Treaty of Tordesillas gives Saharan coast north of Boujdour to Spain (June 7)
1496	Alonso Fajardo reconstructs Santa Cruz de Mar Pequeña
1497	The Catholic kings, Fernando II and Isabel I, ban slave-raiding on Saharan coast in order to promote peaceful trade
1498	Santa Cruz de Mar Pequeña sacked by a Portuguese fleet
1499	Alonso Fernández de Lugo appointed Captain General of Africa by the Spanish crown and instructed to establish more forts on the Saharan coast
16th century	Sidi Ahmed Reguibi and Sidi Ahmed el-Arosi flourished
1500	Battle of the Assaka River—de Lugo defeated by local tribes
1505	Spanish crown lifted ban on slave-raiding
1509	Portuguese-Spanish Treaty of Cintra— Spain renounces rights to Saharan coast

except for Santa Cruz de Mar Pequeña (September 18)

1524   Santa Cruz de Mar Pequeña sacked by local tribes and abandoned by Spanish, who, since their attention had shifted to the Americas, do not attempt another settlement on the Saharan coast until the end of the 19th century

1572   Spanish crown once again bans slave-raiding on Saharan coast

1578–1603   Reign of Moroccan Saadian sultan Ahmed el-Mansour, who, to take control of trans-Saharan trade, sends several military expeditions across the desert but does not control the main Saharan tribes, though the Tekna provide him with military contingents

1590–91   Pasha Judar leads Moroccan army across the HAMMADA en route to Timbuctoo

1644–74   War of Char Bouba in Mauritania leads to subjugation of many Sanhaja tribes by the Beni Hassan

1664–1727   Reign of Moroccan ALAWITE sultan Moulay Rachid, who revives active Saharan policy; Tekna again provide troops for the sultanate

1675   Moulay Rachid sends expedition to Ouadane and Tichit

1672–1727   Reign of powerful Moroccan Alawite sultan Moulay Ismail, who sends expeditions to Sahara to recruit slaves for his army

1679   Moulay Ismail leads expedition to Mauritania, traveling by way of the hammada

c. 1696–97	Battle of Oum Abana—Sanhaja tribes inflict defeat on Beni Hassan
late 17th and early 18th centuries	Sidi Ahmed Bou Ghambor flourished; the OULAD TIDRARIN at their zenith
early 18th century	Migration of the OULAD BOU SBAA to Western Sahara from Morocco after a rebellion against Moulay Ismail
1760s	Creation of independent states in Tazeroualt and Goulimine to the immediate north of Western Sahara; they remain independent of the Moroccan government until the 1880s
end 18th century	Oulad Tidrarin, in decline, are forced to start paying the HORMA (tribute) to the rising OULAD DELIM
1764	George Glas sets up ''Hilsborough'' at Puerto Cansado and is then jailed in the Canaries
1765	Carlos III of Spain sends Bartolomé Girón to Morocco in unsuccessful bid to get Sultan Mohammed Ben Abdallah's support for reestablishment of Santa Cruz de Mar Pequeña
1767	Spanish-Moroccan Treaty of Marrakesh (May 28) in which the sultan disclaims ability to control tribes of and beyond the Oued Noun
19th century	Rise to predominance of the REGUIBAT; the AIT OUSSA leave Ait Jmel bloc of Tekna tribes to join the rival Ait Atman
c. 1820	Start of war between the Reguibat and the Tadjakant

1852	TINDOUF founded by the Tadjakant
1864	Joaquín Gatell explores the coastal regions between Oued Noun and Boujdour
c. 1866	Oulad Bou Sbaa and Reguibat defeat and kill Sidi Ahmed el-Kounti
1874	Donald Mackenzie founds North-West Africa Company
1876	Mackenzie starts negotiations with Tekna chiefs at TARFAYA
1878	War between the Ait Jmel and the Ait Atman prompts the IZARGUIEN to build a fort at DAORA
1879	Mackenzie establishes a trading post at Tarfaya (April) and makes an agreement with Cheikh Mohammed Beyrouk (July 26)
1880	The Reguibat defeat the Oulad el-Lab; Mackenzie explores the RIO DE ORO bay, and the Moroccan sultan Moulay HASSAN I offers to buy out his post at Tarfaya
1881	The Compañía de Pesquerías Canario-Africanas establishes a pontoon at DAKHLA
1882	Hassan I restores the Moroccan sultanate's control over the Oued Noun, appointing Caids among the Tekna during an expedition to Tiznit (May-July)
1883	Founding of the Compañía Comercial Hispano-Africana; Mackenzie explores Saguia el-Hamra; founding in Madrid of the Sociedad de Africanistas y Colonistas (December)

1884   The Compañía Comercial Hispano-
                    Africana sets up a trading pontoon at
                    Dakhla (February); Emilio Bonelli lands at
                    Dakhla and signs agreements with local
                    tribes (November); the Spanish govern-
                    ment declares a "protectorate" over Río
                    de Oro, Angra de Cintra, and CAPE
                    BLANC (December 26)

1885   The Oulad Delim attack the Spanish settle-
                    ment of VILLA CISNEROS at Dakhla,
                    forcing its evacuation (March 9); Bonelli
                    reoccupies Dakhla (June); the Spanish
                    government proclaims a protectorate over
                    the coast from Boujdour to Cape Blanc and
                    appoints Bonelli its royal commissioner
                    (July 10)

1886   Hassan I's second expedition to the Oued
                    Noun reaches Goulimine, where a Moroc-
                    can garrison is established (March–April);
                    Julio Cervera Baviera, Felipe Rizzo and
                    Francisco Quiroga sign Treaties of IDJIL
                    with the emir of Adrar and Saharawi chiefs
                    (July 12)

1887   Hassan I names Cheikh MA EL-AININ his
                    khalifa (deputy) in the Sahara; Villa
                    Cisneros is again attacked by Saharawis
                    (March 24); Río de Oro becomes a Spanish
                    colony, extending from Boujdour to Cape
                    Blanc and up to 150 miles inland, and is
                    placed under the administration of a politi-
                    comilitary subgovernor responsible to the
                    captain general of the Canaries (April 6),
                    but Spanish settlement remains limited to
                    Dakhla until 1916

1888   In an attempt to free themselves from the
                    horma, the Oulad Tidrarin begin a war

against the Oulad Delim with Reguibat aid;
Moroccan troops from Goulimine raid Tarfaya, killing the manager of Mackenzie's
trading post, and clash with Izarguien,
Yagout and AIT LAHSEN; Baron Lahure
visits Tarfaya on behalf of King Leopold II
(September)

1892   Saharawis again attack Villa Cisneros
            (March 4); end of the war between the
            Oulad Delim and the Oulad Tidrarin

1893   Companìa Comercial Hispano-Africana
            goes into liquidation, handing over its installations at Villa Cisneros to the Compañìa Transatlàntica

1894   Attacks on Villa Cisneros by Oulad Delim,
            AROSIEN, and Oulad Bou Sbaa (November 2 and 13)

1895   Villa Cisneros left at peace after agreement
            on trade signed with Ma el-Ainin; AN-
            GLO-MOROCCAN   AGREEMENT
            (March 13) leades to Tarfaya's being
            handed over to Morocco for £50,000 and
            Britain's recognizing Moroccan sovereignty to as far south as Boujdour; the
            Reguibat sack Tindouf, massacring its
            Tadjakant inhabitants

1897   The Reguibat begin a long war with the
            Oulad Jerir

1898   Ma el-Ainin begins construction of
            SMARA; beginning of a war between the
            Oulad Bou Sbaa and the Arosien

1899   Battle at Daora between the Izarguien and
            Moroccan troops

1899–1900	War between the Oulad Delim and the Oulad Ghailan
1900	War begins between the Reguibat and the Oulad Ghailan; a FRANCO-SPANISH CONVENTION defines the southern border of Spain's Saharan colony (June 27)
1901	The military-political subgovernor of Río de Oro has his title changed to politicomilitary governor (November 7)
1902	Ma el-Ainin settles in Smara after the completion of most of the construction work
1903	The Oulad Bou Sbaa almost exterminate the Arosien at Tislatin; Ma el-Ainin arranges a peace between the Reguibat and the Oulad Ghailan; Francisco BENS ARGANDONA is appointed politicomilitary governor
1904	Bens arrives in Dakhla (January) and begins to pursue "sugar-lump policy"; a FRANCO-SPANISH CONVENTION (October 3) extends the demarcation of the border northward
1905	War breaks out between the Oulad Bou Sbaa and the Reguibat; Saharawi and Moor resistance to France's northward expansion into the Sahara spreads after the assassination of Xavier Coppolani at Tidjikja in Tagant (May); the Moroccan sultan, Moulay ABDELAZIZ, sends Moulay Idriss Ben Abderrahman Ben Souleiman to Smara to aid the anticolonial forces led by Ma el-Ainin
1906	The Reguibat inflict a serious defeat on the Oulad Bou Sbaa; Moulay Idriss attacks the

French positions in Tagant but withdraws in December

1907   War between the Ait Jmel and Ait Atman wings of the Tekna; the Ait Oussa join the Oulad Bou Sbaa in their war with the Reguibat, but the Reguibat win a major victory over the Oulad Bou Sbaa at Foucht, in Adrar; Moulay Idriss is recalled to Morocco (May); Ma el-Ainin supports the rebellion by Moulay Hafid against Moulay Abdelaziz (September)

1908   Ma el-Ainin mediates between the Oulad Bou Sbaa and the Reguibat, ending the war that began in 1905

1909   The conquest of Adrar by the French prompts Ma el-Ainin to abandon Smara and settle in Tiznit; the Reguibat win a victory over the Oulad Jerir, ending the war that began in 1897

1910   War briefly breaks out again between the Oulad Bou Sbaa and the Reguibat and ends in a decisive Reguibat victory at Lemden el-Hauat; Ma el-Ainin proclaims himself sultan of Morocco and marches north from Tiznit with an army of Saharawis and Soussis but is defeated by General Moinier on the Plain of Tadla (June 23); Ma el-Ainin dies at Tiznit (October 28) and is succeeded by AHMED EL-HIBA

1912   El-Hiba proclaims himself sultan and seizes Marrakesh (August) but is routed by Col. Mangin at Sidi Bou Othman (September 6); a FRANCO-SPANISH CONVENTION completes the demarcation of the border (November 14)

1912–19	El-Hiba continues resistance to the French in the Anti-Atlas and Oued Noun
1913	A Saharawi GHAZZI massacres a French camp at El-Boirat (January 10); Lt. Col. Muret leads a retaliatory raid into the Spanish zone of the desert, occupying and sacking Smara (February)
1914	Bens lands at Tarfaya but is ordered by the Spanish government to withdraw to Villa Cisneros (October–November)
1916	Bens finally succeeds in occupying Tarfaya (June 29)
1919	El-Hiba dies and is succeeded by Merebbi Rebbu (May 23)
1920	Bens occupies LA GUERA (November 30)
1921	Merebbi Rebbu helps to lead an anti-French insurgency in the Anti-Atlas
1923	The title of politico-military governor is changed to governor
1924–26	From sanctuaries in Western Sahara, Merebbi Rebbu organizes *ghazzis* against the French in Mauritania
1925	Bens leaves Western Sahara (November 7); the title of governor is changed to governor-general; the Dirección General de Marruecos y Colonias is set up (December 5)
1926	Spain establishes first unit of nomad troops; Merebbi Rebbu returns to Morocco, continuing to skirmish intermittently with French troops until 1934

1929   An Izarguien *ghazzi* inflicts heavy losses on the Ait Oussa; Mohammed el-Mamoun becomes principal leader of the anticolonial resistance, using sanctuaries in Western Sahara from which to attack French positions in Mauritania in 1929–34

1932   Oulad Delim and Reguibat inflict serious losses on French troops at Oum Tounsi (August 18)

1934   Ait Oussa attack Ait Jmel tribes at Tarfaya; with French support, the Ait Oussa also attack the Reguibat, the Oulad Bou Sbaa, and the Oulad Delim; the final stage of French pacification of the Moroccan-Mauritanian-Algerian border regions is highlighted by the occupation of Tindouf (March) and the junction of French troops from all three countries at Ain ben Tili (April 6); Merebbi Rebbu gives himself up to the Spanish at Tarfaya (March 15); as a result of French pressure on the Madrid government, Spanish troops occupy points in the Western Saharan interior, including Smara and Daora, for the first time (May–July); the Spanish high commissioner in Morocco is made governor-general of Ifni and Western Sahara and a *delegado gubernativo* (governmental delegate) is appointed to administer Western Sahara (August 29); a Franco-Spanish conference at Bir Moghrein coordinates plans for policing the Saharan border regions (December)

1936   Cheikh EL-OUELI gives himself up to the French in Mauritania (April); the governmental delegate in Western Sahara sides with the Francoists at the start of the Spanish civil war (July)

1940   EL-AYOUN is made capital

1943   Manuel Alia Medina begins the research
               that leads to the discovery of PHOS-
               PHATES

1946–50   A severe drought decimates the nomads'
               herds

1946   AFRICA OCCIDENTAL ESPANOLA is
               created, incorporating Ifni and Western
               Sahara under a governor-general resident
               in Sidi Ifni and with a subgovernor heading
               the administration of Western Sahara (July
               20)

1949   Tarfaya is named Villa Bens upon Bens's
               death

1950   General FRANCO visits Western Sahara

1952   Adaro, a subsidiary of the Spanish INSTI-
               TUTO NACIONAL DE INDUSTRIA, is
               entrusted with phosphate research

1956   BENHAMOU MESFIOUI is given com-
               mand of the southern sector of the ARMY
               OF LIBERATION (January) and begins to
               organize guerrilla nuclei for offensive
               against the Spanish in Ifni and Western
               Sahara and against the French in northern
               Mauritania and the Algerian Sahara; AL-
               LAL EL-FASSI begins claiming Western
               Sahara as part of "GREATER MO-
               ROCCO" immediately after Morocco's in-
               dependence (March); the Army of Liber-
               ation begins attacks on French in the
               Algerian Sahara (June); the Moroccan
               nationalist newspaper Al-Alam publishes a
               map of Greater Morocco, which includes

Western Sahara (July 7); Spain sets up the Dirección General de Plazas y Provincias Africanas (August 21); Morocco claims Western Sahara at the UNITED NATIONS for the first time (October 10)

1957   The Army of Liberation stages its first attack in Mauritania (February 15), and the Spanish government quickly allows French troops to stage hot pursuit raids across the border into Western Sahara; General Mariano GOMEZ ZAMALLOA is appointed governor-general of AOE (June) and orders gradual retrenchment of Spanish troops to a few coastal enclaves, abandoning Smara and other inland points; MOKHTAR OULD DADDAH lays claim to Western Sahara in the name of Mauritania in order to counter the influence of the Army of Liberation (July 1); MOHAMMED V of Morocco appoints ABDEL-KEBIR EL-FASSI to head new Direction des Affaires Sahariennes et Frontalieres (November 12); a Spanish convoy is ambushed near El-Ayoun (November 26); the French government learns of a major split in the Army of Liberation when KHATRI OULD SAID OULD JOUMANI flees from its base at Tan-Tan and rallies to the French post at Bir Moghrein (December); the Army of Liberation attacks Boujdour (December 3); the French cabinet approves plans for a joint Franco-Spanish counterinsurgency campaign, Operation OURA-GAN (December 30)

1958   AOE is dissolved, and Western Sahara is converted into a "PROVINCE" of Spain (January 10); General Josè Hector Vasquez is appointed governor-general (January

10); 51 Spanish troops are killed and wounded in a battle with guerrillas at Edchera (January 13); the Army of Liberation is decimated in Western Sahara during Operation Ouragan (February 10–24); Mohammed V formally lays claim to Western Sahara in a speech at M'hamed (February 25); Spain and Morocco sign the Agreement of CINTRA (April 1), by which the TEKNA ZONE is handed over to Morocco; the Moroccan army moves into the Tekna Zone but is briefly barred at the Oued Chebeika by Saharawi irregulars of the Army of Liberation (April 10); many Saharawis settle in southern Morocco, and the FAR begin to disband most of the remaining guerrillas; General Mariano Alonso Alonso is appointed governor-general (July 22); Spain informs the UN that it has no non-self-governing territories since its African possessions are Spanish "provinces" (October 11)

1959–63   A severe drought wipes out an estimated 60 percent of the livestock, encouraging sedentation

1960   A Spanish decree on oil exploration in Western Sahara is issued (June 25)

1960–61   Eleven international consortia acquire 40 onshore blocks for oil exploration

1961   A group of oil prospectors is kidnapped by Army of Liberation irregulars (March 11–21); law on organization and juridical framework of the Province of the Sahara (April 19)

1962   Creation of the EMPRESA NACIONAL

MINERA DEL SAHARA by INI; decree on local government (November 29)

1963   UN includes Western Sahara on list of non-self-governing territories; the first local elections are held for the AYUNTAMIENTOS of El-Ayoun and Villa Cisneros and for the CABILDO PROVINCIAL, and Khatri Ould Said Ould Joumani becomes president of the Cabildo Provincial (May); Franco and King HASSAN II of Morocco hold a summit at BARAJAS (July 6), which leads to warmer Moroccan-Spanish relations and the downplaying of the Moroccan claim to Western Sahara for 11 years; three PROCURADORES from Western Sahara take their seats in the Spanish Cortes for the first time (July 17)

1964   Most oil companies are by now withdrawing from Western Sahara though several traces of oil have been found; the first secondary school is opened; the UN Special Committee on Decolonization adopts its first-ever resolution on Western Sahara (October)

1965   Hassan II sets up a Ministère des Affaires Mauritaniennes et Sahariennes under Moulay Hassan BEN DRISS; the second elections to the Cabildo Provincial are held (June), and Saila Ould Abeida becomes president, replacing Khatri; the UN General Assembly adopts its first resolution calling on Spain to decolonize Western Sahara and Ifni (December 16)

1966   Offshore oil exploration starts; Spain launches a P250 million emergency DEVELOPMENT PLAN; the FRENTE DE

LIBERACION DEL SAHARA is set up in Morocco; Spain informs the UN that it accepts the principle of self-determination but claims that the territory's backwardness and the nomadic character of its population will necessitate a delay in applying it (April); Morocco and Mauritania support the right of the people of Western Sahara to self-determination and independence at meeting of the UN Special Committee on Decolonization (June), and the Moroccan ISTIQLAL PARTY protests this tactical shift in Moroccan policy (July); the OAU Council of Ministers adopts its first resolution on Western Sahara, calling for the "freedom and independence" of Western Sahara (October–November); for the first time the UN General Assembly adopts a resolution calling for self-determination to be exercised through a referendum (December 20)

1967   The number of *procuradores* in the Cortes from Western Sahara is raised to six; a decree is issued announcing the creation of the Asamblea General del Sahara, or DJEMAA (May 11); a minority of the Djemaa's seats are filled by elections within the tribes (July 14–August 20); the Djemaa is inaugurated and Saila Ould Abeida elected its president (September 11); MOHAMMED SIDI IBRAHIM BASSIRI returns to the territory and starts organizing the HARAKAT TAHRIR SAGUIA EL-HAMRA WA OUED ED-DAHAB (December)

1969   The Moroccan Ministère des Affaires Mauritaniennes et Sahariennes is dissolved as a result of the defrosting of Moroccan-

Mauritanian relations; Ifni is returned to Morocco (June 30); the DIRECCION GENERAL DE PROMOCION DEL SAHARA is set up; FOSBUCRAA is founded by INI

1970

Gregorio López Bravo unsuccessfully attempts to persuade Morocco to participate in the exploitation of phosphates at BOU-CRAA (May); several anticolonial demonstrators are killed at ZEMLA in El-Ayoun (June 17); Mohammed Sidi Ibrahim Bassiri is detained (June 18) and mysteriously disappears; Hassan II, Mokhtar Ould Daddaha, and President HOUARI BOUMEDIENNE of Algeria call for the decolonization of Western Sahara in line with UN resolutions at a summit at Nouadhibou (September 14)

1971

Saharawi students set up an "EMBRYONIC MOVEMENT FOR THE LIBERATION OF THE SAHARA" in Morocco; the second elections to the Djemaa are held (January), and Khatri Ould Said Ould Joumani becomes its president; General Fernando de Santiago y Díaz de Mendivil is appointed governor-general (March 4)

1972

Anti-Spanish demonstrations held by Saharawi students in TAN-TAN, Morocco, are repressed by the Moroccan authorities (March and May); the OAU Council of Ministers, meeting in Rabat, calls on Spain to allow the Western Saharans to "exercise their right to self-determination and independence" (June); MOREHOB is founded in Rabat (July); for the first time the UN General Assembly adopts a resolution upholding the right of the Western Saharan people to independence as well as self-determination (December 14)

1973   The Djemaa requests Franco to allow greater Saharawi participation in the territory's administration (February 20); MOREHOB is allowed to set up an office in Algeria after leaving Morocco (March); phosphate exports begin (May); the POLISARIO FRONT is founded under the leadership of EL-OUALI MUSTAPHA SAYED (May 10) and stages its first attack on a Spanish post at EL-KHANGA (May 20); the third elections to the Djemaa are held (June 10); the MUNATHIMAT 21 GHUSHT is set up in Morocco (July); Hassan II, Mokhtar Ould Daddah and Houari Boumedienne call for self-determination to be exercised in Western Sahara in line with UN resolutions at a summit conference in Agadir (July 23–24); MOREHOB is forced to leave Algeria for Europe (August or September); Franco replies to the Djemaa's request of February 20, promising to introduce internal self-government and convert the Djemaa from a purely consultative body into an assembly with limited legislative powers (September 21)

1974   Spanish and Polisario forces clash at Galb Lahmar (January 26) and at Aoukeyra (March 13); Col. Eduardo BLANCO RODRIGUEZ is appointed Director General de Promoción del Sahara (April 22); the coup in Portugal (April 25) accelerates the Spanish government's plans for internal self-government; General Federico GOMEZ DE SALAZAR is appointed governor-general (May 31); Col. Luis RO-

DRIGUEZ DE VIGURI is appointed secretary-general of the Spanish colonial administration (June); the Spanish government formally announces plans for internal autonomy (July 4); Hassan II protests to Franco about the plans (July 4); the Djemaa approves Madrid's ESTATUTO POLITICO on internal autonomy (July 4–6), but it is not implemented; Hassan launches major diplomatic campaign to lobby for support for Moroccan claim, sending political leaders, including leaders of the Istiqlal Party, the USFP, and the PPS, to world capitals (July 16); after a meeting of the Moroccan National Defence Council (July 16), Col. Ahmed DLIMI is appointed chief of staff of Moroccan troops on Western Saharan frontier; Algeria begins for first time to give some low-key support to the Polisario Front (July); Ahmed OSMAN and Ahmed LARAKI fail to persuade Spanish government to drop plans for internal autonomy during talks in Madrid (August 13); Hassan II says that he cannot accept a referendum that includes the option of independence and warns that Morocco will go to war to annex Western Sahara if diplomatic means fail (August 20); Spain announces plan to hold a referendum in the first six months of 1975 (August 21); the Polisario Front holds its second congress (August 25–31); Hassan II proposes submitting the Western Saharan dispute to the INTERNATIONAL COURT OF JUSTICE (September 17); Ahmed Laraki, in a speech to the UN General Assembly, offers Mauritania a deal over the future of the territory (September 30); the Spanish colonial authorities help to set up a short-lived Partido

Revolucionario Progresivo (October); Polisario supporters sabotage two control stations of the Fosbucraa conveyor belt (October 20); Hassan II and Mokhtar Ould Daddah reach an understanding over the future partition of the territory during an Arab League summit in Rabat, and Houari Boumedienne indicates approval of the arrangement (October 26–27); the Spanish colonial administration scraps the PRP and sets up a new party, the PARTIDO DE LA UNION NACIONAL SAHARAUI (November); the Djemaa approves a NATIONALITY LAW and laws on the judiciary and the civil service (November 19–22); Brahim el-Leili, the Qadi of El-Ayoun, pledges allegiance to Hassan II after leaving Western Sahara (December 3); The UN General Assembly adopts a resolution requesting an advisory opinion from the ICJ on the precolonial ties between Western Sahara and both Morocco anad Mauritania and requesting Spain to postpone its planned referendum (December 13)

1975   Phosphate exports reach 2.4 million tons during the year, making Western Sahara the sixth major phosphate exporter in the world; MOREHOB declares its support for the Moroccan claim (January); Spain announces a postponement of the referendum (January 16); the Djemaa elects the four members of the governing council to which it is entitled under the *estatuto político* and elects a 16-member permanent commission to liaise with the governor-general (February); the PUNS holds its first congress and elects KHALIHENNA OULD RACHID secretary-general (February 16); the pro-Moroccan FRONT DE LIBERA-

TION ET DE L'UNITE is founded in Morocco (March 21); the Algerian foreign minister, Abdelaziz BOUTEFLIKA, contests the Moroccan claim at a meeting of ARAB LEAGUE foreign ministers (April 21–27); FLU guerrillas, mainly FAR soldiers under a new guise, stage a series of sabotage attacks, including in El-Ayoun (May–June); two units of TROPAS NOMADAS mutiny, take 15 Spanish officers and soldiers prisoner, and join the Polisario Front with their arms and equipment (May 10 and 11); a UN VISITING MISSION tours the country, witnessing unprecedented pro-Polisario demonstrations (May 12–19) and later reporting that the overwhelming majority of Western Saharans want independence and reject the territorial claims of Morocco and Mauritania; Polisario guerrillas seize the commander of the POLICIA TERRITORIAL post at GUELTA ZEMMOUR (May 14); Khalihenna Ould Rachid flees to Morocco as a result of the PUNS's poor showing during the UN Visiting Mission's tour and pledges allegiance to Hassan II (May 18); El-Ouali Mustapha Sayed visits Ould Daddah in Nouakchott and proposes a federation between Mauritania and Western Sahara under Ould Daddah's federal presidency, but the idea is rejected by Ould Daddah (June); an FLU unit surrenders to Spanish troops at Mahbes (June 8); Houari Boumedienne upholds the right to self-determination (June 19); the ICJ holds its sessions in The Hague on the Western Saharan problem (June 25–July 30); Abdelaziz Bouteflika negotiates with Hassan II over Western Sahara in Rabat (July 1–4); serious riots break out in El-Ayoun between PUNS and Polisario supporters (July 7); 16 Moroccan soldiers, claiming to be FLU guerrillas, are captured by Spanish troops at Hagounia (July 22); Khalifa Boudjemaa Mohammed, the treasurer of the PUNS, flees to Morocco (August 16); the PUNS holds its second congress and elects DUEH SIDNA NAUCHA as secretary-general (August 16–18); the Spanish foreign minister, Pedro CORTINA Y MAURI, meets El-Ouali Mustapha Sayed in Algeria, agreeing to hand power progressively to the Polisario Front in return for major concessions to Spain over phosphates and fisheries, and the front releases 13 Spanish prisoners (September 9); the FLU holds its first congress, electing Rachid Mohammed Douihi secretary-general; Spain releases 23 Polisario prisoners (September 17); Spanish troops are withdrawn from several small outlying posts (October); talks are held between leaders of the PUNS and the Polisario Front on unity to meet the growing threat from Morocco, but the PUNS leaders are reluctant to accept the Polisario leaders' insistence on the party's dissolution (October 10 and 20); many of the traditionalist CHIOUKH in the Djemaa declare their support for the Polisario Front at a conference at AIN BEN TILI (October 12); the ICJ publishes its advisory opinion, affirming the primacy of the principle of self-determination (October 16); Hassan II responds by announcing a GREEN MARCH across the border by 350,000 Moroccans (October 16); Franco begins his long final illness (October 17); Spain calls for an urgent meeting of the UN Security Council (October 18); the UN Security Council meets and asks Kurt

WALDHEIM to consult all interested and concerned parties (October 20 and 22); José SOLIS RUIZ, a Spanish cabinet minister, visits Hassan II in Marrakesh, hinting at a deal over the territory's future, urging postponement of the Green March to allow time for negotiations, and suggesting that both governments could save face by allowing the marchers to proceed up to a Spanish "dissuasion line" 14 km south of the border (October 21); Spanish and Polisario officials exchange more prisoners (October 21); Gómez de Salazar and El-Ouali Mustapha Sayed hold talks in Mahbes on the transfer of powers to the Polisario Front, and Polisario leaders are given authority to enter El-Ayoun (October 22); Ahmed Laraki, the Moroccan foreign minister, pursues the themes discussed by Hassan II and Solís, during talks in Madrid (October 24–25); Kurt Waldheim visits Spain, Morocco, Mauritania, and Algeria, discussing the possibility of transferring administration of Western Sahara temporarily to the UN (October 25–28); 12,000 Saharawis demonstrate in support of the Polisario Front in El-Ayoun (October 26–27); Ahmed Laraki visits Mauritania (October 27); Ahmed Laraki and the Mauritanian foreign minister, HAMDI OULD MOUKNASS, hold talks with Spanish officials in Madrid (October 28–30); an Algerian minister, Mohammed Benahmed Abdelghani, arrives in Madrid to warn Spain against making a trilateral agreement with Morocco and Mauritania (October 29); as Franco's condition deteriorates, Prince JUAN CARLOS becomes acting head of state in Spain (October 30); the Moroccan army crosses the Western

Saharan border, clashing with the Polisario Front as it tries to occupy Farsia, Haousa, and Jdiriya (October 31); the PUNS, after several months of decline, finally collapses (early November); Juan Carlos flies to El-Ayoun to bolster the sagging morale of Spanish officers (November 2); Khatri Ould Said Ould Joumani, after fleeing to Morocco, makes the BAYAA to Hassan II in Agadir (November 3); the Spanish authorities launch Operation GOLON-DRINA, a compulsory evacuation program for Spanish civilians (November 3); the Green March enters Western Sahara and is deplored by the UN Security Council (November 6); the Moroccan government threatens to order marchers beyond the dissuasion line (November 6); after a cabinet meeting in Madrid (November 7), a Spanish minister, Antonio Carro Martinez, visits Hassan II in Agadir, offering to open talks to resolve the Western Sahara conflict on terms broadly acceptable to Morocco (November 8); Hassan II announces that the march has achieved its objectives and orders marchers to return to the Moroccan side of the border (November 9); Houari Boumedienne meets Mokhtar Ould Daddah at Bechar and threatens dire consequences for Mauritania if he partitions Western Sahara with Morocco (November 10); Negotiations open in Madrid between Spanish, Moroccan, and Mauritanian officials (November 12), culminating in the signing of the MADRID AGREEMENT (November 14); the FLRSM is founded in Mauritania (November 16); Franco dies (November 20); a transitional TRIPAR-TITE ADMINISTRATION, headed by the Spanish governor-general, is set up, following the arrival in El-Ayoun of a Moroccan deputy governor, Ahmed BEN-SOUDA, (November 25) and a Mauritanian deputy governor, ABDELLAHI OULD CHEIKH (November 27); Moroccan troops enter Smara (November 27); 67 of the 102 members of the Djemaa sign the PROCLAMATION OF GUELTA ZEMMOUR, declaring the assembly's dissolution and the creation of a pro-Polisario PROVISIONAL SAHARAWI NATIONAL COUNCIL (November 28); Saharawi refugees begin to leave the cities (November–February), many settling first in the desert hinterland but all eventually arriving in Algeria; the UN General Assembly adopts two resolutions advocating UN involvement in an act of self-determination (December 10); Moroccan troops arrive in El-Ayoun (December 11); Mauritanian troops occupy Tichla and La Guera (December 20)

1976   The Polisario Front attacks the Fosbucraa conveyor belt, forcing a halt to phosphate mining for several years (January); Moroccan troops arrive in Dakhla (January 9); Spanish troops are withdrawn from El-Ayoun (January 9); Mauritanian troops arrive in Dakhla, and the last Spanish troops leave the territory, departing from Dakhla (January 12); Lt. Col. Rafael de Valdes Iglesias is appointed governor-general (January 27); Moroccan troops capture AMGALA after clashing with Algerian troops, who had arrived there to help the Polisario Front to evacuate refugees to Algeria (January 29); Olof RYDBECK visits the territory on behalf of Kurt Waldheim (February 7–12) and reports back that present conditions make a genuine consultation of the Western Saharan people impossible; the Mauritanian army captures AOUSSERT from the Polisario Front (February 8); Moroccan troops capture Mahbes but are decimated by Polisario guerrillas at Amgala (February 14); a rump of the Djemaa (57 of its members) votes to support integration with Morocco and Mauritania, but the UN refuses to send an observer to the meeting, and Spain refuses to accept its vote as a valid act of self-determination (February 26); Spain officially terminates its administration in Western Sahara (February 26); the Provisional Saharawi National Council proclaims the founding of the SAHARAN ARAB DEMOCRATIC REPUBLIC (February 27); the SADR's first government, under the premiership of MOHAMMED LAMINE OULD AHMED, is announced (March 4); Morocco and Mauritania partition Western Sahara (April 14); the governors of Morocco's three new Western Saharan provinces take office (April 15); Moroccan troops seize Guelta Zemmour from the Polisario Front (end of April); Col. Abdenbi BRITEL replaces Col. Ahmed DLIMI as chief of staff of the Moroccan forces in the Sahara (April 26); having completed the refugee evacuation, the Polisario Front begins offensive military actions, spreading the war beyond Western Sahara's borders into southern Morocco and, above all, Mauritania (May); the SAHARAWI RED CRESCENT claims that there are 100,000 Saharawi refugees in Algeria (June), though the Algerian government puts the figure at 50,000 in October; a column of Polisario guerrillas crosses 1,500 km of desert and shells Nouakchott, the Mauritanian capital (June 8), but, during its retreat northward, some of the guerrillas are surrounded and El-Ouali Mustapha Sayed is killed (June 9); Col. AHMED OULD BOUCEIF is appointed chief of staff of the Mauritanian armed forces (June 24); elections to the Mauritanian National Assembly are held under a one-party system in Tiris el-Gharbia (August 8); the Polisario Front holds its third congress, electing MOHAMMED ABDE-LAZIZ secretary-general and BACHIR MUSTAPHA SAYED deputy secretary-general and adopting a constitution for the SADR (August 26–30); France and Mauritania sign a military agreement (September 2, 1976); Morocco holds communal elections in its sector of the territory

1977   Three provincial assemblies are elected in the Moroccan sector (January 25); guerrilla attacks on Spanish fishing boats start (April); Moroccan troops reoccupy Amgala (May); Polisario guerrillas raid ZOUERATE, killing two French citizens and taking six others captive (May 1); Morocco and Mauritania sign a defense pact (May 13) under which 9,000 Moroccan troops arrive in Mauritania by mid-1978; elections to the Moroccan Chamber of Representatives are held in Morocco's three provinces in the territory (June 3 and 21); the Polisario Front shells Nouakchott for the second time (July 3); Col. M'BAREK OULD MOHAMMED BHOUNA, the Mauritanian defense minister, becomes chief of staff of the Mauritanian armed forces (July 15); Moroccan troops suffer heavy casualties at OUM

DROUSS (October 14); Polisario guerrillas capture two more French expatriates in Mauritania, this time on the ZOUERATE-NOUADHIBOU RAILWAY, one of the Front's principal targets (October 25); c. 200 French troops fly out to Dakar, Senegal (November 1–2) to prepare French military aid for the Ould Daddah regime; Hassan II threatens hot pursuit strikes into Algeria (November 6); guerrillas board the *Saa,* capturing three Spanish fishermen (November 13), who are released on November 28; French air force Jaguar jets bomb and strafe Polisario guerrillas for the first time, near Boulanour, Mauritania (December 2); French Jaguars attack the guerrillas again, near Choum, Mauritania, (December 14–15) and near Tmelmichatt, Mauritania (December 18); the Polisario Front releases its eight French prisoners in Algiers (December 23)

1978

Col. MUSTAPHA OULD MOHAMMED SALEK is appointed chief of staff of the Mauritanian armed forces (February 20); guerrillas board a Spanish fishing boat, *Las Palomas,* and capture eight of its crew (April 20); French Jaguars attack Polisario guerrillas again (May 4–5); Ould Daddah is deposed in a coup in Nouakchott led by army officers who set up a COMITE MILITAIRE DE REDRESSEMENT NATIONAL under Col. Mustapha Ould Mohammed Salek and pledge to restore peace (July 10); the Polisario guerrillas declare a cease-fire in Mauritanian territory (July 12) but are soon disillusioned by the CMRN's refusal to negotiate a definitive bilateral peace agreement and its attempts to persuade the front to accept concessions (notably the creation of a Saharawi ministate in Tiris el-Gharbia) as part of a global peace settlement; the OAU summit in Khartoum decides to set up an ad hoc committee of at least five African heads of state to examine the Western Saharan problem (July 18–22); Hassan II warns Mauritania not to set up a Saharawi ministate in Tiris el-Gharbia (August 20); talks between the Polisario Front and the CMRN in Libya (August) and Paris (September 9–16) end in failure, but the front decides to maintain its ceasefire at its 4th congress (September 25–28); Spain's ruling Union de Centro Democrático recognizes the Polisario Front (October 12), partly in order to secure the release of the crew of *Las Palomas* (October 14); further talks between the CMRN and the Polisario Front in Bamako (October 17–18) and Tripoli (October 18) also fail, as do unprecedented talks between Polisario and Moroccan officials in Bamako (October 20–21)

1979   The Polisario Front announces the launching of the HOUARI BOUMEDIENNE OFFENSIVE after the Algerian president's death on December 27, 1978 (January 4); the guerrillas fight their way into TAN-TAN (January 28); CHADLI BENJEDID continues Algerian aid to the Polisario guerrillas after being elected Algerian president (February 7); a CONSEIL NA-TIONAL DE SECURITE is set up in Morocco as a result of the Tan-Tan attack (March 8); Col. Mohammed ABROUQ is appointed chief of staff of the Moroccan armed forces in the Sahara (March 12); Maati BOUABID succeeds Ahmed Osman as Moroccan prime minister (March 27);

Ahmed Ould Bouceif becomes prime minister of Mauritania, reducing Mustapha Ould Mohammed Salek to merely titular president, as the COMITE MILITAIRE DE SALUT NATIONAL replaces the CMRN (April 6); the CMSN and the Polisario Front hold talks in Tripoli (May 21–23); Ahmed Ould Bouceif is killed in an air crash (May 27) and succeeded as Mauritania's premier by Lt-Col. MOHAMMED KHOUNA OULD HEYDALLAH (May 31); Mustapha Ould Mohammed Salek resigns from the Mauritanian presidency and is succeeded as titular head of state by Lt. Col. MOHAMMED MAHMOUD OULD AHMED LOULY (June 3); the Polisario guerrillas stage another attack on Tan-Tan (June 13); the Polisario Front rescinds its cease-fire with Mauritania and attacks Tichla in Tiris el-Gharbia (July 12); the OAU summit in Monrovia approves the report submitted by the OAU ad hoc committee, proposing a cease-fire and a referendum (July 20); the CMSN and the Polisario Front sign the ALGIERS AGREEMENT, by which Mauritania renounces its claim to Western Sahara and promises to withdraw completely within seven months (August 5); the guerrillas attack BIR ENZAREN, inflicting heavy casualties on the FAR (August 11); Moroccan troops take control of Dakhla (August 12); Morocco unilaterally annexes Tiris el-Gharbia, giving it the name of OUED ED-DAHAB (August 14); the Polisario Front overruns the Moroccan base of LEBOUIRATE (August 24); the guerrillas fight their way briefly into Smara (October 6); the guerrillas overrun a Moroccan base at Mahbes (October 14); a

6,000-strong Moroccan force, code-named OHOUD, crosses the territory to bolster the Moroccan garrison in Dakhla (November); the General Assembly adopts a resolution urging Morocco to withdraw from Western Sahara and negotiate directly with the Polisario Front (November 21)

1980   The United States, relaxing a previous partial arms ban, announces a $235 million aircraft sale to Morocco (January 24); the guerrillas attack Akka (January 25); Operation IMAN, an attempt to break a Polisario siege of Zaag, ends in disaster in the Ouarkziz mountains (March 1–11); Hassan II reaffirms that "the Sahara in its totality is Moroccan and that is an irreversible historical reality" (March 3); Hassan II visits Dakhla on his first-ever trip to Western Sahara (March 4); 38 Spanish fishermen are captured by guerrillas in a series of offshore attacks (May–September); the FAR finally break the siege of Zaag (May); guerrillas seize a Moroccan freighter off Khneifis (May 3); an INI bulletin announces the formal closure of the Bou-Craa phosphate mines (June 14); 15 Portuguese fishermen are captured by guerrillas (June 10) and released (June 23); 30 South Korean fishermen are captured by guerrillas (July); a majority of states attending the OAU summit in Freetown (26 out of 51) declare their support for the SADR's admission to the OAU as a full member-state, but a decision on the matter is delayed after Morocco and several allies threaten to quit the OAU (July 1–4); 12,000 Moroccan troops, many from the LARAK force, begin a campaign to take control of the Zini mountains and the road from Abbateh to

Smara (August); the guerrillas seize another Moroccan ship, capturing 42 seamen
(August 25); the guerrillas attack Akka and
Tata, both deep inside Morocco (September 3); the OAU ad hoc committee meets in
Freetown and urges a cease-fire by the end
of December, to be supervised by a UN
peacekeeping force, and the holding of a
referendum under OAU auspices (September 9–12); guerrillas stage repeated attacks
against the Moroccan positions at RAS EL-
KHANFRA (September–February); guerrillas capture another 15 Portuguese fishermen
(end of September), but they are released
(October 8); guerrillas attack M'hamed el-
Ghizlane in Morocco (October 9); the remaining 36 Spanish fishermen in Polisario
hands are released (December 17)

1981   The Polisario Front gives up harassing the
Moroccan positions around Ras el-Khanfra
(February); the Algerian FLN reaffirms its
full support for the Polisario Front (February 11); guerrillas attack Moroccan positions at Hagounia (February 27 and March
3); guerrillas stage major attacks on Moroccan base at Guelta Zemmour (March
24–27); guerrillas and Moroccan troops
clash at Oum Ghreid (March 30); the Libyan leader, Col. Muammar El-Qadaffi calls
for a federation between Mauritania and
the SADR (April 13); the guerrillas attack
the Moroccan defense positions around
Smara (April 20); Morocco claims to have
built a continuous defensive line from the
Zini mountains to the Atlantic, protecting a
"useful triangle" including El-Ayoun,
Smara, and Bou-Craa (May); Morocco or-
ganizes communal elections in Western
Sahara (May 8) and parliamentary elec-

tions in Oued ed-Dahab (May 29); Hassan
II accepts the holding of an internationally
supervised referendum in a speech to the
OAU summit in Nairobi (June 26); the
OAU summit decides to set up a seven-
nation Implementation Committee to negotiate a cease-fire and, with the UN, to
organize a referendum of self-determination (June 27); Hassan II makes a nonag-
gression pact with President Mohammed
Khouna Ould Heydallah of Mauritania at
Taif, Saudi Arabia (June 28), but, upon his
return to Morocco, Hassan II arouses Polisario fears by stating, "I see the referendum as an act of confirmation" (July 2)
and reaffirming his past refusal to allow
direct Polisario-Moroccan negotiations;
the Polisario Front responds by demanding
direct talks with Morocco and insisting
that, as conditions for a fair referendum, all
Moroccan troops and the Moroccan civilian administration be withdrawn, all refugees allowed to return, and an international
interim administration set up (July 4); the
French foreign minister, Claude Cheysson,
says in Algiers that France is prepared to
mediate in Western Sahara "if all the
parties request it to do so" (August 9);
Hassan II repeats that the referendum "can
only be a confirmation of the return of the
Saharan provinces to the mother country"
(August 20) and sets up a Consultative
Council in Moroccan-controlled Western
Sahara (August 21); the OAU Implementation Committee meets in Nairobi and, after
interviewing Hassan II, Presidents Chadli
Benjedid and Mohammed Khouna Ould
Heydallah, and the secretary-general of the
Polisario Front, Mohammed Abdelaziz,
adopts a set of detailed guidelines for the

projected referendum, among them the explicit inclusion of the option of independence on the ballot, the enfranchisement and repatriation of all genuine refugees, the participation of the UN in the conduct of the referendum, the establishment of an impartial interim administration, the arrival of a UN peacekeeping force, and the restriction of Moroccan and guerrilla forces to their bases, but the committee is unable to arrange an immediate cease-fire or even to set target dates for the cease-fire or the referendum, apparently because of Hassan II's refusal to talk directly with the Polisario Front (August 24–25); the USFP implicitly accuses Hassan II of "naïveté" in a communiqué opposing the OAU Implementation Committee's peace plan, leading to the arrest of the party's secretary, Abderrahim BOUABID (September 8) and his being sentenced to one year's imprisonment (September 21); the Polisario Front stages one of its biggest-ever attacks, briefly overrunning the Moroccan base at Guelta Zemmour and shooting down several Moroccan aircraft (October 13); King Hassan accuses Mauritania of allowing the Polisario attackers to use its territory and alleges that "non-Africans" must have launched the Sam-6 missiles that he claims shot down Moroccan planes (October 13); the Algerian FLN's political bureau counters by accusing Morocco of wanting to scuttle the OAU peace plan (October 14); Morocco announces that its air force crossed into Mauritania on October 19 to bomb Polisario guerrillas (October 21), but Mauritania denies that the Polisario Front uses its territory and claims that the Moroccan air force never carried out its raid in Mauritania (end October); Morocco, seeing the vulnerability of Guelta Zemmour and another garrison at Bir Enzaren further southwest, abandons Guelta Zemmour (November 7) and Bir Enzaren (November 9), leaving the enclaves of Boujdour and Dakhla/Argoub as the only areas of Western Sahara under Moroccan control outside the "useful triangle" in Saguia el-Hamra (end November)

1982   U.S. Secretary of State Alexander Haig visits Morocco and proposes to King Hassan transit rights for U.S. forces at five locations in Morocco (February 12); OAU Secretary-General Edem Kodjo formally admits the SADR to the OAU (February 22), resulting in a split in the organization and the collapse of an OAU ministerial meeting (February 23); King Hassan releases jailed USFP head Bouabid and several others who had been imprisoned since September 1981 (February 26); the Moroccan foreign minister, M'HAMED BOUCETTA, asks the OAU to hold an extraordinary summit to reverse the decision to admit the SADR (March 23); the United States announces that military sales to Morocco in fiscal year 1983 will rise to $100 million from $30 million the year before (April 20); this amount is later cut substantially by Congress due to criticism of Morocco's Western Sahara policy; the U.S.-Moroccan military commission meets for the first time in Fez: the session is attended by more than 80 U.S. officials (April 26–27); Morocco says its DEFENSIVE WALLS in Saguia el-Hamra have been extended from Bou-Craa to the settlement of Boujdour (May 6); King Hassan pays a week-long visit to Washington and signs a transit rights agreement with the Reagan Administration (May 27); Morocco announces that the Bou-Craa phosphate mines have reopened (July 9); the Polisario Front holds its fifth congress, which results in Mohammed Abdelaziz's being made head of state of the SADR (October 12–16); a socialist victory in the Spanish elections brings FELIPE GONZALEZ MARQUEZ to power as prime minister but results in no basic shift in Spanish policy on Western Sahara (October 28); the Polisario Front says it will "voluntarily and temporarily" absent itself from the forthcoming OAU summit conference in Tripoli (October 29); Morocco and the U.S. hold their first-ever joint military maneuvers (November 9); the OAU summit in Tripoli collapses despite the SADR's absence due to a dispute over the situation in Chad (November 25); the UN General Assembly passes a resolution (37/28) that is supportive of the OAU's efforts to hold a referendum in Western Sahara (November 23); French and Moroccan naval forces hold joint exercises leading to protests from Polisario and Algeria (November 25–26); the SADR's foreign minister, IBRAHIM HAKIM, says that in future the SADR will no longer absent itself from OAU meetings (December 20)

1983   A warship, believed to be Moroccan, briefly shells the Western Saharan settlement of La Guera, occupied by Mauritania (January 20); in an interview, King Hassan II states that no fewer than 80,000 Moroccan troops are present in Western Sahara (January 23); Gen. Ahmed Dlimi is reported killed in an auto accident in Marrakesh (January 25), but there is immediate speculation that he was assassinated after allegedly plotting a coup; King Hassan and Chadli Benjedid meet for the first time on the Algerian-Moroccan border to discuss the Saharan war (February 26); Algeria signs a treaty of fraternity and concord with Tunisia (March 20); representatives of Morocco and the Polisario Front meet secretly in Algiers for the first time since 1978 (April); Morocco and Algeria reopen their common border as part of a thaw in relations (April 7); an OAU summit conference in Addis Ababa fails to begin due to a boycott over the membership status of the SADR (June 6); breaking the deadlock, the SADR delegation again agrees to withdraw voluntarily from the session (June 8); the summit then goes forward and adopts by consensus resolution 104 (XIX), which names Morocco and the Polisario Front explicitly as parties to the conflict for the first time and directs the OAU Implementation Committee on Western Sahara to prepare for a referendum in the territory by the end of the year (June 10); the Libyan leader, Muammar El-Qadaffi, indicating a change in policy, says that "Libya has finished carrying out its duty with respect to Western Sahara. There is no longer any dispute between Morocco and Libya about this region" (June 16); Col. Qadaffi then goes to Rabat for talks (beginning June 30) and tells King Hassan that Libya is "neutral" on the Saharan conflict; in a sharp reversal of previous pronouncements, King Hassan states, "Even if, impossible as it may be, the consultation [referendum] should result in a negative response, nothing could force us to offer our Sahara as a gift to a group of mercenaries'' (July 8); in response, the Polisario Front ends an 18-month de facto truce by attacking FAR positions in southern Morocco (July 10); the new commander of Moroccan forces in Western Sahara, General ABDELAZIZ BENNANI, later says that a large Polisario force attacked Lemseied, mounting a "colossal'' bombardment with Soviet-made multiple rocket launchers; fighting continues in the area for the next month, with the Polisario Front claiming that 767 Moroccan troops had lost their lives since the beginning of the campaign (end August); the Polisario Front attacks the Smara vicinity with five mechanized battalions along a 50-km. front (September 1); the fighting is of such intensity that Morocco admits the deaths of 37 of its soldiers (September 10); an OAU Implementation Committee meeting in Addis Ababa collapses due to a Moroccan-led walkout (September 22); a Moroccan Mirage F-1 fighter-bomber is shot down east of Smara (October 6); the UN General Assembly adopts by consensus, resolution 38/40, which supports the OAU's efforts to settle the Western Sahara conflict (December 7); Mauritanian president Mohammed Khouna Ould Heydallah visits Algiers and becomes a party to the Algerian-Tunisian treaty signed on March 20 (December 13); a Moroccan troop column captures Amgala from the Polisario Front (December 20) as the FAR extends Morocco's defensive walls to the southeast of Smara

1984

Mauritania, ending months of speculation, announces its formal recognition of the

SADR (February 27); a new "defensive wall" is constructed by Moroccan troops in the eastern Saguia el-Hamra, between Amgala and Zaag (April 19–May 13); the Polisario Front claims that it mounted a seaborne raid against the port facilities at El-Ayoun Playa, deep within the Moroccan-occupied Western Sahara (May 15); U.S. Secretary of Defense Caspar Weinberger visits Rabat to take part in a meeting of the U.S.-Moroccan Joint Military Consultative Commission (May 16–18); in an unusual incident, two Moroccan soldiers are killed and 31 taken prisoner in a clash with Algerian troops south of Bechar when a Moroccan unit strays into Algerian territory (June 15); the incident heightens tensions between Rabat and Algiers; Morocco announces that its "defensive walls" have been extended to encompass the settlement of Haousa, the former provisional capital of the SADR (June 17); Polisario continues to attack FAR positions near Dakhla and Argoub (July 13 and 19); in reaction, King Hassan threatens hot pursuit of the front's forces into Mauritania, which he accuses of harboring Polisario bases (July 20); in a surprise move, Libya and Morocco sign a treaty of "union" at Oujda (August 13); implicitly, this means Libya will end its material and diplomatic support of the Polisario Front; Nigeria withdraws from the OAU Implementation Committee because of its failure to make progress in arranging a referendum of self-determination in Western Sahara (September 21); Polisario launches its "Greater Maghreb" offensive south of Zaag in southern Morocco (October 13); King Hassan, angered by this military escalation, states that he will not speak directly with the Polisario Front's representatives (November 6); Nigeria recognizes the SADR (November 11); the 20th OAU summit conference is held in Addis Ababa (November 12–16); the SADR takes its seat as a full member of the OAU with no serious opposition, but Morocco announces its withdrawal from the organization; only Zaire withdraws from the OAU in support of Morocco, and then only for six months; after the summit, the SPLA attacks FAR positions near Dakhla and Haousa (November 27); Yugoslavia recognizes the SADR, becoming the first European country to do so (November 28); heavy fighting breaks out south of Zaag (December 1), as the Moroccan armed forces build a further extension of the "defensive walls" to enclose the settlement of Mahbes; the new wall passes within 20 kilometers of the Algerian frontier and is completed by mid-January; the UN General Assembly adopts resolution 39/40, calling for direct Morocco-Polisario talks (December 5); in Mauritania, Mohammed Khouna Ould Heydallah is overthrown by Colonel MAAOUIYA OULD SID 'AHMED TAYA (December 12)

1985 In the midst of fierce fighting in Western Sahara, Morocco admits losing a Mirage fighter aircraft but claims that the missile that destroyed it was launched from "a neighboring country," a reference widely interpreted to mean Algeria (January 14); two Belgians in a private aircraft flying over Western Sahara are killed when their plane is shot down by the Polisario Front (January 21); Polisario's number-two official, Bechir Mustapha Sayed, meets secretly with the Moroccan minister of the interior, Driss Basri, in Lisbon (January 27); three West Germans are killed when their private plane is destroyed by a Polisario missile after apparently having been mistaken for a Moroccan Dornier spotter plane (end February); King Hassan pays his first visit to El-Ayoun accompanied by his cabinet and the entire Moroccan parliament (March 13–18), which passes a resolution stating that "the territorial integrity of Morocco is first and foremost among the sacred values of the entire Moroccan people"; the king states also that Rabat would spend $1 billion in the following five years on modern military equipment (March 18); Morocco and Mauritania resume diplomatic relations after a four-year break (April 13); the ruling Algerian party, the FLN, says that its Saharan policy is unchanged and states that direct Morocco-Polisario negotiations are the only way to end the war (April 29); Moroccan troops extend their "berms" south into Río de Oro from Amgala to Guelta Zemmour and Dakhla (May–September); the 21st OAU summit is held in Addis Ababa without incident (July 18–20); the SADR's president, Mohammed Abdelaziz, is elected to serve as one of the organization's vice presidents; serious fighting is reported near Mahbes and Aoussert (August); the foreign ministers' conference on the NON-ALIGNED MOVEMENT, meeting in Luanda, Angola, passes a resolution endorsing OAU resolution 104 (September 2–8); a Spanish fishing boat, the *Junquito,* is attacked by Polisario (September 20), killing a crewman; a Spanish navy patrol boat goes to investigate the next day and is fired upon in turn by Polisario, resulting in the death of a Spanish sailor (September 21); in retaliation, Spain expels all Polisario representatives from the country (September 30); India recognizes the SADR, bringing the total number of states doing so to 63 (October 1); the Moroccan prime minister, Karim Lamrani, offers the United Nations a cease-fire and a referendum in Western Sahara by early 1986 (October 23), but Morocco later withdraws a draft resolution from the UN's Fourth (Decolonization) Committee after failing to prevent it from being amended to conform to OAU resolution 104 (November 12); King Hassan visits France for talks with president FRANÇOIS MITTERRAND (November 27–29) but fails to obtain advanced Mirage-2000 fighter aircraft; the UN General Assembly passes resolution 40/50 (December 2), endorsing the OAU's settlement efforts; Polisario holds its 6th General Popular Congress under the motto of ''all the homeland or martyrdom' (December 7–10); the Front announces that MAHFOUD ALI BEIBA will replace Mohammed Lamine Ould Ahmed as prime minister of the SADR (December 17)

1986

UN Secretary-General JAVIER PEREZ DE CUELLAR says he will hold ''proximity talks'' with Polisario and Morocco in New York (April 8); the first round of these indirect discussions ends (April 12) without positive results; in May the talks resume, but the gap between the two sides remains wide; the Polisario Front responds to this by attacking Moroccan military positions in the region of Guelta Zemmour and Farsia (June 1–2); a Spanish ship, the

Sinbad, is attacked and destroyed by the front's naval units (June 17); Pérez de Cuéllar discusses Western Sahara with King Hassan in Rabat (July 15–16); Polisario attacks another Spanish ship, the *Andes,* leaving one crewman dead (July 21); a few hours later, a Soviet factory ship, the *Tito Uncriak,* is also fired upon by Polisario but fires back, wounding three of the front's guerrillas; Israeli prime minister Shimon Peres visits Morocco for talks with King Hassan (July 21–22), leading to Libyan protests and the king's abrogation of the 1984 treaty of union with Libya (end August); a Spanish sailor is killed when the *Puente Canario* is attacked by the Polisario Front while the Moroccans and the front clash near Haousa and Jdiriya (October 16–17); the UN General Assembly passes resolution 41/16 by a vote of 92 to 2 (with 46 abstentions), reendorsing the referendum concept, supporting the mediation efforts of the secretary-general, and calling for direct talks between Morocco and Polisario "as soon as possible" (October 31); a Romanian fishing boat is attacked by Polisario off Western Sahara (November 8)

1987   Moroccan troops construct a new defensive wall in the south of Western Sahara, enclosing more of Río de Oro (February–April); the new wall extends southward from Bir Enzaren to the Mauritanian border and then westward along the border to reach the Atlantic north of La Guera, cutting the Polisario Front's forces off from access to the coast, but to mark the 11th anniversary of the founding of the SADR, the Polisario Front stages a series of attacks on FAR positions between Mahbes and

Farsia (February 25); Morocco claims that the guerrillas used approximately 110 armored personnel carriers and SAM-6 antiaircraft missiles; the Front claims that 213 Moroccan troops were killed; Polisario announces (March 4) that an attempt was made on the life of Mohammed Abdelaziz on February 27; the alleged assailant, a Saharawi who formerly lived in France, is arrested along with several others; Morocco's General Bennani says that only 12,500 square kilometers of Western Sahara have not yet been enclosed by Morocco's defensive wall system (April); King Hassan and Chadli Benjedid meet at Oujda on the Moroccan-Algerian border to discuss the Saharan dispute at talks sponsored by Saudi Arabia's King Fahd (May 4); a UN team, led by UN Under-Secretary-General for Special Political Questions ABDERRAHIM FARAH, visits the region and proposes sending a mission to plan for a referendum (end June); the U.S. announces plans to sell 100 M-48 tanks to Morocco (July 29); the Polisario Front attacks Moroccan positions near Aoussert (August 21); the SADR's president, Mohammed Abdelaziz, says that Morocco is repopulating Western Sahara with Moroccans (end August); Pérez de Cuéllar issues a report on the Western Sahara situation to the General Assembly (see Bibliography), which outlines plans to send a UNITED NATIONS TECHNICAL MISSION to the territory and neighboring countries (October 1); the General Assembly passes a resolution on Western Sahara (October 21), which, inter alia, urges direct negotiations between Morocco and Polisario; the UN Technical Mission travels to Western

Sahara, Mauritania, Morocco, and the Tindouf region of Algeria (November 21–December 9); the mission is composed of a civilian section, led by Abderrahim Farah, and a military group, led by a Canadian general, TERENCE LISTON.

1988   The Polisario Front alleges that 25 persons were "arrested or kidnapped" by Moroccan police in the occupied areas of Western Sahara during the visit by the UN Technical Mission (late January); the front stages a major attack on the "defensive wall" in the Oum Dreiga region (January 31); Morocco and Algeria, after a 12-year hiatus, resume full diplomatic relations (May 16), leading to speculation that Algeria's interest in Maghreb unity may now outweigh its commitment to Polisario (June); Morocco and the Polisario Front hold secret talks in Taif, Saudi Arabia (July 12); King Hassan, in an interview with *Le Monde,* says he opposes independence for Western Sahara but would grant its inhabitants a degree of "autonomy" if they voted in a referendum to remain a part of Morocco (August 2); Pérez de Cuéllar, in separate meetings with Polisario and Moroccan delegations in New York, presents proposals for a ceasefire and referendum and requests a response within two weeks (August 11); Polisario gives Bechir Mustapha Sayed, its second-ranking official, responsibility for all of the front's external relations (August 16); Morocco and Polisario accept the UN peace proposal in principle (August 30); the Polisario Front làunches attacks on Moroccan troops near Oum Dreiga (September 16), a clash later confirmed by Morocco; the UN Security Council passes resolution 621, authorizing the secretary-general to appoint a special representative for Western Sahara charged with the oversight of the referendum and its preparations (September 20); Pérez de Cuéllar appoints Hector GROS ESPIELL as special representative (October 19); by a vote of 86 to 0, the UN General Assembly passes resolution 43/33, once again calling upon the two parties to the conflict to engage in direct negotiations and endorsing the secretary-general's efforts (November 22); Polisario antiaircraft missiles hit two private U.S.-based DC-7 planes flying over Western Sahara on their way from Senegal to Morocco (December 8); one of the planes crashes, killing all five Americans on board, but the other, badly damaged, manages to land at Ifni in southern Morocco; the bodies of the Americans are recovered by Polisario and handed over to U.S. officials in Algiers (December 16); the Polisario Front says it will send a delegation to Marrakesh in early January to meet with King Hassan for the first time (December 24); the king confirms this, saying that "the doors to the palace are always open"; the front announces the start of a unilateral cease-fire in the territory pending further progress toward peace (December 30)

1989   King Hassan II of Morocco meets in Marrakesh with a Polisario delegation composed of Bechir Mustapha Sayed, SADR prime minister Mahfoud Ali Beiba, and defense minister IBRAHIM GHALI OULD MUSTAPHA (January 4–5); the Polisario Front states that it will observe a truce until the end of February in order to improve the political climate for direct negotiations (end January) but then announces that King Hassan had indefinitely postponed further direct talks (February 13); the front calls off its cease-fire in Western Sahara as a sign of its displeasure (March 10); after Polisario's seventh congress in the "liberated territories" (April 28–May 1), it is announced that the long-serving defense minister, Ibrahim Ghali, is to be replaced by MOHAMMED LAMINE OULD BOUHALI; Ghali retains his place on the front's Executive Committee and is given command of an important military region; Polisario announces that as a gesture of goodwill, it will release 200 Moroccan prisoners of war (May 8), but despite the intervention of the International Committee of the Red Cross, Morocco refuses to accept the prisoners back, obliging the front to continue holding them; Morocco formally ratifies the 1972 border agreement with Algeria (May 14); Pérez de Cuéllar visits Morocco, Mauritania, and Algeria (June 17–24); he also visits Mali to discuss Western Sahara with the OAU chairman, President Moussa Traoré; one of the Polisario Front's leading members, OMAR HADRAMI, who had been assigned to Washington as the front's U.S. representative, defects to Morocco (August 8); the Polisario Front launches numerous attacks on FAR positions along the "defensive wall," notably at Guelta Zemmour (October 7–15 and November 16) and Amgala (November 8)

1990   JOHANNES MANZ of Switzerland is appointed special representative for Western Sahara by the UN secretary-general, replacing Hector Gros Espiell (January 19);

the Polisario Front announces a unilateral cease-fire until the end of March; Pérez de Cuéllar visits Morocco and Algeria and meets with Saharawi officials in the Tindouf region (March 23–26); upon his return to New York, he expresses optimism about the chances for a settlement (March 27); he also says that Rabat accepts the principle of partial troop withdrawal from Western Sahara prior to a referendum in the territory but gives no numbers; a UN-sponsored meeting of Saharawi tribal elders takes place in Geneva (week of June 3) to discuss voter eligibility in a referendum; the new African nation of Namibia recognizes the SADR (June 11); Pérez de Cuéllar formally presents his plan for a cease-fire and referendum in Western Sahara (June 18); this proposes the formation of the UNITED NATIONS MISSION FOR THE REFERENDUM IN WESTERN SAHARA (MINURSO), which would include military, civilian, and police units to oversee the withdrawal or confinement of Moroccan and Polisario forces and the holding of a plebiscite after a short campaign; the 1974 Spanish census is to be updated and used as a basis for determining eligibility for voting; the choice to be offered to the Saharawi voters shall be between independence and integration with Morocco; the secretary-general states that "the United Nations operation in Western Sahara will be large and complicated"; the UN Security Council thereafter meets and by a unanimous vote adopts resolution 658 (June 27), approving the report and requesting that the secretary-general send a second UNITED NATIONS TECHNICAL MISSION to the territory in

1990 to ascertain the exact nature and cost
of MINURSO; Pérez de Cuéllar travels to
Geneva, where he continues his efforts to
mediate between the Polisario Front and
Morocco (July 5–9), but Morocco still refuses to speak directly with the Polisario
delegation; Pérez de Cuéllar's efforts to
bring peace to Western Sahara are aborted
by Iraq's invasion of Kuwait (August 2)
and the Gulf crisis and war that follow; a
second UN technical mission travels to
northwest Africa (July 29) and concludes
its work approximately two weeks later;
SADR president Mohammed Abdelaziz, in
an interview with *Le Monde,* says that the
primary remaining point of disagreement
between Polisario and Morocco concerns
the scale of the Moroccan military forces
and civil service to remain in Western
Sahara prior to the referendum (November
1); he also states that the front has unilaterally refrained from attacking Moroccan
forces since April; King Hassan, in a
speech to Moroccan citizens (November
6), says he envisions a referendum in Western Sahara in which there would be "neither winner nor loser," and he calls upon
his "sons and subjects living beyond the
eastern and southern frontiers of Morocco" to return to Morocco and accept
integration; the UN General Assembly
passes resolution 45/21, urging the secretary-general and the chairman of the OAU
to intensify their efforts toward holding a
plebiscite and encouraging both parties to
the dispute to give their cooperation to the
UN (November 20)

1991   At the height of the U.S.-led war against
Iraq, French radio reports that about 2,000

Moroccan soldiers stationed in Western Sahara deserted their positions on February 4, allegedly to protest the Moroccan government's anti-Iraq stance in the Gulf War; the incident is denied by Morocco and also by Polisario and Algeria (February 6); UN Secretary-General Pérez de Cuéllar, in a report to the UN's Special Committee on Decolonization, states that a solution to the conflict is now within reach (February 21); after consulting with the members of the Security Council on his efforts to resolve the dispute (April 10), he submits his final detailed report on the modalities of the referendum and the structure of MINURSO (see Bibliography); the report outlines a 36-week schedule for a cease-fire, insertion of the peacekeeping force, and the conduct of the voting process—the cost is estimated at $180 million for MINURSO itself plus $34.5 million for the repatriation of Saharawi refugees prior to the voting (April 19); the UN Security Council unanimously approves resolution 690, approving Pérez de Cuéllar's report and formally establishing MINURSO (April 29); the General Assembly approves MINURSO's budget (May 17); King Hassan visits Western Sahara, stopping at Smara before returning to Morocco (May 17–18); Pérez de Cuéllar commences a visit to the region to consult with the parties, seeking agreement as to the date the permanent cease-fire will enter into force (May 25); King Hassan announces that he has pardoned all Saharawis who were opposed to his Western Sahara policy (June 12); the Polisario Front holds its 8th general popular congress, inter alia, adopting a new constitution, forming a new parliament and na-

tional secretariat, and abolishing the
front's Political Bureau and Executive
Committee (June 18–20); Maj. Gen. Ar-
mand Roy of Canada is appointed military
commander of MINURSO (June 25); Morocco and Polisario, after consultations
with the UN, accept September 6 as the
date on which the referendum process
should begin (June 28); Amnesty International states that dozens of Saharawi prisoners detained by Morocco for up to 15
years have been released (end June); Polisario announces a new government as a
result of decisions taken during the recent
congress (July 5); breaking a de facto truce
that had lasted since early 1990, Morocco
conducts bombing attacks against Polisario
positions in Western Sahara beyond its
"defensive walls" in the vicinity of Tifariti (August 4–5); Morocco says its actions
are intended to prevent Polisario infiltration of Western Sahara, asserting that the
front intended to disrupt the referendum;
Polisario claims 16 persons were killed and
65 missing in the raids and that two Moroccan fighter aircraft were shot down and one
pilot captured, whereas other sources report further Moroccan attacks at other locations in Saguia el-Hamra, causing the
forced dispossession of hundreds of civilians into the surrounding desert without
food or water; Polisario requests the "urgent intervention" of the UN (August 7);
Pérez de Cuéllar expresses "deep concern" at the renewed clashes and calls
upon the parties to cease hostilities (week
of August 12); Morocco, having earlier
submitted to MINURSO's Identification
Commission a list of nearly 40,000 persons
it says are eligible to vote, expands the list

to 120,000 (week of August 19); Morocco demands a delay in the referendum process, accuses the UN of failing to adhere to its procedures and timetables for the plebiscite, and rejects any role for the OAU in the referendum (August 21); Polisario reports large Moroccan troop movements toward the Mauritanian and Algerian borders of Western Sahara (August 22); a MINURSO spokesperson confirms that Morocco has refused permission for two UN vessels, carrying advance equipment and personnel for MINURSO, to offload their cargo in Western Sahara to prepare for the September 6 cease-fire date, and Moroccan troops apparently withdraw behind the "defensive walls" in the territory (end August); King Hassan accuses Polisario of deploying military forces in the Tifariti area, an accusation that Polisario denies (September 4); MINURSO's referendum and cease-fire effort officially begins (September 6); about 240 UN personnel arrive in Western Sahara and take up positions at 10 locations (September 7–8); a UN liaison office is also set up at Tindouf; a MINURSO officer states that the UN force is suffering from logistical problems (September 9); the Polisario Front announces that its fighters are assembling in locations supervised by MINURSO observers (September 11); additional MINURSO units travel to Smara and take up positions there (September 12); Polisario accuses Morocco of violating the cease-fire by conducting flights by aircraft over locations where UN observers were positioned from September 18 to 20 (September 21); Morocco and the Polisario Front continue to accuse one another of breaking the truce, and the long-standing dispute over voting qualifications continues (week of September 23); the Moroccan newspaper *L'Opinion* reports that Rabat is sending more than 160,000 refugees, supposedly Saharawis, to Western Sahara, where they can take part in the referendum, and it also says that 20,000 have already arrived in El-Ayoun (October 5); Pérez de Cuéllar reports to the UN General Assembly on developments related to the referendum process (October 23); although the report makes little reference to delays and other difficulties, MINURSO is conceded to be considerably behind schedule (end October); the secretary-general issues new regulations on the identification of Saharawis to ascertain voter eligibility (November 8); the Security Council receives them for review (November 11); it is reported that Pérez de Cuéllar has decided to modify the voting criteria in that the list contained in the 1974 Spanish census will be expanded to include any Saharawi with a father born in Western Sahara and anyone who can prove residence in the territory either for 6 years continuously or for 12 years intermittently (November 15); the Polisario Front warns that any attempt to change voter qualification requirements will constitute a "serious and unjustifiable violation" of the UN plan and would only lead to a ratification of Moroccan control over Western Sahara (November 17); the UN promises an investigation into a November 15 report by the British newspaper, *The Independent,* that UN employees gave to Morocco computer disks containing census data, which were confidentially entrusted by Polisario to the world body (end

November); the front again accuses Morocco of importing its citizens into Western Sahara in an attempt to prevail in any referendum (December 10); Spanish television reports that secret Morocco-Polisario discussions are under way to avoid a referendum in favor of a "federation" arrangement with Morocco (December 13); Polisario denies reports of the talks (December 14); Pérez de Cuéllar submits a report on Western Sahara (see Bibliography) in which he acknowledges difficulties in MINURSO's mission and the disputes over voter eligibility (December 19); he also announces the resignation of Special Representative Johannes Manz effective January 1, 1992, warning that "serious efforts will have to be made at the political and technical levels to keep the process going"; the Polisario Front, reacting to the secretary-general's report, rejects any delay in the conduct of the plebiscite as favoring Morocco and again strongly protests the widening of voter eligibility criteria (December 22); the UN Security Council unanimously passes resolution 725, supporting UN efforts so far and calling upon the new UN secretary-general, BOUTROS BOUTROS GHALI of Egypt, to submit a further report within two months (December 31)

1992

Boutros Boutros Ghali takes office as UN secretary-general, replacing Javier Pérez de Cuéllar (January 1); the Polisario Front alleges that more than 200 persons sympathetic to the organization have been arrested by Morocco since the beginning of 1992 (January 15); a report written by a staff member of the U.S. Senate's Foreign

Relations Committee, George Pickart, details serious problems with the UN's cease-fire and referendum effort in Western Sahara; inter alia, it describes the lack of cooperation with MINURSO by both Polisario and Morocco, the primitive conditions faced by the UN peacekeeping troops, the violations of the cease-fire by Morocco, and budgetary irregularities; the report concludes by recommending that the United States, which had contributed 30 soldiers to MINURSO, withdraw its contingent if the problems are not corrected (January 27); the SADR's president, Mohammed Abdelaziz, travels for the first time to New York and Washington for discussions with the UN's top leadership and with some Americans, respectively (February 20); the secretary-general issues a report reciting the circumstances of MINURSO's deployment and difficulties with both cease-fire violations and voter eligibility criteria; he recommends persevering with settlement efforts and promises to make a further report in May 1992 (February 28); King Hassan II says he is optimistic about progress toward a referendum in Western Sahara, and adds, "We do not have the slightest doubt that the outcome of the referendum will confirm the Sahara as Moroccan territory" (March 3); Polisario accuses Morocco again of violating the cease-fire, saying that it fired its weapons for three hours near Farsia (March 11); Morocco denies this accusation (March 12); Polisario urges France to take a more active mediatory role in the conflict and to respond more forcefully to cease-fire violations (March 18); a Pakistani diplomat, SAHABZADA YAQUB KHAN, is appointed as new UN special representative for Western Sahara, replacing Johannes Manz (March 23); Mohammed Abdelaziz, in an interview with the Algerian daily, *El-Watan,* rejects efforts to settle the Western Sahara question outside of the UN and spurns any talk of federation with Morocco (April 1); Polisario calls for the deployment of additional UN troops in Western Sahara, particularly in border regions where it alleges extensive breaches of the cease-fire by Morocco (April 29); in an interview with *Le Monde,* Mohammed Abdelaziz says the Polisario Front is open to compromise on the question of which Saharawis are eligible to vote in the referendum while maintaining that Morocco's 200 percent increase in proposed voters beyond the number in the 1974 Spanish census is unacceptable (May 20); the UN secretary-general releases his report, attributing 97 of the 102 cease-fire violations in Western Sahara since September 1991 to Morocco (May 29); he states that problems over voter eligibility persist and recommends that the Security Council extend MINURSO's mandate at least until the end of August 1992, at which time, he suggests, the Security Council "might wish to consider a different approach" to settling the problem

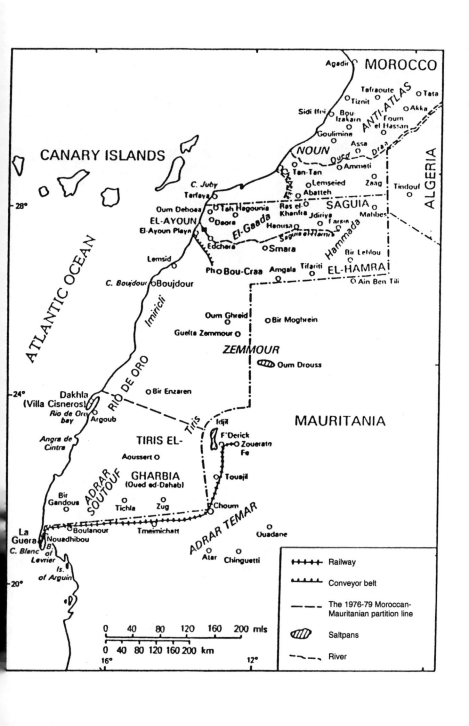

INTRODUCTION

Western Sahara is one of the most arid and thinly populated countries in the world. It is an inhospitable place, whipped by sandstorms and afflicted by dramatic shifts in temperature, which can soar to 50° C in the middle of the day and descend to zero at night. Annual rainfall seldom attains 50 mm. and is often much less. However, this 266,000 sq. km. slab of desert (which is about half the size of Spain but does not boast a single oasis of consequence) has some of the richest deposits of phosphates in the world and, since 1975, has become one of the hottest flashpoints on the African continent.

By virtue of the Madrid Agreement of November 14, 1975, Spain handed over its desert colony to Morocco and Mauritania, which were rapidly enmeshed in a bitter war with nationalist guerrillas of the Front Popular para la Liberación de Saguia el-Hamra y Río de Oro, who had been fighting Spain for independence since 1973. Though Mauritania subsequently withdrew from the country in 1979, after making peace with the guerrillas, the war between the Polisario Front and Morocco remained a major source of tension in the Maghreb and became one of the gravest challenges to the Organization of African Unity.

The country's internationally recognized land borders (i.e., those predating the attempted annexation by Morocco, whose claim of sovereignty over Western Sahara has not been recognized by any foreign governments) extend for 2,045 km., of which 435 km. border Morocco in the north, 30 km. border Algeria in the northeast and 1,570 km. border Mauritania in the east and the south. The country is bounded in the west by 1,062 km. of Atlantic coastline.

The history of this parched land is as fascinating as it is complex and at times controversial. It was not always desert. Through the ages, dry periods have alternated with relatively

1

humid times. Between about 5500 B.C. and 2500 B.C., for example, there was a landscape of bush and savannah on which roamed animals that have long since vanished from this part of Africa, including the elephants, rhinoceroses, and giraffes depicted in the rock engravings of the time.

Western Sahara's inhabitants during the Neolithic period (which began about 5000 B.C.) are thought to have been a people of largely negroid stock. They gradually migrated southward or took refuge in the oases as the savannah gave way to desert from about the middle of the third millennium B.C. During the first millennium B.C., however, a new people arrived from the north. They were Berbers, whose chariots, drawn by horses or oxen, are depicted in numerous rock drawings. The Berbers' use of horses and iron gave them the upper hand against the remnants of the previous population, but it was not until the arrival of the camel from the east in the 1st century A.D. that they acquired the means to guarantee their survival in this increasingly arid land.

The camel, which can survive without drinking for several days (or even weeks in winter if it enjoys good pastures), can cover at least 60 km. a day and carry loads of up to 150 kg. It became the Saharans' basic source of food, served as an ideal pack animal for both trade and nomadic migrations, and was used as a means of exchange and an instrument of war.

The Berbers who dominated the western stretches of the Sahara were a branch of the Sanhaja, the ancestors of, among others, the Tuareg of the central Sahara and the mountain peoples of Kabylia, the Rif, and the Middle Atlas. The Saharan Sanhaja were gradually, but superficially, converted to Islam from about the mid-8th century, following the first Arab expeditions to the Maghreb early that century. It was during the Almoravid period, however, that Islam, of an orthodox Sunni stamp, became firmly implanted in the nomads' culture. Then, under the inspiring leadership of men like Abdallah Ibn Yacin, Yahya Ibn Omar, and his brother Abu Bakr, the Saharan Sanhaja tribes (the Lemtouna, the Gadala, and the Massoufa) rallied under a religious banner against their main rivals, the Zenata Berbers to their north and the Soninke to the south, and by seizing the main trading towns of the time, Sijilmassa (southeastern Morocco) and Aoudaghost (southern Mauritania) became masters of the Saharan trade routes in 1056. They then extended their conquests northward into Morocco, capturing Fez in 1069, and then into Algeria and Muslim Spain, which was brought under Almoravid control by 1110, while another wing of the Almoravid movement destroyed the Soninke kingdom of Ghana to the south of the Sahara in 1076. However, the Almoravids never really created a unified empire. The Almoravid state established in Morocco, western Algeria, and Spain, under Yusuf Ibn Tashfin, did not control the Sanhaja who remained in the desert or followed Abu Bakr Ibn Omar against Ghana. Their fragile unity behind the Almoravid cause repeatedly dissolved into mutual conflict. Moreover, by the mid-12th century, the northern Almoravid state had collapsed as a result of the rise of the Almohad movement in Morocco (1125–50) and the resumption of the Christian *reconquista* in Spain.

The disunited Saharan Sanhaja tribes faced a new challenge in the 13th century from the Beni Hassan, a branch of the bedouin Maqil Arabs, a people who had migrated from Yemen, across North Africa, skirting the fringes of the desert. They arrived in the valley of the Draa and on the Atlantic coast in about 1218, and, after most of them had been barred by the Merinids (the successors to the Almohads) from thrusting through the Atlas ranges to Morocco's fertile plains, many began migrating south into what is now Western Sahara and Mauritania, from the end of the 13th century. The Beni Hassan gradually vassalized or fused with the Sanhaja, giving rise to the caste system that characterized the nomadic society of Western Sahara and Mauritania. The victorious *arab* or *hassan* tribes became the caste of free warriors, the *ahel mdafa*, or "people of the gun." Some of the Sanhaja, defeated in battle, "gave up the sword for the book," becoming *zawiya* tribes dedicated to religious study and teaching, while the weakest became *znaga* (significantly a corruption of Sanhaja), forced to pay the *horma* or other forms of tribute to powerful warrior tribes.

The actual process of interaction between tribes of Sanhaja and Maqil origin was more complex and uneven than this neat schema implies. There were considerable variations between regions, and in what is now Western Sahara many of the Sanhaja recuperated their social position—both by arms and by astutely manipulating their genealogies to claim Arab, indeed *cherifian,* ancestry. The Reguibat, the Arosien, and the Oulad Bou Sbaa are the largest of the tribes of *chorfa* claiming descent from the prophet Mohammed despite their overwhelmingly Sanhaja ancestry. The main tribes of *arab* status are the Oulad Delim and the Tekna tribes, though the latter appear to be the product of a fusion of Beni Hassan and Sanhaja peoples. The most significant example of *znaga* in Western Sahara in the precolonial period was the Oulad Tidrarin, who were vassalized by the Oulad Delim toward the end of the 18th century. At the bottom of the social structure were the castes of *maalemin* (craftsmen) and *iggauen* (bards), who did not form tribes of their own, and, finally, the *abid* (slaves) and *haratin* (freed slaves). In fact, the exploited or subjugated castes were not numerically large. Very few Saharawis were wealthy enough to own slaves; slave labor was not well suited to the Saharawis' almost entirely pastoral economy; and few tribes were so weak as to be obliged to pay tribute or, through opportune alliances or rebellions, to be unable to escape it. In addition, the distinction between the *ahel mdafa* and *chora* was an uneasy one. The 19th century was marked by the rise of the Reguibat, a tribe of essentially Sanhaja extraction, as the most powerful people of the region. They were as much *ahel mdafa* as the purest Arabs, the Oulad Delim.

Moreover, as supposed *chorfa,* the tribes of basically Sanhaja origin thought of themselves as Arabs. This was reinforced by their adoption of Hassaniya, the Arabic dialect of the Beni Hassan, and the gradual disappearance of their former Berber dialect, whose existence was noted in the 15th and 16th centuries by such writers as Alvise da Ca da Mosto, Leo Africanus, and Mármol y Carvajal but which had died out completely by the 19th century.

The Western Saharan tribes remained entirely nomadic until the middle of the 20th century. Despite the rich fishing resources of the coast, which were exploited by the Canary Islanders from the 15th century, only a few small impoverished tribes engaged in fishing—by wading with nets in shallow waters, never by going out to sea in boats. Additionally, there was virtually no agriculture, Western Sahara not having important date palm oases of the kind to be found in southern Morocco and parts of Algeria and Mauritania.

The Saharawis called themselves the ''sons of the clouds,'' for their economy hinged on the constant search for pastures and water sources for their herds. But their economy was not a self-sufficient closed one. They traded with the sedentary societies to the north (the Maghreb) and the south (the blacks) and sometimes, from the 15th century, with Europeans on the coast, exchanging their surplus livestock or salt from the Saharan salt-pans (the *sebkhas*) for such "imports" as cereals, tea, sugar, cloth, weapons, and carpets.

They took part also in the trans-Saharan caravan trade, as guides or traders, taking (according to the epoch) manufactured goods from Europe and the Maghreb to black Africa and, in the opposite direction, slaves, gold, gum, and ostrich feathers.

Besides herding and trading, another element in the nomads' economy was livestock-raiding. The *ghazzis* (raids) were a permanent feature of Saharawi life, though they could debilitate as well as enrich those that practiced them. They were staged as commercial enterprises, with fixed rules governing the distribution of the booty, but the motives were not always economic: The responsibility of agnates for payment of the *diya,* or blood-debt, could spark off a vendetta.

Pastures were usually so scarce that only in times of great insecurity did a tribe assemble in one large group. Usually Saharawis nomadized in small groups, the *friq* (camp) rarely having as many as 100 tents, or *khaimat.* Under these circumstances, the *fakhd* (fraction) often had more immediate importance in day-to-day life than the *gabila* (tribe) as a social unit. Political decisions were made by the *djemaas,* assemblies of free adult men, at fraction or tribal level, and military decisions were the province of a tribal war council known as the *ait arbain.* No supratribal state authority existed to regulate the relations between these wandering and fiercely independent tribes. The Almoravid movement was only briefly a unifying force. The emirates of Mauritania, which were created in the 16th century and were strengthened by their control of much of the trade with the Europeans, were barely more than embryonic supratribal states, and they did not hold sway over the Western Saharan tribes. Nor did the sultans of Morocco, the most powerful rulers in northwest Africa. Until the 20th century, Morocco was not a fully unified nation-state, much of the country (notably the Rif and the three Atlas ranges) being most of the time beyond the effective control of the sultan's government, the *makhzen,* and thus part of what was known as the *bilad es-siba,* or "land of dissidence."

Few Moroccan sultans were sufficiently powerful to pacify all the dissident areas of Morocco itself, let alone attempt to bring the anarchic tribes of the Sahara under their control, and many were preoccupied also with the need to fend off external threats from the Spaniards, the Portuguese, the Turks, and later the French. When Moroccan sultans did pursue an active Saharan policy, it was usually designed to bring the trans-Saharan caravan trade under their control. The aim was most often to secure control of strategic trading towns, salt mines, and oases in order to orient the caravans toward Morocco rather than, for example, the Turkish-controlled Mediterranean cities or the Europeans on the Atlantic coast. Though Moroccan sultans at times made opportune alliances with Saharan tribes in order to facilitate the achievement of these objectives, no attempt was ever made, or could have been made, to bring the nomads under the direct control of the *makhzen*. Moreover, Moroccan intervention in the Sahara was ephemeral and more or less entirely bypassed the region now known as Western Sahara because it had neither oases nor trading towns. The sultans who intervened most significantly in the Sahara were Ahmed el-Mansour (1578–1603), who sent an army across the desert to seize Timbuctoo in 1591, and Moulay Ismail (1672–1727), who personally led an expedition to Mauritania in 1679, mainly to recruit black slaves for his famous slave army, the cornerstone of his iron rule. During the reigns of these unusually powerful monarchs, the Tekna tribes, or at least some of them, appear to have become *guish* tribes; that is to say, they provided the *makhzen* with military contingents in return for the provision of some land in Morocco. After Moulay Ismail's death, Morocco was plunged into anarchy, and from the 1760s the Oued Noun region (southwest Morocco), to the north of present-day Western Sahara, was independent of the *makhzen* under principalities at Tazeroualt and Goulimine. This lasted until the expeditions to Tiznit (1882) and Goulimine (1886) by Moulay Hassan I, who wanted to prevent attempts by the Oulad Beyrouk, the rulers of Goulimine, to trade with the Europeans and who hoped to counter the growing European pressure on the fringes of his empire. He did not intervene in Western Sahara, though his successor, Moulay Abdelaziz, did briefly (1905–7) send his cousin, Moulay Idriss Ben Abderrahman, to assist Saharawi forces, led by Cheikh Ma el-Ainin, against the Europeans.

European explorers first charted the Western Saharan coast in the 14th and 15th centuries. Portugal and Spain, the two great mercantile powers of that time, were the pioneers, defining their respective "rights" along the coast in a series of treaties at the end of the 15th century and early in the 16th century, sometimes following papal arbitration. In 1476, a Castilian noble began construction of a fort, baptized Santa Cruz de Mar Pequeña, on the Saharan coast opposite the Canaries, most of which had by then been colonized by Castile. It alternated as a trading post and a slave-raiding base until it was sacked by local tribes in 1524.

The Spaniards, whose imperial ambitions were then diverted to the Americas, were not to return to the Saharan coast until the end of the 19th century. Then, the Spanish government was prodded and pushed into a colonial adventure in the Sahara by a well-organized commercial and ideological lobby, headed by the Sociedad de Africanistas y Colonistas and the Compañía Comercial Hispano-Africana, which in 1884 set up the trading post at Dakhla on the Río de Oro bay that was to become the settlement of Villa Cisneros. After Emilio Bonelli, a representative of the Sociedad de Africanistas y Colonistas, had signed treaties with local chiefs in November 1884, the Madrid government declared a 'protectorate' over part of the coast the following December. By April 1887, the coastal region from Boujdour to Cape Blanc—up to 150 miles into the interior—was (in theory) under the administration of a politicomilitary subgovernor responsible to the captain general of the Canaries. The borders of the Spanish colony were subsequently extended by three Franco-Spanish conventions in 1900, 1904, and 1912, which gave Spain full sovereignty over Río de Oro (184,000 sq. km.) in the south and Saguia el-Hamra (82,000 sq. km.), a slice of territory between the parallels 26° and 27° 40', which is named after the country's principal river. The conventions specified, however, that the Tekna Zone (25,600 sq. km.), the northernmost strip of Spain's Saharan territory between parallel 27° 40' and the Oued Draa, was part of Spain's protectorate zone in Morocco.

Despite all this arbitrary frontier-drawing, the Spanish presence remained confined in practice to the tiny enclave of Villa Cisneros until 1916. Francisco Bens, who was governor from 1903 to 1925, established a reasonably cordial modus vivendi with the nomads by leaving them alone (unlike the French, who were aggressively trying to "pacify" their part of the Sahara at this time). He took control of Tarfaya (in the Tekna Zone) in 1916 and La Guera (in the extreme south of Río de Oro) in 1920, but no attempt was made to occupy points in the interior until 1934, 50 years after the initial announcement of a "protectorate." This was finally done on the prompting of the French, who wanted Spain to stop allowing its Saharan territory to be used as a sanctuary by anticolonial forces staging *ghazzis* against French positions in the neighboring territories. These forces had been led by Cheikh Ma el-Ainin until his death in 1910, and then by his sons, Ahmed el-Hiba, Merebbi Rebbu, and Mohammed Laghdaf. In 1913, French forces crossed into the "Spanish Sahara" to sack Smara in reprisal for a *ghazzi* that had decimated a French nomad unit in Mauritania.

After the occupation of Smara, Daora, and other inland points by Spanish troops in 1934, Western Sahara was unified administratively with the Spanish zone of Morocco by being placed under the ultimate responsibility of the Spanish high commissioner in Tetuan, who took the additional title of governor-general of Ifni (occupied also in 1934 for the first time) and the Sahara. This arrangement proved embarrassing to Spain when Moroccan nationalism became a powerful force after World War II, so in 1946, a new entity, Africa Occidental Española, comprising both Western Sahara and Ifni, was set up under its own governor-general.

A serious challenge to Spanish rule in both Ifni and Western Sahara followed Morocco's accession to independence in 1956. The Army of Liberation, a radical guerrilla movement that had played a role in the Moroccan independence struggle, sent forces to Bou-Izarkan, Tiznit, and Goulimine in Morocco's far south in 1956 and, the following year, launched guerrilla campaigns against the Spanish in Ifni and Western Sahara and against the French in southwestern Algeria and northern Mauritania. The guerrillas initially had considerable success against the weak Spanish forces, and toward the end of the year Spanish troops again abandoned all points in the interior, including even Smara, falling back on the coastal enclaves of El-Ayoun, Dakhla, and Tarfaya. However, in January 1958, the Spanish government indicated that it had no intention of quitting either Ifni or Western Sahara when it dissolved AOE and turned both of its components into Spanish "provinces." Then, the following February, 9,000

Spanish troops and 5,000 French troops, backed by scores of aircraft, staged a counterinsurgency sweep through Western Sahara (Operation Ouragan), routing the guerrilla bands, whose survivors fled north to take refuge in Morocco. There the regular Moroccan army, the Forces Armées Royales, was by then sufficiently strong in the south of the country to disarm and disband the remnants of the guerrilla movement, whose radical leadership had been distrusted by Mohammed V. With the threat from the Army of Liberation largely removed, the Spanish government finally agreed to hand over to Morocco the Tekna Zone, which Madrid had always recognized as part of its protectorate zone in Morocco.

While disbanding what remained of the Army of Liberation, Mohammed V nonetheless endorsed the territorial claims to Western Sahara, Ifni, Mauritania, and the Algerian Sahara, which formed part of the "Greater Morocco" policy elaborated since 1956 by Allal el-Fassi, the leader of Morocco's nationalist Istiqlal Party. In consequence, Rabat refused to recognize Mauritania when it became independent in 1960 and briefly went to war with Algeria in 1963. Mauritania's President Mokhtar Ould Daddah countered by claiming Western Sahara as part of Mauritania.

King Hassan II, who succeeded Mohammed V in 1961, finally settled Morocco's territorial disputes with Algeria and Mauritania (on their terms) in 1969–72. A pragmatist, Hassan II also put more store on economic cooperation with Francoist Spain than challenging it over Western Sahara. The détente between Spain and Morocco (as a result of which Ifni was finally ceded to Morocco in 1969 but the Western Saharan issue was by and large downplayed) was dubbed the "spirit of Barajas" following a historic summit between Franco and Hassan at Barajas airport near Madrid in 1963. Hassan mounted no serious challenge to Spain over Western Sahara until 1974, but the irridentists in Morocco were further dismayed when, from 1966, his government decided to endorse the calls for self-determination being made at the UN, where the General Assembly adopted its first resolution on Western Sahara in 1965.

Ironically, the downplaying of the Saharan question by the Rabat regime from the early 1960s until 1974 was one of the main causes of the emergence of a new phenomenon, Western Saharan nationalism. Anticolonial Saharawis began to learn to count on their own strength. Moreover, rapid social change in the Sahara encouraged the birth of a new, more modern form of opposition to the Spanish than the old tribal forms of resistance. Phosphates were discovered, and in 1969 Fosbucraa was set up by Spain's state-owned Instituto Nacional de Industria to exploit a huge deposit of 1.7 billion tons of very high-grade ore at Bou-Craa. By 1975, exports were running at 2.6 million tons a year, making Western Sahara the sixth-largest phosphate exporter in the world; there were plans to raise exports ultimately to 10 million tons (second only to Morocco). To service this new industry and the prospecting for other resources (including oil), the Spanish government rapidly expanded administrative and economic infrastructure. Twenty thousand Spaniards had settled in the territory by 1974, and most of the Saharawis abandoned nomadism to settle in the small, growing towns of both Western Sahara itself and the neighboring territories (notably in Tan-Tan, Morocco; Tindouf, Algeria; and Zouerate, Mauritania, the center of a major iron ore industry) in order to escape droughts and take advantage of opportunities for relief, employment, or trading. Thus, by 1974, when the Spanish government carried out a census, 55 percent of the 74,000 Saharawis counted were living in the three main towns (El-Ayoun, Smara, and Dakhla), though many of those who were still engaged in a nomadic way of life may not have been included. At least as many Saharawis (that is, Saharans from tribes or fractions with migratory-pastoral traditions in the Western Sahara) were in the neighboring territories, as a result of either refugee movements after Operation Ouragan in 1958 or the sedentation process described above.

As sedentation occurred, modern education suddenly became available to a large number of Saharawis for the first time, and, whereas there had not been a single secondary school in Western Sahara until 1964, there were more than 50 Saharawis in higher education in Spain by the early 1970s and as many in Moroccan universities. It was from this new elite of well-educated Saharawis, who were greatly influenced by nationalist movements elsewhere in the Third World and by the resolutions on self-determination adopted annually by the UN, that the leadership of a modern Saharawi nationalist movement began to emerge. Nationalism was further encouraged, moreover, by the growing awareness on the part of the Saharawis of the mineral wealth of their country and, ironically, also by the Spanish government's rhetorical and paternalist pledges of commitment to self-determination (from 1966), which were designed both to keep the UN at bay and to rebuff Morocco's territorial claim (which, despite being downplayed, remained official policy). In fact, the Spanish government had no intention of quitting Western Sahara, especially after the discovery of the Bou-Craa phosphates, and continually pleaded to the UN that application of the principle of self-determination would have to be delayed because of the low level of development of the territory and the nomadic character of much of its population.

The first movement to challenge the colonial status quo after the collapse of the Army of Liberation was the Harakat Tahrir Saguia el-Hamra wa Oued ed-Dahab, led by a graduate of the universities of Cairo and Damascus, Mohammed Sidi Ibrahim Bassiri, in 1967–70. This first urban-based political organization, albeit weak and clandestine, was crushed in June 1970, when the Foreign Legion shot dead several demonstrators in the Zemla district of El-Ayoun, and the movement's leaders, including Bassiri, were arrested. Bassiri has never since reappeared and was probably murdered in jail. A group of students from Mohammed V University in Rabat were instrumental in founding the next anticolonial movement, the Polisario Front, on May 10, 1973. It opted for guerrilla warfare from the start and launched its first attack on a Spanish post, at El-Khanga, only ten days later. Under the leadership of El-Ouali Mustapha Sayed, the front led a small-scale guerrilla war against Spain with virtually no external aid except for a small arms consignment from Libya and the ambivalent connivance of (ironically) Mauritania.

In 1973, however, the Franco regime finally decided to plan steps for the gradual introduction of internal self-government. The idea was to devolve limited legislative powers to the Djemaa, a hitherto purely consultative assembly of traditionalist and loyalist *chioukh* (chiefs) and set up a partially-Saharawi governing council under the guiding hand of the governor-general. The devolution of powers became an urgent priority for Madrid in the wake of the April 1974 coup in Portugal, which spelled the collapse of Lisbon's African empire, leaving Spain virtually alone in the colonial field. So, in July 1974, the Djemaa formally approved proposals for internal autonomy contained in a "political statute" drafted by the Franco regime, and in November 1974 a political movement, the Partido de la Unión Nacional Saharaui (PUNS), was founded with Madrid's blessing to challenge the Polisario Front for popular support and provide the leadership of a Saharawi government that could steer the country through a stage of internal self-government toward eventual independence—of a kind that would not threaten Spain's substantial interests in the phosphate industry and offshore fishing. On August 21, 1974, the Madrid government promised finally to implement UN calls for a referendum during the first six months of 1975.

All of a sudden, Western Sahara seemed destined to head toward independence. This presented an immediate challenge to Hassan II. He had endorsed UN calls for a referendum in the past in the belief that the Saharawis would opt for integration with Morocco, but now, Western Saharans had strong nationalist inclinations and it seemed that if the referendum were allowed to proceed, it would endorse the creation of an independent state. That would have enraged the irridentist parties in Morocco, for whom Western Sahara was all that remained after the abandoning of the claims to Mauritania and parts of Algeria. Hassan's regime was extremely weak in the early seventies, moreover. There had been constant conflicts with the opposition parties, unions, and students, and in 1971 and 1972, the armed forces had tried twice to depose him. What better idea under the circumstances, the king calculated, than to spearhead a national crusade for the recovery of Morocco's "amputated Saharan provinces"? By whipping up an atmosphere of *jihad*, with the king at its head, against the European infidel and its dastardly plans to create a "puppet state" on Moroccan land, Hassan succeeded in rallying the Moroccan people, including all the main opposition parties, behind the throne in an unprecedented display of national unity.

This came to a head in the Green March of November 1975, when 350,000 Moroccans briefly crossed the Western Saharan border in an extraordinary display of Moroccan determination. This finally forced Spain to yield—despite the report by a UN Visiting Mission, which had concluded after a tour of the country in May 1975 that the overwhelming majority of the population wanted independence, and despite an advisory opinion from the International Court of Justice (October 16, 1975), which rejected Moroccan and Mauritanian claims to precolonial sovereignty in

Western Sahara and upheld the primacy of self-determination. On November 14, 1975, the Spanish government, which was by then preoccupied with domestic affairs as Franco struggled through his long final illness (he died six days later), signed the Madrid Agreement with Morocco and Mauritania, which had harmonized their conflicting claims in 1974 on the basis of a deal to partition the territory. A transitional tripartite administration was set up, Spanish troops were rapidly withdrawn, and thousands of Moroccan and Mauritanian troops began to arrive in the territory. On February 26, 1976, the Spanish flag was pulled down for the last time, and on April 14, the country was formally partitioned, Morocco receiving the lion's share (170,000 sq. km., including El-Ayoun and the phosphate mines) and Mauritania the crumbs, a virtually resourceless slice of desert in the south known as Tiris el-Gharbia (96,000 sq. km.).

However, both Hassan II and Mokhtar Ould Daddah underestimated the determination of the Saharawis to resist the takeover and of the Algerian government (which had its own grounds to fear Moroccan irredentism) to support them. From the spring of 1975, the Polisario Front received substantial Algerian aid. At the end of the year, Saharawi refugees began arriving by thousands in the Tindouf region of Algeria, where there were at least 100,000 Saharawis (many from southern Morocco, northern Mauritania, and southwestern Algeria as well as Western Sahara itself) in Polisario-run camps by 1993. The Algerian government also provided arms, bases, and training for the Polisario guerrilla army, which had swollen into a well-equipped force of approximately 15,000 men by the early 1980s. To rally diplomatic support, the front proclaimed the founding of the Saharan Arab Democratic Republic (SADR) on February 27, 1976, one day after the Spanish withdrawal, and 74 states, most of them from the Third World, had granted this new desert state-in-exile diplomatic recognition by 1990. Meanwhile, both the UN and the OAU adopted increasingly strong-worded resolutions upholding the Saharawis' right to self-determination.

On the military front, the guerrillas' first priority was to knock Mauritania out of the war. Mauritania had a very small army and was one of the poorest countries in the world, battered by the Sahelian drought and precariously dependent on its exports of iron ore from the mines of Zouerate by way of an exposed 650 km.

railway to the port of Nouadhibou, which, flanking the Western Saharan border, the guerrillas made one of their major targets. Moreover, the annexation of part of Western Sahara did not arouse the kind of passion it engendered in Morocco. In July 1978, a war-weary Mauritanian army deposed Mokhtar Ould Daddah, and immediately the Polisario Front declared a cease-fire in Mauritanian territory. After one year of intermittent negotiations, Mauritania and the front formally made peace by signing the Algiers Agreement (August 5, 1979) by which Mauritania renounced its claim to Western Saharan territory. However, on August 14, Morocco unilaterally annexed Tiris el-Gharbia too, renaming it Oued ed-Dahab (Arabic for Río de Oro), in order to prevent the Polisario flag's flying in its main city, Dakhla.

With Mauritania out of the war, the conflict thereafter pitted the guerrillas of the Polisario Front alone against Morocco. Between the late 1970s and 1981, the Moroccans held only the main towns, whereas Polisario occupied most of the hinterland. The front's fighters, moreover, could attack—and sometimes briefly occupy—areas within southern Morocco itself with relative impunity. Faced with the high cost in lives and equipment that went along with maintaining small, exposed bases highly vulnerable to attack, the Moroccan army retrenched and concentrated on attempting to clear Polisario out of southern Morocco and an area in northwestern Saguia el-Hamra encompassing El-Ayoun, Smara, and the Bou-Craa phosphate mines. Known as the "useful triangle," this zone, which represented only about 25 percent of the total land area of Western Sahara, was protected by an expanding series of defensive walls made up of earthen barriers, minefields, detection devices, and Moroccan troop garrisons. Although these "berms" were reasonably successful in holding off the guerrillas, Moroccan losses continued and the cost of the war did not abate. With or without the walls, Polisario's military prowess was simply too great, and the motivation of the Moroccan army too uncertain, for any decisive victory to be achieved by King Hassan. Morocco's retrenchment policy in the Sahara was to be given a sharp, added incentive in October 1981, when a large Polisario force attacked Guelta Zemmour, one of only two Moroccan outposts outside the "useful triangle." In several days of action, the FAR was to lose control of the garrison and suffer hundreds of casualties. Most ominously for King Hassan, his air force was temporarily neutralized due to Polisario's acquisition of surface-to-air missiles. Although Morocco a few days later managed to recapture Guelta Zemmour, it was badly bruised by the experience and withdrew from both Guelta Zemmour and Bir Enzaren further to the southwest by early November 1981. Morocco's military fortunes hit a low point, and the Polisario position was greatly enhanced.

On the diplomatic front too, Polisario had grounds for feeling confident. Although Morocco had up to that point rejected the concept of a referendum in the Sahara to decide the future of the territory, King Hassan relented in June 1981, when he announced at the annual OAU summit conference in Nairobi that his country was amenable to an internationally supervised plebiscite. At the time, this appeared to be a significant concession to world opinion, and Polisario could take some comfort in the fact that one of its key demands had been met in principle. In addition, the front was enjoying an increasing degree of support from other African countries. Polisario's reputation was to advance in Africa when King Hassan, almost immediately after his overture at Nairobi, began to equivocate on his pledge to hold a referendum by making clear that his own concept of a plebiscite differed from that of the international community. He said that he saw the vote as providing "confirmation" of Moroccan sovereignty over the territory and that the refugees living in Polisario's Tindouf-area camps in Algeria would be allowed to return only if they agreed not to press for independence. In the African community, these statements engendered much resentment, generated much added support for Polisario, and impelled the OAU to act to uphold three of the organization's most central principles: self-determination and freedom from outside domination, the proposition that conflicts on the continent should be resolved peacefully, and a rule that was to serve the Polisario cause especially well—the inviolability of the national boundaries inherited from the days of European colonialism.

At a meeting of the OAU Council of Ministers held in Addis Ababa on February 22, 1982, the then secretary-general of the organization, Edem Kodjo, formally admitted the SADR to membership on the basis that a simple majority of the OAU's member states had assented to its entry under the relevant provisions of the OAU Charter. The reaction by Morocco and its allies was immediate. The following day, the organization's proceedings were boycotted in protest by Morocco and more than a dozen other states, which demanded that the decision be rescinded. Attempts in 1982 to hold the OAU's annual summit conferences were to falter due to boycotts by opponents of the SADR and a concurrent row over the representation of Chad. The OAU was saved from total paralysis only by the SADR's decision to "voluntarily and temporarily" absent itself from the councils of the organization. Although this was a diplomatic victory of sorts for the Moroccans, it was largely dissipated by King Hassan's continued temporizing over a referendum and his continued refusal to negotiate directly with the Polisario Front, whom he considered merely as Algerian surrogates. In fact, at the 1983 OAU summit in Addis Ababa, the organization adopted by consensus a measure (resolution 104) that for the first time explicitly named Morocco and Polisario as "parties to the conflict," in stark contrast to King Hassan's position that the Western Saharan dispute was between Morocco and Algeria. Support for Rabat had dwindled to such an extent by the time of the 1984 summit, held again in the Ethiopian capital, that the SADR took its seat as a member of the OAU with only very mild opposition. Morocco, making good on its prior threats, promptly withdrew from the organization, but no other state followed suit. Diplomatically, Polisario's triumph was complete, an achievement all the more remarkable in that the SADR could not at this stage be considered fully independent or in control of much of its territory.

Ironically, while Polisario was advancing diplomatically, it began to suffer rather serious reverses on the ground. Beginning in early 1982, the Moroccan army began aggressively extending its system of defensive walls much further into Western Sahara. The perimeters soon grew to encompass more and more of Saguia el-Hamra in the north and were then extended further south into Río de Oro as well. Moroccan troop strength in the territory had grown to at least 120,000 by the late 1980s. The Polisario Front was powerless to stop construction of the new walls, choosing instead to engage in no major attacks against Moroccan forces (between January 1982 and July 1983) in order to reflect on future strategy and to emphasize its interest in a diplomatic solution to the conflict. When it did resume attacks, the front took advantage of the fact that its highly mobile forces were able to confront an enemy that was continuously manning static defensive positions in an extremely harsh environment. The new walls were ultimately to enclose about 80 percent of the territory by mid-1987, but they neither achieved for King Hassan and his army a decisive victory in the war nor forced Polisario to abandon its military campaign, much less result in international acceptance of his conquest of Western Sahara.

The OAU's diplomatic efforts to end the war having come to naught due to the failure of its Implementation Committee and by the SADR membership imbroglio, attention was to shift toward the United Nations, whose efforts had been at a lower level since the events of 1974–76. This phase of the settlement effort, which extends from the end of 1985 to the time of writing, may possibly have begun at the instigation of the Moroccans, who saw the UN as a more hospitable forum than the OAU and thus as a vehicle for recouping lost diplomatic prestige. Early in 1986, the UN secretary-general, Javier Pérez de Cuéllar, announced plans to hold indirect "proximity" talks with Morocco and Polisario. In April and May 1986, two rounds of such discussions took place in New York but made no substantial progress. Although no doubt disappointed, the secretary-general began preliminary work on a comprehensive UN peace proposal, and in 1987 he sent the under-secretary-general for special political questions, Abderrahim Farah, to northwest Africa to solicit support for an overall settlement and propose a visit to Western Sahara by a UN-OAU technical mission so it could survey the situation in the territory preparatory to a plebiscite. After a certain amount of hesitation on the part of both Morocco and the Polisario Front, the technical team, composed of both civilian and military personnel, toured the region in November and December 1987. However, Morocco and Polisario remained far apart. Morocco refused to accept Polisario's calls for direct negotiations, and the two sides disagreed over the scale of the Moroccan forces that could remain in the territory during the period leading up to the referendum. Such issues would have to be resolved before a UN-OAU interim administration could finally arrive in Western Sahara and organize a referendum. Without this (or a drastic internal political change in either Morocco, Algeria, or Polisario itself), the UN's diplomatic efforts ultimately could not succeed.

Just such a political change seemed imminent to some observers in May 1988. Following a gradual thaw during the mid-1980s, Algeria announced that it was resuming diplomatic relations with Morocco after a 12-year break caused by Algeria's recognition of the SADR in 1976. Since the state most closely associated with Polisario's efforts to win independence for Western Sahara had chosen rapprochement with Morocco, the front's adversary and occupier of the Sahara, many saw the move as portending a cutback of Algerian assistance to the Saharawis, or even its complete cessation, perhaps to concentrate on addressing North Africa's serious economic and social problems. However, this did not happen; there was little if any diminution in Algerian material aid to Polisario following the resumption of relations. The Algerians and the Polisario Front both denied that any change of policy was contemplated, and a consensus of sorts emerged that Algiers was attempting to induce Morocco to use the new spirit of Maghrebi détente as a way to save face and engage in substantive negotiations with Polisario.

Pérez de Cuéllar saw opportunities in this new atmosphere of concord and redoubled his efforts to present a peace proposal to the parties for their perusal and comment. In two separate meetings with Moroccan and Polisario delegations on August 11, 1988, he formally presented the plan, which was accepted in principle by both sides on August 30. It called for a cease-fire, substantial troop withdrawal on the part of both combatants, and the insertion of UN civilian administrators and military forces to prepare for a referendum. The Saharawi voters would be given a choice between independence and integration with Morocco. The acceptance of Pérez de Cuéllar's blueprint was hailed as a major breakthrough in the long history of the dispute. In the months following the acceptance of the plan, however, the traditional pattern reasserted itself, with Morocco still reluctant to meet Polisario directly and with the Saharawi organization breaking a lull of some months by attacking Moroccan positions near Oum Dreiga in mid-September 1988, perhaps to show that it would not abandon its military option until its demand for negotiations was met. Facing pressure from many sources, King Hassan finally agreed to meet with Polisario representatives. The front announced a unilateral cease-fire in December and sent three of its top leaders to meet King Hassan in January 1989 in Marrakesh.

This further raised hopes for peace, but 1989 turned out to be much like other years; the January Marrakesh meeting was not to be repeated. King Hassan stated that he met the Polisario leaders only because, as he put it, they were citizens who had "gone astray" and because the king wanted to induce them to return to the Moroccan fold. In reaction to this, the Saharawi guerrillas renewed their attacks against Morocco's defensive walls, inflicting significant casualties. A personal visit to the region by Pérez de Cuéllar in June, moreover, failed to produce any progress to speak of, and the secretary-general had to content himself with further refining his 1988 plan. But to keep the process alive, he did get the parties to agree early in 1990 to refrain from further military actions. This de facto cease-fire was to hold throughout the year.

Further steps were taken by the UN to pave the way for an eventual settlement if and when the parties agreed to negotiate with one another. Pérez de Cuéllar announced in March that Morocco had accepted in principle the prospect of withdrawing a substantial number of troops from Western Sahara in advance of a plebiscite. In January, Pérez de Cuéllar appointed a new special representative for Western Sahara, Johannes Manz, who stayed active by working to compile a credible list of Saharawis eligible to vote in the referendum, a daunting task. To that end, a meeting of tribal elders and chiefs from both the Moroccan-held zone and the Polisario camps in Algeria took place in early June in Geneva with UN officials present.

Later that month, Pérez de Cuéllar formally presented a detailed plan to the UN Security Council on the proposed referendum and its modalities, to be conducted under the auspices of a body known as the United Nations Mission for the Referendum in Western Sahara (MINURSO) made up of civilian and military personnel from the UN's member states. On June 27, another diplomatic watershed was reached when the Security Council unanimously passed resolution 658, approving the secretary-general's report. The resolution asked for further refinement of the plan, including a cost estimate, and gave approval for a second technical mission to be sent to Western Sahara (which was done in July and August). Armed with this mandate, Pérez de Cuéllar once again tried to reconcile the parties in Geneva in July, but Morocco continued to reject direct negotiations with the Saharawi nationalists. Further efforts by the secretary-general had to be postponed due to Iraq's invasion of Kuwait in August and the heavy demands placed on the United Nations by that crisis and by the subsequent Gulf war. And when the process finally began, in September 1991, a variety of political and logistical difficulties made themselves apparent, further slowing the process. As this book went to press, in late 1993, it was still too early to predict whether, or how soon, UN efforts to negotiate a peaceful settlement of the Western Sahara conflict might finally yield tangible results.

THE DICTIONARY

- A -

AAIUN see EL-AYOUN

ABD see SLAVERY

ABDELAZIZ, MOULAY, SULTAN OF MOROCCO. Ruler of Morocco from 1894 to 1908, he supported the attempts by Cheikh Ma el-Ainin (q.v.) to stem the French advance northward into the Sahara from southern Mauritania. When he ascended the throne at the age of 14, at a time of mounting pressure on Morocco from the European powers, he came under considerable influence from Ma el-Ainin, who had been appointed *khalifa,* or deputy, in the Sahara by his father, Moulay Hassan I (q.v.), and was to visit Abdelaziz seven times during his reign. On the first occasion, Abdelaziz provided Ma el-Ainin with a consignment of arms, which were shipped from Mogador to Tarfaya, and, when Ma el-Ainin began the construction of Smara (q.v.) in 1898, Abdelaziz supplied craftsmen and building materials. In 1905, he sent his uncle, Moulay Idriss Ben Abderrahman Ben Souleiman, to Smara to aid Ma el-Ainin's *jihad* against the French. However, he recalled Idriss to Morocco in May 1907 under French diplomatic pressure, an example of his tendency toward compromise with the colonial powers—a failing that provoked a revolt against his rule in September 1907, led by his brother Moulay Hafid in favor of whom he abdicated in 1908. Ma el-Ainin supported the revolt.

ABDELKADER TALEB OMAR. One of the top leaders of the Polisario Front (q.v.), he was appointed to the front's political bureau (q.v.) at its 4th congress, held in September

21

1978. At Polisario's 5th congress (October 12–16, 1982), he was appointed to the council of ministers of the Saharan Arab Democratic Republic (qq.v.), assuming the interior portfolio. In a reshuffle of the SADR's government, announced on August 16, 1988, Abdelkader left the interior ministry and was appointed minister of equipment and transport. He held this post only briefly, however, as he was appointed minister of information and culture at Polisario's 7th congress, held on April 28–May 1, 1989. He held the information portfolio until the front's 8th congress, held in June 1991, when he was named minister of interior.

ABDELLAHI OULD CHEIKH. A leading member of the Parti du Peuple Mauritanien (q.v.), he was Mauritania's deputy governor of Western Sahara during the period of tripartite administration (q.v.) after the Madrid Agreement (q.v.) of November 14, 1975. Arriving in El-Ayoun (q.v.) on November 27, he worked alongside a Moroccan deputy governor and the Spanish governor-general until the final Spanish withdrawal at the end of February 1976. He had been Mauritania's minister of trade and transport until 1975, when he became minister of labor and public works, a post which he retained while deputy governor of Western Sahara. He left the Mauritanian government in August 1977.

ABDERRAHMAN OULD ABDELLAHI. One of the first leaders of the Polisario Front (q.v.), he was active in the guerrilla war against Spain, which the movement launched in May 1973. The movement's second martyr, he was killed in the battle of Aoukeyra on March 13, 1974.

ABDERRAHMAN OULD LEIBAK. A native of Dakhla (q.v.), he was born in 1948 and was one of the first Saharawis to receive higher education, becoming a mining engineer for the phosphate-mining company Fosbucraa (qq.v.). In 1975 he joined the pro-Moroccan Front de Libération et de l'Unité (q.v.), being elected to its executive committee at its first congress in Agadir on September 13–14, 1975. On June 3, 1977, he was elected as Istiqlal (q.v.) deputy for Boudjour (q.v.) in the Moroccan parliamentary elections and, on

January 2, 1979, he was appointed governor of the province (q.v.) of Boujdour by King Hassan II (q.v.). However, taking advantage of a trip to Spain, he suddenly defected from the Moroccan cause, flying to Algeria, where he announced his support for the Polisario Front (q.v.) on February 1, 1979.

ABID see SLAVERY

ABROUQ, MOHAMMED. Col. Mohammed Abrouq was appointed chief of staff of the Moroccan forces in Western Sahara on March 12, 1979, replacing Col. Abdelaziz Bennani (q.v.) after a humiliating attack on Tan-Tan by the Polisario Front (q.v.) on January 28, 1979. He was the fifth officer to take on the command of the Moroccan troops in the Sahara since the start of the war in 1975. Later in the year, Abrouq lost his overall command when the unified general staff in the Sahara was replaced by a more decentralized command structure. He was then given command of the Zellagha force (q.v.), which was severely mauled in the Ouarkziz Mountains during Operation Iman (q.v.) in March 1980.

ADRAR SOUTOUF. A mountain range in the extreme south of the country.

AFKHAD. Plural of *fakhd* (q.v.).

AFRA. Plural of *fara* (q.v.)

AFRICA OCCIDENTAL ESPANOLA. On July 20, 1946, a Spanish decree established Spanish West Africa, incorporating Ifni and Western Sahara. Previously (since 1934), both territories had been assimilated administratively into the Spanish protectorate zone of Morocco, a setup that proved inconvenient to Madrid after World War II, when Moroccan nationalism became a powerful force. AOE had its own governor-general (q.v.), resident in Sidi Ifni, with a *subgobernador* (q.v.) in Western Sahara. The governor-general was directly responsible to the presidency of the government in Madrid, through the Dirección General de

Marruecos y Colonias (q.v.). In the Tekna Zone (q.v.), the northernmost strip of Spain's Saharan territory, which was considered part of Spain's protectorate zone in Morocco, the governor-general acted as *delegado* (q.v.) of the Spanish high commissioner in Morroco. AOE was dissolved in 1958, when Western Sahara and Ifni were converted into two Spanish provinces (January 10) and the Tekna Zone was ceded to Morocco by the Agreement of Cintra (q.v.) in April.

AGADIR SUMMIT (July 23–24, 1973). A summit meeting between King Hassan II, President Houari Boumedienne, and President Mokhtar Ould Daddah (qq.v.) in the Moroccan city of Agadir, it was the second of such summits devoted to the Western Saharan problem, the first having been held in Nouadhibou (q.v.) in September 1970. A joint communiqué stated that the three heads of state ''reaffirmed their unwavering attachment to the principle of self-determination and their concern that this principle was implemented in a framework which guaranteed that the will of the inhabitants was given free and genuine expression, in conformity with the UN decisions on this question.'' King Hassan's unequivocal support for self-determination aroused opposition from such hard-line Moroccan nationalists as the Istiqlal Party (q.v.), but the king, who knew that Algeria and Mauritania would not support an outright Moroccan claim to Western Sahara, apparently believed at the time that the Saharawis would be likely to opt for integration with Morocco. Little was done by the three heads of state to bring pressure to bear on Spain after the summit, but when, a year after the summit, King Hassan dropped the self-determination line and insisted on outright annexation, he was accused by both Algeria and the Polisario Front (q.v.) of reneging on the stand he took there.

AGRICULTURE. Agriculture has never been more than marginal to the Western Saharan economy. Soil conditions are poor, there is very little water (and what there is often contains too much salt), and there are such additional impediments as locusts and sandstorms. Traditionally, moreover, Saharawis tended to despise agricultural work, considering it fit only for slaves (q.v.). There are no real oases, Spanish statistics indicating that there are less than 4,000 palm trees in the entire country. The main crop, grown in very small quantities, is barley. The area sown has rarely exceeded 1,000 ha. and was only 600 ha. in 1976. The record annual crop (1974) was 7,000 tons of barley and 210 tons of wheat. Traditionally, barley was grown in water-collecting depressions, known as *graras* (q.v.), the grain being stored in collective granaries. The bulk of cereal needs was, and still is, imported. The country may have better agricultural prospects if underground water sources are tapped on a large scale. In 1963, Spanish geologists discovered one of the world's largest subterranean freshwater lakes near Dakhla (q.v.).

AGUERA see LA GUERA

AHEL. An Arabic term for "people." Thus, the Ahel es-Sahel are the people of the Sahel; the Ahel Cheikh Ma el-Ainin are the descendants of Ma el-Ainin (qq.v.).

AHEL BERIKALLAH. A *zawiya* tribe, the Ahel Berikallah traditionally lived mainly in Mauritania, but some have lived in the far south of Western Sahara. A total of 1,810 were counted there in the 1974 Spanish census, which generally underestimated the population.

AHEL BRAHIM OU DAOUD. One of the most important Reguibat groups, they are a subtribe of the Reguibat es-Sahel (q.v.). Their numbers inside Western Sahara in 1974, according to the Spanish census of that year, which generally underestimated the nomadic population, were almost 8,000, more than half of them settled in El-Ayoun, Smara, and some of the smaller townships of the Saguia el-Hamra (qq.v.). Traditionally, their zone of nomadism had extended from the Saguia el-Hamra in the north to Bir Moghrein, Mauritania, in the south, and from Smara and Guelta Zemmour to the hammada (q.v.).

The Ahel Brahim Ou Daoud claim to be the descendants of Qacem, one of the three sons of Sidi Ahmed Reguibi, the supposed common ancestor of the Reguibat. Their principal fractions are the Ahel Sidi Allal, Ahel Belqacem Ou Brahim,

Sellam, Selalka, Ahel Lahsen Ou Hamad, Lehmeidenet, Oulad Sidi Hamad, and Jenha.

AHEL CHEIKH MA EL-AININ. The descendants of Cheikh Ma el-Ainin (q.v.), the principal leader of the anticolonial resistance in the 1890s and 1900s. They have formed a small, prestigious tribe of their own. Ma el-Ainin had 33 sons, of whom the most celebrated were Ahmed el-Hiba, El-Oueli, Merebbi Rebbu, and Mohammed Laghdaf, who also played important roles in the anticolonial struggle. Ma el-Ainin's descendants settled in Morocco and Mauritania as well as Western Sahara, where the Spanish authorities counted 363 members of the family in their last census in 1974. With an illustrious past, a claim to cherifian ancestry and a reputation for learnedness, the family has had considerable prestige in Morocco and Mauritania as well as in Western Sahara.

AHEL ES-SAHEL. The people of the west, or littoral, of the desert, this was a collective name for the Saharawis of the Western Sahara. In a more restricted sense, it referred to the small fishing tribes of the coast.

AHMED BABA MISKE. Once a leading Mauritanian politician and diplomat, Ahmed Baba Miske threw in his lot with the Polisario Front (q.v.) in 1975, in opposition to the Moroccan-Mauritanian plans to annex and partition the territory. Born in c. 1932–33 in the Tiris region of northern Mauritania, his tribe of origin was the Ahel Berikallah (q.v.), who traditionally straddle the Western Saharan-Mauritanian border. After his primary and secondary education in Mauritania, he studied at the University of Dakar and then went to France. He became a leader of the most militant anti-French movement, An-Nahda al-Wataniya al-Mauritaniya (Mauritanian National Awakening), which was founded in 1958 and opposed Mauritanian participation in the French Community in the September 1958 referendum. The party was banned on the eve of Mauritania's first National Assembly elections in May 1959, and Ahmed Baba Miske, along with other Nahda leaders, was arrested and detained in the eastern Hodh. After Mauritania's independence (November 28, 1960), he was released from detention (February 1961), and a process of reconciliation began between President Mokhtar Ould Daddah (q.v.) and the Nahda leaders, culminating in a roundtable conference on October 4, 1961, that led to the fusion of the country's four main parties into a single party, the PPM (December 12, 1961). Ahmed Baba Miske became the PPM's organizational strongman, as party secretary. This allowed him to build up a power base within the party apparatus (1961–64), but in 1964, Ould Daddah attempted to curtail his growing influence by posting him abroad, as ambassador to the U.S. and permanent representative at the UN. Recalled home in 1966, he was arrested on corruption charges, but after one month in jail, he was acquitted and went into exile for more than 12 years. He lived mainly in Paris in this period and founded the magazine *Africasia*.

Years later, in 1974–75, when Mokhtar Ould Daddah decided to abandon Mauritania's claim to the whole of Western Sahara in favor of partition with Morocco, Ahmed Baba Miske accused Ould Daddah of betraying the Western Saharans and encouraging Moroccan nationalists who had not forgotten the old Moroccan claim to Mauritania. "Mauritania has no interest in aiding the dismembering of the Sahara and the dispersal of its people," he wrote in an open letter to the PPM's 4th congress (August 15–20, 1975). "Not only would that be to fail gravely in the duty of solidarity toward its kin: but, in abetting annexationism between neighbors, it would create for itself a dangerous precedent, of which it runs a strong risk of being the next selected victim." At about this time, he joined the Polisario Front, moving from Paris to Algiers, where he became a prominent spokesman for the movement in the crisis months at the end of 1975. He was elected to the front's political bureau (q.v.) at its 3rd congress (August 26–30, 1976), and wrote a book to popularize the Saharawi cause (see Bibliography). However, his attention shifted once again to the Mauritanian political scene after the military coup of July 10, 1978. He was not reelected to the political bureau at the front's fourth congress (September 25–28, 1978). After reentering Mauritania's confused political scene, he was detained in December 1980, allegedly having participated in a "Libyan plot" against the ruling Comité Militaire de Salut National (q.v.), then headed by Mohammed Khouna Ould Heydallah (q.v.). He was freed on March 3, 1981, and for a time devoted himself to his business interests. However, Ahmed Baba Miské continued to drift away from his previous pro-Polisario stance, apparently objecting to Ould Heydallah's decision in February 1984 to recognize the Saharan Arab Democratic Republic (q.v.). On April 24, 1984, he was arrested by the government, probably as part of a sweep by the CMSN against Libyan influences. Libya was at this time moving closer to Morocco, and its agents were active in the CMSN's Mass Education Structures (SEM) in the country. He was not freed until a general amnesty for political detainees was declared by Ould Heydallah's successor, Colonel Maaouiya Ould Sid 'Ahmed Taya (q.v.). Once freed from detention (on December 16, 1984), Ahmed Baba Miské publicly praised Ould Taya's more neutral stance on the Western Sahara conflict.

AHMED EL-HIBA. A son of Cheikh Ma el-Ainin (q.v.), he was one of the leaders of the anticolonial resistance in both the Sahara and Morocco at the beginning of this century. Born in c. 1875, he was named as Ma el-Ainin's successor by the *cheikh*'s supporters after his death at Tiznit in 1910. El-Hiba appointed his brother Merebbi Rebbu as his *khalifa,* or deputy. In the summer of 1912, his followers proclaimed him sultan of Morocco after the imposition of the Franco-Spanish protectorate (March 1912). With an army of 15,000 Saharawis and Berbers from the Souss and the Anti-Atlas, El-Hiba and Merebbi Rebbu marched on Marrakesh, which they entered in August, imprisoning the French officials they found there. However the "blue sultan," as he was later to be known, was forced to abandon Marrakesh and seek refuge in the Souss when his army was decisively defeated at Sidi Bou Othman on September 6, 1912, by a French force led by Col. Mangin, who entered Marrakesh the next day. From Taroudant, El-Hiba continued the resistance struggle in the Souss. However, French forces occupied Taroudant on May 23, 1913, and Agadir on May 31, 1913. The southern Souss was brought under French control in 1914. In September 1915, El-Hiba took refuge in the Anti-Atlas. During World War I, the Germans tried to make contact with him to provide arms for his struggle against the French. In 1916, a German UC20 submarine surfaced in the mouth of the Oued Draa after a 30-day voyage from Heligoland, with a consignment of arms and, in the hands of a Turkish officer, a message from the Ottoman sultan. However, the crew was in difficulty and could land only some of the arms before going for help to Tarfaya (q.v.), where the Spanish authorities detained them and sent them to the Canaries. Very little German aid reached El-Hibá before the end of the war. El-Hiba died in the Anti-Atlas on May 23, 1919.

AHMED MOHAMMED MAHMOUD, SIDI. A leader of the Polisario Front (q.v.), he was elected president of the Saharawi National Council (q.v.) after its creation as a legislative and consultative assembly of the SADR (q.v.) by the front's 3rd congress, in August 1976. Although he was replaced in this position subsequently, he was elected to the front's political bureau (q.v.) at Polisario's 6th congress, held in December 1985. He retained his place on the political bureau at the 7th congress in April-May 1989, and, as of 1990, was the front's representative to the Arab countries.

AHMED OULD BOUCEIF. Born in 1934 at Kiffa (Mauritania), he was one of Mauritania's senior military commanders during the war with the Polisario Front (q.v.). He entered the Mauritanian army in 1962 and trained in France. On June 24, 1976, President Mokhtar Ould Daddah (q.v.) appointed him chief of staff of the armed forces, to coordinate the war against the Polisario guerrillas. He was promoted to the rank of lieutenant colonel the following October. After a devastating Polisario attack on Zouerate (q.v.) on May 1, 1977, he was appointed commander of the 2nd military region (Zouerate) on July 15; the defense minster, Col. M'Barek Ould Mohammed Bouna Mokhtar (q.v.), became chief of staff. In his new post, he was responsible for planning the resistance to the increasingly audacious Polisario attacks against the vital Zouerate-Nouadhibou railway (q.v.) at this time. Like other Mauritanian officers, he gradually became convinced of the need to restore peace. He supported the military coup that toppled the Ould Daddah regime on July 10, 1978, and was appointed minister of fishing and industry in the new military regime headed by President Mustapha Ould Mohammed Salek (q.v.). He held this post until April 6, 1979, when, as a result of factional infighting in the ruling Comité Militaire de Redressement National (q.v.), he became prime minister in a bloodless palace coup that reduced Mustapha Ould Mohammed Salek to titular president without real powers and replaced the CMRN with a new Comité Militaire de Salut National (q.v.), of which he became first vice president. Though he did not order the immediate withdrawal of the several thousand Moroccan troops still in Mauritania, he continued to search for a way to extract Mauritania from the Western Saharan conflict. During his brief leadership of the country, the guerrillas' unilateral cease-fire (declared on July 12, 1978) held, and his foreign minister, Ahmed Ould Abdallah, held talks with the Polisario Front in Tripoli on May 21–23, 1979. However, Ahmed Ould Bouceif died in an air crash near Dakar on May 27, 1979.

AHMED OULD BRAHIM OULD EL-BACHIR. Born on May 1, 1918, in El-Ayoun (q.v.), Ahmed Ould Brahim Ould el-Bachir became one of the most important traditional leaders to collaborate closely with the Spanish colonial authorities. A trader and a *cheikh* (q.v.) of the Izarguien (q.v.), he was a member of the Djemaa (q.v.) for several years, until its dissolution after the Madrid Agreement (q.v.) in 1975. He was also a *procurador* (q.v.) in the Spanish Cortes in 1970–75, serving as a representative of "family interests" under the Francoist electoral system. He was a member of the Spanish-inspired PUNS (q.v.) after its founding in November 1974, and, like other Saharawi members of the Djemaa and the Cortes, he was a vocal opponent of the Moroccan claim to Western Sahara. On July 12, 1975, an explosive device attached to his car blew up, killing his eight-year-old son. Polisario emblems were later found at the site of the explosion, but the attack was widely believed to have been part of an attempt by the pro-Moroccan FLU (q.v.) to increase friction between the PUNS and the Polisario

Front (q.v.). After the Madrid Agreement, he attended the meeting of the Djemaa, held under Polisario auspices on November 28, which issued the Proclamation of Guelta Zemmour (q.v.), dissolving the Djemaa and establishing a pro-Polisario Provisional Saharawi National Council (q.v.). He spent a few weeks with the front and visited President Houari Boumedienne (q.v.) in Algeria in December 1975, but shortly afterward, he decided to switch his allegiance to Morocco, where he arrived to make the traditional act of allegiance, the *bayaa* (q.v.), to King Hassan II (q.v.) on January 14, 1976. He then took part in the rump Djemaa meeting on February 26, which approved the territory's integration with Morocco and Mauritania. On November 12, 1976, he was elected to the municipal council of El-Ayoun, of which he then became president. On June 21, 1977, he was elected to the Moroccan Chamber of Representatives in the indirect stage of Morocco's general elections, being selected by the provincial assembly of the province of El-Ayoun. His loyalty to Morocco since 1976 appears to have mirrored that which he gave to Spain in earlier years.

AHMED OULD CAID. A veteran of the Saharawi anticolonial movement, he joined the Army of Liberation (q.v.) in 1957 and took part in its guerrilla campaign against Spain and France in 1957–58. Later he joined the Harakat Tahrir Saguia el-Hamra wa Oued ed-Dahab (q.v.) in the late sixties, and, after the massacre of Zemla (q.v.) on June 17, 1970, he was imprisoned, first in the Canary Islands and then in Dakhla (q.v.). He was released in 1971 and became one of the first militants of the Polisario Front (q.v.) after its founding in 1973. He was one of the front's political bureau members who met the UN Visiting Mission (q.v.) during its tour of Saharawi camps in the Tindouf (q.v.) region of Algeria in May 1974. He was also one of the front's leading military commanders during its 1973–75 war with Spain and in the early stages of the later war with Morocco and Mauritania. He was not included in the political bureau elected at the front's 4th congress in September 1978 but served as deputy *wali* of the SADR's *wilaya* (qq.v.) of Smara in the late 1970s and early 1980s. Since 1982, he has been

adviser for social affairs to the SADR's president, Mohammed Abdelaziz (q.v.).

AHMED OULD RACHID. Pseudonym of Bachir Figuigui, leader
of the AOSARIO (q.v.).

AIDAR. A mountainous region, about 100 km. long, which
straddles the border between Western Sahara and Morocco.
To the north, in Morocco, are the Zini mountains; to the
west, along the border, is the plateau of El-Gaada (q.v.); to
the east is the *Hammada* (q.v.). Its accessibility for vehicles
is difficult.

AIN BEN TILI CONFERENCE (OCTOBER 12, 1975). A conference held under the auspices of the Polisario Front but
involving many of the country's most prominent traditional
tribal leaders, it took place four days before King Hassan II's
announcement of the Green March (qq.v.) and was intended to
unite Saharawis of diverse political backgrounds behind the
Polisario Front to meet the growing threat from Morocco. The
conference, which was attended by such prominent *chioukh* as
Saila Ould Abeida, a member of the Cortes, as well as by the
Polisario Front's deputy secretary-general, Mahfoud Ali Beiba
(q.v.), reflected the front's success at this time in rallying the
support of traditional leaders who had previously cooperated
closely with the Spanish colonial authorities and given support
to the PUNS (q.v.). This was due to the disintegration of the
PUNS (whose leaders were engaged in concurrent talks with
Polisario leaders), the rapprochement between Spain and the
Polisario Front at this time, and the widespread feeling of a
need to close ranks against the threat of Moroccan invasion.
This rallying of the traditionalists behind the Polisario banner
culminated in the dissolution of the PUNS early in November
and the dissolution of the Djemaa at Guelta Zemmour (q.v.) on
November 28.

AINI SAYED see MOHAMMED OULD SIDATI

AIT ARBAIN. The *ait arbain* (assembly of 40) was normally a
tribal council, set up in time of war or to organize a *ghazzi*

(q.v.). It is to be distinguished from the more usual peacetime assembly, the *djemaa* (q.v.), which was usually held at fraction or subfraction level. Its name is Berber in origin, suggesting the retention of a pre-Arab political institution—which was, in fact, also found among the Moroccan Berbers of the Souss, the Anti-Atlas, and the Rif. Among Saharawi tribes that are known to have had such a body are the Reguibat and the Izarguien (q.v.), the two largest in Western Sahara. In both cases, it was presided by a *moqadem.* The ait arbain appointed the *dahman,* the leader of the troops entrusted with the tribe's defense or the execution of a ghazzi, and sometimes appointed an ambassador, or *sorba,* to engage in peace negotiations.

AIT LAHSEN. Along with the Izarguien (q.v.), the Ait Lahsen are the main Tekna (q.v.) group to be found in Western Sahara. Their traditional zone of nomadism extended from the Oued Noun region of southern Morocco along the coast to the Saguia el-Hamra (q.v.). Though some Ait Lahsen were traditionally sedentary in southern Morocco, the majority were nomadic. The tribe's fractions are the Injouren, the Ait Bou Meghout, the Ait Yahya, the Rouimiat, the Ait Bou Guezzaten, the Ait Hassein, the Ait Saad, and the Id Daoud Ou Abdallah. By means of the *debiha,* a number of fractions of the Reguibat (q.v.) and other tribes traditionally enjoyed friendly relations with the Ait Lahsen and gained their protection when migrating north of the Saguia el-Hamra into Tekna territory to seek pasturage or visit the markets of the Oued Draa (q.v.) and the Oued Noun.

The origins of the Ait Lahsen, like those of most Saharawi tribes, are shrouded in myth. According to legend, the tribe's founder was a 16th-century fugitive from a Moroccan sultan, known by the Saharawis as Sultan El-Kahal. The legend, which is typical of a number of stories illustrating the role of the desert as a place of sanctuary and refuge, has it that a mischievous child in Tafilalet (southeast Morocco) was sentenced by the sultan to have his hand amputated and, to avoid the punishment, was taken by his mother to the region of the Oued Chebeika, to the southwest of the Oued Draa, where they met and requested protection from Sidi Ahmed

Reguibi, the saintly founder of the Reguibat (q.v.). However, a little later, Sultan El-Kahal is said to have arrived in person in Farsia (q.v.), meeting Sidi Ahmed Reguibi and demanding a pile of gold coins in return for the child's pardon. Sidi Ahmed, it is said, threw to the ground the only three gold coins in his *draa* (q.v.). Instantly, they were transformed into a heap of gold coins. The child was free, and he went on to engender the Ait Lahsen.

The Ait Lahsen became the leading tribe in the Ait Jmel, one of the two rival blocs of Tekna tribes. Thus, in 1907, the Ait Lahsen played a prominent part, along with the Izarguien and the Ait Moussa ou Ali, in a war with the Azouafid, one of the leading tribes of the rival Ait Atman, which was sparked off by an Azouafid *ghazzi* (q.v.) against the Izarguien. As the war developed, it spread north as far as Ifni, as each side sought and won allies, even among the sedentary Berbers, whose own divisions were exploited by the warring Tekna.

Earlier, at the end of the 19th century, the Ait Lahsen had been at war with the Reguibat and the Oulad Tidrarin (qq.v.), notwithstanding their esteem for Sidi Ahmed Reguibi (without whom, as the legend has it, the Ait Lahsen would not exist at all) and the traditional protection pacts between them and several Reguibat fractions. It was in 1888 that the Oulad Delim, badly mauled by a joint ghazzi of Reguibat and Oulad Tidrarin, persuaded the Ait Lahsen to join their struggle. The Ait Lahsen aided the Oulad Delim until the end of the war in 1892.

After the imposition of colonial rule, the ghazzis halted, and in the 1960s and 1970s, most of the Ait Lahsen settled in the small towns growing up in southern Morocco, notably Tan-Tan and in Western Sahara. The 1974 Spanish census, which generally underestimated the Saharawi population, counted about 3,500 Ait Lahsen in the territory, about two thirds of them in the capital, El-Ayoun (q.v.).

AIT OUSSA. One of the main tribes of the Tekna (q.v.), the Ait Oussa live primarily in the extreme south of Morocco, but in the old nomadic days they would also migrate south into what is now Western Sahara, on to the *hammada* (q.v.) in search of pastures. A partly sedentary, though primarily nomadic, tribe in these times, their center was Assa, an oasis town in the valley of the Oued Draa (q.v.), whose *moussem,* or annual fair, is one of the most important in southern Morocco. The palm groves at Assa were worked by black *haratin* (q.v.). The Ait Oussa also had buildings at Aouinet Ait Oussa, which was used mainly as a storage center. Their nomadic wanderings would take them throughout the lower Draa valley, the Ouarkziz mountains and the hammada.

Their alliances and conflicts with other Saharawi tribes were determined by shifting circumstances. With the Reguibat, tension and conflict alternated with mutual assistance and protection. Reguibat fractions needed the protection of the Ait Oussa and other Tekna tribes to get to the Tekna-controlled markets of the Oued Draa and the Oued Noun, and they made pacts with the Ait Oussa and other Tekna in order to be able to do so. Reciprocally, the Ait Oussa sometimes required tacit Reguibat agreement to be able to drive their herds south on to the hammada. However, there was also a history of reciprocal camel-raiding between the Ait Oussa and the Reguibat.

As a result of the expedition to Tiznit by Moulay Hassan I (q.v.) in 1882, the Ait Oussa accepted the nomination of caids (q.v.) for their tribe by the sultan, but these were chiefs already recognized by the tribe, and their formal allegiance to the Alawite (q.v.) sultan did not prevent them from joining the Reguibat in 1895 to sack Tindouf (q.v.), the center of the Tadjakant, another tribe which at this time recognized the sultan's sovereignty. In 1907, the Ait Oussa went to war with the Reguibat, aiding the Oulad Bou Sbaa (q.v.) in their long conflict with the Reguibat.

Until some time in the 19th century the Ait Oussa were part of the Ait Jmel bloc of Tekna tribes. However, after a dispute with the Ait Lahsen (q.v.), they deserted the Ait Jmel alliance to join the rival Ait Atman bloc, giving it a strong nomadic element for the first time. Thereafter they were repeatedly in conflict with the Ait Lahsen and the Izarguien until the mid-1930's. Toward the end of this period, when the French protectorate government in Morocco began to extend its control to the valley of the Draa, the Ait Oussa and the French allied to advance their mutual interests. With French encouragement, they staged *ghazzis* (q.v.) against the Reguibat, the Oulad Delim, and the Oulad Bou Sbaa (qq.v.) in 1934. In the same year, they also staged their last ghazzi against the Izarguien, to avenge heavy losses inflicted on them by the Izarguien in 1929. Setting out from Assa, the Ait Oussa attacked the Izarguien at Tarfaya (q.v.), then a Spanish post. The Spanish soldiers there watched as the two tribes fought it out, until, when the Spanish mail plane arrived on the horizon, the Ait Oussa fled, fearing they were about to be bombed.

Along with the Reguibat and other Saharawis, the Ait Oussa played a prominent part in the Army of Liberation (q.v.) in 1957–58. Thereafter many joined the FAR (q.v.). Their center of Assa, which had been in the French zone, became part of independent Morocco in 1956, and most of their traditional grazing lands had become Moroccan by 1958 as a result of Spain's cession of the Tekna Zone (q.v.), though some Ait Oussa still migrated into the Spanish zone and some settled in the Spanish-ruled territory. Friction between the Ait Oussa and the Reguibat was reported in the 1960s, a factor that seems to have played a role in encouraging a large part of the tribe to side with the Moroccan government against the Polisario Front (q.v.) in 1975. In this they were almost alone among the large Saharawi tribes. They have furnished many of the Moroccan army's best desert troops.

ALAWITES. The dynasty that has ruled Morocco since the mid-17th century. In precolonial times, only three of the Alawite sultans—Moulay Rachid, Moulay Ismail, and Moulay Hassan I (qq.v.)—really attempted to pursue active Saharan policies. The others were too preoccupied with fending off external threats, palace rivals, or dissident Moroccan tribes of the *bilad es-siba* (q.v.) to be able to attempt an active policy in the western Sahara. Moulay Ismail (1672–1727), the most powerful of the Alawite sultans, sent expeditions to parts of Mauritania, probably skirting the present Western Sahara in order to recruit slaves for his *abid* (slave) army. After his death, Morocco was plunged into anarchy, and for 120 years, from the 1760s until 1882, the Alawite sultans were unable to control the Oued Noun (then part of the bilad es-siba), to the north of Western Sahara. Moulay Hassan I (1873–94) brought the Oued Noun back under the control of the *makhzen,* the sultanate's government, as a result of two expeditions there in 1882 and 1886, but failed to extend his authority to most of the Western Saharan tribes. Sultan Moulay Abdelaziz (q.v.) sent limited military support to Cheikh Ma el-Ainin (q.v.) in 1905–6 to support the *cheikh*'s struggle against the French. After Morocco's independence, King Mohammed V (q.v.), formally endorsed the Moroccan nationalists' claim to Western Sahara, as well as Mauritania and much of the Algerian Sahara, and the claim was upheld by his son, Hassan II (q.v.), after Mohammed V's death in 1961.

AL-CHAAB. A clandestine journal published by Saharawi nationalists in southern Morocco in 1973, *Al-Chaab* (*The People*) was edited by Bachir Mustapha Sayed (q.v.), a future leader of the Polisario Front (q.v.).

AL-CHIHAB. *Al-Chihab* (*The Torch*) was a Saharawi nationalist and cultural journal, which was published for several months in Rabat, Morocco in 1967. Its editor was Mohammed Sidi Ibrahim Bassiri (q.v.), the future leader of the Harakat Tahrir Saguia el-Hamra wa Oued ed-Dahab (q.v.).

AL-CHIRAH. A bulletin produced by Saharawi students in Rabat, Morocco, in 1970, *Al-Chirah* (*The Consensus*) reflected the views of the students who formed the "embryonic movement for the liberation of the Sahara" (q.v.) in 1971–72.

ALGIERS AGREEMENT (AUGUST 5, 1979). An agreement between the Polisario Front (q.v.) and Mauritania, which finally ended Mauritania's involvement in the Western Saharan war. The agreement stated notably that "the Islamic Republic of Mauritania solemnly declares that it does not have and will not have territorial or any other claims over Western Sahara" and that "the Islamic Republic of Mauritania decides to withdraw from the unjust war in Western Sahara." This amounted to the renunciation by Mauritania of its claim to Tiris el-Gharbia (q.v.), the sector of the territory it had received under the April 1976 partition treaty with Morocco. A secret part of the agreement, which was published several weeks later, added that "the Islamic Republic of Mauritania undertakes to put an end to its presence in Western Sahara and to hand over directly to the Polisario Front the part of Western Sahara that it controls within 7 months from the date of the signing of the present agreement." In fact, this never happened. On August 12, 1979, Moroccan troops took control of Dakhla (q.v.), and on August 14, Morocco unilaterally annexed Tiris el-Gharbia, declaring it to be the Moroccan province of Oued ed-Dahab (q.v.).

AL-HIZB AL-MOUSLIM. The Muslim Party. A name sometimes given to the Harakat Tahrir Saguia el-Hamra wa Oued ed-Dahab (q.v.).

ALI OULD MAHMOUD. A leader of the Polisario Front (q.v.), he was the first president of the Saharawi Red Crescent (q.v.) after its founding in 1975. He played an important part in assisting the thousands of refugees who fled from Western Sahara to Algeria in 1975–76. After the front's 4th congress, in September 1978, he became a member of the SADR's council of ministers (qq.v.) with the post of secretary-general of the ministry of education. The post's title was later changed to minister of education. He held this position until Polisario's 5th congress (October 12–16, 1982), when he was replaced by Mohammed Lamine Ould Ahmed (q.v.). In 1990, he was serving as the front's representative in Austria.

AL-JANOUB AL-MUNADIL. *Al-Janoub al-Munadil* (*The Fighting South*) was an anticolonial journal published clandestinely by students in El-Ayoun (q.v.) in 1972.

AL-MASSIRA AL-KHADRA. Arabic for the Green March (q.v.).

ALMONTE, ENRIQUE D'. Following a scientific expedition to Western Sahara in October 1913 on behalf of the Sociedad de Geografía de Madrid, d'Almonte made a series of recommendations regarding Spanish policy in Western Sahara, notably the installation of the capital at El-Ayoun (q.v.)—and a policy of indirect rule through influential local leaders like Ahmed el-Hiba (q.v.).

ALMORAVIDS. A religious movement that rallied the Sanhaja (q.v.) nomads in the 11th century and led to the founding of an empire that, in theory, stretched from the Senegal River to Spain.

When the founder of the Almoravid movement, the Soussi preacher Abdallah Ibn Yacin, arrived in the Sahara in c. 1039 at the invitation of Yahya Ibn Ibrahim, a chief of the Gadala, one of the Sanhaja tribes, the Sanhaja had suffered a considerable erosion of power in the desert. They had lost Aoudaghost, a key trading town to the south, to the Soninke, and rival Zenata Berbers were in control of the main northern center of the desert caravan trade, Sijilmassa, in Tafilalet. Through their control of Tafilalet and the Oued Draa (q.v.), moreover, the Zenata appear to have blocked the traditional Sanhaja migration routes to the Atlas mountains. It was the Almoravid movement that allowed a Sanhaja revival under the banner of holy war.

The attachment of the Sanhaja to Islam prior to the Almoravid period was superficial, and animist notions retained much of their hold; according to tradition, it was Yahya Ibn Ibrahim's shame at the ignorance of his people that prompted him, upon his return from a pilgrimage to Mecca, to invite Abdallah Ibn Yacin to follow him to the desert to start preaching.

Though the Gadala at first listened politely, they soon came to resent his austere disciplinarian message and chased him away (c. 1041). After a brief visit to the Souss, he then withdrew with a handful of followers to an island, possibly Tidra off the northern Mauritanian coast, where they gathered a growing armed band of disciples in c. 1041–42. At this *ribat,* or retreat, the *murabitun* (Almoravids) meditated, learned the precepts of orthodox Malekite Sunni Islam, and mastered the techniques of conversion. They aroused the interest of neighboring nomadic groups, from whom many new *telamid* were recruited. When they finally ventured out of their ribat, they were a large and effective armed force, dedicated to the propagation of the true faith and the waging of a *jihad* against all who refused to follow them in their struggle against animism, superstition, and heresy. By c. 1042, both the Gadala and the Lemtouna had accepted the leadership of Abdallah Ibn Yacin, who appointed a Lemtouna chief, Yahya Ibn Omar, as commander of the Almoravid army. Another Sanhaja people, the Massoufa, also rapidly submitted.

In 1054, Yahya Ibn Omar seized Aoudaghost, asserting Sanhaja revenge on the Soninke in the name of God. In the same year, Abdallah Ibn Yacin seized Sijilmassa from the Maghrawa Zenata after receiving a call for help from a Sanhaja holy man there. The Maghrawa ruler of Sijilmassa, Masoud, was killed. The Sanhaja had, by virtue of these two victories, gained control of both ends of the trans-Saharan trade routes at the expense of their historic rivals.

However, the Tafilalet region rebelled against Almoravid domination in 1056, massacring the garrison at Sijilmassa. At the same time, the Gadala, smarting under the ascendancy of the Lemtouna, tried to withdraw from the movement. Recalled from the south to meet these challenges, Yahya Ibn Omar was killed in a battle with the Gadala at Tebferilla later in the year. The command was now handed to his brother, Abu Bakr Ibn Omar, who, with Abdallah Ibn Yacin, was to start the Almoravid invasion of Morocco, capturing Taroudant in the Souss later in 1056, shortly before the recapture of Sijilmassa. The invaders continued their advance, into the Atlas mountains, where they were able to muster the support of Sanhaja kinfolk. However, as the northward invasion proceeded, the Almoravids eventually met determined opposition from the Berghwata, then led by a prophet of their own. Abdallah Ibn Yacin was killed fighting them in 1059 about 30 km. south of present-day Rabat. Nonetheless, the conquest of Morocco went on, Abu Bakr leading a campaign as far north as Meknes in 1060.

However, once again, the Almoravids faced a challenge in their home base, the desert, which was once more the scene of internecine strife between the Sanhaja tribes, who, despite the leadership of the Almoravids, proved unable to maintain their loose unity more than temporarily. In 1061, faced by revolts by the Gadala and the Massoufa, Abu Bakr returned to the Sahara, leaving his cousin, Yusuf Ibn Tashfin, in command of the primarily Lemtouna forces in Morocco. After restoring order among the Sanhaja in the desert, Abu Bakr tried to instill a sense of unity among them by launching a jihad against pagan Ghana, which besides satisfying Islamic duty, promised the pillage of this empire famed for its gold. After astutely winning suppport from the Muslim rulers of Ghana's small vassal kingdoms of Tekrur, Galam, Sosso, and Kaniaga, Abu Bakr launched a military offensive in 1062, which led eventually, in 1076, to the sacking of Kumbi, Ghana's capital, the collapse of the empire, and the flight of its last *tunka* (king). However, Ghana was to be reborn, though without its former power, after the death in battle of Abu Bakr Ibn Omar in Tagant in 1087. The immediate consequence of the Almoravid victories in the south was the conversion of the Soninke aristocracy to Islam, Abu Bakar's condition for the retention of their privileges.

Meanwhile, to the north, Yusuf Ibn Tashfin completed the conquest of Morocco, founding Marrakesh in 1062 and subduing the Zenata, who tried to block the Almoravid advance in northern Morocco. Having seized Fez in 1063, Yusuf Ibn Tashfin lost this strategic city to the Zenata later in the same year. It was not until 1069 that he was able to recapture it. However, by 1082, his empire stretched as far east as Algiers. Moreover, by then, he was beginning to receive appeals from the Muslim rulers of Spain to help them ward off the attacks of Alfonso VI of Castile, then spearheading the Christian *reconquista*. Since the collapse of the Umayyad caliphate of Cordova in 1031, Muslim Spain had been gravely weakened by its division into 23 small, quarrelsome city-states, the *muluk al-tawaif,* or "kings of the parties." In 1085, after Alfonso's capture of Toledo, the emir of Seville, Al-Mutamid, issued an urgent plea to Yusuf Ibn Tashfin for help. After crossing the Strait of Gibraltar, the Almoravid leader inflicted a crushing defeat on Alfonso's army in a battle near Badajoz on October 23, 1086. He returned then to Morocco, but, resummoned to meet a renewed Christian threat, he landed again in Spain in 1090. This time he decided to impose his own rule over Muslim Spain, ending the independence of the cultivated but bickering emirates. By 1106 he had seized all of them with the exception of Saragossa, which was taken in 1110. He died in 1106, leaving his vast empire to his son, Ali Ibn Yusuf, a man of much weaker leadership capabilities.

Yusuf Ibn Tashfin laid the basis of the Moroccan state and checked the progress of the reconquista in Spain. Acquiring the title of *Amir al-Muslimin* (Prince of the Muslims) after his victory in 1086 in Spain, he was spiritual as well as secular ruler of his empire. Rival Islamic sects were rooted out during his rule, and Sunni orthodoxy and Malekism became firmly established. A puritanical and austere man, he saw that the Malekite law was firmly applied. The *fuqaha,* the interpreters of Muslim law, held an influential position in his state, along with his Lemtouna counselors and commanders. Though the rigidity and scholasticism of the Almoravid fuqaha stultified intellectual life during his rule, the conquest of Spain opened Morocco to the refined culture of Al-Andalus, most notably to its architects and craftsmen.

However, the Almoravid empire was not a unified one. From the time of Abu Bakr's departure from Morocco to the Sahara in 1061, there were really two empires—one in the Sahara under Abu Bakr, who led the Sanhaja (primarily Gadala and Massoufa) against the Soninke kingdom of Ghana, the other in Morocco, western Algeria, and Spain, under Yusuf Ibn Tashfin and his successors. When, upon hearing of the latter's conquests, Abu Bakr returned to Morocco in 1062 to claim his command there, he was politely rebuffed by Ibn Tashfin and returned to the Sahara. There, after his death, tribal rivalries rapidly gained the upper hand over Almoravid unity. In the north, the Almoravid dynasty founded by Ibn Tashfin was under serious challenge less than 20 years after his death. The Christian armies in Spain resumed their offensive and, in 1125, Ibn Tumart, Mahdi of the Masmouda of the High Atlas, began a rebellion that was to establish a new Moroccan dynasty, the Almohads. They had gained control of most of Morocco by 1143 and seized Marrakesh in 1147. Muslim Spain, meanwhile, rebelled in 1143. By 1150, the northern Almoravid empire had collapsed.

AL-MURABITUN see ALMORAVIDS

ALTO COMISARIO. The Spanish high commissioner in Morocco during the Franco-Spanish protectorate (1912–56), under a Spanish decree of August 29, 1934, he became also the governor-general of Ifni and Western Sahara. Since he was resident in Tetuan in northern Morocco, he had two *delegados gubernativos* (q.v.) in Ifni and the Sahara to oversee their administration. This assimilation of Western Sahara and Ifni into the Spanish protectorate zone of Morocco for administrative convenience proved embarrassing to Madrid, however, when Moroccan nationalism became a powerful force after World War II. So a decree of July 20, 1946, ended the link by creating Africa Occidental Española (q.v.), incorporating both Ifni and Western Sahara, under a governor-general resident in Sidi Ifni. However, the Tekna Zone (q.v.), the northernmost strip of Spain's Saharan territory, continued to be considered part of Spain's zone of the Moroccan protectorate, and so the governor-general of AOE acted as the high commissioner's delegado there.

AMGALA, BATTLES OF. A water source in the east of Saguia el-Hamra (q.v.), about 180 miles from the Algerian frontier, Amgala was one of the most important battle sites in the early stages of the war between Morocco and the Polisario Front (q.v.). It had been under the effective control of the Polisario Front since October 1975, when the Spanish army withdrew from all points east of Smara (q.v.), and it later became a key staging point in the front's evacuation of Saharawi civilians to refugee camps (q.v.) in Algeria. Regular troops of the Algerian National People's Army were in Amgala, assisting with the refugee exodus, when the Moroccan army attacked in the last week of January 1976. On January 29, Moroccan troops, under the command of Col. Ben Othman, seized the locality, capturing 99 Algerian soldiers and killing dozens more. The incident might have sparked off an all-out war between Morocco and Algeria, but

Algerian troops were then withdrawn from Western Sahara and did not play a direct part in the Polisario struggle thereafter, limiting their role to the provision of bases, arms, and training for the guerrillas. However, less than three weeks after the Moroccan capture of Amgala, Polisario guerrillas massacred a large part of the 300-strong garrison left there by Col. Ben Othman. A day later, on February 15, King Hassan II (q.v.) wrote bitterly to President Houari Boumedienne (q.v.) of Algeria, accusing the Algerian army of "causing dozens of victims among my sons and the combatants of my country." The Algerian Council of the Revolution and cabinet, meeting jointly on February 16, replied categorically: "There is no unit of the National People's Army on Western Saharan territory. International observers can verify this on the spot. On January 29, when battalions of the Moroccan army staged a treacherous attack on the units which had the task of taking provisions of food and medicines to the Saharan refugees in Amgala, Algeria resolved not to yield to provocation and to avoid a comprehensive confrontation between the two sister peoples." Moroccan forces reoccupied Amgala in May 1977 and stayed there, at times harassed by the guerrillas, until 1979, when as part of a retrenchment policy the Moroccan forces pulled out of all their bases east of Smara. The area remained under Polisario control until mid-1985, when an extension of Morocco's "defensive walls" (q.v.) encompassed it.

ANGLO-MOROCCAN AGREEMENT (March 13, 1895). An agreement by which the British government ceded Tarfaya (q.v.), where Donald Mackenzie's North-West Africa Company had established a trading post in 1879. The post was handed to Morocco for £50,000, and it was further agreed that "no one will have any claim to the lands that are between Oued Draa and Cape Boujdour (qq.v.), and which are called Tarfaya above-named, and all the lands behind it, because this belongs to the territory of Morocco." The *makhzen,* the Moroccan government, had become worried by Mackenzie's trading activities and asserted a claim to this part of the Sahara because of the diversion of trade from the sultanate's own ports (where the makhzen derived considerable revenue from duties) and its anxiety over the growing European pressures on Morocco's frontiers. Correspondence between Moroccan and British officials prior to the agreement reveals that the British government did not believe the region between the Oued Draa and Boujdour to be Moroccan, but, in agreeing to sell the Tarfaya trading post, which Mackenzie no longer saw as a viable commercial enterprise, the British government wanted to bar rival colonial powers, such as France and Germany, from staking a claim to the area. Indeed, another clause of the agreement stated, "It is agreed that this [Moroccan] government shall give its word to the English government that they will not give any part of the above-mentioned lands to any one whatsoever without the concurrence of the English government."

AOSARIO see ASSOCIATION DES ORIGINAIRES DU SAHARA ANCIENNEMENT SOUS DOMINATION ESPAGNOLE

AOUSSERT. About 200 km. southeast of Dakhla (q.v.), Aoussert was traditionally an important water source for the nomads. Its water supply prompted the Spaniards to establish a post there, which became one of two outlying administrative centers for the *Delegación Regional del Sur* (Regional Delegation of the South), based at Dakhla (q.v.), after Western Sahara's conversion into a Spanish "province" (q.v.) in 1958. In 1974, 2,448 Saharawis were settled there. Flanked by steep-rising black hills, it became a sanctuary of the Polisario Front (q.v.) in the last weeks of 1975. It was captured by the Mauritanian army on January 23, 1976, but was quickly recaptured by the guerrillas. It was seized again by the Mauritanian army on February 8. It became part of the Mauritanian sector of the territory under the April 14, 1976, partition treaty and was later occupied by Morocco after the August 5, 1979, Algiers Agreement (q.v.). As an isolated garrison outside the first of the "defensive walls" constructed by the FAR (qq.v.) in the 1980s, it was vacated by Morocco in about 1981. However, by April 1987, the Moroccans had extended the wall to encompass Aoussert as well as much of the rest of Río de Oro (q.v.). The Polisario

Front responded with a major attack near Aoussert in August 1987. As of 1990, it remained under Moroccan control, although the vast majority of its inhabitants had departed.

ARAB LEAGUE. Most Arab states supported the Moroccan-Mauritanian annexation of Western Sahara in 1975–76, but Arab support for the Moroccan cause waned somewhat as the war dragged on and Mauritania came to terms with the Polisario Front (q.v.) in 1979. Initially, Arab monarchies tended to support King Hassan II's claim to Western Sahara from a standpoint of monarchical solidarity, whereas fear of separatism and pan-Arabist ideals prompted some republican Arab regimes (Iraq in particular) to back the king's claim. Moreover, Hassan II's prestige in the Arab world had been enhanced by the participation of a Moroccan armored brigade on the Golan Heights in the 1973 Arab-Israeli war and by the king's role in reconciling the Palestine Liberation Organization and Jordan's King Hussein at the October 1974 summit of the Arab League. This same summit adopted a resolution on Western Sahara, which congratulated Morocco and Mauritania for harmonizing their contradictory claims to the territory and declared support for their decision to submit their dispute with Spain over the territory to the ICJ (q.v.). Even Algeria's President Houari Boumedienne (q.v.) declared his support at the summit for the joint Moroccan-Mauritanian stand on the territory. When Algeria later, in the spring of 1975, decided to oppose the Moroccan-Mauritanian claims, it was virtually isolated in the Arab world, apart from Libya, which had given support to the Polisario Front since its founding in 1973. Some Arab countries, notably Saudi Arabia and Jordan, sent token delegations to take part in the November 1975 Green March (q.v.). After the founding of the SADR (q.v.) on February 27, 1976, Algeria was the only Arab state to recognize it immediately (March 6). South Yemen followed suit a year later, on February 2, 1977, but it was not until April 15, 1980, that Libya and Syria recognized the SADR. Saudi Arabia continued to assist Morocco's war effort by financing some of its arms imports. Some military aid also came from Egypt. As for Libya, it did furnish substantial amounts of assistance to Polisario in the early 1980s, but this gradually dried up as its leader, Muammar El-Qadaffi, moved closer to Morocco in an effort to end his international isolation. On August 13, 1984, Libya—in a surprise move—signed an agreement of unity with Morocco in Oujda, thus aligning himself formally with King Hassan. As part of the diplomatic bargain, Libya agreed to end all material aid to the SADR, although some contact with Polisario was maintained. Although the Oujda agreement was abrogated in 1986, Libyan support for the Saharawi cause has since been muted. The only other Arab League member to recognize the SADR has been Mauritania, which did so on February 27, 1984.

AREILZA, JOSE MARIA DE, COUNT OF MOTRICO. Born in Bilbao in 1909, he had a long career as a politician and diplomat under General Franco (q.v.) and was Spanish foreign minister during the last months of Spanish rule in Western Sahara. Shortly after the start of World War II, when the Madrid government hoped that a German-Italian victory would allow Spain to expand its colonial empire at the expense of France, he wrote a book with Fernando María Castiella, *Reivindicaciones de España* (1941), which advocated the enlargement of Spain's colony in the Sahara as well as the extension of Spanish rule to the French sector of Morocco and to western Algeria. In quite different circumstances 34 years later, he was appointed foreign minister in King Juan Carlos's first post-Franco government, in December 1975. As foreign minister, he played on the ambiguities of the Madrid Agreement (q.v.), which had been signed the previous November, arguing that Spain was transferring its administrative powers in Western Sahara to Morocco and Mauritania, but not sovereignty over the territory, which he said was vested in the Western Saharan people. He was anxious not to damage Spain's important economic relations with Algeria.

Following a meeting with Kurt Waldheim, the secretary-general of the UN (qq.v), on February 23, 1976, he joined the UN in refusing to accept the rump Djemaa (q.v.) meeting three days later, which voted to approve integration with Morocco and Mauritania, as a genuine act of self-determination. A Spanish government memorandum, published on February 26, 1976, the date of Spain's final withdrawal from the territory, simply stated that "the decolonization of Western Sahara will reach its climax when the views of the Saharan population have been validly expressed." However, he was also careful not to offend Morocco, in order to prevent retaliation against Spanish fishing interests or the enclaves of Ceuta and Melilla on Morocco's Mediterranean coast. Spanish arms shipments to Morocco continued, and Areilza visited Morocco in May 1976, declaring that the Western Saharan problem was a closed matter.

ARIAS NAVARRO, CARLOS. Born in 1908, Carlos Arias Navarro became Spain's prime minister in 1974 after a long political career under the Francoist regime. During his term of office, which ended in July 1976, Spain finally ended its colonial rule in Western Sahara, after his government had engineered a 180-degree turnaround in its Saharan policy and agreed to hand the territory to Morocco and Mauritania.

The Franco regime had first begun to formulate plans for limited internal autonomy in Western Sahara in 1973; then, after the coup in Portugal in April 1974, Arias Navarro's government began to speed up these plans as a step toward eventual independence. A weak independent Western Saharan government, he calculated, would be unlikely to challenge Spain's important fishing and phosphate interests in the territory. In July 1974, his government announced plans to establish internal self-government through an *estatuto político* (q.v.), which would have transformed the hitherto purely consultative Djemaa (q.v.) into a legislature and established a partially-Saharawi governing council. On August 21, 1974, his government announced that a referendum on the territory's future would be held in accordance with UN (q.v.) resolutions during the first six months of 1975; and in November 1974, the colonial authorities encouraged the launching of the Partido de la Unión Nacional Saharaui (q.v.) in the hope that it would counter the influence of the Polisario Front (q.v.) and lead the country to independence in close association with Spain.

However, Arias Navarro came under intense pressure from Morocco to abandon the commitment to a referendum and to hand the territory over to Morocco and Mauritania through trilateral negotiations. After the UN voted in December 1974 to accept the Moroccan-Mauritanian proposal to submit the Western Sahran dispute to the ICJ (q.v.), his government announced on January 16, 1975, that it would postpone the referendum until after the ICJ had issued its advisory opinion. It did so with great reluctance, and when, in May 1975, the pro-Moroccan FLU began bomb attacks in El-Ayoun (q.v.) and the Polisario Front held large demonstrations during the visit of the UN Visiting Mission (q.v.), outflanking the PUNS, his government became increasingly anxious to quit the colony. On May 23, it told the UN that it would set a date for withdrawal if the neighboring countries (Morocco, Mauritania, and Algeria) did not join Spain in a quadripartite conference and agree to allow the decolonization process to proceed peacefully.

With the demise of the PUNS in the summer of 1975, his government began to consider the possibility of handing power to the Polisario Front, which was judged unlikely to threaten major Spanish interests. His foreign minister, Pedro Cortina y Mauri (q.v.), therefore met El-Ouali Mustapha Sayed (q.v.) in Algeria on September 9 and reached an understanding on the territory's future, the protection of Spanish interests there, and the mutual release of prisoners. However, after King Hassan II announced the Green March (qq.v.) on October 16, Arias Navarro was under strong pressure to settle the Saharan dispute on terms acceptable to Morocco. When Franco entered his final illness the next day, the future of Western Sahara became overshadowed by that of Spain itself. The prime minister did not feel that he could risk a long, drawn-out conflict with Morocco while trying to steer Spain into the unknown terrain of post-Francoism. The memory of the turmoil in Portugal after the overthrow of Salazarism was still fresh in his mind. Moreover, there was pressure from the United States and France to come to terms with Morocco, and there was the danger that, if an agreement was not reached, Morocco might start to threaten the Spanish enclaves of Ceuta and Melilla on Morocco's Mediterranean

coast. The crisis was defused in a series of negotiations—
first between José Solís Ruíz (q.v.) and King Hassan in
Marrakesh (October 20); then between Moroccan and Spanish officials, including Arias Navarro, in Madrid on October
24–25 and 28–30; then between Hassan and Antonio Carro
Martínez (q.v.) in Agadir (November 8); and finally between
Moroccan, Mauritanian, and Spanish officials, including
Arias Navarro, in Madrid (November 12–14), culminating in
the Madrid Agreement (q.v.) on November 14, 1975.

His government then established a tripartite administration (q.v.) in Western Sahara and gradually withdrew its
troops from the territory. The Spanish flag was pulled down
for the last time on February 26, 1976, but Arias Navarro
claimed that Spain had transferred only its administrative
powers and not sovereignty to Morocco and Mauritania. It
refused to recognize the rump meeting of the Djemaa on
February 26, which voted approval of integration with
Morocco and Mauritania as a genuine act of self-
determination.

ARIFA. Pl. *arifat.* The head of a cell of the Polisario Front (q.v.),
he is responsible for the activities of eleven other cell
members. The entire adult Saharawi refugee population that
settled in Polisario camps in Algeria from 1975–76 was
organized into cells.

ARMY OF LIBERATION. The guerrilla war launched in 1957 by
the Army of Liberation (Jaich at-Tahrir) was the most
serious challenge to the Spanish authorities in Western
Sahara since the early years of the colony, forcing the
government to withdraw all its garrisons from the interior,
including even Smara (q.v.), in order to defend a few
strategic enclaves on the coast until the arrival of reinforcements and the launching of a Franco-Spanish counterinsurgency campaign, Operation Ouragan (q.v.), in February
1958, which finally crushed the guerrilla movement.

It was Morocco's independence, on March 3, 1956, which
inspired many Saharawis to take up arms against both the
Spanish regime in Western Sahara and the French in northern Mauritania, and it was a Moroccan-led movement, the

Army of Liberation, which provided the leadership and the arms. The Army of Liberation was formed in mid-1955 from the numerous small guerrilla groups that had sprung to life in Morocco after the French government's decision in August 1953 to depose and exile the sultan, Mohammed V (q.v.). Complementing a number of urban resistance groups, its main support came initially from Berber peasants in the Rif and Middle Atlas mountain ranges. A while later, the French government, which was also confronted by the rebellion in Algeria, decided to rethink its Moroccan policy and allow Mohammed V to return home (November 16, 1955). After this initial victory, the movement rapidly grew in influence and strength, increasing pressure on the French as the negotiations between Mohammed V and the French government on Morocco's future unfolded. In January 1956, at a conference in Madrid, its leaders divided the country into three zones, the Rif, the Middle and High Atlas, and the south, each with its own command.

In the last few weeks of the Franco-Spanish protectorate, thousands of new recruits enrolled, and large tracts of the countryside, especially in the mountain areas and the south, fell effectively under the partisans' control. This was facilitated by an agreement reached by the sultan's government and the French on February 11, 1956, whereby the Moroccan auxiliaries of the French army were relieved of their French commanders. Thousands of the auxiliaries joined the Army of Liberation, bringing their weapons with them, often after raiding their local armories.

The growth of this movement was viewed with alarm not only by the French, who kept several thousand troops in the country after independence in March, but also by Mohammed V and the Istiqlal Party (q.v.) leaders. Rural men for the most part and leaders of a kind of peasant *jacquerie,* the commanders of the Army of Liberation had a different background and outlook from those of the urban bourgeois intellectuals in the leadership of the Istiqlal Party, and, of the 50 members of the Conseil National de la Résistance (National Council of the Resistance), set up after the return of Mohammed V from his exile in Madagascar, only one, Allal el-Fassi (q.v.), was also a member of the executive committee of the Istiqlal Party. Though most of the partisan leaders joined the party and later, in 1959, the Union Nationale des Forces Populaires (q.v.), they remained by and large suspicious of the political elite.

Whereas the Istiqlalians wanted to bring the partisans within their fold, Mohammed V wanted to disband the Army of Liberation. At first he faced great difficulties. A new regular army, the FAR (q.v.), composed mainly of Moroccan soldiers who had served in the French and Spanish armies, was founded on May 14, 1956, and received aid from c. 2,000 French officers. About 10,000 former members of the Army of Liberation had heeded calls from the government to lay down their arms and join the FAR by the end of the year, bringing its total troop strength to some 30,000, but many others refused to join the regular army, especially in the regions south of Agadir, where the Army of Liberation remained effectively in control until early in 1958.

Many of the partisan leaders were disillusioned by the government's failure to bring radical changes after independence. "Some people are beginning to ask themselves whether our revolution did not run aground after the declaration of independence," noted the Conseil National de la Résistance after its first, and only, session in August 1956. "The victories which we have obtained so far are only victories to the extent that they have had the effect of liberating Moroccan sovereignty in the diplomatic and juridical spheres. As to the internal situation, the expected transformations have not been achieved and no change worthy of note has appeared." There was particular resentment at the failure to expropriate the landholdings of the *colons* and at the decision to allow several thousand French troops to remain provisionally in the country, a decision that was interpreted by some as a betrayal of the Algerian FLN, which had begun its rebellion in 1954. The Army of Liberation's radical leaders had a pan-Arab outlook and believed that they had a duty to aid the liberation struggle in the rest of the Maghreb, by helping the FLN to smuggle arms into Algeria and organizing rebellions by the peoples of the territories to Morocco's south—Ifni, Western Sahara and Mauritania.

At the January 1956 conference of Army of Liberation leaders in Madrid, Benhamou Mesfioui (q.v.), a partisan leader from the Rif, was entrusted with the command of the south. Though a guerrilla nucleus had been established in Tiznit in 1954 by Ibrahim Namri (Ibrahim Tizniti), it was not until the arrival of Rifian partisans under Benhamou's command and the mass desertions of the auxiliaries in the spring of 1956 that the Army of Liberation became a mass force in the regions south of Agadir. There, in the Souss, the Anti-Atlas, and the valley of the Oued Draa (q.v.), it became a virtually unchallenged power, as the last French *officers d'affaires indigènes* were withdrawn and their armories raided. Summary justice was meted out to former collaborators with the French authorities, and two of the last French officials in the south of Morocco, Captain René Moureau and Lt. Perrin, were kidnapped (June 23 and October 20, 1956).

Mohammed V turned a blind eye to the activities of Benhamou's men. He deeply distrusted the Army of Liberation and saw their refusal to join the FAR as an affront to his authority, but he was not unhappy to see them concentrate far away in the extreme south of his kingdom, leaving the more populated areas to the north untroubled. The new royal army did not have the means at this time to bring the south under central government control. Though Mohammed V was anxious to maintain good relations with France, he was not prepared to risk alienating nationalists by authorizing military action against the Army of Liberation by the French troops still in Morocco.

In June 1956, the Army of Liberation started a series of raids against French positions in the frontier zone with Algeria. After an attack on the French post of Oum el-Achar in the first week of June, the French evacuated an oil-prospecting group from Hassi Sidi el-Mounir in the valley of the Oued Zemoul. Later in June, there were clashes at Ain Chair and at Beni Ounif and a terrorist attack at Colomb-Bechar. In July, a French convoy traveling between Colomb-Bechar and Tindouf was ambushed on the *hammada* (qq.v.) near Tinfouchy. Further attacks were made on the French posts of Oum el-Achar and Hassi Sidi el-Mounir in 1957, and as late as June 1958, French troops are said to have clashed with guerrillas at Hassi Beida, in the Draa valley, near Tinjoub.

Meanwhile, the Army of Liberation was also turning its attention, in 1957, to the Spanish enclave of Ifni. After the assassination of a Spanish officer there on June 16, 1957, the Spanish authorities arrested scores of nationalists and closed down the local offices of the Istiqlal Party (q.v.). On July 8 and July 25, two policemen were murdered; then, on August 10 and 16, there were clashes between guerrilla groups and Spanish military units near the enclave's frontiers. Finally, on November 23, hundreds of guerrillas invaded the enclave, attacking seven Spanish frontier posts during the night, some of them falling into rebel hands. Reinforcements were rushed to the enclave, and a flotilla of warships arrived in the Canary Islands. In an ensuing counteroffensive, the Spanish succeeded in recapturing some of the positions that had been lost to the guerrillas, but on December 11, the Spanish government suddenly announced that "all the isolated posts held by small garrisons in the territory of Ifni have been evacuated to allow coordinated action by the Spanish troops against the bands of aggressors." At the same time, Madrid announced that 62 Spanish troops, including 5 officers, had been killed and 115 wounded. After abandoning all the small outlying garrisons, the Spanish army fell back to a strip of territory about 20 km. wide around the capital, Sidi Ifni. There, some 7,000–8,000 Spanish troops dug into fortified defense positions to deter the Army of Liberation from trying to stage an assault on Sidi Ifni itself. No such attempt was made. For the following eleven and a half years, the Spanish made no attempt to move out of the small fortified zone around Sidi Ifni and reoccupy the rest of the enclave, which was finally ceded in its entirety to Morocco in 1969.

While these events were unfolding in Ifni, the Army of Liberation was active on another front, in the Sahara, against the French in Mauritania and the Spanish in Western Sahara. To the Saharawis, the achievement of independence by Morocco in 1956 was an inspiration, a spur to revolt. Saharawis began to enroll in the Army of Liberation, which had its main bases in Goulimine and Bou-Izarkan, from mid-1956, among the first to join being Abba el-Cheikh, who became a key leader of the Saharawi guerrilla forces.

The young Moroccan commanders of the Saharawi guerrilla movement at first adopted a two-stage strategy based on their own experience in the Rif: The initial goal was to liberate Mauritania from the French, using Western Sahara (like the Spanish protectorate zone in northern Morocco in 1955) as a sanctuary and zone of transit, and then, as in Spanish-ruled Morocco beforehand, the Spanish would have no option but to hand over Western Sahara. So the first attacks were in Mauritania. On February 15, 1957, a French patrol was ambushed by a force of 200 guerrillas at El-Amar, about 100 km. northeast of Fort Trinquet (Bir Moghrein). Of the 40 members of the French patrol, 23 (including three officers) were killed. The rebels reportedly slipped back across the border into Western Sahara.

The French were alarmed by the incident. A guerrilla war in northern Mauritania threatened plans then afoot to invest in the development of the huge iron ore deposits near Fort Gouraud (Zouerate) and created an inauspicious climate for the implementation of French plans for internal autonomy in Mauritania. A strategy meeting was immediately held in Tindouf (q.v.), Algeria, bringing together General Gabriel Bourgund (q.v.), commander of the French forces in French West Africa; General René Cogny, commander of the French troops still remaining in Morocco; and General Ely, chief of staff of the French armed forces.

The biggest problem facing the French was the Spanish army's weakness in Western Sahara, where the guerrillas could roam almost at will. "The Spanish authorities in Río de Oro," said Gaston Cusin, high commissioner of French West Africa, on February 28, "have given us their full cooperation in the recent Mauritanian events, but they have only been able to do so to the extent of their military means which are very limited." After consultations between the French and Spanish governments, Cusin had received authorization from Gaston Defferre (q.v.), minister for overseas territories in Guy Mollet's socialist government, on February 20, to stage cross-border raids into Western Sahara.

Meanwhile, the Moroccan government washed its hands

of responsibility for the Army of Liberation's activities. "They are elements which we have called uncontrolled and difficult to control that have created these incidents," said Ahmed Balafrej, the Moroccan foreign minister, in Dakar on March 7.

In June, Madrid appointed a new governor-general of Africa Occidental Española (q.v.), General Mariano Gómez Zamalloa (q.v.), who quickly showed a readiness to cooperate with the French to tackle the guerrilla threat. At a meeting with General Bourgund in Dakhla (q.v.) on July 12, he pleaded insufficient men and equipment for effective policing action in Spanish territory but agreed to hold regular consultations with the military officers in Mauritania and to extend the previous limit on French cross-border raids to 60–80 km. and the limit on French reconnaissance flights to 100 km. Bourgund and Cusin were dismayed, however, by Madrid's failure to send reinforcements to Western Sahara and by Gómez Zamalloa's almost inevitable decision in the circumstances to withdraw the isolated Spanish garrisons in the interior to bolster the defenses of the more important Spanish settlements on the coast, at El-Ayoun, Dakhla, and Tarfaya (qq.v.), between August and October. Even Smara (q.v.) was abandoned to the guerrillas.

Toward the end of the year, clashes between the Army of Liberation and Spanish forces became more frequent. On November 26, a guerrilla group ambushed a Spanish convoy at Arbaa el-Mesti, near El-Ayoun. A Spanish communiqué issued on December 4 spoke also of the successful relief of an isolated garrison defending communications installations and of a nine-day battle between guerrillas and Spanish paratroopers in which five Spanish troops were killed. On December 3, a guerrilla group attacked the lighthouse at Cape Boujdour (q.v.), capturing the Spaniards who worked there. The same day, two Spanish soldiers were killed when a guerrilla group ambushed another convoy near El-Ayoun. The most serious incident of all came on January 13, 1958, when 51 Spanish troops were killed or wounded in a daylong battle at Edchera (q.v.), 20 km. southeast of El-Ayoun.

These events and the invasion of Ifni by Army of Liberation guerrillas in November 1957 strengthened Madrid's resolve. In September, Bourgund had drawn up the outlines of a joint Franco-Spanish counterinsurgency sweep through Western Sahara, to which he had given the code name Ouragan (q.v.), and at a meeting in Dakar on September 20, he had got Gómez Zamalloa's personal support for the idea. Finally, on December 30, in Paris, the new government headed by Félix Gaillard gave its assent and in the first week of January 1958, the Spanish government gave its approval too. Operation Ouragan got under way on February 10, involving 5,000 French troops and 9,000 Spanish troops, as well as 70 French and 60 Spanish aircraft. The French maneuvers were code-named Ecouvillon, the Spanish part of the operation Teide. In the first stage of the campaign, on February 10–19, rebel positions in Sagula el-Hamra came under attack; the second stage, on February 20–24, was a sweep through Río de Oro. The guerrilla forces were decimated, their remnants fleeing to the north, and the Spanish were able to reestablish garrisons at key points in the interior, including Smara.

The Army of Liberation had already been weakened, even before Operation Ouragan, by serious internal dissension between some of its Moroccan commanders and the Saharawi guerrilla fighters. The condescending attitudes and allegedly non-Islamic conduct of the young radical Moroccans associated with Benhamou apparently alienated many of the austere and puritanical nomads who made up the overwhelming majority of the guerrillas. The first signs of friction came to the attention of the French authorities when a leader of the Lebouihat, a major fraction of the Reguibat ech-Charg (q.v.), arrived in Fort Trinquet at the end of December 1957 and told the French officials there that he had defected from the Army of Liberation and wanted arms from France to fight against it. The Lebouihat chief was Khatri Ould Said Ould Joumani (q.v.). The friction between the Army of Liberation's Moroccan commanders and Saharawi guerrillas apparently came to a climax with a full-scale mutiny, known as the "raiding of the armoury," in Tan-Tan, during which several Moroccan commanders were detained.

The destruction of the Army of Liberation in Western Sahara and the gradual extension of the royal government's control over southern Morocco satisfied the condition laid down by Spain in 1957 for the cession to Morocco of the Tekna Zone (q.v.), the northernmost strip of Spain's Saharan territories, between the Qued Draa and parallel 27° 40' north, which had been defined as the southern sector of the Spanish protectorate in Morocco in 1912. So, on April 1, by the Agreement of Cintra (q.v.), Spain agreed to cede the zone on April 10. However, some Saharawi guerrillas of the Army of Liberation were fearful of this southward extension of Moroccan governmental authority and decided to block a force of 1,000 regular Moroccan troops trying to reach Tarafaya, the only Spanish base in the Tekna Zone, for the hand-over ceremony. An attempt at reconciliation was later made at a conference between Saharawi leaders of the Army of Liberation and Moroccan officials, including Crown Prince Moulay Hassan, the future Hassan II (q.v.), at Boukhchebia, near the Oued Chebeika.

The guerrilla movement was, by then, in a state of disintegration. Many of its supporters had lost much of their livestock and become virtually destitute refugees, dependent on handouts from the Moroccan authorities for survival. On March 18, 1958, Morocco announced that it had received 13,000 Saharawi refugees (q.v.) as a result of Operation Ouragan. Naturally, the offer of permanent employment in the regular Moroccan army was an attractive one to many former Army of Liberation men, and several thousand of them signed up with the FAR in 1958–59. Others drifted back to Western Sahara. Forty Spanish prisoners captured in Western Sahara and Ifni in 1957 were released in Rabat on May 6, 1959. However, a group of former Army of Liberation guerrillas was apparently responsible for kidnapping a group of eleven oil prospectors (five Spaniards, three Americans, two Canadians, and a Frenchman) 20 km. south of the Moroccan-Western Saharan frontier on March 11, 1961. The men, all employees of Union Oil, were released on March 21 in Rabat.

The disintegration of the Saharawi component of the Army of Liberation was accompanied by the dissolution of the last Moroccan partisan bands further north. The Moroccan government combined carrot-and-stick techniques to stamp out the last pockets of the movement. A *dahir* (q.v.) of March 11, 1959, gave the "resistance fighter" an official status and a certificate, which often gave its holder privileges with respect to the acquisition of government jobs and *colon* farmland. The certificates became so valuable that corrupt officials started selling them. The Office National des Résistants (National Office of Resistance Fighters), set up in August 1961, supervised the dissolution of the few remaining Army of Liberation groups, and the government arrested and in some cases executed the most militant and recalcitrant veterans of the guerrilla struggle.

AROSIEN. One of the main tribes of Western Sahara, their ancestral founder was Sidi Ahmed el-Arosi, who is said to have lived in the first half of the 16th century, Sidi Ahmed's ancestry supposedly going back to the Prophet Mohammed. According to the Arosien, Sidi Ahmed was a saintly figure, a marabout, who arrived in the Sahara from Tunis by way of Marrakesh, where he was jailed by the reigning sultan. His three sons founded the three fractions of the tribe, the Oulad Khalifa, Oulad Sidi Bou Mehdi, and Ahel Sidi Brahim. At the end of the 19th century, their principal enemy was the Oulad Bou Sbaa, who practically exterminated them in a battle at Tislatin in 1903. The survivors emigrated to Morocco, from where they slowly returned to Western Sahara when the Oulad Bou Sbaa entered their period of decline, after a serious defeat at the hands of the Reguibat (q.v.) in 1906. In the mid-20th century, their main zone of nomadic migration was around Bir Enzaren (q.v.). Their sedentation occurred primarily in Bir Enzaren and Dakhla (q.v.).

ASAMBLEA GENERAL DEL SAHARA see DJEMAA

ASSEMBLEE PROVINCIALE. Provincial assemblies were set up by Morocco in the three provinces (q.v.) that it created in the sector of Western Sahara that it annexed in 1975–76 (El-Ayoun, Boujdour, and Smara), and another provincial assembly was set up in Tiris el-Gharbia after its annexation and conversion into the province of Oued ed-Dahab (qq.v.) in August 1979. The provincial assemblies are not elected by universal suffrage but by the *conseils communaux* (q.v.) in each respective province. In El-Ayoun, Smara, and Boujdour, the first provincial assemblies were elected in January 1977 by communal councils elected the previous November. The assemblies have virtually no real power.

ASSOCIATION DES ORIGINAIRES DU SAHARA ANCIEN-NEMENT SOUS DOMINATION ESPAGNOLE. The "Association of Natives of the Sahara formerly under Spanish Domination" was founded in Morocco after the annexation of the northern part of the territory in 1975–76. A very small grouping of pro-Moroccan Saharawis, its leader was Ahmed Ould Rachid, alias Bachir Figuigui, who was best known under the strange, Christian pseudonym of Edouard Moha, which he had used as president of the Mouvement de Résistance "les Hommes Blues" (q.v.). Its principal activity was to lobby for foreign backing for the Moroccan cause during the war with the Polisario Front (q.v.), though in 1979, it also started to issue communiqués, published prominently in the Moroccan press, which boasted of fictitious guerrilla raids by its members against targets deep inside Algeria.

AUGUST 21 MOVEMENT see MUNATHIMAT 21 GHUSHT

AUSERT see AOUSSERT

AYOUB LAHBIB. A leader of the Polisario Front (q.v.), he was elected to the front's executive committee (q.v.) and thus, in accordance with the constitution of the SADR (q.v.), also to the Council for the Command of the Revolution (q.v.), at the 3rd and 4th congresses of the front, held in August 1976 and September 1978. As one of the front's senior military commanders, he led the guerrilla forces that attacked Zouerate (q.v.) on May 1, 1977. His membership in the front's executive committee (and the CCR) was most recently confirmed at Polisario's 7th congress, held in April-May 1989.

AYUNTAMIENTO. A city council during the Spanish colonial

period, it was not until Western Sahara's conversion into a Spanish province (q.v.) in 1958 that the Spanish authorities considered establishing *ayuntamientos* on the peninsular model. Until then there had simply been two appointed *juntas locales* in El-Ayoun and Dakhla (qq.v.). These two growing urban settlements were upgraded to the rank of *términos muncipales* (q.v.) and hence granted the right to select ayuntamientos as a result of a decree enacted on November 29, 1962. Article 19 established that El-Ayoun would have a council consisting of an *alcalde* and 12 *concejales* (q.v.) and that Dakhla's council would consist of a mayor and eight councillors. The mayors were appointed by the government, and, though the councillors were elected, the electoral system was modeled on the corporatist method of election then current in Francoist Spain. Only committed allies of the colonial authorities were represented in the councils. Half were elected by male heads of families and the rest by corporate groups representing commerce, industry, cultural interests, and the professions. With respect to the latter, the 1962 law required the governor-general (q.v.) to draw up lists of candidates, three times more than the number of seats to be filled. The councillors' mandate lasted four years, half being reelected every two years. The bylaws (*reglamentos*) and ordinances (*ordenanzas*) adopted by the councils were subject to the governor-general's power of veto (within 60 days of their adoption). The first municipal elections were held in May 1963. In El-Ayoun, seven Spaniards and five Saharawis were elected councillors, and a Spaniard became mayor. In Dakhla, there were four Spanish and four Saharawi councillors and a Saharawi mayor, Souilem Ould Abdellahi (q.v.). By 1967, the mayor of El-Ayoun too was a Saharawi. That year, the mayors of both councils became ex officio members of the new Djemaa (q.v.).

- B -

BABA OULD HASSENA. Born in 1926 at Togba in the south of the country, he was a prominent supporter of the Spanish administration during the last years of colonial rule. A *cheikh* of the Oulad Delim (qq.v.), he was elected vice president of the Djemaa (q.v.) at its inauguration on September 11, 1967. He was reelected vice president of this conservative assembly of tribal *chioukh* in 1971 and later became a member of the Spanish Cortes. However, when Spain capitulated to Moroccan pressure in 1975 and signed the Madrid Agreement (q.v.), he decided to support the Polisario Front (q.v.). He chaired the session of the Djemaa held under Polisario auspices on November 28, 1975, which issued the Proclamation of Guelta Zemmour (q.v.), and, after arriving in Algiers, addressed the press conference held on December 6, 1975, to announce the Djemaa's decision to dissolve in favor of a new pro-Polisario Provisional Saharawi National Council (q.v.).

BACHIR MUSTAPHA SAYED. A longtime leader of the Polisario Front (q.v.), he was the brother of the front's first secretary-general and early charismatic leader, El-Ouali Mustapha Sayed (q.v.). A Reguibi of the Thaalat fraction (qq.v.), his parents were extremely poor, especially after they settled, in semidestitution, in Tan-Tan (Morocco) after the crushing of the Army of Liberation (q.v.) by the French and Spanish armies in Operation Ouragan (q.v.) in 1958. Bachir Mustapha Sayed had been born c. 1950–52 and had spent his early childhood in a nomadic environment. In Tan-Tan, he completed primary school. He then attended secondary schools in Bou-Izakarn and Tiznit before moving on to the lycée in Agadir, as a boarder under a government scholarship. While there, he joined the "embryonic movement for the liberation of the Sahara" (q.v.), the circle of Saharawi students, living primarily in Rabat, which his brother, El-Ouali, had played a key part in founding with Mohammed Lamine Ould Ahmed (q.v.), in 1971–72. It was in this period that Bachir Mustapha Sayed was briefly detained by the Moroccan police in Tan-Tan after an unauthorized anti-Spanish demonstration held there by supporters of the movement in March 1972. Early in 1973, in Agadir, he started editing a Saharawi newsletter, *Al-Chaab* (q.v.). Several months after the founding of the Polisario Front in May 1973, he decided to leave the Agadir lycée, without taking the baccalaureate, in order to join the guerrilla movement.

He became an influential leader of the front during its last year of anti-Spanish activity (1974–75) and then during the ensuing wars with Morocco and Mauritania. After the death of his brother, he was elected deputy secretary-general of the front at its 3rd congress, held on August 26–30, 1976. As such, he was one of the nine members of the front's top leadership body, the executive committee (q.v.), and of the Council for the Command of the Revolution (q.v.), the supreme executive organ of the Saharan Arab Democratic Republic (q.v.). As one of the Polisario Front's top leaders, he has played a major part in the elaboration of its military and diplomatic strategy. It was he who, on behalf of the front, signed the Algiers Agreement (q.v.) on August 5, 1979, ending the war with Mauritania. He also took an active part diplomatically in the early 1980s in attempting to gain full membership for the SADR in the Organization of African Unity (q.v.). At the front's 5th congress (October 12–16, 1982), he was confirmed as a member of Polisario's executive committee with responsibility for foreign affairs, but, as part of a general reorganization of the SADR's government related to its effort to win recognition as a sovereign state, he lost his position as deputy secretary-general of the front after the post itself was abolished. In reality, little change was portended by this shift, as he continued to tour foreign capitals seeking support for Polisario and sometimes engaging in high-level secret diplomacy. For example, in April 1983, he held secret, though unsuccessful, talks in Algiers, which included Minister of Interior Driss Basri, Royal Counsellor Ahmed Reda Guedira, and then Foreign Minister M'Hamed Boucetta (qq.v.). Two years later, Bachir Mustapha Sayed met with Driss Basri in Lisbon, Portugal, on January 27, 1985—again, nothing came of the encounter. At Polisario's 6th congress in December of the same year, his membership in the executive committee was reconfirmed, and from that time forward, he headed delegations to the United Nations (q.v.) in New York and Geneva to try to resolve the conflict. In 1988, he was named head of the foreign affairs department of Polisario's executive committee. On August 11, 1988, he received on behalf of the front a comprehensive UN cease-fire and referendum proposal authored by secretary-general Javier Pérez de Cuéllar (q.v.), and on August 30, he accepted this proposal in principle along with the Moroccan foreign minister, Abdellatif Filali (q.v.). Hopes for a settlement to the dispute were raised still further when, on January 4, 1989, he met with the Moroccan monarch, Hassan II (q.v.), in Marrakesh. Accompanying him were the SADR's prime minister, Mahfoud Ali Beiba, and then defense minister, Ibrahim Ghali Ould Mustapha (qq.v.). His hopes of a follow-up meeting with the king failed to materialize, but Bachir Mustapha Sayed continued to act as Polisario's principal negotiator at the United Nations in 1989–90.

BACHIR OULD LAHLAOUI. The first martyr of the Polisario Front (q.v.), he died in a clash with Spanish forces at Hassi Maitalla on March 8, 1974.

BARAJAS SUMMIT (JULY 6, 1963). A historic meeting at Barajas airport, near Madrid, between General Franco and King Hassan II (qq.v.), which ushered in more than a decade of détente between Spain and Morocco, it was the first Spanish-Moroccan summit meeting since a visit to Madrid by Mohammed V (q.v.) in April 1956 to sign a treaty ending Spanish rule in northern Morocco. Since then, relations had been soured by the armed conflict in both Ifni and Western Sahara between the Army of Liberation (q.v.) and the Spanish in 1957–58. However, the disarming of the Army of Liberation by the Moroccan government at the end of the fifties and then Hassan II's accession to the throne in 1961 and the departure of the ultranationalist ministers of the Istiqlal Party (q.v.) from the Rabat government in January 1963 opened the way for a rapprochement between the two countries, a rapprochement in which territorial bones of contention like the Ifni and Western Saharan questions were relegated to second place in favor of growing economic cooperation. The summit was prepared by visits to Madrid by Ahmed Balafrej, then Moroccan foreign minister, on October 24–28, 1962, and by Captain General Muñoz Grandes, vice president of the Spanish government, to Rabat on November 16–22. Ideological affinities cemented the ties between Hassan and Franco: "Spain and Morocco are the two columns of Hercules which guard the entrance to the Mediterranean. It is upon our two countries that depends, in great part, the destiny of the free world," said Hassan in Paris on July 6, 1963, before flying to Barajas. A joint communiqué issued after the summit stated that "the two heads of state are in accord to study all the problems of common interest with a view to reaching solutions which could serve as a basis for later agreements." Though the details of the Barajas summit remained a closely guarded secret, Morocco did not thereafter pursue its claims to Ifni and Western Sahara with great vigor. Ifni was not returned to Morocco until 1969, and Franco's refusal to negotiate with Morocco over Western Sahara met with little response from Hassan beyond Moroccan support for the anti-Spanish resolutions adopted by the UN (q.v.) from 1965. Economic relations between the two states grew in importance, the Barajas summit being followed closely (in March 1964) by a visit to Morocco by the Spanish industry minister, Gregorio López Bravo. Détente between the two countries was symbolized, moreover, by a second visit to Spain by Hassan on February 11–13, 1965, when the Moroccan monarch joined Franco at a hunting party in Andalucía. The more nationalist-minded Moroccan parties, notably the Istiqlal Party and the PCM (q.v.), were highly critical of Hassan's downplaying of the Western Saharan question in this period, which did not end until Hassan's launching of a major diplomatic campaign to assert the Moroccan claim to the territory in the summer of 1974.

BARAKA. A qualilty of special blessedness, which Saharawis traditionally believed to be imparted by God to individuals of outstanding wisdom and holiness. It was thought that such *baraka* gave its holders unique powers of healing and spirit exorcism and could be hereditarily transmitted.

BASSIRI, MOHAMMED SIDI IBRAHIM see MOHAMMED SIDI IBRAHIM BASSIRI

BATAL SIDI AHMED. One of the leaders of the Polisario Front (q.v.), he was elected to the front's executive committee (q.v.) and hence, under the SADR's constitution, also to the SADR's Council for the Command of the Revolution (qq.v.) at the front's 3rd congress in August 1976 and 4th congress in September 1978. Although he left the executive committee at the time of Polisario's 5th congress (October 12–16, 1982), he was appointed minister of education at the 6th congress, held in December 1985. He was confirmed as minister of education at the front's 7th congress held in April–May 1989, but on December 4, 1989, he was replaced in that post by Mohammed Salem Ould Salek (q.v.), and was named minister of health. He continued to hold that position in 1992.

BAYAA. The traditional act of allegiance to the sultans and kings of Morocco. It was usually made in precolonial Morocco by tribal chiefs on behalf of their peoples. The institution has been retained in postindependence Morocco to bolster the legitimacy of the monarchy and was much encouraged at the time of Morocco's bid to annex Western Sahara in 1974–76. The *bayaa* made in Fez on December 5, 1974, by the *qadi* of El-Ayoun Cheikh Brahim el-Leili, for example, was given considerable publicity in the Moroccan press and interpreted by the Rabat government as an indication of Saharawi loyalty to the Moroccan throne. The bayaa made by the president of the Djemaa, Khatri Ould Said Ould Joumani (qq.v.), in Agadir on November 3, 1975, on the eve of the Green March (q.v.), was likewise interpreted in Morocco.

BENI HASSAN see MAQIL

BENJEDID, CHADLI. Born in 1929 at Sebaa near Annaba, Chadli Benjedid became president of Algeria in February 1979 after the death of Houari Boumedienne the previous December. He had been commander of the 2nd military region (Oran) uninterruptedly since 1964 and a member of the Council of the Revolution since Boumedienne's coup deposing Ahmed Ben Bella in 1965. Contrary to hopes expressed by King Hassan II (q.v.) after Boumedienne's death, President Benjedid rapidly revealed that Algeria's commitment to the Polisario Front (q.v.) would not falter.

The Saharawi nationalist movement's considerable diplomatic and military success, and notably the August 1979 Algiers Agreement (q.v.) ending the war between the guerrillas and Mauritania, virtually ruled out the option of diminishing or ending Algerian support for the movement that Algeria had done so much to assist. The continuity of Algerian policy toward Western Sahara under Benjedid was aptly expressed by the ruling Front de Libération Nationale on February 11, 1981, in a communiqué that reaffirmed "the total and unconditional commitment of the Algerian Revolution alongside the struggle of national liberation which the Saharawi people is waging under the leadership of its sole and legitimate representative, the Polisario Front."

Throughout the 1980s, Benjedid repeatedly rebuffed propositions from King Hassan to negotiate a settlement of the Saharan conflict bilaterally over the heads of the Saharawi nationalists. He always maintained that Morocco should negotiate directly with Polisario with a view toward holding an internationally supervised referendum of self-determination. However, bilateral relations with Morocco underwent somewhat of a thaw, and Benjedid and King Hassan met with one another at Akid Lotfi, on the Moroccan-Algerian border, on February 26, 1983. This marked the first time that the heads of state of the two countries had met since the beginning of the Western Saharan war but resulted in no bilateral "deal" at Polisario's expense. And although Benjedid said afterward that he would "spare no effort" to reconcile the Moroccans and the Saharawis, he declared, "I was very clear about Algeria's position on the question of Western Sahara. I explained to the Moroccan king that I had no mandate to speak in the name of the Saharawis and that I would not arrogate to myself the right to speak in their name or to assume their trusteeship." In the following several years, the Algerian government continued its material and diplomatic support for Polisario, even increasing it when aid to the Saharawis from Libya was curtailed in 1983 as part of a temporary warming of relations between Rabat and Tripoli. Personal relations between Hassan and Benjedid were probably improving, but the Algerian president still refused to consider any proposal that would submerge the Saharawi cause in the name of either bilateral or Maghrebi harmony. On May 4, 1987, he met again with the Moroccan king near Oujda, on the border, as part of a mediation effort sponsored by King Fahd of Saudi Arabia, but this produced no appreciable change in either Algerian or Moroccan policy. In a far-reaching move, however, he agreed to restore diplomatic relations with Morocco on May 16, 1988, after a 12-year break. Although many observers believed at the time that this act portended a softening or even a withdrawal of support by Algiers for Polisario, this did not happen. Instead, Benjedid believed that the Saharan conflict could best be solved in an atmosphere of unity among the countries of North Africa, in which the SADR would eventually take its rightful place. His supportive attitude toward the Saharawis continued right up until he was obliged to resign the presidency, for domestic political reasons, on January 11, 1992.

BENNANI, ABDELAZIZ. A general in the FAR (q.v.), he was appointed chief of staff of the Moroccan forces in Western Sahara in 1977. He faced increasing military pressure from the Polisario Front (q.v.) after the July 10, 1978, coup in Mauritania, which allowed the guerrillas to concentrate their attacks against the Moroccans, in both Western Sahara and southern Morocco. His prestige as chief of staff suffered a very serious knock when a Polisario force succeeded in battling its way briefly into the city of Tan-Tan, a provincial capital in southern Morocco, in January 1979. This humiliating setback led to Bennani's replacement by Col. Mohammed Abrouq (q.v.) on March 12, 1979. He was then appointed Inspector General of Infantry. Abdelaziz Bennani again became commander of the troops in Western Sahara following the death of General Ahmed Dlimi (q.v.), on January 25, 1983. In early 1985, he was promoted to the rank of brigadier general, a mark of King Hassan II's (q.v.) increasing confidence in him. Regarded as nonpolitical and professional in outlook, he was responsible in the 1980s for the planning and construction of the series of ''defensive walls'' (q.v.), which eventually succeeded in restricting the Polisario guerrillas' access to much of the territory.

BENS ARGANDONA, FRANCISCO. Governor for 22 years, from 1903 to 1925, Francisco Bens personified Spain's role in the Sahara in the first decades of the 20th century. His aim was to extend the Spanish presence on the coast, which had been restricted to Villa Cisneros (Dakhla) (q.v.) at the time of his appointment, while leaving the interior, which the Spanish did not have the means at the time to control, to the nomads. The careful cultivation of friendly relations with the Saharawi tribes ensured the relative security of the Spanish enclaves on the coast.

Bens was born in Havana in 1867. After graduating from the Academia Militar in Cuba in 1885, he was made a second lieutenant and posted to the infantry garrison in Madrid. However, two years later, in September 1887, he was back in Cuba, then seething with discontent at Spanish rule. After six years there, he was transferred to Melilla, the Spanish-ruled enclave on Morocco's Mediterranean coast, where local tribes fought a small-scale war in 1893 to prevent Spanish attempts to expand the enclave's borders. After a few months in Melilla, Bens went back to Cuba in 1894, this time to spend four years in full-scale war fighting the Cuban nationalists. When, in 1898, Spain was forced to acknowledge Cuba's independence, Bens returned once again to the peninsula, but he was soon dispatched to the Canary Islands, where he became fascinated by Africa.

The chance to satisfy his urge for adventure came when the ministry of state in Madrid asked the military authorities in the Canaries to name a captain for the post of "politico-military governor" of the colony of Río de Oro (q.v.). Bens was chosen (1903) and on January 17, 1904, he arrived in Villa Cisneros. His first preoccupation there was to win the confidence of the nomads, who had intermittently harassed the tiny Spanish settlement at Villa Cisneros since its establishment in the 1880s. He assured the Saharawis that Spain guarded no hostile intentions toward them and had no ambition to extend its presence into the interior as the French had then started to do in the Mauritanian Sahara. The "sugar-lump policy" was the name given to Bens's combination of appeasement and friendliness. Characteristic of Bens's style was his decision to import 200 sheep for a giant feast soon after his arrival in Villa

Cisneros, his guests being Oulad Delim, Oulad Bou Sbaa, and Arosien (qq.v.) from the enclave's vicinity. In 1906, Bens persuaded *chioukh* (q.v.) from the same tribes, plus the Reguibat (q.v.), to travel by steamer, with their camels, and take part in a pageantry in Las Palmas de Gran Canaria during a visit to the city by King Alfonso XIII.

By virtue of his careful nurturing of relations with the Saharawis, Bens was able to travel widely in the interior at a time of fierce Saharawi resistance to the northward thrusts of the French. His primary objective in this was to prepare the way for the establishment of a string of Spanish posts along the coast, from Cape Blanc to Ifni, and so prevent another European power from establishing itself along the coast. In fact, Bens's ambition to extend the Spanish presence along the coast from the enclave of Villa Cisneros was repeatedly frustrated by the vacillations of successive governments in Madrid, which were either under diplomatic pressure from their chief European rivals, the French, until the final border demarcations of 1912, or were fully absorbed by the difficulties of imposing Spanish rule over northern Morocco, where the semiconstant conflict between Spaniards and Moroccans culminated in the great Rif war of 1921–26.

Bens's first extensive expeditions into the interior were in 1907–8, but the most ambitious came in 1911 when he spent 42 days on an exploratory mission in the region around Tarfaya. He then suggested to the Spanish government that new settlements should be established to the north of Villa Cisneros. To this end, reconnaissance of the coast was carried out by a Spanish vessel, *El Parchel,* following which Bens proposed that Boujdour and Tarfaya (qq.v.) should be occupied. With the border questions with France still not resolved, however, Madrid hesitated, and Bens's suggestions were not put into effect. The same fate befell Bens's attempt to take possession of Ifni in 1911. Two previous Spanish attempts to land there, in 1878 and 1883, had already failed; this time, French pressure on the Moroccan sultan, Moulay Hafid (q.v.), led to the Moroccan foreign minister, El-Mokri, withholding the Moroccan delegations, which was to have met Bens at Sidi Ifni and arranged the hand-over. Spain was too weak to act on its own.

In 1912–13, there were further studies to prepare the occupation of Tarfaya. One of the most important was that made by Enrique d'Almonte (q.v.), an explorer dispatched by the Sociedad de Geografía de Madrid, who traveled widely in the territory in October 1913. By then, the French government was actively encouraging the extension of the Spanish presence within the zones allocated to Spain by the 1912 treaty, to complement France's own attempt to "pacify" the desert. Romanones, the Spanish prime minister, therefore gave Bens the go-ahead in 1914 for the occupation of Tarfaya. The onset of World War I delayed execution of the plans, but on October 15, Bens set sail with a band of Spanish soldiers, a few Saharawis, and enough supplies to last three months. However, as they sailed up the coast from Villa Cisneros, the steamship *Antónico* transmitted to Bens an order from the ministry of the navy to suspend the operation. Bens and his men then disembarked at La Sarga, a small bay about 50 km. south of Boujdour, and, ignoring the admiralty's instructions, set off overland, with an escort of 36 Saharawis, to Tarfaya. It took him 17 days to arrive, but, after taking possession of the buildings left there in the 1890s by Donald Mackenzie's North-West Africa Company, he was promptly ordered by a Spanish cruiser, the *Cataluña,* then lying offshore, to "embark with all personnel and return to Río de Oro." It was not until June 29, 1916, that Bens, by then a lieutenant colonel, finally ran up the Spanish flag over Tarfaya with Madrid's assent.

The next step was to take control of La Guera (q.v.) at Cape Blanc. On October 30, 1920, Bens received instructions from the ministry of state to occupy La Guera and set up fish-processing installations there. Preparations were made in the Canaries, from where Bens set sail on November 27 aboard the *Infanta Isabel,* with 3 other officers, 50 soldiers of the 66th Infantry, and some construction workers. After picking up some Saharawi allies near Dakhla, they landed at La Guera on November 30 and raised the flag, almost 36 years after the government of Antonio Cánovas del Castillo had declared a Spanish "protectorate" over Río de Oro, from La Guera to Boujdour (December 1884).

The occupation of Tarfaya, which lay in what the 1912

Franco-Spanish convention had defined as the southern zone of the Spanish protectorate in Morocco, led to Bens's receiving the title of *delegado* of the Spanish *alto comisario* (q.v.) in Morocco. Further south, in the Saguia el-Hamra and Río de Oro, where the 1912 convention gave Spain full sovereignty, Bens remained governor, the title losing its "politico-military" qualification in 1923.

When Bens left the governorship in 1925, handing it over to Lt. Col. de la Peña, the Spanish presence remained confined to the three little coastal enclaves of Villa Cisneros, Tarfaya, and La Guera. Even Villa Cisneros was still only a settlement of about 1,000 people, almost all Saharawis, camped around a fort and the fishing installations of the Compañía Transatlántica. La Guera, where the Sociedad Marcotegui set up a fish factory, and Tarfaya had even smaller settlements. "As a colony or dependency, and in part a Protectorate of Spain," a handbook on Spanish Sahara published by the British Foreign Office in May 1919 commented, "the country is, to all intents and purposes, still in its infancy, and does not show sign of growing into maturity." The first posts in the interior to be set up by the Spanish were not established until 1934, nine years after Bens's departure.

Later promoted to the rank of general, Bens died in 1949. Tarfaya was renamed Villa Bens in his memory, until 1958, when, following the Treaty of Cintra (q.v.), it was handed over to Morocco.

BENSOUDA, AHMED. One of the closest advisers of King Hassan II (q.v.), Ahmed Bensouda was appointed Morocco's deputy governor of Western Sahara in the tripartite administration (q.v.) set up after the Madrid Agreement (q.v.) of November 14, 1975. He arrived in El-Ayoun (q.v.) on November 25, 1975, to take up office alongside the Spanish governor-general and a deputy governor nominated by Mauritania. The tripartite administration came to an end on February 26, 1976, when Spain finally withdrew from the territory. Bensouda continued to play an important role in the Saharan problem, however. On October 20–21, 1978, he was one of the Moroccan officials who took part in unprecedented, though unsuccessful, talks with the Polisario Front (q.v.) in Bamako, Mali. He remains one of those closest to King Hassan, holding the position of royal adviser.

BERMS see DEFENSIVE WALLS

BILAD ES-SIBA. In defending its annexation of Western Sahara, the Moroccan government argued that Western Sahara historically constituted in precolonial times part of the *bilad es-siba* (land of dissidence), the parts of Moroccan territory that often or usually lay outside the effective control of the sultan's government, the *makhzen,* and hence were distinguished from the *bilad el-makhzen,* the areas that were directly controlled by the central government. Western Sahara was in a state of *siba* in the sense that there was no supratribal state authority maintaining law and order in this desert region before 1935, but the claim that it was part of the Moroccan bilad es-siba, which was otherwise normally constituted by Morocco's mountainous areas (the Atlas ranges and the Rif), has been hotly contested.

The Moroccan bilad es-siba escaped the makhzen's control in the sense that taxes were not paid, troops could not be levied for the sultan's armies there, and administration was carried out by *caids* (q.v.) chosen by the tribes even if the sultan's authority was delegated to them formally by *dahir* (decree). However, there was not a rigid distinction between bilad es-siba and bilad el-makhzen. Tribes often passed from dissidence to submission and vice versa, and the extent of the bilad el-makhzen, in relation to the bilad es-siba, recognized the spiritual, if not the temporal, authority of the sultan as *amir al-muminin* (commander of the faithful).

A typical example of the bilad es-siba was the region of the Anti-Atlas and the Oued Noun (to the north of Western Sahara in southwestern Morocco) during most of the three centuries preceding Morocco's colonization. A virtually independent statelet was established at Tazeroualt in the Anti-Atlas early in the 17th century, and, though it was brought under Alawite (q.v.) control by Moulay Rachid and Moulay Ismail (qq.v.), it was reborn in the 1760s, when a small state was also set up in Goulimine by a largely sedentary Tekna (q.v.) tribe, the Ait Moussa Ou Ali. Under the rule of the Beyrouk family, Goulimine's degree of independence was such that the Beyrouks negotiated with several French, Spanish, and English representatives during the 19th century. Nonetheless, these regions did at times come under the direct control of the makhzen–for example, during the reign of the Saadian sultan Ahmed el-Mansour at the end of the 16th century, when some of the Tekna tribes were *guich* tribes (i.e., provided military contingents in return for land); later under the first Alawite sultans, when they resumed their role as guich tribes, and then, following 150 years of *siba,* after the expeditions to the Oued Noun in 1882 and 1886 by Moulay Hassan I (q.v.), who once more reappointed *caids* among some of the Tekna tribes and established a garrison in Goulimine.

Taken to extremes, the concept of bilad es-siba shaded into that of tribes' full and permanent independence. There was inevitably a gray area in between. However, there was generally a rather clear distinction between the sedentary and seminomadic peoples of the Oued Noun, the Anti-Atlas and the Oued Draa (all now within southern Morocco) and the full-scale camel-rearing nomads further south in the Sahara. In the former, as noted above, direct rule by the makhzen, however short-lived, did punctuate the long periods of virtual independence; in Western Sahara, however, the absence of villages and oases (by contrast, for example, to the Touat-Gourara-Tidikelt regions of the Algerian Sahara, which were at times administered by officials of the Moroccan makhzen), the purely nomadic character of the population, the harshness of the climate and terrain, and the fiercely independent traditions of the main tribes effectively placed these peoples beyond the bilad es-siba.

BIR. An Arabic term for a well. See WATER RESOURCES.

BIR ENZAREN. An important water source in the south of the country, it is about 120 km. northeast of Dakhla (q.v.). Its deep well was a permanent source of good drinking water in precolonial times, and a small settlement grew up there during the Spanish colonial period. It had c. 1,300 residents in 1974. After the April 1976 Moroccan-Mauritanian partition, it fell within the Moroccan sector, forming a commune of the province of Boujdour (qq.v.). The Moroccan base there was the target of a major attack by the Polisario Front (q.v.) on August 11, 1979. Bir Enzaren remained one of the few Moroccan garrisons outside the "useful triangle" in Saguia el-Hamra (q.v.) until a major Polisario attack took place against one of Morocco's other exposed outposts, Guelta Zemmour (q.v.), on October 13, 1981. After that attack, Morocco elected to withdraw its 1,500–man garrison from Bir Enzaren, which was equally vulnerable; the pullout was completed by November 9. It did not come under Moroccan control again until 1985–86, when it was enclosed by one of the final stretches of the "defensive walls" (q.v.) that Rabat was constructing in the territory in an attempt to secure Western Sahara against Polisario raids.

BLANCO RODRIGUEZ, EDUARDO. A Spanish career officer, Col. Blanco was appointed head of the Dirección General de Promoción del Sahara (q.v.) on April 22, 1974, in order to oversee the plans then being made by the Franco regime (q.v.) to introduce internal self-government in the territory under an *estatuto político* (q.v.) as a first step toward independence in close association with Spain. He had previously worked for many years in the Francoist security service, the Dirección General de Seguridad (General Directorate of Security), first as director of information services (from 1959) and then as director general (from 1965). Working closely with the new governor-general, Gen. Gómez de Salazar, and the new secretary-general, Col. Rodríguez de Viguri (qq.v.), who were both appointed at about the same time, he planned to devolve some legislative powers to the Djemaa (q.v.), previously a purely consultative body, and establish a governing council composed partly of Saharawis chosen by the Djemaa. The estatuto político, which codified these constitutional changes, was approved by the Djemaa in July 1974, and the following November, a Saharawi political party, the PUNS (q.v.), was created with his approval to rival the Polisario Front (q.v.) and lead the country toward independence in a framework that would not threaten Spain's important interests in the territory's fishing and phosphate resources (qq.v.).

However, the estatuto político was never implemented because of the protests it elicited from Morocco, and in May 1975, the PUNS began to collapse as a result of the massive display of popular support for the Polisario Front during a tour of the territory by a UN Visiting Mission (q.v.). Later, in November 1975, the Spanish government abandoned completely its plans for internal self-government and eventual independence and signed the Madrid Agreement (q.v.) with Morocco and Mauritania. Testifying at a special hearing held by the foreign relations committee of the Cortes on March 13–16, 1978, Col. Blanco said he supported this 180-degree switch in Spanish policy at the end of 1975 because Polisario supremacy in Western Sahara would have threatened the security of the Canary Islands (because, he said, the front might have given bases to the Movement for the Self-Determination and Independence of the Canary Archipelago), and a failure to satisfy King Hassan II (q.v.) over Western Sahara would have prompted Morocco to threaten the Spanish enclaves of Ceuta and Melilla on its Mediterranean coast and the government's overriding priority had been to avoid war with Morocco, which he said had been a real danger at the time of the Green March (q.v.). Spain, he said, would have won a war but it "would have been Europe's last colonial war" and would have ruined Spain's carefully nurtured relations with the Arab world. Remarkably, Blanco told the Cortes hearing that "our information services, which I know, did not reveal anything about the preparations of the Green March, despite the enormous logistical apparatus which it was necessary to deploy." After the Madrid Agreement, Col. Blanco flew to El-Ayoun (q.v.) on November 26, 1975, to oversee the establishment of the tripartite administration (q.v.), which governed the territory until Spain's formal withdrawal on February 26, 1976.

BOJADOR. Spanish spelling of Boujdour (q.v.).

BOUABID, ABDERRAHIM. A leading Moroccan social-democratic politician, he has for long embraced strong irridentist views on Western Sahara. Though he did not support the Moroccan government's similar claim to Mauritania during the 1960s, he tended at that time to criticize the Moroccan government for failing to advance its claim to Western Sahara with sufficient vigor. When finally, in 1974, King Hassan II (q.v.) began to mount a strong challenge to Spain's plans to introduce internal autonomy and hold a referendum, Bouabid agreed in July to act as his special envoy on a mission to India, China, and other Asian countries in a (largely unsuccessful) bid to win international support for the Moroccan claim to the territory. Later, in September 1974, he took part in the Moroccan delegation to the UN (q.v.), along with the foreign minister, Ahmed Laraki (q.v.), and the leader of the Istiqlal Party, M'hamed Boucetta (q.v.), and played an important part there in convincing the Mauritanian foreign minister, Hamdi Ould Mouknass (q.v.), to harmonize Mauritania's embarrasing counterclaim by agreeing to the idea of eventual partition. Bouabid's full support for the Moroccan government's action over Western Sahara in 1974–75 was prompted both by an appreciation of the depth of popular support for the Saharan claim in Morocco and also by a calculation that an alliance with the monarchy on this issue would allow his long-harassed Union Socialiste des Forces Populaires (q.v.) to widen its freedom of action. After the start of the war with the Polisario Front (q.v.), he attempted to differentiate himself from the Moroccan government by taking an ultratough line, advocating crossborder raids into Algeria and the arming of an anti-Polisario militia of irregulars. After King Hassan announced in June 1981 that Morocco would thenceforth cooperate with the efforts of the Organization of African Unity (q.v.) and hold a referendum to decide the future of Western Sahara, Bouabid dissented. On September 8, 1981, the USFP issued a communiqué attacking the king's new, more accommodating stance on the Sahara, and he, along with several other party leaders, was detained the same day, charged with, inter alia, "demonstrations contrary to public order and attacks on the respect due to authority.'' On September 21, he was sentenced to one year in prison but was released after only a few months (February 1982), perhaps under pressure from the socialist government in France headed by François Mitterrand (q.v.). Preparatory to King Hassan's holding of new parliamentary elections, Bouabid was made one of several ministers of state without portfolio in an interim government on November 30, 1983. He served in that position until elections were held on September 14, 1984, and has continued since then to espouse a strongly pro-annexationist policy on Western Sahara.

BOUABID, MAATI. Born in 1927, he was appointed prime minister of Morocco by King Hassan II (q.v.) on March 27, 1979. As such, he was head of the Rabat government at a time when the war in Western Sahara was his country's main preoccupation. A member of the UNFP (q.v.), he had served as labor minister in 1958–60 and as justice minister in the government of Ahmed Osman (q.v.) in 1977–79. He remained premier until November 19, 1983, when he was replaced by Mohamed Karim Lamrani.

BOUCETTA, M'HAMED. As Morocco's foreign minister between 1977 and 1984, he played a major role in attempting to garner international support for Morocco's claim to Western Sahara. However, his term of office saw Morocco's diplomatic support diminishing, notably in the Third World and in such international forums as the UN and the OAU (qq.v.). Born in Marrakesh in 1925, he became a leader of the nationalist Istiqlal Party (q.v.), joining its political bureau in 1956 and becoming secretary-general in 1974 after the death of Allal El-Fassi (q.v.). He had served as secretary of state for foreign affairs in 1956 and as minister of justice in 1961–63. During the late sixties and early seventies, when the Istiqlal Party was out of office, he was vocal in urging King Hassan to take a tougher line against Spain over Western Sahara. In July 1974, he served as an envoy of the king in a major diplomatic campaign to win foreign support for Rabat's claim to Western Sahara. He was appointed minister of state without portfolio in March 1977, an office he held until his appointment as foreign minister under Prime Minister Ahmed Osman in October 1977. He retained this portfolio after Osman's replacement by Maati Bouabid (q.v.) in March 1979. Periodically during his tenure as foreign minister, he reiterated his country's unyielding stance on the Saharan issue, in particular refusing to negotiate directly with the Polisario Front (q.v.). At the height of the crisis caused within the OAU in February 1982 by the issue of whether to grant membership status to the Saharan Arab Democratic Republic (q.v.), Boucetta stated, "For us the Polisario does not exist either legally or internationally" and avowed, "There is no way that the Moroccan administration will leave the Western Saharan territory." He served as foreign minister until 1983, and from 1983 to 1985 was minister of state without portfolio in the Moroccan government. He was succeeded as foreign minister by Abdelouahed Belhaziz and thus left the government. However, Boucetta remained secretary-general of the Istiqlal Party, being elected to that position for the fourth consecutive time at the party's 12th congress in May 1989.

BOU-CRAA (variant: Bu-Craa). The site of a deposit of 1.7 billion tons of phosphates (q.v.), Bou-Craa is about 100 km. southeast of El-Ayoun (q.v.). Mining began there in 1972. After the April 1976 partition, it became part of the Moroccan zone. The small town there has remained in Moroccan hands, but all mining stopped in 1976 because of guerrilla attacks on the power lines and ore-carrying conveyor belt that link Bou-Craa with El-Ayoun *playa* (q.v.). Following construction of the first of Morocco's "defensive walls" (q.v.) in 1981–82, the town became less vulnerable to attacks by the Polisario Front (q.v.), and mining resumed on a very modest scale in July 1982.

BOUELA OULD AHMED ZINE. A leading militant of the Polisario Front (q.v.), he was appointed secretary-general for health, education, and social affairs in the first government of the SADR (q.v.), appointed on March 4, 1976. However, he died a few weeks later, on April 24, 1976, at Guelta Zemmour (q.v.) while Moroccan troops were closing in on this sanctuary from which he was helping to evacuate thousands of refugees who had gathered there since the Madrid Agreement (q.v.).

BOUJDOUR (variant: Bojador). About 170 km. south of El-Ayoun (q.v.), Cape Boujdour, or Cabo Bojador as it was known to the Spaniards, has been a familiar coastal landmark since the first Portuguese navigators reached it in the mid-15th century. Later, in the 20th century, Spanish colonial authorities built a lighthouse there to assist Canary fishing boats and other shipping along this dangerous stretch of coast. The lighthouse was attacked in December 1957 by a unit of the Army of Liberation (q.v.), which kidnapped its Spanish staff. They were eventually released in May 1959. When Spain withdrew from Western Sahara in 1975–76, Boujdour became part of the Moroccan zone. Though it still had no buildings besides the lighthouse and a small barracks, it was chosen as the "capital" of one of the three new Moroccan provinces created in Western Sahara at this time. A governor arrived, a desalination plant was built (1976), and neighboring nomads were enrolled in a house-building program. Until the early 1980s, Boujdour was protected from Polisario (q.v.) attack by only a small defensive perimeter in the immediate area. However, in May 1982, Morocco completed an extension of its "defensive wall" in Saguia el-Hamra (qq.v.) westward from the vicinity of Bou-Craa (q.v.) to enclose Boujdour.

BOUMEDIENNE, HOUARI. President of Algeria from 1965 until his death in 1978, Houari Boumedienne (born 1927) gave all-out military and diplomatic support to the Polisario Front (q.v.) after the entry of Moroccan and Mauritanian troops into Western Sahara in 1975.

He had been distrustful of Moroccan irredentism since the October 1963 Moroccan-Algerian border war, when, under President Ahmed Ben Bella, he was head of the Algerian army. However, he welcomed the decision by King Hassan II (q.v.) at the end of the sixties to improve Morocco's relations with Algeria and Mauritania and settle the lingering frontier disputes. On January 15, 1969, Hassan and Boumedienne signed a treaty of friendship at Ifrane, Morocco, and on May 27, 1970, at a summit in Tlemcen, Algeria, they decided to set up a commission to examine the Algerian-Moroccan border question. Two years later, on June 15, 1972, during an OAU (q.v.) summit in Rabat, they signed a convention that formally ended the border dispute by recognizing the de facto border. Boumedienne did not, however, recognize the Moroccan claim to Western Sahara in return for this concession on King Hassan's part. The Boumedienne government had consistently supported the UN General Assembly resolutions that, since 1966, had called on Spain to hold a referendum in the territory under UN supervision; after the start of the period of détente between Morocco and both Algeria and Mauritania in 1969, Boumedienne joined Hassan and President Mokhtar Ould Daddah (q.v.) in two tripartite summits, in Nouadhibou, Mauritania, on September 15, 1970, and Agadir, Morocco, on July 23–24, 1973, where all three heads of state voiced their support for self-determination in the territory in accordance with the UN resolutions. Like Hassan II, Boumedienne may have believed at this time that a referendum in Western Sahara would lead to unification with Morocco, because there was seemingly no strong nationalist movement there.

In March 1973, he allowed the Mouvement de Résistance "Les Hommes Blues" (q.v.) to establish an office in Algiers, but its leader, Edouard Moha, soon created a poor impression and was obliged to leave for Europe a few months later. One result of Moha's stay in Algiers was that the Boumedienne government refused to give support to the Polisario Front when it was founded in May 1973. Its secretary-general, El-Ouali Mustapha Sayed (q.v.), was even arrested and deported from Algeria that year. Unaware that the Polisario Front was a more serious organization than MOREHOB and believing that the Saharawi nationalist movement was small and factionalized, the Boumedienne regime regarded the front with suspicion until at least the summer of 1974 and did not provide substantive support until the spring of 1975. For these reasons, and also to avoid rupturing the good relations that had been established with Morocco since 1969, Boumedienne reacted cautiously to Hassan's sudden decision in

July 1974 to drop his support for self-determination and mount an all-out diplomatic campaign for annexation. At an Arab League summit in Rabat in October 1974, at which Hassan and Ould Daddah came to an understanding over Western Sahara, hinged on a commitment to the territory's future partition, Boumedienne actually voiced support for this papering over of the antagonistic Moroccan and Mauritanian claims. "We are with Morocco and Mauritania for the liberation of each piece of its land, not only the Western Sahara or the Sahara still under Spanish rule, but also Ceuta, Melilla, and all the islands still occupied by Spain," he told the summit. "Those are then historical attitudes which must be recorded." The following December, Algeria voted at the UN General Assembly in favor of the resolution, backed by Morocco and Mauritania, which submitted the Western Saharan problem to the International Court of Justice (q.v.) and requested Spain to postpone the referendum it had announced the previous August.

It was in the spring of 1975 that the Boumedienne government first showed signs of a change of heart. Boumedienne's foreign minister, Abdelaziz Bouteflika (q.v.), spoke out against the Moroccan claim to the territory at a meeting of Arab League foreign ministers held on April 21–27, and, when the UN Visiting Mission (q.v.) toured Saharawi camps in the Tindouf (q.v.) region of southwestern Algeria in May 1975, the Polisario Front was well installed there. In the same month, favorable mention of the movement in the government-controlled press began. Moreover, Boumedienne sent his ambassador in Paris, Mohammed Bedjaoui, to The Hague to argue the primacy of the principle of self-determination during the ICJ's proceedings in June-July. And, in a major speech on June 19, 1975, he affirmed that "the principle of self-determination has become a constant theme of Algerian policy which cannot be questioned as long as it is true that it constitutes a fundamental basis of our political philosophy." Boumedienne now began to make up for lost time. He condemned Morocco's Green March (q.v.) and began providing substantial military support for the Polisario Front. On October 29, he sent his interior minister, Mohammed Benahmed Abdelghani, to Madrid to try to stop

Spain from agreeing to hand the territory over to Morocco and Mauritania, and, on November 10, in a meeting at Bechar, Algeria, he warned Mauritania's President Ould Daddah of dire consequences if he tried to partition the territory with Morocco. When, however, Morocco, Mauritania, and Spain did come to terms, signing the Madrid Agreement (q.v.) on November 14, Boumedienne was not prepared to accept a fait accompli. "I am not like Christ," he said. "I will not turn the other cheek." On November 14, his government informed the UN secretary-general, Kurt Waldheim (q.v.), that it considered the agreement "null and void." Military aid to the Polisario guerrillas was stepped up, and the Algerian army briefly entered Western Saharan territory itself, to help organize the evacuation of refugees to Algeria, clashing with Moroccan troops at Amgala (q.v.) in January 1976. An open war between Morocco and Algeria was narrowly averted. On March 6, 1976, the Boumedienne government officially recognized the Saharan Arab Democratic Republic (q.v.) and pledged that it would "lend to its government all the political, moral, and material support necessary to the accomplishment of her people's national aspirations." By October 1976, it estimated that there were 50,000 Saharawi refugees on Algerian soil.

Military support to the guerrillas was gradually increased, as they became capable of handling more and more sophisticated material; when, in November 1977, King Hassan threatened retaliatory military strikes into Algeria, Boumedienne's Council of the Revolution warned Hassan that that would lead to all-out war between their two countries, a warning sufficient to make Hassan desist. He also strongly opposed France's military intervention against the guerrillas in 1977–78 and ordered Algerian state-owned companies to retaliate by refusing to place contracts with French firms. His commitment to the Polisario cause remained undiminished until his death on December 27, 1978, at the end of a long illness.

BOURGUND, GABRIEL. The architect of Operation Ouragan (q.v.), the Franco-Spanish counterinsurgency campaign against the Army of Liberation (q.v.) in February 1958, Gen.

Bourgund first became alarmed by the growing strength of the Army of Liberation when he was appointed supreme commander of the French forces in Morocco on November 15, 1955, the eve of the return of Mohammed V (q.v.) from his enforced exile in Madagascar. The French government had been forced, in fact, to let Mohammed V return to Morocco by the insurrection led by the Army of Liberation in the Rif in October. In the ensuing months, as Moroccan auxiliaries of the French army enrolled with partisans, the Army of Liberation became a powerful irregular army, especially in the south of Morocco. After Morocco's independence on March 3, French troops remained in the country, with General Bourgund still in command, but he became frustrated by Mohammed V's unwillingness to take the political risks of authorizing a French military operation in southern Morocco to destroy a movement of irregulars, which not only refused to submit to the royal government or to join the new regular army, the FAR (q.v.), but also threatened the security of French officials still in the south (a French captain, René Moureau, was kidnapped by the Army of Liberation on June 23) and was known to be preparing a Saharawi insurgency in the desert against both the French and the Spanish. The general's poor relations with the Moroccans prompted the French government to replace him on July 2, 1956, with Gen. René Cogny. He was then posted to Dakar, as commander of the French forces in French West Africa, an assignment that once again brought him up against the Army of Liberation, when its guerrillas staged their first attack in Mauritania, on February 15, 1957, about 100 km. northeast of Fort Trinquet (Bir Moghrein). A few days later, Bourgund held a strategy meeting in Tindouf (q.v.), Algeria, with General Cogny and General Ely, chief of staff of the French armed forces, and Spain was persuaded to allow French forces to stage hot-pursuit raids across the border into Western Sahara, where the guerrillas were able to move almost at will because of the weakness of the Spanish forces there.

On July 12, 1957, General Bourgund met the new governor-general of Africa Occidental Española (q.v.), Gen. Mariano Gómez Zamalloa, who agreed to extend the limit on

French cross-border raids to 60–80 km. Bourgund was dismayed, however, by the Spanish government's failure at this stage to reinforce the weak Spanish forces in Western Sahara and by Gómez Zamalloa's inevitable decision in the circumstances to withdraw the exposed Spanish garrisons in the interior to a few well-defended enclaves on the coast in August–October. However, at a second meeting with Gómez Zamalloa on September 20 in Dakar, he won support for the idea of a joint Franco-Spanish counterinsurgency campaign, for which he had already drawn up a rough outline and given the code name Ouragan. It was the high commissioner in Dakar, Guy Cusin, and his diplomatic councillor, Roger Chambard, who finally (December 30) persuaded the government of Félix Gaillard (q.v.) to adopt Bouraud's plan in principle and approach the Spanish authorities for support. When Spain's foreign minister, Fernando Maria Castiella (q.v.), gave the green light in the first week of January 1958, Bourgund attended a series of strategy meetings later in the month in Las Palmas and Dakar. The operation was finally launched on February 10, Bourgund committing 5,000 French troops, 600 vehicles, and 70 aircraft to the French wing of the campaign, known as Ecouvillon. Unfolding in two stages, on February 10–19 in Saguia el-Hamra (q.v.) and February 20–24 in Río de Oro (q.v.), the campaign decimated the Army of Liberation's forces in the Spanish colony, its remnants taking refuge to the north. Gen. Bourgund returned to France by steamer in April, being decorated with the Order of Christ by the captain general of the Canary Islands during a stop en route at Las Palmas. Later in the year, he became a Gaullist deputy in the French National Assembly.

BOUTEFLIKA, ABDELAZIZ. Born in 1937 and educated in Morocco, Abdelaziz Bouteflika joined the Front de Libération Nationale in 1956 and became Algeria's foreign minister in 1963. He supported the coup that brought Houari Boumedienne (q.v.) to power in June 1965, became a member of Boumedienne's Council of the Revolution, and remained foreign minister until after Boumedienne's death in December 1978. As foreign minister, he played a prominent part in bringing about the honeymoon in Algerian-

Moroccan relations in 1969–74, a success that may have influenced his initial inclination not to challenge Morocco's sustained diplomatic campaign in 1974 to promote its claim to Western Sahara. In the autumn of 1974, while Boumedienne formally endorsed the Moroccan-Mauritanian decision to harmonize their claims to the territory at the Arab League summit in Rabat (October), Bouteflika's delegation at the United Nations voted in favor of the successful Moroccan-Mauritanian bid to have the UN request an advisory opinion on Western Sahara's precolonial status from the International Court of Justice (q.v.). It was only in the spring of 1975, when Algerian leaders began to fear that the resurgence of ultranationalist sentiment in Morocco over Western Sahara might lead to the revival of the old Moroccan claim to parts of the Algerian Sahara that Bouteflika began to criticize publicly Morocco's claim to Western Sahara, most notably at a meeting of Arab League foreign ministers in Cairo in April, when he infuriated the Moroccan delegation by stating that Western Sahara "does not belong to Morocco." Algeria was by then beginning to give significant logistical support to the Polisario Front (q.v.) for the first time, but Algerian policy toward Western Sahara remained ambiguous in the summer of 1975. During a visit to Morocco on July 1–4, 1975, Bouteflika apparently made a deal with King Hassan, promising Algeria's tacit support for a Moroccan-Mauritanian takeover of Western Sahara in return for ratification by Morocco of the 1972 Moroccan-Algerian convention, which settled the two countries' old border dispute (Morocco dropping its claims to parts of Algeria) but which Morocco had refused to ratify. However, the agreement was either a ruse or rapidly rescinded in Algiers. From July 1975, Algeria's support for the Polisario Front was clear and unambivalent. Belatedly but with determination, Bouteflika mounted a strong diplomatic challenge to the Moroccan-Mauritanian claims to Western Sahara and tried to prevent the Spanish government from succumbing to King Hassan's pressure. He insisted on a self-determination referendum supervised and guaranteed by the UN (q.v.). "The opinion of the population directly concerned will always remain the primary and decisive element in any settlement," he argued in a speech to the UN General Assembly on October 9. However, he failed to prevent the Spanish government from executing a 180-degree turnaround in its Western Saharan policy and handing Western Sahara over to Morocco and Mauritania without the holding of a referendum. Bouteflika denounced the Madrid Agreement (q.v.) of November 14, 1975, as "null and void" and devoted himself to rallying international support for the Polisario cause, especially from Third World countries and in world bodies like the UN and the OAU (q.v.). He did much to win diplomatic recognition for the SADR (q.v.), which Algeria itself recognized on March 6, 1976, and he strongly condemned France's decision to send its air force into action against the Polisario guerrillas in Mauritania in December 1977. However, a year later, when President Boumedienne died (December 1978), Bouteflika left the foreign ministry after the failure of his own attempt to become president. One month after the election of Chadli Benjedid (q.v.) to the presidency (February 1979), Bouteflika was appointed one of two counselor ministers to the president, a post he held until January 1980. Thereafter, he did not hold any office in the government, though he remained a member of the FLN's political bureau. After a period of (apparently) self-imposed exile in France during the 1980s, Bouteflika returned to Algeria, where he was elected to the 268-member FLN central committee in November 1989.

BRAHIM OULD DERWICH see IBRAHIM HAKIM

BRITEL, ABDENBI. A colonel in the Moroccan Forces Armées Royales (q.v.), hc was appointed chief of staff of the Moroccan troops in Western Sahara on April 26, 1976, relieving Col. Ahmed Dlimi (q.v.), who had commanded the Moroccan troops that marched into the territory in 1975. He remained commander in the Saharan war zone until 1977.

BU-CRAA see BOU-CRAA

BUDGETS. Though heavily subsidized by the Spanish government, the territory's budget was minuscule until the mid-

1960s, when, as a result of the growing interest in Western Saharan minerals, the budget's administrative and economic infrastructure was rapidly expanded. In 1961–64, the annual budget was around P200–250 million. By 1966 it had reached P552 million; by 1972, P1,277 million; and by 1974, P2,460 million. In this last year, more than two thirds of the budget was covered by subsidies from Spain, but it was anticipated that this dependence would soon be over as a result of the rapid expansion of phosphate exports, which were expected to become the main source of government revenue if the territory proceeded to independence. Since the Spanish withdrawal in 1976, few reliable figures on Moroccan and Mauritanian government expenditure or revenue in Western Sahara have been published. Recurrent expenditure in the Mauritanian sector in 1977 was 162 million ougiyas, and total tax revenues were only 9 million ougiyas. State investment spending there in 1976–77 was set at 600 million ougiyas. Morocco launched a Dh1.5 billion emergency plan in its sector in 1976–78, financed partly by a Dh1 billion Saharan loan floated in Morocco in 1976. Whatever the true figures of recurrent and investment spending in Western Sahara after Spain's withdrawal from the territory, there is no doubt that, for Morocco and initially Mauritania too, it became a huge drain of resources. Not only were there huge military outlays to finance the war with the Polisario Front (q.v.), but there was no revenue from the phosphate industry, which was at a standstill from 1976 to 1982. As for the war itself, it has been variously estimated to cost Morocco between $1 million and $4 million daily. In addition, the cost of building and maintaining the system of "defensive walls" (q.v.) in Western Sahara must have been staggering. And finally, the Moroccan government claims to have spent over $1 billion on developing its "Saharan provinces" since 1976.

- C -

CABILDO PROVINCIAL. The Provincial Council of Western Sahara was established under a decree of April 19, 1961, on the organization of the "province" (q.v.) created in 1958. Theoretically, it was responsible for the administration of the province in matters ranging from industrial development to health and education. In fact, it had little real power over the governor-general (q.v.) and other provincial officials. A decree of November 29, 1962, laid down that the council would have 14 members, made up of a president, who thereby also became an exofficio member of the Cortes, and 13 *consejeros provinciales* (provincial councillors). Two members were to be elected by the *ayuntamientos* and *juntas locales* (qq.v.), six by the *fracciones nómadas* (q.v.), and six by industry, commerce, the professions, and cultural bodies. This was typical of the corporatist electoral system employed in Francoist Spain. The government kept a tight rein over the elections, the governor-general personally drawing up lists from which the six representatives of industry, commerce, the professions, and cultural bodies were chosen. In the first elections, in May 1963, seven Spaniards and seven Saharawis were elected. Khatri Ould Said Ould Joumani (q.v.) became the council's first president. With half of the seats coming up for reelection every two years, further elections were held in June 1965, after which Khatri Ould Said Ould Joumani was replaced as president by Saila Ould Abeida. However, by 1967, the Spanish authorities were not satisfied with the Cabildo. It did not give adequate representation to the traditionalist *chioukh* (q.v.) on whom the colonial authorities knew they would have to depend to counter the deepening politicization of the Saharawis as sedentation, urbanization, and modern education developed. So, by a decree of May 11, 1967, a new, exclusively Saharawi assembly, the Djemaa (q.v.), was created. The president of the Cabildo Provincial became an ex officio member.

CABO BLANCO. Spanish for Cape Blanc, the promontory in the extreme southwest of the territory where La Guera (q.v.) is sited.

CABO BOJADOR. Spanish for the cape at Boujdour (q.v.).

CABO YUBY. Spanish for Cape Juby, where Tarfaya (q.v.) is located.

CADI see QADI

CAID. In precolonial Morocco, a caid was a tribal chief appointed by royal *dahir* (q.v.), or decree. The appointment of *caids* in Western Sahara was extremely rare, since almost no sultans attempted or were able to assert significant influence in these remote desert regions. After his expeditions to the Oued Noun region of southern Morocco in 1882 and 1886, Moulay Hassan (q.v.) appointed a number of caids among the Tekna (q.v.), though primarily the more sedentary Tekna tribes of the Oued Noun. Of the nomadic Tekna, the Ait Oussa (q.v.) appear to have accepted the nomination of a caid at this time, but this did not prevent the Ait Oussa from joining the Reguibat (q.v.) in sacking Tindouf (q.v.) in 1896 despite the close links between that city's traders and Morocco. No caids were appointed among the main nomadic tribes of Western Sahara, such as the Reguibat and the Oulad Delim (q.v.). In postindependence Morocco—and, by extension in the three Moroccan provinces (q.v.) created in Western Sahara in 1976 and in Oued ed-Dahab (q.v.) from 1979—a caid is the official who heads the local government structure in a rural commune or *caidat* (q.v.). He is responsible to the *supercaid* of the *cercle* (qq.v.) of which his caidat forms part.

CAIDAT. The local administrative unit of the Moroccan state, corresponding to a municipal or rural commune (q.v.). Several *caidats* were created in the three provinces (q.v.) established in the Moroccan sector of Western Sahara after the 1976 partition and in Oued ed-Dahab (q.v.) after its annexation by Morocco in 1979. Each caidat is headed by a *caid* (q.v.) in rural areas or by a *pasha* (q.v.) in municipalities. In both cases, they are civil servants, appointed by and responsible to the ministry of the interior. Several caidats make up a *cercle,* which is headed by a supercaid (qq.v.).

CAMELS see LIVESTOCK

CAPE BLANC (variant: Cabo Blanco). A cape in the extreme south, it is the site of La Guera (q.v.).

CAPE BOUJDOUR see BOUJDOUR

CAPE JUBY (variant: Cabo Yuby). A cape about 35 km. north of the post-1958 Moroccan-Western Saharan border, it is the site of Tarfaya (q.v.).

CERCLE. A subdivision of a Moroccan province (q.v.), a *cercle* comprises several urban and rural *caidats* (q.v.). Several cercles were established in the part of Western Sahara annexed by Morocco under the 1976 partition and in Oued ed-Dahab (q.v.) after its occupation in 1979. Cercles are headed by *supercaids* (q.v.), who are appointed by and responsible to the Moroccan ministry of the interior.

CHARIA see SHARIA

CHEICH see SHAYSH

CHEIKH (variant: *shaykh*). Pl. *chioukh*. A "notable" in traditional Saharawi society, of either religious or political character. The head of a religious brotherhood or *zawiya*, or of a tribe, fraction, or subfraction (qq.v.).

CHENAGLA. A small tribe that traditionally lived near the coast and engaged in fishing.

CHIOUKH. Pl. of *cheikh* (q.v.).

CINTRA, AGREEMENT OF (APRIL 1, 1958). The agreement by which Spain handed over to Morocco the northernmost strip of its Saharan territory, the Tekna Zone (q.v.), which had been defined by the Franco-Spanish Convention of November 11, 1912, (q.v.), as being the southern sector of the Spanish protectorate zone in Morocco. The 25,600 sq. km. region, which includes the Ouarkziz and Zini mountains and the settlements of Tan-Tan, Tarfaya (q.v.), and Zaag, was bordered in the north by the Oued Draa (q.v.), in the east by the 11th meridian west of Paris, and in the south by the parallel 27° 40′ north. The Moroccan government had been demanding that Spain hand the region over in compliance with its commitment to recognize the ''territorial unity of the (Moroccan) empire, which the international treaties recognize,'' made in the Spanish-Moroccan Declaration of Madrid (April 7, 1956), by which Madrid ended its protectorate in northern Morocco and recognized Morocco's independence. The Spanish government's delay in handing over the southern sector of its protectorate zone was due to the activity there of the Army of Liberation (q.v.), the insurrectionary movement that then controlled much of southern Morocco and was at war with the Spanish in both Ifni and Western Sahara and with the French in southwest Algeria and northern Mauritania. The Spanish government informed Morocco in 1957 that it was prepared to hand over the Tekna Zone, but only after the Moroccan government and its regular army, the FAR (q.v.), had taken control of the regions to its north from the irregulars of the Army of Liberation. The success of the joint Franco-Spanish counterinsurgency campaign in Western Sahara in February 1958, known as Operation Ouragan (q.v.), and the gradual extension of the Moroccan government's control of the regions south of Agadir paved the way for the reopening of Spanish-Moroccan negotiations about the hand-over of the Tekna Zone. These started on March 18, 1958, when Felipe de Alcover Sureda, the Spanish ambassador in Rabat, began talks with the Moroccan foreign minister, Ahmed Balafrej. Then, on April 1, 1958, Balafrej met his Spanish counterpart, Fernando María Castiella, in Cintra, Portugal, and reached an agreement that the Tekna Zone would be handed over to Morocco on April 10, 1958. No joint communiqué was issued after the agreement, however, because of the differences between Spain and Morocco over the rest of Spain's Saharan territories. ''Mr. Balafrej refused to recognize the southern frontiers of the said zone and expressed in that respect the strongest reserves,'' the Moroccan foreign ministry stated on April 2. There was also disagreement in the ensuing weeks about the continued presence of 1,500 Spanish troops at Tarfaya, who remained on the same provisional basis as the 35,000 Spanish troops still in northern Morocco two years after the ending of the Spanish protectorate there. The Tarfaya garrison was withdrawn a few weeks later. A difficulty of a quite different order prevented the FAR from reaching Tarfaya in time for the hand-over ceremony set for April 10. One thousand Moroccan regulars set out from Goulimine to make their way there; but a large force of Saharawis, ex-supporters of the Army of Liberation, blocked their path at the Oued Chebeika. Crown Prince Moulay Hassan, the future Hassan II (q.v.), who was then chief of staff of the FAR and had planned to attend the April 10 ceremony, eventually visited Tarfaya on July 22, 1958, for the first official celebration of its integration with Morocco.

CLIMATE. The harshness of the Saharan climate is legendary. Its principal characteristics are the extreme variations in temperature and the very low rainfall. Inland, temperatures can reach 50°C during the day and then fall below zero at night. The coastal regions, which include the main population settlements, enjoy a somewhat more moderate climate, the mean temperature being around 20°–25°C and maximum and minimum temperatures around 0°–15°C and 35°–42°C in El-Ayoun and Dakhla (qq.v.). Annual rainfall seldom rises above 50 mm. and is often much less. Rains usually come in the autumn, from September onward, but there is great irregularity in both time and space. Another characteristic of the climate is represented by the strong winds that sweep across the territory, usually in a northeast-to-southwest direction. The *irifi* (q.v.), which comes from the east or southeast, gathering sand particles as it crosses the vast desert, constitutes perhaps the worst affliction—a searing sandstorm that impairs visibility and destroys vegetation.

COMITE MILITAIRE DE REDRESSEMENT NATIONAL. The Military Committee of National Recovery was the military junta that came to power in Mauritania as a result of the overthrow of President Mokhtar Ould Daddah (q.v.) on July 10, 1978. Its principal objective was to extract Mauritania from the war in Western Sahara and rebuild Mauritania's war-shattered economy. Fortunately for the CMRN and its president, Col. Mustapha Ould Mohammed Salek (q.v.), the Polisario Front (q.v.) responded to the coup by declaring two days later a "temporary halt in military operations in Mauritanian territory." Much less easy was the negotiating of a definitive end to Mauritania's involvement in the Saharan conflict. Though the CMRN wanted peace above all, it was anxious not to antagonize Morocco, which had 9,000 troops in Mauritania at the time of the coup. It did not want to replace one enemy with another, and it was also under strong pressure from France not to make a unilateral peace agreement with the Polisario guerrillas. The CMRN hoped, somewhat naively, that its coup would set in motion a "peace dynamic" that would infect the other parties to the conflict, and it banked on France's using its influence over both Morocco and Algeria to encourage a global peace settlement. Within this framework, the CMRN held a series of negotiations with the Polisario Front—in August 1979 in Libya; on September 9–16, 1979, in Paris; on October 17–18, 1979, in Bamako, Mali; and on October 18, 1979, in Tripoli. But these talks ended in failure, as did the CMRN's whole attempt to bring about a global peace settlement involving all the parties to the conflict. The CMRN, with French encouragement, suggested to the Polisario negotiators that they accept the creation of a Saharawi "ministate" in Tiris el-Gharbia (q.v.), the Mauritanian sector of Western Sahara, leaving Morocco in control of the phosphate-rich northern region of the territory. King Hassan II (q.v.) spoke out forcefully against the creation of such a ministate in a speech on August 20, 1978. He might have been persuaded to accept the idea if he had been assured that the Polisario Front would drop its claim to the rest of the territory, but this was something that the guerrilla movement was adamant that it would never contemplate. The front became increasingly frustrated by the CMRN's refusal to renounce its Western Saharan claim unilaterally, and it was partly to placate the guerrilla movement (and keep it from rescinding the cease-fire) that President Mustapha Ould Mohammed Salek announced in January 1979 that all remaining Moroccan troops (then about 7,000) would be withdrawn from Mauritania by the end of March. But the pledge was not carried out, and the CMRN appeared to be in a quandary over how to proceed over the Saharan problem. It was also wracked by internal factional conflicts and was facing heightened tension between Mauritania's two main communities, the blacks and the Moors. On April 6, 1979, it was dissolved as a result of a palace coup led by Ahmed Ould Bouceif (q.v.), who established a new Comité Militaire de Salut National (q.v.).

COMITE MILITAIRE DE SALUT NATIONAL. The Military Committee of National Salvation was the military junta that came to power in Mauritania on April 6, 1979, replacing the Comité Militaire de Redressement National (q.v.), as a result of an internal struggle in the CMRN. It was the CMSN that, after several changes in policy and leadership, eventually, on August 5, 1979, ended Mauritania's involvement in the Western Saharan war by signing the Algiers Agreement (q.v.) with the Polisario Front (q.v.). It came to power as a result of serious internal faction-fighting in the CMRN and the failure of the CMRN and its president, Col. Mustapha Ould Mohammed Salek (q.v.) to extract Mauritania definitively from the Western Saharan conflict (its principal pledge when it came to power on July 10, 1978) and to resolve serious domestic problems, notably a heightening of tension between Mauritania's blacks and Moors. Mustapha Ould Mohamnmed Salek remained president under the new regime, but his office was now a purely titular one. The new strongman was Ahmed Ould Bouceif, the prime minister, but, before he could seriously set about finding a solution to the Western Saharan problem, he was killed in an air crash, on May 27, 1979. He was succeeded by his defense minister, Mohammed Khouna Ould Heydallah (q.v.), an officer of Saharawi origin, on May 31, while Mustapha Ould Mohammed Salek resigned on June 3, to be succeeded as titular president by Lt. Col. Mohammed Mahmoud Ould Ahmed Louly (q.v.), he in turn giving up the presidency in January 1980 to Ould Heydallah, who then combined all three posts of president, premier, and defense minister. After becoming premier at the end of May 1979, Ould Heydallah was determined to end Mauritania's involvement in the Western

Saharan conflict once and for all, but, like his predecessors, he feared how Morocco might react to a unilateral peace agreement with the Polisario guerrillas, so his policy was at first cautious and ambiguous. Out of frustration, the guerrillas rescinded their cease-fire on July 12, 1979, exactly one year after its proclamation, and immediately they staged a successful attack on Tichla, a small settlement in the Mauritanian sector of Western Sahara, Tiris el-Gharbia (q.v.). This rapidly brought the CMSN to the negotiating table. On August 5, 1979, the CMSN and the Polisario Front signed the Algiers Agreement, Mauritania formally renouncing its claim to Western Saharan territory. Mauritanian troops were then withdrawn from Tiris el-Gharbia, and the remaining Moroccan troops in Mauritania were also withdrawn, but Morocco unilaterally annexed Tiris el-Gharbia on August 14, and relations between Morocco and the CMSN became increasingly strained.

The CMSN retained a garrison in La Guera (q.v.) in the extreme south of Western Sahara, out of fear of seeing Moroccan forces in the vicinity of Nouadhibou, a port city upon which Mauritania depends for both its fishing industry and its iron ore exports. The Moroccan government repeatedly accused the CMSN of allowing Polisario guerrillas to stage attacks from Mauritanian territory, and on May 16, 1981, there was an unsuccessful coup attempt in Nouakchott, which the CMSN accused Morocco of masterminding. Diplomatic relations with Rabat were severed the same day, and the coup plotters were rounded up, summarily tried by a military court, and executed. Relations with Morocco remained poor, and King Hassan continued to accuse the CMSN of allowing Polisario to transit through northern Mauritania and establish bases there. Ould Heydallah always denied these charges, but as time went on, he tilted further toward Polisario and became less inclined to follow the cautious advice of his colleagues.

On January 20, 1983, a Moroccan gunboat shelled Mauritanian-held La Guera. Although the incident was a minor one, Ould Heydallah then threatened to formally recognize the SADR in 1984 if no progress was made in ending the Saharan war under the auspices of the Organization of

African Unity (q.v.). No diplomatic headway was forthcoming in 1983, and so Mauritania recognized the Saharawi state on February 27, 1984. This move was reportedly made by Ould Heydallah without any consultations with the rest of the CMSN and was met with considerable reservations from many in the ruling group, notably Maouiya Ould Sid 'Ahmed Taya (q.v.), the prime minister and defense minister who was soon demoted to army chief of staff for his objections. Faced with this action and by Mauritania's other serious problems, the CMSN decided to act, and so it restored the collegial decision making that had been its watchword. On December 12, 1984, while Ould Heydallah was out of the country, he was deposed and replaced by Ould Taya in a bloodless palace coup. Upon his return, Ould Heydallah was placed under house arrest, where he remained until late 1988. The reconstituted CMSN, although it did not revoke its recognition of the SADR, was quick to reassert a more neutral position on the Western Sahara issue. Relations were soon restored with Morocco, and Polisario activities in Mauritania were somewhat curtailed.

COMMANDOS DE LA MARCHE VERTE. Special commando groups named after the Green March (q.v.), the CMVs were set up by the Moroccan army in 1979 to engage in commando-type operations against the Polisario Front (q.v.).

COMMERCE. In traditional Saharawi society, the nomads were not self-sufficient economically. They depended on trade (almost entirely in the form of barter) with the Maghreb to the north, the black peoples to the south, and, from the 15th century, European traders on the Atlantic coast. Indeed, trade was an important axis of their economy, along with live-stock-herding and raiding. Their main ''exports'' were their livestock, wool, and the salt mined in the Sahara's salt-pans, while they depended on ''imports'' of cereals (mainly barley from the Maghreb and millet from the blacks), dates (from the oases of southern Morocco or Mauritania), sugar and tea (both of which were introduced in the 18th-19th centuries), cloth and other necessities, armaments, and such luxuries as Moroccan carpets. In particular, the Saharawis would frequent the markets, fairs and *moussems* (religious fairs) of such southern Moroccan towns as Goulimine and Assa. The Saharawis also participated in the centuries-old trans-Saharan caravan trade, acting either as traders themselves or as guides and military escorts, or alternatively pillaging the caravans of others. To the black peoples of the Senegal River, the bend of the Niger, and beyond they sold salt from the Saharan salt-pans, as well as cloth and other manufactured goods brought from Europe and the Maghreb, while (depending on the epoch) slaves, gold-dust, and ostrich feathers were brought back to the cities and ports of the Maghreb and to the European traders on the coast.

Markets tended to be controlled by tribes or states by virtue of their donation of areas in which vital trading cities, wells, oases, and salt-pans were located. Inevitably this lucrative commercial system aroused ethnic and political rivalries. One of the most important was the struggle of the Sanhaja (q.v.), under the leadership of the Almoravids, to gain control of the northern trading city of Sijilmassa from the Zenata (q.v.) and of the southern trading city of Aoudaghost from the Soninke of Ghana in the 11th century. Commercial interests were usually the principal motive for the occasional direct intervention in the Sahara by Moroccan dynasties. Thus, the struggle between the Saadians and the Songhay of Gao for control of the salt-mines of Teghazza and the trans-Saharan trade in gold and slaves culminated in the seizure of Timbuctoo in 1591 by an army dispatched by Ahmed el-Mansour, though Moroccan control of Timbuctoo was ephemeral. Trade routes tended to shift through the centuries, as wells, cities, and oases shifted from the control of one ethnic group or state to another. Also, the arrival of the Europeans on the Atlantic coast gradually shifted much of the trade to the coast, especially in the 18th and 19th centuries.

It was the hope of tapping the trans-Saharan trade that prompted the Compañia Comercial Hispano-Africana to establish the trading post at Dakhla (q.v.) in 1884, which gave birth to the Spanish colony in Western Sahara. It failed as a commercial venture, however, since few caravans were attracted and the price on the world market of the most important commodity brought there, ostrich feathers, plummeted as a result of the sharp increase in exports from South Africa at that time. For several decades thereafter, exports were limited to the fish-meal produced at a small factory in La Guera (q.v.), livestock, skins, and seaweed, and imports consisted of cloth, sugar, tea and other basic consumer items sold to the Saharawis, and the needs of the handful of Spaniards in the coastal enclaves. Imports slowly rose, however, as the Spanish civilian and military presence gradually increased from the 1930s. By the 1950s, imports were about double exports, though trade remained minuscule. In 1958, for example, P21.4 million worth of goods were imported, whereas total exports reached only P0.9 million.

However, as the economic and administrative infrastructure was expanded in the 1960s and early 1970s to service the prospecting for and exploitation of minerals, imports of investment goods started to expand dramatically. At the same time, thousands of Europeans began to arrive to work in the territory, and the majority of Saharawis abandoned their nomadic traditions, settling in the small but growing towns. The market expanded and the importing of luxury consumer goods was encouraged by the creation of a ''free zone,'' which allowed Spanish and Saharawi traders to import goods from the Canary Islands at import duties far below those imposed in Spain. TV sets, radios, watches, and household electrical appliances poured into the country, many of them to be smuggled across the border into neighboring territories. The recorded number of Saharawi businessmen rose from 79 in 1960 to 981 in 1974. By 1971, total imports had reached P1,618 million. Exports remained negligible until the start of phosphate mining in 1972. In 1974, phosphate sales brought in P2,411 million, and for the first time there was a trade surplus.

After Spain's withdrawal in 1976, both Morocco and Mauritania decided to maintain the free-zone system. Indeed, they extended it by abolishing import duties entirely in order to buy the loyalty of the Saharawi trading class. Most of the Saharawi traders remained in the towns to maintain their businesses, only a minority joining the exodus of refugees (q.v.) to Algeria. From Dakhla and La Guera, the flow of smuggled goods into Mauritania became even greater than it had been during Spanish rule, most of the smuggling being done by Mauritanian army officers and civil servants. The same thing went on in the Moroccan zone, where imports of Mercedes-Benz cars for sale to Moroccan army officers and civil servants at half the after-duty price then current in the rest of Morocco had become a matter of public scandal by 1978. However, in 1978–79, the Moroccan authorities finally placed restrictions on the importers in El-Ayoun (q.v.) on account of Morocco's severe balance of payments problems. In the years since, despite this, many duty-free goods continued to flow into the parts of the territory controlled by Morocco, mostly from the Canary Islands. Regardless of the cost of this state of affairs to Rabat, however, it was no doubt politically expedient to let it continue.

COMMUNE. The basic unit of local government in Morocco. Communes were set up in the Moroccan sector of Western Sahara after the 1976 partition and in Oued ed-Dahab (q.v.) after its annexation in 1979. There are both rural and municipal communes, which have elected *conseils communaux*. The latter have little real power, being effectively subservient to the local state administration, which is run by *caids* and *pashas* (qq.v.) appointed by the ministry of the interior. Several communes make up a province (q.v.).

CONCEJALES. *Concejales* (councillors) were the members of the *ayuntamientos* (q.v.), the city councils set up after Western Sahara's conversion into a Spanish province (q.v.) in 1958. Two ayuntamientos were set up in El-Ayoun and Dakhla (qq.v.) by a decree of November 29, 1962. This stated that El-Ayoun's ayuntamiento would have 12 concejales plus an *alcalde* (mayor) and that Dakhla's would have eight concejales and a mayor. The alcaldes were nominated by the governor-general; the concejales were elected, under the strict state supervision of the Francoist system, half being elected by the male heads of families

living in the municipality, the other half by groups representing commerce, industry, the professions, and cultural interests according to the corporatist principles of the Francoist
system. With regard to the latter, the 1962 decree required
the governor-general to draw up lists of candidates (three
times as great as the number of seats to be filled) for each
corporate group. The concejales' mandate lasted for four
years, half being reelected every two years. The first municipal elections were held in May 1963. In El-Ayoun, seven
Spaniards and five Saharawis were elected concejales. In
Dakhla, four Saharawi and four Spanish concejales were
elected.

CONSEIL COMMUNAL. A communal council in the Moroccan
system of local government, which was introduced into the
Moroccan-held sector of Western Sahara in 1976 and extended to Oued ed-Dahab (qq.v.) after the Moroccan annexation of the previously Mauritanian sector of the country in
August 1979. Communal councils are known as *conseils
ruraux* in rural areas and as *conseils municipaux* in towns. In
both cases, they have very little real power: Their budgets are
almost entirely dependent on subsidies from the central
government; they are closely supervised by the heads of the
caidats (q.v.), the local administrative unit of the state, to
which they correspond; and their formal powers are limited
to discussion of the budget and minor proposals that have
prior government approval. According to the Moroccan
government, free elections were held in Western Sahara to
select councillors on November 12, 1976. In fact, the elections were tightly controlled by the ministry of the interior.
The Polisario Front (q.v.) naturally did not take part; not
even the Moroccan opposition parties, such as the USFP and
the PPS (qq.v.), which supported the annexation of Western
Sahara, were allowed to present candidates. Only the conseils
municipaux, which were set up in El-Ayoun, Smara, Boujdour,
Tarfaya (qq.v.), and, after the annexation of Tiris el-Gharbia,
Dakhla (q.v.), really functioned in any sense at all.

CONSEIL MUNICIPAL see CONSEIL COMMUNAL

CONSEIL NATIONAL DE SECURITE. The National Security Council was set up in Morocco by King Hassan II (q.v.) in March 1979 to associate the parliamentary opposition parties more closely with the war effort against the Polisario Front (q.v.). The establishment of the council followed bitter criticism of the conduct of the war, notably from the Istiqlal Party, the USFP, and the PPS (qq.v.), after the successful guerrilla raid into the southern Moroccan provincial capital of Tan-Tan (q.v.) on January 28, 1979. This dramatic Polisario success jolted Moroccans, and on March 8, the Moroccan parliament met in extraordinary session to hear an address from King Hassan. After announcing that "Morocco is faced, in its southern territory, with an ever-increasing difficult situation which, if allowed to continue, would place the country in serious danger," the king said that he had "deemed it necessary to associate the whole nation, through its representatives, with the decision-making process" and that "in this perspective, we have decided to create, next to us, and parallel to our government, a council composed of representatives of all organized political tendencies, whose role will be to assist us in the determination and the conduct of our policy with regard to safeguarding our national territory and the security of the nation." However, this was more of a palliative to temper nationalist criticism than the start of real involvement by the parliamentary opposition in determining war policy, which remained firmly in the king's hands. Though the Istiqlal Party (which had been in the government since 1977) and the USFP and the PPS (which had remained in opposition) were all included in the new council, it hardly ever met and had no real decision-making powers. It rapidly fell into abeyance.

CONSEIL RURAL see CONSEIL COMMUNAL

CONSEJEROS PROVINCIALES. These were the provincial councilors who sat in the Cabildo Provincial (q.v.) set up by the decrees of April 19, 1961, and November 29, 1962, on the organization of the new Spanish "province" (q.v.) of the Sahara. According to article 59 of the latter of these two laws, there were 14 *consejeros provinciales,* of whom two represented *ayuntamientos* and *juntas locales* (qq.v.), i.e., the councils set up in the urban settlements; six represented the *fracciones nómadas* (q.v.), the administrative units for the nomadic part of the population; and six represented such corporate interest groups as industry, commerce, the professions, and cultural groups. Their term of office lasted four years, half of the councillors being elected every two years. The first elections to the Cabildo Provincial were held in May 1963, with seven Spaniards and seven Saharawis being elected.

CORTINA Y MAURI, PEDRO. Born in 1908, Pedro Cortina y Mauri had a long diplomatic career before serving as Spain's foreign minister in 1974–75, when he played a major role in the evolution of Spanish policy toward Western Sahara. He was firmly convinced of the need to end Spanish colonial rule in the territory—not only because the collapse of Portugal's African empire after the April 1974 coup in Lisbon showed that the days of direct colonial rule were over but also because the Spanish campaign at the United Nations (q.v.) over Gibraltar could only be credible if Spain accepted decolonization in Western Sahara. On July 4, 1974, he informed the ambassadors of Morocco, Mauritania, and Algeria in Madrid of the Spanish government's decision to pave the way for self-determination by granting the territory internal autonomy. When the Spanish-created Partido de la Unión Nacional Saharaui (q.v.), the government's favored candidate for the leadership of an independent Western Sahara, began to disintegrate in the summer of 1975 as a result of the mushrooming of popular support for the Polisario Front (q.v.), Cortina y Mauri became convinced of the need to come to terms with the guerrilla movement. On September 9, 1975, he met the front's secretary-general, El-Ouali Mustapha Sayed (q.v.), in Algeria, arranging for a swap of prisoners and, according to El-Ouali, agreeing upon terms for a hand-over of power to the Polisario Front. Only a few weeks later, however, the Spanish government, under intense pressure from Morocco, executed a sharp about-face in policy and, against Cortina y Mauri's advice, signed the Madrid Agreement (q.v.) on November 14, 1975, opening the way to a Moroccan-Mauritanian occupation without a referendum. It was, he thought, a dishonorable betrayal of Spain's pledges to proceed toward self-determination. He left the foreign ministry in December 1975.

COUNCIL FOR THE COMMAND OF THE REVOLUTION (OF THE SADR). The former constitution of the Saharan Arab Democratic Republic (q.v.), adopted by the 6th general popular congress of the Polisario Front (qq.v.), which was held on December 7–10, 1985, stated that "the Council for the Command of the Revolution [CCR] is the supreme organ of executive power in the SADR." From 1976 to 1991, the members of this body doubled as members of the front's executive committee, the two leading organs of state and party having been collapsed into one as a temporary wartime measure. At Polisario's 8th congress, held on June 18–20, 1991, the CCR, along with the Executive Committee and the Political Bureau (qq.v.), were abolished as part of the sweeping government changes instituted at that gathering.

For a list of the members of the last CCR (as of 1990), see EXECUTIVE COMMITTEE.

COUNCIL OF MINISTERS (OF THE SADR). The announcement of the first council of ministers of the Saharan Arab Democratic Republic (q.v.) was made on March 4, 1976, a few days after the proclamation of the republic on February 27. According to the new constitution of the SADR, adopted provisionally at the Polisario Front's 8th general popular congress (qq.v.), held in June 1991, the council of ministers is the primary body comprising the government of the Saharawi state (Article 89), subject to the supervision of the president of the SADR (Article 88) and the national parliament (Article 33). The council of ministers as of early 1992 is as follows (see individual entries where indicated):

Prime Minister	Mahfoud Ali Beiba (q.v.)
Ministers	
Interior	Abdelkader Taleb Omar (q.v.)
Foreign Affairs	Mohammed Salem Ould Salek (q.v.)

Defense	Mohammed Lamine Ould Bouhali (q.v.)
Information	Mohammed Ould Sidati (q.v.)
Justice	Abeida Cheikh
Education	Khalil Sidi M'Hamed
Health	Batal Sidi Ahmed (q.v.)
Economic Development	Mohammed M'Barek Rahal
Equipment and Transport	M'Hamed Mustapha Tlaimidi
Commerce	Salek Baba Hassana
Culture	Tami Mohammed
Secretary-General at the Presidency	Malainine Ould Saddick (q.v.)

- D -

DAHIR. A Moroccan decree, issued by the sultan or, since Morocco's independence, by the king.

DAHMAN. A tribal military leader, usually appointed by the *ait arbain* (q.v.).

DAIRA. The *dairat* are subdivisions of the three *wilayat* (q.v.) of the Saharan Arab Democratic Republic (q.v.). Though intended by the leaders of the Polisario Front (q.v.) to become the regional and local administrative units of an independent country after the end of the war with Morocco, the wilayat and dairat have in fact been the units of administration of the rcfugccs (q.v.) in thc Tindouf (q.v.) region of southwestern Algeria since their creation in 1976. Since 1976, mass assemblies, known as popular base congresses (q.v.), have been held periodically in each camp or daira to elect both the daira's delegates to the general popular congress (q.v.) and the members of the daira popular council. This council, which oversees the administration of the refugee camp, is headed by an administrative official who is an *ex officio* member of the wilaya popular council. Since the holding of the second popular base congresses, in March-April 1977, it has had five other members, each responsible for heading one of the five daira committees supervising education, health, justice, food, and crafts. Every adult member of the daira is assigned to one of these committees. Administration has been the sole responsibility of the five specialized committees of the daira popular council. For purposes of "political orientation," the entire adult population of each daira has also belonged since 1976 to eleven-member cells, headed by an *arifa* (q.v.), responsible to the respective wilaya's Department for Training and Orientation.

DAKHLA. The Dakhla peninsula protrudes some 38 km. from the Atlantic coastline, enclosing Río de Oro (q.v.) bay, the only real bay along the 875 km. coast. In 1881, the Sociedad de Pesquerías Canario-Africanas (q.v.) set up a pontoon there. Then, in 1884, the Compañía Comercial Hispano-Africana arrived and, following negotiations between Emilio Bonelli and local tribes in November of that year, founded the settlement to be known as Villa Cisneros. However, on March 9, 1885, this little trading settlement was attacked by the Oulad Delim (q.v.), who killed several Spaniards and forced the rest to set sail for the Canaries. Bonelli returned the following June with a force of 20 Spanish soldiers who thereafter formed a permanent garrison. However, the attacks continued, notably on March 24, 1887; September 4, 1890; March 4, 1892, when a Syrian disciple of Cheikh Ma el-Ainin (q.v.), Ayoub, led the attackers; and on November 2 and 13, 1894, when the attackers were a combined force of Oulad Delim, Arosien, and Oulad Bou Sbaa (qq.v.). Finally, the Spaniards were left at peace in their tiny enclave after a trade concession agreement was signed with Cheikh Ma el-Ainin (q.v.) on March 2, 1895. However, the settlement at Dakhla was not a commercial success. Very few caravans arrived there to trade with the Spaniards. The Saharawis sold only wool and skins and some ostrich plumes, whose prices on the world market were falling dramatically by then on account of the rapid expansion of exports from South Africa. In 1893, the Compañía Comercial Hispano-Africana went into liquidation, its installations at Vila Cisneros being taken over by the Compañía Transatlántica. No attempt was made in these early years to extend the Spanish presence into the hinterland, and, until 1916, when La Guera (q.v.) was occupied, Villa Cisneros was Spain's only coastal settlement. It remained little more than a minor outpost for decades. "The native population does not reach 150 persons," wrote a doctor in the Spanish colonial health service, Guillermo Rocafort, in 1926. "To that must be added a military detachment (35 soldiers), a captain governor, a lieutenant, a doctor, a policeman, a chaplain, and the manager of the Transatlántica, and that is the entire breakdown of the population of Villa Cisneros." In the 1930s, Spanish governments started sending political prisoners there, and in March 1937, a group of political detainees made a daring and successful breakout, escaping down the coast to Dakar, Senegal, by fishing boat. As the administrative center for Río de Oro (q.v.), Dakhla slowly expanded, and, by 1974, there were 5,413 Saharawis and at least 3,000 Europeans living there. In 1963, the first elections for the city's *ayuntamiento* (q.v.) were held, with four Spaniards and five Saharawis being elected and a Saharawi *alcalde* (q.v.), or mayor, Souilem Ould Abdellahi (q.v.), appointed. In 1963, one of the world's largest underwater deposits of potable water was discovered near the city, a factor that could one day spur the region's economic development, particularly with regard to agriculture.

After the Madrid Agreement (q.v.), Moroccan troops arrived in the city on January 9, 1976. Mauritanian troops first arrived three days later, on January 12, when the last Spanish troops were evacuated. Under the Moroccan-Mauritanian Agreement of April 14, 1976 (q.v.), which partitioned Western Sahara, Dakhla (as Villa Cisneros was renamed) became part of Tiris el-Gharbia (q.v.), the Mauritanian sector of the territory. However, a large Moroccan military force remained in the city alongside Mauritanian troops. After the Algiers Agreement (q.v.) of August 5, 1979, by which Mauritania made peace with the Polisario Front (q.v.), Moroccan troops seized control of Dakhla on August 12, and the Moroccan government formally annexed Tiris el-Gharbia two days later. Most of the city's Saharawi inhabitants had fled to Algeria at the end of 1975 and early in 1976. Until the completion of Morocco's final extension of its "defensive walls" (q.v.) in the Sahara in 1987, Dakhla, along with the much smaller nearby settlement of Argoub, was enclosed by a small defensive perimeter, at most encompassing a few hundred square kilometers. In addition, the location of the town, at the end of a long peninsula, ensured its relative invulnerability to Polisario attack.

DAORA. About 40 km. northeast of El-Ayoun (q.v.), Daora has a plentiful water supply. The Izarguien (q.v.) built a fortified sanctuary there in 1878 during a war between the two wings of the Tekna (q.v.), the Ait Atman and the Ait Jmel—the Izarguien being part of the Ait Jmel bloc. The small fort was attacked the same year by the Ait Oussa (q.v.). In 1899, a small force of Ait Moussa Ou Ali (q.v.) and Moroccan troops, led by Dahman Ould Beyrouk, the *caid* (q.v.) of the Ait Moussa Ou Ali of Goulimine, seized the fort to punish the Izarguien, reportedly on the orders of Sultan Moulay Abdelaziz (q.v.), for their dealings with the Christians. The Izarguien, led by their chief, Baba Ahmed Ould Sidi Yusuf, finally retook the fort, after killing a number of Moroccan and Ait Moussa Ou Ali troops. Later, during the Spanish colonial period, Daora became the site of a small Spanish outpost, around which a minor settlement grew up. It was occupied by the Moroccan army at the end of 1975 and remained under Moroccan control as of 1993.

DEFENSIVE WALLS. The term most often used to describe the system of earthen defenses, about 1,500 kilometers long, constructed by Morocco in 1980–87 to attempt to close off roughly 80 percent of Western Sahara from attacks by the Polisario Front (q.v.). They are also known popularly as "berms" (meaning, essentially, a narrow ledge typically at the top of a slope in the terrain, whether natural or artificial). Manned by tens of thousands of Moroccan troops and equipped with electronic sensors and heavy artillery, the series of walls as it existed by the late 1980s had antecedents in similar, but much less extensive, barriers built by Morocco in the period immediately following its annexation of Western Sahara. These early perimeters were built around the towns of El-Ayoun, Smara, Dakhla, and Boujdour, as well as the phosphate mines at Bou-Craa (qq.v.). By the end of 1980, walls had been built in southern Morocco, too, to seal out Polisario guerrillas from Morocco proper, where the FAR had suffered serious reverses in the late 1970s. The FAR then proceeded to build a continuous wall to enclose the main towns and the phosphate industry in the northwest of Western Sahara (El-Ayoun, Smara, and Bou-Craa). The wall surrounding this "useful triangle," which included the territory's main population centers and economic resources, was completed in March 1981, and by April 1982, it had been extended south to incorporate Boujdour. The FAR gradually abandoned all isolated garrisons outside this well-defended, consolidated zone, except for an enclave around Dakhla and Argoub in the south. In 1983–85, however, the Moroccan armed forces extended the wall system deep into Saguia el-Hamra (q.v.), enclosing Echderia, El-Farsia, Mahbes, Haousa, and Amgala (q.v.), which had previously been under Polisario control. The wall ran within 20–30 kilometers of the Algerian border, the Moroccan objective being, apparently, to cut Western Sahara in two, denying the Saharawi guerrillas easy access to the territory from their rear bases in the Tindouf (q.v.) region of Algeria. Polisario forces could still transit Mauritanian territory to reach Río de Oro, however. So, between 1985 and 1987, the FAR extended the wall system southward to enclose much of Río de Oro, including Dakhla, Argoub, Aoussert, Bir Enzaren, and Guelta Zemmour (qq.v.). By April 1987, 80 percent of Western Sahara was effectively sealed off from Polisario. The guerrillas could no longer roam most of the territory at will, as they had in the first few years of the war, and they could no longer easily reach the coast, where they had earlier staged numerous attacks on foreign fishing boats and other shipping. Significantly, however, Morocco made no attempt to enclose the settlement of La Guera (q.v.), which was still occupied by Mauritanian troops. Despite this massive level of construction activity by the FAR, however, the war was not over, and the wall itself became a principal target of the Polisario forces.

Rarely did the FAR venture beyond the berm for patrols or interdiction operations, and maintaining this vast defensive structure required stationing at least 120,000 Moroccan soldiers in Western Sahara by the late 1980s. Physically, the walls were bulldozed out of gravel and rock from the desert floor into a double line of embankments 3–4 meters in height and several meters apart. Between the double line and behind it, roads and parking facilities were available for Moroccan tanks and armored personnel carriers. Along the walls there were foxholes and revetments for the troops, equipped with mortars and artillery, as well as radar to detect the enemy. On the outer flank of the wall, there were mine fields, barbed wire entanglements, and sensing devices supposedly capable of detecting a person on foot at 30 kilometers or a truck at 60 kilometers. The sensors and radar seem to have had only limited utility, however, as Polisario had little difficulty approaching the wall and staging scores of attacks against it. Every 10 kilometers or so, the wall was garrisoned by stone blockhouses (*postes avancés*) manned by 600–800 FAR troops; 3–4 kilometers between them, there were additional detachments (*sonettes*) of 100–200 troops commanding a view in front (and to each side) of a specific location. Each *sonette* and *poste avancé* was responsible for its sector, and in time of need could call upon reserve forces positioned behind the wall, such as the FAR's *Détachements d'Intervention Rapide* (q.v.), especially created for this purpose. As time went on, though, the increase in the number of *sonettes* and *postes avancés* caused by the wall's extension entailed a thinning of troop strength along the berm, so that there were fewer troops in any given sector to deal with a Polisario attack.

More than any other factor, the construction and extension of the defensive walls by Morocco in the 1980s changed the character of the Saharan war. Freed of the necessity of defending widely scattered and exposed outposts in the territory, Morocco was able to some degree to concentrate its defenses and to react and intervene more quickly when Polisario attempted to penetrate them. Indeed, confronted with this new challenge, Polisario staged no major military attacks between January 1982 and July 1983, choosing instead to gather intelligence about the walls and mount minor harassment raids against them from a distance. By mid-1983, however, Polisario was sufficiently confident to mount large, semiconventional attacks against the wall, often sending up to 2,000 men into battle with multiple rocket launchers and other heavy weaponry. The secretary-general of Polisario, Mohammed Abdelaziz (q.v.) said, "We can consider the wall an advantage because, since it is static and very long, the Moroccan soldiers are obliged to be in a static position. So it allows our freedom fighters to attack those points where and when we want, and to determine before an attack what we want to achieve." After the Saharawi nationalists had mastered the wall's characteristics, they were in fact able to approach it undetected, briefly overrun the Moroccan positions, and capture or destroy weapons and equipment as well as take prisoners, usually before the FAR's reserve units were able to react. Numerous such attacks took place between 1983 and 1989, until a de facto cease-fire took effect in 1990. Although the sheer weight of the FAR's numbers, coupled with the power and sophistication of the equipment massed along the wall, had rendered the specter of Polisario marching on El-Ayoun quite improbable, periodic attacks threatened to tie down and demoralize the Moroccan forces. The wall strategy had turned the conflict into a long and costly war of attrition.

DELEGADO; DELEGADO GUBERNATIVO. The titles of "delegate" and "governing delegate" designated several different official roles during the various phases of the Spanish colonial administration in the Sahara. When Francisco Bens Argandoña (q.v.), then politicomilitary governor of Río de Oro (qq.v.), occupied Tarfaya (q.v.) in 1916, he acquired the additional title of *delegado* of the *alto comisario* (q.v.), or high commissioner, of Spain in Morocco. As the delegate of the Spanish high commissioner in Tetuan, he was responsible for the Tekna Zone (q.v.), the southern zone of the Spanish protectorate in Morocco, whose borders had been defined by the Franco-Spanish Convention of November 27, 1912 (q.v.), and of which Tarfaya was part. Later, after the occupation for the first time, in 1934, of Ifni and a number of inland points in the Sahara, the Spanish government adopted a decree (August 29, 1934) by which the high commissioner in Morocco also became governor-general of Ifni and the Sahara. The administration of the two territories, however, was entrusted to two *delegados gubernativos,* one in Ifni, the other in the Sahara, who were responsible to the high commissioner in his capacity as governor-general of Ifni and the Sahara, in Tetuan. In 1946, a decree (July 20) set up Africa Occidental Española (q.v.) (Spanish West Africa), with its own governor-general distinct from the high commissioner in Morocco. AOE comprised both Ifni and the Spanish Sahara, the latter being defined by an ordinance of February 8, 1947, as including the "zone" of Saguia el-Hamra and the "colony" of Río de Oro. The Tarfaya region, which was the southern sector of the Spanish protectorate zone in Morocco, was not officially part of AOE, but the governor-general of AOE, who was based in Ifni, was made the delegado of the high commissioner there. The *khalifate* (q.v.), a wing of the Moroccan sultan's government, which represented the sultan's interests in the Spanish protectorate zone and was based in Tetuan, also had a *delegación* in Tarfaya, headed for many years by Mohammed Laghdaf. Meanwhile, in El-Ayoun (q.v.), there was a subgovernor (q.v.), who was responsible to the governor-general in Sidi Ifni and was in charge of the administration of Saguia el-Hamra and Río de Oro. Under him came a delegado gubernativo, based in Dakhla (q.v.), who was the senior Spanish official heading the colonial administration in Río do Oro. This chain of command remained unaltered until 1958, when first, in January, AOE was abolished and in its place two separate "provinces" (q.v.) were set up in Ifni and Spanish Sahara, and then, in April, by the Agreement of Cintra (q.v.), the Tarfaya region was handed over to Morocco. Thereafter, there was a governor-general of the province of the Sahara, based in El-Ayoun, and under him two delegados gubernativos heading *delegaciones regionales* (regional delegations) in the north and the south, based respectively in El-Ayoun and Dakhla. Subordinate to them were local administrative offices in Smara and Daora (qq.v.) in the north and in La Guera and Aoussert (qq.v.) in the south. This system remained operative until the end of Spanish rule.

DETACHEMENT D'INTERVENTION RAPIDE. The Rapid Intervention Detachments (DIR) were units of the Moroccan army, each comprising about 200 men, set up in Western Sahara in 1977 to intercept guerrilla groups of the Polisario Front (q.v.). However, they were used primarily in fixed positions guarding the Moroccan-controlled towns and later were positioned largely along the "defensive walls" (q.v.) built in the territory in 1980–87.

DEVELOPMENT PLANS. There was very little investment, public or private, in Western Sahara until the territory's potential mineral wealth began to be appreciated. In order to explore for and exploit this wealth, major infrastructural investments were begun in the 1960s—in roads, ports, administrative services, housing, water supplies, electricity, and many other sectors. Virtually all investment since the introduction of the first investment budget in 1961 has been by the state and parastatals like the phosphate-mining company Fosbucraa (q.v.). In November 1964, a commission was set up to examine the territory's development needs. In February 1965, an extraordinary budget of P225.7 million for urgent public works projects was adopted. In November 1965, a director of economic and social development was appointed, and in 1966, a P250 million emergency development plan was launched for 1966–67. By 1972, the annual investment budget had reached P702 million. Shortly before Spain's withdrawal (1976), a five-year capital expenditure program, set at P20 billion, was launched for 1974–78. P8.3 billion of this was to have been spent by Fosbucraa in the phosphate industry, and almost all the rest was to have been provided by the state, half of the total investment being slated for social services (housing, health, and education) and most of the rest for infrastructural projects and industrial development. After its annexation of most of the country in 1976, the Moroccan government adopted a Dh1.5 billion emergency plan for its three new Western Saharan provinces for 1976–78, with the accent on infrastructural projects such as road-building, the construction of a new airport at Smara (q.v.), the building of a desalination plant at Boujdour (q.v.), and the tapping of water resources at Foum el-Oued to supply El-Ayoun (q.v.). Another priority in the plan was housebuilding, in order to encourage the permanent settlement of former nomads in the Moroccan-controlled towns, as well as to accommodate the thousands of Moroccan settlers who were induced to move to the disputed region. In the years since the annexation, the emphasis on development appears to have been oriented toward highly capital-intensive projects, relatively few in number, in or near the major population centers of Western Sahara. Improved airports were constructed to serve El-Ayoun and Smara, although they were used primarily for military purposes since there is little civilian air traffic. A new sports stadium, a large mosque, hotels, and a hospital were also built in El-Ayoun. At nearby El-Ayoun *Playa,* a new fishing (qq.v.), and general cargo pier, costing about $42 million, was opened in 1987, replacing the by-now dilapidated pier inherited from Spanish colonial times. A much smaller fishing pier was also constructed at the settlement of Boujdour. The pier at El-Ayoun *Playa* also contains an industrial park (see Ports). Some new sewers and water and electricity lines were also installed in the towns, and there was much new building of roads (q.v.) between some of the key areas of the territory that Morocco administered. Nonetheless, by 1989, the level of development had progressed little, and Western Sahara could not remotely be considered self-sufficient. The level of Moroccan subsidy was probably extremely high, and Morocco's own economic troubles meant that by the late 1980s, many projects had to be scaled back or abandoned. Although the phosphate mines had formally reopened in 1982, production was much lower than at the end of the colonial period. Tourist development also moved at a slow pace, although a Club Méditerranée resort was built near El-Ayoun in 1985. The Moroccan government had plans to build a railway from El-Ayoun to Agadir, but as of 1990, implementation of this project still seemed far off.

DIRECCION GENERAL DE PROMOCION DEL SAHARA. The General Directorate for the Advancement of the Sahara was set up in 1969 as a subbody of the Spanish prime minister's office, the presidency of the government. Replacing the former Dirección General de Plazas y Provincias Africanas, which was dissolved after the Spanish withdrawal from Ifni and Equatorial Guinea in 1969, it was responsible for overseeing policy in Spain's only remaining African colony, Western Sahara.

DJEMAA (variants: *jemaa, yemaa*). (1) The assembly of notables of a tribe, or a tribal *fakhd* (q.v.), or fraction, which, in traditional Saharawi society, acted as a legislative, executive, and judicial body. It applied the *orf* (q.v.), the body of customary law used to deal with criminal cases. Anyone who refused to obey its decisions could be expelled from the tribe or fraction. The practice of collective decision making through *djemaas* indicated that Saharawi society was relatively democratic, though only the elder, free men generally took part. Women, slaves, and the members of the lowly castes of craftsmen and bards, as well as younger men, were excluded.

(2) In line with their version of "indirect rule," the Spanish colonial authorities tried to make use of the traditional political leaders and institutions of Saharawi society, albeit under government supervision, in their system of colonial administration. Thus, a decree of November 29, 1962, on the local government of the territory stated that the *fracciones nómadas* (q.v.) would be governed by *djemaas,* and the urban settlements would be represented by *ayuntamientos* and *juntas locales* (qq.v.). The law established that each djemaa would set up a council, whose size depended on the number of heads of families in the fraction. Its president was the chief of the fraction, whose election by the heads of families was subject to the approval of the governor-general (q.v.).

(3) A territorial Djemaa, or Asamblea General del Sahara (General Assembly of the Sahara) was set up by Spanish decree on May 11, 1967, to provide a framework for more

effective consultation of the traditional tribal leaders than had proved possible through the Cabildo Provincial (q.v.), which had only six Saharawi members, alongside several Spaniards, in 1967. The Djemaa, by contrast, was to have 82 Saharawi members and only two (nonvoting) Spaniards (a secretary and the colonial administration's secretary-general, who was to act as adviser). The president of the Cabildo Provincial and the *alcaldes* (mayors) of El-Ayoun and Dakhla were to be ex officio members, along with 39 prominent tribal *chioukh* (q.v.); 40 members were to be elected by the djemaas of the nomad fractions. The number of representatives was roughly proportional to the size of the tribes, the Reguibat having 45 seats (the Reguibat ech-Charg with 22 and the Reguibat es-Sahel with 23), the Izarguien 9, Oulad Delim 12, Arosien 5, Oulad Tidrarin 4, Ahel Cheikh Ma el-Ainin 2, Ait Lahsen 2, Ait Moussa Ou Ali 1, and Filala 1 (qq.v.). The president and vice president of the Djemaa were to be chosen by the assembly's members from among the nonelected members.

The first elections were held between July 14 and August 20, 1967, when the tribal fractions held their respective djemaa meetings. The assembly was formally opened on September 11, 1967. Its members, who had a four-year mandate, elected Saila Ould Abeida (q.v.), who was then president of the Cabildo Provincial, as president and Baba Ould Hassena (q.v.), a *cheikh* of the Oulad Delim from Dakhla (q.v.), as vice president. "We are men who have the duty to join together to work for greater unity with Spain and for the welfare of our land," Saila Ould Abeida told the opening session on April 30.

The second elections for the 40 elected seats were held in January 1971. Saila Ould Abeida was then replaced as president by the Reguibi cheikh, Khatri Ould Said Ould Joumani (q.v.); Baba Ould Hassena remained vice president. Specialized commissions for education, agriculture, livestock, trade, housing, public works, water, and tourism were created in 1973, and the colonial authorities increased the number of seats to 102 (40 *chioukh* elected by the djemaas of the nomad fractions; 40 representatives elected by male

Saharans holding identity cards in polls held in "family units," i.e., subfractions; 16 representatives of "corporate groups" such as salaried workers, craftsmen, etc.; and, finally, the president of the Cabildo Provincial, the 2 alcaldes of El-Ayoun and Dakhla, and 3 other representatives elected by the Cabildo Provincial and the ayuntamientos of El-Ayoun and Dakhla, respectively). Their term of office lasted four years, elections being held every two years to fill half of the elected posts. The next elections were duly held on July 10, 1973.

Saharawi nationalists decried the Djemaa, partly because most of its members were not directly elected and because most of those who were elected were chosen in tribal constituencies. The body was clearly weighted in favor of the older, more traditionalist element of Saharawi society and consisted overwhelmingly of Saharawis who were openly prepared to collaborate with the colonial authorities. Moreover, the assembly had no legislative powers. It was essentially a consultative and advisory body, able to examine and give opinions on questions affecting the territory, examine and suggest alterations to laws and decrees drawn up by the colonial authorities, and propose laws to the latter. It did not control the territory's budget, though it could examine it and submit recommendations regarding it.

However, in 1973–74, when the Spanish government finally began to envisage a gradual transition to independence through an intermediary stage of internal autonomy, it considered converting the Djemaa into a parliament with legislative powers over internal affairs. The process began with the Djemaa's being prompted to send a letter to General Franco (q.v.) on February 20, 1973, stating that "only the people of the Sahara have the right to determine their future, without outside coercion and interference" and requesting that "existing legal institutions be gradually developed in order to secure greater participation by the people of the Sahara in the functions and responsibilities relating to the internal administration of their territory." Franco replied on September 21, 1973, promising the Saharawi people progressive participation in the "management of its own affairs" and the conversion of the Djemaa into a territorial parliament with legislative powers. This was to have been enacted by the *estatuto político* (q.v.), which was drafted by the Spanish government early in 1974, approved by the Djemaa in July 1974, but never implemented because of Moroccan protests and pressure. At first shelved and then completely abandoned, it would have given legislative powers to the Djemaa and set up a governing council, four of whose eight members were to be elected by the Djemaa. In February 1975, the Djemaa did elect its four members to the council (though the body never met) and also elected a permanent commission, which, with 16 members, was to act as a link with the government. In November 1974, the Djemaa had also started adopting *normas,* which were then promulgated as laws by the governor-general, on such important matters as Saharan nationality, the creation of a unified judicial system, and the establishment of a Saharan civil service.

Most members of the Djemaa joined the Partido de la Unión Nacional Saharaui (q.v.), which was set up in November 1974 to lead the country to independence in close association with Spain. However, after the PUNS had been decisively outflanked by the Polisario Front (q.v.) during the tour by the UN Visiting Mission (q.v.) in May 1975, the Spanish authorities began to consider coming to terms with the nationalist guerrilla movement, and, in consequence, many Djemaa members too began to make contact with the movement. The assembly's president, Khatri Ould Said Ould Joumani, traveled to Tindouf (q.v.), the movement's main center abroad, at the end of May 1975 to hold talks with its secretary-general, El-Ouali Mustapha Sayed (q.v.). Later, as the threat of Moroccan intervention mounted, more and more of the Djemaa members started to sink their differences with the youthful radicals of the front. Many, including Khatri, attended the conference of Ain Ben Tili (q.v.), held by the front on October 12, 1975, to unify Saharawi ranks against the Moroccan threat.

The Madrid Agreement (q.v.) of November 14, 1975, pledged that "the views of the Saharan population, expressed through the Djemaa, will be respected." Apparently, the Spanish, Mauritanian, and Moroccan governments expected this hitherto docile and loyalist body to endorse annexation by Morocco and Mauritania. However, most Djemaa members were opposed to the Moroccan-Mauritanian takeover, and on November 28, 1975, 67 of them (an absolute majority of the 102 members) signed the proclamation of Guelta Zemmour (q.v.), dissolving the assembly, to avoid its being used to legitimize the planned annexation, and declaring their support for the Polisario Front. The following day in El-Ayoun, only 32 members of the assembly showed up at a session called to introduce the Moroccan and Mauritanian deputy governors of the new tripartite administration (q.v.). Then, some Djemaa members later switched their allegiance to Morocco or Mauritania, and on February 26, 1976, 57 members attending a rump session of the assembly voted to support integration with Morocco and Mauritania. However, the Djemaa's credibility had reached such a nadir by then that the UN (q.v.) refused to send an observer to the session, and the Spanish government issued a statement saying that it could not accept its vote as a genuine consultation of Saharawi opinion.

DLIMI, AHMED. Born in 1931, he became King Hassan II's (q.v.) most trusted senior military commander in the 1970s and led the Moroccan forces that entered Western Sahara in the autumn of 1975. He had achieved notoriety when, as deputy director of the Moroccan intelligence service, the Direction Générale d'Etudes et de Documentation (DGED), he was accused of complicity in the murder in Paris in October 1965 of the radical Moroccan exile Mehdi Ben Barka, but he was acquitted by a Paris court in October 1966; however, his boss, Gen. Mohammed Oufkir, was sentenced in absentia to life imprisonment. In May 1970, he was appointed director of the DGED; in August 1972, he became the king's personal security chief as director of his aides de camp following the death of Gen. Oufkir. In the summer of 1974, as Hassan launched his diplomatic blitzkrieg to stop Spain from holding a referendum in Western Sahara, he was named commander of the third military region (Tarfaya), with full civil and military powers. There, on the northern border of Western Sahara, he assembled a force of 20,000 men, poised to march into the territory. During 1975, the guerrillas of the Front de Libération et de l'Unité (q.v.) were selected from his units in Morocco's far south and sent over the border into the Spanish colony. Meanwhile, he was responsible for the secret logistical preparations for the Green March (q.v.). On October 31, two weeks before the signing of the Madrid Agreement (q.v.), some of his forces began the Moroccan invasion of Western Sahara, moving toward Haousa, Jdiriya, and Farsia, which they captured after clashes with the Polisario Front (q.v.), these former Spanish bases having already been evacuated by the Spanish army. Dlimi arrived in El-Ayoun (q.v.) on November 26, one day after the arrival there of the Moroccan deputy governor in the tripartite administration (q.v.) set up by the Madrid Agreement, Ahmed Bensouda (q.v.); a day later, he led a column of Moroccan troops into Smara (q.v.). He proceeded to coordinate the occupation of other strategic points throughout the territory, including Dakhla (q.v.), which his troops entered on January 9, 1976. As the Moroccan troops arrived in ever greater numbers, the Spanish forces were slowly withdrawn, the last units leaving the territory on January 12. The occupation of the main towns and settlements completed (but the war with the guerrillas just beginning), Dlimi was relieved of his Saharan command and promoted to the rank of colonel major on April 26, 1976. He was succeeded in the Sahara by Col. Abdenbi Britel (q.v.). However, as one of King Hassan's closest advisers and senior commanders, he continued to be closely involved in both the military and political planning of Morocco's Western Saharan strategy. On October 20–21, 1978, for example, he was one of the royal advisers who met top leaders of the Polisario Front for unprecedented but unsuccessful talks in Bamako, Mali. In October–November 1979, he commanded the Ohoud Force (q.v.), a 6,000-man column that traversed the Sahara to bolster the Moroccan garrison in recently annexed Dakhla, and in 1980 he was intimately involved in the major counterinsurgency operations of the Ohoud, Zellagha, and Larak Forces (qq.v.). Dlimi remained as the unchallenged head of the DGED and the Moroccan armed forces in the early 1980s despite a series of rather serious military setbacks against the Polisario Front. However, on January 25, 1983, the Moroccan government announced that Ahmed Dlimi was killed in an automobile accident near Marrakesh, reportedly after a meeting with King Hassan. Immediately, the foreign press was rife with speculation that he had been assassinated, possibly because he was dissatisfied with the conduct of the Saharan war or because he was feared by King Hassan as a potential rival. The Polisario Front said that the general had secretly been in contact with its representatives and that he favored a negotiated settlement of the long war. Ahmed Rami, a dissident former Moroccan army officer who was living in exile in Europe, claimed that Dlimi had been plotting a coup d'état against the king. Whatever the true situation, it was clear that Dlimi had accumulated an unusual degree of power, unmatched since the days of Gen. Oufkir. After Dlimi's death, his numerous responsibilities were split among several other high-ranking officers. Among them was Abdelaziz Bennani (q.v.), who shortly thereafter took over command of the FAR's "southern zone," which encompassed Western Sahara and southern Morocco.

DRAA. The flowing cotton robe traditionally worn by Saharawi men. Similar to the West African *boubou,* it is large and light and falls to the ankles, the perfect garment for the dry, hot climate of the desert. The *draa* is normally white when worn by marabouts (q.v.), teachers, and political leaders. Otherwise, it is blue, the cloth traditionally dyed with indigo that sometimes stains the skin, a fact that led Europeans to name the Saharawis "blue men."

DRAA, OUED. This 1,000-mile-long river, which drains the Anti-Atlas and reaches the Atlantic a little north of Tan-Tan, formed the northern border of Spain's Saharan territory—by virtue of the Franco-Spanish Convention of November 27, 1912 (q.v.)—until the cession of the Tekna Zone (q.v.) in April 1958 under the Agreement of Cintra (q.v.).

DUEH SIDNA NAUCHA. A leader of the Partido de la Unión Nacional Saharaui (q.v.), a short-lived party set up in

November 1974 with Spanish encouragement and that advocated independence in close association with Spain. As the PUNS's assistant secretary-general, he represented the party in talks with the three members of the UN Visiting Mission (q.v.), which toured the country on May 12–19, 1975. It was during the visit of this UN mission that the rival Polisario Front (q.v.) held mass demonstrations throughout the territory, outflanking the PUNS decisively in terms of popular support and eroding its credibility in the eyes of the Spanish colonial administration that had given it extensive organizational and financial support in the hope that it would become the governing party of an independent Western Sahara. The party's disastrous performance during the UN mission's tour prompted the secretary-general, Khalihenna Ould Rachid (q.v.), to switch his allegiance to Morocco, where he fled before the UN mission had even completed its tour of the territory. The party rump was then reorganized at the end of May by an ad hoc executive committee of four members, among them Dueh Sidna, who went on to be elected secretary-general at the PUNS's second congress, held in El-Ayoun August 16–18, 1975. Conscious of the erosion of popular support for the party and worried that the Spanish government was now considering coming to terms with the Polisario Front, Dueh favored the formation of a coalition with the front. The program adopted at the 2nd congress was very similar to the front's, but a stumbling block to unity between the two movements was the PUNS's insistence on maintaining its own separate identity. Talks held between Dueh Sidna and El-Ouali Mustapha Sayed (q.v.), the secretary-general of the Polisario Front, in Ain Ben Tili and Amgala the second week of October 1975 broke up in disagreement on this score, El-Ouali insisting that PUNS dissolve and its members join the front. However, as the threat of Moroccan intervention grew, after the announcement by King Hassan (q.v.) on October 16 of plans for the Green March (q.v.), and as the Spanish resolve to resist the Moroccan pressure started to waver, the need for Saharawi unity became the overriding consideration for Dueh Sidna and most of the other remaining members of the PUNS, who were now incapable of serious action on their own. On

October 20, he announced that the PUNS would hold a countermarch to the Moroccan border to oppose the Green March. "Our wish is to go armed," he told the press, "because we expect that after the civilian population that will head the Moroccan march will come the army of Hassan II to invade our country. We are ready to die for our country if that is necessary, but we need arms to fight." The countermarch was never held, but, also on October 20, Dueh Sidna held another round of talks with the Polisario Front leaders in El-Ayoun (q.v.). "At this time," he said afterward, "there are no political parties, only Saharawis who want to defend our people from the enemy invasion." Shortly afterward, the PUNS dissolved, and most of its remaining members, including Dueh Sidna, joined the Polisario Front.

- E -

ECOUVILLON, OPERATION see OURAGAN, OPERATION

EDCHERA, BATTLE OF. Fought on January 13, 1958, this was one of the most serious clashes between Spanish troops and guerrillas of the Army of Liberation (q.v.) during the 1957–58 uprising. The Spanish Foreign Legion (q.v.) admitted that 51 of its men were killed or wounded during the daylong battle, about 20 km. southeast of El-Ayoun (q.v.), but claimed that 241 guerrillas were killed.

EDUCATION. Until the 1960s, modern education was virtually nonexistent. In 1954, there were only seven primary schools in the entire country. They had only 8 teachers between them, 6 of them Spanish and 2 Saharawis. There were only 132 Saharawi pupils and 127 Spanish. There were no secondary schools at all until 1964, when 217 Spanish and 23 Saharawi children were enrolled in the first state secondary school. Education became more widespread in the sixties and early seventies as a result of the sedentation and urbanization of much of the Saharawi population, the arrival of large numbers of Spanish families in the growing urban settlements, and the expanding needs of both the colonial administration and companies for more and better-trained personnel. The latter needs led to the creation of technical schools under the auspices of the Promoción Profesional Obrera (PPO) in the late sixties, about 1,500 students passing through its courses by 1972. By 1974, the education situation was as follows. There were 6,160 Saharawi students in school (out of a school-age population almost certainly underestimated at 16,459). There were also 2,979 European children in school.

Among the Saharawis, there was a huge dropout rate between primary and secondary education: There were 6,059 Saharawis in primary school but only 111 in the country's two secondary schools in El-Ayoun and Dakhla (qq.v.), which had almost five times as many European pupils (542). Moreover, fewer than 1 in 8 school-age girls were in school—only 909 in primary school and just 3 in secondary school. Very few Saharawis went on to higher education: Out of 75 Saharawi students in Spain on government scholarships in 1975, only 52 were studying in institutions of higher education. Another salient feature was that, apart from teachers of Arabic and Islamic studies, nearly all the teaching staff (184 at primary level and 60 at secondary level) were Spaniards. The school curriculum contained a good dose of procolonialist Francoist propaganda, but this was almost certainly counterproductive, for students were, by the early 1970s, militantly nationalist. Literacy figures for 1974 show that about 70 percent of the Saharawi population (over 5 years old) was illiterate. After the Moroccan-Mauritanian occupation of Western Sahara in 1975–76, some schools closed down as a result of the considerable fall in the school-age population—following the departure of practically all of the Spanish population and the exodus of Saharawi refugees (q.v.) to Algeria. However, the number of pupils gradually increased during the 1980s, due to the influx of Moroccan settlers into the territory. In the refugee camps near Tindouf (q.v.), the Polisario Front (q.v.) established primary schools in all *dairat* (q.v.) and three primary boarding schools at *wilaya* (q.v.) level. A "national" vocational school for women was established in 1978, and a technical training school for men and women was opened in 1984. By 1987, almost 100 percent of children aged 6–12 years were attending school, a substantial accomplishment. By 1985, the boarding schools, which offered both the last years of primary schooling and the beginning of secondary education, had 5,500 pupils. In 1984, preprimary schools for children aged 3–6 years were opened in all the *dairat*. Saharawi pupils were mostly sent to Algerian schools for secondary education and to Algeria, Cuba, and (until 1983) Libya for postsecondary studies. Finally, literacy campaigns were held every year in the refugee camps, and by the late 1980s, virtually all adults could read and write.

EL-AAIUN see EL-AYOUN

EL-AIOUN see EL-AYOUN

EL-AYOUN (variants: El-Aaiun, El-Aioun, Laayoune). The capital of Western Sahara, El-Ayoun is situated on the banks of the Saguia el-Hamra (q.v.), about 30 km. from the Atlantic coast. Its Arabic name means "water sources"; it was the discovery of potable water there in 1938 by the *delegado gubernativo* of Western Sahara, Lt. Col. de Oro Pulido, which led to a military garrison being established and the first buildings erected. By the early 1970s El-Ayoun had been transformed into a small, but modern, capital city, with scores of bars, a luxurious state-owned *Parador* (tourist hotel) and even a striptease club. A decree of January 10, 1958, named El-Ayoun the capital of the new "province" of Western Sahara, and, as mineral prospecting and infrastructural investments proceeded in the 1960s, the town rapidly grew. A jetty was built 30 km. away at El-Ayoun *playa* (beach) to provide the first port facilities, in 1961; later, in 1972, a 3-km. pier for phosphate exports was completed there, along with a phosphate treatment plant. The European population of the city grew from 3,545 in 1963 to 5,842 in 1967 and was almost certainly over 10,000 by 1974. The Saharawi population, which had totaled only 5,021 in 1963, grew to 9,676 and reached 28,499 in 1974. Many Saharawis had moved into houses, though some still camped in tents or shanties on the city outskirts. Though there was no official racial discrimination, the city seemed segregated de facto residentially, with the Saharawi population crowded in such suburbs as Colominas and Casas de Piedras. The city also always looked like a garrison town, with one Spanish soldier for perhaps every four or five civilians in the early 1970s. This military aspect did not change, of course, when Spanish rule ended in 1975–76. Moroccan troops entered El-Ayoun on November 25, 1975, and gradually took over the barracks and military installations left by the Spaniards. The city became part of the Moroccan zone of Western Sahara under the Moroccan-Mauritanian Agreement of April 14, 1976, and in the same year, the city became the capital of one of the three Moroccan provinces created in the territory. As many as two thirds of the city's Saharawi residents are estimated to have fled to Algeria in 1975–76 but the arrival of thousands of Moroccans gradually restored the city's population. Though the Polisario Front (q.v.) staged a few hit-and-run attacks on the capital in the early years of its war with Morocco, the city was increasingly well-guarded by a series of heavily armed "defensive walls" (q.v.). By the mid-1980s, the city had not only become practically invulnerable to Polisario attack due to the walls' extension ever deeper into Saguia el-Hamra but had also become a centerpiece of sorts for Morocco's development plans (q.v.) for its new Saharan provinces. El-Ayoun became the preferred destination for thousands of Moroccan immigrants from the country's impoverished north, attracted by subsidized housing, higher wages, and other inducements offered to them so the kingdom could consolidate its hold over the area. By 1984, the population of the city was apparently more than 90,000, of whom only a minority seemed to be Saharawi. To improve the city's infrastructure, Moroccan authorities installed new electricity lines and built much new housing. However, most development seemed designed on a grandiose scale in order to impress outsiders and residents alike. For example, a large, new international airport terminal was constructed, though it handled only a very few flights per day. A 35,000-seat sports stadium was built, in addition to an exhibition hall, a zoo, a hospital, a large mosque, and several parks and hotels. The hotels remained largely empty, as the influx of visitors that Morocco had hoped to attract failed to materialize.

EL-AYOUN PLAYA. El-Ayoun Beach, which is about 30 km. southwest of the capital, is the site of the 3-km. phosphate-loading pier completed in 1972 for Fosbucraa (qq.v.), as well as a phosphate treatment plant, a power station, and military installations. The Fosbucraa pier also includes an unloading berth for general cargo. There is a good tarmac road between the *playa* and the capital, which cuts through the coastal dune belt. In the years since the Moroccan takeover of Western Sahara, the original Fosbucraa pier has fallen into disrepair, party because the conveyor belt to the mines and the loading facility have never resumed operation. A new pier was opened in 1987 at a cost of $42 million and includes an adjoining industrial park.

EL-FASSI, ALLAL. The main leader of the Istiqlal Party (q.v.), he was the originator of the Moroccan claim to Western Sahara, as well as to Mauritania, much of the Algerian Sahara, and other parts of "Greater Morocco" (q.v.). He began to advance these territorial claims almost immediately after Morocco's independence in March 1956. On March 27, 1956, he declared: "So long as Tangiers is not liberated from its international statute, so long as the Spanish deserts of the south, the Sahara from Tindouf to Atar, and the Algerian-Moroccan borders are not liberated from their trusteeship, our independence will remain incomplete, and our first duty will be to carry on action to liberate and unify the country." On June 19, 1956, he made even more extravagant claims: "The Moroccans will continue the struggle until Tangiers, the Sahara from Tindouf to Colomb-Bechar, the Touat, Kenadza, and Mauritania are liberated and unified. Our independence will only be complete with the Sahara! The frontiers of Morocco end in the south at Saint Louis du Sénégal!" El-Fassi's "Greater Morocco" ideology and its associated claims to Western Sahara, Mauritania, and much of Algeria were adopted by King Mohammed V (q.v.) and his government in 1957–58 and later by King Hassan II (q.v.). In consequence, Morocco briefly went to war with Algeria in 1963 and refused to recognize Mauritania after its independence in 1960. El-Fassi was horrified by Hassan II's decision in 1969 to settle these disputes with Algeria and Mauritania. He opposed the ensuing Moroccan-Mauritanian treaty of friendship and cooperation (1970) and Moroccan-Algerian border convention (1972) by which Hassan II formally renounced the Moroccan claims to Mauritanian and Algerian territory. Only the claim to Western Sahara remained, but el-Fassi died in 1974, one year before Morocco marched into the Spanish colony.

EL-GAADA. A plateau, which is of easy access to vehicles, lying between the Moroccan border and the Saguia el-Hamra and bordered to the east by a more hilly region, Aidar. It includes the localities of Daora, Tah, and Hagounia.

EL-HIBA see AHMED EL-HIBA

EL-KHANGA RAID. This first attack launched by the Polisario Front (q.v.), on May 20, 1973, ten days after the front's founding. El-Khanga, a tiny Spanish military outpost in the northeast of the territory, had a small garrison of Saharawi troops, commanded by a Spanish officer, who was absent at the time of the attack. The Polisario group consisted of only seven men, among them the front's secretary-general, El-Ouali Mustapha Sayed (q.v.), and was armed with a motley collection of ancient rifles and one small submachine gun. Success was to hinge totally on the advantage of surprise, as the group had about enough ammunition to keep firing for five minutes. The operation almost turned into a fiasco before it had begun. After camping near El-Khanga, the little guerrilla group sent two of their number, including El-Ouali, to find water. On their way back, they ran into a group of soldiers from El-Khanga, who were making one of their routine patrols. They were arrested and taken back to the post. After realizing what had happened, the remaining five guerrillas decided to attack that evening, after sunset. Despite holding two suspicious-looking youths, about whose arrest they had already alerted the nearest Spanish base, the

Saharawi garrison had no idea that an attack was imminent; when it came, they surrendered without firing a shot. The two prisoners were released, a valuable new collection of firearms stolen, and the Saharawi soldiers who were arrested lectured on the front's political objectives and were then freed.

EL-OUALI MUSTAPHA SAYED. The first secretary-general of the Polisario Front (q.v.) and its charismatic leader from its founding in May 1973 until his death in action in Mauritania in June 1976, El-Ouali Mustapha Sayed was born somewhere on the *hammada* (q.v.) in c. 1948. A Reguibi of the Thaalat fraction of the Reguibat es-Sahel (q.v.), El-Ouali, or "Lulei," as he came to be known, spent the first few years of his childhood in a nomadic environment, traveling with his parents and their livestock in search of pastures. However, the family's traditional way of life was destroyed when war broke out in 1957 between the Army of Liberation (q.v.) and the Spanish and French in Western Sahara and Mauritania, culminating in the devastating Franco-Spanish counterinsurgency campaign, Operation Ouragan (q.v.), in February 1958, and as successive droughts in the late fifties killed off a good part of the herds. El-Ouali's family moved north, first to Zaag and then to Tan-Tan, a water-point and small settlement in the Tekna Zone (q.v.), the territory handed over to Morocco by Spain in April 1958 after the Agreement of Cintra (q.v.). Here, El-Ouali lived with his father, Mustapha Sayed; his mother, Mbarka; his five brothers, Mohammed, Labat, Ibrahim, Bachir (q.v.) (later to become assistant secretary-general of the Polisario Front), and Baba; and his single sister, Miriam. His family was utterly destitute. His father was suffering from a mental disorder and was unable to work, his mother brought in some income from occasional work as a seamstress, and Labat made some money from joining road-building gangs. For much of this period, the family was surviving largely on charity, and, though he began attending a primary school in Tan-Tan in 1962, El-Ouali often had to skip school to tend the family's remaining goats. Despite these handicaps, he eventually managed to obtain his primary school certificate and, with the aid of a Moroccan government scholarship, attend the Lycée Ben Youssef, in Marrakesh, as a boarder. A fellow pupil at the time was Mohammed Salem Ould Salek (q.v.), who was later to become minister of information of the Saharan Arab Democratic Republic (q.v.). It appears that El-Ouali was expelled from the Lycée Ben Youssef and returned home to Tan-Tan for a few months, in 1965, working there briefly as a road-builder. Later in 1965, he was back in school, once again under a government scholarship, this time in Taroudant, where a classmate and one of his closest friends was Mohammed Lamine Ould Ahmed (q.v.), who was to become the SADR's first premier in 1976. It was in Taroudant that El-Ouali began to take a deep interest in politics, especially the fate of the Spanish-ruled Sahara. He was excited to hear of the creation, in 1966, of the Frente de Liberación del Sahara (q.v.), a group established in Rabat with royal support to press Morocco's claim to Western Sahara in international forums. It was this growing political awareness that prompted him to move to Rabat, where he was able to gain admission in 1967 to the Groupement Scolaire Mohammed V, one of the oldest lycéees in Morocco, set up as a "free school" by Moroccan nationalists in the early years of the French Protectorate. By all accounts, he was a brilliant student, passing the baccalaureate exams in 1970 with distinction. With another scholarship, he entered the law faculty of Mohammed V University, Rabat, along with his old friend Mohammed Lamine.

While he was vacationing in Tan-Tan in the summer of 1970 before starting college, news arrived in Morocco of the bloody events in Zemla (q.v.), a suburb of El-Ayoun (q.v.), where Spanish Foreign Legionnaires shot dead a number of Saharawi demonstrators on June 17, 1970. On June 25, El-Ouali and a group of fellow students set out by car from Tan-Tan to the border, to meet refugees arriving from the Spanish colony. Back in Rabat, he became a tireless activist in the cause of Saharawi liberation—though in these still early days it had apparently not occurred to him to seek the creation of an independent state. Most politically active Saharawis in Morocco, such as those in the officially sanctioned FLS (which dissolved in 1969), had expressed support for the territory's integration with Morocco. In his student days in Rabat, El-Ouali seems not to have questioned this established outlook. Indeed, he and other Saharawi students in Morocco at this time turned for support to the very parties that proclaimed the "Moroccanity" of the Sahara and criticized the monarchy for its collaborationism with Francoist Spain. El-Ouali maintained close contact with Ali Yata and the pro-Moscow Parti de Libération et du Socialisme (qq.v.) and contributed to a lengthy study of the situation in Western Sahara, "The Reality of Our Usurped Saharan Province," which was published in the party's journal *Al-Mabadi* in May 1972. He also maintained relations with the Istiqlal Party (q.v.), which, along with the PLS was the most vocal advocate of Morocco's claim to Western Sahara. He became increasingly disillusioned, however, by the failure of these parties to translate their verbal militancy on the Saharan question into practical aid for the creation of a new liberation movement. After the Zemla events, El-Ouali was convinced of the need for armed action against Spain, and it was with this in mind that he requested support from the leaders of the PLS, the Istiqlal Party, and the Union Nationale des Forces Populaires during 1972. Nothing came of these approaches. A meeting with Allal el-Fassi (q.v.), the Istiqlalian leader, was reportedly a "dialogue of the deaf." Like Yata and the UNFP leader, Abderrahim Bouabid (q.v.), he apparently told El-Ouali to await first the transformation of Morocco itself. Only the labor federation, the Union Marocaine du Travail (q.v.), offered any practical support, organizing a series of public rallies in support of the Saharawi cause in several Moroccan cities, beginning in March 1972.

It was in this period that El-Ouali and other Saharawi students in Morocco began to organize themselves into what came to be known as the "embryonic movement for the liberation of the Sahara" (q.v.). The contacts with the established nationalist Moroccan parties were part of the group's work. But increasingly the emphasis began to shift elsewhere, to the recruitment of support from the large Saharawi community of southern Morocco, from which these students themselves sprang, and to making contact with Saharawis living within Western Sahara and in other neighboring territories. In the summer of 1971 El-Ouali, along with Mohammed Lamine and Mohammed Salem Ould Salek, made a pioneering trip to El-Ayoun to sound out the political situation there. In March 1972, he was detained for two or three days by the Moroccan police after taking part in an unauthorized anti-Spanish demonstration in Tan-Tan. As the summer of 1972 approached, he gave up his law studies entirely and began to devote himself full-time to preparing the groundwork for the formation of a new liberation organization. Between then and the founding of the Polisario Front on May 10, 1973, he was traveling constantly, visiting the main centers of Saharawi settlement, including Zouerate and Tindouf, and lobbying the Algerian, Libyan, and Mauritanian governments for support.

At the end of 1972, he traveled overland from Morocco to Tindouf, where he received a cold response from the Algerian authorities, and went on to Zouerate, where he met M'hamed Ould Ziou (q.v.), a veteran of the anticolonial struggle, who had good relations with the Mauritanian regime. It was in Mauritania that El-Ouali therefore began to assemble the nucleus of the new movement. Financial support and a small quantity of arms were obtained from Libya, but Algeria, which allowed Edouard Moha's MORE-HOB (qq.v.) to set up an office in Algiers in March 1973, remained distrustful and even briefly detained El-Ouali at one point during the year.

The Zouerate-based nucleus decided from the start to embark on a guerrilla campaign against Spain. The first operation, launched with almost no weapons at all ten days after the front's founding conference, was almost a disaster. Seven men, including El-Ouali, planned to raid a small Spanish post at El-Khanga (q.v.), but before the attack had even begun, El-Ouali and one of his comrades fell into the hands of an enemy patrol, which detained them. However, that evening, May 20, the remaining five members of the group surrounded the post, its all-Saharawi garrison surrendered without a fight, and El-Ouali was freed. Over the next two years, El-Ouali's preoccupation was the organization of the front's small-scale guerrilla war, but much was also done to make contact with and recruit support within the towns of the Spanish colony and among the Saharawi troops in the Spanish armed forces. The diplomatic work went on, too, El-Ouali finally winning some low-key support from the Algerian government after a meeting with Algerian officials in July 1974. A month later, at the front's 2nd congress (August 25–31), when the objective of full independence was explicitly stated for the first time, he was reelected secretary-general.

Over the following year, the front was transformed from a small vanguard group into a movement with a real mass following, partly as a result of El-Ouali's tireless organizing and great leadership skills. By the time of the arrival in El-Ayoun in May 1975 of the UN Visiting Mission (q.v.), whose members El-Ouali met later (May 29–30) during their tour of the Saharawi camps in Tindouf, it was visibly the dominant political force in Western Sahara. The Spanish government decided in the ensuing weeks to try to come to terms with the front, and to this end, Pedro Cortina y Mauri (q.v.), the Spanish foreign minister, met El-Ouali in Algeria on September 9, 1975. The negotiations were successful, leading not only to the release of prisoners by both sides but also to an agreement in principle that Western Sahara would be given independence under a Polisario government in return for Spanish privileges in the vital phosphate and fishing industries (qq.v.) for 15–20 years.

However, since mid-1974, pressure on Spain from Morocco had been intense, and after the announcement of the Green March (q.v.) on October 16, Spanish policy started to waver. On November 14, Spain came to terms with Morocco and Mauritania, signing the Madrid Agreement (q.v.), which El-Ouali saw bitterly as a betrayal of the pledge made to him only two months earlier by Cortina y Mauri. "Our people who are at present facing the Moroccan invasion consider the agreement concluded in Madrid between Spain, Morocco, and Mauritania as null and void and as an act of aggression and brigandry," he declared in Algiers on November 15. He felt betrayed by Mauritania's President Mokhtar Ould Daddah (q.v.), as well as by Spain. He had held a two-hour meeting with Ould Daddah in June 1975, reportedly suggesting a federation between Western Sahara and Mauritania and offering the federal presidency to the Mauritanian president, who had decided at the end of 1974 to strike a deal with Morocco's King Hassan II (q.v.), hinged on a promise of eventual partition of the Spanish colony.

However, El-Ouali was heartened by the Algerian government's decision in 1975 to give all-out support to the Polisario Front, whose main external base of operations shifted to Tindouf. In the months preceding the Madrid Agreement, he was also involved in negotiations with several leaders of the dying Partido de la Unión Nacional Saharaui (q.v.) and *chioukh* (q.v.) in the Djemaa (q.v.), persuading many of these men, who had collaborated closely with the Spanish authorities in the past, to throw in their lot with the Polisario Front in order to meet the growing common threat from Morocco. The PUNS dissolved early in November, and a majority of Djemaa members voted the assembly out of existence in favor of a new pro-Polisario Provisional Saharawi National Council (q.v.) at a meeting in Guelta Zemmour (q.v.) on November 28. On the military front, El-Ouali's attention was focused on organizing resistance to the first Moroccan incursions, which began on October 31, two weeks before the Madrid Agreement, in the region of Farsia, Haousa, and Jdiriya, from which Spanish troops had already been withdrawn. Besides hectic diplomatic activity at the end of 1975, El-Ouali also had to cope with the huge and sudden refugee exodus (q.v.) and the recruitment of thousands of new volunteers into the previously tiny guerrilla force, the SPLA (q.v.).

On February 27, 1976, the day of the proclamation of the founding of the SADR, El-Ouali made a final plea to Mauritania to break its alliance with Morocco. "Logic and the truth mean that the brotherly Mauritanian people must be at the side of the Saharawi people, given the objective links between them, whether they be historical or racial links or even the inevitable unity of interests and destiny." A week later, on March 6, he wrote similarly to King Hassan, demanding the "recognition of our independent and neutral state." He even offered the king a share in the phosphate wealth: "Do not have any fear about our phosphate; we are ready to cooperate, even if we give more than we get from it.'' Events had already gone too far for these appeals to make much impact. In May, with the drama of the refugee exodus nearing its end, the Polisario Front decided to move on to the offensive. Mauritania, the weaker of the front's two adversaries, was to become the principal target. Within a few weeks, El-Ouali was dead. He chaired the executive committee (q.v.) for the last time on June 2 and then set out, with several hundred guerrillas, on what was to become an epic but tragic *ghazzi,* across 1,500 km. of desert to the very edge of the Mauritanian capital, Nouakchott. By June 7, El-Ouali and his men had reached Oum Tounsi, just 80 km. north of the city, but two days earlier they had been spotted further north, near Tourine, by one of the Mauritanian air force's ancient Defenders, whose pilot raised the alarm that something was afoot. On June 8, early in the morning, El-Ouali dispatched a group of his Land Rovers to advance to the outskirts of Nouakchott, where for 30 minutes they lobbed mortar shells around the presidential palace. In the evening, there was another 15-minute bombardment. His mission accomplished, El-Ouali ordered the whole of his force to retreat northward on June 9, but by now Mauritanian troops were beginning to close in. As his men moved northward, El-Ouali led a small group away from the main column to a place near Benichab, where they planned to blow up water installations that served the copper-mining city of Akjoujt; but there they were cornered by enemy troops and planes. El-Ouali was shot dead, a bullet passing through his head. (For a detailed account of the June 1976 Polisario attack on Nouakchott, see NOUAKCHOTT RAIDS.)

EL-OUELI, CHEIKH. One of the sons of Cheikh Ma el-Ainin (q.v.), he was one of the main leaders of the anticolonial resistance in the early part of the 20th century. He gave himself up to the French authorities in Mauritania in April 1936 but later settled in Río de Oro (q.v.).

EMBRYONIC MOVEMENT FOR THE LIBERATION OF THE SAHARA. A nucleus of Saharawi activists, it laid the basis for the founding of the Polisario Front (q.v.) in 1973. It was formed by a group of Saharawi students in Morocco in 1971–72 and included such prominent future Polisario leaders as El-Ouali Mustapha Sayed, Mohammed Lamine Ould Ahmed, Bachir Mustapha Sayed, Mohammed Ali Ould el-Ouali, Mohammed Salem Ould Salek, and Mohammed Ould Sidati (qq.v.). They were representative of a new well-educated generation of Saharawis who had settled as children in southern Morocco in the late fifties and early sixties and made their way through the Moroccan education system, several of them gaining admission to Moroccan universities. They were influenced by the radicalization process then occurring on Moroccan campuses, which were in an almost permanent state of effervescence in 1970–73, and by the examples set by national liberation movements in other parts of the world, in particular Palestine. The anticolonial movement led by Mohammed Bassiri (q.v.) until the massacre of Zemla (q.v.) and the UN (q.v.) resolutions on Western Sahara were also impetuses for their political activity.

There were probably at first about 40 Saharawi students, many of them from the Mohammed V University in Rabat, in their group, which was originally more of a loose collective than a structured organization. At first they were not explicitly dedicated to the achievement of Western Sahara's independence. Their focus was on driving out the Spanish rather than specifying the future status of the territory, and ironically, in hindsight, they concentrated in the early days on trying to lobby support for their cause from the main nationalist opposition parties in Morocco, which had criticized the Moroccan government for its collaboration with Spain. Meetings were held with leaders of the Istiqlal Party, the Parti de Libération et du Socialisme, the Union Nationale des Forces Populaires, the Union Marocaine du Travail (qq.v.), and the Union Nationale des Etudiants Marocains (UNEM—National Union of Moroccan Students). Some members of the embryonic movement were militants or sympathizers of these Moroccan parties and unions. However, with few exceptions, the Moroccan opposition forces were not prepared to translate their verbal criticisms of the government's inactivism over Western Sahara into practical and effective support for the Saharawi students' plans to start a new liberation movement. As frustration with the Moroccan opposition groups grew, the Saharawi students in Morocco began to strike out on their own. In the summer of 1971, El-Ouali Mustapha Sayed visited Western Sahara to gain a firsthand impression of conditions in the territory. The following October, a clandestine meeting of Saharawi youth was organized in Tan-Tan, the main center of Saharawi settlement in southern Morocco, to start to build support there; this was followed by anti-Spanish demonstrations in Tan-Tan (q.v.) in March and May 1972, which led to several students, including El-Ouali and Mohammed Lamine, being briefly detained by the Moroccan authorities. This experience reinforced the students' belief that the Moroccan government was complicit with Spain and would never allow an independent liberation movement to organize from Moroccan territory. Leaders of the student group made new visits to Western Sahara in 1972–73, as well as further afield, to such other centers of the Saharawi diaspora as Zouerate, Mauritania, and Tindouf (q.v.), Algeria. El-Ouali was particularly involved in this traveling, dropping his studies at Mohammed V University in 1972 and visiting Libya as well as Algeria and Mauritania in search of support. Letters explaining the movement's aims and requesting aid were sent to the Algerian government on March 24, 1972; to the Libyan government on March 20, 1972, and June 6, 1972; to the Mauritanian government on March 23, 1972, April 4, 1972, and March 14, 1973; and to the Iraqi government on March 24, 1972. Algeria refused support, but Libya provided a very small consignment of arms (1973), and Mauritania agreed to allow some of the movement's militants to settle on its territory. At Zouerate, moreover, El-Ouali and his colleagues received enthusiastic support from another Saharawi grouping around M'hamed Ould Ziou (q.v.). As the nucleus of a real organization was created, recruiting from within and beyond Western Sahara, it began to take an overtly pro-independence line. In May 1973, the Polisario Front was born.

EMIGRATION. Though never a large-scale phenomenon, there was some emigration by Saharawis to Spain in the 1960s and early 1970s. They settled primarily in Barcelona, Madrid, the

Canary Islands, Oviedo, and León and were employed mainly in road-building and mining. Most left for Algeria in 1975 to join the Polisario Front (q.v.). A pro-Polisario Unión de Obreros Saharauis en España (q.v.) was active among them in 1974–75.

EMPLOYMENT. Until the 1950s, there was not more than a handful of either Saharawi or Spanish wage and salary earners in the country. During the first half of this century, a few Saharawis found employment in the Spanish army or on construction gangs building airports, roads, and other public works projects. Paid employment began to expand significantly in the 1960s, when large-scale oil and mineral prospecting began and concomitantly investments were made to expand infrastructure and basic administrative services. Several thousand Spaniards took jobs in the territory and virtually monopolized skilled trades. Most Saharawis were employed in the army, construction, transport, and mining, though the capital-intensive phosphate industry did not provide jobs for more than about 1,200 Saharawi workers (1975). In addition, about 1,400 Spaniards were employed by Fosbucraa (q.v.). Saharawis filled only 19 percent of the company's technical and supervisory jobs. Statistics for 1974 indicate that 5,465 Saharawis were employed that year as unskilled laborers, 1,341 as soldiers, 707 as drivers, 190 as office workers, 141 as teachers, 111 as craftsmen, 149 as fishermen, 119 as health workers, 345 as industrial workers, 148 as unskilled workers, and 358 as "various skilled employees." There were 27 "senior officials" and 13 "middle-ranking officials." There were also 981 traders, reflecting the fact that the retail-wholesale trades had expanded greatly as a result of the influx of Europeans, the duty-free import rights granted by the Spanish authorities under their "free-zone" policy, and the large-scale smuggling to neighboring countries. Most urbanized, employed Saharawis were strong supporters of the Polisario Front (q.v.) by 1975 and so joined the refugee exodus to Algeria in 1975–76. The vast majority of Spanish workers also left, though 200-300 remained by 1978, working mainly in the phosphate industry. Several thousand Moroccan workers arrived, to work in the administration, phosphate (despite the halt in mining in 1976), construction, and other sectors, whereas unskilled Saharawis were employed in public works programs.

EMPRESA NACIONAL MINERAL DEL SAHARA, SA. Founded in 1962, the National Mining Company of the Sahara was a subsidiary of the huge Spanish state-owned firm, Instituto Nacional de Industria (q.v.). It was set up after the discovery of phosphates (q.v.) in Western Sahara and had the job of studying the possibility of exploiting the deposits. ENMINSA first made a geological survey to determine the most favorable areas for exploitation and eventually concluded that it would be feasible to exploit the deposits at Bou-Craa (q.v.), where 1.7 billion tons of high-grade ore were found. The company then attempted unsuccessfully to involve non-Spanish firms in a joint venture. The first attempt to form a consortium, involving Gulf, W. R. Grace, Texaco, and Standard Oil, failed in 1967. A second, involving International Minerals and Chemical Corporation (25 percent), European interests (20 percent), and INI (55 percent), failed, too, in 1968. The non-Spanish companies were apparently worried about the territory's political future and objected to Spain's insistence on shipping the ore to Spain for processing by the new phosphoric acid industry in Huelva. As a result of these rebuffs by foreign companies, INI decided to proceed alone. To do this, ENMINSA was replaced by a new company, Fosfatos de Bu-Craa (Fosbucraa) (q.v.), another INI subsidiary, in 1969.

EN-NAS EL-MAALUMIN. The notables, or persons enjoying the greatest respect, in traditional Saharawi society. In each tribe or fraction (qq.v.), *en-nas el-maalumin* were those men who enjoyed a high degree of respect on account of their age, wisdom, valor, or wealth. Their political influence was felt in the *djemaa* (q.v.), the assembly of the tribe or fraction, and it was from their ranks that the *chioukh* (q.v.), or chiefs, were drawn.

ENTIDADES LOCALES MENORES. The administrative units set up by the Spanish colonial authorities for the smaller towns after the conversion of the territory into a Spanish "province" (q.v.) in 1958. A decree on the new province's organization, issued on April 19, 1961, divided the territory for administrative purposes into *términos municipales* (q.v.) or municipalities for the larger towns, *entidades locales menores* (minor local entities) for the smaller towns, and *fracciones nómadas* (q.v.) for the nomadic population. Whereas two cities, El-Ayoun and Dakhla (qq.v.), became municipalities, the two towns of Smara and La Guera (qq.v.) were designated minor local entities by a decree of November 29, 1962. This also stated that they would be administered by *juntas locales* (q.v.) composed of four members, elected by male heads of families, and a president who was nominated by the governor-general (q.v.).

ERG. An Arabic term designating a dune zone. Western Sahara does not have the huge dune zones that are found in some parts of the Sahara desert, for example in Algeria, but much of the coastline is fringed by a narrow dune belt.

ESTATUTO POLITICO. The Political Statute, which was drafted by the Spanish government in 1974, was intended to establish internal self-government in Western Sahara as a first step toward independence in close association with Spain. It was shelved and then completely abandoned because of Morocco's hostile reaction. The first indication that the Spanish government planned to move toward internal autonomy in the territory came in a letter to the Djemaa from General Franco (q.v.) on September 21, 1973, which promised that a law would be enacted to allow the Saharawi people to play a progressively greater part in the administration of their own affairs and to convert the Djemaa, previously a purely consultative body, into an assembly with legislative powers, albeit subject to the power of veto by the governor-general. The Spanish government believed by 1973–74 that its interests in the territory, especially its investments in the phosphate industry (q.v.) and considerable fishing (q.v.) interests off the coast, could better be defended by establishing an independent Saharawi government, whose very weakness would dictate a need for close cooperation with Spain, than by handing the territory to the Moroccan government (which could have been expected to take nationalist economic measures against Spain's interests in the territory, as it had done in Morocco itself) or by maintaining Spanish colonial rule and so incurring the risk of international diplomatic embarrassment. The revolution in Portugal in April 1974 made a switch in Spain's Saharan policy especially urgent. A new governor-general, General Gómez de Salazar (q.v.), was appointed on May 31, and a new secretary-general of the colonial administration, Col. Rodríguez de Viguri (q.v.), was appointed the following June, with instructions to prepare the country for internal autonomy and eventually independence. The plan was to convert the Djemaa into a legislature; establish a governing council, composed partly of Saharawis; and launch a political party that, under the leadership of Saharawis who had proved their loyalty to Spain, could outbid the Polisario Front (q.v.) in terms of popular support and lead the country toward independence without jeopardizing Spanish interests. This party was the Partido de la Unión Nacional Saharaui (q.v.), set up with the colonial authorities' encouragement in November 1974.

The Spanish government informed Morocco, Mauritania, and Algeria of its plan to establish internal self-government on July 4, 1974, and during a session on July 4–6, 1974, the Djemaa endorsed the Political Statute. Under the latter, the Djemaa was to cease being a tribally-based assembly and consist of 40 members elected from constituencies and up to 12 members designated by the Spanish governor-general either to represent special interests or because they possessed particular personal attributes. The Djemaa was to be empowered to enact laws relating, among other things, to the territory's budget and taxation; natural resources; civil, penal, and social law; local administration; and the organization of Koranic justice. The laws adopted by the Djemaa were to be promulgated by the governor-general, though he could refer them back to the Djemaa for reconsideration or, if they affected the powers reserved to Spain (primarily external defense and internal security), refuse to enact them. Under the statute, the governing council, which was to take over the administration of the territory, was to consist of the governor-general, four members of the Djemaa elected by its members, and three members designated by the governor-general.

The statute's endorsement by the Djemaa in July 1974 was followed by the Spanish government's announcement on August 21 of plans to hold a referendum on independence in the first six months of 1975. However, both the statute and the plans for the referendum were postponed and later abandoned because of Moroccan protests and pressure. The statute was never published in the Spanish government's *Boletín Oficial*. Certain preparatory steps in the direction of internal autonomy were taken over the following months. At an important session on November 19–22, 1974, the Djemaa adopted *normas* (regulations), which were later promulgated as law by the governor-general, on the criteria of Saharawi nationality (see NATIONALITY LAW), the creation of a unified judicial system, and the creation of a Saharan civil service (there being very few Saharawis in senior administrative positions, though five of the province's 30 services had Saharawis as assistant heads by 1975). In February 1975, the Djemaa elected its 4 members of the governing council and also elected a permanent commission of 16 members, under its president, Khatri Ould Said Ould Joumani (q.v.), which was to act as a link with the government. However, the political statute was forgotten once and for all when, in the autumn of 1975, Spain decided to abandon completely its plans for internal autonomy and eventual independence and, following the Madrid Agreement (q.v.), handed the country over to Morocco and Mauritania.

EXECUTIVE COMMITTEE (OF THE POLISARIO FRONT). Formerly, the top leadership body of the Polisario Front (q.v.), the executive committee was, until 1991, elected by the front's general popular congress (q.v.) and was headed by Polisario's secretary-general. The executive committee, whose membership was identical to that of the Council for the Command of the Revolution (q.v.), was abolished as part of the governmental and constitutional changes adopted at the front's 8th congress (June 18–20, 1991). The following is a list of the membership of the final executive committee, elected at Polisario's 7th congress in April–May 1989 (see individual entries on each):

Mohammed Abdelaziz, secretary-general of the Polisario
   Front and president of the SADR
Bachir Mustapha Sayed
Mohammed Lamine Ould Ahmed
Mahfoud Ali Beiba
Ibrahim Ghali Ould Mustapha
Mohammed Lamine Ould Bouhali
Ayoub Lahbib

- F -

FAKHD. The fraction of a tribe in traditional Saharawi society. A patrilineal clan, a *fakhd* has a supposed apical ancestor, usually an immediate descendant of the tribe's founder. In precolonial times, it was a key social unit, whose affairs were regulated by an assembly of notables, the *djemaa* (q.v.). Marriage was endogamous within the fakhd. During the Spanish colonial period, the djemaa was maintained but brought under government supervision. With the ending of the *ghazzis* (q.v.), there was no need for an entire fraction to be grouped together for purposes of security, and the average size of a nomad camp, the *friq* (q.v.), was reduced to five or six tents, involving a few dozen persons, by the 1950s. Though of greater import than the tribe as a whole, the fakhd therefore began to lose some of its practical meaning as a sociopolitical unit during the mid-20th century.

FARAH, ABDERRAHIM. Of Somali nationality, Abderrahim Farah, in his capacity as under secretary-general for special political questions of the United Nations (q.v.), headed the first UN technical mission (q.v.), which toured Western Sahara and neighboring countries in November-December 1987. The technical mission consisted of a military group, led by Gen. Terence Liston (q.v.) of Canada, and a civil group, led by Farah. After being received by King Hassan II (q.v.) in Fez, Farah and the rest of the civil group traveled to areas of Western Sahara controlled by Morocco, namely, El-Ayoun, Boujdour, Smara, and Dakhla (qq.v.), meeting with people and gathering documentation regarding the population and administration of the territory. Subsequently, the civil group of the technical mission traveled briefly to northern Mauritania and to areas of Western Sahara controlled by the Polisario Front (q.v.), as well as to the refugee (q.v.) camps in the region of Tindouf (q.v.), Algeria. Consultations with Polisario's leadership were also held, and the mission then returned to New York. The information gathered, although it was not made public, served as a basis for the detailed and comprehensive peace plan put forward by the UN secretary-general in August 1988.

FIGUIGUI, BACHIR see MOUVEMENT DE RESISTANCE "LES HOMMES BLEUS" and ASSOCIATION DES ORIGINAIRES DU SAHARA ANCIENNEMENT SOUS DOMINATION ESPAGNOLE

FILALA. A very small tribe of traditionally religious vocation, they consider themselves to be *chorfa,* the descendants of a cherif of Tafilalet, Sidi Bou Beker, though they are probably descended in fact from the Gadala. As a *zawiya* tribe, with many marabouts and men of learning, they played an important role as educators in traditional society. They were centered on Hagounia, the site of Sidi Bou Beker's tomb, in the region of El-Gaada (q.v.). They have three fractions: the Oulad Sidi Ahmed Filali, the Ahel Ben Mehdi, and the Ahel Faki Ben Salah.

FILALI, ABDELLATIF. Since his appointment as foreign minister of Morocco in 1985 (he also held the post of minister of information in 1985–86), Abdellatif Filali has played a major role in articulating and executing Morocco's policies on Western Sahara, although King Hassan II (q.v.) himself has remained the chief architect of his country's external policy. Born in 1928 in Fez and educated at the University of Paris, Filali joined the foreign ministry in 1957 and represented Morocco in various countries before becoming foreign minister in 1985, succeeding Abdelouahed Belhaziz. As the head of the Moroccan foreign service, he received, on his country's behalf, the comprehensive settlement proposal for the territory put forward on August 11, 1988, by the secretary-general of the United Nations, Javier Pérez de Cuéllar (qq.v.), and also accepted the plan in principle a fortnight later. Since that time, he has held numerous meetings with UN officials relating to the terms for a settlement of the Saharan conflict.

FISHERIES. Though Western Sahara has a 1,200-km. coastline, which is acknowledged to be among the richest fishing zones in the world, the main Saharawi tribes traditionally did not engage in fishing, and most Saharawis even today do not care much to eat fish. Only a few impoverished small coastal tribes, which had very little livestock, depended for their survival on fishing, and their methods were very primitive. They did not use boats but fished in shallow waters using large nets and wading techniques. There was little wood for boat-building, and the steep cliffs, the lack of natural harbors, and the dangerous stormy coastline were further impediments to the development of fishing.

Spanish fishermen from the Canary Islands, however, began fishing off Western Sahara from the late 15th century, and they would occasionally land on the Saharan coast to dry their fish and mend nets. Later, at the end of the 19th century, the idea of establishing bases to assist fishing operations, on the part of the Sociedad de Pesquerías Canario-Africanas, for example, was one of the factors that led to the creation of Spain's little colonial enclaves at Dakhla and La Guera (qq.v.). Dried fish, of extremely poor quality, was the territory's main export in the early years of this century, the main market being Spanish-ruled Equatorial Guinea. The industry remained minuscule and archaic until the creation of IPASA by Spain's state-owned Instituto Nacional de Industria (q.v.) in 1948 and its ensuing investments in refrigeration and processing plants. By 1975, there were two fish-meal plants at La Guera, which processed most of the territory's catch, producing about 9,000 tons of fish-meal a year. In 1974, there were about 120 vessels operating wholly or partially from La Guera and Dakhla, the two main fishing ports, though most also served the processing industries in the Canaries too.

This small fishing industry was simply an extension of the huge fishing industry in the Canary Islands. The companies involved were Spanish and so were the crews. Moreover, the tonnage of fish being landed in Western Sahara was marginal compared to the huge quantities being scooped up off the coast by the world's fishing fleets. An extension of the Senegal-Mauritania coast, which, along with the Gulf of Guinea, is the richest fishing zone in Africa, Western Sahara's waters attract trawlers from Japan, Russia Korea, Poland, Italy, Greece, and many other countries, as well as the Canary Islands and metropolitan Spain. In recent years, the estimated annual catch has been about 1.5 million tons, of which about 225,000 tons are taken by fishing boats based in the Canary Islands.

Naturally, these considerable Saharan fisheries resources were of great interest to Morocco when it annexed the greater part of Western Sahara in 1975–76. The Moroccan government's Office National de Pêche estimated in 1976 that, whereas the total annual potential sardine catch in its waters north of Ifni was only 200,000 tons, it was 400,000 tons along the coast from Ifni to El-Ayoun and another 100,000 tons from El-Ayoun to Boujdour. To increase its benefits from these resources, the Moroccan government began building two new fishing ports in the south, at Tan-Tan and Tarfaya (q.v.), in 1977.

The Madrid Agreement (q.v.) of November 14, 1975, was widely opposed in the Canary Islands, where there were fears that Morocco would sooner or later place restrictions on fishing in its newly acquired Saharan waters, just as it had progressively controlled Spanish fishing activities off Morocco itself during the 1960s and early seventies. The Madrid Agreement gave 800 Spanish fishing boats the right to fish unrestricted in Western Saharan waters without paying license fees for 5 years and to fish for 15 years thereafter paying preferential license fees; 640 boats were eventually licensed. However, the 1975 agreement did not hold. In 1977, the Spanish government negotiated a fishing agreement that gave fishing rights to Spanish trawlers in return for Moroccanization of part of the Spanish fleet and about $44 million of Spanish government investment in the Moroccan fishing industry. Bitterly denounced in the Canaries, where it was feared that the agreement would lead to a run-down of the islands' fishing industry and boost already high unemployment, the agreement was approved in the Cortes on February 15, 1978, by 174 votes to 142, but it was never ratified by the Moroccan parliament and so never took effect. A new, temporary, six-month agreement was signed by Spain and Morocco on June 30, 1979. Most of the Canaries' fleet refused, however, to recognize it, insisting that they had been given rights to fish without restrictions in Western Saharan waters, and they continued fishing in violation of the agreement's clauses. On November 19, 1979, a trawler from the Canaries was seized by a Moroccan naval patrol, and thereafter the Canaries fleet found itself facing the same restrictions in Western Saharan waters as boats from mainland Spain—despite the concessions granted in the Madrid Agreement. A series of temporary fishing agreements was eventually signed. In 1983, the new Spanish socialist government of Felipe González Marquez (q.v.) negotiated a permanent agreement with Rabat, but this was replaced by a multilateral fishing agreement between the European Community (EC) and Morocco. It was signed in 1988 following Spain's accession to the EC two years previously.

A challenge of a different kind came meanwhile from the Polisario Front, which started in 1977 to send squads of guerrillas out to sea in pneumatic launches to machine-gun or hijack Spanish and other trawlers, accusing them of violating the territorial waters of the SADR (q.v.). Several crews were arrested, their release often hinging on the extraction of diplomatic concessions from their governments. The first attack was in April 1977, when two Spanish fishing boats were strafed from the shore. Then, on November 13, 1977, a Spanish boat, the *Saa,* was seized, and three crew members taken off to captivity by the guerrillas. They were released after the intercession of the main Spanish opposition parties, on November 28. Another Spanish fishing boat, *Las Palomas,* was boarded on April 20, 1978, and its eight crew members were imprisoned until October 14, when they were released after an official of Spain's ruling Unión de Centro Democrático, Javier Rupérez, signed a communiqué with Polisario recognizing the movement as "the sole legitimate representative of the struggling Saharan people." Several Spanish boats were machine-gunned in May–September 1978. In October 1978, six black South African crew members of a Dutch fishing boat, *Zuiderster-9*, were shot dead after their boat was boarded off Nouadhibou, and three Spanish fishermen were wounded in an attack on the *Genesis*. Seven Spanish fishermen were then massacred aboard the *Cruz del Mar* on November 28, 1978, though this time the Polisario Front denied responsibility for the incident, and it was widely believed in Spain that the attack was carried out by a special Moroccan force to discredit the guerrilla movement, whose relations with Spain were then improving. During 1980, the guerrillas staged numerous attacks, capturing 38 Spanish fishermen between May and August, though all were released by mid-December after a Spanish official signed a statement declaring "support of the right of the Saharawi people to self-determination as a basis for a political solution englobing the totality of the territory of Western Sahara." Thirty Portuguese fishermen, from two trawlers, were also captured during 1980, in addition to 30 South Koreans. After diminishing somewhat in 1981–84, attacks on Spanish and other ships sharply increased in 1985, perhaps as a sign of the front's displeasure with the pro-Moroccan policies being pursued by Madrid. On September 20, 1985, a Spanish trawler, the *Junquito,* was raked by Polisario gunfire from several small boats and later capsized, killing a fisherman. A patrol boat of the Spanish navy was sent to the area to investigate, and it too was fired upon; one sailor was killed. The incident created an uproar in Spain, and the González government retaliated by expelling all of the front's representatives and closing its three Spanish offices. But the attacks did not end; in June 1986, a Spanish ship, the *Sinbad,* which was flying the Moroccan flag, was machine-gunned, as were ships from Portugal and the U.S.S.R., although the Soviet ship fired back. Undaunted, the front attacked the Spanish merchant ship *Puente Ca-*

nario, killing one crewman. On November 8, a Romanian ship was set upon, and in a more serious incident in January 1987, three Moroccan soldiers who were escorting a Portuguese fishing trawler were killed. At about the same time, a British ship and a luxury yacht were also attacked. After 1987, however, Morocco's extensions of its "defensive walls" (q.v.) in Western Sahara cut Polisario off almost entirely from access to the Atlantic, and the attacks ceased.

FORCES ARMEES ROYALES. Morocco's Royal Armed Forces (FAR) entered Western Sahara on October 31, 1975, a fortnight before the Madrid Agreement (q.v.). By the end of that year, most of the 20,000 troops that had been massed on the Western Sahara border since mid-1974 had moved into the territory, taking over the bases and barracks vacated by the departing Spanish troops. As the war with the Polisario Front (q.v.) developed, spilling into southern Morocco itself, as well as Mauritania, with which Morocco had signed a defense pact in 1977, the FAR rapidly expanded. From 65,000 troops in 1975, the FAR grew to 90,000 in 1976 and 120,000 in 1979, of which at least 30,000 were then stationed in Western Sahara and probably almost as many in the war zones of southern Morocco. During 1979, the FAR completed the withdrawal of 9,000 troops sent to Mauritania in 1977–78, but the continuation of the Saharan war and the construction of a series of "defensive walls" (q.v.) to keep the Polisario Front at bay forced the government to expand the Moroccan armed forces to over 192,000 men by 1989. At least 120,000 were committed to Western Sahara; the rest were positioned along the Algerian border or were specially picked units charged with protecting King Hassan II (q.v.). The increase in the size of the armed forces and the enormous costs incurred in the Sahara took a heavy toll on the Moroccan budget (q.v.). By 1987, it was estimated that the security ministries (defense and interior) were being allocated more than 40 percent of the total recurrent budget. As chief of staff of the FAR, King Hassan set overall military strategy, and some defense analysts noted that the FAR's top-heavy command structure, under which all major decisions are made by the king, hampered effective counterinsurgency techniques and frustrated senior officers. It was, however, the experience of two serious coup attempts in 1971 and 1972 that had prompted the king to assume personal control over the FAR by permanently abolishing the post of defense minister and becoming chief of staff. Despite these precautions, however, there was always speculation that a failure to end the war, coupled with Morocco's domestic economic troubles, could revive the political ambitions of the officer corps and pose a new threat to the throne. This view was given some credence when, on January 25, 1983, General Ahmed Dlimi (q.v.), commander of Moroccan forces in Western Sahara, died under circumstances that led the foreign press to theorize that he had been planning to overthrow King Hassan. Dlimi's successor as commander of the FAR's "southern zone" (Western Sahara and southern Morocco) was Abdelaziz Bennani (q.v.), a career officer who was not thought to have political ambitions. It was Bennani in subsequent years who supervised the extension of the "defensive walls" in Western Sahara eastward and southward to encompass 80 percent of the territory by mid-1987. Although these walls did shut Polisario forces out of much of Western Sahara, they necessitated permanent garrisons along a 1,500-km.-long front line, at which the troops lived under harsh and demoralizing conditions. The defensive positions were also difficult and expensive to resupply and were frequently attacked by Polisario's armed wing, the Saharawi Popular Liberation Army (q.v.).

FORCES AUXILIARES see MAKHZANI

FOSBUCRAA. Fosfatos de Bu-Craa, or Fosbucraa for short, was set up as a wholly owned subsidiary by the Spanish state firm Instituto Nacional de Industria (q.v.) in August 1969 to exploit the 1.7 billion tons of phosphate (q.v.), which had been discovered at Bou-Craa (q.v.). Production began in 1972, and exports reached 2.6 million tons in 1975. As a result of the Madrid Agreement (q.v.) of November 14, 1975, Morocco's state-owned Office Cherifien de Phosphates acquired 65 percent of the company's shares, leaving INI with only 35 percent. However, mining ground to a halt early in

1976 as a result of the war between Morocco and the Polisario Front (q.v.), whose guerrillas repeatedly sabotaged the company's 100-km. conveyor belt (which evacuates the ore to the coast) and the power supply lines (which bring electricity to the mines from a coastal power station). As a result, the company suffered a loss of P1,772 million in 1976. Small quantities of previously stockpiled ore were exported in 1976-79, but production at the mine remained at a complete standstill. The mine was officially closed in 1980 due to the war and did not reopen until July 1982, after completion of the first "defensive wall" (q.v.) around the northwest portion of Western Sahara in 1981. Mining operations were hindered, however, by the deteriorated state of the infrastructure, including the conveyor belt to the coast, which was still out of operation in 1989. In 1985, production levels reached 963,878 tons, a little over one third of the 1974 level.

FOUIKAT. A very small tribe that traditionally engaged in fishing along the coast. In precolonial times, they paid tribute to more powerful tribes, notably the Izarguien (q.v.), for protection. Grouped primarily along the northern stretch of the coast, they were divided into four fractions, the Ahel Cheheb, the Ahel Abdahou, the Aila Ould Said, and the Ahel Lagoueyed. Their common ancestor is said to have been Moussa Ibn Fouikat.

FRACCION NOMADA. Based on the traditional fractions, or *afkhad* (q.v.), of Saharawi society, the "nomad fraction" became an administrative concept in the system of government set up after the conversion of Western Sahara into a Spanish "province" (q.v.) in 1958. A law of April 19, 1961, on the organization of the province drew an administrative distinction between the towns and small desert settlements, which were given the status of *terminos municipales* and *entidades locales menores* (qq.v.), respectively, and the nomadic population, which was divided into *fracciones nómadas*. Article 10 of the law stated that "the nomad fractions will follow the system established by norms of a customary character and by ordinances consistent with the latter.'' The law reflected that, despite the formal conversion of the territory into a Spanish province, it was impossible to apply the norms of Spanish provincial administration to the nomadic population, who were left to run their day-to-day affairs through the customary *djemaas* (q.v.). It was a kind of Spanish version of ''indirect rule.'' However, the colonial authorities could and did intervene to ensure that the leaders of these traditional organizations were men inclined to cooperate with the Spanish. A decree of November 29, 1962, which set out the details of the system of government enunciated in the 1961 law, laid down that ''the nomad fractions will be administered by a djemaa, and this will be represented by a council whose president will be the head of the fraction; its members will be proportionate to the number of heads of family.'' Article 18 of the decree stated that, whereas the heads of the fractions would be elected by heads of families in accordance with established tradition, ''their nominations will be recommended by the governor-general (q.v.).'' When the Asamblea General del Sahara, better known as the Djemaa (q.v.), was set up in 1967 as an advisory body to the colonial government, the 40 elected seats (initially out of 82) were divided up by the government between the nomad fractions, the male heads of family being entitled to vote at meetings of the fraction djemaas. This system remained unaltered in essentials until the withdrawal of the Spanish in 1976.

FRACTION see FAKHD; FRACCION NOMADA

FRANCO BAHAMONDE, FRANCISCO. General Franco (born 1893) played an important personal role in setting Spanish policy on Western Sahara during his long period of rule, from the 1936–39 Spanish civil war until his death on November 20, 1975, just six days after the Madrid Agreement (q.v.). His attention had been drawn to the territory's mineral wealth by Manuel Alia Medina, the discoverer of its phosphates (q.v.), whom he met during a visit to El-Ayoun and Dakhla (qq.v.) in 1950. This, along with his deeply ingrained notion of Spain's imperial African mission, a belief in Spain's historic ''rights'' in the desert sands opposite the Canaries, a need to find a new stamping ground for the Spanish Foreign Legion (q.v.) after Morocco's independence in 1956, and a calculation that the country's small and nomadic population would not be able to force the Spanish out, gave him the resolve to maintain this colonial outpost after being obliged to end Spain's "protectorate" in northern Morocco in April 1956 and in the Tekna Zone (q.v.) in April 1958. Nonetheless, he had to accept French military aid—in Operation Ouragan (q.v.) in February 1958—to stamp out the guerrilla threat posed by the Army of Liberation (q.v.) and reoccupy the points in the interior, including Smara (q.v.), which his troops had been forced to abandon in 1957. In January 1958, he indicated his resolve to retain control of the colony by transforming it into a full-blown Spanish "province" (q.v.), and, on October 11, 1958, his government informed the UN (q.v.), in reply to a request for information on its colonies, that "Spain possesses no non-self-governing territories, since the territories subject to its sovereignty in Africa are, in accordance with the legislation now in force, considered and classified as provinces of Spain." In December 1960, he said that the Spanish flag would fly in Western Sahara forever.

To keep the UN at bay, however, his government hinted in 1964 that it would eventually accept self-determination in the territory. This was explicitly spelled out in 1966, in response to the adoption of the first resolution on Western Sahara by the UN General Assembly in 1965, though with the rider that it would take time to prepare for the territory's self-determination because of its low level of development and the small size and nomadic character of its population. Though the Franco government voted against the UN General Assembly resolutions on Western Sahara in 1965, 1966, and 1972 and refused to implement the UN calls for the holding of a referendum under UN supervision, it abstained on the General Assembly resolutions of 1967, 1968, 1969, 1970, and 1973 and continued to plead that the territory's special conditions made it premature to apply the principle of self-determination. It argued that its good intentions were shown by the granting of independence to Equatorial Guinea in October 1969 and the retrocession of Ifni to Morocco in June 1969.

These shifts in policy were designed to reduce Spain's international isolation and drum up Third World support for its claim to Gibraltar, which the Franco government first presented to the UN in 1963. For economic reasons too, it particularly desired friendly relations with Arab states and remained the only Western European government to deny recognition to Israel. At the same time, Franco had no intention of actually allowing self-determination in Western Sahara, especially after plans were made in the late sixties to exploit the huge phosphate deposits at Bou-Craa (q.v.). Although the principle of self-determination was upheld and conveniently pitted against the territorial claims and "external interference" of Morocco and Mauritania, the low level of development and the small, nomadic nature of the population provided handy excuses for failing to apply it. Though the UN resolutions were invariably passed with huge majorities, there was no serious challenge to the Spanish presence in the territory from its Maghrebian neighbors because of their own rivalries, which Franco encouraged, and because Morocco, Mauritania, and Algeria were all keen to bite the economic carrot dangled before them by the *caudillo* and his ministers, most notably Gregorio López Bravo (q.v.). In 1969, Franco even tried to get King Hassan II (q.v.), during a visit that year to Madrid, to accept the Spanish presence in the territory by offering Morocco the chance to participate in the exploitation of the phosphates at Bou-Craa, a proposition that the king did not accept. However, Spanish-Moroccan relations were pragmatically warm throughout this period, from the summit of Barajas (q.v.) in 1963 until the dramatic and sudden shifts in Spanish and Moroccan policy toward Western Sahara in 1974.

Within Western Sahara, moreover, the Franco government did not face any serious challenge after the disintegration of the Army of Liberation in 1958. The Harakat Tahrir Saguia el-Hamra wa Oued ed-Dahab (q.v.) was crushed in 1970 before it had time to organize a powerful political movement, and support for the Spanish connection was carefully cultivated among the conservative *chioukh* (q.v.), many of whom were induced to lobby and petition the UN in support of unity with Spain in 1966 and 1967. They were given a consultative forum, the Djemaa (q.v.), in 1967, and many were impressed by the Franco regime's decision to launch a special development plan (q.v.) in 1966. They were, moreover, led to believe that Spain was protecting their interest, against the expansionist designs of hostile neighbors, and preparing the country for eventual self-determination. By 1973, however, Franco had come to believe that Spanish interests in the territory, above all the phosphate and fishing (q.v.) interests, could be ensured, and embarrassment abroad removed, by preparing the territory gradually for internal self-government and then independence. An independent state, he calculated, would be too weak to risk challenging Spain's interests, whereas, if Morocco took control of the territory, it would be likely to reduce or end Spain's involvement in the phosphate industry and restrict Spain's offshore fishing rights (as it had already done in Moroccan waters). In a letter to the Djemaa on September 21, 1973, Franco promised that "self-determination will take place when the population freely so requests," pledged to institute a "system of gradually increasing participation" by the Saharawi people "in the management of its own affairs," and suggested that the Djemaa should acquire limited legislative powers for the first time ("drawing up general provisions concerning the internal affairs of the territory, without prejudice to the power of sanction vested in the governor-general"). The implementation of this new strategy became urgent when, in April 1974, the Marcello Caetano regime was overthrown in Lisbon, and Portugal's African empire began to collapse. An *estatuto político* (q.v.), establishing internal autonomy, was drawn up by the Franco government and endorsed by the Djemaa in July 1974, while plans for the holding of a referendum in the first half of 1975 were announced on August 21, and a party, the PUNS (q.v.), was set up in November 1974 to counter the growing influence of the Polisario Front (q.v.) and provide the leadership for the new governmental institutions to be created. The whole plan got frozen, however, as a result of the loud protests made by Morocco. When the UN requested Spain in December 1974 to postpone its planned referendum while the Western Saharan problem was examined by the International Court of Justice (q.v.), the Franco government reluctantly complied (January 16, 1975). In May 1975, after almost a decade of stalling, it allowed a UN Visiting Mission (q.v.) into the territory, and, when its arrival revealed the extent of popular support for the Polisario Front and shattered the credibility of the PUNS, Franco began seriously to consider coming to terms with the guerrilla movement, which he did not believe would endanger basic Spanish interests if it were allowed to take power.

However, his government came under intense pressure to abandon completely its plans to prepare the territory for independence when, on October 16, 1975, King Hassan announced plans to send 350,000 Green Marchers across the border. Franco became seriously ill at a cabinet meeting held the next day to examine Spain's response to this challenge, and on October 21–24, he suffered a series of heart attacks. Thereafter, he was unable to direct the government, and on October 30, Prince Juan Carlos (q.v.) became acting head of state. As Franco's condition continued to deteriorate, his ministers became preoccupied with preparing the transition to a new post-Francoist order at home and, desperate to avoid conflict with Morocco, engineered a 180-degree turnaround in policy on the Sahara, signing the Madrid Agreement on November 14. Franco died six days later.

FRANCO-SPANISH CONVENTION (JUNE 27, 1900). This was the first of several Franco-Spanish conventions at the beginning of the 20th century defining these countries' respective zones of influence in the Sahara. The 1900 convention defined the southern and southeastern frontiers of Spain's Saharan territory with French Mauritania but left its northern borders deliberately vague, possibly because Britain had recognized Moroccan territory as extending as far south as Boujdour (q.v.) in the March 13, 1895, Anglo-Moroccan Agreement (q.v.). Significantly, the 1900 convention gave France both the famous Idjil salt-pans and the important Bay of Levrier, to the east of the peninsula of Cape Blanc (q.v.). However, Spanish fishermen were given the right to fish, land, and even erect buildings in the Bay of Levrier (article 2), and salt exported from Idjil through the Spanish zone was not to be subject to French export duties.

Article 1 defined the frontier from the coast at Cape Blanc to the intersection of the Tropic of Cancer and the meridian 14° 20′ west of Paris but then vaguely said that it would "continue on that latter meridian in a northerly direction." The following is the main part of its text:

> On the coast of the Sahara, the limit between the French and Spanish possessions will follow a line which, departing . . . on the western side of the Cape Blanc peninsula, between the extremity of that cape and the Bay of the West [Bay of Levrier], will reach the middle of the aforesaid peninsula, then, in dividing the latter in half as much as the terrain will permit, will go to the north as far as the point of encounter with the parallel 21°20′ north latitude. The frontier will continue to the east along 21°20′ until the intersection of this parallel with the meridian 15°20′ west of Paris (13° west of Greenwich). From that point, the line of demarcation will run in the direction of the northeast by making a curve, between the meridians 15°20′ and 16°20′ west of Paris (13° and 14° west of Greenwich), which will be traced in a way to leave to France, with their dependencies, the salt pans of the region of Idjil, from whose external bank the frontier will be kept at a distance of at least 20 km. From the intersection of the aforesaid curve with the meridian 15°20′ west of Paris (13° west of Greenwich), the frontier will reach as directly as possible the intersection of the Tropic of Cancer with the meridian 14°20′ west of Paris (12° west of Greenwich), and will continue on that latter meridian in a northerly direction.

FRANCO-SPANISH CONVENTION (OCTOBER 3, 1904). This was one of a number of conventions signed by France and Spain at the beginning of the century to demarcate their colonial spheres of influence in Morocco and the Sahara. A convention of June 27, 1900 (q.v.), had defined the southern frontiers of Spain's Saharan territory with Mauritania. A draft convention of November 8, 1902 (q.v.), had extended the border northward as part of a division of Morocco into French and Spanish spheres of influence, but it had not been signed as a result of Spanish hesitations to proceed without the agreement of Britain. The signing of the October 3, 1904, convention was made possible by the Anglo-French Declaration of April 8, 1904, which gave France and Spain a free hand in Morocco in return for French recognition of Britain's "rights" in Egypt. The convention included a public declaration, which stated that France and Spain "remain firmly attached to the integrity of the Moroccan empire under the sovereignty of the sultan" and, of much greater importance, a set of secret accords, whose contents were not to be published until 1911. These, like the 1902 draft convention, stated that France and Spain could intervene in their respective spheres of influence in Morocco in the event of a breakdown of the status quo there. As in 1902, Spain was to receive both northern and southern spheres of influence, though they were less extensive than those proposed in 1902. In the south, the Spanish zone was defined as follows by article 5:

> In order to complete the delimitation set out in article 1 of the convention of June 27, 1900, it is understood that the line of demarcation between the French and Spanish spheres of influence will start from the intersection of the meridian 14°20′ west of Paris with 26° latitude north, which it will follow eastward as far as its intersection with the meridian 11° west of Paris. It will follow this meridian as far as the Oued Draa, then the thalweg of the Oued Draa until its meeting with the meridian 10° west of Paris, and finally the meridian 10° west of Paris until the crest-line between the basins of the Oued Draa and the Oued Souss and then follow in a westerly direction the crest-line between the basins of the Oued Draa and the Oued Souss, and then between the basins of the Oued Mesa and the Oued Noun as far as the nearest point to the source of the Oued Tazeroualt.

Article 4 fixed the frontiers of what was later to become Ifni. Article 6 was of special importance with respect to Western Sahara. Unlike the 1902 draft convention, which defined the territory to the north of parallel 26° latitude north as part of Morocco (albeit the Spanish sphere of influence in Morocco), article 6 of the 1904 convention recognized that "Spain has henceforward full liberty of action in regard to the region comprised between 26° and 27°40′ latitude north and the meridian 11° west of Paris, which are outside Moroccan territory." Confirmed in the later convention of November 14, 1912 (q.v.), this clause was to mean that Spain later considered the region of Saguia el-Hamra (q.v.) a full colony rather than part of what was to become in 1912 the Spanish protectorate zone in Morocco. After Morocco's independence in 1956, the Moroccan government was to protest that this clause violated the 1906 Act of Algeciras, by which both France and Spain had committed themselves to upholding the territorial integrity of Morocco, the public declaration contained in the 1904 convention (which contained the same pledge), and the Anglo-Moroccan Agreement of March 13, 1895 (q.v.), which recognized Moroccan territory as extending as far south as Boujdour (q.v.), which is just north of parallel 26°. However, France and Spain appear to have chosen parallel 27°40′ as the southern limit of Morocco because of the presence of an officially nominated Moroccan *caid* (q.v.) at Tarfaya (q.v.), a little to the north.

FRANCO-SPANISH CONVENTION (NOVEMBER 14, 1912). This was the last of a series of conventions signed by France and Spain at the beginning of the 20th century, which defined the frontiers of their respective colonial spheres of interest in Morocco and the Sahara. It followed the Franco-German Agreement of November 4, 1911, by which Germany became the last of France's major European rivals to accept French predominance in Morocco (in return for the cession of part of the French Congo to Germany), and the Treaty of Fez between France and Moulay Hafid, the sultan of Morocco, on March 30, 1912, setting up the French "protectorate" in Morocco. It was by virtue of the latter that France was permitted to hand over part of Morocco to be administered by Spain. However, though British pressure ensured that Spain, rather than France, would control the northern Moroccan Mediterranean coast opposite Gibraltar (with the exception of Tangiers, which became an "international" zone), France was less generous toward Spain than in the previous, secret convention of October 3, 1904 (q.v.), because, after the British and German endorsement of France's Moroccan ambitions, Spain had little bargaining power and France wished to compensate for its losses in the Congo by getting more of Morocco. So the Spanish zones of the Moroccan protectorate were much smaller, in both the north and the south, than the Spanish spheres of influence agreed to in 1904. With regard to southern Morocco and the Sahara, article 2 of the convention stated that:

> The frontier of the French and Spanish zones will be defined by the thalweg of the Oued Draa (q.v.), which it will follow from the sea as far as its intersection with the meridian 11° west of Paris; it will follow this meridian southward until its intersection with the parallel 27°40' latitude north. To the south of this parallel, articles 5 and 6 of the convention of October 3, 1904, will remain applicable.

Thus, the territory between the parallels 27°40' and 26° latitude north, that is, what became known as Saguia el-Hamra (q.v.), was to be considered (as article 6 of the 1904 convention put it) as "outside Moroccan territory." Spain was to have "full liberty of action there." By contrast, the reduced Spanish zone to the north of parallel 27°40', that is, the "Tekna Zone" (q.v.), between that parallel and the Oued Draa, was to be considered part of the Moroccan protectorate. It was for that reason that the Spanish government agreed to hand over the Tekna Zone to Morocco in 1958 (two years after the rest of Morocco had become independent) but refused steadfastly to do likewise with regard to the rest of its Saharan territory.

FRANCO-SPANISH DRAFT CONVENTION (NOVEMBER 8, 1902). By contrast to the earlier Franco-Spanish Convention of June 27, 1900 (q.v.), which defined the southern frontiers of Spain's Saharan territories (with Mauritania), this draft convention demarcated "zones of influence" in Morocco, which extended into the Sahara, linking up with the border defined in 1900. Article 2 stated that in the event of a disturbance of the status quo in Morocco, both Spain and France would have an "exclusive right" of intervention in two spheres of influence. By article 3, the Spanish sphere was defined as including a large part of northern Morocco, including the Rif mountains, Fez, Taza, and, in the south, part of the Souss, the Anti-Atlas range, and the territories to its south, including the region of the Saguia el-Hamra (q.v.). Two aspects of the convention are of special interest. First, it defined the territory to the north of 26° latitude north as being part of the Spanish sphere of influence in Morocco, whereas in the later conventions of October 3, 1904, and November 14, 1912 (qq.v.), the territory between 26° and 27°40' latitudes north (i.e., what became Saguia el-Hamra) were defined as being outside Moroccan territory. Second, Spain was offered far more territory in Morocco than it was to be offered by France in 1904 and 1912. Spain did not sign this draft convention, however—out of fear of acting without the accord of Britain, which was not to give France and Spain a free hand in Morocco until the Anglo-French Declaration of April 8, 1904, by which France in return recognized Britain's "rights" in Egypt.

FRENTE DE LIBERACION DEL SAHARA (BAJO DOMINACION ESPANOLA). The Front for the Liberation of the Sahara (under Spanish Domination) was a small Moroccan-based group of Saharawi supporters of the Moroccan claim to Western Sahara, which was active in 1966–69 with the Rabat regime's backing. The group had no presence in Western Sahara itself, concentrating on publishing literature in Morocco, with the aid of the Ministère des Affaires Mauritaniennes et Sahariennes (q.v.), and on lobbying international organizations like the UN (q.v.). It was, in fact, the adoption of the first UN General Assembly resolution on Western Sahara (resolution 2072 of December 16, 1965), which prompted King Hassan II (q.v.) to re-create the old Ministry of Mauritanian and Saharan Affairs and to sanction the establishment of a Saharawi political organization that could buttress the Moroccan claim to Western Sahara at the UN and the OAU (q.v.). The front published a Spanish-language journal, *Nuestro Sahara* (q.v.), edited by Brika Zaruali, a member of the Istiqlal Party (q.v.), between March 1967 and June 1968. Besides Zaruali, its most prominent member was Ma el-Ainin el-Abadila Ould Cheikh Mohammed Laghdaf, a grandson of Cheikh Ma el-Ainin (q.v.). He led an FLS delegation that lobbied the UN General Assembly in December 1966. The delegation's principal success was to win over a rival group of pro-Mauritanian lobbyists led by Mohammed Ma el-Ainin Mohammed Boya (q.v.). The movement's other notable action was a rally held in Tan-Tan, southern Morocco, in May 1967, at which the

Moroccan minister of the interior, General Mohammed Oufkir, made a strongly worded anti-Spanish speech which led to the Spanish foreign minister, Fernando María Castiella, lodging a formal protest with the Moroccan ambassador in Madrid. However, the movement did not attempt to start political activity in Spanish Sahara. Its close links with the royal government in Morocco, which wanted to maintain friendly relations with Madrid at the time, prevented that. "It did not undertake any activity against colonialism in the practical sphere, that is, the arming of the popular masses and their placing in the context necessary to allow them to determine their future in a real way," wrote El-Ouali Mustapha Sayed (q.v.), founder of the Polisario Front (q.v.), in January 1973. "When it reached a dead end, its members returned to their jobs." The FLS's fate was sealed by the sudden détente between Morocco and Mauritania in 1969, when King Hassan finally recognized Mauritania (after claiming for the first nine years of Mauritania's independence that it was historically part of Morocco) and as a result the Ministry of Mauritanian and Saharan Affairs, on which the FLS was financially and organizationally dependent, was dissolved.

FRENTE POPULAR PARA LA LIBERACION DE SAGUIA EL-HAMRA Y RIO DE ORO (Polisario Front). The Popular Front for the Liberation of Saguia el-Hamra and Río de Oro was founded on May 10, 1973, by a group of anticolonial militants who had previously been active in a loose preparatory body known as the "embryonic movement for the liberation of the Sahara" (q.v.), which had brought together a nucleus of Saharawi students from Morocco, a few veterans of the anticolonial struggle who had settled in Zouerate, Mauritania, and a number of relatively well-educated youth from within Western Sahara. The front was founded at a clandestine congress held somewhere in the Western Saharan-Mauritanian border region. The congress elected El-Ouali Mustapha Sayed (q.v.) as the front's secretary-general and also appointed an executive committee, which issued a manifesto announcing the front's creation. "The Polisario Front," it proclaimed, "is born as unique expression of the masses, opting for revolutionary violence and the armed struggle as the means by which the Saharawi Arab African people can recover total liberty and foil the manoeuvres of Spanish colonialism.'' Just ten days later, the front staged its first guerrilla raid, against a Spanish post at El-Khanga (q.v.), which narrowly avoided turning into a disaster. The following October, the front began publishing a monthly journal, *20 de Mayo* (q.v.).

The front received virtually no material support from foreign sources during its first two years fighting against the Spanish. The Algerian government, which was to give the movement substantial support from 1975, had decided to assist a tiny rival faction, the MOREHOB (q.v.), in March 1973 and, when MOREHOB rapidly proved lacking in seriousness, resolved not to support other Saharawi groups until they could prove they were of greater mettle. El-Ouali was briefly detained and deported from Algeria in 1973. The front did, however, get a better hearing from Libya, which gave it broadcasting facilities and sent a very small consignment of arms. The Mauritanian regime of Mokhtar Ould Daddah (q.v.) allowed some of the front's leaders to live in Mauritania, issued a few of them passports, and tacitly connived in their activity, though it did not directly assist their guerrilla exploits.

The 1973–75 guerrilla campaign against Spain was a small-scale affair, involving a very small number of armed militants, who staged occasional hit-and-run raids and ambushes, sometimes taking refuge across the border in the vast and largely unpoliced desert regions of northern Mauritania. Among the better-known incidents were a battle at Galb Lahmar on January 26, 1974, when five Polisario guerrillas were captured by the Spanish and jailed; a sabotage attack on two of the control stations of the Fosbucraa (q.v.) conveyor belt on October 20, 1974; the kidnapping of a Spanish businessman, Antonio Martín, on March 11, 1975; mutinies by pro-Polisario Saharawi soldiers in two units of the *Tropas Nómadas* (q.v.) on May 10 and 11, 1975, which resulted in 1 Spanish soldier being killed and 15 others, including 4 officers, being taken into captivity; and a raid on the *Policía Territorial* post at Guelta Zemmour (qq.v.) on May 14, 1975, when the post's commanding officer, a Saharawi, was captured.

Though the May 1973 manifesto did not explicitly specify independence as the front's objective, referring vaguely to "total liberty," it is probable that most, if not all, its founders had set their sights on independence as their ultimate goal by the time that the movement was born. At the 2nd congress, held on August 25–31, 1974, this objective was clearly spelled out in a new manifesto. Replying to the announcement by Spain the previous July that it would institute an *estatuto político* (q.v.) to establish internal autonomy, the manifesto declared:

> Regarding internal autonomy, the popular masses, convinced of the legitimacy of the people's war of long duration, regard it as a maneuver to save colonialism in a state of weakness and as an attempt to dupe the people to prolong its domination over our soil and natural wealth. In the face of these maneuvers, the Saharawi people have no alternative but to struggle until wresting independence, their wealth, and their full sovereignty over their land.

The congress also sent a letter to King Hassan II (q.v.) warning of fierce Saharawi resistance to any Moroccan attempt to annex Western Sahara and elected a 7-member executive committee, which consisted of 4 military leaders (including El-Ouali, who was reelected secretary-general) and 3 "political" leaders, and a 21-member political bureau (qq.v.).

A few weeks before the congress, in July, the Algerian government decided to give the movement some low-key support, though substantial aid was not to begin until the following spring. Within Western Sahara, support for the front began to mushroom from mid-1974 as a result of Spain's announcement then of plans to establish internal autonomy and hold a referendum and the ensuing disappointment and frustration when Spain shelved these plans because of Moroccan protests and pressure. Disillusionment with Spain grew by leaps and bounds toward the end of 1974 and early in 1975, especially among young students and workers. Typical of the front's recruits were the skilled Fosbucraa employees, mainly electricians and graduates of the technical courses of the Promoción Profesional Obrera (PPO—Workers Professional Advancement) in El-Ayoun (q.v.), who staged the sabotage attack on the Fosbucraa conveyor belt in October 1974. Urban youth shared the front's distaste for the conservative *chioukh* (q.v.) in the Djemaa (q.v.) who loyally supported the colonial authorities, and they shared its modernizing, reformist social policies—notably its opposition to slavery, polygamy, caste inequalities, and tribal divisions and its advocacy of women's involvement in the political and military struggle against colonialism. The front gradually won majority support in all parts of the country and from all tribes, though its implantation remained somewhat weaker in the south, where the Spanish-backed Partido de la Unión Nacional Saharaui (q.v.) had some initial success after its creation in November 1974.

The front's popular support was dramatically revealed in May 1975, when the arrival of a United Naitons Visiting Mission (q.v.) brought pro-Polisario demonstrators onto the streets in the thousands wherever the mission members went. In their report, the UN team noted that the front, "although considered a clandestine movement before the mission's arrival, appeared as a dominant political force in the territory." The mission members met leaders of the front during a subsequent visit at the end of May to the Tindouf (q.v.) region of southwestern Algeria, where the movement was by then receiving considerable assistance from the Algerian authorities. They told the UN team that they saw no need to hold a referendum, since the people evidently wanted independence, but said that, if the UN insisted on one's being held, they would go along with it on condition that the Spanish administration had previously been withdrawn and replaced by a temporary "national" administration, the Spanish armed forces had been withdrawn and replaced by the front's guerrilla army, the political exiles and refugees had been allowed to return home, and the front had been allowed to participate in any body set up to screen and determine the authenticity of the refugees—acceptable criteria for the latter, according to the front, being membership of a subfraction (q.v.) existing within the territory and an intention to settle in the territory regardless of the outcome of the vote.

The front's outflanking of the PUNS during the UN mission's visit prompted the Spanish authorities to try to come to terms with the guerrilla movement. The Spanish government doubted that an independent Western Saharan government, under Polisario leadership, would be strong enough to challenge Spain's important economic interests in the territory, in particular its interests in phosphate-mining and fishing (qq.v.). The front responded favorably to Spanish overtures, and on September 9, 1975, El-Ouali held talks in Algeria with the Spanish foreign minister, Pedro Cortina y Mauri (q.v.). A deal was struck. The guerrillas freed 13 Spanish prisoners and promised Spain a 15- to 20-year transition period with respect to its fishing and phosphate interests in return for a Spanish commitment to transfer power to the front in preparation for independence. Twenty-three Polisario prisoners were then released from Spanish jails on September 17, and on October 21, 1975, at a meeting in Mahbes (q.v.), there was a further prisoner exchange, a Spanish official handing over all but five of Spain's remaining Polisario prisoners and Ibrahim Ghali (q.v.) handing over the front's last two Spanish prisoners. The next day at Mahbes, El-Ouali met the Spanish governor-general, General Federico Gómez de Salazar (q.v.), who agreed to allow several senior Polisario leaders, including Ibrahim Ghali and Mahfoud Ali Beiba (q.v.), to enter El-Ayoun at the end of the month. Meanwhile, Spanish troops withdrew from a number of their smaller outlying posts, allowing Polisario guerrillas to take control of such places as Mahbes, Guelta Zemmour, and Tifariti at about this time.

The Spanish government's attempt to come to terms with the front forced the conservative *chioukh* in the Djemaa and the remnants of the PUNS to do likewise. At the end of May 1975, the president of the Djemaa, Khatri Ould Said Ould Joumani (q.v.), traveled to Tindouf to hold talks with El-Ouali and other Polisario leaders. In July, there was serious rioting between Polisario and PUNS supporters in El-Ayoun, but the PUN's 2nd congress, held on August 16–18, voted to attempt to reach an understanding with the front. A series of meetings between the two groups' leaders was held, notably on October 10 between El-Ouali and the PUNS secretary-general, Dueh Sidna Naucha (q.v.). The Polisario leaders, however, refused to form an alliance with the PUNS, which by then was on the verge of collapse, and insisted that the remaining PUNS members simply join the front. This most of them had done by the beginning of November. On October 12, moreover, the front organized a conference, at Ain Ben Tili (q.v.), at which many of the country's most prominent *chioukh* pledged to unite with the movement to resist the growing threat of invasion from Morocco.

After King Hassan's announcement of the Green March (q.v.) on October 16, virtually all Saharawis, whatever their tribal, social, or political background, rallied behind the front as the Moroccan threat intensified and the Spanish government's commitment to self-determination began to waver. On October 26–27, for example, up to 12,000 pro-Polisario supporters demonstrated in El-Ayoun, prompting the Spanish authorities to impose a curfew.

On October 31, Moroccan troops crossed the border, advancing toward Jdiriya, Haousa, and Farsia and clashing with Polisario guerrillas. The front's long war with Morocco was beginning . . . a fortnight before the signing of the Madrid Agreement (q.v.) on November 14. The agreement itself was denounced as "null and void" by the front, and on November 28, the front succeeded in making nonsense of one of its key clauses (that pledging respect for the will of the Saharawi people as expressed by the Djemaa) by getting an absolute majority of the Djemaa's members (67 out of 102) to sign the Proclamation of Guelta Zemmour (q.v.), dissolving the assembly and creating a pro-Polisario Provisional Saharawi National Council (q.v.).

Over the following few months, the front's principal preoccupation became the evacuation of tens of thousands of refugees (q.v.) from the cities—first mainly to encampments in the desert hinterland and then to the Tindouf region of Algeria. The assistance given the refugees by the Algerian government was, by then, just one facet of its substantial aid to the Polisario cause. Algeria provided quantities of arms, as well as rear bases and training, and lobbied strenuously abroad on the front's behalf. On December 3, 1975, the front began broadcasting "The Voice of Free Sahara" from Algerian radio transmitters.

With most of the refugees safely in Algeria by May 1976, the front was finally able to turn its attention to offensive military action against Morocco and Mauritania. By then it had lost control of most of the small desert outposts it had occupied in the autumn of 1975 (one of the last to be lost was Guelta Zemmour, captured by the Moroccans in April), but by using highly flexible and mobile guerrillas tactics, adapting the techniques of the traditional *ghazzi* (q.v.) to the age of the Land Rover and the SAM missile, the guerrillas rapidly proved very effective, pinning down most of the Moroccan and Mauritanian forces in defensive positions in a handful of towns and bases and spreading the war across the territory's borders into the desert regions of southern Morocco and Mauritania. In an especially audacious initiative, the guerrillas crossed 1,500 km. of desert to attack the Mauritanian capital, Nouakchott (q.v.), in June 1976, though some of the raiders were surrounded by Mauritanian forces and El-Ouali was killed.

Meanwhile, on February 27, 1976, the Provisional Saharawi National Council proclaimed the founding of a pro-Polisario republic, the SADR (q.v.), whose first government was announced on March 4. At the front's 3rd general popular congress (q.v.), held near Tindouf on August 26–30, 1976, a constitution for the new state was approved, and Mohammed Abdelaziz (q.v.) was elected secretary-general to succeed El-Ouali. The latter's brother, Bachir Mustapha Sayed (q.v.), was elected deputy secretary-general, and seven other members were elected to the front's supreme executive committee, which, under the SADR's constitution, also constituted the SADR's Council for the Command of the Revolution (q.v.). A new 21-member political bureau was also elected. The fulfilling of the role of the SADR's CCR by the front's executive committee was typical of the extensive overlapping of "party" and "state." Another feature of the front by this time was that it had become a mass movement, of which all adult Saharawis, excepting "traitors" who had sided with Morocco or Mauritania, were members as of right; it was not a "vanguard party" with a small or politically homogenous membership but a broad movement including traditionalist elders as well as socialist-influenced ex-students.

Militarily, the front's principal target at first was Mauritania, which it correctly identified as the weak link in the enemy chain. The June 1976 attack on Nouakchott was followed by a second, more successful, raid on the Mauritanian capital in July 1977, and on May 1, 1977, the front fought its way into Zouerate (q.v.), the center of Mauritania's key iron-mining industry. There were also repeated attacks against the iron-ore railway from Zouerate to the port of Nouadhibou (q.v.). The aim was to undermine the Mauritanian economy by crippling the iron ore industry, on which Mauritania depended for 80–90 percent of its exports. In particular, the front hoped to force an evacuation of the hundreds of French expatriate mine personnel, on whom the industry largely depended for its smooth running. In its May 1977 attack on Zouerate, two French citizens were killed and six more were captured, and, the following October 25, two more French expatriates were seized on the Zouerate-Nouadhibou railway. Instead of ordering an evacuation, however, the French government decided to boost Mauritania's hitherto feeble defenses by sending military experts to the country and, in December 1977 and April 1978, sending sophisticated Jaguar jets of the French air force into action against the guerrillas.

This French aerial intervention forced the front to switch to smaller-scale operations in Mauritania, but it could not drive the guerrillas from Mauritania's vast desert expanses, and, on July 10, 1978, the war-weary Mauritanian army staged a coup in Nouakchott, overthrowing the regime of Mokhtar Ould Daddah (q.v.) and promising to restore peace. Two days later, the front unilaterally declared "a temporary halt in military operations in Mauritanian territory."

The front was rapidly disillusioned, however, by the new Mauritanian military government's refusal to reach a definitive bilateral peace agreement, a refusal prompted by its hope of bringing all the parties together to negotiate a global settlement to the war in which the front would be obliged to compromise on its goal of full independence, perhaps by accepting a "ministate" in Tiris el-Gharbia (q.v.). The front would have none of this. At its 4th congress on September 25–28, 1978, it decided to continue the cease-fire but adopted a manifesto that demanded of Mauritania:

1. Official recognition of the sovereignty of the SADR over the whole of the territory of Western Sahara;
2. The restitution of the part which it occupies to the authorities of the SADR;
3. The withdrawal of Mauritanian forces to their internationally recognized frontiers (frontier of 1960).

The congress also adopted a "national general program" (see below), reelected Mohammed Abdelaziz as secretary-general and Bachir Mustapha Sayed as deputy secretary-general, reelected the other 7 members of the executive committee, and elected a new 21-member political bureau.

Negotiations with Mauritania continued unsuccessfully for several months—notably in Libya in August 1978, in Paris on September 9–16, in Bamako, Mali, on October 17–18, in Libya on October 18, and in Libya again on April 21–23, 1979. There was also an unsuccessful but unique round of talks between the front and Moroccan officials in Bamako on October 20–21, 1978. As the talks with Mauritanian officials spanned on without result, the front became increasingly frustrated and threatened to lift its cease-fire. Finally, on the cease-fire's first anniversary, July 12, 1978, it did so, attacking the Mauritanian-held post of Tichla in Tiris el-Gharbia. This immediately forced the Mauritanian authorities to come to heel, and on August 5, 1979, the front scored a major victory when Mauritania signed the Agreement of Algiers (q.v.), renouncing its claims to Western Saharan territory and agreeing to hand over the parts of Tiris el-Gharbia under its control.

After the July 1978 cease-fire in Mauritania, the front was able to give undivided military attention to the Moroccan forces, both within Western Sahara and in southern Morocco. It achieved considerable success on this score, especially during its Houari Boumedienne Offensive (q.v.) in 1979–80. The front also received greater international support during this period, especially from Third World governments that were impressed by the guerrillas' staying power. Algerian military and diplomatic support remained constant, and the movement was in no mood to compromise with Morocco. It demanded direct talks with Morocco to prepare for a complete Moroccan withdrawal and recognition of the country's independence.

In 1981–87, however, Morocco built a series of ''defensive walls'' (q.v.), which gradually pushed Polisario forces out of about four fifths of the territory. Polisario switched to semiconventional tactics, repeatedly sending large numbers of troops, equipped with multiple rocket launchers and other powerful equipment, into battle against the 1,500-km.-long defense line established by the Moroccans. Polisario could no longer hope to win the war in purely military terms, but it was engaged in a war of attrition that would eventually require attempts at a political solution.

Diplomatically during the 1980s, the front remained firm on basic principles but increasingly flexible on the details of a settlement. Even so, Polisario's continued calls for direct negotiations were continually rebuffed by Morocco. Though there were informal meetings between the two sides in April 1983, January 1985, and January 1989, these did not lead to real negotiations. Instead, Polisario acquiesced in practice to speak indirectly with Morocco through the ''good offices'' of the United Nations secretary-general, Javier Pérez de Cuéllar (qq.v.), who, in April 1986, initiated ''proximity talks'' to try to reach a settlement. In August 1988, Polisario, along with Morocco, agreed in broad outline to a peace plan proposed by the secretary-general. The front showed flexibility by accepting that Morocco could keep a portion of its forces, and some of its administration, in Western Sahara before and during the UN-OAU referendum. As of the end of 1990, Polisario was hopeful that final details of the UN plan would soon be agreed upon, but despite considerable progress concerning the modalities of the referendum, due in part to strenuous efforts by the UN secretary-general, the situation in the middle of 1993 remained clouded.

The front has not spelled out in detail the policies that it would aim to pursue in an independent Western Sahara, though its broad political orientation was outlined in a "national general program" adopted at the 4th general popular congress in 1978. This document proclaimed that the Saharawis are an Arab, African, and Islamic people, who are part of the Third World and who oppose colonialism, imperialism, and exploitation. Socialism and the promotion of the Arabic language are supported. The program advocates a "republican, democratic system," the unification of the Arab world, and "the mobilization of the masses and the liberation of their spirit of initiative." It goes on to propose social equality, suppression of all forms of exploitation, provision of housing for all, "protection of the family . . . given that it constitutes the fundamental cell of society," "the achievement of women's political and social rights and the favoring of her access to all domains so that she assumes her responsibilities in national construction, this in accordance with our national realities and our religion," "the protection of the (Saharawi) civilization and religious heritage," free and compulsory education, the complete Arabization of education, health care, the guaranteeing of "the fundamental liberties of the citizens," and balanced economic development. The program says nothing specific about future economic policy, remaining mute on such issues as the possibility of nationalizations, but the SADR's foreign minister, Ibrahim Hakim (q.v.), said in September 1977, "The Sahara will be a primary commodity-producing country, it is necessary to develop these primary resources, and it is obligatory to cooperate with the industrialized countries." Regarding foreign policy, the programmatic document adopted by the front's 6th congress (December 7–10, 1985) stated, "Our foreign policy is based on the conviction that . . . freedom and independence are the natural and irreplaceable rights of peoples and fundamental in contemporary international relations based on mutual respect for the national sovereignty of each country." Turning to intra-Maghrebi relations, it said, "Unity can be achieved only through cooperation and respect between peoples in the region and therefore with the effective participation of the six entities that compose it," a reference to Western Sahara's hoped-for status as the sixth Maghreb state, alongside Algeria, Libya, Mauritania, Morocco, and Tunisia. What was most remarkable about the Polisario Front in the 1980s was not only its strength on the battlefield despite Morocco's massive system of "defensive walls" or even the widespread support it enjoyed in the world community (74 countries had recognized the SADR by mid-1990) but also the fact that the Saharawi organization remained relatively cohesive, compared with most other liberation movements in Africa or elsewhere. The only high-level official of the front to have switched sides and defected to the opposing camp was Omar Hadrami (q.v.), who flew to Morocco in August 1989 after being removed from his positions of high responsibility with Polisario. It would appear that the exigencies of survival in the face of difficult conditions have kept the Saharawi nationalist movement united.

FRIQ. A nomad encampment. The size of the normal *friq* appears to have diminished during the mid-20th century as a result of the ending of the *ghazzis* (q.v.), which allowed the nomads to travel in smaller groups, thus taking better advantage of the limited pastoral resources. By the 1950s, the average Reguibat (q.v.) friq had about five or six *khaimat* (tents).

FRONT DE LIBERATION ET DE L'UNITE. The Front for Liberation and Unity (FLU) was set up on March 21, 1975, with the goal (according to a Radio Rabat announcement that day) of "destroying Spanish colonialism in order to reunite the territory with the Moroccan motherland." The group was virulently opposed to the Polisario Front (q.v.), which it described (September 2, 1975) as a "puppet grouplet, which is trying desperately to open the door to international communism in our occupied Sahara." It held its first and only congress on September 13–15, 1975, in the Moroccan city of Agadir, electing a 79-member central committee and a 17-member permanent executive committee headed by a young pro-Moroccan Saharawi, Rachid Mohammed Douihi (q.v.), as secretary-general. The Moroccan government was instrumental in settling up FLU, apparently because it expected Western Sahara's fate to be settled by the end of the year and so

urgently needed to boast a "liberation front" that supported
the Moroccan claim to the territory. A considerable number of
regular Moroccan troops (about 1,500 according to Spanish
intelligence sources at the time) were converted in the spring of
1975 into FLU "guerrillas" and sent across the Western
Saharan border to attack isolated Spanish outposts and place
bombs in El-Ayoun (q.v.). Most of them were Saharawis, then
numerous in the Moroccan Forces Armées Royales (q.v.)
because of the poverty of most of the Saharawis of southern
Morocco, and their commanders were a group of Saharawi
officers of the FAR, among them Commandant Abba el-
Cheikh, Captain Mohammed Ould Khir, and Captain Ahmed
Ould Moulay. It did not take the Spanish authorities in
Western Sahara long to obtain proof that the FLU forces were
a wing of the regular Moroccan army: On June 8, 1975, an
entire FLU unit surrendered to Spanish forces at Mahbes (q.v.),
after being surrounded by a Spanish patrol, and documents
found on the soldiers showed that all of them were members of
the FAR. Sixteen other regular Moroccan soldiers, claiming to
be FLU militants, were captured by the Spanish army near
Hagounia on July 22, 1975. The FLU attacks were designed to
pressure Spain to abandon its plans for self-determination in
Western Sahara and hand the territory over to Morocco. They
also had an important propaganda value when they were
launched in May 1975, on the eve of the arrival in El-Ayoun of
the UN Visiting Mission(q.v.), which the Rabat regime hoped
would conclude that a genuine pro-Moroccan Saharawi guer-
illa group was actively fighting the Spanish. The first incidents
were on May 4, eight days before the UN team's arrival, when
shots were fired at the Spanish military posts at Jdiriya and
Amgala, and May 5, when there were three separate bombing
incidents in El-Ayoun. Troop reinforcements were rushed
from the Canary Islands when a FLU unit tried unsuccessfully
to shoot down a Spanish helicopter near Tah (q.v.), on May 14,
right in the middle of the UN mission's visit (May 12–19). The
next day, a Saharawi businessman was shot dead by a FLU
group when his vehicle was ambushed near Haousa. The
attacks continued into June and July, and five Spanish soldiers
were killed on June 22 when their vehicle detonated a mine
laid by FLU near Tah. Later, on October 31, 1975, when the

Moroccan army crossed into Western Sahara, two weeks before the Madrid Agreement (q.v.), to try to take control of Farsia, Haousa, and Jdiriya, bases that had already been evacuated by Spanish forces, the Moroccan government claimed that FLU, rather than the FAR, was involved, but the claim convinced neither Spain nor the Polisario Front. After the Madrid Agreement, no more was heard of FLU.

FRONT DE LIBERATION ET DU RATTACHEMENT DU SAHARA A LA MAURITANIE. The Front for the Liberation and Unification of the Sahara with Mauritania was founded by pro-Mauritanian Saharawis, with the backing of the Nouakchott government, on November 16, 1975, two days after the Madrid Agreement (q.v.). It thus did not take part in the anti-Spanish struggle. Really an appendage of the Parti du Peuple Mauritanien (q.v.), Mauritania's ruling and single legal party at the time, its purpose was to organize those few Saharawis that opposed both the Polisario Front (q.v.) and Morocco and thereby facilitate the integration into Mauritania of what was to become Tiris el-Gharbia (q.v.). Its most prominent members were Mohammed Lamine Ould Horomtalla, who became its president; Souilem Ould Abdellahi, the mayor of Dakhla (qq.v.); and Saila Ould Abeida, who had been a member of the Cortes. However, most of the population of Tiris el-Gharbia joined the refugee (q.v.) exodus to Algeria, and the FLRSM remained a weak and largely inactive group. It had already virtually died by the time of the July 10, 1978, coup that toppled the regime of Mokhtar Ould Daddah (q.v.). Some of the group's original supporters later joined the Polisario Front, among them Souilem Ould Abdellahi, who left Mauritania to join the guerrilla movement early in 1979.

- G -

GAFER see GHAFFER

GAILLARD, FELIX. It was during his period in office as France's prime minister, from November 1957 to April

1958, that French forces joined the Spanish army in a major counterinsurgency sweep, Operation Ouragan (q.v.), against Army of Liberation (q.v.) guerrillas in Western Sahara in February 1958. Gaillard came under pressure from Gaston Cusin, high commissioner of French West Africa, to intervene in Western Sahara, which was being used as a sanctuary by guerrillas attacking the French in Mauritania, and agreement was given to the idea of a joint Franco-Spanish operation at an interministerial council meeting in Paris, attended by Cusin, on December 30. Gaillard shared Cusin's view that the Army of Liberation threatened plans for investment in the development of Mauritania's iron ore resources near Zouerate and created inauspicious conditions for the experiment in internal self-government in Mauritania under Mokhtar Ould Daddah (q.v.), who had become vice president of the colony's government council the previous May. Since Spain was too weak to clear the guerrillas from its territory on its own and had been forced to evacuate all points in the interior, including even Smara (q.v.), in August-October in order to bolster the defenses of its main enclaves on the coast, the Gaillard government decided on December 30 to propose a joint operation to the Spanish authorities. Gaillard instructed the French ambassador in Madrid, Baron Guy de la Tournelle, to put the idea directly to the Spanish foreign minister, Fernando María Castiella (q.v.). His assent was rapidly given, and a series of joint strategy meetings was held. Gaillard, however, wanted a pretext for the operation's launching. It was provided by a clash between French troops and guerrillas at the end of January near Fort Trinquet (Bir Moghrein), and the operation then took effect on February 10, ending successfully on February 24. It was carried out in the greatest secrecy, since Gaillard did not want to admit openly to a military alliance with the Franco regime (a sensitive matter to French socialists) and feared increasing France's diplomatic difficulties after the embarrassing French air raid on Sakiet Sidi Youssef in Tunisia (said to be a base of the Algerian FLN) on February 8, two days before the launching of Ouragan.

GAZI see GHAZZI

GENDARMERIE ROYALE. A Moroccan paramilitary security force, numbering about 10,000 men in 1989, the Gendarmerie Royale took an active part, alongside the regular Moroccan army, the FAR (q.v.), in the war against the Polisario Front (q.v.). It established a special counterinsurgency wing of "auxiliaries," former guerillas who, after being captured, were recruited to this force instead of remaining in jail. The force as a whole consists of one brigade, two mobile groups, an air squadron, and a coastguard unit.

GENEALOGIES. All Saharawi tribes have given themselves intricate genealogies, tracing their descent back to their supposed founders and often beyond them to the prophet Mohammed. Even tribes with a predominantly Berber ethnic origin, such as the Reguibat (q.v.), have claimed *cherifian* (q.v.) descent in order to attain the high status this is held to bestow. Few of the genealogies have much historical value beyond the most immediate generations. The origins of most of the tribes are shrouded in mystery and myth, and most tribes are not "pure," having absorbed outsiders and immigrant groups. Genealogies had great practical value in traditional Saharawi society, for they established the exact inherited social status of every individual and hence also of his or her rights, duties, and obligations in such matters as the choice of marriage partners and the payment of blood debts.

GENERAL POPULAR CONGRESS. The name given to the congresses of the Polisario Front (q.v.) since 1976. All general popular congresses are preceded by "popular base congresses" in the front's refugee camps located in the Tindouf (qq.v.) region of Algeria. These popular base congresses, along with the SPLA, the UNMS, UGTS, and Ugesario (qq.v), elect delegates to the general popular congress. The congress elects the executive committee and political bureau (qq.v.) of the front, the former body then assuming also the mantle of the Council for the Command of the Revolution of the SADR (qq.v.). Besides electing the leadership, the congress usually adopts one or more general programmatic documents. All the general popular congresses are held, to the extent possible, in the "liberated territories'' of Western Sahara under Polisario's control and are attended, to varying degrees, by foreign guests.

Since 1976, there have been six general popular congresses:

—the 3rd congress, held on August 26–30, 1976;
—the 4th congress, held on September 25–28, 1978;
—the 5th congress, held on October 12–16, 1982;
—the 6th congress, held on December 7–10, 1985;
—the 7th congress, held on April 28–May 1, 1989; and
—the 8th congress, held on June 18–20, 1991.

Since the 1976 general popular congress, there has been a remarkable stability in the top ranks of the Polisario Front and the SADR, with Mohammed Abdelaziz (q.v.) remaining the front's secretary-general (and the SADR's president) throughout the entire period. Reshuffles in the top ranks are usually announced at the congresses.

GENERAL UNION OF SAHARAWI WORKERS see UNION GENERAL DE TRABAJADORES SAHARAUIS

GENERAL UNION OF STUDENTS OF SAGUIA EL-HAMRA AND RIO DE ORO see UNION GENERAL DE LOS ESTUDIANTES DE SAGUIA EL-HAMRA Y RIO DE ORO

GHAFFER (variant: *gafer*). A collective form of tribute (q.v.) in traditional Saharawi society, to be distinguished from the individual (family-linked) form of tribute known as the *horma* (q.v.). It was paid by an entire tribe or fraction to another in order to establish or maintain an alliance. It usually consisted of a gift of one or two dozen camels and did not generally have the derogatory connotations of the horma. A celebrated example was the annual gift of eight camels given to the Izarguien (q.v.) by the emirs of Trarza (Mauritania), until early this century, in recognition of the military assistance given by the Izarguien chief Hammou Said to Emir Ali Chandora during a war at the beginning of the 18th century.

GHALI, BOUTROS BOUTROS. Born in 1922, Boutros Boutros Ghali, from a prominent Egyptian family, was educated at Cairo University and at the University of Paris (Sorbonne). He served in many positions with the Egyptian government, including minister of state for foreign affairs from 1977 to 1991. Effective January 1, 1992, he became secretary-general of the United Nations (q.v.), succeeding Javier Pérez de Cuéllar (q.v.). The Western Sahara question was one of many unresolved disputes he faced immediately upon assuming office, and by the middle of 1993, he had already held many meetings with both Morocco and the Polisario Front (q.v.) and issued six reports concerning the status of the deployment of the United Nations Mission for the Referendum in Western Sahara (MINURSO) (q.v.).

GHAZZI (variants: *razzi, gazi*). A raid. Raiding was such an intrinsic part of traditional Saharawi society that it sometimes ranked in economic importance with livestock-herding and trading. The methods, rules, and obligations associated with it were virtually institutionalized. The harsh desert environment and the pastoral nomadic way of life of the Saharawis encouraged raiding. There was no supratribal state to maintain order. The segmentary nature of Saharawi societies and the responsibility of agnates for the payment of the bloodwit, or *diya,* tended to encourage vendettas, which could often degenerate into a vicious cycle of counterraids. Moreover, the very practice of nomadic livestock-raising provided a ready supply of animals suited to military use (camels) and provided skills and techniques (knowledge of terrain, riding skills, great mobility) of obvious military application. Finally, the competition between groups for livestock encouraged violence, though the almost endless raiding could ruin as well as enrich those that practiced it. Saharawi society in general was militarized by the *ghazzi,* for all tribes had to organize militarily to defend their own livestock, irrespective of their involvement in stealing the livestock of others. Whether motivated by a blood debt or purely by considerations of loot, the ghazzi was always a commercial affair. It was primarily among the youth, men with ambition to make their fortune, that the ranks of the *ghazzia* (raiding party) were recruited. They often had to rent much of the equipment, *selb*, needed for the ghazzi (camel or horse, rifle, ammunition) from wealthier, elder men of their fraction or *fakhd* (q.v.), who, according to long-established rules, received a fixed share in the booty, according to the investment they made in the venture. The rental, or *atila*, for a camel, for example, was normally a third of the booty received by the borrower. The head of the ghazzia, who was often appointed by the *ait arbain* (q.v.) when major military operations were involved, was known as the *dahman* (q.v.). The booty was divided among the participants in the ghazzi according to precise rules. All participants had a right to an ordinary share. Additional extraordinary shares went to the dahman, the guide, any holy men who accompanied the raiders to bring good fortune, and any warrior who had distinguished himself by his bravery or skill in battle. These shares were known respectively as *oud tadamanet, tannert, said,* and *el-rih.*

Though the frequency of the ghazzis encouraged the philosophy of "might is right" among the Saharawis, there were countervailing factors that favored the maintenance or establishment of peace among the tribes. Often a *sorba* (q.v.), a sort of ambassadorial group, would follow after a group of successful raiders to negotiate a deal by which some of the booty might be returned to its rightful owners. The practice of the *meniha* (q.v.), by which the wealthier herd-owners lent out much of their livestock and with it the right to usufruct, to those without herds, minimized—through dispersal—the risk of great losses and also increased—through mixing up herds—the risk to the raider of creating additional or unexpected enemies. Moreover, the sharing of blood-debt obligations through the creation of alliances and protection pacts, such as those established by the *debiha* (q.v.), were defensive mechanisms that increased the risks facing potential or actual enemies.

The techniques of the ghazzi were used with effect by the Saharawi tribes against the first Spanish enclave on the Western Saharan coast, at Dakhla (q.v.), at the end of the 19th century, and later, during the first decades of the 20th century against the French and their tribal allies during the

French pacification of northern Mauritania, southern Morocco, and southwestern Algeria. The French, in turn, allowed their tribal allies to stage punitive ghazzis against their enemies, sometimes deep into "Spanish" territory, which the anti-French forces often used as a sanctuary. The Spanish did not occupy points in the interior until 1934, when the French also completed the pacification of the border regions and the age of the ghazzi finally came to an end. Many young Saharawis who would in earlier times have engaged in ghazzis to make their wealth or reputations then bore arms in the Spanish and French armies. The tradition of the ghazzi, however, did not die. Indeed, the guerrilla raids of the Army of Liberation (q.v.) in 1957–58 and then of the Polisario Front (q.v.) from 1973 owed much, in method and technique, to the tradition, despite the replacement of camels and horses with Land Rovers and the adoption of modern weapons.

GISCARD D'ESTAING, VALERY. During his presidency of France between 1974 and 1981, Valéry Giscard d'Estaing (born 1926) gave discreet support to the Moroccan-Mauritanian annexation of Western Sahara in 1975–76 and then ordered direct military intervention by the French air force against the Polisario Front (q.v.) in 1977–78. In May 1975, one year after taking office, he made a state visit to Morocco, whose ruler, King Hassan II (q.v.), he regarded as one of France's most important allies in Africa. Aware of the instability of the king's regime in the early seventies, he appreciated that a strengthening of Hassan's internal position was likely to hinge on success in his campaign to annex Western Sahara (a campaign launched in 1974). Prior to the Madrid Agreement (q.v.), Giscard is thought to have advised the Spanish government to settle the Saharan dispute on terms acceptable to Morocco and to have assured President Mokhtar Ould Daddah of French support for the idea of a Moroccan-Mauritanian partition.

Moreover, under the Marrakesh Plan (q.v.), drawn up after Giscard's visit to Morocco, his government assisted the large rearmament program launched by Morocco in 1975. In an interview published in *Le Monde* (February 2, 1976), he said that he was opposed to the creation of an independent

Western Sahara because he was against "the multiplication of microstates."

However, Giscard was dismayed by the repercussions of the war, particularly in Mauritania, whose small army proved little match for the highly mobile and audacious guerrillas of the Polisario Front (q.v.). On September 2, 1976, the Giscard government signed a Franco-Mauritanian military agreement by which French officers were dispatched to Mauritania to work as instructors in the military academy at Atar. After the guerrillas' raid into the iron-mining center of Zouerate (q.v.) on May 1, 1977, in which two French citizens were killed and six others captured, and then, on October 25, 1977, the seizure of two more French citizens by guerrillas during an attack on the vital Zouerate-Nouadhibou railway (q.v.), Giscard had a pretext to order more direct intervention to shore up Mauritania's defenses. After a strategy meeting at the Elysée Palace on October 27, 1977, he instructed the Centre Opérationel des Armées, a special military planning unit, to draft plans to aid the Mauritanian armed forces. Then, on the night of November 1–2, about 200 elite troops flew out to the French air base at Cap Vert, outside Dakar (Senegal), to join the 1,100 French troops already stationed there under the 1974 Franco-Senegalese military agreement. The commander of the special force, Gen. Forget, moved on with about 75 military specialists to Mauritania, where they installed vital telecommunications equipment, supervised the arrival of French arms, and assisted the Mauritanian general staff plan operations against the guerrillas. Meanwhile, a squadron of French Jaguars, sophisticated "electronic warfare" jets, arrived in Dakar, along with Transall and Noratlas transports and Breguet-Atlantic reconnaissance planes. While the latter flew missions into northern Mauritania to spot guerrilla columns, the Jaguars were readied for action. Their first strike mission came on December 2, when Jaguars bombed and strafed guerrillas withdrawing after a raid on Boulanour, a small settlement on the Zouerate-Nouadhibou railway. On December 14–15, they attacked again, after another Polisario attack on the railway, near Choum. A third attack took place on December 18, after a guerrilla raid on Tmeimichatt, another point along the railway. The Polisario Front liberated its eight French prisoners five days later, but the Jaguars staged further air strikes against the guerrillas on May 4–5, 1978, near Oum Dreiga inside Western Sahara according to the guerrillas, in Mauritania according to the French authorities.

This direct French intervention was an example of Giscard's broader strategy of intervention in defense of beleaguered pro-French African regimes at this time. In 1977 and 1978, he helped to quell the rebellions in the Shaba province of Zaire (significantly with Moroccan assistance), and in 1978, Jaguars based at Cap Vert flew strike missions against anti-French forces in Chad. However, Giscard's military intervention against the Polisario Front in 1977–78 failed to stabilize Mauritania and proved damaging to France's important relations with Algeria. President Houari Boumedienne accused Giscard of harboring neocolonial designs and ordered economic retaliation against France by denying lucrative contracts to French firms. Thereafter, Giscard became increasingly anxious to restore friendly relations with Algeria. At the same time, he came to realize that, despite French military assistance, the Mauritanian armed forces could not hope to police their vast frontiers effectively and that a continuation of the conflict in Mauritania could lead to internal political upheavals as serious as those in Chad. After the military coup in Mauritania on July 10, 1978, he appreciated the desire of the country's new rulers to restore peace, though he urged them to seek a global settlement between all the parties to the conflict, hinging possibly on the creation of a Saharawi ministate in Tiris el-Gharbia (q.v.). However, when he saw that such a general compromise solution was not possible, he did not oppose the decision of the Comité Militaire de Salut National (q.v.) to make a unilateral peace agreement with the Polisario Front, at Algiers (q.v.) on August 5, 1979. Earlier in the year (February 15, 1979), he had for the first time publicly described the Saharan conflict as "a decolonization problem," and he had claimed that France was neutral and ready to mediate between the main parties. Nonetheless, he remained anxious to avoid Hassan's humiliation, and France continued, along with the United States, to be Morocco's principal arms supplier, delivering 50 Mirage F-1 jets in 1979–80, as well as Alpha jets, Franco-Austrian SK-105 tanks, and Panhard armored cars. Giscard continued his generally pro-Moroccan policies until he was defeated in France's general elections in the spring of 1981. He was succeeded by François Mitterrand (q.v.).

GOATS see LIVESTOCK

GOLONDRINA, OPERATION. Launched on November 3, 1975, less than a fortnight before the Madrid Agreement (q.v.), Operation Golondrina was a compulsory evacuation program for the bulk of the civilian Spanish population in Western Sahara. Prepared several weeks in advance, as the political uncertainty in the territory grew, it affected almost 20,000 Spanish civilians. Only skeleton staffs were left in essential public services, though the Spanish work force at the Bou-Craa phosphate mines (qq.v.) was allowed to stay so that mining could continue without interruption. Most of the evacuees were taken, along with their cars and belongings, to the Canary Islands. Government files and equipment were shipped out, and even the collection of Saharan animals at the El-Ayoun (q.v.) zoo was sent off to a Spanish zoo, in Almería.

GOMEZ DE SALAZAR, FEDERICO. After a long career in the Spanish armed forces, General Gómez de Salazar was appointed governor-general (q.v.) of Western Sahara on May 31, 1974, with a brief to prepare the territory for independence after a transitional period of internal self-government and the holding of a self-determination referendum. His aim was to set up a governing council, responsible to the Djemaa (q.v.), a hitherto purely consultative assembly, which was to be converted into a legislature. In November 1974, the Partido de la Unión Nacional Saharaui (q.v.) was established with his encouragement in the hope that it would prove an effective counterweight to the Polisario Front (q.v.) and lead Western Sahara to independence in close association with Spain. However, when, in the summer of 1975, the Polisario Front emerged as the clearly dominant political force in the territory and the PUNS started to disintegrate, he began to favor a political settlement with the Polisario Front and a rapprochement between the guerrilla movement and the more conservative Saharawis in the Djemaa and the PUNS. In October 1975, he met Polisario leaders on a number of occasions. There was a cease-fire between the guerrillas and the Spanish forces, while both sides released prisoners and a number of senior Polisario officials were allowed into El-Ayoun (q.v.). However, in October-November 1975, the Spanish government's commitment to self-determination first wavered and then collapsed under pressure from Morocco, notably as a result of the Green March (q.v.). Gómez de Salazar found himself obliged in the circumstances to place tight controls over the Saharawi population in the capital at the end of October 1975 by imposing a curfew, banning petrol sales to Saharawis, and placing military cordons and barriers around all their neighborhoods, while Spanish troops pulled back 14 km. from the Moroccan border to a "dissuasion line" to allow the Green Marchers to cross into Western Saharan territory on November 6. The governor-general still hoped, however, that the Madrid government would remain true to its pledge of self-determination. "Our withdrawal should be carried out after a referendum on self-determination and the creation of a Saharawi army in a position to defend the integrity of the territory," he said on November 13, 1975, just one day before the Madrid Agreement (q.v.), which placed him in the invidious position of having to work with Moroccan and Mauritanian deputy governors in a transitional tripartite administration (q.v.). He left Western Sahara at the end of December, leaving Rodríguez de Viguri (q.v.) in charge of the tripartite administration, and became captain general of the 1st military region (Madrid) in 1976. Giving evidence on Spain's withdrawal from Western Sahara before a special hearing held by the foreign relations committee of the Cortes on March 13, 1978, he revealed great bitterness about the 180-degree switch in Spanish policy in October–November 1975. He claimed that he had never even been consulted before the Madrid Agreement. "The desire for independence on the part of the Saharawi people was unanimous," he said.

"In the end the Polisario Front was representative of the Saharawi people. The Djemaa had lost prestige, and it was the Polisario that directed the politics of the Saharawi people." Moreover, "if there had been an attack by the Moroccans, we would have been in a position to destroy the Alawite army in 48 hours. The Moroccans had 20,000 men deployed near the Saharawi frontier. We had approximately the same number in the Sahara, but our potential was superior to that of Morocco."

GONZALEZ MARQUEZ, FELIPE. Born in 1942 and a longtime Spanish lawyer and socialist politician, he became prime minister of Spain in October 1982 as the head of the Partido Socialista Obrero Español (PSOE). While in opposition, he had expressed sharp criticism of the Moroccan takeover of Western Sahara. He had also denounced the Madrid Agreement of November 14, 1975 (q.v.), and expressed sympathy for the Polisario Front, most notably when he visited the front's refugee camps located in the Tindouf (qq.v.) region of Algeria in November 1976. Upon his accession to power in 1982, however, he showed much greater sensitivity to Spain's strategic interests, primary among them the defense of Spain's position in the *presidios* of Ceuta and Melilla on Morocco's Mediterranean coast and the protection of Spanish fishing interests off the Moroccan and Western Saharan coasts. Therefore, after gaining power, he made his first foreign trip to Morocco as a gesture of Spain's continuing friendship. In the years that followed, the PSOE government sold naval patrol craft and other arms to Rabat and failed to rescind the Madrid Agreement. In 1983, the Spanish and Moroccan governments signed a fishing agreement that covered the waters off Western Sahara as well as Morocco. Spain even conducted occasional military exercises with the Moroccan armed forces, much to the displeasure of Polisario and its main backer, Algeria. Madrid's relations with the Saharawi nationalists remained poor during the 1980s. There were frequent guerrilla attacks on Spanish fishing boats along Western Sahara's Atlantic coast, and after one of these incidents on September 20–21, 1985, Spain expelled all Polisario representatives from the country. However, the

Saharan diplomats were later allowed to return, and the PSOE did reiterate diplomatic support for Saharawi self-determination at the United Nations (q.v.). Relations also improved over time with Algeria, a major supplier of natural gas for Spain. In addition, the Polisario Front could count on the continued sympathy of a substantial part of Spanish public opinion, which manifested itself in protests during a state visit to Madrid by King Hassan II (q.v.) in September 1989. But there was no real change in the PSOE's policies, which, like those of its predecessors, were based mostly on the strategic importance of friendly relations with Morocco.

GOVERNOR; GOVERNOR-GENERAL. The title of the senior Spanish official in Western Sahara, and with it often also the chain of command, changed frequently during the Spanish colonial period. By a royal decree of July 10, 1885, the Spanish enclaves on the coast were placed under the administration of a *comisario regio* (royal commissioner), who was directly responsible to the ministry of overseas affairs in Madrid. By another royal decree of April 6, 1887, the title was changed to *subgobernador políticomilitar* (politico-military subgovernor). He was now responsible to the captain general of the Canaries. The title was upgraded to *gobernador políticomilitar* (politico-military governor) by a royal ordinance of November 7, 1901. In 1923, the title became simply *gobernador,* and in 1925, it was made *gobernador general.* However, on August 29, 1934, a decree unified the administration of Ifni and Western Sahara under the Spanish *alto comisario* (q.v.) (high commissioner) in Tetuan, who took the title of *gobernador general de Ifni y Sahara.* Under him were two *delegados gubernativos* (q.v.) in Ifni and Western Sahara. After the creation of Africa Occidental Española (AOE) (q.v.) by a decree of July 20, 1946, Western Sahara was administered by a *subgobernador* responsible to the *gobernador general* of AOE, who was resident in Sidi Ifni. When eventually Western Sahara became a Spanish "province" by a decree of January 10, 1958, its administration was placed in the hands of a governor-general responsible directly to the presidency of the government in Madrid. He had very wide-ranging powers. Besides controlling all aspects of the provincial administration, he appointed the president of the Cabildo Provincial (q.v.), the mayors of the two cities of El-Ayoun and Dakhla (qq.v.), and the presidents of the smaller *juntas locales* (q.v.). He also had the right to veto the choice of chiefs of the *fracciones nómadas* (q.v.). In command of all the Spanish military forces in the territory, he was responsible in military matters to the captain general of the Canaries. After the Madrid Agreement (q.v.) of November 14, 1975, two deputy governors, one Moroccan, the other Mauritanian, were appointed by the Moroccan and Mauritanian governments to work with the Spanish governor-general in a tripartite administration. This arrangement continued until the final Spanish withdrawal on February 26, 1976. Then, after the Moroccan-Mauritanian Agreement of April 14, 1976 (q.v.), which formally partitioned the country, three governors were appointed by King Hassan II (q.v.) to administer the three new Moroccan provinces of El-Ayoun, Smara, and Boujdour (qq.v.). A Mauritanian governor was appointed to administer the new Mauritanian region of Tiris el-Gharbia (q.v.). When the latter was occupied by Morocco in August 1979, it too became a Moroccan province under a Moroccan governor. For its part, the Polisario Front (q.v.) divided the Saharan Arab Democratic Republic (q.v.) into three *wilayat* (q.v.) in 1976. Each is, in theory, under the authority of a *wali* (q.v.), or governor.

GRARA. An Arabic term for a basin or depression that, by collecting water, forms a cultivable piece of land. The small amount of agriculture (q.v.) that was traditionally practiced by Saharawis usually involved the growing of barley in such depressions.

GREATER MOROCCO. The notion of "Greater Morocco," of which the Moroccan claim to Western Sahara was originally a component, along with claims to such territories as Mauritania and much of the Algerian Sahara, was the brainchild of Allal el-Fassi (q.v.), the historic leader of the Istiqlal Party (q.v.). Almost immediately after Morocco's independence in March 1956, he began to urge the reconstitution of what he claimed had been Morocco's precolonial empire. Besides

Tangiers and Ifni (incorporated into Morocco in 1956 and 1969, respectively), he claimed for Morocco such disparate and far-flung regions as Bechar, Tindouf, and the Gourara-Touat-Tidikelt oases in Algeria, the whole of Mauritania, the northwestern tip of Mali, including Timbuctoo (on account of its brief capture by a Moroccan army in 1591), and even Saint Louis du Sénégal, as well as Spanish-ruled Western Sahara. A map of Greater Morocco, illustrating these claims, was drawn by his cousin Abdelkebir el-Fassi (q.v.) and published in the Istiqlal Party's daily newspaper, *Al-Alam,* on July 7, 1956; and, at a congress the following August, the Greater Morocco line was formally endorsed by the party.

Though directed at the time against the colonial powers still ruling these supposedly Moroccan territories, the Greater Morocco propaganda of Allal el-Fassi and the Istiqlal Party represented a shift from the internationalist and pan-Arabist stance of the early Moroccan nationalist movement, which, from the late 1940s, had preached Maghrebian unity and mutual assistance against colonialism rather than the aggrandizement of Morocco at the expense of its Maghrebian neighbors. And it was a desire to spread the anticolonial struggle to the rest of the Maghreb, rather than the Greater Morocco notion, which inspired the radical Moroccan nationalists of the Army of Liberation (q.v.) who led the guerrilla campaign against Spain and France in Western Sahara and northern Mauritania in 1957–58.

Moreover, while King Mohammed V (q.v.) deeply distrusted the irregulars of the Army of Liberation, whom he saw as a potential threat to the security of his own regime, and later (1958–59) disbanded and disarmed its remaining units, he was happy, after initial amazement at the extravagance of Allal el-Fassi's claims, to endorse the Greater Morocco rhetoric and turn it to his own advantage. He could not allow the largest party in Morocco to outstrip his nationalist credentials, and he was aware that Allal el-Fassi's ideology, with its glorification of the military exploits and victories of past Moroccan sultans, could be used to boost the prestige of the monarchy. The territorial demands were given some credibility, moreover, by the actions of the Army of Liberation and by the defection to Morocco of such leading Mauritanian oppositionists as Horma Ould Babana, a one-time Mauritanian deputy in the French National Assembly who arrived in Morocco in 1956, and the Emir of Trarza, who made the *bayaa* (q.v.) to Mohammed V after fleeing to Morocco with three other opponents of Mokhtar Ould Daddah (q.v.), including two Mauritanian ministers, in April 1958. Later, after the victorious conclusion of Algeria's war of independence in 1962, the territorial demands directed against Algeria were astutely employed by King Hassan II (q.v.) to lessen the political impact in Morocco of the Algerian Revolution and weaken the radical government of Ahmed Ben Bella.

It was in the autumn of 1956 that the Moroccan government first formally endorsed Allal el-Fassi's territorial demands. On October 15, a Moroccan delegate claimed Mauritania, Western Sahara, and Ifni at the United Nations, and on November 12, 1957, a royal decree named Abdelkebir el-Fassi head of a new Direction des Affaires Sahariennes et Frontalières (q.v.) in the Moroccan ministry of the interior. A few days later, the Rabat government started broadcasting *La Voix du Sahara Marocain* to Western Sahara and Mauritania. Mohammed V himself first publicly embraced the claim to Western Sahara and Mauritania in a famous speech at M'hamed, a small oasis in the south of Morocco, on February 25, 1958. In signing the Agreement of Cintra (q.v.) of April 1, 1958, by which Spain handed over to Morocco the Tekna Zone (q.v.), the northernmost strip of its Saharan territory, the Moroccan government was adamant that this did not imply Moroccan recognition of parallel 27°40', the border between the Tekna Zone and Saguia el-Hamra (q.v.), as its southern frontier. During the same month, Mohammed V established a consultative commission, including the main leaders of the Istiqlal Party, to examine the frontier question.

The claim to parts of Mali was dropped after the creation of the Casablanca Group, a forerunner of the OAU (q.v.) of which both Mali and Morocco were members, in 1961. The claim to Saint Louis du Sénégal was also quietly forgotten. However, the claim to Mauritania was upheld throughout the 1960s. On November 4, 1960, a few days before the French colony's independence, the Moroccan government published a "white book" setting out its claim to the country, and for the following year, it did its best to prevent Mauritania's gaining admission to the UN (q.v.). Moreover, when Morocco formally adhered to the OAU charter in September 1963, the Moroccan foreign ministry informed Emperor Haile Selassie that this did not mean that Morocco "intended to renounce its legitimate rights in regard to the achievement and preservation of the territorial integrity of the Kingdom within its rightful frontiers." The point was made because the OAU insisted on the maintenance of the borders inherited from the colonial era. A month later, in October 1963, Morocco was to be at war for four weeks along its frontier with Algeria in an unsuccessful bid to force the Ben Bella regime to negotiate a revision of the de facto borders inherited from France. A cease-fire was arranged by the OAU.

The Greater Morocco notion was supported throughout the sixties by the Parti Communiste Marocain (q.v.), which, though banned in 1959, was able to continue publishing a legal journal. However, the Union Nationale des Forces Populaires (q.v.) opposed this chauvinist ideology from the time of its founding, following a split from the Istiqlal Party in 1959. At its 2nd congress, in Casablanca on May 25, 1962, the UNFP decided: "Favorable to the principle of independence of the peoples and to their free choice of collective destinies, the UNFP will not make the blunder of creating an exception for Mauritania. It will publicly contest the annexationist propaganda of Allal el-Fassi." The main Moroccan trade union federation, the Union Marocaine du Travail (q.v.), took the same view. Moreover, the UNFP's principal leader, Mchdi Ben Barka, openly condemned the October 1963 war with Algeria. Then in exile, he issued an appeal on October 16, 1963, decrying the conflict as "downright treachery not only regarding the dynamic Algerian revolution but, in a general sense, against the whole Arab revolution for freedom, socialism, and unity and against the entire world movement for liberation."

Though Hassan II met Ben Bella in May 1965, a real thaw in Morocco's relations with Mauritania and Algeria did not begin until 1969. In the Moroccan town of Ifrane on January

15, 1969, Hassan II and President Houari Boumedienne (q.v.) signed a treaty by which they resolved to submit their bilateral disputes for resolution by joint commissions. A frontier commission was duly set up when the two heads of state met again on May 27, 1970, in the Algerian city of Tlemcen. Two years later, on June 15, 1972, during an OAU summit meeting in Rabat, Hassan II and Boumedienne signed two conventions, one formally recognizing the existing de facto Moroccan-Algerian frontier, the other establishing a joint company for the transportation of iron ore from the huge deposits at Gara Djebilet in southwestern Algeria through southern Morocco to the Atlantic and its sale on the world market. Détente with Mauritania began in September 1969, when Ould Daddah was allowed to take part in an Islamic summit conference in Rabat. On June 8, 1970, Ould Daddah and Hassan II signed a treaty of friendship and cooperation in Casablanca by which Morocco finally granted formal diplomatic recognition to Mauritania.

The dropping of these claims to Mauritania and parts of Algeria, which left only the claim to Western Sahara (besides the little Spanish enclaves of Ceuta and Melilla on Morocco's Mediterranean coast), was bitterly resented by the Istiqlal Party—and the successor to the PCM, the Parti de Libération et du Socialisme. In settling its territorial disputes with Algeria and Mauritania, the Moroccan government did not get Algerian or Mauritanian endorsement of the Moroccan claim to Western Sahara, and in 1970–73, most notably at the tripartite summits of Nouadhibou on September 14, 1970, and Agadir on July 23–24, 1973 (qq.v.), Morocco joined its Maghrebian partners in pledging support for self-determination in Western Sahara in line with UN resolutions. Rabat undoubtedly believed that, in Western Sahara, self-determination would lead to integration with Morocco, but when, in 1974, this suddenly appeared not to be likely, the Moroccan government abandoned its commitment to self-determination and once again asserted its right to direct annexation. Still suspicious of Algeria, the Moroccan government failed, moreover, to ratify the 1972 Moroccan-Algerian border convention (which was ratified by Algeria on May 17, 1973), a factor that almost certainly contributed to Algeria's decision in 1975 to resist the Moroccan takeover of Western Sahara by backing the Polisario Front (q.v.). The 1972 border convention was not ratified by Morocco until May 14, 1989, a dividend of the improving relationship between Morocco and Algeria, which had resulted in the restoration of diplomatic relations between the two countries the previous year.

GREEN MARCH. A march by 350,000 Moroccan civilians into Western Sahara in November 1975, the Green March (al-Massira al-Khadra) brought to a climax the Moroccan government's campaign to force Spain to hand over Western Sahara to Morocco and Mauritania and led rapidly to the Madrid Agreement (q.v.) of November 14, 1975.

Plans for the march, which was named after the holy color of Islam, were first announced by King Hassan II (q.v.) on October 16, 1975, a few hours after the International Court of Justice (q.v.) had published its advisory opinion on the territory, affirming the primacy of the principle of self-determination. Brushing aside the court's conclusions, the king, who had been planning the march in secret for several months, said that he would personally lead 350,000 Moroccans into the territory, of whom 306,500 would be volunteers from the general public and 43,500 government officials. Ten percent were to be women, and quotas were assigned to each province almost in the manner of the tribal levies raised by the sultans in precolonial days for a *mahalla* (campaign). The king announced that ten special trains a day would be laid on to take the marchers to Marrakesh, from where they would be ferried to the border of Western Sahara by 7,813 trucks. The marchers were to be accompanied by 470 doctors and nurses, 220 ambulances, 23,000 tons of water, 17,000 tons of food, and 2,590 tons of motor fuel.

Recruiting offices were opened throughout the country, and by October 20, as many as 524,000 volunteers were said to have registered. Indeed, the march caught the imagination of the Moroccan people. It was portrayed as a holy march, a *jihad,* and its participants, who were told that they would be armed only with the *Koran,* were led to consider themselves as *mujahhidin,* or holy warriors, in a campaign to reclaim

Islamic territory from the European infidel. On October 23, Hassan even compared the march to the prophet Mohammed's return to Mecca. The announcement of the march was greeted with wild enthusiasm by the strongly irridentist Moroccan political parties, in particular the Istiqlal Party, the USFP, and the PPS (qq.v.), which hailed it as a popular mobilization to recover Moroccan territory that had been amputated from the rest of the nation by colonialism. Ironically, however, the king did his utmost to prevent the parties from capitalizing on the march, notably by keeping a tight governmental and military grip on its organization and ensuring that most of the marchers were drawn from the rural areas, where support for the monarchy was strongest and the implantation of the parties weakest. As a royal initiative, moreover, the march was effectively used by radio, TV, and pro-government newspapers to boost the prestige of the monarchy, which had been considerably eroded by domestic upheavals in the early seventies.

"Go then under divine protection, helped by your unshakable faith, your true patriotism, and your total devotion to the guide of your victorious march, King Hassan II," the prime minister, Ahmed Osman, told the first convoy of marchers, 20,00-strong, when they left Ksar es-Souk, a poor rural province in eastern Morocco, for the border on October 21. As the marchers gradually assembled in a vast tent city near Tarfaya (q.v.), about 40 km. north of the border, it became evident, to the Spanish government as much as to other observers of this remarkable mobilization, that King Hassan would not be able to call off the march or fail in his pledge to send the marchers across the border without endangering his throne. "I cannot turn the 350,000 Moroccans who have responded to my call with enthusiasm into 350,000 frustrated Moroccans," he said at the end of the month.

The Saharawis reacted with open hostility to the march. The Polisario Front (q.v.) denounced it as an "invasion," and the remnants of the Partido de la Unión Nacional Saharaui (q.v.) asked the Spanish government for arms and threatened to stage a countermarch to the Moroccan border, though this never materialized. The Spanish government reacted initially by requesting on October 18 an urgent meeting of the UN (q.v.) Security Council "so that the Moroccan government may be dissuaded from carrying out the announced invasion." The Security Council met on October 20 and 22 but failed to condemn the march and merely requested the UN secretary-general, Kurt Waldheim (q.v.), to consult the Spanish, Moroccan, Mauritanian, and Algerian governments, which he did during a visit to all four countries on October 25–28.

Waldheim suggested that the tension could be lessened by establishing a temporary UN administration in Western Sahara, and, though the Spanish government reacted favorably to the idea, it was already beginning to recognize that a trilateral settlement with Morocco and Mauritania was the only way to avoid a direct confrontation with Morocco. Hassan's timing could not have been better. General Franco, then 82, fell seriously ill on October 17, just one day after the announcement of the march, and, as hopes for his eventual recovery slowly dwindled, the Spanish government became preoccupied with the domestic challenge of securing a stable transition to a new post-Francoist era. A conflict with Morocco was the last thing needed at such a delicate time. So, on October 21, a Spanish minister, José Solís Ruíz (q.v.), visited Hassan in Marrakesh to try to defuse the crisis. He urged the postponement of the march (then set to cross the border on October 26) to allow time for negotiations, on both the future of Western Sahara and a way to allow both governments to save face with respect to the march itself. Solís returned to Madrid happy to report, "I believe that we have left the doors open for further conversations in an ambience of extraordinary friendliness," and talks soon began in Madrid, on October 24, at first involving Spanish officials and Ahmed Laraki (q.v.), the Moroccan foreign minister, (October 24–25), and then broadening to include the Mauritanian foreign minister, Hamdi Ould Mouknass (q.v.). One result of these talks was that a formula was arranged to allow the Green March to proceed as a kind of scenario. To avoid disappointing the marchers, Hassan was allowed to send them across the border, while, to prevent an affront to the Spanish army, whose loyalty had to be carefully nurtured at this crucial turning point in internal

Spanish politics, the Spanish negotiators insisted that the marchers should not be allowed to make more than a symbolic penetration. They were not to march all the way to El-Ayoun (q.v.) but to halt before a "dissuasion line," about 14 km. south of the border, to which Spanish troops were withdrawn. If they tried to proceed beyond the line, Spanish officials claimed, the marchers would enter an area sown with mines.

Despite the understanding, the Spanish government put on a facade of condemnation of the march, in particular at the UN, where, at Spanish request, the Security Council was once again urgently convened on November 2 and vaguely urged "all the parties concerned and interested to avoid any unilateral or other action which might further escalate the tension in the area." Significantly, the Spanish government did nothing about the fact that regular Moroccan troops had already crossed the frontier, in the remote northeast, on October 31, clashing with Polisario guerrillas near Farsia, Haousa, and Jdiriya. Their aim was probably to divert the guerrillas' attention from the march itself, which, on November 5, Hassan finally ordered to cross the border the following day. "When you have crossed the border," he told the marchers in a radio broadcast, "you must perform your duties; turn toward Mecca to render thanks to the Almighty." But he said he would not personally lead the marchers across the border. After a meeting during the night of November 5–6, the president of the Security Council cabled an "urgent request" to Hassan to "put an end forthwith to the declared march." However, early the next morning, Osman led the first contingent of marchers across the border to the abandoned Spanish border post at Tah. Thousands swarmed in Osman's wake, under a sea of red Moroccan flags, waving portraits of King Hassan and copies of the Koran. They continued down the road from Tah toward Daora (q.v.), eventually camping in the Sebkha Oum Deboaa, 9 km. south of the border and 5 km. north of the dissuasion line. Fifty thousand entered the territory on the first day. That evening, the Security Council "deplored" the march and called on Morocco to withdraw the marchers immediately. But the same day, the Moroccan government presented Spain with an ultimatum, warning that it would order the marchers to remain in the territory and move on across the dissuasion line, sparking war if the Spanish troops there tried to stop them, unless it agreed to start formal negotiations on the hand-over of the territory. On November 7, when the number of marchers in the Sebkha Oum Deboaa rose to 120,000 and a second wave of marchers crossed the frontier 80 km. to the east, from Abatteh, the Spanish cabinet met to consider the Moroccan ultimatum and decided to send another minister, Antonio Carro Martínez, to meet Hassan, then in Agadir. After their talks on November 8, Hassan made another nationwide broadcast, announcing, "Our march has borne more fruit than expected," and ordering the marchers to withdraw back across the border. "We will establish relations with Spain on a new basis," he said. The next day, the marchers started withdrawing to Moroccan territory, it was announced that talks would soon open in Madrid, and Morocco warned that the marchers would remain in Tarfaya so that, if the talks failed, "the 350,000 Moroccans will once again cross the border." Trilateral talks opened in Madrid on November 12 and culminated in the signing of the Madrid Agreement on November 14, six days before Franco's death. The last Green Marchers had left Western Saharan territory on November 13.

GROS ESPIELL, HECTOR. A Uruguayan judge and diplomat who also sat on the Inter-American Court of Human Rights, he was appointed as the first special representative of the United Nations (q.v.) for Western Sahara by the organization's secretary-general, Javier Pérez de Cuéllar (q.v.), effective October 19, 1988, that is, about a month after Morocco and the Polisario Front (q.v.) accepted in principle a comprehensive settlement proposal put forward by the UN. As special representative, he would exercise substantial powers in the territory once a transition process to a referendum commenced. However, due to a lack of progress in resolving outstanding issues between Morocco and Polisario, Gros Espiell met separately with the parties to the conflict (as well as with Mauritania and Algeria) in the final weeks of 1988. On January 10, 1989, he traveled to the region for further talks, meeting with both King Hassan II and the SADR's president, Mohammed Abdelaziz (qq.v.). The visit did not produce any substantive breakthrough, but Gros Espiell continued his mediation efforts until his resignation in late 1989. He was succeeded as UN special representative by Johannes Manz (q.v.) of Switzerland on January 19, 1990.

GUELTA. Arabic term for a rocky hollow that collects rainwater. An important source of drinking water for the nomads, the *guelta* is a sort of natural cistern. The most famous of its kind in Western Sahara is Guelta Zemmour (q.v.), which often holds water throughout the year.

GUELTA ZEMMOUR. An important *guelta* (q.v.) c. 225 km. southeast of El-Ayoun (q.v.) and 35 km. west of the Mauritanian border. It is a natural reservoir formed by a steep rocky gully, which, after good rainfall, often retains water for as long as one year. As one of the territory's most important water sources, it used to attract the nomads, especially during the dry summer, as well as passing caravans. Later, the Spanish established a military post and administrative center there. After their withdrawal from Guelta Zemmour in 1975, it became an important base for the Polisario Front (q.v.) for several months. The Djemaa issued its proclamation of Guelta Zemmour (q.v.) there on November 28, 1975, and thousands of refugees from the cities took refuge there over the following weeks. However, they were eventually forced to leave for Algeria after attacks from Moroccan forces, which succeeded in capturing Guelta Zemmour in April 1976. The Moroccan base there was heavily attacked by Polisario guerrillas on March 24–27, 1981, and again on October 13–16, 1981. This last attack was the most intense and costly of the entire war. Using a force of about 3,000 men, the Polisario Front overran the heavily fortified Moroccan garrison and claimed, over the next few days, to have wiped out most of the Moroccan army's 4th Régiment d'Infanterie Motorisée, to have taken 200 prisoners, and to have captured large amounts of matériel. For its part, Morocco admitted to losing 100 soldiers. Most ominously for the FAR (q.v.), its air force was temporarily neutralized in the course of the battle: shot down were at least two Mirage F-1 aircraft and two C-130 Hercules transport planes, one of which was apparently serving as a sophisticated airborne command and control post. Nearby, a Puma helicopter and a Northrup F-5E fighter plane were also downed. Although Morocco reoccupied Guelta Zemmour after the battle, its exposed position brought home to King Hassan II (q.v.) the costs of maintaining a garrison there, and it was abandoned on November 9. The area stayed under Polisario control until mid–1985, when the settlement was enclosed by an extension of the FAR's "defensive walls" (q.v.), then being constructed in the territory. But due to its proximity to Western Sahara's border with Mauritania, it remained quite vulnerable. On October 7, 1989, it was attacked again in force by the Saharawi guerrillas, killing at least 50 Moroccan troops.

GUELTA ZEMMOUR, PROCLAMATION OF (NOVEMBER 28, 1975). A declaration signed by 67 of the 102 members of the Djemaa (q.v.) a fortnight after the Madrid Agreement (q.v.), it dissolved the Djemaa, declared support for the Polisario Front (q.v.), and established a pro-Polisario Provisional Saharawi National Council (q.v.). Among those signing it were three members of the Spanish Cortes—Ahmed Ould Brahim Ould el-Bachir, Baba Ould Hassena, and Souilem Ould Abdellahi (qq.v.). The proclamation embarrassed the Spanish, Moroccan, and Mauritanian governments, which had pledged in the Madrid Agreement to respect the "views of the Saharan population expressed through the Djemaa." They had expected this assembly of generally elderly and conservative *chioukh* (q.v.) to endorse their plans for Western Sahara's integration with Morocco and Mauritania, but as the conference of Ain Ben Tili (q.v.) six weeks earlier (October 12) had shown, many traditionalist notables were by then sinking their differences with the youthful radicals of the Polisario Front out of fear of Morocco. The following is the full text of the proclamation:

In the name of Allah the Merciful, may blessings be upon his prophet. El-Guelta, November 28, 1975.

We the undersigned of this historic document, meeting under the chairmanship of His Excellency Baba Ould Hassena Ould Omar Ould Cheikh, vice president of the Saharan General Assembly which was set up by the Spanish colonialist authorities, hereby declare:

We were willing in the past to take part in this colonialist institution (the Djemaa), for Spain had promised to make of this body an authority working for the Saharawi people and to strengthen its independence in the shortest possible time. However, Spain many times refused to recognize the prerogatives originally granted to the Assembly, which has no real authority and is an Assembly in name only.

Recently Spain has started to hatch avowed plots against the independence of our homeland by publicly selling off our country to Morocco and Mauritania, thus achieving the most far-reaching colonialist pact that history has ever known. In doing this, Spain put forward a justification of its treason of the Saharawi people by claiming to have consulted them through the General Assembly.

We the members of the General Assembly, meeting on November 28, 1975, in El-Guelta, unanimously reassert that:

1. The only way to consult the Saharawi people is to enable them to decide on their own future and obtain their independence with no pressures being exerted upon them and no foreign intervention. The General Assembly, which was not democratically elected by the Saharawi people, cannot therefore decide on the self-determination of the Saharawi people.

2. So that there can be no utilization by Spanish colonialism of this puppet institution (the Djemaa) and following the maneuvers attempted by the enemies of the Saharawi people, the General Assembly, by the unanimous decision of its members present, is hereby definitively dissolved.

3. The sole legitimate authority of the Saharawi people is the Polisario Front, recognized by UNO, according to the conclusions of the United Nations fact-finding mission (q.v.).

4. Within the framework of a solution for national unity and outside any foreign intervention, a Provisional Saharawi National Council is hereby set up.

5. We the signatories of the El-Guelta document reassert our unconditional support for the Polisario Front, the sole legitimate representative of the Saharawi people.

6. We reassert our determination to pursue the struggle for the defense of our homeland until total independence is obtained and our territorial integrity safeguarded.

GUERA see LA GUERA

- H -

HADDAD, SLIMANE. The first Moroccan governor of the province of Smara (q.v.), he was appointed by King Hassan II on April 12, 1976. He remained governor until January 1979.

HAKIM ADEL see IBRAHIM HAKIM

HALIL MOHAMMED SALEM. A leader of the Partido de la Unión Nacional Saharaui (q.v.), a short-lived party set up in November 1974, which favored independence in close association with Spain. Along with the party's first secretary-general, Khalihenna Ould Rachid (q.v.), he fled to Morocco on May 14, 1975, after the Polisario Front (q.v.) had shattered the party's credibility by organizing large demonstrations to greet a United Nations Visiting Mission (q.v.), which toured the country on May 12–19. He was later appointed Moroccan ambassador to Cuba.

HAMDI OULD MOUKNASS. Born in 1935 at Port Etienne (Nouadhibou), Hamdi Ould Mouknass was Mauritania's foreign minister under President Mokhtar Ould Daddah (q.v.) from 1968 until the military coup of July 10, 1978. In the first few years of his term of office, he promoted his government's traditional claim to the whole of Western Sahara. In the summer of 1974, when the tension between Spain and Morocco over the territory first began to mount, he continued to lobby support internationally for Mauritania's claim, causing considerable embarrassment to Morocco. However, during a visit to New York in September–October 1974 to address the UN (q.v.) General Assembly, he reacted favorably to the idea of a Moroccan-Mauritanian partition of the territory when this was proposed to him there by a

Moroccan delegation headed by Ahmed Laraki (q.v.), the Moroccan foreign minister. A deal along these lines was later worked out in October by King Hassan II (q.v.) and President Ould Daddah. Thereafter, Hamdi Ould Mouknass supported the joint Moroccan-Mauritanian bid at the UN to have the Western Saharan problem submitted to the International Court of Justice (q.v.). He coordinated policy closely with Morocco and took part in the negotiations in Madrid on October 28–30 and November 12–14, 1975, that culminated in the signing of the Madrid Agreement (q.v.) on November 14. Over the following three years, he was the principal defender in such international forums as the UN and the OAU (q.v.) of Mauritania's role in the Western Saharan war. He was attending an OAU foreign ministers' meeting in Khartoum when the Ould Daddah government was overthrown in July 1978. He flew home to Nouakchott on July 13, 1978, but was immediately arrested.

HAMMADA. Arabic term designating a flat rocky plain. The term usually refers, in a Western Saharan context, to the *hammada* of Tindouf (q.v.), a large plateau, excellent for vehicles, which extends from the Oued Draa (q.v.), to the sources of the Saguia el-Hamra and the Zemmour massif (qq.v.).

HAMOUD OULD ABDEL WEDOUB. The first Mauritanian governor of Tiris el-Gharbia (q.v.), the sector of Western Sahara annexed by Mauritania, he was appointed by President Mokhtar Ould Daddah (q.v.) on January 15, 1976, three months before the formal partition treaty with Morocco on April 14, 1976.

HARAKAT TAHRIR SAGUIA EL-HAMRA WA OUED ED-DAHAB. The Movement for the Liberation of Saguia el-Hamra and Oued ed-Dahab (MLS) was founded clandestinely in El-Ayoun (q.v.) in December 1967, under the inspiration of Mohamed Sidi Ibrahim Bassiri (q.v.), a young Saharawi who had been influenced by radical Arab nationalist ideas while a student in Cairo and Damascus. It became the first serious anticolonial challenge to the Spanish authorities since the crushing of the Army of Liberation (q.v.) in 1958, though, unlike the latter, it engaged in peaceful forms of protest rather than guerrilla warfare. Also known as al-Hizb al-Mouslim (the Muslim Party), the MLS wanted the Spanish authorities to prepare the country gradually for independence, according to two of the group's leaders who were interviewed by the Algerian daily, *La République* (January 21, 1971). They stated that the movement's program included three main points: internal autonomy, an "agreement between the organization and the Spanish government fixing a time limit for the proclamation of the independence of the Sahara and the evacuation of the Spanish troops," and "no exploitation of the natural riches [of the country] without the organization's consent." They made no mention of the Moroccan or Mauritanian claims to the territory, stating simply that "our first objective is to drive out colonialism; afterward we will reflect on all the other questions." Finally, they said that they favored the holding of a referendum on the country's future, but only on condition that the MLS was recognized by the administration and that "there is no military garrison between the population and the ballot boxes."

Though Bassiri and a handful of supporters had been seeking recruits to the organization since the end of 1967, it was not until the spring of 1970 that its influence began to be widely felt in the Saharawi population. It was then, too, that its existence came to the attention of the Spanish authorities. An intelligence report prepared early in June 1970 by the *delegado gubernativo* (q.v.) of the northern region of the territory, López Huertas, noted that "the members of the party were very numerous, being found among them a considerable number of soldiers of the Tropas Nómadas (q.v.), policemen, interpreters, drivers, administrative auxiliaries, and teachers of the *Koran*, that is to say, practically all the personnel in the confidence of the *jefes de puesto*." It was, in other words, among those Saharawis who had received some education and found employment in the urban settlements that the MLS was finding recruits. It was perhaps because of this social composition and the radical influence of Bassiri that the movement advocated a series of modernizing social reforms as well as internal autonomy and eventual independence. According to Huertas, it wanted to break the authority of the *chioukh* (q.v.), the traditional tribal leaders, and the whole system of tribal loyalties, as well as to reform the Djemaa (q.v.), the powerless assembly of conservative *chioukh* set up by the Spanish authorities in 1967. It was, in fact, the territory's first modern, urban-based political party, though it was too weak to withstand the severe repression to which it was exposed in June 1970, when it emerged from clandestinity to present a petition to the Spanish authorities and hold a demonstration in Zemla, a suburb of El-Ayoun.

According to Huertas, the MLS's recruits swore an oath of loyalty and paid dues to the movement but it was evidently loosely structured and neither held a congress nor published propaganda material, relying entirely on word-of-mouth contact to summon support. In the spring of 1970 it decided to seek aid from the governments of the neighboring Arab states, but the Spanish repression, unleashed in June, cut short these plans. All that the organization was able to do before the axe fell was to draft a document requesting support from the Algerian authorities, which was handed over to Algerian officials in Tindouf (q.v.) on May 8, 1970. The leadership had been arrested and the organization crushed before having time to submit similar planned documents to the Moroccan and Mauritanian authorities.

Within the movement there were differences over tactics: A radical tendency believed that only armed action would force the Spanish to concede independence, but the more cautious majority advocated peaceful protest and the petitioning of the colonial authorities, an approach the radicals thought, correctly in retrospect, would lay the movement open to repression. Matters came to a head when the colonial administration announced plans to hold an official demonstration, in support of the colonial status quo, in El-Ayoun on June 17, 1970, and the MLS decided to use the occasion to hold a counterdemonstration and present to the government a petition listing its demands. The radicals, among them Bassiri, went along with the decision to emerge from clandestinity, having failed to convince the majority that the whole movement might thereby open itself to repression.

The MLS's petition was handed over to the Spanish authorities in Smara (q.v.), on June 16, a day before the rival demonstrations in El-Ayoun. It was moderate in tone, calling for internal autonomy rather than independence. The next day, while the pro-government demonstration assembled in the Plaza de Africa in the center of El-Ayoun, a much larger crowd assembled in the poor Saharawi neighborhood of Zemla, on the city's outskirts, and demanded that the governor-general, General José María Pérez de Lema y Tejero (q.v.), come personally to receive a copy of the MLS petition and respond to its demands. Eventually, General Pérez de Lema arrived and took the document. However, later, in the evening, Spanish Foreign Legion troops arrived in Zemla, with instructions from the governor-general to disperse the demonstrators. When the demonstrators started stoning the Spanish troops, the order was given by their commander, Capt. Arcocha, to open fire. Officially, 2 Saharawis were said to have been killed and 20 wounded. Reports from Arab sources, reaching Morocco and Mauritania over the following few days, spoke of more than 10 dying. The real death toll may never be known, but the "massacre of Zemla," (q.v.) was a turning point in the evolution of the Saharawi anticolonial movement. The MLS was destroyed by the ensuing arrests of its militants, and its strategy of peaceful protest was discredited. The young nationalists who launched the next anti-Spanish movement, the Polisario Front (q.v.), three years later, took up arms from the start, launching their first guerrilla attack only ten days after the front's formation in May 1973.

But there was to be a long period of demoralization and disorganization before this new movement was created. Several hundred Saharawis were detained for a few days after the demonstration. A few were jailed for several months, among them ten militants who were held in the Alcandi prison in Dakhla (q.v.) until January 5, 1971, and six soldiers who were detained in the Canary Islands until January–May 1971. Bassiri himself was detained a few hours after the events in Zemla, at 3 a.m. on June 18.

According to the Spanish government, he was then deported to Morocco on June 29. However, there has been no trace of him, in Morocco or anywhere else, since his detention.

HARATIN see SLAVERY

HARTANI see SLAVERY

HASSAN I, MOULAY. Alawite (q.v.) ruler of Morocco from 1873 to 1894, he tried to halt trade between the Tekna (q.v.) and Europeans on the Atlantic coast as part of a broader attempt to stem the growing European pressure on his kingdom, prevent the diversion of trade from his own ports (notably Mogador), and strengthen the Moroccan state by bringing dissident regions under control. He was alarmed by Spain's declared intention to reestablish Santa Cruz de Mar Pequeña (q.v.) as a result of the April 1860 Treaty of Tetuan and his own agreement to fix the site of this Spanish coastal enclave (the later territory of Ifni) between the Oued Souss and Oued Noun. Another potential risk was created by the British trading post of Donald Mackenzie at Tarfaya (q.v.). The problem facing the sultan was that the whole region south of the Oued Souss had effectively been independent of the sultanate's control since the mid-18th century. Two principalities, at Tazeroualt and Goulimine (where the Beyrouk family ruled), actively fostered trade with the Europeans. So, in May–July 1882, the sultan personally led an expedition, which reached as far south as Tiznit, bringing the main tribes of the Oued Noun and the Beyrouk family under the control of the *makhzen,* the sultan's government. A governor was based at Tiznit and *caids* (q.v.) appointed among such tribes as the Ait Moussa Ou Ali (the tribe of the Beyrouk family), the Ait Oussa (q.v.) and the Tadjakant. In March–April 1886, Moulay Hassan led a second expedition to the Oued Noun, this time reaching Goulimine, where a military garrison was installed. In 1887, he named Ma el-Ainin (q.v.) his *khalifa,* or deputy, in the Sahara when the *cheikh* (q.v.) visited him in Marrakesh, and in 1888, his forces at Goulimine raided Mackenzie's post at Tarfaya, killing the manager there. However, Moulay Hassan did not succeed in bringing the main Western Saharan tribes under his control. Although the sedentary Tekna accepted the nomination of caids, the principal nomadic Tekna remained independent, with the exception of the Ait Oussa, who, nonetheless, were not thereby hindered from joining the Reguibat (q.v.) in sacking Tindouf (q.v.), the center of the Tadjakant, in 1895. The Izarguien, the Yagout, and the Ait Lahsen (q.v.), three of the main nomadic groups of Tekna, refused to stop trading with Mackenzie and in 1888, defeated a Moroccan force sent out from Goulimine to chastise them. Other Saharawi tribes, such as the Reguibat, remained completely beyond the control of Moulay Hassan, though the sultan claimed to be the ruler of all the Muslims of the western belt of the Sahara.

HASSAN II. Born in 1929 and Morocco's king since 1961, King Hassan first came to grips with the Western Saharan problem when, as crown prince and chief of staff of the Forces Armées Royales (q.v.), he took possession of the Tekna Zone (q.v.) after the Agreement of Cintra (q.v.) and disbanded the remnants of the Army of Liberation (q.v.). His purpose was to end the presence of armed irregulars in Morocco's far south, which he and Mohammed V (q.v.) saw as a potential security risk to the new and still weak royal government. Distrustful Saharawi guerrillas barred his troops at the Oued Chebeika in mid-April 1958 as they tried to make their way to Tarfaya (q.v.), the remaining Spanish base in the Tekna Zone, and, later, Hassan had to intercede personally with the Saharawis. His task was facilitated, however, by the demoralization that had set in among the Saharawi guerrillas as a result of Operation Ouragan (q.v.) and divisions within the guerrilla ranks; by 1960, the last guerrillas had been disarmed, many of them in fact joining the FAR to escape destitution.

After becoming king in 1961, Hassan formally upheld the Moroccan claims to Western Sahara, Ifni, Mauritania, much of the Algerian Sahara, and the rest of "Greater Morocco" (q.v.). When, belatedly, he signed the OAU (q.v.) charter in September 1963, he expressed reservations regarding the OAU principle of the sanctity of the borders inherited from colonialism. In October 1963, moreover, he ordered Moroccan troops to cross the Algerian border, astutely using the Greater Morocco cause to minimize the influence of the Algerian Revolution on the Moroccan people and weaken the radical regime of Ahmed Ben Bella, who had come to power at the time of Algeria's independence in 1962. The war was brought to an end in November 1963 under the auspices of the OAU, and Moroccan troops then withdrew from Algerian territory, but Hassan maintained his claim to large parts of the Algerian Sahara, including Tindouf (q.v.), until the end of the decade. He also upheld the claim to Mauritania, creating a ministry of Mauritanian and Saharan affairs in 1966. In the same year, his government responded to the growing interest in Western Sahara at the United Nations (q.v.) by helping to set up (in Morocco) the Frente de Liberación del Sahara (q.v.), which lobbied support for Morocco's claim to the territory, mainly at the UN.

However, Hassan buried his territorial disputes with Mauritania and Algeria in 1969–72, and, having disbanded the Army of Liberation's remaining guerrilla groups in 1958–59, he did little during his reign to cause serious alarm to the Spanish government over Western Sahara until 1974. It was at a summit meeting with president Houari Boumedienne (q.v.) at Ifrane, Morocco, on January 15, 1969, that Hassan agreed to resolve his border dispute with Algeria amicably, and on June 15, 1972, in front of OAU heads of state attending a summit in Rabat, he and Boumedienne signed a convention formally recognizing the de facto Moroccan-Algerian frontier. Meanwhile, relations with Mauritania, which had been nonexistent since its independence in 1960, were established when Hassan invited President Mokhtar Ould Daddah (q.v.) to an Islamic summit held in Rabat in September 1969. On June 8, 1970, he and Ould Daddah signed a treaty of friendship and cooperation, formally establishing normal state-to-state relations.

From 1962, Hassan had pragmatically worked to ensure friendly and cooperative relations with the Spanish government. He had no desire to harbor anti-Spanish guerrillas and had a high regard for General Franco (q.v.), whose anticommunism and authoritarian style of rule he found easy to embrace. Franco, moreover, offered economic aid and cooperation and even returned two prominent political refugees to Morocco in 1970. The friendship between Hassan and Franco was dubbed the "spirit of Barajas," after their historic summit at Barajas (q.v.), an airport near Madrid, on July 6, 1963, and was epitomized by Hassan's joining Franco at a hunting party in Andalucía in February 1965. Secret negotiations continued during the late sixties, culminating in the return of Ifni to Morocco in 1969, but no real pressure was placed on Spain to hand over Western Sahara. The king's pragmatic relationship with the Spanish regime and his concessions to Algeria and Mauritania in 1969–72 were bitterly resented by the nationalist opposition, most notably the Istiqlal Party (q.v.).

Ironically (in view of his later stand), Hassan also began to endorse the United Nations stand on Western Sahara, which hinged on the Saharawis' right to attain self-determination and independence by means of a referendum, from the mid-sixties. His delegates at the UN voted for all the UN General Assembly resolutions on Western Sahara from 1965 onward, with the single exception of that adopted in 1972, when Morocco abstained. On July 30, 1970, he even told a press conference that, in negotiations with Spain, "instead of going purely and simply to claim the territory of the Sahara, I went to demand precisely that a popular consultation take place there, assured as I was that the first result would be the departure of the non-Africans and that then one would leave to the people of the Sahara the possibility of choosing whether to live under the Moroccan aegis or their own aegis or any other aegis." At the two tripartite summits of Nouadhibou and Agadir (q.v.), held on September 9, 1970, and July 3–24, 1973, respectively, he joined the presidents of Mauritania and Algeria in backing UN calls for self-determination. He was criticized by the ultranationalists of the Istiqlal Party for taking these stands, but he clearly thought that it was better to swim with the UN tide rather than against it and that, since there was no strong indigenous nationalist movement in Western Sahara, its population would probably decide to join Morocco if a UN-supervised referendum were held. In any case, Hassan's stance on Western Sahara remained, until 1974, a purely verbal one.

In the summer of 1974, Hassan's policy suddenly changed. He renounced his former support for UN decolonization principles, overtly opposed the holding of a referendum that included the option of independence, and insisted that Western Sahara should be integrated with Morocco whether the Saharawis approved or not. The turnabout in policy came when he learned in July that the Spanish government planned to grant internal autonomy to the territory as a first step toward independence. On July 4, 1974, he wrote a letter of protest to Franco about the internal autonomy plan, and, four days later in a public speech, he recalled the he had in the past offered Franco economic concessions and the right to maintain military bases in the Sahara in return for the hand-over of the territory. But his alarm grew when, on August 21, the Spanish government announced that it would hold a referendum during the first six months of 1975. Hassan knew that, if held, it would lead to a vote for independence.

He also knew that if he allowed Western Sahara to slip from Morocco's grasp, he would come under intense political fire from the main Moroccan opposition parties. The Istiqlal Party and the communists, in particular, had been incensed by his abandoning of the claims to Mauritania and parts of Algeria and his endorsement of the UN calls for self-determination in Western Sahara. He had been at loggerheads with the main opposition parties on domestic policies too, while the armed forces had attempted two coups in 1971 and 1972, a group of leftists had tried to launch a guerrilla campaign in the Atlas mountains in 1973, and both students and workers were becoming increasingly militant. By launching a vigorous campaign to take over Western Sahara, Hassan was able to cement an alliance with the urban opposition parties, provide a useful focus for the distrusted army, and rally unprecedented popular support behind his regime. He ended up riding a wave of nationalism. The campaign was presented to Moroccans as a holy *jihad* and the culmination of a long struggle against colonialism to reunite a divided country. So much popular enthusiasm was aroused, in fact, that Hassan would have been virtually unable to retreat, and failure on his part might have cost him his throne.

On August 20, 1974, he threatened to go to war if diplomatic means failed, and he explicitly rejected the "question of the Saharawi people's independence" being included as an option in Spain's planned referendum. The latter, he insisted, had to be limited to a straight choice between remaining under Spanish rule or joining Morocco. The previous July, the opposition party leaders, Abderrahim Bouabid, M'hamed Boucetta, and Ali Yata (qq.v.), had all been dispatched abroad as special envoys to plead Morocco's case, and Col. Ahmed Dlimi (q.v.) was sent south to command a force of 20,000 troops massed on the Western Saharan border. On September 17, the king lambasted the "secessionists" led by El-Ouali Mustapha Sayed (q.v.), i.e., the Polisario Front (q.v.), and stated that "I have already asked the Spaniards either to police their own territory, since it is still theirs, or else to give me the freedom to prevent the secessionsts." He was not ready, however, for a total showdown with Spain, because he needed time to come to terms with Mauritania, which had reacted to the launching of his campaign with a countercampaign of its own. So, also on September 17, he proposed that the Western Saharan problem be submitted to the International Court of Justice (ICJ) (q.v.). During a summit of the Arab League in Rabat in mid-October, he finally came to an understanding, based on the promise of eventual partition, with Ould Daddah. In December, the UN General Assembly agreed to request the ICJ for an advisory opinion on Western Sahara's precolonial ties with Morocco and Mauritania. During the ensuing months, while the ICJ was examining these historic questions, Hassan kept up the pressure on Spain. A pro-Moroccan "liberation movement," the Front de Libération et de l'Unité (q.v.), was set up and started carrying out urban bomb attacks in Western Sahara, while Spanish fishing boats were harassed off the Moroccan coast and the claims to Cueta and Melilla, the Spanish enclaves on Morocco's Mediterranean coast, were revived. Whatever the outcome of the ICJ's deliberations, Hassan let it be known he was prepared to go to war to annex Western Sahara by the end of 1975. "It will be in October or November at the latest that we will know whether we are going to enter our Sahara by peaceful means or arms," he said on August 20, 1975.

On October 16, the day that the ICJ published its advisory opinion, Hassan broadcast to the Moroccan people in order to announce that 350,000 Moroccans would be mobilized to stage a Green March (q.v.) across the Western Saharan border. Through this remarkable display of national determination, he gambled, Spain would be forced to capitulate. It did, partly because the crisis engendered by the Green March coincided with Franco's long final illness, the accession to the Spanish throne of Juan Carlos, and the Spanish government's preoccupation with the problems of transition to the post-Francoist domestic political order. On October 21, a Spanish minister, José Solís Ruíz (q.v.), arrived in Marrakesh to inform Hassan of the possibility of a deal and arrange a face-saving formula by which the Green Marchers would be allowed to enter Western Sahara as far as a "dissuasion line" 14 km. south of the border. The king ordered the marchers across the border on November 6 but then threatened to keep them there and order them on beyond the dissuasion line. Another Spanish cabinet minister, Antonio Carro Martínez, flew out to Morocco to meet Hassan on November 8, and a day later, Hassan declared that Morocco had gained its objectives and ordered the marchers to return home. He sent his prime minister, Ahmed Osman (q.v.), to Madrid, and, on November 14, the Madrid Agreement (q.v.) was signed. The king, proclaimed a hero in Morocco, claimed on November 25 that "the dossier is closed."

But that was to be far from true. Hassan had made two fatal miscalculations. He had underestimated the degree of Saharawi determination to resist the Moroccan takeover, and he had not expected Algeria to give full-scale military and diplomatic support to the Polisario guerrillas. His army was rapidly bogged down in an unwinnable war, while the guerrillas spread the conflict by striking into southern Morocco and much of Mauritania. His ally, Ould Daddah, with whom he signed a partition agreement on April 14, 1976, had to turn to Morocco for military aid, and in 1977–78, 9,000 Moroccan troops arrived in Mauritania. As the war developed, Hassan occasionally threatened to stage hot pursuit or reprisal raids across the Algerian border, but being enough of a pragmatist to appreciate the dangers of sparking off an open war between Morocco and Algeria, he never implemented the threat. Meanwhile, Hassan and his government became increasingly isolated internationally, in particular at the UN and the OAU, while the Moroccan economy suffered from the high cost of the conflict and the enthusiasm of the days of the Green March gave way to frustration at the inability to bring the conflict to an end. The biggest blow was the overthrow of Ould Daddah on July 10, 1978, and the ensuing Polisario-Mauritanian cease-fire. On August 20, 1978, Hassan warned the new Mauritanian military regime not to allow the creation of a Saharawi ministate in Tiris el-Gharbia (q.v.), but he could not prevent Mauritania from signing a peace agreement with the guerrillas a year later, on August 5, 1979, in Algiers (q.v.). He described the agreement as a "document signed at a picnic," which "had no validity" and, on August 14, 1979, he unilaterally announced Morocco's annexation of Tiris el-Gharbia. As the possibility of the SADR's admission to the OAU increased, in 1980–81, he threatened to quit the OAU. Boxed into a policy that had originally aroused almost unanimous domestic popular support and on which he had effectively staked the credibility of his regime, Hassan could not make major concessions to the Polisario Front without courting the risk of losing his throne. He often appealed to Algeria's leaders to settle the dispute bilaterally, but both Boumedienne and his successor, Chadli Benjedid (q.v.), insisted that they would not negotiate over the heads of the Saharawi nationalists. Hassan, though, would not negotiate directly with the Polisario guerrillas, and he repeatedly warned that Morocco would never renounce any part of Western Sahara. "Though we are favorable to any agreement susceptible of putting an end to the conflict," he said on March 3, 1981, "we cannot accept that such an agreement be made to the detriment of an integral part of our national territory." In what was at the time billed as a major reversal of policy, however, he finally announced at an OAU summit conference in Nairobi in June 1981 that he would accept the principle of an internationally supervised referendum. Almost immediately after this, though, the king made statements indicating that his concept of a referendum differed substantially from that of the African and international community. On July 2, 1981, he said he saw the referendum as providing "confirmation" of Moroccan sovereignty over Western Sahara and rejected a plebiscite in which the Saharawis would be offered the option of becoming independent. "Moroccan citizens of the Sahara will not go back on all the manifestations of loyalty they have shown," he added. On top of this, the king seemed reluctant to allow the Saharawi refugees in the Tindouf region to return to the territory to vote ("we have no need of troublemakers") and ruled out participation by the Polisario Front in the referendum if it pressed for independence ("Morocco will not tolerate foreign publicists campaigning for such a secession, because that would be to ask too much of us"). He also maintained his position that Polisario was nothing more than a surrogate for the Algerians and that as "mercenaries," they were unworthy of direct negotiations. The Moroccan monarch appeared to hope that the Saharan conflict could be settled by means of a bilateral deal with Algeria. Meanwhile, within Western Sahara, the king's armed forces built a series of "defensive walls" (q.v.) in 1980–87, which gradually evicted Polisario from about four fifths of the territory. But despite this success, the king had to station up to 120,000 troops in Western Sahara by the late 1980s to maintain this huge defensive system. The conflict turned into a seemingly endless war of attrition, as Polisario forces continued to attack the Moroccan "walls," often in great strength.

Much as King Hassan wanted to see his control of Western Sahara somehow legitimized by the international community, support for Polisario in the OAU continued to build, after his concession in Nairobi in 1981 began to be widely interpreted as a ploy to block the SADR's admission as a member of the organization. When the SADR was indeed admitted to the OAU in February 1982, the king embarked on a strategy of boycotting the OAU until it reversed its decision. By persuading a large minority of OAU member-states to follow suit, he brought the OAU to a virtual standstill. No OAU meetings could achieve a quorum until June 1983, when the SADR delegation "voluntarily and temporarily" absented itself from an OAU summit in Addis Ababa, enabling the meeting to proceed. This was a short-lived victory for the king, however. His pledge at Nairobi had gone unfulfilled, and most African leaders were fast losing patience with what they saw as the king's delaying tactics. As a result, more and more African states recognized the SADR. In November 1984, at an OAU summit held in Addis Ababa, the SADR took its seat as a member without substantial opposition. King Hassan made good on his earlier threat to quit the OAU, but he was joined only by Zaire, which withdrew from the organization only for a few months.

While facing increasing isolation in Africa and elsewhere in the Third World, the king did manage to retain the support of key Western powers, such as France and the U.S., which continued to furnish considerable military and economic assistance to Rabat. He also retained important allies in the Arab world, notably Saudi Arabia, which provided large-scale financial aid. More surprisingly, King Hassan succeeded in neutralizing one of the Polisario Front's main sources of support, Libya. On August 14, 1984, he signed the Treaty of Oujda with Libya's controversial leader, Muammar El-Qadaffi, who was anxious at the time to break out of his own isolation. The treaty, which was supposed to "unify" the two countries, was viewed by the king as a counterweight to an Algerian-Tunisian-Mauritanian "treaty of concord" signed the previous year, which he believed was directed against Morocco. The accord obliged Qadaffi to end all material and most political support for Polisario. As with most such Arab unionist ventures, the Treaty of Oujda was rather short-lived: Hassan II canceled the accord in August 1986 after Libya denounced his meeting, on July 22, with the then Israeli prime minister, Shimon Peres.

Relations with Morocco's main regional rival, Algeria, also gradually improved, although President Chadli Benjedid (q.v.), who came to power in 1979, was steadfast in his refusal to settle the Saharan dispute over the heads of the Saharawis. Hassan and Benjedid met on the Moroccan-Algerian border on February 26, 1983, and again on May 4,

1987, and although bilateral relations improved somewhat, neither country altered its Western Sahara policy appreciably. On May 16, 1988, however, Rabat and Algiers restored diplomatic relations with one another after a 12-year hiatus. As part of this rapprochement, King Hassan finally agreed to ratify the agreement on their common border reached at Ifrane in June 1972. The agreement took effect on May 14, 1989, resolving any lingering irredenta by Morocco for certain areas of Algerian territory.

Having left the OAU in 1984, King Hassan turned increasingly to the United Nations in the hope of reaching a settlement of the Western Sahara conflict. He remained steadfast in his refusal to negotiate directly with Polisario (though he did permit occasional secret contacts) but ended up accepting indirect talks through the UN, whose secretary-general, Javier Pérez de Cuéllar (q.v.), began "proximity talks" with Polisario and Morocco in April 1986. However, he did receive a senior Polisario delegation in January 1989 at his palace in Marrakesh. The king made a number of concessions, accepting that the choice to be put to the Saharawis in a referendum should be between independence or remaining part of Morocco, and acknowledging that some of the Moroccan armed forces in Western Sahara should be withdrawn prior to the plebiscite. Although in August 1988, the king formally accepted the outlines of a comprehensive peace plan proposed by Pérez de Cuéllar, which, inter alia, contained the above components, the outcome of the plan, to be carried out by the United Nations Mission for the Referendum in Western Sahara (q.v.), remained greatly in doubt. King Hassan continued to come under heavy criticism by the Polisario Front and by some independent observers in 1991 and 1992, who alleged a lack of cooperation with the United Nations and carrying out other measures to attempt to influence the outcome of the referendum in Morocco's favor.

HASSANIYA. The Arabic dialect spoken in Western Sahara, Mauritania, southern Morocco, and southwestern Algeria. Close to classical Arabic, it was brought to this part of the Sahara by the Beni Hassan, Bedouin Arabs who began invading the region in the 13th century, and had been adopted by all the tribes of predominantly Sanhaja (q.v.) origin by at least the 19th century, though some words from the Berber dialect of the Sanhaja were absorbed into Hassaniya. An example is the term *"ait"* ("sons of"), which is frequently used in the naming of tribes and fractions. Many geographical terms and place-names are also Berber in origin.

HASSI. A well up to 12 meters deep. See WATER SOURCES.

HEALTH. Statistics from 1972 indicate that there were two general hospitals in El-Ayoun and Dakhla (qq.v.) at that time. There were also 15 dispensaries throughout the country. There were 29 doctors, 2 pharmacists, 25 assistant health technicians, 3 midwives, 57 assistant health workers, and 19 nurses. There was approximately 1 doctor for every 2,150 inhabitants and one hospital bed for every 238. The main diseases are tuberculosis, bronchitis, and intestinal and venereal diseases. After the exodus of refugees (q.v.) to Algeria in 1975–76, there was a measles epidemic in the refugee camps near Tindouf (q.v.), which caused many deaths among children who had been weakened by the hardships endured during their flight from Western Sahara. Health committees and dispensaries were established in all the camps and three small regional hospitals and one national hospital built by the Polisario Front (q.v.) there, greatly improving the health situation by 1989, although facilities were sometimes austere and medicines often in very short supply. Polisario's national hospital was in a position to provide dental, surgical, and prenatal care by the late 1980s, although the most serious of cases still had to be referred to Algerian hospitals.

HEYDALLAH, MOHAMMED KHOUNA OULD see MOHAMMED KHOUNA OULD HEYDALLAH

HORMA. The most humiliating and exploitative form of tribute (q.v.) in traditional Saharawi society, it was paid by low-caste tribes, the *znaga,* to powerful warrior tribes, supposedly in return for protection. The *horma* was paid individually, by each family head in the tribute-paying tribe to a designated family in the warrior tribe. The most notable example of such a tribute relationship was that between the Oulad Tidrarin and the Oulad Delim (qq.v.), which began in the second half of the 18th century. The Oulad Tidrarin, previously a *zawiya* tribe, were obliged, fraction by fraction, with the single exception of the Ahel Taleb Ali, to start paying the horma to fractions of the Oulad Delim, then at the height of their power. Within each Oulad Tidrarin fraction, each family paid the horma to a specific family of the respective fraction of the Oulad Delim. The exact nature of the horma was normally specified in the *orf*, the body of customary law of the tribes involved, but in all cases its payment implied submission and degradation. Still considering themselves to be zawiya, the Oulad Tidrarin were insulted to be labeled znaga. The Delimis had the right to transfer, even to sell, their capitation rights to other families in their fraction and were said to be ruthless in extracting the horma from their tributaries. The tributary, like the slave (q.v.), was barred from carrying arms, which in itself denoted weakness and humiliation in a society where the *ghazzi* (q.v.) was a permanent institution and where strength, through the bearing and use of arms, was seen as one of the highest virtues. Generally, the horma seems to have had its origins in a protection pact (in itself humiliating for the group forced to admit its weakness), which was then turned to advantage, abused, and exploited by the powerful protector group. Not surprisingly, znaga would, if given a chance, attempt to escape such exactions, as did the Oulad Tidrarin in a long war with the Oulad Delim in 1888–92. The horma was officially outlawed by the Spanish colonial administration and then died out gradually as tributaries refused to pay it.

HOUARI BOUMEDIENNE OFFENSIVE. On January 4, 1979, the Polisario Front announced the launching of an offensive against Morocco in honor of the late Algerian president, Houari Boumedienne (q.v.), who had died on December 27, 1978. Launched six months after the July 12, 1978, Polisario cease-fire in Mauritania, the offensive's targets were Moroccan positions in both Western Sahara and the desert regions of southern Morocco. The first attack of the offensive was a raid against two of the control towers of the phosphate conveyor belt from Bou-Craa (q.v.) to the coast. Then, on January 16–17, guerrillas mauled Moroccan convoys at Lemseied, near El-Ayoun (q.v.). For the first time in the war, Polisario guerrillas then succeeded in battling their way briefly into a Moroccan city when a large guerrilla force broke into Tan-Tan (q.v.) on January 28. Tan-Tan was attacked twice again, on June 13 and June 27, 1979. There was another major battle on August 11, when a large guerrilla force attacked Moroccan positions at Bir Enzaren (q.v.): Morocco admitted that 82 of its soldiers were killed in the attack, and the guerrillas later (August 30) showed journalists 175 Moroccan soldiers they had captured there. A more devastating attack came on August 24, when a Polisario force smashed its way into Lebouirate (q.v.), overrunning a Moroccan base there. Journalists taken there later by the guerrillas counted scores of captured Moroccan tanks and armored cars, and 36 of the Moroccan garrison there were later court-martialed. In further battles in the Oued Draa (q.v.) region on September 16–17, the guerrillas captured scores more Moroccan vehicles, including tanks. In another bold move, a large Polisario force attacked the city of Smara (q.v.) on October 6, killing its Moroccan commander, Col. Driss Harti, capturing scores of prisoners, and successfully breaking into a part of the city to evacuate 700 Saharawi residents, among them Mohammed Ali Ould el-Bachir (q.v.), the local deputy in the Moroccan Chamber of Representatives, who were taken back to the Tindouf refugee camps (qq.v). A few days latter, on October 14, an attack was launched against a Moroccan base at Mahbes (q.v.), 30 km. from the Algerian frontier. The Moroccan ministry of information later announced that 141 of the 767 Moroccan soldiers there were killed. The base, the last that Morocco held in the entire region between Smara and the Algerian frontier, was abandoned to the guerrillas. As a result of the offensive, the Moroccan armed forces were obliged to give up scores of small isolated bases, including Tafariti and Jdiriya in the northeast of Saguia el-Hamra (q.v.) and others in southern Morocco, in order to consolidate the defenses of the more important towns and bases nearer the coast.

- I -

IBRAHIM GHALÍ OULD MUSTAPHA. A Reguibi of the Oulad
   Taleb fraction from Smara (qq.v.), Ibrahim Ghali spent
   several years in the Spanish paramilitary Policía Territorial
   (q.v.), where he achieved the rank of corporal, before
   becoming the top military commander of the Polisario Front
   (q.v.). He had made contact in Mauritania with the nucleus of
   anticolonial militants who were to found the front in May
   1973. He was elected to the front's leadership at the founding
   congress on May 10, 1973, and assumed overall responsibility for the front's guerrilla campaign against Spain. As one of
   Polisario's top leaders, he was a member of the delegation
   that met with the UN Visiting Mission (q.v.) during its tour
   of the Saharawi camps in the Tindouf (q.v.) region of
   southwest Algeria in May 1975. He was also involved in the
   negotiations with Spanish officials in September–October
   1975 that led to the release of prisoners by both the front and
   the Spanish authorities. In October 1975, he was allowed by
   the Spanish colonial authorities to enter El-Ayoun because
   the governor-general, Gómez de Salazar (qq.v.), with whom
   he had a number of meetings, was anticipating at this time
   that Spain would soon be handing over the reins of government to the front. He played a central part in large Saharawi
   nationalist demonstrations held in El-Ayoun on October
   26–27 and almost certainly coordinated recruitment into the
   front's guerrilla army of the bulk of the Saharawi members
   of the Tropas Nómadas (q.v.) and the Policía Territorial, who
   were demobilized by the Spanish authorities from October
   26. However, when Spanish policy began to waver under
   Moroccan pressure at the end of October and a strict curfew
   was imposed on Saharawis in the capital on October 28,
   Ibrahim Ghali left El-Ayoun and turned his attention to
   resisting the first incursions by the Moroccan army, which
   began on October 31 in the region of Haousa, Farsia, and
   Jdiriya. His primary tasks over the ensuing few months were
   to enroll, train, and equip the thousands of Saharawi men
   volunteering to fight the Moroccans and to arrange for the
   evacuation of refugees (q.v.) to Algeria. It was not until
   about May 1976 that he was able to go on to the offensive.

Appointed minister of defense of the Saharan Arab Democratic Republic (SADR) (q.v.) on March 4, 1976, a few days after the SADR's proclamation, he was in overall command of the guerrilla forces, now known as the Saharawi Popular Liberation Army (SPLA) (q.v.). The SPLA concentrated its attacks on Mauritania, until the coup d'état in Nouakchott in July 1978. Thereafter, the guerrillas were able to give single-minded attention to their war against Morocco, taking the fighting far across the Western Saharan border into southern Morocco itself. By 1979–80, Ibrahim Ghali had a well-armed, motorized army of about 15,000 men under his command. He was also one of the members of the Polisario Front's top leadership body, the executive committee (q.v.), and hence automatically a member of the SADR's supreme Council for the Command of the Revolution (q.v.), having been elected to these bodies by both the 3rd and the 4th congresses of the front, held in August 1976 and September 1978, respectively. Remaining defense minister until 1989, he held his portfolio for considerably longer than any other member of the SADR's council of ministers (q.v.) since the founding of the Saharawi state. In that post, he reportedly took part in most of the SPLA's military engagements with the Moroccan army. He remained defense minister despite the fact that Polisario's military options were being limited by Morocco's construction of a series of ''defensive walls'' (q.v.), which hampered the SPLA's freedom of movement within the territory. On the diplomatic side, Ibrahim Ghali's role was less prominent, although he was one of the three members of a Polisario delegation that traveled to Marrakesh in January 1989 for a first-ever direct meeting with King Hassan II (q.v.). Reputedly, Ibrahim Ghali, as a career military officer, espoused a primarily military strategy by Polisario against Morocco. At the front's 7th congress, held between April 28 and May 1, 1989, he was replaced as minister of defense by Mohammed Lamine Ould Bouhali (q.v.), another long-serving military commander, and was placed in charge of the SPLA's 2nd military region in Río de Oro near Guelta Zemmour (qq.v.), subsequently the scene of major Polisario attacks in September and October 1989.

IBRAHIM HAKIM. A Reguibi (q.v.), also known as Ibrahim Ould Derwich and Hakim Adel, he was born in Chinguetti, Mauritania. He spent his childhood in Mauritania, attending primary and secondary schools there and later, in 1966, embarking on a career in the country's diplomatic service, which culminated in his appointment as chargé d'affaires at the Mauritanian embassy in Algiers in the early seventies. He also attended Algiers University, graduating in 1974, when he returned to Mauritania to become a senior official of the Banque Internationale de Mauritanie (BIMA). In mid-1975, however, he decided, probably on account of his Reguibat ancestry and ties, to throw in his lot with the Polisario Front (q.v.). He moved to Algeria, where he became a valuable new asset to the movement because of his past diplomatic experience. When the Saharan Arab Democratic Republic (q.v.) was founded in February 1976, he was appointed foreign minister in the new state's first council of ministers (q.v.), on March 4, 1976. In this capacity, he played a key role in achieving major diplomatic successes for the SADR and Polisario, most notably at the Organization of African Unity, the United Nations, and the Nonaligned Movement (qq.v.), all of which were to adopt pro-Polisario resolutions on Western Sahara, and in one case (the OAU) to accept the SADR into full membership. An indefatigable lobbyist and fluent in several languages, he could also take much of the credit for the large number of countries that accorded recognition to the Saharawi state. He was reconfirmed as foreign minister at Polisario's 5th congress, in 1982, but at the front's 6th congress (December 7–10, 1985), he was replaced as foreign minister by Mansour Ould Omar (q.v.) and became minister of information. In late 1988, he left this ministerial post to become the SADR's ambassador to Algeria, Polisario's strongest and most consistent backer. He held this position until August 11, 1992, when, in a surprising move, he defected from Polisario to Morocco. As the highest-ranking official of the front to do so next to Omar Hadrami (q.v.), Ibrahim Hakim stated that he defected to Morocco because he felt that Polisario's struggle had become hopeless and because he was dissatisfied with the Saharawi nationalist movement itself, causing him to abandon it.

IMAN, OPERATION. This was a disastrous campaign, code-named Iman (the Faith) and launched by the Moroccan army on February 27, 1980, to try to relieve the Moroccan garrison at Zaag, in southeastern Morocco, which had been under siege from the Polisario Front (q.v.) for several months. Some 7,000 troops were involved in the operation—about 2,000 from Zaag itself and the rest, assembled at Lemseied, 100 km. to the west, from the Ohoud force (q.v.), under Col. Harchi, and the Zellagha force (q.v.), under Col. Mohammed Abrouq (q.v.). The idea was that the Ohoud and Zellagha groups would move eastward and eventually meet the troops moving westward from Zaag, the Polisario being flushed out in the process, so allowing a large supply convoy to move through to Zaag. The troops from Lemseied covered 60 km. to Ammeti without incident, arriving there on February 29, but between March 1 and 6, Polisario guerrillas routed them as they tried to advance toward Zaag. The Moroccans retreated north into the Ouarkziz Mountains and toward Assa. From there, a second attempt was made to break through to Zaag. Descending from the Ouarkziz Mountains through the pass of N'Gueb into the plain of Tighzert, which leads on to Zaag, the Moroccan troops again came under heavy fire and, after three days of fighting, were finally forced, on March 11, to retreat back into the Ouarkziz. Foreign journalists, brought to the site of these battles a few days later by the guerrillas, were left in no doubt as to the scale of the Polisario victory. "The guerrillas had clearly been left in control on the ground over a large area of southeast Morocco," concluded a correspondent of the London *Observer* (March 23, 1980). However, in May, after assembling a large force of some 20,000 troops, the Moroccan army did finally succeed in breaking the siege of Zaag. A 30-km. corridor was secured between the N'Gueb pass and Zaag in the first week of the month, allowing a supply convoy to reach the town. Its civilian population was then evacuated to Assa and Goulimine.

IMERAGUEN. A fishing people, who lived traditionally along the southern coast of the territory, the Imeraguen are said to have been constituted by "exiles" from other, larger tribes, who turned to fishing on account of their lack of livestock.

INSTITUTO NACIONAL DE INDUSTRIA. A Spanish state-owned holding company, the National Institute of Industry had 100 percent control of the territory's phosphate industry until 1975. In 1962, it set up a subsidiary, the Empresa Nacional Minera del Sahara (ENMINSA) (q.v.), to prospect for and study the country's phosphate deposits. After the discovery of 1.7 billion tons of phosphate in the region of Bou-Craa (q.v.) in 1963 and a later failure on ENMINSA's part to establish a joint venture with foreign companies to exploit the deposits, INI decided to go it alone under the auspices of another subsidiary, Fosbucraa (Fosfatos de Bu-Craa) (q.v.), created in August 1969. The mines started production in 1972, and exports reached 2.6 million tons of dry phosphate in 1975. However, as a result of the Madrid Agreement (q.v.) of November 14, 1975, INI was obliged to give up its controlling share in the company. It retained a 35 percent share, and 65 percent was acquired by Morocco's Office Chérifien de Phosphates.

INTERNATIONAL COURT OF JUSTICE. On December 13, 1974, the United Nations (q.v.) General Assembly passed a resolution (No. 3292) requesting "the International Court of Justice, without prejudice to the application of the principles embodied in General Assembly resolution 1514 (XV)," to give an advisory opinion at an early date on the following questions:

I. Was Western Sahara (Río de Oro and Saguia el-Hamra) at the time of colonization by Spain a territory belonging to no one (*terra nullius*)?
If the answer to the first question is negative,
II. What were the legal ties between the territory and the Kingdom of Morocco and the Mauritanian entity?

The court, which sits in The Hague, responded positively to the request and, after 27 sessions in June–July 1975, at which Spain, Morocco, Mauritania, and Algeria—but not the Polisario Front (q.v.)—were represented, published an advisory opinion on October 16, 1975. The court first defined "the time of colonization" as "the period beginning in 1884, when Spain proclaimed a protectorate over the Río de Oro," and decided unanimously that Western Sahara was not then *terra nullius*, since "at the time of colonization, Western Sahara was inhabited by peoples who, if nomadic, were socially and politically organized in tribes and under chiefs competent to represent them" and that Spain itself did not believe at the time that it was occupying *terra nullius* since the Royal Order of December 26, 1884, establishing a Spanish protectorate in Río de Oro (q.v.) was based on agreements already made with such local chiefs.

Turning to the second question, the court first examined the legal ties between Western Sahara and the Kingdom of Morocco in precolonial times. The court accepted that Morocco was a special sort of state, based on the allegiance of tribes to the sultan, through their *caids* and *chioukh* (qq.v.), rather than on the notion of territory as such, but it concluded that such allegiance had to be shown to involve the acceptance of real political authority in order to establish that Morocco effectively exercised sovereignty in Western Sahara. The court noted that much of the historical evidence on which it was being called to make an opinion was "far-flung, spasmodic, and often transitory." The Moroccan evidence was of two kinds—examples of what was said to be the internal display of Moroccan authority and international treaties that were said to constitute recognition of Moroccan sovereignty by other states. Given as examples of the former were *dahirs* (q.v.) appointing caids and acts of allegiance to sultans. Morocco placed considerable emphasis on the expeditions to the Oued Noun region of southern Morocco by Moulay Hassan (q.v.) in 1882 and 1886, when some Tekna (q.v.) caids were nominated by the sultan, and also stressed the relationship between Cheikh Ma el-Ainin (q.v.) and the Moroccan sultanate in the 1890s and 1900s. Spain, which contested Morocco's claim to precolonial sovereignty over Western Sahara, countered that the 1882 and 1886 expeditions did not reach Western Sahara (Moulay Hassan not going beyond Goulimine), that the nomination of caids was purely formal (being only acts of confirmation of chiefs that had previously been chosen or accepted by their tribes), that there was no evidence that the nomadic Tekna tribes, which have traditionally migrated through Western Saharan territory, as opposed to the sedentary Tekna of southern Morocco, paid allegiance to the sultanate, and, finally, that Ma el-Ainin had not acted as a subject of the sultanate in any real way, being in effect an independent leader who made alliances, as opportune, with the sultans. Spain added that Morocco was unable to provide any proof of Moroccan taxation in Western Sahara. The court concluded:

> The material before the court appears to support the view that almost all the *dahirs* and other acts concerning *caids* relate to areas situated within present-day Morocco itself and do not in themselves provide evidence of effective display of Moroccan authority in Western Sahara. Nor can the information furnished by Morocco be said to provide convincing evidence of the imposition or levying of Moroccan taxes with respect to the territory. As to Cheikh Ma el-Ainin, the complexities of his career may leave doubts as to the precise nature of his relations with the sultan, and different interpretations have been put on them. The material before the court, taken as a whole, does not suffice to convince it that the activities of this *cheikh* should be considered as having constituted a display of the sultan's authority in Western Sahara at the time of its colonization.
>
> Furthermore, the information before the court appears to confirm that the expeditions of Sultan Hassan I to the south in 1882 and 1886 both had objects specifically directed to the Souss and the Noun and, in fact, did not go beyond the Noun so that they did not reach even the Draa (q.v.), still less Western Sahara. Again, although Morocco asserts that the Reguibat (q.v.) tribe always recognized the suzerainty of the Tekna confederation and through them that of the sultan himself, this assertion has not been supported by any convincing evidence. Moreover, both Spain and Mauritania insist that this tribe of marabout warriors was wholly independent.
>
> Consequently, the information before the court does not support Morocco's claim to have exercised territorial sovereignty over Western Sahara. On the other hand, it does not appear to exclude the possibility that the sultan displayed authority over some of the tribes in Western Sahara. That this

was so with regard to the Reguibat or other independent tribes could clearly not be sustained. The position is different, however, with regard to the septs of the Tekna, whose routes of migration are established as having included the territory of the Tekna caids within Morocco as well as parts of Western Sahara. The court considers that, taken as a whole, the information before it shows the display of some authority by the sultan, through Tekna caids, over the Tekna septs nomadizing in Western Sahara.

Thus, even taking account of the specific structure of the Cherifian state, the material so far examined does not establish any tie of territorial sovereignty between Western Sahara and that state. It does not show that Morocco displayed effective and exclusive state activity in Western Sahara. It does however provide indications that a legal tie of allegiance had existed at the relevant period between the sultan and some, but only some, of the nomadic peoples of the territory.

Moving on to the evidence provided by international treaties, the court considered the "shipwreck clauses" of a series of treaties between Morocco and Spain, the United States, and Great Britain in the 18th and 19th centuries, as well as the March 13, 1895, Anglo-Moroccan Agreement (q.v.) and a Franco-German exchange of letters in 1911. The shipwreck clauses obliged the sultans to use their authority in the Oued Noun (and, in some of the treaties, further south) to secure the rescue of shipwrecked sailors who fell into the hands of local tribes. "Morocco," the court felt, "is correct in saying that these provisions would have been pointless if the other state concerned had not considered the sultan to be in a position to exercise some authority or influence over the people holding the sailors captive. But it is quite a different thing to maintain that those provisions implied international recognition by the other state concerned of the sultan as territorial sovereign in Western Sahara." The 1895 Anglo-Moroccan Agreement explicitly stated that the region between the Oued Draa and Boujdour (q.v.) was part of Morocco. But the court concluded: "Numerous documents . . . show that the position repeatedly taken by Great Britain was that Cape Juby [q.v.] was outside Moroccan territory, which in its view did not extend beyond the Draa. In the light of this material, the provisions of the 1895 treaty invoked by

Morocco appear to the court to represent an agreement by Great Britain not to question in future any pretensions to the lands between the Draa and Cape Boujdour, and not a recognition by Great Britain of previously existing Moroccan sovereignty over those lands.'' Finally, the court examined an exchange of letters annexed to a Franco-German Agreement of November 4, 1911, which stated that ''Germany will not intervene in any special agreements that France and Spain may think fit to conclude with each other on the subject of Morocco, it being understood that Morocco comprises all that part of northern Africa that is situated between Algeria, French West Africa, and the Spanish colony of Río de Oro.'' Morocco argued that this definition recognized Saguia el-Hamra as being part of Morocco. Spain countered by pointing to article 6 of the earlier Franco-Spanish Convention of October 3, 1904 (q.v.), which placed Saguia el-Hamra ''outside the limits of Morocco.'' The court concluded that the purpose of these agreements, in their different contexts, was ''to recognize or reserve for one or both parties, a 'sphere of influence' as understood in the practice of that time.'' Thus, ''the court finds difficulty in accepting the Franco-German exchange of letters of 1911 as constituting recognition of the limits of Morocco rather than of the sphere of France's political interests vis-à-vis Germany.'' The court then concluded:

> The inferences to be drawn from the information before the court concerning internal acts of Moroccan sovereignty and from that concerning international acts are, therefore, in accord in not providing any indications of the existence, at the relevant period, of any legal tie of territorial sovereignty between Western Sahara and the Moroccan state. At the same time, they are in accord in providing indications of a legal tie of allegiance between the sultan and some, though only some, of the tribes of the territory, and in providing indications of some display of the sultan's authority or influence with respect to those tribes.

Turning to the precolonial ties between the ''Mauritanian entity'' and Western Sahara, the court noted that Mauritania had accepted that it did not constitute a state at this time. It also noted the definition of the Mauritanian entity as a vast region bordered by the rivers Saguia el-Hamra and Senegal, the Atlantic, and the meridian of Timbuctoo, which constituted a distinct social, linguistic, and cultural entity. In the court's opinion, the evidence it had examined disclosed that

> at the time of Spanish colonization, there existed many ties of a racial, linguistic, religious, cultural, and economic nature between various tribes and emirates whose peoples dwelt in the Saharan region, which today is comprised within the territory of Western Sahara and the Islamic Republic of Mauritania. It also discloses, however, the independence of the emirates and many of the tribes in relation to one another and, despite some forms of common activity, the absence among them of any common institutions or organs, even of a quite minimal character. . . .

The court therefore concluded that "there did not exist between the territory of Western Sahara and the Mauritanian entity any tie of sovereignty, or of allegiance of tribes, or of 'simple inclusion' in the same legal entity." The court did accept, however, that there were legal ties of a different order between tribes living in the Mauritanian-Western Saharan region, "ties which knew no frontier between the territories and were vital to the very maintenance of life in the region," such as agreements over migration routes, the use of wells, and the settlement of disputes.

Finally, while noting that the geographical "overlapping" of the evidence presented by Morocco and Mauritania presented further complications, the ICJ summed up its advisory opinion as follows:

> The materials and information presented to the court show the existence, at the time of Spanish colonization, of legal ties of allegiance between the sultan of Morocco and some of the tribes living in the territory of Western Sahara. They show equally the existence of rights, including some rights relating to the land, which constituted legal ties between the Mauritanian entity, as understood by the court, and the territory of Western Sahara. On the other hand, the court's conclusion is that the materials and information presented to it do not establish any tie of territorial sovereignty between the terri-

tory of Western Sahara and the kingdom of Morocco or the Mauritanian entity. Thus the court has not found legal ties of such a nature as might affect the application of resolution 1514 (XV) in the decolonization of Western Sahara and, in particular, of the principle of self-determination through the free and genuine expression of the will of the peoples of the territory.

Of the 16 judges, 14 concurred with the final conclusion on the nature of the legal ties between Morocco and Western Sahara, and 2 disagreed. They divided 15-1 in support of the final conclusion on the nature of the legal ties between Mauritania and Western Sahara. Twisting beyond recognition the ICJ's advisory opinion, the Moroccan government issued a communiqué on the same day as its publication, claiming that it "can only mean one thing—that the Western Sahara was part of the territory over which the sovereignty of Moroccan kings was exercised and that the people of the territory considered themselves and were considered Moroccans." This remarkable interpretation was used later that same day when King Hassan II (q.v.) announced plans for the Green March (q.v.). The pressure that this then imposed on Spain was such that the final recommendation of the court, the application of the principle of self-determination, was, quite simply, ignored.

IRIFI. A severe sandstorm, the *irifi* is one of the worst afflictions of the desert. It whips up sand and dust as it is blown across the desert by powerful winds from the east or southeast, becoming hotter and drier the farther it travels. It destroys plant life, causes sand drifts on roads, and impedes visibility for ground traffic and low-flying aircraft.

IRON ORE. There are considerable iron ore deposits in Western Sahara, but the mineral has not been exploited to date. In the Agracha region, in the southeast, estimates of iron ore reserves have been as high as 72 million tons, and it is possible that the iron ore there is an extension of the huge deposits being mined near Zouerate across the border in Mauritania. In the early 1960s, the Spanish authorities talked of building a 160-km. railway from Agracha to Dakhla (q.v.) and of mining 3 million tons a year, but in 1964, the Spanish

Instituto Nacional de Industria (q.v.) said that the world iron ore market was too depressed to permit exploitation of the deposits. The ore at Agracha has a 57.3 percent iron content. It also contains 13.6 percent titanium oxide, which is a major component of paint but difficult to separate. The rock also contains 0.6–0.8 percent vanadium, making Western Sahara one of the world's largest potential sources of this strategic metal, which is used in the aerospace industry to make light, heat-resistant metal alloys. In the northeast of the territory, iron ore has since 1947 been known to exist and there is a possibility that the whole Tindouf depression, which includes the massive iron ore deposits of Gara Djebilet in southwestern Algeria, may contain iron ore in commercial quantities. In 1965, an aeromagnetic survey in the center of the country revealed that there may be iron ore there too. Forty-six possible sites were located, some of which are four times as large as those found at Agracha.

ISLAM. Though an Arab army first reached the western Maghreb, under Uqba Ibn Nafi, in A.D. 669–70, it was probably not until the mid-8th century that Islam began to spread gradually into Western Sahara, possibly following an expedition into the desert by an Arab army, sent by one of Uqba's great-grandsons, Abderrahman Ibn Habib, which sunk a series of wells from the Bani oases to Aoudaghost in present-day Mauritania in c. 745. However, it was the Almoravid (q.v.) movement, founded by Abdallah Ibn Yacin in the 11th century, that, by waging a *jihad* against paganism and heresy, firmly rooted Islam, of an austere and orthodox Sunni Malekite brand, in this part of the desert.

In the 15th–16th centuries, mystical Sufi movements reached Western Sahara. Led by holy men, or marabouts (q.v.), who were believed to possess the quality of *baraka* (q.v.) and who were often associated with orders or brotherhoods, the *Zawiya*. Sufism was closely bound up with the popular reaction at this time to the arrival of slave-raiding Christians on the Atlantic coast. The main Sufi orders in Western Sahara were the Qadiriya and the Tijaniya. Certain of the marabouts of this period, e.g., Sidi Ahmed Reguibi and Sidi Ahmed el-Arosi, became "founders" of tribes that, though of primarily Sanhaja (q.v.) origin, were to claim to be descendants of the prophet Mohammed, or *chorfa,* thus buttressing their social position vis-à-vis the *arab* descended from the Beni Hassan (q.v.). Pre-Islamic beliefs, such as the fear of evil spirits (*djenoun*) and the "evil eye," remained and are still in evidence today, but Islam has provided an ardent faith well suited to face the rigors and adversity of nomadic desert life. In traditional Saharawi society, civil law was applied in conformity with the *sharia* (q.v.). Saharawis were strict in observing the daily prayer obligations, though few were wealthy enough to make the *hadj* (pilgrimage) to Mecca. Charity was widespread, particularly in the form of the *meniha,* the lending of livestock by the rich to the poor.

The Spanish colonial authorities were careful not to upset religious sensibilities. They tried to cultivate close relations with marabouts, organized an official annual pilgrimage to Mecca, all expenses paid, from the mid-1930s, and paid stipends to Koranic teachers. However, they never overcame the Saharawis' hostility to foreign Christian rule. The Moroccan government, by contrast, tried to give religious sanction to its entry into Western Sahara in 1975, by claiming that the Saharawis had traditionally recognized the Moroccan sultan (or king) as *amir almuminin* (commander of the faithful), ruler in both spiritual and secular matters, and had traditionally said the Friday prayer in his name. Little evidence has been adduced for these hotly contested claims, though some Saharawis did in certain special times—for example, during the anticolonial struggle led by Cheikh Ma el-Ainin (q.v.) early this century—give nominal recognition to the sultan's rule. What is certain is that attempts by Morocco to win popular support for its occupation of Western Sahara on religious grounds have not met with success since 1975, the majority of Saharawis aligning with the Polisario Front (q.v.). As an essentially secular movement, Polisario has not often used the religious idiom in pressing its policies, but it still finds occasional expression, as at the 6th congress of the front (December 7–10, 1985), when it addressed a letter to King Fahd of Saudi Arabia, a close ally of King Hassan II (q.v.), calling on him to show consideration for "the Muslim Saharawi people, who defend Islam and work ceaselessly for the propagation of its principles and teachings."

ISLAMIC CONFERENCE. The Islamic countries have been divided over the Western Sahara problem in recent years. Some of them have supported the right of the Saharawis to self-determination; other, more conservative, Islamic states have tended to back the Moroccan claim to the territory out of loyalty to King Hassan (q.v.). The 5th Islamic Conference, held in Kuala Lumpur, Malaysia, on June 21–25, 1974, called for the holding of a referendum in accordance with UN (q.v.) resolution 3162 of December 14, 1973, to "allow the indigenous populations to express themselves in full liberty, in conformity with the UN Charter." Since then, Islamic conferences have been either too preoccupied with other matters or too divided on the issue to take any position on the Western Saharan conflict.

ISTIQLAL PARTY. The party that led the Moroccan independence struggle from its founding in 1943 until the ending of the Franco-Spanish protectorate in 1956, the Istiqlal (Independence) Party first began to advance a Moroccan claim to Western Sahara after the return to Morocco in 1956 of its exiled leader, Allal el-Fassi (q.v.). The party newspaper, *Al-Alam,* published a map of "Greater Morocco," including Western Sahara, Mauritania, much of the Algerian Sahara, and even Saint Louis du Sénégal and parts of northwestern Mali, on July 7, 1956, and el-Fassi's call to re-create a supposedly historic Moroccan empire in these far-flung regions was endorsed by the party's congress the following August. This policy was adopted by the government of Mohammed V (q.v.), in which the Istiqlal Party was represented, in the autumn of 1956. As a result of the party's incessant irredentist propaganda and the ability of both Mohammed V and his successor, Hassan II (q.v.), to turn it to their advantage, the Moroccan government refused to recognize Mauritania when it became independent in 1960 and briefly went to war with Algeria in 1963. However, the Istiqlal Party was forced out of Hassan II's government in 1963, and the king gradually began to play down the party's favorite territorial causes. The party criticized the king's pragmatic modus vivendi with Spain, which began with his summit with Franco (q.v.) at Barajas (q.v.) in 1963, and protested strongly when Moroccan officials started declaring their support, from the mid-sixties, for UN (q.v.) resolutions advocating a self-determination referendum and independence in Western Sahara. After a Moroccan official had called for the independence of Spain's African colonies at a session of the UN decolonization committee in Addis Ababa in June 1966, the party protested in July: "We are absolutely opposed to any attitude, even explicable for tactical reasons, which could engender confusion and put in question the integrity of Moroccan territory to the slightest extent." The party was aghast when Hassan II decided in 1969 to settle the territorial disputes with Algeria and Mauritania, signing a treaty of friendship and cooperation with Mauritania in 1970 and a convention with Algeria in 1972 that gave de jure recognition to the de facto Moroccan-Algerian border, but the party was powerless to stop what it regarded as the abandonment of historic Moroccan territories. The party also resented the king's decision to grant important fishing concessions to Spain in 1969 in return for the cession of Ifni.

Not surprisingly, after so many setbacks, the party was ecstatic when Hassan II decided in 1974 to drop his support for self-determination in Western Sahara and launch an all-out campaign to annex it. This was just the kind of action for which the Istiqlal Party had been clamoring for years. M'hamed Boucetta (q.v.), who became the party's secretary-general after Allal el-Fassi's death the same year, became a diplomatic envoy for the king in the summer of 1974. The party enthusiastically backed the Green March (q.v.) and reentered the Moroccan government in 1977, Boucetta becoming foreign minister.

The party has always adamantly rejected any hint of compromise on the Saharan question and at times has been distrustful of King Hassan's tactics. For example, it was intensely skeptical of the king's conditional offer at the June 1981 summit of the Organization of African Unity (q.v.) in Nairobi, Kenya, to hold an internationally supervised referendum in the territory. The Istiqlal Party likewise viewed with unease the January 1989 meeting between the king and three high-ranking Polisario officials in Marrakesh, stating at the time that "nobody can think for one minute about any renunciation of national unity or the installation of a particular entity in the Sahara that is not integrated within national unity." Furthermore, the party reconciled itself only with difficulty to King Hassan's ratification of the Moroccan-Algerian border convention in May 1989: the Istiqlal continued to champion a claim to large tracts of western Algeria, including Tindouf (q.v.).

The party won 13.4 percent of the vote and 41 seats (out of 306) in parliamentary elections held in September 1984. Its longtime secretary-general, Boucetta, who was foreign minister from 1977 to 1983 and then minister of state, left the Moroccan government in 1985, when the party went into opposition. Boucetta was reelected secretary-general (for the fourth time) at the Istiqlal's 12th congress, in May 1989. As might be expected, the party also strongly reaffirmed its ultranationalist stance on Western Sahara.

IZARGUIEN. The largest Tekna (q.v.) tribe in Western Sahara, the Izarguien are also numerous in the extreme southwest of Morocco. Completely nomadic until recent times, unlike most other Tekna, they traditionally migrated in search of pastures along the coast between the Oued Draa (q.v.) and Boudjour (q.v.). Their three fractions are the Echtouka, the El-Guerah, and the Ait Said, each of which customarily received political leadership from three families, the Ahel Sidi Yusuf, the Ahel Yahya, and the Ahel Boudjemaa Ould Jilali, respectively. The fractions rarely coming together, except in times of war, when a tribal *ait arbain* (q.v.) would be formed, decisions were normally taken at the fraction or subfraction level by *djemaas* (q.v.), councils of notables. The tribe's fractions received tribute from a number of small coastal fishing tribes, notably the Mejat, the Fouikat, and the Lemiar (qq.v.). A people of *arab* warrior status, the Izarguien also gave protection to the small *cherifian* tribe of marabouts (qq.v.), the Taoubalt (q.v.).

At one time, during the reign of the powerful Moroccan sultan Moulay Ismail, the Izarguien were closely allied to the

Alawite (q.v.) sultanate. One of their chiefs, Hammou Said, accompanied Ali Chandora, the emir of Trarza (Mauritania) in 1703–27, to Moulay Ismail's court in Meknes to request, successfully, Moroccan troops to help put down a rebellion in Trarza. Hammou Said and a force of Izarguien took part in the ensuing expedition.

However, after Moulay Ismail's death (1727), anarchy reigned in Morocco, and for most of the following 150 years, the regions to the north of the Izarguien (the Oued Noun and the Souss) were in a state of *siba* (q.v.) and more or less independent of the *makhzen,* the government of the sultan-ate. Later, at the end of the 19th century, their divergent interests were to bring them into direct conflict. In 1882 and 1886, Sultan Moulay Hassan I (q.v.) personally led two military expeditions to the Souss and the Oued Noun, appointing *caids* (q.v.) and establishing garrisons in order to bring these regions once again under the control of the makhzen and, in particular, end the collaboration and trading between the local tribes and Europeans—among them Donald Mackenzie at Tarfaya (q.v.)—who, to the sultan, posed both a strategic danger and a commercial threat to his port at Mogador. But the Izarguien, like some other Saharawi coastal tribes, benefited from the trade with the Europeans. When, in 1888, Moroccan soldiers arrived in Tarfaya and attacked Mackenzie's trading station, they failed to force the Izarguien, the Ait Lahsen, and the Yagout to end their relations with Mackenzie. In an ensuing clash, the Izarguien and their allies defeated a Moroccan force near the mouth of the Saguia el-Hamra (q.v.). Again, in 1899, a force of Ait Moussa Ou Ali and Moroccan soldiers, sent by the Ait Moussa Ou Ali caid Dahman Ould Beyrouk to chastise the Izarguien for their dealings with the Christians, was routed by the Izarguien, under Baba Ahmed Ould Sidi Yusuf, at Daora (q.v.).

The Izarguien were one of the leading tribes of the Ait Jmel, one of the two rival blocs of Tekna tribes, the other being the Ait Atman. As a result of one of the wars between these two Tekna alliances, the Izarguien built a fortified sanctuary at Daora in 1878. Conflict between the two blocs, and especially between the Izarguien and the Ait Oussa, continued, punctuated by occasional periods of peace, until 1934, when colonial pacification finally put an end to the *ghazzis* (q.v.). In 1907, for example, the Izarguien, backed by the Ait Lahsen and the Ait Moussa Ou Ali, went to war with the Azouafid, a leading tribe of the Ait Atman, following an Azouafid ghazzi against an Izarguien encampment. The war spread northward to Ifni as both the Izarguien and the Azouafid widened their respective alliances to include tribes in Ifni, some of which were non-Hassaniya-speaking Berbers. There were endless clashes between the Izarguien and the Ait Oussa in the 1920s and early 1930s. In 1929, for example, an Izarguien ghazzi inflicted severe losses on the Ait Oussa. In revenge, a force of Ait Oussa and their allies set out from Assa in 1934 to attack the Izarguien and other Ait Jmel tribes near the coast. The engagement took place at Tarfaya, watched by surprised Spanish soldiers in the little base set up there by Francisco Bens (q.v.). The Izarguien and their allies were saved by the arrival of a Spanish plane from the Canaries, which prompted their enemies to flee.

Thereafter, under the "colonial peace," the Izarguien continued to herd their animals, but more and more they turned to trade. By the early 1970s most had settled in the small, growing towns of Western Sahara and southern Morocco. The 1974 Spanish census, which generally underestimated the population of Western Sahara, reported about 8,000 Izarguien as living in the territory, most of them in the capital, El-Ayoun (q.v.).

- J -

JAICH AT-TAHRIR see ARMY OF LIBERATION

JATRI ULD SAID ULD YUMANI see KHATRI OULD SAID OULD JOUMANI

JEMAA see DJEMAA

JUAN CARLOS. Born in Rome in 1938, Juan Carlos de Borbón became king of Spain on November 22, 1975, two days after

238 / Juan Carlos

the death of Francisco Franco (q.v.) and eight days after the signing of the Madrid Agreement (q.v.). Having been named Spain's future king by Franco in 1969, he had briefly been acting head of state during Franco's serious illness in the summer of 1974, a period of mounting tension with Morocco over Western Sahara caused by Morocco's virulent reaction to the Spanish government's announcement in July 1974 of plans for internal self-government in the territory. Along with the prime minister, Carlos Arias Navarro, and the foreign minister, Pedro Cortina y Mauri, Prince Juan Carlos refused to bow to Moroccan protests brought to Madrid on August 13, 1974, by the Moroccan premier and foreign minister, Ahmed Osman and Ahmed Laraki (qq.v.). However, it was during Juan Carlos's second period as acting head of state in October-November 1975 that the Saharan crisis brought Spain and Morocco into sharpest conflict. Franco fell ill on October 17, one day after the announcement of the Green March (q.v.) by King Hassan II (q.v.). After a series of heart attacks, Franco was hospitalized, and on October 30, Juan Carlos became acting head of state, as Spanish ministers were engaged in negotiations with Moroccan and Mauritanian officials in a bid to resolve the crisis sparked by the Green March. Nobody expected Franco to recover, and Juan Carlos knew that he had the responsibility in these tense moments of laying the basis for a stable transition to a new post-Francoist order. He knew that a war with Morocco would be an inauspicious and highly risky opening to his reign, yet he also appreciated the sense of betrayal that would be felt by many army officers, especially those in Western Sahara, if the desert colony was handed over to Morocco and Mauritania. To reassure the officers in the Sahara, he flew to El-Ayoun (q.v.) on November 2, to give a morale-boosting speech in the barracks. "I am the first soldier of Spain," he proclaimed, promising that "the prestige and honor of the army will be safeguarded" and that "we also wish to protect the legitimate rights of the Saharawi civilian population." However, after the entry of the Green Marchers into Western Sahara on November 6, the Spanish government rapidly came to terms with Morocco and Mauritania, signing the Madrid Agreement on November 14 by which a tripartite administration (q.v.) was set up until Spain's final withdrawal in February 1976. Franco died on November 20, and Juan Carlos became king on November 22. He has since played a part in his governments' attempts to balance between the conflicting pressures on Madrid generated by the ensuing conflict, but in recent years, his sympathies have seemed to drift toward Morocco, in line with the decidedly pro-Rabat policies being pursued by the socialist government led by Felipe González Márquez (q.v.). For example, Juan Carlos was in attendance at the lavish festivities, held on March 3, 1986, in celebration of the 25th anniversary of King Hassan's rule. This underscored the generally close state of Spanish-Moroccan relations in the late 1980s.

JUDICIAL SYSTEM. In traditional Saharawi society, there was a dual judicial system, reflecting the retention of pre-Islamic customary law (of Berber origin) alongside the Muslim judicial code. The latter, known as the *sharia* (q.v.), was the basis of civil law; the former, known as the *orf* (q.v.), which differed in details from one tribe to another, provided a code of criminal law. Civil cases were heard by a *qadi* (q.v.), who was nominated by the tribal *djemaa* (q.v.) and could be overruled or removed by it if his decisions were deemed unjust. The orf law, which was codified and applied by the djemaa, consisted essentially of a set of prescribed punishments for specified crimes and a series of rules regarding the swearing of oaths and the presentation of witnesses in criminal cases. This dual system remained unchanged until at least the 1950s, when the Spanish authorities made their first attempts to streamline and modernize the traditional system of justice. A new national system of courts, both Koranic and customary, was set up to handle civil and criminal cases, respectively. The orf-based system was streamlined by an ordinance of December 16, 1955, which set up *tribunales de demarcación* (composed of the senior local Spanish official, 3 Muslims, and a secretary) at the local level (El-Ayoun, Dakhla, Aoussert, Smara, and La Guera), to try cases in which the maximum sentence was a fine of P5,000 or one month in jail. More serious cases and appeals went to the *tribunal territorial* in Dakhla, which was composed of the *delegado gubernativo* (q.v.) of the city, an *asesor de justicia islámica* (adviser on Islamic justice), 2 practicing Muslims, and a secretary, and to the highest court, the *tribunal superior* in El-Ayoun, which was composed of the secretary-general of the colonial administration, his secretary, and 2 judicial advisers. The system of civil justice was reformed by another ordinance, of March 21, 1956, which set up a series of parallel courts. At local level, *qodat* (q.v.) were set up to hear minor cases. More important cases and appeals from the qodat went to a court in El-Ayoun comprising an official qadi, 2 *adel,* and a secretary. The highest court was the *mejeles,* or *tribunal superior,* which was composed of a president, 3 *vocales* (members), an asesor de justicia islámica, and a secretary.

Another form of duality existed by virtue of the separation of this system of courts for cases involving Saharawis from the system for Europeans. A decree of January 23, 1953, stated that two *juzgados locales* (local courts) would be appointed to try cases involving Europeans in El-Ayoun and Dakhla. They were to be subordinate to a *juzgado territorial* in El-Ayoun, which in turn was subordinate to higher courts in Las Palmas (Canary Islands) and ultimately the supreme court in Madrid. The decree specified that the juzgados locales and the juzgado territorial could hear cases only when "both or one of the two parties are not natives."

In practice, the system established in the 1950s was not as elaborate as it appeared on paper. Saharawis continued to resolve many disputes through recourse to the traditional djemaas and qadis. There were no juzgados locales and only a single juzgado territorial in the country in 1960. Moreover, the juzgado territorial heard only civil cases; criminal cases involving Europeans were submitted to military jurisdiction. The "special nature" of the Sahara, by comparison to metropolitan Spain, meant that the army played a major judicial role, especially regarding matters to do with public order and security. The conversion of Western Sahara into a "province" (q.v.) of Spain in 1958 did not bring any substantive change to the judicial system. The low level of economic and social development of the territory meant that the formal judiciary remained minute, the army retained its role in judicial matters, and, as a law of April 19, 1961, on the organization and juridical regime of the province reaffirmed, the Saharawis' "religion, cause, and consequence at the same time of some special customs and ways of life" made it convenient to retain the dual judicial system. As sedentation and urbanization speeded up in the 1960s and early 1970s, the role of the official orf and sharia courts in the towns assumed growing importance. However, such a system could hardly have been suitable for an independent state. The Spanish authorities became aware of this when, in 1974, they planned to introduce internal self-government through the *estatuto político* (q.v.) as a step toward eventual independence. The estatuto político itself provided for the establishment of a unified and independent judicial system in the territory, and in November 1974, the djemaa, in anticipation of this, approved *normas* (regulations) that set out the principles on which it would be based. The normas specified that justice would be administered by independent and fixed qodat, which would have jurisdiction in civil, criminal, litigious-administrative, and labor cases. An organic law of justice was to have been drawn up by the judicial commission of the djemaa and submitted to the latter for approval. However, none of these reforms were implemented. The estatuto político, which had been approved by the djemaa in July 1974, was never enacted because of Moroccan protests to Spain at the time of its announcement and later the Madrid Agreement (q.v.).

When Spain withdrew from the country in February 1976, handing it over to Morocco and Mauritania, the judicial systems of these two countries were introduced into the zones they controlled. Mauritania withdrew from Western Sahara in August 1979, and Morocco then annexed the erstwhile Mauritanian sector, Tiris el-Gharbia (q.v.). Communal courts were established in the Moroccan-controlled towns to hear minor cases. However, the war with the Polisario Front (q.v.) apparently led to the widespread use of detention without trial and the creation of secret prisons for Saharawis suspected of sympathy for the guerrillas, according to reports published by Amnesty International in 1978 and 1990. For its part, the Saharan Arab Democratic Republic (SADR) (q.v.), founded by the Polisario Front in February

1976, has its own judiciary. The SADR constitution, which was ratified in greatly revised form by the front's 8th general popular congress (q.v.), in June 1991, states that there is a Supreme Court, an intermediate appeals court, and tribunals of first instance (article 66). In addition, a Supreme Council of Juridical Power is established (article 68), consisting of the president of the Supreme Court and 6 other members, either elected or appointed by the president of the SADR, the Supreme Court, or the SADR's parliament. The Supreme Council also recommends who shall occupy the office of attorney general, who is formally appointed by the SADR's president (article 69). In actual practice, committees for social affairs in each refugee (q.v.) camp continued to handle minor differences within the Saharawi community, and the formal court system set forth in the constitution was not fully established. Some provisions of the constitution, especially those relating to judicial matters, seemed designed for use when independence is attained, not for immediate implementation in a refugee camp environment.

JUNTA LOCAL. Local *juntas* were set up during the Spanish colonial period to administer small settlements that were not large enough to warrant the creation of an *ayuntamiento* (q.v.) or city council. Until 1962, there were no ayuntamientos at all, and El-Ayoun and Dakhla (qq.v.) were the only two towns with *juntas locales*. However, after the conversion of the territory into a "province" (q.v.) in 1958, a law on the province's organization (adopted on April 19, 1961) divided the country for administrative purposes into *términos municipales* (q.v.) (municipalities, to be administered by elected ayuntamientos) in the larger towns, *entidades locales menores* (q.v.) (minor local entities) in the smaller settlements, and *fracciones nómadas* (q.v.) (nomad fractions) for the nonsedentary population. A further decree of November 29, 1962, laid down that the entidades locales menores would be administered by juntas locales made up of 4 members elected by male heads of families living in the locality, plus a president nominated by the governor-general (q.v.). The decree designated 2 entidades locales menores, Smara and La Guera (qq.v.), and El-Ayoun and Dakhla were upgraded to municipalities. In the first elections, held in May 1963, 2 Spaniards and 2 Saharawis were elected to each of the two juntas locales. The elections were, of course, no more free than those held in Francoist Spain at this time, and the juntas locales had very few real powers.

- K -

KATIBA. A unit of the Saharawi Popular Liberation Army, the military wing of the Polisario Front (qq.v.).

KHAIMA. Pl. *khaimat*. The traditional Saharawi tent. Made of goat or camel hair, it is sewn communally by a gathering of women from the families who make up the *friq* (q.v.)—a form of collective labor known as the *touiza*. The tent is well suited to the harsh climate of the desert and easy to transport. It can be quickly dismantled or erected and is relatively spacious, isothermic, and waterproof.

KHALIHENNA OULD RACHID. Born in 1948, Khalihenna Ould Rachid was secretary-general of the small Spanish-inspired Partido de la Unión Nacional Saharaui (q.v.) in 1974–75 and then, in a political volte-face, switched his allegiance to Morocco in May 1975. A Reguibi (q.v.), he had trained as an engineer in Las Palmas and Madrid before becoming leader of the PUNS, which was founded in November 1974 with the encouragement of the Spanish colonial authorities. Over the following half-year, he was almost certainly being groomed by the colonial regime to head the pro-Spanish government that the governor-general, Gen. Gómez de Salazar, and his secretary-general, Col. Rodríguez de Viguri (qq.v.), hoped would lead the territory to independence after the referendum to which Spain had been formally committed since the previous August. However, the explosion of popular support for the Polisario Front (q.v.) during the tour of the territory by the UN Visiting Mission (q.v.), on May 12–19, 1975, placed Khalihenna Ould Rachid in a difficult political position. Fearing that the Spanish authorities would abandon the discredited PUNS and seek a political accommodation with the Polisario Front, he fled to Morocco in the middle of the UN mission's visit and on May 18, 1975, pledged allegiance to King Hassan II (q.v.) in Casablanca. He then joined the pro-Moroccan Front de Libération et de l'Unité (q.v.) and accused the Polisario guerrillas of being "communists." He returned to Western Sahara after the Madrid Agreement (q.v.) in an attempt to muster support there for integration with Morocco, and on June 3, 1976, he was elected a deputy for El-Ayoun (q.v.) in the Moroccan Chamber of Representatives, where he joined the pro-royalist "independents" who formed the Rassemblement National des Indépendants (National Assembly of Independents) in 1978. On April 19, 1977, he was appointed secretary of state in the prime minister's office, and on January 3, 1979, he became secretary of state for the Sahara.

KHAN, SAHABZADA YAQUB. A national of Pakistan, he was appointed on March 23, 1992, by the secretary-general of the United Nations, Boutros Boutros Ghali (qq.v.), to be the UN's special representative for Western Sahara. Prior to his appointment, he served in Pakistan's armed forces, rising to the rank of general, and served as Pakistan's foreign minister from 1982 to 1987. Replacing Johannes Manz (q.v.) as special representative, his primary task was to restart the stalled Western Sahara peace process, which by the beginning of 1992 had not resulted in a referendum of self-determination in the territory. His position also involves being in overall charge of the United Nations Mission for the Referendum in Western Sahara (q.v.) and all aspects of the UN peace plan, including the difficult task of maintaining credibility with both parties to the conflict, Morocco and the Polisario Front (q.v.).

KHATRI OULD SAID OULD JOUMANI. A Reguibi (q.v.), of the Lebouihat, born in Smara in 1921, he has led one of the most prominent, but checkered, political careers of any Saharawi politician, aligning in turn with the Army of Liberation (q.v.), France, Spain, and, after a brief flirtation with the Polisario Front (q.v.), Morocco. He first came to prominence in 1957 as a supporter of the Army of Liberation's guerrilla struggle against Spain and France in Western Sahara and northern Mauritania. However, he fell out with the radical Moroccans leading the movement and was placed under house arrest by Army of Liberation commanders in Goulimine, southern Morocco. He managed to escape, dressed as a woman, and reached the French military outpost of Fort Trinquet (Bir Moghrein) in northern Mauritania in December 1957. There he pledged his loyalty to France and requested arms and money with which to combat the guerrillas. "We ask Your Excellency," he wrote on January 16, 1958, to the high commissioner of French West Africa, Gaston Cusin, "to grant us peace and your aid against the Army of Liberation, which is attacking us, in our territory, causing damage to the country, its wealth and people." His arrival at Fort Trinquet, which signified that an important split had occurred in the ranks of the Army of Liberation, encouraged the French government to give the green light, on December 30, 1957, to plans for a joint Franco-Spanish counterinsurgency drive, Operation Ouragan (q.v.), which decimated the guerrilla forces in Western Sahara the following February. After this defeat, more of the Reguibat Lgouacem (q.v.) rallied to the French, with Khatri's encouragement, at ceremonies in Fort Trinquet and Fort Gouraud (Zouerate) on April 10 and 11, 1958. Shortly afterward, on May 2–5, Khatri attended the constitutive congress of the Parti du Regroupement Mauritanien, which, under the leadership of Mokhtar Ould Daddah, was being primed for leadership of the Mauritanian government by France. Shortly thereafter, however, Khatri returned to the Spanish zone, where he became one of Madrid's most trusted allies.

After the first elections to the Cabildo Provincial (q.v.), in May 1963, he was selected to be its first president, a position he held until 1965, when he was replaced by another staunch loyalist, Saila Ould Abeida. On July 17, 1963, he took his seat in the Spanish Cortes, of which he remained a member almost without interruption until 1975. Nonetheless, he showed hesitant sympathy for the anticolonial movement set up by Mohammed Sidi Ibrahim Bassiri (q.v.) at the end of the sixties, and he was briefly placed under house arrest in June 1970 after the Zemla massacre (q.v.). But after the demise of Bassiri's movement, he quickly returned to Spanish favor. After the second elections to the Djemaa (q.v.), in January 1971, he was elected president of this Spanish-created assembly of conservative tribal leaders. He remained president until the assembly's dissolution.

In 1974–75, he emerged as a key figure in Spain's plans to institute territorial autonomy through the *estatuto político* (q.v.). In February 1975, he became president of a new permanent commission of the djemaa, a 16-man body that became a link between the assembly and the colonial authorities. However, Spain's plans for a gradual transfer of power to loyal local traditionalists suffered an irreversible rebuff when overwhelming popular support for the Polisario Front was demonstrated during the tour of the territory by the UN Visiting Mission (q.v.), in May 1975. At the end of the month, Khatri traveled to Tindouf (q.v.), in Algeria, to hold talks with the leader of the guerrilla movement, El-Ouali Mustapha Sayed (q.v.). He and other leaders of the Djemaa began to favor an alliance with the front in order to check Moroccan ambitions, and, until the autumn of 1975, they had support in this from the Spanish colonial administration. On October 12, 1975, Khatri was the most illustrious of the djemaa leaders to attend and speak at the conference of Ain Ben Tili (q.v.), an important gathering organized by the Polisario Front to unite Saharawis of diverse political backgrounds against the mounting Moroccan threat. On October 17, one day after the announcement of the Green March (q.v.) by King Hassan (q.v.), Khatri warned: "The Saharawi people will oppose the march, by force if necessary. The Saharawis will not rest with arms folded in the face of our only enemy, Morocco. We will fight until death for our objective—independence." But, less than two weeks later, he suddenly boarded a plane for Morocco from the Canary Islands. On November 3, he made the *bayaa* (q.v.), the traditional pledge of allegiance, to King Hassan in Agadir. "I have come on behalf of all the inhabitants and tribes of the Sahara to render to Your Majesty the allegiance of our ancestors," he said. "I have come out of patriotism because the Sahara is an integral part of Morocco. We have never ceased to be Moroccans."

On February 26, 1976, he presided at the rump meeting of the djemaa, which endorsed the Madrid Agreement (q.v.) of November 14, 1975. Thereafter a loyal supporter of the Moroccan annexation, he was elected president of the communal council of Guelta Zemmour (q.v.) after the communal elections of November 12, 1976, and then elected president of the provincial assembly of Boujdour (q.v.) after indirect elections to that body on January 25, 1977. The provincial assembly elected him on June 21, 1977, to the Moroccan Chamber of Representatives, of which he became vice president.

- L -

LA GUERA. A small town in the extreme south of the territory on the Cape Blanc peninsula. Though the western strip of this peninsula was given to Spain by virtue of the Franco-Spanish Convention of June 27, 1900 (q.v.), it was not until November 30, 1920, that Francisco Bens (q.v.), the Spanish governor of the territory, landed at La Guera and established a garrison there. With him arrived workers of the Sociedad Marcotegui, which established a fish-processing factory there. The little settlement's importance derived from its proximity to the rich fishing resources of the Bay of Levrier, to which Spanish fishermen had right of access under the 1900 convention despite its lying in the Mauritanian zone. About 6,000 tons of fish were being landed annually at La Guera by the end of the 1960s. However, though it remained a small fishing and administrative center and the site of a military base, La Guera was overshadowed by Port Etienne (present-day Nouadhibou), 3 km. away across the Mauritanian border. In 1974, the census recorded a population of only 1,200. After the Madrid Agreement (q.v.) of November 14, 1975, Spanish troops quickly withdrew from most small settlements, including La Guera, which was left briefly in the hands of the Polisario Front (q.v.). After a spirited resistance by Polisario guerrillas, Mauritanian troops entered the town on December 19, 1975, and under the Moroccan-Mauritanian agreement of April 14, 1976 (q.v.), it became part of the Mauritanian zone of the territory. By the Algiers Agreement (q.v.) of August 5, 1979, Mauritania withdrew from the war with the Polisario Front and dropped its claims to Western Saharan territory, but as a result of Morocco's immediate takeover of all the other small settlements and outposts in Mauritania's erstwhile zone, the Mauritanian government decided to maintain a garrison in La Guera, which still remained under Mauritanian administration in 1993.

LA REALIDAD. The only daily newspaper ever to have been published in Western Sahara, it appeared briefly in 1975. Ninety-nine issues appeared, the last dated October 24, 1975, when it was closed down at the behest of the Spanish authorities. Edited by Pablo Ignacio de Dalmases and published by Prensa y Publicaciones Saharauis SA, *La Realidad* ran articles in both Spanish and Arabic. One of the initiatives taken with the encouragement of the Spanish authorities to prepare the country for independence, the paper proved an embarrassment when, in October 1975, Spanish policy started to waver after the announcement of the Green March (q.v.). Its forthright reporting sowed alarm among the Saharawi population, and the headline of its last front page, "Parece proximo un acuerdo hispano-marroquí" (A Spanish-Moroccan agreement seems near), was the last straw.

LAAROUSSI MAHFOUD. One of the first militants of the Polisario Front (q.v.), he was active in the guerrilla war the front launched against Spain in May 1973. He was one of the first guerrillas to be killed—during a clash with Spanish forces at Aoukeyra on March 13, 1974.

LAAYOUNE see EL-AYOUN

LARAK FORCE. A large, well-equipped force, assembled in 1980 and placed under the command of Col. Ben Othman, the Larak Force was dispatched to southern Morocco by King Hassan II (q.v.) to attempt to gain control of the region between Tan-Tan and Smara (q.v.) where Polisario guerrillas had gained almost total control in 1978–79, preventing overland communications and threatening Tan-Tan. In the summer of 1980, some 12,000 troops, mainly from the Larak Force, were assembled at Abatteh, south of Tan-Tan in the Zini mountains. From there, thousands of Moroccan troops moved south to Ras el-Khanfra (q.v.), at the southern approaches to the Zini range, about 10 km. north of the Western Saharan border, and to Khreibichatt, about 50 km. south of the border, toward Smara. The Moroccan troops engaged in this operation were almost continually harassed by guerrillas until February 1981. However, after taking control of the Zini mountains, they successfully set up a continuous defense line from Ras el-Khanfra, via Khreibichatt, to Smara, and then beyond, to the phosphate mines at Bou-Craa (qq.v.), as part of a plan to establish a defense perimeter around the entire "useful triangle" of the territory's northwest (El-Ayoun, Smara, and Bou-Craa).

LARAKI, AHMED. Born in Casablanca in 1931, he was Morocco's foreign minister at the time of the Madrid Agreement (q.v.) of November 14, 1975. He had a long political and diplomatic career, serving as minister of foreign affairs in 1967–69 and 1974–77 and as prime minister in 1969–71. During his first stint as foreign minister, he played an important role in the negotiations that culminated in the cession of Ifni by Spain to Morocco in 1969. After returning to the foreign ministry in 1974, he was preoccupied with the Western Saharan question. Following King Hassan II's (q.v.) decision in July 1974 to mount a major diplomatic campaign to stall Spain's plans for internal autonomy and to advance the Moroccan claim to the territory, he held talks with Spanish leaders in Madrid on August 13, 1974, though he failed then to persuade the Spanish to drop their internal autonomy plans. On September 23, he communicated to the Spanish government King Hassan's proposal to submit the Western Saharan problem to the International Court of Justice (ICJ) (q.v.), and in a speech to the UN (q.v.) General Assembly on September 30, he proposed that the UN request an advisory opinion from the ICJ if (as was to be the case) Spain refused a contentious recourse to the court. Anxious to resolve the embarrassing dispute with Mauritania over the territory, Laraki also hinted in his UN address that Morocco would be prepared to strike a deal with Mauritania. "Mauritania is interested in the future of the Sahara and cannot but be associated, by virtue of its rights, with the settlement and the outcome of the litigation that opposes Morocco and Mauritania to Spain." Laraki's olive branch was to lead to the "understanding" on partition reached the following October by King Hassan and President Mokhtar Ould Daddah (q.v.) at the Arab League (q.v.) summit in Rabat. A year later, Laraki was in the thick of the negotiations that followed King Hassan's announcement of the Green March (q.v.) on October 16 and culminated in the Madrid Agreement. He was engaged in talks with Spanish officials in Madrid on October 24–25, October 28–30, and November 12–14, and, besides helping to work out the compromise formula by which the Green Marchers were allowed to cross the Western Saharan border symbolically on November 6 up to a Spanish dissuasion line 14 km. to the south, he played a major role in negotiating the terms of the Madrid Agreement. He remained foreign minister until October 1977, when his place was taken by M'Hamed Boucetta (q.v.).

LEBOUIRATE, BATTLE OF. An army base in southeast Morocco, Lebouirate was overrun by the Polisario Front (q.v.) on August 24, 1979, after one of the most devastating attacks launched by the guerrillas since the start of their war with Morocco in 1975. Journalists taken to Lebouirate by guerrillas a few days later, on September 2, were shown documents captured there that revealed widespread demoralization in the Moroccan ranks. They showed that the post had already been attacked twice, on July 6 and August 10, before the final Polisario assault on August 24, and that its commander, Mohammed Azelmat, of the 3rd Armored Squadron, had been pleading with his superior officers for reinforcements. After the second attack, on August 10, he reported that "the men of the 3rd Armored Squadron, traumatized and demoralized, are no longer operational, and a catastrophe grave in consequences can be expected if the general staff do not take this force's situation into consideration." No reinforcements arrived, and at 5:30 a.m. on August 24, the guerrillas struck again. "We suddenly saw dozens of headlights in the distance," recalled a Moroccan soldier captured in the ensuing battle. "The Polisario land rovers reached us at top speed, firing with all their automatic arms and shooting rockets. The noise was infernal. It was terrifying." He put the size of the attacking force at 1,200 men, with 150–200 vehicles. Within an hour, the base was in Polisario hands. Two days later, the Moroccan ministry of information admitted that Lebouirate had fallen. "Surprised, squadron leader Azelmat, commanding the garrison of Lebouirate and responsible for the defense of this locality, did not oppose the appropriate resistance to the enemy, abandoning even its defensive positions as well as a large part of its equipment, so allowing the enemy to seize the attacked locality." Meanwhile, a relief column that set out for Lebouirate from Zaag fell into a guerrilla ambush. In a communiqué issued on August 27, Polisario claimed to have killed 562 Moroccans and captured 92 during both the attack on Lebouirate and the ensuing ambush of the relief column from Zaag. The guerrillas also claimed to have evacuated 166 Saharawi civilians from the hamlet and taken them to the refugee camps (q.v.) near Tindouf (q.v.). Whatever the true death toll, the loss of Lebouirate, which had a garrison of about 1,000 men, was a serious setback for the Moroccans. A correspondent of the London *Observer,* Shyam Bhatia, who was taken to Lebouirate by the Polisario Front on September 12, reported: "The amount of Moroccan armour visibly lost to the Polisario is a defence arsenal which many small countries would be delighted to own. It includes 37 Russian T-54 tanks, 13 French armoured troop carriers and 12 armoured cars." The Moroccan ministry of information announced on August 26, "An inquiry has been ordered with a view to determining responsibilities and punishing those guilty." In February 1980, 36 members of the garrison were given jail terms after a court-martial, but they were immediately pardoned by King Hassan II (q.v.). Lebouirate remained under Polisario control for over a year after this engagement, until the front evidently withdrew its forces from southern Morocco. Somewhat later, Morocco's construction of its "defensive walls" (q.v.) around this region rendered Lebouirate effectively beyond the reach of Polisario's guerrillas.

LEMANASIR see MENASIR

LEMIAR. A small fishing tribe, subordinate traditionally to the Izarguien (q.v.), to whom they paid tribute (q.v.) for protection, their fractions are the Ahel Sidi Amar, the Ahel Brahim, and the Ahel Ahmed. The Lemiar traditionally lived along the northern coast.

LEMOUEDENIN. A subtribe of the Reguibat es-Sahel (q.v.), the Lemouedenin trace their ancestry to Moueden, who was either a son of Ali Ould Sidi Ahmed Reguibi, the supposed ancestor of several of the subtribes of the Reguibat es-Sahel, or a disciple of his father, Sidi Ahmed Reguibi. In the 1960s and early 1970s, many Lemouedenin settled in El-Ayoun and Smara (qq.v.).

LISTON, TERENCE. A division general in the Canadian armed forces, Terence Liston headed the Military Group of the first United Nations technical mission (q.v.) to Western Sahara and the adjacent region in November and December of 1987. Gen. Liston, along with several other military experts from various countries, toured Western Sahara, visiting areas occupied by Morocco and those areas "liberated" by the Polisario Front (q.v.). The technical mission, sent to the area pursuant to resolution 104 of the Organization of African Unity (q.v.) and General Assembly resolution 41/16 of the United Nations (q.v.), which was passed on October 31, 1986, was also composed of a Civil Group headed by UN Under Secretary-General for Special Political Questions Abderrahim Farah (q.v.) of Somalia. The technical mission presented its report to UN Secretary-General Javier Pérez de Cuéllar (q.v.) and then to the OAU chairman, President Kenneth Kaunda of Zambia, in early 1988. The mission did not make its findings public, but its information served as a basis for a peace plan presented by Pérez de Cuéllar in August 1988.

LIVESTOCK. In 1975, it was estimated that the territory had 63,000 camels, 125,000 goats, 10,000 sheep, 1,600 donkeys, and 350 horses, as well as a few pigs and zebu cattle. In traditional nomadic society, the camel was the axis of the pastoral economy, though the goat was also an important source of meat and milk. With a stomach capacity of up to 245 liters, the camel can go for days without drinking—five days in the hottest weeks of the summer or even several weeks in the autumn or winter if pastures are good. Its ability to travel at least 69 km. a day, and in exceptional cases as much as 120 km., allows it to take the best advantage of the dispersed and limited pastures. As a pack animal, the camel can take loads of up to 120–150 kg., making it ideal for long-distance trade in the days of the trans-Saharan caravans. It was also a military asset, being well suited for the *ghazzi* (q.v.). Camel's milk was the foundation of the nomad's diet, the females being able to produce usually abut 5–7 liters a day or, at a maximum (six months after giving birth), 15 liters. The animal's hair was used to weave the *khaima* (q.v.), the Saharawi tent. Finally, the camel was traditionally a means of exchange and the main "export" of the nomads, being sold for cereals, sugar, tea, cloth, and other necessities in the markets of southern Morocco, notably at Goulimine.

Camels and other animals were privately, not communally, owned, but the largest herd-owners used to lend some of their animals to poor families, a practice known as *meniha*. This gave the borrower the right to use the products (milk, hair) of the borrowed animals, and the owner benefited from the spreading of risks (of robbery) and a more rational exploitation of pastoral resources.

Prolonged droughts were feared by the Saharawis like biblical plagues. One or two years without rain could decimate the herds, as happened during the great droughts of 1946–50 and 1956–63. Since the onset of the war between the Polisario Front (q.v.) and Morocco (and, for a while, Mauritania), nomadic migrations have been impossible, and the territory's remaining nomads have either joined the Polisario camps in Algeria or, in a minority of cases, settled in the Moroccan-controlled towns. Under these conditions, livestock herds have greatly diminished.

LULEI see EL-OUALI MUSTAPHA SAYED

- M -

MA EL-AININ, CHEIKH. The great leader of the Saharawi resistance to colonialism at the beginning of the 20th century, the founder of Smara (q.v.), and an influential marabout (q.v.), Mohammed Sidi el-Mustapha, or Ma el-Ainin ("water of the eyes"), as he was nicknamed as a child, was born in the Hodh, in southeastern Mauritania, in c. 1830–31. He was one of 32 sons of Mohammed Fadel, a great marabout of the Ahel Taleb Mokhtar and founder of the Fadeliya wing of the Qadiriya movement. He was given prominent attention by his father from an early age because of his remarkable intellectual capacities and physical endurance. He was later said to have learned the *Koran* by heart at the age of 7, and in c.1847–48, he was sent to Marrakesh, Morocco, to complete his education, possibly establishing at this time the friendships with members of the ruling Alawites (q.v.), which were to stand him in good stead later in his life.

In c. 1858, he returned to Morocco and embarked from Tangiers, with some of Sultan Abderrahman's sons, on a steamer to the Middle East to undertake the pilgrimage to Mecca. Returning the following year to Morocco, he went back to the desert, where he enjoyed considerable prestige as a result of his *hadj* and erudition, as well as his physical strength. Invested as a *cheikh* by his father, he rapidly acquired influence among the Tadjakant, who had founded Tindouf (q.v.) in 1852, and in Adrar (Mauritania), he spent several years in the region between Adrar and the Oued Draa (q.v.), engaging in trade, and in 1860, married Maimouna Mint Ahmed Ould Alien, the woman who was to bear his most important sons, including Ahmed el-Hiba, Merebbi Rebbu, and Mohammed Laghdaf. In all, he was to have 68 children, 33 of them sons, by 26 women, giving rise to a new tribe, the Ahel Cheikh Ma el-Ainin (q.v.). After a brief visit to the Hodh, to see his father, in 1864, he returned to the desert, but in 1873, he was back in Marrakesh to visit Sultan Sidi Mohammed, and in 1877, he once again visited the Hodh to see his widowed mother shortly before her death.

His religious zeal inspired his determination to resist the growing incursions into the desert by Europeans at the end of the 19th century. In 1886, he urged opposition by the Saharawi tribes to the expedition to Idjil (q.v.) by the Spanish explorers Julio Cervera Baviera, Felipe Rizzo, and Francisco Quiroga, though he could not prevent the treaties they signed with the emir of Adrar and several Saharawi chioukh (q.v.). He approved or inspired some of the attacks against the Spanish enclave at Dlahla (q.v.) in the early 1890s. Thereafter, however, he became more and more worried by the aggressive military expansion of the French into Trarza and Brakna (southern Mauritania). He was appalled when, in 1902, his greatest marabout rival, Cheikh Sidiya Baba of the Oulad Birri in Trarza, allied with the French. Meanwhile, he began to be obsessed by the ambition of building a Saharan city.

It was to the Alawite rulers of Morocco, with whom he retained close relations, that he turned for aid. Moulay Hassan I (q.v.), who became sultan in 1873, was eager to assist, since he wanted to resist the encroachments of the colonial powers by bringing the fringes of his empire under royal control. Thus, in 1887, shortly after his expeditions to the previously de facto independent region of the Oued Noun (southwestern Morocco) in 1882 and 1886, Hassan nominated Ma el-Ainin his khalifa, or deputy, in the Sahara, when the cheikh visited him in Marrakesh. Ma el-Ainin retained a strong influence over his successor, Moulay Abdelaziz (q.v.), who became sultan in 1894 at the age of 14. Ma el-Ainin, then aged 64, acted almost as the boy's uncle. He visited him seven times during his reign (1895–1908), four times in Marrakesh and three times in Fez. He was able to establish two zawiyas in Morocco, in Fez and Marrakesh, and the sultan himself became one of his telamid. With Moroccan help, Ma el-Ainin was able to start constructing his Saharan city, at Smara, on a tributary of the Saguia el-Hamra (q.v.), in 1898. It was a good site—near a good source of water, on the route between Adrar and the Oued Noun, and close to good pasture lands. Thousands of Saharawis, aided by Moroccan craftsmen, took part in its construction, most of the materials arriving by ship from Morocco and Spain at Tarfaya (q.v.) and then being transported overland by camel. The main part of the city had been built by 1902.

Meanwhile, refugees from the south of Mauritania began to warn Ma el-Ainin of the danger posed by Xavier Coppolani, the new French commissioner general sent to Mauritania in 1901. After taking control of Trarza and Brakna, he began to threaten Tagant, whose emir appealed to Ma el-Ainin for aid. After defeating the Idou Aich of Tagant and killing the emir in February 1905, however, Coppolani was assassinated at Tidjikja on May 12. This emboldened the anticolonial resistance and momentarily brought the French advance to a halt. The same year, Ma el-Ainin appealed again for aid to Moulay Abdelaziz, who decided to dispatch his uncle, Moulay Idriss Ben Abderrahman Ben Souleiman (q.v.), to Smara to assist the *cheikh's* forces. Ma el-Ainin now called for a *jihad* against the French and in October 1905, sent a letter to Cheikh Sidiya urging him to recognize the suzerainty of the sultan and join the anti-French camp. However, the religious leaders of southern Mauritania, who benefited from the French presence, refused to heed the call. It was in Western Sahara and in Adrar, where Ma el-Ainin's son Cheikh Hassena was acting as regent to the child-emir, Ould Aida, that the resistance movement was centered. However, in December 1906, an anti-French campaign led from Adrar into Tagant by Moulay Idriss finally ended in failure, and in May 1907, Moulay Abdelaziz recalled his uncle to Morocco under French pressure. Ma el-Ainin, too, returned to Morocco to visit the sultan and was accused by the French government of stirring up the anti-French riots that led to the landing of French and Spanish troops in Casablanca in August 1907. Ma el-Ainin, dismayed by Abdelaziz's compromises with the colonial powers, supported the revolt by the sultan's brother Moulay Hafid, who forced Abdelaziz to abdicate in his favor in 1908. Back in the Sahara, however, Ma el-Ainin faced a new challenge when Col. Gouraud began an invasion of Adrar in December 1908, finally routing the forces of Ould Aida and Ma el-Ainin's sons Hassena and El-Oueli (q.v.) in July 1909.

Ma el-Ainin now abandoned Smara and took refuge in Tiznit (southern Morocco). Morocco was on the verge of anarchy, Moulay Hafid proving as incapable a ruler and as willing to compromise with the French as his brother. In 1910, Ma el-Ainin decided he would try to fill the vacuum of leadership. Proclaiming himself sultan, he assembled an army of Soussi and Saharawi tribesmen and marched north but was defeated by a French force under the command of Gen. Moinier in the Plain of Tadla on June 23, 1910. He returned to Tiznit, where he died on October 28, 1910.

MA EL-AININ EL-ABADILA OULD CHEIKH MOHAMMED LAGHDAF. A grandson of Cheikh Ma el-Ainin (q.v.), he was born in El-Ayoun in 1927 and after a traditional Koranic education, went to Tetuan, the capital of the Spanish zone of northern Morocco, in 1936 to enter secondary school. He became a Moroccan nationalist and upon his return to Western Sahara, urged support for the Moroccan Istiqlal Party (q.v.). After Morocco's independence in March 1956, he helped to organize the Congress of Oum Achkak, a gathering of Saharawis in April 1956 that decided to send a delegation, under his leadership, to Rabat, where he made the traditional *bayaa* (q.v.), or act of allegiance, to King Mohammed V (q.v.). During the 1957–58 Saharawi insurrection led by the Army of Liberation (q.v.), to which he gave his support, he organized the evacuation of 300 Saharawi children from the war zone to schools in Morocco. After the guerrilla movement's defeat in 1958, he became an important adviser to the Moroccan government on Saharan affairs, and when the semiofficial FLS (q.v.) was set up in 1966, he became one of its chief spokesmen, leading an FLS delegation that lobbied the UN (q.v.) in New York in December 1966. He remained a staunch supporter of the Istiqlal Party and of the Moroccan claim to Western Sahara until his death in May 1976.

MAAOUIYA OULD SID 'AHMED TAYA. Mauritania's military ruler since 1984, Maaouiya Ould Sid 'Ahmed Taya was born in 1943 and received his military training in France. He

was reputed to be an apolitical, diligent, and highly professional soldier during Mauritania's 1975–78 war against the
Polisario Front (q.v.). Like other leading officers, however,
he joined the Comité Militaire de Redressement National
(CMRN) (q.v.), which overthrew the regime of Mokhtar
Ould Daddah (q.v.) in July 1978, and he was later a member
of the CMRN's successor ruling body, the Comité Militaire
de Salut National (CMSN) (q.v.), which was formed in April
1979 and which reached a peace agreement with Polisario in
August 1979 under which Mauritania gave up its share of
Western Sahara.

As a member of the ruling group, he served as chief of
military operations, commander of the strategic garrison at
Bir Moghrein, and commander of the gendarmerie. Mohammed Khouna Ould Heydallah (q.v.), who became president
of Mauritania in January 1980, appointed Ould Taya army
chief of staff, a position he held until a major reshuffle of
government and military posts that followed an unsuccessful
coup attempt on March 16, 1981, in which Ould Taya was
briefly captured by the Moroccan-based putschists of the
Alliance pour une Mauritanie Démocratique. In April 1981,
he was appointed prime minister and minister of defense,
becoming second in rank only to Ould Heydallah. As time
went on, however, Ould Taya and other members of the
CMSN began to fall out with Ould Heydallah for a variety of
reasons, most notably among them the increasingly pro-
Polisario tilt in Ould Heydallah's policies on Western
Sahara. Ould Taya, an instinctively cautious man, is believed
to have expressed reservations about policies he thought
would undermine the country's delicate neutrality in the
Saharan war and damage relations with critical aid donors in
the West and the Arab world. On February 27, 1984, in a
move that apparently caught the CMSN by surprise, Ould
Heydallah recognized the Saharan Arab Democratic Republic (SADR) (q.v.), which worsened already poor relations
with Morocco. Perhaps due to his disagreements with this
move, Ould Taya was demoted back to his old post as army
chief of staff in another reshuffle on March 8. Incensed by
this turn of events, and wearying of Ould Heydallah's
increasingly autocratic style of rule, the rest of the CMSN

decided to act. On December 12, 1984, while Ould Heydallah was out of the country attending a Franco-African summit conference in Burundi, he was overthrown in a bloodless coup and replaced by Ould Taya, who became head of state, prime minister, and minister of defense. This turn of events was greeted positively by Morocco and certain other states, who saw the possibility of more moderate and less unpredictable policies.

Ould Taya reasserted his country's neutrality in the Western Sahara conflict, though he did not revoke Mauritania's recognition of the SADR. He also restored diplomatic relations and airline links with Morocco, toned down his predecessor's rhetoric, and mended fences with the conservative Gulf monarchies. In an interview with the *New York Times* (February 28, 1985), Ould Taya said, "What we really want is to have relations with all countries in the region." Indeed, Mauritania remained a party to the Algerian-Tunisian-Mauritanian "treaty of fraternity and concord," which it had signed in December 1983, and Ould Taya also worked to improve relations with Libya. In walking this delicate path, however, he had not only to be mindful of the various factions within the CMSN but also to cope with his country's basic vulnerabilities, namely, long frontiers his weak army could not effectively police, persistent social and racial tensions that exploded into bloody interethnic riots in April 1989, and almost continuous Moroccan pressures on his regime to clamp down on Polisario's activities in the north of Mauritania.

King Hassan II (q.v.) periodically threatened to stage cross-border operations into Mauritanian territory to pursue Polisario forces. But the king did not carry out these threats, probably for fear of triggering a reaction from Algeria, with whom Ould Taya always maintained good relations. Ould Taya was especially concerned about the Saharan war in the spring of 1987, when Morocco completed its series of "defensive walls" (q.v.), which came to within a few kilometers of Mauritania's border and the vital railway link between the iron ore mines at Zouerate and the port of Nouadhibou. Emphasizing his neutrality, however, he declined an offer by Algeria to send its own troops to Nouadhibou, fearing such a move would be too provocative.

In the late 1980s, Ould Taya's attentions were increasingly directed toward the deteriorating domestic situation and away from the Western Saharan problem. He faced acute economic difficulties, ethnic unrest, tensions with Senegal, and a succession of "plots" by his political opponents. Possibly in an attempt to balance these competing factors, he cultivated increasingly close ties with Iraq. As a result, Mauritania lost substantial aid from the U.S. and conservative Arab states after Baghdad's invasion of Kuwait on August 2, 1990.

MADRID AGREEMENT (NOVEMBER 14, 1975). An agreement between Morocco, Mauritania, and Spain, this established a temporary tripartite administration in Western Sahara and committed Spain to withdraw from the territory by the end of February 1976. The agreement itself was and remains secret. All that was published was a brief declaration of principles, which read as follows:

> On November 14, 1975, the delegations lawfully representing the governments of Spain, Morocco, and Mauritania, meeting in Madrid, stated that they had agreed in order on the following principles:
>
> 1. Spain confirms its resolve, repeatedly stated in the United Nations, to decolonize the territory of Western Sahara by terminating the responsibilities and powers it possesses over that territory as administering power.
>
> 2. In conformity with the aforementioned determination and in accordance with the negotiations advocated by the United Nations with the affected parties, Spain will proceed forthwith to institute a temporary administration in the territory, in which Morocco and Mauritania will participate in collaboration with the Djemaa (q.v.) and to which will be transferred all the responsibilities and powers referred to in the preceding paragraph. It is accordingly agreed that two deputy governors nominated by Morocco and Mauritania shall be appointed to assist the governor-general of the territory in the performance of his functions. The termination of the Spanish presence in the territory will be completed by February 28, 1976 at the latest.
>
> 3. The views of the Saharan population, expressed through the Djemaa, will be respected.

4. The three countries will inform the secretary-general of the United Nations of the terms set down in this instrument as a result of the negotiations entered into in accordance with article 33 of the Charter of the United Nations.

5. The three countries involved declare that they arrived at the foregoing conclusions in the highest spirit of understanding and brotherhood, with due respect for the principles of the Charter of the United Nations and as the best possible contribution to the maintenance of international peace and security.

6. This instrument shall enter into force on the date of publication in the *Boletín Oficial del Estado* of the Sahara Decolonization Act authorizing the Spanish government to assume the commitments conditionally set forth in this instrument.

The Sahara decolonization law was approved in the Cortes by 345 votes to 4, with 4 abstentions, on November 18.

A notable feature of the declaration is that Spain purported only to be transferring temporary administrative powers to Morocco and Mauritania in the framework of the tripartite administration. It did not transfer sovereignty to Morocco and Mauritania, and it stated that "the views of the Saharan population, expressed through the Djemaa, will be respected." The Djemaa had not generally been accepted, in the UN in particular, as a genuinely representative body, since most of its members were not elected by universal adult suffrage and the assembly was known to be disproportionately representative of the older, more conservative tribal *chioukh* (q.v.). The Djemaa was obviously thought more likely to approve a Moroccan-Mauritanian annexation and partition than would a popular referendum, the formula for self-determination that had been consistently advocated by the UN since 1966 but to which the declaration of principles made no reference. However, the Spanish, Moroccan, and Mauritanian governments found the rug pulled from under their feet when, on November 28, 67 members of the Djemaa, an absolute majority of its 102 members, signed the Proclamation of Guelta Zemmour (q.v.), formally dissolving the body "so that there can be no utilization by Spanish colonialism of this puppet institution" and declaring their support for the Polisario Front (q.v.). The credibility of the Djemaa fell so low that, when the UN refused to send an official observer to a rump meeting of the assembly on February 26, 1976, which formally endorsed annexation by Morocco and Mauritania, the Spanish government declared that it could not accept its vote as a genuine consultation of the Saharawi people of the kind required by the Madrid Agreement.

Nonetheless, the practical effect of the Madrid Agreement was to hand the territory, or at least its major population centers, to Morocco and Mauritania. Thousands of Moroccan and Mauritanian troops started to arrive in the main cities within a fortnight of the agreement, while Spanish troops were all withdrawn by mid-January 1976. King Hassan II (q.v.) was in no doubt that the reference in the declaration of principles to respect the views of the Saharan population was a mere formality, included only for purposes of show. "The Sahara has been handed back to you," he bluntly told Moroccans in a speech on November 17. For the Spanish government, the Madrid Agreement represented the outcome of a remarkable 180-degree turn in policy, engineered in the space of only one month following King Hassan's announcement on October 16 of the Green March (q.v.) and the start of Franco's (q.v.) long, final illness on October 17. The 350,000-strong Green March, which crossed the Western Saharan frontier on November 6, was symbolic of the depth of feeling in Morocco about Western Sahara and the extent to which Hassan II had committed himself to its annexation. Refusal to allow him victory not only would have brought a real risk of armed conflict between Morocco and Spain, but also would have imperiled his throne and perhaps brought to power a more left-wing, or nationalist, regime on Spain's doorstep. After receiving assurances from a Spanish minister, Antonio Carro Martínez, on November 8, King Hassan ordered the Green Marchers to return to Morocco on November 9. Negotiations resumed in Madrid on November 12, leading to the agreement two days later.

Franco's illness made the Spanish cabinet especially anxious to avoid the risk of conflict with Morocco. Nobody expected the *caudillo* to recover, and he died on November

20, just six days after the agreement. The prime minister, Carlos Arias Navarro (q.v.), and his cabinet colleagues, as well as Prince Juan Carlos (q.v.), who became acting head of state on October 30, did not want to be lumbered with a colonial dispute while steering the country into the unknown terrain of post-Francoism. The disorders that had followed the collapse of the Marcello Caetano regime in Portugal in 1974 were a warning of what might happen in Spain, and there is no doubt that the United States and France, which had a keen interest in the stability of both Morocco and Spain, advised the Madrid government to abandon its previous commitment to a self-determination referendum and come to terms with Morocco. This was the message that was apparently brought to Madrid a few days before the agreement by Vernon Walters, then deputy director of the Central Intelligence Agency. Those members of the Spanish government, such as Pedro Cortina y Mauri (q.v.), the foreign minister, who feared that reneging on the commitment to self-determination would embarrass Spain in the United Nations and undermine its lobbying there on the Gibraltar question, were very much out on a limb.

In securing the agreement, moreover, the Moroccan government was able to threaten reprisals against Spanish fishing interests and the Spanish enclaves of Ceuta and Melilla on Morocco's Mediterranean coast if it did not get its way. Likewise, it offered concessions on these matters as well as Spain's interests in the Western Saharan fishing and phosphate industries in return for an acceptable agreement. King Hassan evidently agreed to keep quiet about Ceuta and Melilla (though not to drop his country's formal claim to them) in return for Western Sahara. Morocco and Mauritania also agreed to allow up to 800 Spanish fishing boats to fish in Western Saharan waters for 20 years, paying license fees only from the sixth year, and, with regard to minerals, it was agreed that Morocco and Spain would establish joint companies in which Spain would hold 35 percent of the capital. In the case of Fosbucraa (q.v.), the previously 100 percent Spanish-owned phosphate mining company, Morocco's Office Chérifien de Phosphates acquired 65 percent of the shares, apparently paying for them with free deliveries of

Moroccan phosphate ore for Spain's phosphoric acid plants at Huelva after mining at Bou-Craa (q.v.) ground to a halt in 1976 as a result of the guerrilla war. Despite speculation by a few observers that Spain's support in the United Nations (q.v.) for diplomatic efforts to achieve self-determination for the Saharawis in the 1980s constituted an effective repudiation of the spirit, it not the letter, of the Madrid Agreement, Spain to date has not yet published it, let alone formally renounced it.

MAHBES. About 30 miles from the Algerian frontier, in the northeastern corner of the Saguia el-Hamra (q.v.), this was the site of an important military base in the last years of the Spanish colonial period. Some Saharawi families, mainly Reguibat ech-Charg (q.v.), started to settle around the base, and in 1974, there were about 1,400 civilians living there. Spanish troops pulled out of Mahbes in October 1975, leaving it in the hands of the Polisario Front (q.v.), which used the post as an important staging area in its refugee evacuation operation after the Madrid Agreement (q.v.). The Moroccan army finally took control of Mahbes on February 14, 1976, but the isolated Moroccan garrison there later became a frequent target of the guerrillas, who finally recaptured it in a bloody battle (see MAHBES, BATTLE OF) on October 14, 1979. It remained under Polisario control until December 1984, when it was enclosed by one of Morocco's "defensive walls" (q.v.) in the territory.

MAHBES, BATTLE OF. After fierce fighting with its Moroccan defenders, the Polisario Front captured the base of Mahbes (q.v.), 30 miles from the Algerian frontier, on October 14, 1979. The battle was one of the bloodiest in the Polisario-Moroccan war, and the guerrillas' capture of the base was a serious reverse for the Moroccan army. According to a Polisario Front communiqué (October 18), 767 Moroccan troops were killed and 59 captured. The Moroccan ministry of information (October 14) admitted that 141 soldiers had been killed, almost one fifth of the entire garrison, which the ministry said had 780 men.

MAHFOUD ALI BEIBA. Of Izarguien (q.v.) ancestry, Mahfoud Ali Beiba, who is also often known as Mahfoud Laroussi, was born c. 1953, in the Mzick area, near El-Ayoun (q.v.). Though his parents seem to have settled briefly in the Tan-Tan area after the crushing of the Army of Liberation (q.v.) in 1958, he spent most of his later childhood in El-Ayoun. It was here that he met El-Ouali Mustapha Sayed (q.v.), who was to become the first secretary-general of the Polisario Front in May 1973, during his trips to Western Sahara in 1971–73. El-Ouali persuaded Mahfoud Laroussi to move to Zouerate, in Mauritania, where the nucleus of the new liberation movement was being assembled. There he became one of the movement's top leaders. At the second congress, on August 25–31, 1974, he was elected assistant secretary-general and, as such, a member of the executive committee (q.v.). He was put in charge of the political, as opposed to the military, wing of the front's work. He was one of the Polisario leaders who met the UN Visiting Mission (q.v.) members on their tour of the Saharawi camps in the Tindouf (q.v.) region of southwestern Algeria in May 1975. As the head of the political department, he played a major part in the Conference of Ain Ben Tili (q.v.), on October 12, 1975, at which a wide range of traditional Saharawi notables, fearful of the growing Moroccan threat, declared their allegiance to the front, considerably broadening its base of support. Later in the month, he was allowed by the Spanish authorities, who were then expecting to hand power eventually to the front, to enter El-Ayoun, where he held meetings with the governor-general (q.v.), Gómez de Salazar (q.v.) and organized large anti-Moroccan demonstrations on October 26 and 27. However, when Spanish commitments to Saharawi independence started to weaken under Moroccan pressure and a curfew was imposed on the Saharawi population of El-Ayoun on October 28, he left the Saharan capital.

After the Madrid Agreement (q.v.), he played a major role in the dissolution of the Djemaa on November 28 at Guelta Zemmour and in the subsequent creation of the Provisional Saharawi National Council (q.v.), the body that proclaimed the founding of the Saharan Arab Democratic Republic

(SADR) (q.v.) on February 27, 1976. A few days later, on March 4, 1976, when the first SADR council of ministers (q.v.) was appointed, Mahfoud Laroussi was named minister of the interior and justice. However, he resigned the post to assume the responsibilities of caretaker secretary-general in June 1976 after the death in action of El-Ouali Mustapha Sayed. Two months later, at the 3rd congress of the Polisario Front, Mohammed Abdelaziz was elected secretary-general and Bachir Mustapha Sayed assistant secretary-general. However, Mahfoud Ali Beiba remained a member of the top leadership body, the executive committee, whose members also became members of the Council for the Command of the Revolution (q.v.), the supreme executive organ of the SADR, under the constitution for the new republic that was adopted by the congress. In the reshuffled council of ministers, whose composition was announced after the congress, he was given responsibility for the ministry of the interior, the justice portfolio being handed to M'hamed Ould Ziou (q.v.). In these capacities, which were confirmed at the 4th congress, in September 1978, he played a key role in elaborating the front's political strategy and overseeing the organization of the Saharawi refugee population in the Tindouf region during the extremely arduous early years of the Saharawis' forced exile.

At Polisario's 5th congress (October 12–16, 1982), he was appointed prime minister of the SADR, retained his place on the front's executive committee, and also took responsibility for the ministry of information and culture, replacing Mohammed Salem Ould Salek (q.v.). He kept both portfolios until Polisario's 6th congress, in December 1985, when he relinquished both, with the premiership going for a time to Mohammed Lamine Ould Ahmed (q.v.) and the ministry of information to Ibrahim Hakim (q.v.). Mahfoud Ali Beiba, however, was reconfirmed as a member of Polisario's governing body, the executive committee. In a reshuffle of the SADR's top leadership announced on August 16, 1988, he was again named prime minister and at the same time became minister of justice (replacing Hametti Abdelaziz Rabbani) and minister of interior. Soon afterward, on January 4–5, 1989, in the company of Bachir Mustapha Sayed and Minister of Defense Ibrahim Ghali (qq.v.), he traveled to Marrakesh to meet with King Hassan II (q.v.) in the first-ever direct and mutually acknowledged talks between Morocco and the Polisario Front. Mahfoud Ali Beiba was reelected to the executive committee of the front at its 7th congress (April 28–May 1, 1989), and remained prime minister and minister of justice and interior until Polisario's 8th congress, in June 1991, when he relinquished the justice and interior posts while remaining prime minister.

MAHFOUD LAROUSSI see MAHFOUD ALI BEIBA

MAKHZANI. Also known as the Forces Auxiliaires (Auxiliary Forces), they are a paramilitary branch of the Moroccan security forces. In Western Sahara, they have taken part in the war against the Polisario Front (q.v.), alongside the FAR (q.v.). At the national level, they are administered by an inspector general in the ministry of the interior. In 1988, the Forces Auxiliaires consisted of about 30,000 men, including 5,000 in a Mobile Intervention Corps.

MAKIL see MAQIL

MALANINE OULD SADDICK. A leader of the Polisario Front (q.v.), he first became active in the Saharawi movement while a student in Morocco. He was active in the "embryonic movement for the liberation of the Sahara" (q.v.) in the early seventies and was detained by the Moroccan authorities in Casablanca in 1972 after the anti-Spanish demonstrations organized by the movement in Tan-Tan in March and May 1972. He joined the Polisario Front after its founding in May 1973. He was one of the 21 members of the political bureau elected by the front's 4th congress, in September 1978, and was the SADR's ambassador to Algeria in this period. His membership in the Polisario Front's political bureau was confirmed in subsequent years, but in June 1991 when the political bureau was abolished at the front's 8th congress, he became secretary-general at the presidency of the SADR, part of the Saharawi state's council of ministers (q.v.).

MANSOUR OULD OMAR. A leader of the Polisario Front (q.v.), he became a member of the SADR's council of ministers (qq.v.) after the SADR's founding on February 27, 1976. In the first cabinet, announced on March 4, he held the post of secretary-general of the ministry of energy and communications. He held the post until the 3rd congress of the Polisario Front, in August 1976. He was one of the 21 members elected to the front's political bureau at the 4th congress, in September 1978. At Polisario's 5th congress, held on December 7–10, 1985, he was reelected to the political bureau and appointed minister of foreign affairs, a post he held until August 18, 1988, when he was replaced by Mohammed Salem Ould Salek (q.v.).

MANZ, JOHANNES. A Swiss diplomat, he was named by United Nations Secretary-General Javier Pérez de Cuéllar (qq.v.) as the UN's second special representative for Western Sahara on January 19, 1990, replacing Hector Gros Espiell (q.v.), who had resigned at the end of 1989. Manz's brief was essentially the same as his predecessor's: to meet with and attempt to reconcile the two parties to the dispute, Morocco and the Polisario Front (q.v.); to meet with other "interested parties"; and to prepare for an interim administration to be set up in the territory prior to a referendum under UN auspices. To this end, Manz embarked on a tour of the region in February 1990 to attempt to narrow the differences that existed between Morocco and the Saharawi nationalists and in June set up a meeting in Geneva between Saharawi tribal elders from both the Moroccan-controlled areas of Western Sahara and the Polisario camps in Algeria to discuss voter eligibility for the referendum.

After achieving a relative degree of success in these and other related efforts, Manz could attend to overseeing the emplacement of the United Nations Mission for the Referendum in Western Sahara (q.v.), known as MINURSO, in 1991. Once the MINURSO administration was established, he would exercise extensive powers over issues in the territory, including verification of troop withdrawals by both sides, release of prisoners of war, voter eligibility, cease-fire violations, and the actual conduct of the plebiscite in order to ensure that the referendum was conducted "without any military or administrative constraints." However, after the arrival of the initial MINURSO personnel in Western Sahara in early September 1991, Johannes Manz confronted a situation in which Morocco refused to withdraw any of its thousands of troops from the territory, proposed to vastly increase the number of persons entitled to vote in the referendum (in the process greatly burdening MINURSO, which had to decide these eligibility questions), and often restricted the movements and activities of UN troops and administrators. By the latter part of 1991, it was apparent that the referendum would not take place in January 1992 as planned, that MINURSO's strength was far below the projected level, and that allegations of dishonesty and budgetary irregularities were being leveled against some UN personnel. In addition, MINURSO seemed powerless to prevent or sanction the constant Moroccan reconnaissance flights over Western Sahara in violation of the cease-fire. On December 19, 1991, Pérez de Cuéllar announced that Manz would resign effective January 1, 1992, reportedly out of frustration at the slow pace of the referendum effort. Manz was succeeded as special representative by Sahabzada Yaqub Khan (q.v.) effective March 23, 1992.

MAQIL (variant: *Makil*). An Arab Bedouin people of Yemeni origin, the Maqil migrated westward across North Africa, from Egypt to Libya and then, skirting along the northern edge of the Sahara desert, reached the Oued Draa (q.v.) and the Atlantic in c. 1218, thereby cutting across the traditional migratory routes of the Sanhaja (q.v.) Berbers between the Atlas mountains and the desert. They had left havoc in their path, raiding as they went and chasing away or vassalizing some of the peoples of the oases—notably the Zenata of Touat. Their soldiering abilities were sometimes harnessed, with the promise of loot, by others, notably the Beni Merin, a Zenata group that had conquered its way to power in Morocco in the 13th century, ending Almohad rule and establishing the Merinid dynasty, which ruled Morocco until the mid-15th century. It was likewise upon the Maqil that the Zayanid ruler of Tlemcen, Taghmorasan (1235–1283), depended to gain control of Sijilmassa in 1265 and hold it until its capture by the Merinids in 1274. But both Merinids and Zayanids needed to keep the pillaging Maqil tribes at bay. Taghmorasan is said, somewhat improbably, to have conducted 72 expeditions against Arab Bedouin tribes, principally a Maqil group, the Dawi Ubaid Allah. The Merinid sultans, faced with repeated attempts by the Maqil to break through the Atlas ranges into Morocco's fertile Atlantic plains, settled some Maqil tribes in northern Morocco and tried to keep out the rest by establishing military posts overlooking the main mountain passes. In 1271 and 1284, the Merinid sultan, Abu Yusuf Yaqub (1258–86), sent punitive expeditions to the Souss and the Draa to try to bring them to heel. Not surprisingly, Maqil warriors were often recruited by enemies of reigning Moroccan sultans. In 1320–22, for example, the governor of Sijilmassa, Abu Ali, used Maqil troops in an unsuccessful revolt against his father, the Merinid sultan Abu Said. The Maqil were the soldiers of another virtually independent Merinid prince in Sijilmassa in the 1360s, and they were allies of the Alawites (q.v.) during their rise to power in Morocco in the mid-17th century.

The Maqil group that left the greatest mark on the Western Sahara was the Beni Hassan, who, after arriving in the regions of the Oued Draa and the Oued Noun, fused with Berbers to give rise to the Tekna (q.v.) tribes, which came to claim *arab* caste status on account of their Maqil ancestry.

From the end of the 13th century, Beni Hassan tribes started migrating southward into the regions now known as Western Sahara and Mauritania—to escape the punitive expeditions of the Merinids or to seek new pasture lands or both. As they spread southward into the desert, over the following two centuries, they subdued or fused with the nomadic Sanhaja tribes there. Among them, for example, were the Oulad Delim (q.v.), the "purest" Arab tribe in Western Sahara today, who established themselves eventually in the southern part of the future Spanish colony. They claim descent from Delim, said to be one of the sons of Hassan, the apical ancestor of the Beni Hassan. Other tribes migrated further south, into what is now Mauritania.

There, Sanhaja resistance to the Beni Hassan culminated in a 30-year war, *Char Bouba,* in 1644–74. Led by Nacer ed-Din, a marabout (q.v.) of the Lemtouna, a large number of Sanhaja tribes, from Tiris to the River Senegal, fought against the Arabs, until, weakened by internal divisions, they submitted at Tin Yedfad in 1674. This has often been said to have consecrated the system of castes characteristic in this part of the Sahara. The victorious Beni Hassan tribes came to be known as arab or *hassan*, synonymous with "warrior." Many of the defeated Sanhaja became tributaries, or *znaga* (a corruption of Sanhaja), forced to pay the *horma* (q.v.). But this was no uniform process. Some allied or fused with the Beni Hassan, and others maintained or recuperated their social position by their devotion to religion and teaching—the *zawiya*—or, as was common in the region now known as Western Sahara, by manipulating genealogies to claim Arab, indeed *cherifian*, ancestry. Moreover, the conflicts within and between Maqil tribes, as within and between Sanhaja tribes, complicated the picture. There were great regional variations. In Adrar, for example, it was not until the 1740s that the Maqil ensured their supremacy over the Sanhaja, who, at the end of the 19th century, rose against their Maqil emir and murdered him. In this they were aided by the Idou Aich, a Sanhaja tribe that had successfully ended Maqil domination in Tagant at the end of the 18th century. In Western Sahara, Sanhaja warriors imposed a severe defeat on the Maqil in the battle of Oum Abana in c. 1696–97, and, though the Maqil Oulad Delim were to play a powerful role in this part of the desert in the 18th and 19th centuries, it was, above all, the rise of the Reguibat, a tribe of essentially Sanhaja origin, though claiming to be *chorfa*, which marked the 19th century.

As a result of these complex and varying historical processes, virtually all the tribes of Sanhaja origin in the desert regions extending from the Oued Draa to the Senegal River ended up considering themselves to be Arabs, whether as a result of alliance or fusion with the Beni Hassan or the adoption of a cherifian genealogy. All of these tribes adopted the language of the Beni Hassan, Hassaniya (q.v.), which had completely displaced the Sanhaja language by at least the 19th century.

MARABOUT. A French corruption of *murabit*. A marabout is a holy man, usually blessed with *baraka* and often associated with a Sufi order or *zawiya*.

MARRAKESH PLAN. A name commonly given to a series of agreements in 1975 on French arms sales to Morocco, which followed the sudden increase in tension in the spring of 1975 between Algeria and Morocco over Western Sahara. Morocco was becoming increasingly worried that its plans to take over Western Sahara (which had begun later in the year) would meet resistance, from Algeria as well as Saharawi nationalists, and so decided to try to speed up a rearmament program, which had been drawn up in 1974 with the aid of U.S. officials. King Hassan II (q.v.), who knew that France can often deliver arms to its clients much faster than the U.S., discussed the matter with President Valéry Giscard d'Estaing (q.v.) during his state visit to Morocco in May 1975. Then, in June 1975, a large Moroccan team attended the French arms exhibitions at Le Bourget and Satory. Soon after, the Moroccan government signed an arms agreement with the Direction des Affaires Internationales (Directorate of International Affairs) of the Délégation Ministérielle à l'Armament (Ministerial Delegation for Armaments) covering a series of individual contracts to be signed by Morocco with French arms manufacturers. According to *Le Nouvel Observateur* (Paris, No. 591, March 8–14, 1976), radar equipment was then acquired from Thompson, Milan missiles and Puma helicopters from SNIAS, 50 Mirage F-1 jets from Dassault, AMX tanks from GIAT, and light machine guns from Panhard. The magazine also claimed that unusual measures were taken by the French authorities to speed up delivery of some of this military equipment. The French ministry of defense reportedly permitted certain arms manufacturers to repaint in Moroccan colors vehicles already delivered to the French armed forces, and VAB vehicles under construction by Renault for the French armed forces were allegedly diverted to Rabat instead. As for the pilots of the Mirage F-1 jets, whose delivery did not commence until 1979, they were reportedly trained at the French air force base at Tours.

M'BAREK OULD MOHAMMED BOUNA MOKHTAR. Appointed Mauritania's minister of defense in March 1977, Col. M'Barek made little headway in fending off increasingly audacious attacks by the Polisario Front (q.v.), which was then striking deep inside Mauritanian territory, notably on May 1, 1977, when its guerrillas attacked Zouerate (q.v.), and on July 3, 1977, when Nouakchott (q.v.) was the target. After this second humiliation, he became chief of staff of the armed forces while retaining his position as minister of defense. However, he left the government on January 28, 1978, and the following month was replaced as chief of staff, becoming instead inspector general of the armed forces. He did not take part in the coup against President Mokhtar Ould Daddah (q.v.) on July 10, 1978.

MEJAT. A small tribe that lived traditionally along the northern stretch of the coast, the Mejat had little livestock, engaged in fishing, and were tributaries of the Izarguien (q.v.). They originally split away from the Mejat of the western Anti-Atlas, who arrived from the Haouz in the 16th century under Sidi Ahmed Ou Moussa. The founder of the group that settled along the northern stretch of the Saharan coast is thought to have been El-Garm, whose tomb is at Chebeika, north of Tarfaya (q.v.).

MENASIR. A once large tribe, the Menasir had become a very small group of fishing people by the 20th century. They lived primarily along the coast between the mouth of the Saguia el-Hamra and Dakhla (qq.v.). They are divided into two wings, the Oulad Mohammed Aidi and the Oulad Ali Serg.

MESFIOUI, BENHAMOU. A Rifian, he was one of the leaders of the Army of Liberation (q.v.) and the mastermind of its campaign against the Spanish and French in the Sahara in 1957–58. After taking part in the insurrection against France in the western Rif in October 1955, he was selected at a conference of leaders of the Army of Liberation in Madrid in January 1956 to take command of its operations in the south of Morocco. Though a small armed nucleus had been set up in Tiznit in 1954 by Ibrahim Namri (Ibrahim Tizniti), it was only in the spring of 1956, on the eve of Morocco's independence (March 3, 1956) that the Army of Liberation gathered strength in this region. However, its ranks were rapidly swollen by thousands of volunteers when, in accordance with an agreement between the sultan's government and France on February 11, 1956, the Moroccan auxiliaries of the French forces were relieved of their French command. Benhamou Mesfioui's forces effectively took control of much of southern Morocco, with their headquarters in Bou-Izarkan and Goulimine. After independence and the creation of the Forces Armées Royales (FAR) (q.v.) in May 1956, his men retained their autonomy and their power. They refused to join the FAR and were critical of the continued presence of French troops in postindependence Morocco. As a member of the Conseil National de la Résistance (National Council of the Resistance), Benhamou Mesfioui attended the council's first and only meeting, on August 18, 1956, which condemned the government's failure to root out the French presence in the country. In the zones under their control in the south, his men wrought vengeance on past collaborators with the French and kidnapped two French officers, Captain René Moureau (June 23, 1956) and Lt. Perrin (October 20, 1956).

Benhamou Mesfioui was also passionately committed to the extension of the liberation struggle to the rest of the Maghreb. His men began attacks on the French posts in the southern Moroccan-Algerian frontier zone in June 1956. Meanwhile, a large guerrilla force invaded the Spanish enclave of Ifni in November 1957, forcing the Spanish to withdraw a month later to a small zone around its capital, Sidi Ifni, from which they did not venture for the remaining eleven and a half years of their stay there. From mid-1956, Benhamou Mesfioui began assembling a large Saharawi guerrilla force as well, in the valley of the Oued Draa (q.v.). It began operations in February 1957, clashing first with French forces in northern Mauritania and using Western Sahara, then poorly reconnoitered by the Spanish, as a zone of transit. Attacks against the Spanish army in Western Sahara started in November 1957. However, the leadership given by Benhamou Mesfioui and his radical Moroccan comrades was challenged by many of the Saharawi guerrillas, and from December 1957, the movement was seriously weakened by internal conflict and defections. The joint Franco-Spanish counterinsurgency campaign, Operation Ouragan (q.v.), in February 1958, decimated the Army of Liberation's forces in Western Sahara, and later in the year, the FAR began to establish control over most of southern Morocco, recruiting many of Benhamou Mesfioui's former partisans. Benhamou Mesfioui was now politically isolated. Like other radical veteran leaders of the Army of Liberation, he was distrusted by the conservative Moroccan monarchy, and when treason trials started against many of them in 1961–63, he fled abroad, settling in Algeria. He later returned to Morocco, living quietly in Casablanca.

M'HAMED OULD ZIOU. M'hamed Ould Ziou first joined the anticolonial struggle as a militant of the Army of Liberation (q.v.) during its guerrilla campaign against France and Spain in 1957–58 in northern Mauritania and Western Sahara. After the movement's defeat, early in 1958, he was briefly imprisoned in Morocco, when he opposed the demobilization of the guerrilla forces and turned down an offer to become a captain in the Forces Armées Royales (q.v.). He later settled in Zouerate, Mauritania, where he is said to have established cordial relations with the Mauritanian regime, relations that later proved of considerable value when a small nucleus of anti-Spanish militants started to gather around him there in the early seventies, after the Zemla massacre in El-Ayoun (qq.v.) in June 1970. It was with M'hammed Ould Ziou and his comrades in Zouerate that El-Ouali Mustapha Sayed and Mohammed Ali Ould el-Ouali (qq.v.), two leaders of the "embryonic movement for the liberation of the Sahara," a Rabat-based group of Saharawi students, held discussions about the formation of a new anticolonial movement when they visited the city on a support-seeking mission at the end of 1972. M'hamed Ould Ziou readily backed the idea and suggested that the new group, which became the Polisario Front (q.v.) in May 1973, establish its headquarters in Zouerate. He helped to arrange for tacit support from the Mauritanian authorities. Later, after the Madrid Agreement (q.v.) in November 1975, he played a major role in organizing the Saharawi resistance to the Moroccan-Mauritanian annexation. He was elected president of the Provisional Saharawi National Council (q.v.), set up by the proclamation of Guelta Zemmour (q.v.) on November 28, 1975. It was in the name of this Saharawi ''parliament'' that he read out the proclamation of the founding of the Saharan Arab Democratic Republic at a ceremony near Bir Lehlou on February 27, 1976. He remained president of the provisional council until its replacement by a council, under the presidency of Sidi Ahmed Mohamed Mahmoud (q.v.), elected at the Polisario Front's 3rd congress, in August 1976. After the congress, he was appointed to the SADR's council of ministers (q.v.), receiving the justice portfolio, a post he retained after the 4th congress of the front, in September 1978, as well as at Polisario's 5th congress, on October 12–16, 1982. However, at the 6th congress, in December 1985, he was replaced as minister of justice by Hametti Abdelaziz Rabbani, and he left the front's executive committee and political bureau (qq.v.).

MINERALS. Since 1972, Western Sahara has been one of the world's largest exporters of phosphates (q.v.). Production, under the auspices of Fosbucraa (Fosfatos de Bu-Craa) (q.v.), has been at Bou-Craa (q.v.), where deposits are officially estimated at 1.7 billion tons; exports reached 2.6 million tons in 1975. Exports would have gradually expanded to 5 million tons a year had production not ground to a halt in 1976 as a result of the war between Morocco and the Polisario Front (q.v.). However, mining was resumed on a modest scale in 1982. An estimated 72 million tons of iron ore (q.v.) have been found, but not yet exploited, at Agracha. Besides iron (57.3 percent), the ore there contains titanium oxide (13.6 percent), a major component of paint, and vanadium (0.4–0.6 percent), a strategic metal used in the aerospace industry. Iron ore may also exist in the northeast (part of the Tindouf depressions, which includes the huge deposits at Gara Djebilet in southwestern Algeria) and in the center, where an aeromagnetic study revealed 46 possible sites in 1965. The existence of radioactive materials was announced in 1956; uranium oxide is normally associated with phosphates. Other minerals whose existence has been confirmed include tungsten, platinum, gold, chrome, tin, beryl, manganese, and corindum. Hornblende, a mixture of calcium, magnesium, and iron silicates, exists in 67 percent concentrations in the southeast, where there is also known to be copper, nickel, kyanite, epidote, staurolite, hyperstene, ilmenite, magnetite, and rutile as well as such precious and semiprecious stones as garnets, tourmalines, and zircons. Besides phosphates, however, none of Western Sahara's mineral wealth has yet been exploited.

MINURSO see UNITED NATIONS MISSION FOR THE REFERENDUM IN WESTERN SAHARA

MITTERRAND, FRANCOIS. Born in 1916 and a veteran socialist politician, François Mitterrand was elected president of France in 1981. Before that time, while he was in opposition, he had been critical of many aspects of the foreign policy of his predecessor, Valéry Giscard d'Estaing (q.v.), including Giscard's strong support for Morocco during and after the takeover of Western Sahara. When Mitterrand triumphed in the French presidential elections and assumed office in May 1981, many observers expected a substantial change in France's policy on Western Sahara. Many socialist deputies were openly in sympathy with the Polisario Front (q.v.), favored French recognition of the SADR (q.v.), and wanted France to halt all arms sales to Rabat. But French strategic interests, which had traditionally involved close ties with the Moroccan monarchy, continued to override whatever sympathies Mitterrand and other French socialists may have had for the Saharawis. French weapons sales continued through the 1980s, and Paris remained, along with the United States, Morocco's main source of arms. Joint military maneuvers were held with Morocco in November 1982, after a visit by the king to Paris the previous January. The French socialist government did, however, soon announce that Polisario would be allowed to open an office in Paris, and direct contacts were initiated for the first time between the front and the French government. In addition, Mitterrand attached more importance than Giscard to relations with Algeria. He visited Algiers on November 30–December 1, 1981, and thereafter concluded several major economic agreements, notably regarding French purchases of Algerian natural gas. This paved the way for a short visit by Algerian President Chadli Benjedid (q.v.) to Paris on December 17, 1982, the first such visit by an Algerian leader since that country's independence. A full state visit followed about a year later. Although all of this was generally pleasing to Polisario and its supporters, the fact remained that France was still trying to delicately balance its relations with both Algiers and Rabat. President Mitterrand continued this balancing act through the 1980s.

MOHA, EDOUARD. Pseudonym of Bachir Figuigui, the leader of the Mouvement de Résistance "Les Hommes Bleus" (q.v.).

MOHAMMED V. Sultan of Morocco from 1927, during the Franco-Spanish protectorate, he supported the irredentist demands of the Moroccan nationalists after his country's independence in 1956 but did his best to control and eventually disband the irregulars of the Army of Liberation (q.v.) who launched attacks from southern Morocco against the Spanish in Western Sahara and Ifni and against the French in northern Mauritania and southwestern Algeria in 1957–58. During the last decade of the Franco-Spanish protectorate, he was closely allied to the Moroccan independence movement and was punished with banishment to Madagascar by the French in 1953–55. After Morocco's independence, however, his aim was to consolidate monarchical power at the expense of the nationalist Istiqlal Party (q.v.) and such allied forces as the trade unions and the Army of Liberation. Ironically, he was not displeased to see the latter move its focus of activity after independence to the far south of Morocco and the Sahara, far away from Morocco's main populated centers, where a new regular army, the Forces Armées Royales (q.v.), was created, with French aid, from the Moroccan troops of the French and Spanish armies. The kidnapping of some of the remaining French officials in southern Morocco in 1956–57 was a cause of embarrassment for Mohammed V, who changed his title to king in 1957, but he could claim, justifiably, that he did not control most of the area south of Agadir. He certainly gave no active support to the Army of Liberation's guerrilla campaign in Ifni and the Sahara. Indeed, he was almost certainly appreciative of the successful Franco-Spanish counterinsurgency campaign, Operation Ouragan (q.v.), which, in February 1958, decimated the guerrilla forces in Western Sahara. The operation, which he never publicly criticized, decisively weakened a radical movement that had potentially threatened the security of his own regime. In 1958–59, his army gradually disbanded, disarmed, and in certain cases absorbed the remnants of the guerrilla movement. However, Mohammed V did endorse the Greater Morocco (q.v.) ideology of the Istiqlalian leader, Allal el-Fassi (q.v.), both because it was popular among Moroccans and because it played up the historic role of the monarchy. Perhaps he also overestimated the degree of popular support in Mauritania for the Moroccan claim to Mauritania as a result of the arrival in Morocco in this period of such Mauritanian opposition leaders as Horma Ould Babana, once Mauritania's deputy in the French National Assembly. In 1957, he set up the Direction des Affaires Sahariennes et Frontalières (q.v.), and on February 25, 1958, he formally spelled out his kingdom's claim to Western Sahara and Mauritania in a famous speech in the little oasis town of M'hamed on the edge of the Sahara. "We will continue to do everything in our power to recover our Sahara and all that which, by historical evidence and by the will of its inhabitants, belongs as of right to our kingdom." He died in 1961, to be succeeded by Hassan II (q.v.).

MOHAMMED ABDELAZIZ. A longtime leader of the Polisario Front (q.v.), Mohammed Abdelaziz was educated in Moroccan primary and secondary schools, in Bou-Izakarn, Casablanca, and Rabat, having settled with his parents in Tan-Tan at the time of the 1957–58 uprising against Spain and France in Western Sahara and northern Mauritania by the Saharawi wing of the Army of Liberation (q.v.). A Reguibi (q.v.), of the Foqra group, he became a supporter of the "embryonic movement for the liberation of the Sahara'' (q.v.) in the early seventies in Rabat. Along with other members of the movement, he participated in the founding of the Polisario Front in May 1973, becoming one of the front's main military leaders during the guerrilla war against Spain. It was after the death in action in Mauritania of the front's first secretary-general, El-Ouali Mustapha Sayed (q.v.), in June 1976, that Mohammed Abdelaziz emerged as the movement's most important leader. Though the assistant secretary-general at the time, Mahfoud Ali Beiba, assumed the temporary leadership of the movement, Mohammed Abdelaziz was elected secretary-general at the front's 3rd congress, held on August 26–30, 1976. As such, he was also one of the nine members of the front's top leadership body, the executive committee (q.v.), and, under the new constitution of the Saharan Arab Democratic Republic (SADR) (q.v.), which was adopted by the congress, he became president of the Council for the Command of the Revolution (CCR) (q.v.), the supreme executive organ of the SADR. At the Polisario Front's 4th congress, in September 1978, he was reelected secretary-general of the front and president of the CCR. In these leading positions, he has played a major role in the formulation of both military and diplomatic strategy. He took part in several stages of the protracted peace negotiations with Mauritania that began after the July 1978 Nouakchott coup and culminated in the Algiers Agreement (q.v.) of August 5, 1979. He represented the Polisario Front at the talks held in Freetown, Sierra Leone, on September 9–12, 1980, between the parties to the Western Saharan conflict and mediation committee of African heads of state designated by the OAU (q.v.).

At Polisario's 5th congress (October 12–16, 1982), article 13 of the SADR constitution was amended to give Mohammed Abdelaziz the position of president of the SADR. He remained secretary-general of Polisario, and his influence was further enhanced by the abolition of the post of deputy secretary-general. That post's incumbent, Bachir Mustapha Sayed (q.v.), however, was given other duties, which conformed his overall position as a senior leader of the front. As the de jure head of state, Mohammed Abdelaziz played a central role in the OAU summit conferences in 1982–84, which would finally settle the question of SADR membership. Significantly, he served a term as an OAU vice president in 1985–86. His position as president of the SADR has been reaffirmed at each of the subsequent congresses of the front, most recently at Polisario's 8th congress, held on June 18–20, 1991.

MOHAMMED ALI OULD EL-OUALI see OMAR HADRAMI

MOHAMMED CHEIKNA OULD LAGHDAF. A prominent Mauritanian businessman, he was appointed foreign minister by the Comité Militaire de Redressement National (CMRN) (q.v.) which came to power in a military coup on July 10, 1978. While foreign minister, he tried to extract Mauritania from its ruinous involvement in the Western Sahara conflict. Contacts were made with the Polisario Front (q.v.), which unilaterally declared a cease-fire with Mauritania two days after the coup, but no conclusive peace agreement was reached with the guerrillas, essentially because the CMRN hoped at this stage to encourage all the parties to the conflict, including Morocco, to work out a global settlement. There was probably strong pressure from France against a unilateral settlement with the Polisario Front. He gave up the foreign affairs portfolio on January 16, 1979, to take up the post of minister in the premier's office, and on March 6, 1979, he left the government.

MOHAMMED KHOUNA OULD HEYDALLAH. Born at Port Etienne (Nouadhibou) into a Saharawi tribe—the Arosien (q.v.)—in 1940, he joined the Mauritanian army in 1962 and later was both one of the senior Mauritanian commanders during the war against the Polisario Front (q.v.) and the prime minister of the government that finally, in 1979, extracted Mauritania from its ruinous involvement in the Western Saharan conflict. He was military commander in Zouerate (q.v.) when the Polisario Front (q.v.) fought its way into this crucial iron-mining city and captured six French citizens there on May 1, 1977. After this debacle, he was transferred to the 5th military region (Nema) in the extreme southeast of Mauritania. Disillusioned by the war, he became one of the members of the Comité Militaire de Redressement National (q.v.), which deposed President Mokhtar Ould Daddah (q.v.) on July 10, 1978. Immediately after the coup, he was appointed chief of staff of the armed forces. He later became a member of the Comité Militaire de Salut National (CMSN) (q.v.) after the palace coup led by Ahmed Ould Bouceif (q.v.), on April 4, 1979. He joined the latter's cabinet as minister of defense. On May 31, 1979, he was appointed prime minister after Ahmed Ould Bouceif's death in an air crash. He retained the defense portfolio. He was determined to negotiate a definitive end to Mauritania's involvement in the Western Saharan conflict, though he did not proceed immediately toward a unilateral peace agreement with the Polisario Front, probably out of fear of Morocco's possible reactions to such a move. Frustrated by Mohammed Khouna Ould Heydallah's delays and hesitations, the Polisario Front announced on July 12, 1979, that it was ending the cease-fire it had proclaimed exactly a year earlier vis-à-vis Mauritania. Its guerrillas immediately attacked the small settlement of Tichla in the Mauritanian sector of Western Sahara, Tiris el-Gharbia (q.v.). This had a salutary effect. On July 30, Ould Heydallah said that Mauritania had no claim to Tiris el-Gharbia and wanted to reopen talks with the Polisario Front. The negotiations began almost immediately, and on August 5, his government finally made peace with the guerrillas, with the signing of the Algiers Agreement (q.v.), by which Mauritania dropped its claim to Western Saharan territory. Ould Heydallah's government then withdrew its troops from Tiris el-Gharbia, which Morocco unlaterally annexed on August 14.

Ould Heydallah kept a contingent of Mauritanian troops, however, in the Western Saharan settlement of La Guera (q.v.) to keep Moroccan forces away from the nearby Mauritanian town of Nouadhibou. Relations with Morocco were thereafter very tense. Ould Heydallah eventually forced the last Moroccan troops to leave Mauritania (from a base at Bir Moghrein) toward the end of 1979. After this, Morocco often claimed that his government was allowing the Polisario guerrillas to establish bases in northern Mauritania, but Ould Heydallah repeatedly denied this. In January 1980, he suc-

ceeded in removing the (titular) president, Lt. Col. Mohammed Mahmoud Ould Louly (q.v.), and so become head of
state while keeping his previous positions as premier and
defense minister.

On March 16, 1981, Ould Heydallah's government was
challenged by a coup attempt, which he claimed had the
logistical backing of Morocco. Rabat denied complicity. The
plotters were immediately arrested, tried, and executed.
Relations between Morocco and Mauritania fell to a new
low. Diplomatic ties were severed and were not resumed
until three years later after a change of regime in Nouakchott.
Ould Heydallah's government thereafter assumed an increasingly pro-Polisario stance, although it kept reiterating
its protestations of neutrality. Ould Heydallah threw his
weight behind the attempts of the Organization of African
Unity (OAU) (q.v.) to resolve the conflict by means of a
referendum, an endeavor that foundered upon Morocco's
refusal to negotiate directly with the Polisario Front.

Mauritania came under Moroccan pressure periodically,
as evidenced by the shelling, on January 20, 1983, of the
Western Saharan settlement of La Guera, which was still
occupied by Mauritanian forces. Ould Heydallah moved
closer to Algeria, and on December 13, 1983, Mauritania
became a signatory to a "treaty of fraternity and concord"
signed by Tunisia the previous March. Also in the latter half
of 1983, Ould Heydallah threatened several times to formally recognize the Saharan Arab Democratic Republic
(q.v.) if Morocco continued to refuse to implement OAU
resolution 104, adopted in June 1983, which called for a
cease-fire, direct Morocco-Polisario negotiations, and a referendum of self-determination. He finally carried out his
threat: on February 27, 1984, Mauritania recognized the
Saharawi state.

Internally, Ould Heydallah's regime was being undermined by the combined effects of the Saharan war (which
continued to necessitate a massive defense expenditure),
drought and desertification, a prolonged economic crisis,
divisions between the dominant Arabic-speaking Beydanes
and black African groups, and chronic factionalism within
the armed forces. Additional problems presented themselves,

too: controversy over the persistence of slavery in parts of the country despite its abolition in 1980, and the influence of foreign Arab states, especially Libya and Iraq, over rival factions within Mauritania. Confronted by all these pressures, Ould Heydallah oscillated between accommodating and imprisoning opponents. In addition, reports of mismanagement and corruption became commonplace. There was opposition from some members of the CMSN to Ould Heydallah's recognition of the SADR, which some believed could tilt Mauritania into direct involvement in the Saharan war once again, with calamitous consequences. Within the CMSN, Ould Heydallah was also seen as demonstrating an inordinate degree of independence and unpredictability. On December 12, 1984, he was deposed as president while attending a Franco-African summit meeting in Burundi. The army chief of staff, Col. Maaouiya Ould Sid 'Ahmed Taya (q.v.), became the new president. Despite his ouster, Ould Heydallah chose to return to Nouakchott and was placed under house arrest in a military barracks. Although there were suggestions that he would be placed on trial for corruption, this did not occur. He remained in detention until December 1988, when he was released.

MOHAMMED LAMINE OULD AHMED. Born in the late 1940s, Mohammed Lamine Ould Ahmed became one of the top leaders of the Polisario Front (q.v.) and, after the creation of the Saharan Arab Democratic Republic (SADR) (q.v.) in February 1976, became its prime minister. He was born into a small tribe of *chorfa,* the Taoubalt (q.v.), and in c. 1956, his father was one of the first to settle in Tan-Tan, setting up shop there as a tailor. Mohammed Lamine himself was staying further south when the Army of Liberation (q.v.) began its war against the Spanish in Western Sahara and the French in Mauritania in 1957, but in September 1957, he was evacuated by an Army of Liberation convoy that took several hundred children to Morocco. Mohammed Lamine was taken to Tafraout, where he entered primary school. After completing his primary education there and at Tarfaya, he received secondary schooling at Bou-Izakarn and Taroundant, where, between 1965 and 1967, one of his classmates was El-Ouali Mustapha Sayed (q.v.), who was later to become the Polisario Front's first secretary-general. The two pupils formed a solid friendship and began to develop a common commitment to the anticolonial cause during their days in Taroudant. In 1969, Mohammed Lamine moved to Rabat, entering the lycée to which El-Ouali had transferred in 1967. After passing the baccalaureate exams, he entered the law faculty of Mohammed V University in Rabat, along with El-Ouali, at the end of 1970. During the previous summer, however, he had traveled south to Western Sahara to take stock of what had happened in the massacre of Zemla (q.v.), on June 17, 1970. At the university, he joined with other Saharawi students in a network of discussion groups that evolved into the "embryonic movement for the liberation of the Sahara" (q.v.) in 1971–72. During summer vacation in 1971, he traveled with El-Ouali and Mohammed Salem Ould Salek (q.v.), at the group's bidding, to Western Sahara to sound out the political situation there. The following year he was active in the group's attempts to organize support among the large Saharawi population of southern Morocco, taking part in anti-Spanish demonstrations in Tan-Tan in March and May. He was arrested by the Moroccan police on both occasions, spending several days in jail in Agadir after the May demonstrations. Toward the end of 1972, he was off on another exploratory mission to Western Sahara, this time with Mohammed Ali Ould El-Ouali, returning to Morocco to report to his Saharawi student comrades.

After graduating with a law degree in June 1973, he left Morocco to settle in Zouerate, where the initial nucleus of the Polisario Front (which had been formally founded the previous May) had been assembled. He then became a central leader of the group. In 1974–75, he was head of the front's foreign relations committee. Later, after the start of the war with Morocco and Mauritania and the creation of the SADR, he was appointed president of the SADR's council of ministers (q.v.), i.e., premier of the SADR government, on March 4, 1976. At the 3rd congress of the Polisario Front, held on August 26–30, 1976, he was one of nine members elected to the front's top leadership body, the executive committee, and thus also to the SADR's supreme executive organ, the Council for the Command of the Revolution (q.v.). He was reelected by the 4th congress, held in September 1978. As a member of these leadership bodies and as premier, he played a key role in setting the political, diplomatic, and military orientation of the movement in the course of the guerrilla war. He remained premier of the SADR until Polisario's 5th congress (October 12–16, 1982), when he relinquished the office to Mahfoud Ali Beiba (q.v.) and became minister of education. Despite taking this less prominent portfolio, he retained his seat on the front's executive committee. Three years later, at the 6th congress, held in December 1985, he was reappointed prime minister of the SADR. In another governmental change announced on August 16, 1988, however, he was again replaced as premier by Mahfoud Ali Beiba. He was then appointed minister of health, a post he held until 1989.

MOHAMMED LAMINE OULD BOUHALI. A leader of the Polisario Front (q.v.), he was elected to the movement's executive committee (q.v.) and thus automatically to the SADR's Council for the Command of the Revolution (qq.v.) at the front's 4th congress, in September 1978. With a primarily military background, he continued to sit on the SADR's highest policy-making body, being reelected to the executive committee at the 5th congress (October 1982) and 6th congress (December 1985). At Polisario's 7th congress, held in April–May 1989, he was elevated to the SADR's highest military position, minister of defense, replacing Ibrahim Ghali Ould Mustapha (q.v.), who had held the defense portfolio since the founding of the Saharawi state, in February 1976. Ould Bouhali continued to hold that post after the front's 8th congress, held on June 18–20, 1991.

MOHAMMED MAHMOUD OULD AHMED LOULY. President of Mauritania when his country finally signed a peace agreement with the Polisario Front in 1979, he was born in Tidjikja in 1943 and joined the Mauritanian army in 1960. After the outbreak of war with the Polisario guerrillas in 1975, he played a major part in the fighting but, like many other Mauritanian officers, became convinced that the war was ruining his impoverished country. He supported the military coup that deposed President Mokhtar Ould Daddah (q.v.) on July 10, 1978, becoming a member of the new Comité Militaire de Redressement National (CMRN) (q.v.). On January 16, 1979, he was appointed minister in charge of the permanent secretariat of the CMRN and then, on March 21, 1979, minister of the civil service and higher, technical, and vocational education. When Ahmed Ould Bouceif's Comité Militaire de Salut National (CMSN) (qq.v.) staged a palace coup on April 6, 1979, he became a member of the CMSN and minister of general employment. Then, after the resignation of Col. Mustapha Ould Mohammed Salek (q.v.) from the presidency on June 3, 1979, he became president, but with the truncated powers to which his predecessor had been reduced as a result of Ahmed Ould Bouceif's accession to the premiership the previous April. During his term of office, when real power was in the hands of his premier, Mohammed Khouna Ould Heydallah (q.v.), who had succeeded Ahmed Ould Bouceif after his death on May 27, negotiations proceeded with the Polisario Front, culminating in the signing of the Algiers Agreement (q.v.) on August 5, 1979, by which Mauritania formally dropped its claim to Western Saharan territory. He was replaced in the presidency by his powerful prime minister, Ould Heydallah, on January 4, 1980.

MOHAMMED OULD BAH OULD ABDEL KADER. A senior officer in Mauritania's minuscule air force, he played a major part in the war against the Polisario Front (q.v.). He had strong affections for Morocco and was not one of the officers who deposed President Mokhtar Ould Daddah (q.v.) on July 10, 1978, setting up the Comité Militaire de Redressement National (CMRN) (q.v.). He did not become a member of the CMRN, though he was appointed minister of culture, information, and communications on March 21, 1979. Two weeks later, on April 6, 1979, he emerged as a leading member of the new Comité Militaire de Salut National (CMSN) (q.v.), which, under the leadership of Ahmed Ould Bouceif (q.v.), stripped the president, Mustapha Ould Mohammed Salek (q.v.), of most of his powers. He became a member of the CMSN and the minister responsible for the CMSN in Ahmed Ould Bouceif's cabinet. However, after the latter's fatal air crash on May 31, 1979, and his succession by Mohammed Khouna Ould Heydallah (q.v.), he suddenly lost political influence. Demoted to the post of minister of education, he fled to Morocco on June 17, 1979. There he declared himself the leader of a "free officers movement" and later became a supporter of the Alliance for a Democratic Mauritania, an opposition group in exile. He strongly condemned the August 5, 1979, Algiers Agreement (q.v.), by which the Mauritanian government finally came to terms with the Polisario guerrillas by dropping its claim to Western Saharan territory, and he urged a return to the old alliance with Morocco. On March 16, 1981, he attempted unsuccessfully to overthrow the Mauritanian government in a coup that President Ould Heydallah blamed on Morocco. He was captured and on March 26, was shot by a firing squad.

MOHAMMED OULD SAAD BOU. A founding member of the Polisario Front (q.v.), he was one of the seven participants in its very first guerrilla raid, against a Spanish post at El-Khanga (q.v.) on May 20, 1973. He was killed in February 1977 during the war with Morocco and Mauritania.

MOHAMMED OULD SIDATI. Also known as Mohammed Ma el-Ainin, he was a leader of the Polisario Front (q.v.). A member of the prestigious Ahel Ma el-Ainin and a grandson of Ahmed el-Hiba (qq.v.), one of the most prominent anti-colonial leaders of the early 20th century, he was born in c. 1950. Like many Saharawis of his generation, he settled as a child in southern Morocco after the crushing of the Army of Liberation (q.v.) in 1958. After attending Moroccan primary and secondary schools, he was admitted to Mohammed V University in Rabat, where he became active in a circle of about 40 Saharawi students known as the "embryonic movement for the liberation of the Sahara" (q.v.) in 1971–72. Along with El-Ouali Mustapha Sayed (q.v.), he maintained close relations at this time with the Moroccan Parti de Libération et du Socialisme (q.v.). Meanwhile, in March

1972, he was one of several Saharawi students arrested briefly in Tan-Tan (q.v.) during an anti-Spanish demonstration held there without the authorization of the Moroccan government. After graduating from Mohammed V University with a *licence* in economics, he went to France, where he began work on a doctorate at Grenoble University. However, as the storm clouds gathered over Western Sahara in the summer of 1975, he left for Algeria, where he became an important leader of the Polisario Front. His activity thereafter was primarily in the diplomatic field. Going under the name Aini Sayed, he was the front's representative in Paris in 1977–78 during the tense period when the French air force sent Jaguar bombers to strafe the guerrillas in Mauritania. Later, on October 9, 1978, he was appointed to the council of ministers of the Saharan Arab Democratic Republic (qq.v.) as minister of the presidency of the council, i.e., minister in the office of the premier, Mohammed Lamine Ould Ahmed (q.v.). Ould Sidati remained in this post after Polisario's 5th congress, in October 1982, and continued his energetic diplomacy on behalf of the SADR. At the 6th congress (December 7–10, 1985), he was dropped from this position, but he was elected to the political bureau (q.v.) and promptly took up residence in Paris as the front's principal representative in Europe. On September 24, 1988, he was appointed foreign minister of the SADR, replacing Mohammed Salem Ould Salek (q.v.). He was confirmed as foreign minister at Polisario's 7th congress (April–May 1989). In this position, he traveled widely and often, building support for the SADR and engaging in talks at the United Nations (q.v.) on a peaceful settlement of the Saharan conflict. At the Polisario Front's 8th congress, held in June 1991, however, he was appointed minister of information, the foreign affairs portfolio again going to Mohammed Salem Ould Salek.

MOHAMMED SALEM OULD SALEK. One of the leaders of the Polisario Front (q.v.), he was born in c. 1950, in the coastal region between El-Ayoun and Tarfaya (qq.v.), where his parents, Oulad Tidrarin (q.v.), were nomads at the time. In the late fifties, after the crushing of the Army of Liberation (q.v.) and the cession by Spain of the northern part of its desert territory to Morocco in 1958, his parents settled, semidestitute, in Tarfaya. With financial aid from the Moroccan government, he completed primary school and then went on to the Lycée Ben Youssef in Marrakesh, where one of his fellow pupils was El-Ouali Mustapha Sayed (q.v.), who was later to become the first secretary-general of the Polisario Front. However, family relatives had also settled in Western Sahara itself. One of his brothers was working in El-Ayoun at the time. So, in the mid-sixties, he moved to El-Ayoun, where he took three more years of secondary education. Returning to Morocco, he completed the baccalaureate at the Lycée Ben Youssef in Marrakesh and then enrolled in 1970 in the political science department at Mohammed V University in Rabat, where he was nicknamed Franco by fellow students because of his fluency in Spanish. It was there that he joined the group of 40 or so Saharawi students from which evolved the "embryonic movement for the liberation of the Sahara" (q.v.) in 1971–72, under the inspiration of El-Ouali Mustapha Sayed, then also a student at the same university. During the 1971 summer vacation, he returned to El-Ayoun with El-Ouali and Mohammed Lamine Ould Ahmed (q.v.) on a mission decided upon by the Rabat student group to sound out the situation there. They met participants in the then-defunct MLS (q.v.) and members of the Djemaa (q.v.) and returned full of enthusiasm for the launching of a new liberation movement. After graduating from Mohammed V University with a *licence* in political science in the summer of 1973, a few weeks after the founding of the Polisario Front in Mauritania, he went to Paris, where he started work on a doctorate and sought to popularize the Saharawi liberation cause among political groups. A year later he returned to Morocco, where he married, and then, at the end of 1974, he left for Algiers, where he became one of the main leaders of the Polisario Front. After the proclamation of the Saharan Arab Democratic Republic (SADR) (q.v.), in February 1976, he was appointed a member of the SADR's first council of ministers (q.v.), with the title of secretary-general of the ministry of information, on March 4, 1976. His position was upgraded to that of minister of information on October 9, 1978. In that ministerial post, he was responsible for, and successful in, gaining sympathetic coverage for Polisario's cause in the foreign press, and hundreds of journalists were taken on tours of the Tindouf refugee camps (qq.v.) and the "liberated territories" of the Saharawi state. Ould Salek held the information portfolio until the front's 5th congress, in October 1982. At that time, he left the council of ministers and was appointed head of Polisario's external relations committee. He remained a member of the political bureau. At the front's 6th congress, held on December 7–10, 1985, he rejoined the council of ministers, becoming secretary-general at the presidency, and at the same time left the political bureau. He continued his extensive and far-ranging diplomatic activities, among them, secretly meeting with a Moroccan delegation in July 1988 in Taif, Saudi Arabia, although without discernible results. In August 1988, Ould Salek was restored to the political bureau and named foreign minister of the SADR. However, a month later (September 24, 1988) he left the foreign ministry and became minister of information once again after a hiatus of six years, replacing Omar Hadrami (q.v.). At the front's 7th congress, held from April 28 to May 1, 1989, he was moved again, leaving the information ministry to become head of the Latin America department of Polisario's external relations committee, residing in Caracas, Venezuela. He remained a member of the political bureau. He stayed in this diplomatic position until December 3, 1989, when he returned to Tindouf to become minister of education, a post he held until June 1991, when he was again named foreign minister in the critical run-up to the activation of MINURSO, the United Nations Mission for the Referendum in Western Sahara (q.v.).

MOHAMMED SIDI IBRAHIM BASSIRI. The leader of the first modern anticolonial movement in Western Sahara, the Harakat Tahrir Saguia el-Hamra wa Oued ed-Dahab (Movement for the Liberation of Saguia el-Hamra and Oued ed-Dahab, or MLS), Mohammed Bassiri was born in c. 1942–44 in the vicinity of Tan-Tan, then (and until its cession to Morocco in 1958) under Spanish rule. A Reguibi, he was a member of the Lemouedenin, a subtribe of the Reguibat es-Sahel (qq.v.). During the 1957–58 Saharawi uprising led by the

Army of Liberation (q.v.), he was one of many Saharawi children evacuated from the war zone and given a school place in Morocco. In October 1957, he started attending school in Casablanca. He did well, passing the baccalaureate and then leaving Morocco for the Middle East, where he studied at the Universities of Cairo and Damascus, finally graduating with a diploma in journalism. He was, in fact, one of the first in a new generation of educated Saharawis who were strongly influenced by the nationalist movements of the Third World. When he returned to Morocco from Syria in 1966, he founded a journal, *Al-Chihab* (q.v.), which combined radical political analyses and articles on Saharawi culture. A year later, he moved to Western Sahara, where he managed to persuade the Spanish authorities to grant him a residence permit and started to teach the Koran in the mosque at Smara (q.v.). It was in December 1967 that he started to form the nucleus of what was to become the MLS. Though at first he had few contacts and little influence, he slowly gathered supporters, partly as a result of his work as a Koranic teacher.

By the spring of 1970, the movement had attracted considerable support, mainly from better-educated and employed Saharawis in the small towns. Though loosely structured, the MLS was becoming the country's first modern political party, with the goal of achieving independence after an intermediate stage of internal autonomy. It also wanted to reform Saharawi society and challenge the authority of the conservative and generally pro-Spanish *chioukh* (q.v.). Bassiri has been said to have favored the maintenance of clandestinity, to avoid repression, but in the spring of 1970, he went along with a majority decision to hold a demonstration and present a petition to the colonial authorities on June 17, 1970. "The situation is dangerous, very dangerous," he noted in his last letter, written on June 16, on the eve of the demonstration, which was held in Zemla, a Saharawi suburb of El-Ayoun (q.v.). Indeed it was. The rally was broken up by the Foreign Legion (q.v.), and several demonstrators were killed (see ZEMLA, MASSACRE OF). Scores of Saharawis were arrested, and at 3 a.m. on June 18, Bassiri himself was seized. He was, wrote the *delegado gubernativo* (q.v.) of the northern region, López Huertas, in a report dated June 23, a "classic agitator." What happened to him remains a mystery. According to the Spanish authorities, he was deported from Western Sahara to Morocco on June 29. The Moroccan government has since claimed to have no knowledge of his return to Morocco, and both Moroccan and Saharawi observers have suspected that he was murdered by his Spanish jailers. The riddle of his disappearance was brought five years later to the attention of a UN Visiting Mission (q.v.), which toured the country in May 1975—both by supporters of the Polisario Front (q.v.), who, the mission's report stated, "regarded him as a hero of the liberation movement," and by three of Bassiri's brothers, whom the mission members met in Tan-Tan during their ensuing visit to Morocco. The Spanish authorities in El-Ayoun, however, restated to the mission that he had been deported to Morocco.

MOKHTAR OULD DADDAH. Born in 1924 at Boutilimit, Mokhtar Ould Daddah was Mauritania's head of state from its independence in 1960 until, as a result of his disastrous alliance with Morocco over Western Sahara, which dragged his country into an unwinnable and costly involvement in the war with the Polisario Front (q.v.), he was overthrown by disillusioned war-weary army officers in July 1978.

Ironically, he had fiercely contested Morocco's claim to Western Sahara, advancing a rival claim on behalf of his own country, until 1974. He had first spelled out this claim in a famous "Greater Mauritania" speech in Atar on July 1, 1957, shortly after his selection as vice president of a new government council (May 1957) established by France after the 1956 *loi-cadre,* which established internal self-government in France's African colonies. "Henceforth, an increasingly strong tie of solidarity unites all the Mauritanians who are conscious of belonging to a single community from the Atlantic to the Sudan," he proclaimed. "But this solidarity goes beyond our frontiers; it encompasses the Moorish populations of Spanish Sahara and the borders of Morocco." Addressing himself to "our brothers of Spanish Sahara," he went on: "I cannot help evoking the innumerable ties which unite us: we bear the same names, we speak the same language, we conserve the same noble traditions, we honor the same religious leaders, graze our herds on the same pastures, give water to them at the same wells. In a word we are referring to that same desert civilization of which we are so justly proud. So I invite our brothers of Spanish Sahara to dream of this great economic and spiritual Mauritania. . ..'' This was not just a counterclaim to Morocco's claim to Western Sahara. It was a reaction to Morocco's claim to Mauritania itself. If Mauritania had the right to existence, Ould Daddah believed, then it was logical that the Hassaniya-speaking peoples of Western Sahara and even the extreme south of Morocco should become part of independent-to-be Mauritania. By contrast, if Morocco had a valid claim to Western Sahara, the identical premises of its claim to Mauritania could not be rebuffed. The idea that Western Sahara itself might develop a specific national identity and proceed eventually to independence was never conceived to be a serious possibility at the time. The immediate objective of the Atar speech was to appeal to the tribes of both Western Sahara and northern Mauritania to halt their support for the Army of Liberation (q.v.), a Moroccan-led guerrilla movement that initiated a large-scale insurrection against both the French and the Spanish in the Sahara in 1957. It was thus in the name of Moorish unity that Ould Daddah, with the support of the French colonial authorities, attempted to undermine support for a radical and uncompromisingly anticolonial movement that alarmed the French, because it threatened to destabilize Ould Daddah's loyalist regime.

Though the Army of Liberation was crushed by the Franco-Spanish Operation Ouragan (q.v.) in February 1958 and its remnants were then disarmed by the Moroccan government, Morocco officially asserted its claim to Mauritania when it was granted formal independence by France in 1960. Morocco tried to prevent Mauritania's admission to the United Nations (q.v.) and harbored a number of prominent exiled Mauritanian oppositionists. Thus, it was once again to defend its own right to existence as an independent government that the Ould Daddah regime countered the

Moroccan claim to Western Sahara during the 1960s with its own claim to the territory, notably at the United Nations, where the General Assembly started to debate the Western Saharan problem in 1965. It was not until 1969 that a new period of détente opened between Morocco and Mauritania. Aware, after nine years of independence, that Mauritania was unlikely ever to be annexed by Morocco, King Hassan II (q.v.) decided to break the ice by inviting Ould Daddah to the Islamic summit held in Morocco in September 1969. A few months later, on June 8, 1970, the two countries signed a treaty of friendship by which Morocco formally recognized Mauritania. After the signing of the treaty in Fez, a joint communiqué was published stating that Ould Daddah and King Hassan had "examined the situation in the Sahara under Spanish domination and have decided to collaborate closely to hasten the liberation of this territory in accordance with the pertinent resolutions of the United Nations." During the ensuing four years, Ould Daddah, like King Hassan, formally endorsed UN policy on Western Sahara, which hinged on the principle of self-determination. This principle was explicitly endorsed by Ould Daddah, along with King Hassan and President Boumedienne of Algeria, at two tripartite summits, at Nouadhibou on September 14, 1970, and at Agadir on July 23–24, 1973 (qq.v.). But, despite this facade of unity, both King Hassan and Ould Daddah maintained their distinct claims to Western Sahara. Ould Daddah did not renounce the Mauritanian claim to the territory in gratitude for Morocco's recognition of Mauritania.

But, despite his formal claim to Western Sahara, Ould Daddah did nothing to cause alarm to the Spanish in 1960s and early 1970s. Their presence in Western Sahara really provided a convenient buffer between Morocco and Mauritania, and Ould Daddah maintained very friendly relations with the Spanish government, visiting Madrid in 1971 and 1973. Paradoxically, however, it was again to keep Morocco at bay that Ould Daddah gave some support to the Polisario Front in 1973–74, though his anxiety to maintain warm relations with Spain meant that the support was limited and at times withdrawn, most notably in October 1973 when the Mauritanian authorities arrested six Polisario guerrillas who were detaining members of a Spanish army patrol ambushed on September 30. The guerrillas' POWs were handed back to Spain.

When the tension between Morocco and Spain over Western Sahara's future began to mount in the summer of 1974, Ould Daddah reacted to Morocco's wide-ranging diplomatic offensive by launching his own countercampaign to assert Mauritania's claim. This caused great embarrassment to Morocco, for the Ould Daddah regime had acquired considerable prestige in the Third World. In September 1974, Morocco first broached the idea of a joint approach to the International Court of Justice (ICJ) (q.v.) and (regardless of the ICJ's conclusions) an eventual partition of the territory between Morocco and Mauritania. Ould Daddah readily agreed to King Hassan's proposition when he arrived in Rabat for the Arab League (q.v.) summit of October 26–27, 1974. Thereafter, he coordinated his policy closely with King Hassan, who promised substantial economic aid to Mauritania when Ould Daddah visited Morocco again on December 9–10, 1974. At the ICJ in 1975, Ould Daddah's representatives claimed historic sovereignty over the south of Western Sahara, while admitting Moroccan rights in the north. In June 1975, he received El-Ouali Mustapha Sayed (q.v.), the secretary-general of the Polisario Front, for a two-hour discussion in Nouakchott, turning down the guerrilla leader's offer to federate Western Sahara with Mauritania under the presidency of Ould Daddah and resist jointly the Moroccan bid to annex the territory. Later, on November 10, 1975, in Bechar, Algeria, he met President Boumedienne to persuade the Algerian leader, an old friend who had done much to bring Mauritania and Morocco together in 1969, to give his support to a tripartite Spanish-Moroccan-Mauritanian agreement on Western Sahara, the broad brush strokes of which were already being worked out in Madrid. Instead, Boumedienne warned him that Algeria would support the Polisario guerillas in a war that would be ruinous to Mauritania. Four days later, on November 14, his government signed the Madrid Agreement (q.v.), by which Spain set up a tripartite administration (q.v.) in the territory until its final withdrawal in February 1976. Ould Daddah appointed a Mauritanian deputy governor, and between December 1975 and February 1976, Mauritanian troops occupied the main towns and settlements in the south of the territory. Later, on April 14, 1976, Ould Daddah visited Rabat for the signing of the Morrocan-Mauritanian convention, which formally partitioned the territory, Mauritania receiving a virtually resourceless slab of desert in the extreme south, Tiris el-Gharbia (q.v.).

Why did Ould Daddah switch his Western Saharan policy so dramatically in 1974–75 and end up engulfed in the war with the Polisario Front? It seems certain that he assumed that Morocco's diplomatic-military blitzkrieg at this time was unassailable—and he judged rightly insofar as Spain did finally submit to the Moroccan pressure, which reached a climax with the Green March (q.v.). He thought that it was better to join the winning side, get a small part of the spoils, and cement his hard-won friendship with Morocco than to watch a once-more hostile Morocco extend its border right up to Mauritania's existing borders within striking distance of the vital iron ore mines of Zouerate (on which Mauritania then depended for some 85 percent of its exports), the key port of Nouadhibou, and the long railway which links them. But Ould Daddah made a fatal misjudgment. He underestimated the determination of the Polisario Front, and, despite the personal warning he received from Boumedienne, he did not appreciate the scale of support that Algeria would give the guerrillas. By joining Morocco in the occupation and partition of Western Sahara, he plunged his country into a war that was unpopular at home, militarily unwinnable, diplomatically indefensible to most of his Third World allies, and disastrous for Mauritania's fragile, drought-hit economy. With an army totaling only about 2,000 men at the start of the war (and rapidly expanded to some 20,000 by 1978), the Ould Daddah regime could not possibly prevent the guerrillas from counterattacking into Mauritania's 420,000 sq. mi. of largely desert territory. The guerrillas had some stunning successes, most notably in June 1976 and July 1977 when they succeeded in shelling Nouakchott and in May 1977 when they fought their way into Zouerate (qq.v.). After signing a defense pact with Morocco in May

1977, Ould Daddah suffered the humiliation of seeing 9,000 Moroccan troops arrive in his country to ensure its defense against the guerrillas, while France sent military advisers and eventually, in December 1977, its air force to help stem the guerrilla threat. Meanwhile, the economy was being undermined. The constant guerrilla attacks on the Zouerate-Nouadhibou railway (q.v.) interrupted iron ore exports, which fell to 8.4 million tons in 1977 compared to 11.7 million tons in 1974, and, whereas the country had had a slight trade surplus in 1973, imports were double exports by 1977. By mid-1978, Mauritania's public external debt was over $700 million, equivalent to about 150 percent of its GNP.

As the scale of the disaster came to be appreciated, almost the whole Mauritanian elite—military officers, businessmen, technocrats, and politicians—realized the urgency of restoring peace. On July 10, 1978, Ould Daddah was deposed in a bloodless coup by the Comité Militaire de Redressement National (q.v.) led by Col. Mustapha Ould Mohammed Salek (q.v.), who immediately promised to extract Mauritania from the conflict.

Ould Daddah was then detained for one and a half years, mainly at Oualata. He was freed in August 1979 and allowed to go into exile in France in October 1979. In November 1980, he was condemned in absentia to life imprisonment with hard labor for "high treason, violation of the constitution, and attack on the economic interests of the nation." He later took up residence in Tunisia and, on December 21, 1984, shortly after the accession to power of Col. Maaouiya Ould Sid 'Ahmed Taya (q.v.), was amnestied by the new Mauritanian leader along with many other political prisoners and persons under sentence in exile.

MOROCCAN-MAURITANIAN CONVENTIONS OF APRIL 14, 1976. Signed in the presence of King Hassan II and President Mokhtar Ould Daddah (q.v.) in Fez, these conventions partitioned Western Sahara and committed Morocco and Mauritania to cooperation in exploiting its minerals and fish resources. Article 1 of the partition convention stated that "the frontier between the two countries shall be drawn by a straight line from the intersection of the 24th parallel north and the Atlantic coast to the intersection of the 23rd parallel north and the 13th meridian west, the intersection of this straight line with the present frontier of the Islamic Republic of Mauritania constituting the southeast limit of the frontier of the Kingdom of Morocco.'' From there the new Moroccan-Mauritanian border went due north, following the border between Mauritania and Spanish Sahara until the Algerian frontier. The partition increased the land area of Morocco from 458,000 sq. km. to 635,000 sq. km. Its Atlantic coastline was increased by 600 km. Morocco received the capital, El-Ayoun; the second-largest city, Smara; and, most important of all, the phosphate mines of Bou-Craa (q.v.). By contrast, Mauritania's share was a virtually resourceless slab of desert in the extreme south, though it did include the third city, Dakhla (q.v.). Mauritania's land area was increased from 1,030,000 sq. km. to 1,120,000 sq. km., and its coastline was extended by 460 km. In the second convention, the two countries promised to cooperate in the exploitation of Western Sahara's economic resources. Article 1 stated that Mauritania would be able to take a share in the capital of Fosbucraa (q.v.), the company exploiting the phosphates at Bou-Craa, in which Morocco's Office Chérifien de Phosphates had already taken a 65 percent share, leaving Spain's Instituto Nacional de Industria (q.v.) with 35 percent. This pledge to Mauritania was never honored. Articles 2 and 3, which projected the formation of joint companies to prospect for minerals and engage in fishing, were also never implemented.

MOROCCAN-MAURITANIAN DEFENSE COMMITTEE. Set up under a defense pact signed on May 13, 1977, after the humiliating Polisario (q.v.) attack on Zouerate (q.v.) on May 1, this committee met almost monthly until the overthrow of President Mokhtar Ould Daddah (q.v.), on July 10, 1978. It virtually merged the two countries' high commands under Moroccan control and coordinated the dispatch of thousands of Moroccan troops to Mauritania to shore up its defenses against the audacious attacks deep inside its territory by the Polisario guerrillas. Moroccan troops had remained since

January 1976 in what became the Mauritanian sector of Western Sahara, but in July 1977, 600 troops landed for the first time inside Mauritania's pre-1976 borders, to bolster the defenses of Zouerate. By the end of the year, there were some 6,000 Moroccan troops in the country, reinforcing the Mauritanian garrisons in Zouerate, Atar, Bir Moghrein, Ain Ben Tili, Nouadhibou (where Moroccan F5 jets were also based), and Akjoujt (only 250 km. from the capital) as well as along the Zouerate-Nouadhibou railway (q.v.). However, despite the arrival of these Moroccan troops in addition to assistance at times of the French air force, the Mauritanian army was unable to clear the guerrillas out of Mauritania and eventually decided to prepare the way for a peace settlement by overthrowing the Ould Daddah regime. By that time, Moroccan troop strength in Mauritania had reached 9,000. They were gradually withdrawn, but the last Moroccan troops did not leave the country until several weeks after the Algiers Agreement (q.v.) of August 5, 1979, by which Mauritania formally ended its conflict with the Polisario Front and dropped its claim to parts of Western Sahara.

MOUVEMENT DE RESISTANCE "LES HOMMES BLEUS" (Resistance Movement "the Blue Men"). Also known variously as the Mouvement de Résistance pour la Libération des Terres sous Domination Espagnole and the Mouvement Révolutionnaire des Hommes Bleus, MOREHOB was founded in July 1972 in the Moroccan capital, Rabat, its colorful name coming from the common tourist description of the Saharawis as "blue men" because of their indigo-dyed robes. The group, which remained very small, led a checkered career, moving in turn from Morocco to Algeria, then to Europe and eventually back to Morocco between 1973 and 1975, when it finally died. Initially, it was vehemently pro-Moroccan. In its first public communiqué, issued in July 1972 in Rabat, it declared that its goal was to "lead a struggle against Spanish colonialism," in both Western Sahara and the Spanish-occupied enclaves of Ceuta and Melilla on the Moroccan Mediterranean coast, "to attain their liberty and allow at the same time their return to the mother country." To achieve its goal of "liberation of the occupied Moroccan territories,'' MOREHOB declared that it would carry on its struggle "parallel to the wise policy carried out by the government of the mother country.'' Explicitly royalist, it took as its slogan the official Moroccan motto, "God, Country and King.'' Formed in Morocco at a time when Saharawi students there had already set up a radical activist group called the "embryonic movement for the liberation of the Sahara'' (q.v.), which was later to evolve into the Polisario Front (q.v.), MOREHOB said that "all infiltration for hostile ideological ends will be circumscribed'' and that the group would link up with the resistance groups inside Western Sahara "on the sole condition that the latter are not against the fundamental principles of national unity.''

MOREHOB's president, Bachir Figuigui, who took the curious (because Christian) pseudonym of Edouard Moha, was widely accused, not only by Saharawi radicals but also by Moroccan left-wingers who supported the Moroccan claim to Western Sahara, of being a police agent because he had served once in the Moroccan police in the city of Benguerir.

However, Moha suddenly left Morocco in March 1973 and set up a new MOREHOB headquarters in Algiers. In a communiqué published on March 5, he stated that he "refused categorically'' to play the role of a "fifth column'' for the benefit of the Moroccan authorities. The communiqué warned "public opinion against the maneuvers to enslave the movement for the liberation of areas under Spanish domination.'' The real reasons for Moha's departure from Morocco remain shrouded in mystery. He may have been angered by the lack of practical support he had received from the Moroccan government and the main Moroccan political parties and gone to Algiers in the hope of receiving more concrete aid there. A more Machiavellian interpretation, favored in Polisario circles, is that he was actually sent to Algiers by the Moroccan regime to counter the attempts then being made by El-Ouali Mustapha Sayed (q.v.) to gain Algerian support. Whatever the truth, Moha's success in persuading the Algerian government to allow him to set up an office in Algiers did mean that the government of

President Houari Boumedienne (q.v.) initially refused to support the group led by El-Ouali, which set up the Polisario Front in May 1973. While in Algeria, MOREHOB dropped all references to the Moroccan claim to Western Sahara and came out in favor of self-determination and independence in line with the classic UN and OAU (qq.v.) doctrine on decolonization favored by its new Algerian hosts. However, after the desertion of his only two collaborators in Algiers, a conflict with another foreign political group based there, the Movement for the Self-Determination and Independence of the Canary Archipelago (MPAIAC), and rumors of financial dishonesty, Moha was forced to leave Algeria in August or September 1973. He settled in Brussels, where he spent most of the following year. MOREHOB had left the Algerian authorities with the impression that the Saharawi liberation movement was small, divided, and immature, and so Algeria continued to withhold even minimal support from the Polisario Front until the summer of 1974.

Little was heard of MOREHOB during Moha's stay in Europe, though the Polisario Front accused him of visiting Spain in 1974. Then, in January 1975, he reappeared as a supporter of Morocco's claim to Western Sahara. In a memorandum sent that month to the International Court of Justice (q.v.), which had just been requested by the UN to give an advisory opinion on the precolonial political status of Western Sahara, MOREHOB recognized "the arguments advanced by the Kingdom of Morocco regarding its legitimacy over the territory composed by the so-called Spanish Sahara as well-founded and irrefutable." On July 28, 1975, MOREHOB cosigned with the Front de Libération et de l'Unité (q.v.) a letter to the OAU, the UN, and the Arab League (q.v.), which protested alleged Algerian interference in the Western Saharan question.

There is no evidence that MOREHOB ever engaged in political or military activity within Western Sahara itself. The UN Visiting Mission (q.v.), which toured the territory extensively and then visited all three of its neighbors in May 1975, noted that "the Spanish authorities and the political movements encountered within the territory consider that MOREHOB does not have many members and point to the fact that there is no evidence of its having engaged in armed activities within the territory.'' Though they interviewed Moha during their visit to Morocco, the mission members stated in their report that they ''did not encounter any other members or supporters of MOREHOB either in the territory or elsewhere.'' The Moroccan government, which created another ''Saharan liberation movement,'' the FLU, in 1975, evidently did not take Moha and MOREHOB seriously, though Moha's pronouncements in favor of the Moroccan claim to Western Sahara were publicized in the Moroccan press and put to use in the government's attempts to win international support. After the Madrid Agreement (q.v.) and Morocco's annexation of the territory, no more was heard of MOREHOB. Moha remained in Morocco, however, living in Rabat with his wife, Farida, a journalist on the staff of the pro-government daily, *Al-Maghrib,* and secretary to Ahmed Osman (q.v.), prime minister between 1977 and 1979. Moha formed a new group, the Association des Originaires du Sahara Anciennement sous Domination Espagnole (q.v.), adopting for the purpose a new pseudonym, Ahmed Ould Rachid.

MOUVEMENT DE RESISTANCE POUR LA LIBERATION DES TERRES SOUS DOMINATION ESPAGNOLE see MOUVEMENT DE RESISTANCE ''LES HOMMES BLEUS''

MOUVEMENT NATIONAL DEMOCRATIQUE. A Mauritanian opposition front, the National Democratic Movement gave political support to the Polisario Front (q.v.) in 1973–75. The movement grew up in 1968 among left-wing students and workers and was particularly strong in Zouerate and Nouadhibou, cities with large Saharawi populations. It was closely associated with a strike by workers in the Zouerate iron industry in 1968 in which several workers were shot dead by the army. Its opposition to the regime of Mokhtar Ould Daddah (q.v.), its strong anticolonial line, and the involvement of a considerable number of Saharawis in its ranks encouraged the movement to lend support to the Polisario Front when it was operating mainly from northern

Mauritania in 1973–74. However, nationalist economic measures taken by the Ould Daddah regime in 1973–75 prompted
the majority of the MND leadership to enter the ruling PPM
(q.v.) at its 4th congress in August 1975 and to vote for the
pro-annexation resolution on Western Sahara adopted at it. A
Marxist minority remained outside the PPM, however, and
opposed the ensuing war with the Polisario Front.

MOUVEMENT REVOLUTIONNAIRE DES HOMMES
BLEUS see MOUVEMENT DE RESISTANCE "LES
HOMMES BLEUS"

MOVEMENT FOR THE LIBERATION OF THE SAHARA see
HARAKAT TAHRIR SAGUIA EL-HAMRA WA OUED
ED-DAHAB

MURABIT see MARABOUT

MUSTAPHA OULD MOHAMMED SALEK. Born in 1936 at
Kiffa, he joined the Mauritanian army in 1961 and, after
playing a major role in the war against the Polisario Front
(q.v.), was the leader of the Comité Militaire de Redressement National (CMRN) (q.v.), which overthrew President
Mokhtar Ould Daddah (q.v.) on July 10, 1978, opening the
way to the ending of Mauritania's ruinous involvement in
the Western Saharan war. During the war with the Polisario
guerrillas, he took part in the defense of the Mauritanian
capital, Nouakchott, at the time of the audacious Polisario
attack there in June 1976. Later, on July 15, 1977, he was
appointed commander of the 3rd military region, which
included the cities of Akjoujt, Atar, Ouadane, and Chinguetti. Then, on February 20, 1978, he was appointed chief
of staff of the armed forces. However, he became convinced
of Mauritania's need to extract itself from the war, which he
saw as inherently unwinnable and a terrible drain of resources. So, on July 10, 1978, he deposed President Mokhtar
Ould Daddah in a bloodless coup, becoming president of the
CMRN. His first pledge to the Mauritanian people was to
restore peace. He was given an initial vote of confidence by
the Polisario guerrillas, who unilaterally declared a cease-

fire in Mauritanian territory two days after his seizure of power. However, the search for a definitive peace settlement was to prove much more difficult. He did not want to antagonize Morocco, which had 9,000 troops in Mauritania, and he was under considerable pressure from France also not to make a unilateral peace settlement with the Polisario guerrillas. He hoped that the mere fact of his coup would prompt the other parties, too, to look for a settlement. He was prepared to abandon Mauritania's claim to Tiris el-Gharbia (q.v.) if Morocco and the Polisario Front were prepared to accept the creation of a Saharawi "ministate" there. But this bid for a global peace settlement, which apparently had French backing, was not accepted by the Polisario Front. A series of meetings between Polisario and CMRN representatives in Libya in August 1978, Paris on September 9–16, 1978, Bamako, Mali, on October 17–18, 1978, and Tripoli on October 18, 1978, came to naught, and King Hassan II (q.v.) warned on August 20, 1978, that he would not accept the creation of a Polisario state on Morocco's southern border, probably because he doubted that the Saharawi nationalists could be persuaded to halt their struggle for the independence of the rest of the territory if they were given Tiris el-Gharbia by Mauritania. The Polisario Front got increasingly irritated by Mustapha Ould Mohammed Salek's failure to arrive at a unilateral peace agreement, and it was probably to avert the threat of the guerrillas' ending their cease-fire that he announced in January 1979 that all remaining Moroccan troops, then numbering about 7,000, would be withdrawn from Mauritania by the end of March. However, Moroccan troops were still in Mauritania when the deadline passed. The president seemed unsure of how to proceed over the Western Saharan problem, while tension was rising at home between the Moors and the blacks and his CMRN was being torn by factional infighting. It was in these circumstances that Ahmed Ould Bouceif (q.v.) led a bloodless palace coup, replacing the CMRN with a new Comité Militaire de Salut National (q.v.) and reducing the presidency to a purely titular position. Mustapha Ould Mohammed Salek remained president, stripped of all real power, until June 30, 1979, when he resigned.

- N -

NATIONALITY LAW. This was one of the important set of *normas* (regulations) approved by the Djemaa (q.v.) in a session held on November 19–22, 1974, and then promulgated as law by the Spanish governor-general (q.v.) on December 18, 1974. It set criteria for the issuing of identity cards and was also seen at the time as a preparatory step for the holding of the referendum on the territory's future, which Spain had promised the previous August. The referendum was never held because of Moroccan objections. The nationality law was denounced by the Polisario Front (q.v.) on the grounds that a significant number of Spaniards might receive Saharan nationality and hence be enfranchised at the same time that many Saharawis living abroad as refugees (q.v.) might be refused nationality. Under the law, nationality was conferred on all persons born of Saharan fathers or mothers and persons born in the territory of parents of foreign nationality who were also born in the territory and resident in it at the time of birth. The law also provided, however, that a non-Saharan (e.g., a Spaniard) could be granted Saharan nationality on the recommendation of the appropriate commission of the Djemaa if the applicant had resided in the territory for at least five consecutive years prior to the application, or for three years if the applicant had made a significant contribution to the territory by virtue of having introduced an important industry or by being director of a major agricultural, industrial, or trading enterprise.

NATURAL GAS. Natural gas was discovered in the 1960s at Oudeiat Oum Rekba. However, it has not been exploited.

NOMAD FRACTION see FRACCION NOMADA and FAKHD

NOMAD TROOPS see TROPAS NOMADAS

NOMADISM. The people of Western Sahara were entirely nomadic until the colonial era, there being no significant oases or other centers of settlement, with the limited exception of Smara (q.v.), a city built at the end of the 19th century but never really more than a religious-military base of operations for people of essentially nomadic ways. The nomads' economy was hinged on trading, raiding, and, above all, herding. Their livestock consisted primarily of camels and goats. The camel was a vital ingredient in the nomads' struggle for survival. Its huge stomach (up to 245 liters) allows it to survive for prolonged periods without drinking, while the abundant lactation of the females provides the main food source for the nomads. Its ability to cover enormous distances (at least 60 km. a day when in good health) allows it to take maximum advantage of the limited and dispersed pastures in the desert. Its ability to carry loads of up to 120–150 kg. made it an excellent pack animal, both for the nomads' regular displacements and for use in the trading caravans, and its speed and resilience in covering long distances made it well suited to the military requirements of the *ghazzi* (q.v.). Unlike some nomadic peoples, the Saharawis did not make fixed or regular seasonal migrations, though they tended to concentrate around wells or *gueltas* (q.v.) in the hot and arid summer months while taking advantage of the more abundant pastures after the occasional rains of the autumn. Their way of life involved a constant battle for survival. The slightest misjudgment with respect to the location of pastures or water resources could lead to death. In these conditions, the Saharawis had a highly developed sense of orientation, a remarkable ability to distinguish and recall the most minute details of landscape, great knowledge of the stars, and excellent eyesight. Nonetheless, it is not surprising that the majority of nomads abandoned their harsh way of life in the 1960s and early 1970s—partly because droughts decimated their herds but also because of the growth of employment and relief opportunities in the small developing towns (see SEDENTATION).

NONALIGNED MOVEMENT. Most Third World countries have been favorable to the Polisario Front (q.v.) during its war with Morocco and (briefly) Mauritania. The main principle for which it has been fighting, the right of self-determination, is one held dear by most Third World countries, and its considerable military success and consistent diplomatic lobbying (much aided by Algeria) have made its cause a prominent one in Third World politics. Recently, the 9th summit conference of the movement, held in August 1989 in Belgrade, Yugoslavia, resolved to support the efforts of the United Nations and the Organization of African Unity (qq.v.) to settle the conflict by means of a referendum in the territory, stressing its members' belief "that full and open cooperation by the parties concerned with the secretary-general of the United Nations and the chairman of the OAU in their further efforts is essential for a just and definitive settlement.''

NOUADHIBOU SUMMIT CONFERENCE (SEPTEMBER 14, 1970). A summit meeting between King Hassan II of Morocco, President Houari Boumedienne of Algeria, and President Mokhtar Ould Daddah of Mauritania (qq.v.) in the Mauritanian city of Nouadhibou, it was held to discuss regional matters and notably the situation in Western Sahara, where Spanish troops had killed a number of Arab demonstrators in El-Ayoun (q.v.) a few weeks earlier, on June 17 (see ZEMLA, MASSACRE OF). After a one-and-a-half-hour meeting, the three heads of state issued a communiqué stating, ''After a thorough study of the situation prevailing in the Sahara under Spanish domination, they decided to intensify their close cooperation in order to hasten the decolonization of this region in compliance with the relevant United Nations resolutions. For this purpose, a Tripartite Coordinating Committee was set up to follow the process of decolonization in the territory in both the political and diplomatic fields.''

The summit symbolized a new spirit of détente between Morocco and its Maghrebian neighbors, following closely on the heels of the Treaty of Ifrane, signed on January 15, 1969, by which Morocco and Algeria declared their intent to resolve their long-simmering border dispute, and the Moroccan-Mauritanian Treaty of Friendship and Cooperation of June 8, 1970, by which Morocco finally recognized Mauritania ten years after its independence. These agreements with Algeria and Morocco, by which King Hassan buried the

"Greater Morocco" (q.v.) claims to Mauritania and parts of the Algerian Sahara, were bitterly denounced by the ultranationalists of the Istiqlal Party (q.v.), which likewise had harsh words for the Nouadhibou summit. "It appears that the Nouadhibou summit has not resolved any problem, let alone that of Saguia el-Hamra (q.v.), this incontestably Moroccan territory which the whole people demands," stated the party's daily, *L'Opinion,* on September 16, 1970. The Istiqlal Party had reason to be alarmed. No mention was made in the Nouadhibou communiqué of the traditional Moroccan claim to Western Sahara. Indeed, King Hassan had penned his signature to a declaration of support for the resolutions of the UN (q.v.) on the decolonization of the territory, and these spoke of self-determination through a referendum. If the king had hoped that his renunciation of the Moroccan claims to Mauritania and the Algerian Sahara would be rewarded by a tacit Algerian-Mauritanian acceptance of Morocco's "rights" in Western Sahara, he was disappointed. "We want these territories to become free and independent and even to enjoy the benefits of independence and sovereignty," said Algeria's foreign minister, Abdelaziz Bouteflika (q.v.), right after the summit. "That does not mean that we are leaning toward one solution any more than toward another." Very probably, King Hassan believed that a majority of Western Saharans would have opted to join Morocco if a UN-supervised referendum had been held at this time and that therefore there was nothing to lose by embracing the established UN doctrine and combining with Algeria and Mauritania to put up a common front.

In fact, however, this common front existed only in name. The tripartite coordinating committee projected by the Nouadhibou summit met only twice, on January 4–5, 1972, in Algiers, and on May 8–9, 1973, in Nouakchott. The Agadir summit conference (q.v.) of July 23–24, 1973, brought the three heads of state together again to discuss Western Sahara among other regional matters. But nothing came out of these meetings beyond a repetition of the Nouadhibou summit's call for decolonization in accordance with the UN resolutions on the territory. It was not until 1974, and then ironically to prevent Spain from carrying out its belated decision to implement the repeated UN resolutions and hold a referendum, that King Hassan began to turn his attention seriously to the Western Sahara question. His unilateral decision then to break off the tripartite coordination of policy that had started in Nouadhibou in September 1970 and to advance the Moroccan territorial claim in opposition to the UN decolonization strategy to which he had given his support at the Nouadhibou and Agadir summits naturally aroused great anger from Algeria, as well as the Polisario Front (q.v.).

NOUAKCHOTT RAIDS. In two of its most daring attacks against Mauritania, the Polisario Front (q.v.) sent guerrilla forces across 1,500 km. of desert to attack the Mauritanian capital, Nouakchott, in June 1976 and July 1977. In the first of these epic raids, reminiscent of the old *ghazzis* (q.v.), the secretary-general of the front, El-Ouali Mustapha Sayed (q.v.), lost his life. A force of several hundred guerrillas set out for Nouakchott, in a column of Land Rovers and Berliet trucks, after a meeting of the front's executive committee (q.v.) on June 2, 1976, the last to be chaired by El-Ouali. There were few Mauritanian troops in Nouakchott at the time: most of the country's minuscule army was far to the north, under two commands—G1 (Group One), led by Col. Viah Ould Mayouf (q.v.), based at Aoussert (q.v.), in the Mauritanian sector of Western Sahara, and G2 (Group 2), led by Lt. Col. Ahmed Ould Bouceif (q.v.), based in the mining center of Zouerate. However, on June 5, a Mauritanian pilot, flying an ancient Defender, spotted a concentration of Polisario vehicles near Tourine, to the east of Zouerate. Alerted, Bouceif sent his deputy, Commandant Mohammed Khouna Ould Heydallah (q.v.), to attack them. To his stupefaction, Heydallah learned from prisoners captured in the ensuing fighting that the Polisario *katibas* (q.v.) at Tourine were merely a backup group for a much larger force that was already heading for Nouakchott. Meanwhile other katibas were being sent toward Zouerate, Atar, Chinguetti, Ouadane, and even Tichit in the southeast of Mauritania to divert attention from the main raid on the capital. The prisoners' revelations were not at first taken seriously in Nouakchott, where President Mokhtar Ould Daddah saw no reason to postpone a state visit to the Cape Verde Islands, from which he returned on June 7, the eve of the attack. On June 6, however, the Mauritanian general staff started to take the threat of an attack more seriously when a private French pilot, flying toward Nouakchott, spotted a powerful military column in the region of Touyema, 80 km. west of Atar. The next day, Bouceif set out from Zouerate with 400 men to race to Nouakchott, arriving at Akjoujt, almost 30 km. from the capital, by 4 a.m. on June 8. By then, Viah, too, was en route for Nouakchott from Aoussert, and Lt. Col. Ahmed Salem was bringing up some troops from Rosso in the south. The Polisario forces, meanwhile, had reached Oum Tounsi, 80 km. from the capital, by the evening of June 7. From there, a small group of Land Rovers set off early in the morning to the northern outskirts of the capital, which they began shelling at 9 a.m. After 30 minutes, they retreated, but later, after sunset, at 10 p.m., they returned, firing, with great accuracy, into the compounds of the West German and Soviet embassies and the presidential palace for about 15 minutes, before disappearing once again, into the night. However, the next morning, as the main column, which had spent the day of the attack near Oum Tounsi, started its long retreat to the north, the Mauritanian units arriving under the command of Bouceif, Viah, and Ahmed Salem began to close in. At a place near Benichab, where Polisario planned to blow up the water installations that serve Akjoujt, a part of the guerrilla column, which included El-Ouali, was cornered by an armored squadron under the command of one of Bouceif's deputies, Lt. Ney Ould Bah. After a half-hour shoot-out, the Mauritanian troops found the corpse of the Polisario secretary-general, who had been shot through the head. The main part of the Polisario force continued their retreat, however, toward Tourine, oblivious of the Mauri- tanian attack on the relief force there on June 5. Viah's troops were waiting for them and opened fire on the first Polisario Land Rovers arriving for the appointed rendezvous. The rest of the Polisario column headed on to the northeast, finally reaching a relief force at El-Mreiti.

The second Polisario attack on Nouakchott, staged for

maximum effect in the middle of a summit conference of the OAU (q.v.) in Libreville, was a much greater success. A force of some 45 Land Rovers, accompanied part of the way by some trucks, traveled, night and day for almost a week, from bases near Amgala, in Saguia el-Hamra (q.v.), via Bir Enzaren and Aoussert (qq.v.), to the very edge of Nouak-chott, where they lobbed mortar shells into the grounds of the presidential palace for 45 minutes on the evening of July 3, 1977. Under cover of night, the column then retreated northward, first driving up the main highway to within 35 km. of Akjoujt, and then travelling across the desert, via Tmeimichatt and Agouenit, where there was a brief clash with Mauritanian troops, Oum Dreiga and Guelta Zemmour, to the Polisario bases near Amgala.

- O -

OHOUD FORCE. In November 1979, a force of some 6,000 Moroccan troops, which had been assembled in September in Benguerir, 50 km. from Marrakesh, was led across the desert by Col. Maj. Ahmed Dlimi (q.v.), the chief of staff of the Forces Armées Royales (q.v.), to bolster the defenses of Dakhla (q.v.), the capital of the formerly Mauritanian sector of Western Sahara, to which the Mauritanian government had renounced its claim under the Algiers Agreement (q.v.) of August 5, 1979, and which Morocco had unilaterally annexed on August 14. The force joined the Moroccan troops that had been posted to the city under the May 13, 1977, Moroccan-Mauritanian defense pact. It was one of the largest forces assembled by the Moroccan regime during its war with the Polisario Front. Rolling south in an armada of some 1,500 vehicles, with U.S.-supplied M-113 armored troop carriers, Franco-Austrian SK-105 tanks, and Romanian-supplied Stalin Organs, Dlimi's men took some three weeks to make the journey, 20 miles abreast, to Dakhla. The Polisario guerrillas made no attempt to intercept the column, apparently undisconcerted by King Hassan's (q.v.) decision to send 6,000 of his best-equipped troops to the far south of Western Sahara, far from Polisario's favored zone of operations at the time, in Saguia el-Hamra (q.v.) and southern Morocco. The force was named after a battle in the third year of the Hegira (625 A.D.) between the forces of the prophet Mohammed, then in exile in Medina, and the pagan Meccans. The core of the Ohoud force was constituted by the 8th Infantry Regiment, under the command of Col. Harchi. Its troops, who were mainly Rifians and Ait Oussa (q.v.), were later withdrawn from Dakhla to join another large, newly assembled force, code-named Zellagha (q.v.), in southern Morocco for a disastrous campaign in the Ouarkziz Mountains (q.v.), known as Operation Iman (q.v.), an attempt to relieve a Polisario siege of Zaag (q.v.), in March 1980.

OIL see PETROLEUM

OMAR HADRAMI. The pseudonym of Mohammed Ali Ould El-Ouali, he was for many years one of the foremost leaders of the Polisario Front (q.v.). A Reguibi (q.v.) of the Sellam fraction, he was born in c. 1947 in the Goulimine area of southern Morocco, where his parents, who were of modest means, had settled. His father served for many years in the Forces Auxiliaires after Morocco's independence. After completing primary school and the first stage of his secondary education at Bou-Izakarn, Mohammed Ali went on to a lycée in Agadir, where he passed the baccalaureate exams. He then gained admission in 1969 as a student in the faculty of letters at Mohammed V University in Rabat, where he became a close friend of other future leaders of the Polisario Front, including El-Ouali Mustapha Sayed and Mohammed Lamine Ould Ahmed (qq.v.). With these and other Saharawi students in Rabat, he took an active part in the "embryonic movement for the liberation of the Sahara" (q.v.), the informal grouping of Saharawi students in Morocco that began in 1971–72 to lay the groundwork for the creation of a new Saharawi liberation movement. At the end of 1972, he was selected by the group to travel, with Mohammed Lamine Ould Ahmed, on an exploratory political mission to Western Sahara and Zouerate, Mauritania, where he was joined by El-Ouali Mustapha Sayed at the end of another mission via Tindouf (q.v.). These missions played an important role in assembling the initial nucleus that was to found the Polisario Front in May 1973, and, though Mohammed Ali returned to Rabat after his travels to El-Ayoun (q.v.) and Zouerate and was not present at the front's founding conference, he left Morocco in the summer of 1973 to join the Polisario nucleus in Zouerate. There he became one of the movement's central leaders. At the 2nd congress, held on August 25–31, 1974, he was elected to the executive committee (q.v.), and in May 1975, he was one of the Polisario leaders who met the members of the UN Visiting Mission (q.v.), which toured the Saharawi camps in the Tindouf region after its fact-finding visit to Western Sahara. After the proclamation of the founding of the Saharan Arab Democratic Republic (SADR) (q.v.), on February 27, 1976, he was appointed secretary-general of the ministry of finance, trade, and supplies in the first SADR council of ministers (q.v.). After El-Ouali's death in action, in June 1976, he switched portfolios, becoming minister of the interior and justice, a post he kept until the holding of the front's 3rd congress a few weeks later, on August 26–30, 1976. At the congress, he was reelected to Polisario's executive committee and thus, in accordance with the SADR constitution adopted at this time, also became a member of the SADR's supreme executive body, the Council for the Command of the Revolution (CCR) (q.v.). His membership in the front's executive committee and the SADR's CCR was confirmed at the 4th congress, held in September 1978. He played a major part in the elaboration of the movement's political, military, and diplomatic strategy and was its chief negotiator in the talks with Claude Chayet, a French foreign ministry official, in Algiers on November 3–17 and November 16–19, 1977, on the fate of the eight French prisoners captured by guerrillas during raids on Zouerate (May 1, 1977) and the Zouerate-Nouadhibou railway (October 25, 1977) (qq.v.). Omar Hadrami continued to maintain a high profile within the Polisario leadership, as the executive committee's senior official with responsibility for foreign affairs, a position he held until 1980.

Subsequently, and after a few months' stint as a military commander, he was dropped from the executive committee at the front's 5th congress, held in October 1982, and was made responsible for military security. He retained his place on Polisario's political bureau and remained head of military security until 1988, although he continued from time to time to act as a diplomatic spokesman for the Saharawi organization. In December 1985, he was reelected to the political bureau at Polisario's 6th congress. Then, in August 1988, he was replaced as head of military security and appointed the SADR's minister of information. At the time, it seemed that this was no more than another routine rearrangement in Polisario's top ranks, but apparently some members of the leadership had come to suspect him of pro-Moroccan or at least "accommodationist" leanings and may have felt it wise to remove him from the sensitive security post. On September 24, 1988, he was reassigned once again, becoming the front's ambassador to Algeria. This was still a very critical post, and for the moment, he retained his place on the political bureau. Later, Omar Hadrami would claim that this period was marked by near turmoil within the Polisario leadership and within the refugee (q.v.) camps in the Tindouf region of Algeria, necessitating frequent changes in personnel. He later said (in 1989) that he objected to the front's continued insistence on attaining full independence for Western Sahara, its unwillingness to compromise with Morocco, and what he claimed to be the monopolization of the Polisario leadership by a single tribe, apparently a reference to the Reguibat. Whatever the true situation, it is clear that at the Polisario Front's 7th congress (April-May 1989), he was removed from all positions of responsibility, including the political bureau. He was then named as the front's North American representative, based in Washington. He took up his post in June 1989 but was in Washington for only a matter of weeks before dramatically defecting to Morocco on August 8, becoming the highest-ranking and most prominent member of the Polisario Front ever to switch sides. This was an undoubted propaganda coup for Morocco. In press interviews after his defection, Omar Hadrami said that he and certain other dissidents had been imprisoned by the front between October 1988 and May 1989. In late 1989, he was appointed by King Hassan II (q.v.) to a position in Morocco's ministry of the interior.

OMAR MOHAMMED ALI see OMAR HADRAMI

OREJA AGUIRRE, MARCELINO. Born in 1935, Marcelino Oreja Aguirre became Spain's foreign minister in July 1976 after a long diplomatic career beginning in 1958. Though Spain had withdrawn from Western Sahara a few months before his appointment as foreign minister, the unresolved Saharan conflict was to remain one of his principal preoccupations until leaving the post in 1980. Though his government did not renounce the Madrid Agreement (q.v.) of November 14, 1975, he consistently argued that Spain had merely transferred administrative powers—and not sovereignty—to Morocco and Mauritania and that the decolonization process would not be completed until the Saharawi people were freely consulted about their future. "After withdrawing from the administration of the territory, Spain has not recognized any sovereignty over Western Sahara," he said on May 5, 1977, adding that Madrid wanted "a just agreement between the parties and above all that the expression of the will of the Saharawi people be respected." He claimed that Spain was neutral in the war then raging in the Sahara, though his government continued to allow Spanish arms to be delivered to Morocco and Mauritania until 1977. His ambiguous policy reflected the counterpressures facing his government at the time. The main Spanish opposition parties, the Spanish Socialist Workers Party and the Spanish Communist Party, were mounting vigorous campaigns for the annulling of the Madrid Agreement. Algeria exerted additional pressure by giving strong support to the Movement for the Self-Determination and Independence of the Canary Archipelago (MPAIAC), in particular in the OAU (q.v.), and by reminding Spain of its substantial economic stake in Algeria, Spain's main trading partner in Africa. The Polisario Front exerted considerable influence too by capturing Spanish fishing boats and their crews off the Western Saharan coast, the principal fishing waters of the Canary Islanders for five centuries. The release on November 28, 1977, of the first three Spanish fishermen to be captured by the guerrillas (on November 13, 1977) was followed by an announcement by Oreja on December 12, 1977, that Spanish arms shipments to Morocco and Mauritania had been banned. The release of eight fishermen captured on April 20, 1978, was arranged only after the ruling Center Democratic Union (UCD) had formally declared its recognition of the Polisario Front on October 12, 1978. However, Oreja held back from granting recognition to the SADR (q.v.) and tearing up the Madrid Agreement because there were powerful counterpressures from Morocco, notably the danger that Morocco might clamp down on Spanish fishing rights off the Moroccan and Western Saharan coasts and resurrect its old claim to the Spanish enclaves of Ceuta and Melilla on Morocco's Mediterranean coast.

ORF. The body of customary law by which criminal cases were judged in traditional Saharawi society, the *orf* was distinct from the Islamic *sharia* upon which the administration of civil justice was based. It included both general precepts, known as *adda,* which were common to all the Saharawi tribes, and more detailed laws, many of them specifying fixed penalties for particular crimes, which were adopted and enforced by the tribe, through its *djemaa* (q.v.). The orf had a pre-Islamic, Berber origin. In some cases, the orf was written, Julio Caro Baroja (1955, p. 45) noting that of the Ait Jmel wing of the Tekna (qq.v.), dating from 1717. Usually the orf listed the precise punishments to be inflicted for such crimes as murder, rape, theft, burglary, wounding, threatening behavior, and physical assault. Thus, the orf of the Yagout (q.v.) laid down, for example, that a thief had to hand over one camel and five goats to the person whom he had robbed. If the theft was carried out inside the victim's *khaima* (q.v.) (tent), the payment was one camel and ten goats. Sometimes the orf also included clauses relating to the payment of tribute (q.v.) and very often had something to say about the swearing of oaths and the number of witnesses. For example, a suspect could absolve himself of responsibility for a crime by swearing an oath, but this had to be endorsed by other members of his family, according to criteria that differed between tribes and according to the nature of the crime. Thus, among the Izarguien, a man accused of stealing a camel had to get ten of his relatives to back up his oath of innocence. In traditional society, it was the djemaa of the tribe or the fraction (q.v.) who judged criminal cases and sentenced those found guilty according to the tribe's orf law. This system remained unchanged until at least the 1950s, when the Spanish colonial authorities first attempted to bring the system of orf law under their aegis. An ordinance of December 16, 1955, attempted to reorganize the customary judicial system (q.v.) by setting up Spanish-run courts for criminal cases and establishing a unified system of punishments, including prison terms and fines, for the Saharawi population.

ORGANIZATION OF AFRICAN UNITY. The OAU first adopted a resolution calling on Spain to grant independence to Western Sahara in 1966. At its session in Addis Ababa in October–November of that year, the OAU Council of Ministers voted "its full support to all efforts aimed at the immediate and unconditional liberation of all African territories under Spanish domination (Ifni, the so-called 'Spanish Sahara,' Equatorial Guinea, and Fernando Po)" and appealed to Spain to "initiate resolutely a process giving freedom and independence to all these regions." At subsequent sessions in Addis Ababa in August–September 1969, February–March 1970, and August 1970, the Council of Ministers adopted resolutions urging Spain to implement United Nations (q.v.) resolutions on Western Sahara. Particularly forthright was a resolution adopted by the Council of Ministers at a session held in Rabat, Morocco, in June 1972, which called on Spain to "create a free and democratic atmosphere in which the people of that territory can exercise their right to self-determination and independence without delay in accordance with the Charter of the United Nations." Resolutions in a similar vein were adopted by the Council of Ministers at sessions in Addis Ababa in May 1973 and Mogadiscio in June 1974. The first departure from the tradition of uncontroversial support for the UN resolutions on self-determination came at the OAU summit in Kampala, Uganda in July–August 1975, when, as a result of intense Moroccan pressure, African heads of state were "unable to produce an acceptable resolution of recommendation on the question of the so-called Spanish Sahara" and decided to "await the opinion of the International Court of Justice (q.v.)."

During the following five years, the OAU was torn by conflicting considerations. On the one hand, most African governments were hostile to the open flouting by Morocco and Mauritania of two hallowed principles, the right of self-determination and the sanctity of the frontiers inherited from colonialism (a principle spelled out by the Proclamation of Cairo adopted at the 1964 OAU summit). On the other hand, many African governments were influenced by Moroccan and occasional Mauritanian threats to quit the OAU if it adopted resolutions openly critical of their roles in Western Sahara. The upshot was that until 1979 the OAU shelved the problem. At a meeting of the Council of Ministers in February–March 1976, for example, the issue of recognition of the Polisario Front as a liberation movement was dropped on the pretext that the front had proclaimed the Saharan Arab Democratic Republic (q.v.) on February 27 and that it was up to each member-state whether or not to give it recognition. The following Council of Ministers session, in Mauritius in June 1976, did adopt a strongly worded resolution, calling for the withdrawal of foreign troops from Western Sahara, by 29 votes to 2, with 17 abstaining or absent, but the ensuing threats from both Morocco and Mauritania to leave the OAU succeeded in convincing the following summit of heads of state, in Mauritius in July, not to endorse that resolution and instead to postpone debate on Western Sahara until the convening of an extraordinary summit on the problem. The extraordinary summit never took place. The next ordinary summit, in Libreville in July 1977, shelved the issue once again, leaving it once more for the long-awaited extraordinary summit.

However, by the time of the following ordinary summit, in Khartoum in July 1978, the war had reached an intensity that was difficult to ignore. Indeed, the Mauritanian regime of Mokhtar Ould Daddah (q.v.) was deposed in a coup led by war-weary officers on July 10, on the eve of the summit. The summit therefore passed a resolution setting up an ad hoc committee of African heads of state to examine the problem.

The committee met on November 30–December 1, 1978, and asked two of its members, Presidents Moussa Traoré of Mali and Olvsegun Obasanjo of Nigeria, to visit Morocco, Mauritania, and Algeria, which they did on May 1–5, 1979, while the OAU secretary-general, Edem Kodjo, visited Madrid. Their report was approved by 33 votes to 2, with 13 abstentions, by the next summit, at Monrovia, on July 20, 1979. This called for a cease-fire and a referendum. Among those voting approval of the report was Mauritania, which a few days later, on August 5, signed the Algiers Agreement (q.v.), ending its conflict with the Polisario Front (q.v.). Morocco's subsequent annexation of Tiris el-Gharbia (q.v.) was poorly viewed almost throughout Africa. Increasingly isolated, Morocco decided to boycott a crucial meeting held by the OAU ad hoc committee in Monrovia on December 4–5, 1979, to which all the parties to the conflict had been invited. After lengthy discussions with President Chadli Benjedid of Algeria, the foreign minister of Mauritania, and Mohammed Abdelaziz (qq.v.), the secretary-general of the Polisario Front, the committee adopted a resolution that, besides regretting the absence of Morocco, congratulated Mauritania for its peace agreement with the Polisario Front, called on Morocco to withdraw its troops from Western Sahara, and urged an immediate cease-fire to allow the holding of a referendum. The resolution also suggested that a UN peace-keeping force be dispatched to the territory.

By the time that African heads of state gathered in Freetown, Sierra Leone, for their next summit, on July 1–4, 1980, the strength of support for the Polisario guerrillas had increased still further. Twenty-six African countries, an absolute majority of the OAU's 51 member-states, declared that they had recognized the Saharan Arab Democratic Republic (SADR) (q.v.) and thus favored its admission as a full member-state of the OAU under article 28 of the OAU charter, which requires only a simple majority for admission. Morocco, citing article 27, countered that the SADR was not eligible as it was not a sovereign, independent state (a factor that had not, however, prevented Guinea-Bissau from joining the OAU in 1973, a year before its independence was recognized by Portugal) and, along with a few conservative allies, threatened to withdraw from the OAU if the SADR was admitted. Afraid of a split, the summit shelved the issue of admission of the SADR and once again handed the Saharan issue for further examination to the ad hoc committee. Morocco, by then under considerable pressure, decided to attend the ad hoc committee's next mediation meeting, in Freetown on September 9–12, along with Presidents Benjedid of Algeria, Mohammed Khouna Ould Heydallah (q.v.) of Mauritania, and Mohammed Abdelaziz, but the ad hoc committee's recommendations (a cease-fire by December 1980, the restriction of armed forces to their barracks, a UN peacekeeping force to monitor the cease-fire, and the holding of a referendum under OAU auspices with the assistance of the UN) were not heeded. The December deadline went by, the fighting continuing. However, seven months later, at the OAU summit in Nairobi (June 24–28, 1981), King Hassan publicly pledged to hold an internationally supervised referendum. The king joined other African leaders at the summit in asking the UN to organize a peacekeeping force with the OAU, while Moroccan and Polisario forces were confined to their bases, in preparation for a plebiscite conducted by the UN and the OAU. At the Nairobi summit, therefore, some African leaders saw a newfound magnanimity on the part of Morocco, and the summit as a result postponed consideration of the SADR's OAU membership for another year. The OAU formally thanked King Hassan for his pledge and drafted a resolution that did not explicitly name the Polisario Front as one of the parties to the conflict. Out of deference to Moroccan sensibilities, the parties were referred to only obliquely. It appeared that Morocco, at Nairobi, had scored a substantial diplomatic victory. The resolution reaffirmed the OAU's support for a cease-fire and a referendum, however, and set up an "Implementation Committee," made up of the heads of state of Guinea, Kenya, Mali, Nigeria, Sierra Leone, Sudan, and Tanzania.

The new mood of optimism generated by these events did not last long. After King Hassan returned to Morocco from the summit, he made a host of comments that indicated that he intended to ensure that the referendum in Western Sahara was held under conditions that would ensure an outcome favorable to Morocco. As a result, the OAU peace process failed to make further progress, and suspicion grew among the organization's members that the king's acceptance of a referendum at the Nairobi summit was a cosmetic move designed to keep the SADR membership issue off the agenda. The number of African states recognizing the SADR continued to grow, but a core of pro-Moroccan sentiment remained. And the OAU's latent divisions were brought into high relief by the decision, taken in February 1982, by the OAU secretary-general, Edem Kodjo, to allow the SADR to take its seat as a full member of the OAU just prior to a council of ministers meeting in Addis Ababa, which opened on February 22. Kodjo claimed he was acting in a manner fully consistent with the OAU charter and that in any event his action was a purely ministerial one because a simple majority of members had already assented to the Saharawis' membership under article 28 of the charter. Kodjo said that the relevant charter language "stipulated provisions characterized by an automaticity that requires no political considerations on the part of the secretary-general." His action was taken in spite of the continuing diplomatic activities of the Implementation Committee, although prospects for the consummation of its brief had never been overly bright.

The Addis Ababa conference was instantly thrown into disarray. King Hassan told the then OAU chairman, President Daniel arap Moi of Kenya, that the SADR's admission was a "juridical hold-up and act of banditry" and instructed his delegation to leave the meeting. Eighteen other African countries joined in dissenting from Edem Kodjo's decision and in boycotting the council of ministers meeting. Although these pro-Moroccan states were in a minority, they effectively prevented a quorum from being constituted. For this, a majority of two thirds (34 states) was required. A bid by Morocco in March 1982 to persuade the OAU to hold an extraordinary summit to annul the SADR's membership got nowhere. But for the rest of 1982, the OAU was virtually paralyzed, with some observers predicting its permanent disintegration. Although strenuous efforts were made by many nonboycotting states to resolve the imbroglio in time for the next ordinary summit, scheduled to be held in Tripoli,

Libya, in August 1982, their endeavors were to meet with failure. The boycotting states showed no sign of compromise, and the August meeting also collapsed without a quorum. The summit was rescheduled for November, after the SADR delegation, showing flexibility, had agreed on October 29 "voluntarily and temporarily" to absent itself from the Tripoli summit while not renouncing its membership. However, because of a row over the representation of war-torn Chad and the opposition of some OAU member states to the summit's being held in Libya, the summit was still not held. Three states—Egypt, Somalia, and Sudan—announced they would not attend any OAU summit in Libya because of their distaste for its ruler, Col. Muammar El-Qadaffi, who, under the OAU's rules, would have become the organization's chairman for the following year. The OAU was thus once again without a quorum, and the effort to hold the summit in the Libyan capital was abandoned on November 25, 1982. Clearly exasperated, the Polisario Front's foreign minister, Ibrahim Hakim (q.v.), announced that the SADR was no longer prepared to stay away voluntarily from future OAU meetings, although its presence would have seemed to hold only the prospect of continued and possibly fatal deadlock. At the end of 1982, the only clear winner was King Hassan: the disarray in the ranks of the organization had provided his country with a welcome diplomatic reprieve.

It was not until June 1983 that another attempt was made to hold a summit, this time in the less controversial location of Addis Ababa. Although Morocco had warned repeatedly that it would withdraw from the OAU if the SADR were seated, and the OAU secretariat had invited the Saharawi state to come to Addis Ababa, hopes were high that Morocco and its allies would not stage another boycott. These hopes were dashed on June 6, when Morocco and several other states once again walked out, depriving the summit of the necessary quorum. After intense and complex diplomatic activity on the part of opponents and allies of the SADR, Polisario finally announced on the evening of June 8 that it would once again voluntarily not participate in the summit proceedings. The OAU's 19th summit could thus go forward, but the drama was yet to play itself out fully. Morocco declared that Polisario's abstention was "a victory for legality," but this was dissipated by other, related developments. First, Morocco did not relent from its unyielding refusal to hold direct talks with Polisario and still appeared unwilling to include independence as an option to be put before the Saharawis in the referendum, which Morocco itself had agreed should be held. This attitude squandered what little patience still existed in most of the African community for Morocco. Second, the Polisario Front's stock rose in the OAU as a result of its accommodating attitude over taking its seat and because of the SADR's continuing diplomatic successes elsewhere. For example, more and more states were recognizing the Saharawi state, and the UN had passed a resolution on November 23, 1982, by 78 votes to 15, with 50 abstentions, supporting the OAU's efforts and mentioning Morocco and Polisario by name as the two parties to the conflict—action that the OAU still had not taken. The OAU had also to take account of the fact that its Implementation Committee had come almost to a dead end due to Morocco's lack of flexibility.

So the organization decided to take a stronger stand. On June 10–11, 1983, what was later to become OAU resolution 104 was presented to the summit. Not only did it call for a referendum in Western Sahara "without any administrative or military constraints," and direct the Implementation Committee to resume its work toward that end in cooperation with the United Nations, but it also named—for the first time— Morocco and Polisario explicitly as the parties to the dispute and urged them to meet directly to settle the outstanding issues between them in preparation for the plebiscite, which was optimistically set for December 1983. As a sop to King Hassan, however, nothing was said about Moroccan troop withdrawal from Western Sahara during the prereferendum period. When the resolution was presented to the summit, the Moroccan foreign minister, M'Hamed Boucetta (q.v.), at once demanded an adjournment (no doubt with another boycott in mind), but only 15 states supported him, which was too small a number to stop the proceedings. Resolution 104 was then adopted by consensus without a formal vote, to Polisario's intense satisfaction. Resolution 104 was later noted with approval by both the fourth (decolonization) committee and the General Assembly of the United Nations. The SADR's diplomatic star was clearly rising.

Morocco, after a few days of temporizing immediately after the summit, made clear that it was not prepared to make concessions even in the face of strong pressure from the international community. The efforts of the Implementation Committee, accordingly, ground to a standstill. For its part, the SADR was determined to take its seat at the next OAU summit, which was scheduled to be held in Conakry, Guinea, in mid–1984. Polisario insisted that the venue for the summit be moved to Addis Ababa to prevent Guinea's president, Ahmed Sekou Touré, a strong backer of King Hassan, from assuming the OAU's chairmanship. Bowing to pressure from the Saharawi nationalists and their many backers, the summit was relocated to the Ethiopian capital once again and postponed until November 1984 to give time for efforts to prevent the breakdown of the meeting. A curious calm seemed to settle over the diplomatic battleground at this point. King Hassan stated that although Morocco would quit the OAU if the SADR were seated, it would not ask its allies to follow suit. Perhaps this indicated that the king was resigned to the inevitable. The most populous black African state, Nigeria, recognized the SADR and withdrew from the Implementation Committee just before the summit. Although the committee was now moribund, Nigeria's action was an indication of the direction in which the wind was blowing. The 20th OAU summit was convened in Addis Ababa on November 12–15, 1984, and the SADR at last took its seat without substantial opposition. Although Morocco fulfilled its promise to withdraw from the organization (under article 32 of the charter, its pullout became effective in one year's time), only one other country joined the boycott. This was Zaire, a staunch ally of Morocco. But Zaire was back in the OAU six months later. Not even Libya, with whom King Hassan had signed a treaty of union in August 1984, sided with Morocco. The SADR has since attended all OAU summits and other meetings without incident, and as a gesture of the OAU's determination that the membership issue should henceforth be closed, it named the SADR's president, Mohammed Abdelaziz, as one of the organization's vice presidents at the 1985 OAU summit. On the negative side, the OAU could go no further to reconcile the warring parties due to Morocco's absence. The focus of settlement efforts then shifted to the United Nations, although its subsequent peace proposals merely built upon the foundation laid by the OAU. In recent years, reports have surfaced from time to time that Morocco will reapply for membership in the organization, but this had not occurred by the end of 1993. A suggestion in mid–1989 by Gabon's president, Omar Bongo, a close friend of King Hassan, that the SADR's membership be ''suspended'' garnered no support and was dropped.

OSMAN, AHMED. Moroccan prime minister between 1972 and 1979, Ahmed Osman played a crucial part in the negotiations that led to Spain's cession of Western Sahara to Morocco and Mauritania in 1975 and was head of government during the first three and a half years of the ensuing war with the Polisaro Front (q.v.). Born in Oujda in 1930, he became brother-in-law of King Hassan II (q.v.) when he married Princess Lalla Nezha in 1965. In 1956, he was head of the legal section of the royal cabinet; in 1957, he joined the ministry of foreign affairs; and in 1959–61, he served as secretary-general of the ministry of national defense. He was Moroccan ambassador to the United States in 1967–70 and then director of the royal cabinet in 1971–72 before becoming prime minister in 1972. Western Sahara became his government's major preoccupation from the summer of 1974 when it became clear that Spain planned to allow a process of self-determination in its colony. Osman failed to persuade Spanish leaders to desist from this course during talks in Madrid on August 13, 1974. It was the intensification of Moroccan pressure on Spain at the time of the Green March (q.v.), which forced the Spanish government to make a 180-degree shift in its Saharan policy and yield to Morocco and its ally, Mauritania.

Osman headed the first column of marchers to cross the border on November 6. While the marchers were camped inside the Western Saharan border, the Madrid government decided to cave in. On November 11, Osman flew to Spain to begin the negotiations, which ended in the signing of the Madrid Agreement (q.v.) on November 14. However, Osman's government then found itself confronted by the Polisario Front's tenacious guerrilla campaign. Osman resigned the premiership on March 21, 1979, shortly after a serious wave of strikes in Morocco and the humiliating Polisario attack on Tan-Tan (q.v.) on January 28. Osman then devoted himself to leadership of the pro-royalist Rassemblement National des Indépendants, of which he had become president in 1978. He served as minister of state in 1983–85. In 1986, he became speaker of the Moroccan Chamber of Representatives, where he has also been the member for Oujda since 1977.

OUDEI. An Arabic term for river or stream.

OUED. An Arabic term for river or stream.

OUED ED-DAHAB. "River of gold." This is the Arabic translation of Río de Oro (q.v.), the name given by early European explorers to the bay formed by the Dakhla (q.v.) peninsula because of the gold dust traded there. It later became the name of the southern part of Spain's Saharan colony. Since August 1979, it has also been the name given to the Moroccan province created after the annexation of the previously Mauritanian sector of Western Sahara, Tiris el-Gharbia (q.v.).

OULAD BORHIM. A subtribe of the Reguibat es-Sahel (q.v.). According to the 1974 census held by the Spanish authorities, they numbered only about 700, of whom more than half were settled in El-Ayoun (q.v.), but this was almost certainly an underestimate.

OULAD BOU RAHIM see OULAD BORHIM

OULAD BOU SBAA. "The Sons of the Father of the Lions" received their colorful name from a celebrated legend about their ancestor, Sidi Ahmer Ould Hamel, an Idrisid *cherif* who probably lived in the early 15th century. The legend has it that, while shepherding in the Echtouka region of the Anti-Atlas, in southern Morocco, he used his magical powers to transform his sheep and goats into lions to scare away a Saharawi *ghazzi* (q.v.). By his fourth marriage, he is said to have had four sons, of whom three (Amar, Amaran, and Numer) engendered the tribe of the Oulad Bou Sbaa. Sidi Ahmer was buried in the Echtouka region. Numer settled in the region of the Oued Massa, where he died, and his descendants, the Oulad Numer, live today in the Tiznit region of southern Morocco. Meanwhile, Amar and Amaran settled to the northwest of the High Atlas between Marrakesh and the Atlantic. The Oulad Bou Sbaa first appear in the history of the Western Sahara sometime in the 16th century, when, according to the annals of the Arosien (q.v.), they were sent by a Moroccan sultan in pursuit of the Arosien founder, Sidi Ahmed el-Arosi. After being barred from reaching the saintly fugitive by the full flow of the Saguia el-Hamra (q.v.), many of the Oulad Bou Sbaa and their herds are said to have died, but seven survivors of the force, "the seven of the Oulad Bou Sbaa," then joined Sidi Ahmed and, after being killed fighting the Portuguese, were buried with him 30 km. west of Smara (q.v.).

However, it was not until much later, in the early 18th century, during the reign of the Moroccan sultan Moulay Ismail, that a large part of the tribe migrated into Western Sahara. After a rebellion against the sultan, the Oulad Bou Sbaa feared a massacre at the hands of the *makhzen* and left their traditional lands near Marrakesh. One group, formed by the fraction of the Oulad el-Hadj, marched to the northeast, to the Oran region. Later the makhzen pardoned this branch of the tribe, which returned to the Marrakesh region, where some still live today, among the Srarhna, near Imin-Tanout. Another wing of the tribe, the Oulad Brahim, drove their herds south into the desert, halting first in the region of the Saguia el-Hamra and then moving on to Tiris (q.v.). There they embarked on a war with the Oulad Gandous, a tribe then inhabiting the central coastal belt, the Imirikli from the mouth of the Saguia el-Hamra at Foum el-Oued to the Oued

Graa in the south, a region that, upon their defeat, the Oulad
Gandous were forced to cede to the Oulad Bou Sbaa. In fact,
the tribe became very powerful. Besides its pastoral activities, it engaged in trading. Its caravans would travel north to
the Souss and south to Timbuctoo, Adrar, and Senegal. From
Morocco they brought European goods, including firearms,
into the Sahara, and they are thought to have been the first
to introduce tea, now a key element in the diet and social
life of the Saharawis. Their access to modern firearms made
them a formidable military force, as others, after the Oulad
Gandous, were to discover to their cost during the 19th
century.

One of their adversaries was Sidi Ahmed el-Kounti, a
fanatical marabout (q.v.) from Ouadane, in Adrar (Mauritania),
who arrived in Tiris at the head of a force from Adrar and the
Hodh (southeast Mauritania) and demanded deference and
tribute from all and sundry. Meeting a delegation of 30 elders
of the Oulad Bou Sbaa, who vainly offered him presents in the
hope of being left at peace, El-Kounti insisted that he be
recognized as sultan and that the Oulad Bou Sbaa give their
men as soldiers and their women as slaves. Protesting that their
sultan was Moulay Hassan (q.v.), the ruler of Morocco, the
Oulad Bou Sbaa elders rejected El-Kounti's demands. Hostilities then broke out. The Oulad Bou Sbaa withdrew to
Zemmour (q.v.), where they made a pact with fractions of the
Reguibat (q.v.), who were then approaching the peak of their
power in the Western Sahara. The Oulad Bou Sbaa also foiled
an attempt by El-Kounti to forge an alliance with Dahman
Ould Beyrouk, the ruler of the Ait Moussa Ou Ali, the Tekna
people of Goulimine. In a decisive engagement in c. 1886,
El-Kounti himself was killed, and over the following years, the
Oulad Bou Sbaa enjoyed relative peace, carrying on their
trading activities and herding their animals in the Imirikli and
Tiris. However, in 1898, after one of their number had been
murdered at a well at Taguersimet, in the Imirikli, war broke
out with the Arosien. In 1903, at Tislatin, to the south of the
present-day city of El-Ayoun (q.v.), the Arosien warriors were
exterminated after suffering the defection of their erstwhile
allies, the Oulad Delim (q.v.). Many of the Arosien then
emigrated for safety to Morocco, from which they slowly

returned in the 1920s. After inflicting this crushing defeat on the Arosien, the Oulad Bou Sbaa decimated a large force of Oulad Abieri (a tribe from Adrar) later in 1903. The same year, a force of Oulad Bou Sbaa killed the emir of Adrar. However, this greatly feared tribe found a tougher match in the Reguibat, with whom war broke out in 1905, when a Reguibat ghazzi killed seven of the tribe in Hadada (on what is now Western Sahara's southern border with Mauritania) and set off to Adrar with their looted livestock. A force of Oulad Bou Sbaa give pursuit and fell upon the Reguibat ghazzi at Seriba, killing 70 Reguibat. Both Reguibat ech-Charg and es-Sahel (qq.v.) were horrified when news of the incident spread. An *ait arbain* (q.v.), representing both wings of the confederation, was organized and a force of 1,000 men assembled. A large number of Oulad Bou Sbaa were then wiped out at Foucht (Adrar). The survivors flied northward to the Oued Noun (southern Morocco), where they joined another branch of their tribe. From there they made incursions into the Sahara against the Reguibat, but, after a serious defeat at Oudei el-Guesah, north of Zemmour, they made peace with the Reguibat in 1908, after mediation by Cheikh Ma el-Ainin (q.v.), then the main leader of the Saharawi resistance to the growing European threat. Nonetheless, the Oulad Bou Sbaa staged another ghazzi against the Reguibat in 1910, at Lemden el-Hauat. Surrounded during their retreat, however, they were annihilated by the Reguibat. That marked the end of the tribe's military aspirations. Greatly weakened, they turned their attention to trading and herding, prospering both under the French regime in Mauritania and in the Spanish Sahara.

The Oulad Bou Sbaa established trade relations with the Spanish from the 1880s. On November 28, 1884, they signed a treaty with Emilio Bonelli, the representative of the Sociedad de Africanistas y Colonistas, recognizing Spanish "protection" over Nouadhibou, or Cape Blanc (q.v.), and pledging not to have dealings with "the subjects of any other Christian nation." On July 12, 1886, the Oulad Bou Sbaa signed another treaty with the Spanish explorers, Julio Cervera Baviera, Francisco Quiroga, and Felipe Rizzo, at Idjil.

Today, the Oulad Bou Sbaa are widely dispersed, from southern Morocco to Senegal. The 1974 Spanish census, which generally underestimated the Saharawi population, counted only just over 400 Oulad Bou Sbaa in Western Sahara, most of them in El-Ayoun.

OULAD CHEIKH. A subtribe of the Reguibat es-Sahel (q.v.), their ancestor is said to be Amar, one of the sons of Sidi Ahmed Reguibi. Their fractions are the Ahel Delimi, Ahel Baba Ali, Lemouissat, Lahouareth, Lahseinat, and Ahel el-Hadj. The Spanish census of 1974 counted 3,000 Oulad Cheikh in the territory, but this was almost certainly an underestimate. Most of them were sedentary by then—living primarily in El-Ayoun, Dakhla, Smara, and Bir Enzaren (qq.v.). Those still engaged in a nomadic life were mainly in the region east of Bir Enzaren and Aoussert (q.v.).

OULAD DAOUD. A subtribe of the Reguibat es-Sahel (q.v.), their ancestor is said to be Ali, one of the sons of Sidi Ahmed Reguibi. Their fractions are the Ahel Salem, Ahel Temakha, and Ahel Baba Ammi. According to the 1974 census, which generally underestimated the population, they numbered almost 3,000, most of them settled in El-Ayoun, Smara, and Guelta Zemmour (qq.v.), though some were still nomadic, in the region of Gleiba el-Foula.

OULAD DELIM. The Western Saharan tribe with probably the purest Arab ancestry, the Oulad Delim were a branch of the Beni Hassan (q.v.), the Bedouin Maqil (q.v.) people of Yemeni origin who invaded the regions now known as Western Sahara and Mauritania in the 13th and 14th centuries. Their presence in Western Sahara was recorded early in the 16th century by Leo Africanus and Mármol y Carvajal. Leo Africanus, who crossed the desert somewhat to the east of present-day Western Sahara in 1512, noted that "the Delim live in the desert of Libya [i.e., the Sahara] along with Znaga, an African people." The northernmost of the Beni Hassan tribes to have settled in the western reaches of the Sahara desert, they were, according to Leo Africanus, a people of poor reputation. "They possess neither dominion nor tribute, as a result of which they are reduced to an extreme poverty which obliges them to convert themselves into robbers. They frequently go to the region of the Draa [q.v.] to exchange their livestock for dates.'' However, by the time that Spanish explorers arrived in Western Sahara at the end of the 19th century, the Oulad Delim had acquired a warlike and powerful reputation. They were then living primarily in the southwest of what is now Western Sahara and were divided into five fractions—the Oulad Tegueddi, the Loudeikat, the Oulad Khaliga, the Oulad Ba Amar, and the Serahenna.

The tribe's rise to power began in the 18th century. In the second half of the 18th century, they forced an important tribe of *zawiya* status, the Oulad Tidrarin (q.v.), to submit to their authority. Unable to defend themselves, the Oulad Tidrarin were obliged to become tributaries, paying the *horma* (q.v.) to the Oulad Delim, in return for "protection." Only one fraction of the Oulad Tidrarin, the Ahel Taleb Ali, escaped this exacting and humiliating treatment at the hands of the Oulad Delim. However, the rise of another Saharawi tribe, the Reguibat (q.v.), in the course of the 19th century, undermined the Oulad Delim. In 1888, the Oulad Tidrarin refused to pay the horma, sparking off a war that eventually involved several tribes. The first battle in the conflict was an attack by a *ghazzi* of Oulad Delim on an encampment of Oulad Tidrarin in a *grara* at Tah (qq.v.). After 22 Oulad Tidrarin had been killed in this engagement, 5 Oulad Delim were killed at Tagersimet in the same year (1888). By then, some Oulad Tidrarin had migrated to Morocco to escape the oppression of the Oulad Delim; others had forged an alliance with the Reguibat (angered by the murder of a Reguibi by a Delimi after the battle of the grara) to fight back. The Oulad Delim sought allies in turn, sending a force to the territory of the Tekna (q.v.) in the north. After being rebuffed by the Izarguien (q.v.), who had no wish to arouse the ire of the Reguibat, the Oulad Delim made a pact with the Ait Lahsen (q.v.) in Tan-Tan, from where a joint ghazzi set off south to attack the Oulad Tidrarin and the Reguibat at Raudat el-Hadj in Saguia el-Hamra (q.v.). After losing 40 dead, however, the Oulad Delim returned north, pursued by the Reguibat. The Oulad Delim and their opponents then widened their alliances and staged further raids before establishing a precarious peace. The tribes had been exhausted by the loss of livestock as a result of both the fighting and the scarcity of pastures. Nonetheless, a year later, in 1891, the struggle resumed when a group of Oulad Delim attacked the Ahel Esteila fraction of the Oulad Tidrarin. After six months of fighting, the Oulad Delim finally persuaded the Reguibat to desert their Oulad Tidrarin allies in 1892. The latter, now greatly weakened, entered a grave crisis, some migrating to Morocco, others agreeing to submit once more to the horma. The Oulad Delim too had been weakened by the prolonged conflict, and both prudence on their part and the emigration of many of the Oulad Tidrarin meant that they could now extract far less tribute than in the past.

The Oulad Delim were involved in other tribal conflicts at the end of the 19th century—for example, with the northern Mauritanian tribe, the Oulad Ghailan, in 1899–1900.

Their warlike image was not lost on the early Spanish explorers and settlers who arrived in Western Sahara in the 1880s. On March 9, 1885, they attacked the installations of the Compañía Comercial Hispano-Africana at Dakhla (q.v.), only a few weeks after they had been established. Julio Cervera Baviera, who explored Western Sahara in 1886, wrote of the "fearsome tribe of Oulad Delim" living in the vicinity of Dakhla. While traveling in the interior, he came across the Loudeikat fraction of the tribe, describing them on his return as "dedicated to marauding and theft, famous for their villainy and bloodthirsty instincts." In 1932, the Oulad Delim, along with some Reguibat, were responsible for the ghazzi that inflicted a bloody and humiliating defeat on a French patrol at Oum Tounsi (q.v.), Mauritania, in which a French commander (Lt. MacMahon), 2 French sergeants, and scores of Senegalese and Moor soldiers were killed.

However, despite initial conflicts with the Spanish, the Oulad Delim gradually established a modus vivendi with the little settlement at Dakhla. On March 23, 1895, one of their chiefs signed an accord with Spain promising to collaborate with the Spanish traders there. Like other Saharawi tribes, the Ould Delim saw the Spanish, who were too weak to expand their presence into the interior at this time, as much less dangerous to their interest than the expansive and aggressive French. With the enforcement of the colonial peace (due far more to the French than the Spanish), the Oulad Delim could no longer carry out ghazzis or enforce payment of the horma by their tributaries. A pillar of their economy was destroyed, and ironically, the Oulad Tidrarin, who had thus been freed from such exactions, prospered more than their former exploiters, owning more camels than they by 1950, according to Spanish statistics. However, for many Oulad Delim, it was still possible to lead the life of a "man of the gun," as a soldier in the Spanish army or paramilitary police. Their heavy enrollment in the Tropas Nómadas and the Policía Territorial may have been the cause of their reputation for loyalty to Spain in the last decade or so of Spanish rule. It was in the south, the traditional zone of the Oulad Delim, that the Spanish-backed Partido de la Unión Nacional Saharaui (q.v.) apparently enjoyed its only significant, though limited, support in 1974–75. Like most other Saharawis, however, the great majority of Oulad Delim, including those in the Spanish army and police, gave their support to the Polisario Front (q.v.) when Spain reneged on its promise to grant self-determination and allowed Morocco to enter the territory in 1975.

By then, most Oulad Delim were sedentary. The Spanish census of 1974, which generally underestimated the Saharawi population, counted just under 5,400 Oulad Delim, the greatest concentration being in Dakhla.

OULAD MOUSSA. (1) One of the most important subtribes of the Reguibat es-Sahel (q.v.). They numbered 5,407 in 1974, according to the Spanish-held census of that year, but this was almost certainly an underestimate. The census recorded more than 2,000 of them living in the city of El-Ayoun (q.v.) alone, with more settled in Smara and elsewhere. Those still living a nomadic way of life were to be found at the time in the Guelta Zemmour (q.v.) region, straddling the border with Mauritania. The Oulad Moussa are said to be descendants of Ali, one of the three sons of the Reguibat founder, Sidi Ahmed Reguibi. Their fractions include the Oulad el-Qadi, Ahel Bellao, Oulad Moueya, Oulad Lahsen, and Oulad Hossein.

(2) One of the main fractions of the Oulad Tidrarin (q.v.). They, along with six other fractions, are direct descendants of Sidi Ahmed Bou Ghambor, the tribe's great leader of the early 18th century. In the second half of the 18th century, the Oulad Moussa, like most of the Oulad Tidrarin, were forced to pay tribute to the increasingly powerful Oulad Delim (q.v.). The Oulad Moussa paid the *horma* (q.v.) to the Loudeikat fraction of the Oulad Delim. Payment of the horma died away, however, as a result of the long war of liberation waged by the Oulad Tidrarin in 1888–92 and the social changes occasioned later by the European colonial presence.

OULAD TALEB. One of the subtribes of the Reguibat es-Sahel (q.v.), their ancestry is traced back to Taleb Ali, a son of Amar, whose father, Sidi Ahmed Reguibi, is the supposed ancestral founder of the Reguibat (q.v.). They numbered only 397 according to the Spanish census of 1974 but were almost certainly more numerous. Half of those counted in the census were living in El-Ayoun (q.v.). Their fractions include the Oulad Ben Hossein, Oulad Ba Brahim, Oulad Ba Aaissa, Oulad Ba Moussa, and Ahel Dera.

OULAD TIDRARIN. One of the main tribes of Western Sahara, the Oulad Tidrarin are also to be found in southern Morocco and northern Mauritania. With the rank of *zawiya,* they have traditionally had a reputation for erudition and learning. Their supposed founder was Hannin, alias Tidrarin (the mountain-dweller), who may have lived in the 15th century and is said to have been brought to what is now Western Sahara from the mountainous Adrar (Mauritania) after being captured by a *ghazzi* (q.v.). Most of the tribe's present fractions—with the exception of the Lidadsa and the El-Haseinat, which have been adopted by the tribe—are said to be directly descended from Hannin's great-great-grandson, Ali. Seven of the tribe's numerous fractions, including the two most important in Western Sahara, the Oulad Moussa and the Ahel Taleb Ali, are said to be descendants of Sidi Ahmed Bou Ghambor, the tribe's powerful chief at the end of the 17th century and the beginning of the 18th century, when the Oulad Tidrarin were at their zenith. However, during the 18th century, the tribe entered a long period of decline, and by the end of the century, all of its fractions, with the exception of the Ahel Taleb Ali, had become tributaries of the Oulad Delim (q.v.), then at the height of their expansion. Reduced to the status of *znaga,* the Oulad Tidrarin were obliged for more than a century to pay the *horma* (q.v.) to designated families of the Oulad Delim in return for "protection." They were barred from bearing arms, the ultimate humiliation in the tough world of the desert. However, in 1888, the Oulad Tidrarin tried to free themselves from the burden of the horma. In reprisal, a force of Oulad Delim attacked a large concentration of Oulad Tidrarin at Tah, killing 22 of them. Many Oulad Tidrarin then took refuge in Morocco. Others continued the struggle against the Oulad Delim, with the support of the Reguibat (q.v.), who entered the conflict to avenge the death of a Reguibi who had been killed by the Oulad Delim for giving a camel to a Tidrarini who had been badly wounded in the battle of the grara. The Oulad Tidrarin took revenge on the Oulad Delim in 1888 when they killed 5 Delimis at Tagersimet. Other murders followed during the year. Finally, after a joint ghazzi by a force of Oulad Tidrarin and Reguibat, the Oulad Delim forged an alliance with a Tekna tribe, the Ait Lahsen (q.v.), but in their first joint engagement against the Oulad Tidrarin and the Reguibat, the Oulad Delim and the Ait Lahsen lost 40 dead. After further ghazzis, peace was restored until 1891, when the struggle broke out again, for about six months, with the Ait Lahsen and the Oulad Delim generally coming off worst. However, in 1892, the Reguibat finally came to terms with the Oulad Delim, leaving the Oulad Tidrarin in disarray. New migrations to southern Morocco began, and, much weakened, those who remained in the Western Sahara once again found the Oulad Delim demanding tribute, though with greater prudence than in the past. Under the *pax hispánica,* the Oulad Tidrarin were freed from the horma and prospered relative to their old enemies. The Spanish government published statistics in 1950, which showed the Oulad Tidrarin as owning more camels than their erstwhile oppressors. Like the other Saharawi tribes, the

Oulad Tidrarin were mainly sedentary by the early 1970s. The 1974 Spanish census, which generally underestimated the Saharawi population, counted just under 5,000 Oulad Tidrarin, most of them living in El-Ayoun, Dakhla, and Boujdour (qq.v.). Those still leading a nomadic way of life were concentrated in the central region.

OURAGAN, OPERATION. Operation Hurricane was a joint Franco-Spanish counterinsurgency campaign against the Army of Liberation (q.v.) in February 1958. The idea of a joint operation came from Gen. Gabriel Bourgund (q.v.), commander of the French forces in French West Africa, who was responsible for fending off the guerrilla attacks that began in northern Mauritania in February 1957. The problem facing Bourgund was that the Army of Liberation was able to use Western Sahara, where Spain had few troops at the time, as a sanctuary, and though Spain had agreed as early as February 1957 to French requests for permission to stage hot-pursuit raids across the border into Spanish territory, Spain's own policing of its territory weakened further when, between August and October 1957, the small, exposed garrisons in the hinterland were withdrawn to bolster the defenses of a handful of coastal enclaves. Even Smara (q.v.), the only precolonial city in Western Sahara, was abandoned to the guerrillas. At a meeting with the governor-general of Africa Occidental Española (q.v.), Gen. Mariano Gómez Zamalloa in Dakar on September 20, Bourgund won this senior Spanish official's support for the idea of a joint operation, for which he had already drawn up a rough plan and given the code name Ouragan. The French government of Félix Gaillard (q.v.) gave its support to the plan in principle on December 30 and then won the backing of the Spanish government in the first week of January 1958. For the Spanish regime, decisive action against the guerrillas had become an urgent matter: The Army of Liberation, which had also launched a full-scale invasion of Ifni in November, stepped up its attacks against Spanish targets in Western Sahara between November 1957 and January 1958. For the Gaillard government in France, the principal consideration was the need to restore security in northern Mauritania to provide a more auspicious political framework for the new experiment in internal autonomy in Mauritania, which had begun with the selection of Mokhtar Ould Daddah (q.v.) as vice president in May 1957, and to allow plans for massive international investment in the rich iron ore deposits near Fort Gouraud (Zouerate) to proceed. Both Madrid and Paris were agreed that the Army of Liberation bands could not be flushed out of their Western Saharan sanctuaries by Spanish troops alone.

At joint strategy meetings in January in Las Palmas and Dakar, it was decided that the whole operation would last only a fortnight, sweeping first through Saguia el-Hamra and then through Río de Oro (qq.v.). The French wing of the operation, which was code-named Ecouvillon (Sponge), was to involve 5,000 troops, 600 vehicles, and 70 aircraft, under the overall command of General Bourgund. The French forces were divided into three groups, commanded by Colonels Grall, Vidal, and Cusin. The overall commander of the Spanish maneuvers, code-named Teide, was Lt. Gen. López Valencia, captain general of the Canary Islands, with Gen. José Héctor Vásquez, governor-general of Western Sahara, second in command. The Spanish committed 9,000 troops and 60 aircraft.

D-day, which had originally been set for February 5, was postponed to February 10 because of bad weather. That day, Spanish troops took control of Hagounia while a French force under Grall surrounded Smara. The city was captured the next day by Grall's men and a unit of Spanish paratroopers. Meanwhile, a Spanish force destroyed a large base of the Army of Liberation at Tafudaret. On February 12, Grall's force and French paratroopers clashed with guerrillas at Sidi Ahmed el-Arosi. Later, French forces under Vidal occupied Guelta Zemmour (q.v.), and another French force moved out of Tindouf (q.v.), Algeria, to take control of Farsia. A large number of guerrillas managed to evade the French and Spanish forces and flee northward, but their main bases in Saguia el-Hamra were destroyed and their morale badly shaken. The second phase of the operation, which centered on Río de Oro, started on February 20. While the French force from Tindouf pushed south into the Ain Ben Tili region of northern Mauritania, the Grall and Vidal groups and additional French troops from Atar, Port Etienne (Nouadhibou), and Fort Gouraud linked up with Spanish troops coming from El-Ayoun, Guelta Zemmour, Dakhla, and La Guera (qq.v.). Aoussert, Bir Enzaren, and other points in the interior were occupied. It was all over by February 24, the French forces withdrawing to Tindouf, Fort Trinquet (Bir Moghrein), Fort Gouraud, Atar, and Port Etienne, the Spanish reestablishing permanent bases in the interior, at Smara, Guelta Zemmour, Tafudaret, and elsewhere. The French forces announced later that they had lost 7 killed and 25 wounded while killing 132 guerrillas and taking 51 prisoners. The Spanish government announced on March 2 that 5 Spanish soldiers were killed and 27 wounded.

- P -

PARTI COMMUNISTE MOROCAIN. The Moroccan Communist Party, which was founded in 1943, consistently supported the Moroccan claim to Western Sahara after Morocco's independence in 1956. Indeed, under the leadership of Ali Yata (q.v.), who became secretary-general in 1946, the PCM embraced the ideology of "Greater Morocco" popularized by the Istiqlal Party leader Allal el-Fassi (qq.v.). Though banned in 1959, the PCM survived in semiclandestinity and was able to publish legal journals in the 1960s in which it expressed its views on the "national question." Like the Istiqlal Party, the party argued that Western Sahara, Mauritania, much of the Algerian Sahara, Ifni, and the Spanish enclaves of Ceuta and Melilla on Morocco's Mediterranean coast had historically been part of Morocco before the imposition of arbitrary colonial borders. Thus, Ali Yata described Mauritania after its independence in 1960 as "a Moroccan province in which France has practically conserved its domination" (*La Vie Internationale*, January 1962), and, though the party opposed the brief Algerian-Moroccan border war in October 1963, Ali Yata asserted that "the cities of Tindouf and Colomb Bechar are part of authentically Moroccan territories'' (letter to Hassan II, February 1, 1967). The party's policy toward Western Sahara fell within this irredentist framework. On April 10, 1956, just three days after Spain had recognized Morocco's independence, it issued a communiqué noting that in the joint Moroccan-Spanish Declaration of Madrid (April 7, 1956), "No mention is made of the *presidios* of Ceuta (and) Melilla, the enclave of Ifni [and] the territory of Río de Oro, all governed by particular conventions" and stated that "they must be joined with the whole of the country without any restriction." Later, the PCM accused the Moroccan government of conniving with the French and Spanish governments in crushing the Army of Liberation (q.v.) during and after Operation Ouragan (q.v.), and throughout the 1960s, the party criticized the government for maintaining friendly relations with Spain and failing to aid the Saharawis against their colonial rulers. An editorial in the party paper, *Al-Kifah al-Watani*, spoke, for example, on October 21, 1966, of "the policy of complacency, toward Franco followed by all the Moroccan governments that have followed each other since independence." The PCM also denounced the Moroccan government's decision to support the concept of self-determination in UN debates on Western Sahara from 1966.

In 1968, Ali Yata founded a new party, the Parti de Libération et du Socialisme, though it too was banned a year later. Like the PCM, however, the PLS was able to publish legal journals. It remained loyal to the PCM's irredentist policies, condemning King Hassan II's (q.v.) decision in 1969–70 to recognize Mauritania and the existing Algerian-Moroccan frontier. In 1971–72, El-Ouali Mustapha Sayed (q.v.), the future leader of the Polisario Front (q.v.), collaborated with the party, as a student in Rabat, and contributed to a major study of Western Sahara, "The Reality of Our Usurped Saharan Province," which was published in the PLS journal *Al-Mabadi* in May 1972. However, the unwillingness of the PLS to provide direct support for the launching of a new armed struggle against Spain in the Sahara was one of the factors that prompted El-Ouali and other Saharawi students in Rabat at the time to reduce their relations with the

PLS and other Moroccan nationalist parties and turn their energies to the creation of a new, autonomous Saharawi liberation movement.

In the summer of 1974, the PLS suddenly found itself in de facto alliance with King Hassan II on the Saharan question, when the king launched a major diplomatic campaign to block Spain's plans to hold a self-determination referendum in Western Sahara. In July–August 1974, Ali Yata acted as the king's special envoy on an 18-day mission to Eastern Europe to lobby for support for the Moroccan claim to the territory. This unprecedented collaboration between the monarch and Morocco's veteran pro-Moscow communist opened the way for the relegalization of his movement as the Parti du Progrés et du Socialisme in August 1974. At its first congress, held in Casablanca on February 21–23, 1975, party delegates adopted a resolution that expressed "delight at the realization of national unanimity around the slogan of completing national territorial integrity and refusing the installation of a puppet state on the land of our Western Sahara." The party went on to give full-hearted support to the Green March (q.v.) and the Madrid Agreement (q.v.) of November 1975. With one deputy in the Chamber of Representatives (Yata) after the June 1977 general elections, the PPS and its daily newspaper, *Al-Bayane,* took an ultra-tough line during the ensuing war with the Polisario Front (q.v.), opposing any hint of compromise. In the years since, the PPS has maintained its hard-line stance on Western Sahara but otherwise occupies only a peripheral place on the domestic Moroccan political scene. The PPS fielded 159 candidates in the general elections that took place on September 15, 1984. However, only 2 of them were victorious, and the party's overall share of the nationwide vote was only 2.3 percent.

PARTI DE LIBERATION ET DU SOCIALISME see PARTI COMMUNISTE MAROCAIN

PARTI DU PEUPLE MAURITANIEN. The Mauritanian People's Party, which ruled Mauritania under President Mokhtar Ould Daddah (q.v.) from its creation in 1961 until the military coup of July 10, 1978 (when it was dissolved), advocated the annexation of the whole of Western Sahara by Mauritania until Ould Daddah's compromise with King Hassan II (q.v.) of Morocco over the territory's future, involving a partition, in the autumn of 1974. The new policy was endorsed by the 4th party congress in Nouakchott, on August 15–20, 1975, when a resolution was passed renewing the party's confidence in the president's "wise and lucid policy pursued with a view to the liberation and return to the mother country of that part of our national territory which is still occupied."

PARTI DU PROGRES ET DU SOCIALISME see PARTI COMMUNISTE MAROCAIN

PARTIDO DE LA UNION NACIONAL SAHARAUI. The Party of Saharan National Union, the successor of a short-lived Partido Revolucionario Progresivo, was set up in November 1974, with the encouragement of the Spanish colonial authorities, to provide a counterweight to the Polisario Front (q.v.) and lead the country toward internal self-government and eventually, after a referendum, to independence in close association with Spain. The party, which was formally registered on February 16, 1975, the date of its first congress, appealed for support to the conservative tribal leaders of the Djemaa (q.v.) and other traditionalist-minded and more elderly Saharawis. It opposed radical social change. The 14-point program adopted by the party at its first congress stated that it aimed "to attain Saharan independence through a process of accelerated self-determination" but added that it wanted "to preserve mutual friendship and cooperation with Spain in every field." It rejected the Moroccan and Mauritanian claims to the country. The party also promised to "preserve and strengthen the religious and social traditions, adapting them to the institutions of a modern state," to "reorganize the system of Islamic justice, adapting it to present times," to "consider Islam as the official religion, and Arabic as the national language," to advance the position of women so that they could "actively participate in the political, cultural, and economic life of the country" and to promote economic development, raise the standard of living, provide free, compulsory education, guarantee full employment, set up agricultural cooperatives, and provide social security and health assistance. The congress elected Khalihenna Ould Rachid (q.v.), a young engineer, as the party's secretary-general.

Despite the active support of the colonial authorities, which provided the PUNS with funds and put considerable pressure on students and state employees to join, the party did not win much popular support, except in the south. Young Saharawis were especially suspicious of the party because of its close connections with the colonial authorities. The party's failure to rally significant mass support, except in a few places in the south, during the tour of the territory by the UN Visiting Mission (q.v.) on May 12–19, 1975, was a humiliating blow to its credibility. The Polisario Front held very large demonstrations wherever the UN mission members went, decisively outflanking the PUNS. Fearing that the Spanish authorities would make a deal with the Polisario leaders, Khalihenna Ould Rachid and two of his closest collaborators fled to Morocco while the UN team was still in the country and on May 18 paid allegiance to King Hassan II (q.v.).

The PUNS was then restructured at the end of May by a new, four-member executive committee headed by the assistant secretary-general, Dueh Sidna Naucha. But the party's prospects were by then rather gloomy. Not only did it have very little popular support, but the Spanish colonial authorities decided after the UN mission's visit to try to come to terms with the Polisario guerrillas and urged the rump of the PUNS to do likewise. On July 7, 1975, serious rioting between PUNS and Polisario supporters broke out in El-Ayoun (q.v.), and a few days later, four Saharawis were killed when bombs exploded in the capital. PUNS leaders blamed the Polisario Front for the deaths, though they were more likely to have been the work of the Moroccan-backed Front de Libération et de l'Unité (q.v.). However, the PUNS leaders were in a more conciliatory mood by the time of the party's 2nd congress, held in El-Ayoun on August 16–18. On the opening day of the congress, there was another defection to Morocco, this time by the treasurer, Khalifa Boudjemaa, who allegedly took with him some of the party funds. However, the 250 delegates elected a new, 6-man executive committee, headed by Dueh Sidna Naucha (secretary-general) and Mohammed Lamine (assistant secretary-general), and mandated it to make contact with the Polisario leadership and resolve their mutual differences. The program adopted by the congress mirrored closely that of the front, including commitments to independence, the establishment of a republic with a president and a parliament elected by direct, universal suffrage, religious freedom, free education, the abolition of slavery, and equality for women. A similar orientation was adopted by the PUNS youth congress at Aoussert (q.v.) at the end of September 1975.

At the end of August, PUNS leaders had held talks with a Polisario delegation, which included Bachir Mustapha Sayed (q.v.), the brother of the Polisario secretary-general, El-Ouali Mustapha Sayed (q.v.), in Nouadhibou, Mauritania. Further talks were held on October 10 at Ain Ben Tili between El-Ouali and Dueh Sidna Naucha. As the Moroccan threat loomed, especially after the announcement of the Green March (q.v.) on October 16, the pressure on the PUNS to unite with the Polisario Front became more and more strong. On October 20, there was a further round of negotiations between PUNS and Polisario leaders, this time in El-Ayoun itself, in the presence of Spanish officials. The PUNS appealed to the Spanish authorities for arms and threatened to counter the Green March with a march of its own. While accepting the need for unity with the Polisario Front, however, the remaining PUNS leaders still refused to accept the Polisario demand that the PUNS be dissolved and its members integrated into the front.

However, by November, the party was crumbling. It failed to organize its countermarch to the Moroccan border. Most of the party's traditional supporters in the Djemaa had aligned by then with the Polisario Front. The party's final collapse came early in November 1975, when Polisario forces surrounded and occupied Aoussert, a small settlement in the south, which PUNS had made its principal base. Most of the party's remaining members then joined the front.

PASHA. The head of an urban *caidat* (q.v.), or municipality, in Morocco. *Pashas* were appointed to administer the main towns in the Moroccan sector of Western Sahara in 1976—and in Oued ed-Dahab (q.v.) after its annexation in August 1979. Pashas are subordinate to the governor of the province of which their municipality forms a part. They are appointed by the ministry of the interior, to which they are ultimately responsible. A pasha controls a relatively autonomous municipal administration, and the local police report to him as well as to the provincial governor. In some cases, a pasha may appoint one or more deputies, known as *khulafa* (sing. *khalifa*).

PEREZ DE CUELLAR, JAVIER. Born in 1920 and a career Peruvian diplomat, he became secretary-general of the United Nations (q.v.) in 1982. In this position, he played an increasingly important role in diplomatic efforts to resolve the Western Sahara conflict. Following a period of increasing attention being paid to the war by the UN during late 1985, he attempted to reconcile Morocco and the Polisario Front (q.v.) by holding "proximity talks" at UN headquarters in New York in April and May 1986. Each side met separately with him in order to convey their positions to the other without having to meet face-to-face. It was hoped that Morocco and Polisario would eventually meet directly, but this did not happen. Persistently, Pérez de Cuéllar continued his efforts, meeting with Morocco's King Hassan II (q.v.) in Rabat on July 15–16, 1987. He then commenced work on a comprehensive peace plan in 1988, building upon the work of the first United Nations technical mission (q.v.), which had visited the affected region in late 1987. He presented the plan to the protagonists in separate meetings on August 11, 1988, in New York, and on August 30 was informed by both of their acceptance of his plan in principle. At this time, hopes rose for an early resolution of the Western Sahara conflict, but they were dashed by Morocco's refusal to meet directly with Polisario representatives for substantive talks and by Polisario's resumption of military activity late in 1988 as a sign of its frustration. Nevertheless, Pérez de Cuéllar persisted in trying to reconcile the parties, touring the region in 1989 and meeting as many individuals as possible who were in a position to affect the progress of the peace initiative. On June 27, 1990, the UN Security Council passed a unanimous resolution supporting the secretary-general, further encouraging him. A second technical mission (q.v.) was dispatched to the region in July and August 1990 to assist Pérez de Cuéllar in formulating a final blueprint for the deployment of UN peacekeeping troops and administrators to Western Sahara to prepare for the plebiscite. However, Iraq's invasion of Kuwait on August 2, 1990, forced the postponement of the secretary-general's efforts on Western Sahara due to the heavy demands placed on the UN by the Kuwait-Iraq crisis and the subsequent Gulf war.

After the conclusion of the Gulf conflict in February 1991, Pérez de Cuéllar set to work once again. On April 19, he issued his long-awaited plan for the actual conduct of the referendum (see Bibliography), outlining a 36-week schedule for the withdrawal of Moroccan and Polisario armed forces from sensitive areas, publication of a list of those Saharawis eligible to vote, insertion of the troops and administrators of the United Nations Mission for the Referendum in Western Sahara (q.v.), and the actual voting, in which the choice offered to Saharawis would be between independence and integration with Morocco. But severe problems cropped up almost immediately: a resumption of military activity by Morocco in July and August 1991, just before the planned insertion of the UN forces; a reluctance by Morocco to allow the UN to fully deploy its personnel; and constant disputes over the number of persons allowed to vote in the referendum. Responding to a Moroccan proposal to allow tens of thousands of people to vote who were not counted in the 1974 Spanish census, Pérez de Cuéllar, after much work on the subject, issued a report on December 19, 1991 (see Bibliography), which attempted to clarify the situation. In general, he accepted King Hassan's idea that the voter roll ought to be greatly expanded and laid down a series of rather broad guidelines to that end in his report. This was severely condemned by Polisario, with some outside commentators conceding that the UN had indeed given a clear advantage to Morocco in the voting, since many of those individuals allegedly "imported" to Western Sahara by Morocco would now be entitled to vote, possibly more than balancing the Saharawis from Polisario-administered areas. In addition, the UN Security Council gave only qualified support to this proposal in resolution 725, passed unanimously on December 31, 1991. On this rather lukewarm note, Pérez de Cuéllar finished his tenure in office that day and was succeeded by Boutros Boutros Ghali (q.v.) of Egypt, who inherited the problems of the Western Sahara referendum effort.

PESETA. The currency of Spain, it was used in Western Sahara during the Spanish colonial period. In the sector annexed by Morocco after Spain's withdrawal, the peseta was formally withdrawn in favor of the Moroccan *dirham* on June 1, 1976.

PETROLEUM. Though no crude oil has yet been exploited in Western Sahara, numerous international oil companies have explored the territory since the early 1960s, and several traces of oil have been found. Interest has centered on two large sedimentary basins, one stretching along the northern border area of Saguia el-Hamra (q.v.), the other extending down the coast from the Moroccan border to Cape Blanc (q.v.). Exploration was not possible, however, until the Spanish government liberalized its investment laws to allow foreign oil companies to acquire concessions on Spanish territory. On December 26, 1958, the Spanish government published an oil investment law, which divided Spanish territory into three zones, one of which was Western Sahara, and a decree of June 25, 1960, spelled out the terms on which companies could explore for and exploit oil in the territory. This stipulated that both Spanish and foreign oil companies could acquire permits for six years, renewable for a further three years, the permits being for 125,000 ha. following the division of the territory into 108 rectangles of 70 x 35 km. No company could acquire more than 16 concessions, and a minimum expenditure per block was required. Foreign oil companies were placed under the same fiscal obligations as

Spanish companies, and, upon a decision to exploit oil found in a block, the concessionaire would have the right to exploitation of half of the block, the state receiving 12.5 percent of the oil extracted by the company.

Meanwhile, the territory's Servicio Minero carried out an aeromagnetic survey covering 180,000 sq. km., delimiting 160,000 sq. km. in the north and along the coast, where there were good prospects of finding oil. Copies of the survey were immediately bought up by the world's oil companies for a total of P60 million, and requests for permits covering more than 100,000 sq. km. were made. Eventually, more than 40 onshore concessions were granted to eleven consortia. Spain's state-owned Instituto Nacional de Industria (q.v.) participated through association contracts with Caltex, Gao of Spain, and Pan-American Hispano Oil Company in ten of the permits, covering 23 percent of the total concessions area. Most of the companies involved in this exploration were Spanish subsidiaries of U.S. oil companies.

Drilling began in 1960–61, and by 1964, 27 traces of oil had been found. But by then most of the companies had started withdrawing, two years before the expiry of their six-year exploration permits. Though some oil had been found, none of the companies apparently discovered commercially viable deposits. The low price of oil at this time, as well as the low level of infrastructural development in the territory, may also have influenced the companies' decisions.

However, the Cepsa-Gulf consortium retained its onshore permits, and in 1966, offshore exploration began for the first time. The Cepsa-Gulf group discovered oil offshore in the south of the territory in 1971, but it was said to be of poor quality and difficult to extract. The state-controlled company, Ibérico de Sondeos, appears to have drilled offshore for ENMINSA (q.v.), the INI subsidiary that retained rights to almost 12 million acres of abandoned and unlet concessions, and in 1969, Union Carbide Petroleum acquired a permit to explore 1.6 million ha. offshore. Meanwhile, the Spanish state budget for oil exploration in Western Sahara grew from around P200–240 million a year in 1960–64 to P464 million in 1965 and P1,215 million in 1972.

It is also significant that heavy oil has been discovered in an offshore zone near Tarfaya (q.v.), just north of the Western Saharan border. The first oil exploration in the Tarfaya region had taken place onshore in 1960–63, when the Italian state-owned company ENI drilled at Oum Doul and near the Oued Chebeika. In 1963, ENI withdrew, but in 1965, the Moroccan government granted exploration rights offshore to Esso. Drilling started in 1968, and later that year, heavy oil was discovered. According to Serfaty (see Bibliography), Esso's second drilling revealed a 100-km.-long oil field, which stretched south, crossing the border onto Western Sahara's continental shelf. Serfaty, who visited the Esso installations at Tarfay in 1969, when he was working for the Moroccan Direction des Mines et de la Géologie, claims that Esso decided to keep quiet about its discovery because the field straddled the border and the political future of Western Sahara was then in doubt. The main reason for the failure to develop the field, however, was probably that the oil was very heavy. An eighth wildcat in Esso's offshore zone near Tarfaya in 1972 also struck heavy oil. Interest in the region continued, Esso signing an agreement with Shell in 1974 to drill offshore and, in the same year, oil shale deposits being found onshore near Tarfaya.

By the time that Spain withdrew from Western Sahara (1976), two consortia still held exploration concessions there: the Cepsa-Gulf Conoco group, which held six concessions, three offshore and three onshore, covering 2.5 million ha.; and the Enpasa-Enpensa group (two subsidiaries of INI), with three concessions offshore totaling 170,000 ha. Moreover, since then, Morocco has granted new offshore exploration permits. In 1977, British Petroleum and Phillips Oil Company signed an agreement with the Moroccan state's Bureau de Recherches et de Participations Minières to explore seven offshore blocks covering 35,000 sq. km. between El-Ayoun and Boujdour (q.v.) for a four-year period. By mid-1978, seismic studies had reportedly been carried out, but no drilling followed, and in 1980, the concession was abandoned. In February 1981, however, Morocco signed an agreement with Mobil for the resumption of offshore oil exploration in the Tarfaya area where Esso and ENI had earlier drilled. In September 1980, Shell undertook a feasibility study regarding large, onshore shale oil deposits near Tarfaya, which are thought to extend into Western Sahara. A U.S. company began exploring for oil off the coast of Tarfaya in the 1980s, and Shell signed an agreement to explore for oil off the Tarfaya coast in 1989. As of 1990, no commercially viable discoveries had been made, either in Western Sahara or in the Tarfaya area. Plans to exploit the onshore shale deposits in Tarfaya were abandoned in the mid-1980s because of the decline in world oil prices.

PHOSBOUCRAA. Acronym for Phosphates de Bou-Craa, the large mining company. See FOSBUCRAA, the acronym of the Spanish version of the company's name.

PHOSPHATES. Western Sahara was becoming one of the world's major phosphate exporters when, as a result of the war between the Polisario Front (q.v.) and Morocco, mining suddenly ground to a halt early in 1976.

It was shortly after the occupation by Spanish troops of points in the interior for the first time (1934) that a franchise was granted (to the Compañía Española de Investigación y Fomento SA) to search for phosphates. The real "discoverer" of the territory's phosphates, however, was the geologist Manuel Alia Medina, who carried out his research in the 1940s. In 1952, responsibility for more advanced studies was given to a state-owned firm. After a decade of tests of samples for different parts of the country, a new company, the Empresa Nacional Minera del Sahara (q.v.), was set up in July 1962 by the state holding company, Instituto Nacional de Industria (q.v.), with a brief to carry out a systematic geological survey and examine the feasibility of exploiting known phosphate deposits. ENMINSA soon claimed that the territory had about 10 billion tons of phosphates, including a proven reserve of 1.7 billion tons of very high grade ore at Bou-Craa (q.v.), about 107 km. southeast of El-Ayoun (q.v.). In terms of dried phosphate concentrate, the Bou-Craa deposit has up to 900 million tons. The ore is 75–80 percent bone phosphate of lime (BPL), equivalent to 34.31–36.6

percent P_2O_5, a better grade than that mined in Morocco, the world's largest exporter, where the grade ranges between 68 and 75 percent BPL. It is also particularly easy to mine by open-cast methods, since the deposit lies just below the surface, about 2.5–7 meters in width, extending over 260 sq. km.

ENMINSA at first attempted to involve non-Spanish companies in a consortium to exploit the deposit. Several U.S. companies (Gulf Oil, W.B. Grace, Texaco, and Standard Oil of California) were approached, but in 1967, negotiations broke down. Another attempt, involving International Mining and Chemicals Corp. of Chicago, ended in failure in January 1968. Apparently, these firms were discouraged by the low world phosphate price at this time, the political uncertainty regarding Western Sahara's future, and, above all, the Spanish government's insistence on maintaining full management control and sending the ore to Spain for processing. In 1970, the Spanish foreign minister, Gregorio López Bravo, was equally unsuccessful when, during a visit to Rabat, he tried to persuade Morocco to drop its claim to the territory in return for participation in the Bou-Craa venture.

After the breakdown of the talks with International Mining and Chemicals Corp., the Spanish government decided to go it alone. In August 1969, a new INI subsidiary, Fosfatos de Bu-Craa, or Fosbucraa (q.v.) for short, was set up and investment plans drawn up. Loans were raised from, among others, the First Wisconsin National Bank and the U.S. Export-Import Bank. By 1974, P24.5 billion had been invested in the first phase of the project, which provided an initial capacity of 3.7 million tons a year. At Bou-Craa, strip-mining methods are used. Two giant draglines, each weighing almost 3,000 tons, remove the topsoil. The phosphate is then extracted by bucket-wheel excavators or electric shovels and loaded on to 100-ton bottom-dump trucks, which carry the mineral to a crushing plant. The ore is then stockpiled in a 300,000-ton-capacity storage area before being fed onto Fosbucraa's famous conveyor belt, the longest of its kind in the world and an astonishing feat of engineering. Built by Krupps and the Continental Clouth rubber consortium at a cost of $72.2 million, it carries the ore 98.6 km. across the desert to the coast. Its 113,000 rollers, operated by eleven control stations, which are in turn monitored from a computerized control room at the coast, can carry up to 2,000 tons per hour at 16.2 kph. Arriving at El-Ayoun Playa (q.v.), the ore is stored in another stockpile (capacity 300,000 tons) before being fed into the treatment plant, where the ore is washed with desalinated seawater and dried. It then goes to a third storage area (capacity 300,000 tons). The shallow waters precluded construction of a conventional harbor, and so instead, a 3.2-km.-long pier was built, jutting out to sea at right angles from the coast. At its end are three loading berths, which can receive ships of 100,000 tons, 60,000 tons, and 20,000 tons, respectively, with a loading rate of 4,000 tons per hour at the first two and 2,000 tons per hour at the third. Few jobs were created by this ultramodern mining operation—about 2,550 by 1975, of which three fifths were held by Spaniards. Only 19 percent of supervisory and technical posts were held by Saharawis.

The first shipment of phosphate left for Japan in May 1972, and by 1974, annual production had reached 2.4 million tons. In 1975, exports were 2.6 million tons, making Western Sahara the world's sixth-largest phosphate exporter (after Morocco, the United States, the USSR, Tunisia, and China). With a production capacity of 3.7 million tons a year and plans to raise capacity to 10 million tons a year by 1980, Western Sahara seemed destined to become the world's second-largest exporter (after Morocco, since most U.S. and Soviet output is not exported). Spain, which had previously bought its phosphate from Morocco to meet domestic needs of about 1.65 million tons (1975), had built phosphoric acid plants at Huelva to process some of the ore and expected to recover its investment within ten years. Having prolonged its colonial presence partly in order to take advantage of the territory's phosphate wealth, the Spanish government calculated in 1975 that it would still be able to reap the benefits of its investments if independence were granted to a weak and pragmatic Saharawi government. But Morocco forced Spain to abandon these plans, and instead, Western Sahara was handed over to Morocco and Mauritania in 1975–76. Bou-

Craa ended up in the Moroccan zone of the partitioned territory and, under the Madrid Agreement (q.v.), the INI was obliged to hand over 65 percent of Fosbucraa's shares to Morocco's state-owned Office Chérifien de Phosphates (OCP). Reportedly, INI was to receive compensation in kind—deliveries of phosphate priced at preferentially low rates. For Morocco, the takeover of the Western Saharan phosphate industry was a significant prize, despite the fact that political, rather than economic, considerations were the principal motives for Morocco's bid to annex the territory. Morocco, which depends on phosphates for almost one third of its total export earnings, had no interest in the emergence of a major potential rival in the world phosphate market and expected to add significantly to its own export capacity by taking over the Bou-Craa mines. In fact, though, mining ground to a halt early in 1976 because of the war between Morocco and the Polisario guerrillas. The latter had already, in November 1974, alarmed the Spanish authorities by sabotaging two of the conveyor belt's control stations. After Morocco's entry into the territory, the conveyor belt became one of the guerrillas' principal targets. By 1978, they had burned up five and a half kilometers of it in five places, put two of the control stations out of action, and felled several of the power pylons that take electricity from a power plant at the coast to the mines, where all the mining equipment is electrically powered. Exports slumped to 277,000 tons in 1976 and only 25,000 tons in 1977, as Fosbucraa managed to ship out only small quantities of phosphate, which had been stockpiled before the mines and the conveyor belt were forced to a halt. The company lost P1.8 billion in 1976, and, though a reduced work force was maintained (with OCP employees from Morocco replacing most of the Spanish employees) in the hope of restoring production, the company finally decided in 1980 to close down its operations entirely. In 1982, following a return to relative normalcy in the vicinity of Bou-Craa caused by Morocco's construction of a "defensive wall" (q.v.) around the northwest of the territory, the Moroccan government announced that the mine would reopen and that production would resume. However, the conveyor belt, the most economical way of transporting to the coast the phosphate ore mined at Bou-Craa, remained inoperative as of 1989, forcing Fosbucraa to use trucks, a far more expensive substitute. In 1985, production was 963,878 tons, a little over one third of its 1974 level.

POLICIA TERRITORIAL. A paramilitary police force during the last two decades of Spanish rule, the Territorial Police was composed primarily of Saharawis but mainly officered by Spaniards. Responsible for desert patrols, alongside the Tropas Nómadas (q.v.), it evolved out of the Policía del Africa Occidental Española, a force established in AOE (q.v.) in 1956–57. Almost all its Saharawi members joined the Polisario Front after being demobilized in October–November 1975 on the eve of the Madrid Agreement (q.v.). Along with demobilized soldiers of the Tropas Nómadas, they made up the core of the Polisario guerrilla army in the early months of the war against Morocco and Mauritania.

POLISARIO FRONT see FRENTE POPULAR PARA LA LIB-ERACION DE SAGUIA EL-HAMRA Y RIO DE ORO

POLITICAL BUREAU (OF THE POLISARIO FRONT). Formerly one of the main leadership bodies of the Polisario Front (q.v.), the political bureau membership was elected, until 1991, about once every three years by the front's general popular congresses (q.v.). It was not the top leadership body—that role was played by the executive committee (q.v.)—but it was responsible for handing down political guidelines to the rank and file of the movement. Among the members were the *walis* (q.v.) and the secretaries-general of the "mass organizations"—the UNMS, UGTS, and Ugesario (qq.v.). Before the political bureau was abolished by the front's 8th congress (June 18–20, 1991), it consisted of 27 members, some of whom were also members of the council of ministers of the Saharan Arab Democratic Republic (qq.v.).

POPULAR BASE CONGRESSES. The mass assemblies held in the *dairat* (q.v.), the administrative subdivisions of the Saharawi refugee (q.v.) population in southwestern Algeria, since 1976. These assemblies were first held in April 1976, in March–April 1977, and in April 1978 to elect delegates to the general popular congresses (q.v.) convened shortly thereafter. The meetings of the popular base congresses have been held on roughly a yearly basis since that time and include members of the daira popular councils, who are responsible for administrative matters in the refugee camps. The presidents of the daira popular councils and the members of the popular committees in each *wilaya* (q.v.) are elected by the congresses as well. Thus each person in authority in each camp is subject to a yearly "vote of confidence." As part of the major governmental and constitutional changes undertaken at Polisario's 8th congress, in June 1991, the popular base congresses were to function normally until the "liberation of the country" (i.e., the independence of the Saharan Arab Democratic Republic [q.v.]), when they were to be abolished and replaced by an elected parliament and other forms of local self-government.

POPULAR FRONT FOR THE LIBERATION OF SAGUIA EL-HAMRA AND RIO DE ORO see FRENTE POPULAR PARA LA LIBERACION DE SAGUIA EL-HAMRA Y RIO DE ORO

POPULATION. The most recent but incomplete census, carried out by the Spanish authorities in 1974, recorded a Saharawi population of 73,497; the European population of the territory at that time was 26,126. However, the 1974 census should be consulted with caution. The census authorities reported considerable variation in the degree of cooperation they received from the Saharawi population, and it is therefore almost certain that the census underestimated the number of Saharawis present in the territory in 1974, especially those living outside the urban areas and engaged in a nomadic way of life.

The census naturally did not include the very large numbers of Saharawis with historical ties to the country (through membership of tribes with migratory-pastoral traditions in Western Sahara) who happened to be living outside the territory in 1974—in southern Morocco, southwestern

Algeria, and northern Mauritania. During the 1960s and early 1970s, many Saharawis settled in such growing towns as Zouerate, Tindouf (q.v.), and Tan-Tan as a result of droughts and the availability of employment opportunities or drought relief in these centers. Escape from colonial repression, notably after Operation Ouragan (q.v.) in 1958, also encouraged some Saharawis to settle in neighboring countries. There were certainly more Saharawis, as defined in the above broad terms, living outside the borders of Western Sahara than within them in 1974. The official Moroccan population figure for the province of Tan-Tan, whose population is almost entirely Saharawi, was 81,900 in 1978. The 1977 Mauritanian census gave a population of 47,000 from Regions 8 (Nouadhibou) and 9 (Zouerate and the far north), both of which border Western Sahara and are populated mainly by Saharawis. Finally, there are Saharawis among the 148,000 inhabitants of the Algerian *wilaya* (province) of Bechar, which includes the Tindouf area.

Many Saharawis from all three neighboring countries have enrolled in the Polisario Front (q.v.) since the mid-1970s. This explains the paradox that the number of Saharawis in the Polisario refugee (q.v.) camps near Tindouf by 1990 (about 150,000), was higher than the total number of Saharawis counted by the Spanish census authorities in 1974, a paradox made all the more remarkable when account is taken of the fact that an estimated 20,000 Saharawis remained in the Moroccan-controlled towns of Western Sahara after the departure of the Spanish.

Nonetheless, the 1974 census retains considerable interest as a study of a large ''sample'' of the Saharawi population. A detailed ethnic breakdown shows the preponderance of the Reguibat (q.v.)—37,972 out of 73,497, or 52 percent of the sample. The two branches of the Reguibat, the Sahel (western) and Charg (eastern), are found to be of roughly equal size (18,347 and 19,625, respectively), each therefore constituting about one quarter of the population. Two Tekna (q.v.) tribes, the Izarguien (7,984) and Ait Lahsen (3,540), are the second- and fifth-largest groups. The third is the Oulad Delim (5,382). The other main tribes are the Ould Tidrarin (4,842) and the Arosien (2,858).

According to the 1974 census, 45.18 percent of the population are aged under 15 years old. Most were living in the urban areas—a reflection not only of the census's underestimation of the nomadic population but also of the important process of sedentation and urbanization, which occurred in the 1960s and early 1970s as a result of droughts and the creation of employment opportunities in the towns as administrative services and economic infrastructure were expanded and prospecting and development of the territory's mineral resources began. The Saharawi population of El-Ayoun (q.v.) grew from only 3,378 in 1950 to 28,010 in 1974. This was equivalent to 38 percent of the total Saharawi population recorded in the census. Including also Dakhla (q.v.), with 5,370 Saharawis (compared to 1,120 in 1950), and Smara (q.v.), with 7,280 (compared to 2,688 in 1950), the census recorded 40,660 Saharwis, 55 percent of the total, as living in the three main towns.

Of all the matters of contention between Morocco and the Polisario Front, few are as sharply disputed as the present number of Saharawis who come from Western Sahara and who thus should be counted for voting purposes in a referendum of self-determination conducted by the United Nations (q.v.). Not only did Polisario claim, by the late 1980s, that upwards of 165,000 Saharawis were living in its refugee camps in the Tindouf (q.v.) region of Algeria, but it also alleged that Morocco had "imported" large numbers of Moroccan citizens into the territory to act as a counterweight to the high numbers of Saharawis living in the Tindouf camps. Those newly arrived Moroccans, numbering in the tens of thousands, were drawn to Western Sahara by substantial economic incentives, such as subsidized housing and higher wages. Polisario wanted this group of persons to be removed from the territory before the vote, or at least not placed on the voter register for the referendum. For its part, Morocco claimed that many of the refugees in the camps in southwestern Algeria were non-Saharawi nomads from surrounding countries.

In August 1988, however, both Morocco and Polisario agreed in principle to a UN peace plan under which the 1975 Spanish census would be used as a basis for determining who would be qualified to vote in a referendum. Later on, the United Nations established a Saharan Identification Commission under the supervision of the UN's special representative for Western Sahara, Johannes Manz (q.v.). As described by the secretary-general in a report to the Security Council on June 18, 1990 (see Bibliography), the Identification Commission would "review carefully" the 1974 census and update it to take account of the growth in the population since that time, using information related to births, deaths, and movements in the Saharawi population since that time. The commission also utilized the expertise of Saharawi tribal chiefs or "elders" from both the Polisario- and Moroccan-administered portions of Western Sahara, who were intimately familiar with the social organization of the territory.

But despite the undoubted goodwill on the part of the United Nations and its secretary-general, the renewed effort to finalize the list of those entitled to vote in the plebiscite soon ran into snags. Months after the personnel of the United Nations Mission for the Referendum in Western Sahara (q.v.), known as MINURSO, had begun to arrive in the territory, the list of voters had still not been determined, much less published in the territory. This was due partly to the intrinsic complexity of the task—merely removing the names of those Saharawis who had died since 1974 was an involved process. But shortly after the cease-fire was declared (on September 6, 1991), Morocco allegedly began moving many thousands of inhabitants of the southern part of Morocco into Western Sahara, who were housed for the most part in desert encampments. Morocco claimed that all of them were Saharawis eligible to vote, and their numbers soon climbed to over 120,000. Merely processing and deciding the eligibility of such a large number of persons greatly burdened the Identification Commission and delayed the other parts of the MINURSO plan, much to the anger of the Polisario Front. After an extensive review of the situation, Secretary-General Pérez de Cuéllar issued new instructions to the Identification Commission in an annex to his report to the Security Council of December 19, 1991 (see Bibliography). In this document, Pérez de Cuéllar acknowledged the

complex nature of deciding voter eligibility given the nomadic nature of Saharawi society in years past and the fact
that many live outside Western Sahara itself. But his proposed solution to the problem ignited a firestorm of controversy. He stated that those persons from a Saharawi tribe
who could prove they had resided in the territory for 6
consecutive years (or 12 years intermittently) before December 1, 1974, should be eligible to vote in the referendum.
Polisario immediately denounced this move, saying it bla-
tantly favored Morocco by introducing a substantial number
of new voters into the process who had their origins in
Morocco and who had lived there for many years. These
persons, quite possibly, would outnumber those already in
the territory (either in Morocco- or Polisario-administered
areas) or in the refugee camps in Algeria run by Polisario.
Particularly galling to the Polisario Front (and puzzling to
outside observers) was the contention in the report by the
secretary-general that "it is also appropriate to note that one
of the main tasks of the United Nations has been to promote
decolonization around the world. In that context, people who
fled colonial rule cannot be deprived of the right to decide on
the future of the territory to which they belong." Some felt
that this shifted the issue from one of Moroccan "importa-
tion" of persons into Western Sahara into one concerning
the iniquities of the Spanish colonial period, in the process
opening up a whole new field of possible disputes over voter
qualification. And the statement was cold comfort for Polisario, which had always claimed that Morocco was itself
practicing a form of colonialism in Western Sahara. So
intense was the controversy on this issue that the UN
Security Council, reportedly after pressure by Third World
states, including (among others) Zimbabwe, gave only qualified approval to Pérez de Cuéllar in its resolution 725 of
December 31, 1991—it "welcomed" rather than approved
his report and urged the incoming secretary-general, Boutros
Boutros Ghali (q.v.), to devote added attention to the matter.
In late 1993, matters essentially rested at this point, with
implementation of the UN peace plan stymied by this
population-related problem.

PORTS. Western Sahara has an extremely dangerous coastline. Most of the shore consists of steep cliffs, the coastal waters are generally very shallow, and there are numerous sandbanks. Moreover, there are frequently violent storms. Traditionally, this coast has therefore been hazardous for shipping, and there have not been any good natural harbors. The only fishing port of consequence is at La Guera (q.v.), where there is a small jetty. Though Dakhla (q.v.) lies alongside the large natural bay of Rio de Oro (q.v.) and has a port with a 450-m. quay (completed in 1961), access is limited to vessels of up to 6,000 tons with a 6-m. draught because of sandbanks at the bay's entrance. At El-Ayoun (q.v.), a jetty was first built in 1960–61, and then the phosphate company, Fosbucraa (q.v.), built a remarkable 3-km.-long ore-loading pier, which was completed in 1972. Its two conveyor belts could each carry up to 2,000 tons of ore an hour, and its three loading berths were designed to handle ships of up to 100,000 tons, 60,000 tons, and 20,000 tons, respectively, the first two with loading rates of 4,000 tons per hour, the third 2,000 tons per hour. One and a half kilometers along the pier, which juts out to sea at right angles to the coast, there was an unloading berth for general cargo, which could accommodate vessels of up to 10,000 tons. After the start of the war between Morocco and Polisario, the pier fell into disuse because of the decline and temporary closure of the phosphate mining industry and because of major damage to one of the loading berths by a ship in 1976. The phosphate industry resumed production in 1982. Morocco began work on an entirely new pier, opened for use in 1987, for general cargo and the fishing industry. Built at a cost of $42 million, it consists of two jetties of 2,000 and 750 meters in length, as well as a 50-ha. industrial park in the vicinity. The pier is capable of handling 250,000 tons of fish a year. A small, new port facility has also been constructed by the Moroccan government at Boujdour (q.v.).

PROVINCE. On January 10, 1958, a decree converted Western Sahara into a ''province'' of Spain. Taken at a time of serious challenge from the guerrillas of the Army of Liberation (q.v.), the decision to create the Provincia del Sahara was probably made to underline that Spain had no intention of leaving the territory. It was also a ruse by which to counter pressure from the United Nations (q.v.). Indeed, on November 10, 1958, the Spanish government informed the UN that "Spain possesses no non-self-governing territories, since the territories subject to its sovereignty in Africa are, in accordance with the legislation now in force, considered to be and classified as provinces of Spain." Nonetheless, a law of April 19, 1961, on the organization and juridical regime of the province did not hesitate to note in its preamble the specificities that distinguished Western Sahara from the metropolitan provinces (nomadism, Islam, the low level of economic development). As a Spanish province, Western Sahara was ruled by a governor-general (q.v.), who was responsible in military matters to the captain general of the Canary Islands and in administrative matters to the presidency of the government in Madrid through the Dirección General de Plazas y Provincias Africanas—or, after 1969, the Dirección General de Promoción del Sahara (q.v.). The governor-general had very wide-ranging powers, the Cabildo Provincial (q.v.), which was first elected in 1963, having little role in provincial policy-making. Likewise, the provincial assembly, the Djemaa (q.v.), which was created in 1967, was a purely consultative body. The province elected *procuradores* (q.v.) to the Cortes—three in 1963 and six from 1967—but all elections were as strictly controlled as they were at this time in metropolitan Spain. After Spain's withdrawal from Western Sahara in 1975–76 and the Moroccan–Mauritanian partition in April 1976, the Rabat regime created three provinces—El-Ayoun, Smara, and Boujdour (qq.v.) in the Moroccan sector of the territory. Their first governors took office on April 15, 1976. A fourth Moroccan province was created in Tiris el-Gharbia (q.v.) when this erstwhile Mauritanian sector of the territory was annexed by Morocco in August 1979.

PROVISIONAL SAHARAWI NATIONAL COUNCIL. "Within the framework of a solution of national unity and free of any outside intervention, there is hereby established a Provisional Saharawi National Council," declared one of the clauses of the

Proclamation of Guelta Zemmour (q.v.), a document signed by 67 members of the Djemaa (q.v.), the consultative territorial assembly set up by the Spanish in 1967, 3 of the Saharawi members of the Spanish Cortes (q.v.) and more than 60 other notables and *chioukh* (q.v.), gathered together under the auspices of the Polisario Front in Guelta Zemmour (q.v.) a few days after the Madrid Agreement (q.v.). The proclamation dissolved the Djemaa and set up the Provisional Saharawi National Council, under the presidency of M'hamed Ould Ziou (q.v.), a veteran anticolonial militant, in its place. There was a dual objective in this. One was to remove the one Saharawi institution, of traditionally conservative bent, which the Madrid Agreement had specified would be consulted on the territory's future; the other was to associate some of the elder notables, who had generally collaborated with the Spanish but were by then fearful of Morocco, more closely with the Polisario Front, whose leadership was overwhelmingly young and radical. The council was seen, symbolically, as a kind of national, modern version of the old tribal war council, the *ait arbain* (q.v.), or council of 40. At its first ordinary session, on December 30–31, 1975, the council set up a permanent committee, a series of nine specialized committees responsible for such matters as foreign relations and education, and regional councils. It was the Provisional Saharawi National Council that proclaimed the founding of the Saharan Arab Democratic Republic (q.v.) at Bir Lehlou on February 27, 1976. A few months later, at the Polisario Front's 3rd general popular congress (q.v.), held on August 26–30, 1976, the provisional council was replaced by a new elected Saharawi National Council (q.v.).

- Q -

QABILA. Pl. *qabael*. Arabic for tribe (q.v.) or clan.

QADI. Civil justice was administered in traditional Saharawi society by a *qadi,* an Islamic judge, according to the Muslim judicial code, the *sharia* (q.v.). By contrast, criminal matters were judged by the *djemaa* (q.v.) according to customary law, the *orf* (q.v.). The qadi was traditionally appointed by the djemaa, which could override his rulings or replace him if he was deemed unjust or biased. This system remained unchanged until the mid-1950s, when the Spanish authorities tried to bring the traditional judicial system under their aegis. By an ordinance of March 21, 1956, the Koranic judicial system was streamlined by the establishment of a national system of Koranic courts, from a *mejeles,* or *tribunal superior,* at national level to *qodat* at local level. Under this system, a qadi was appointed for the city of El-Ayoun. He was assisted by two *adel* and a secretary. Since the departure of the Spanish in 1975–76, the term qadi has denoted the judges of the Moroccan judicial system (introduced into the towns controlled by Morocco) and those appointed by the Judicial Council at the SADR (qq.v.).

QAID see CAID

- R -

RAINFALL see CLIMATE

RAS EL-KHANFRA. A small hill, at the foot of the Zini mountains, about 10 km. north of the Western Saharan frontier, Ras el-Khanfra became one of the fiercest fought battle sites of the war between Morocco and the Polisario Front (q.v.). Several thousand Moroccan troops from the Larak force (q.v.) dug in there in August 1980 as part of a drive to gain control of the Zini Mountains and the road through them from Tan-Tan to Smara (q.v.). In a long campaign of harassment, the Polisario guerrillas staged almost continuous raids on the Moroccan troops there until February 1981.

RAZZI see GHAZZI

REFUGEES. The first major refugee movements in recent decades accompanied the war between the Army of Liberation (q.v.) and Spain and France in 1957–58. Several thousand

Saharawis settled at that time in southern Morocco to escape the fighting or join the guerrillas' rear bases. After the cession of the Tekna Zone (q.v.) by Spain to Morocco in April 1958, a few weeks after the decimation of the guerrilla forces during Operation Ouragan (q.v.), many of these Saharawis began to live in settlements in the zone, including Tarfaya (q.v.), Tan-Tan, and Zaag. Others settled further north, for example in Goulimine. A severe drought in 1959–63, which wiped out much of the nomads' livestock, also encouraged sedentation in these southern Moroccan settlements—as it did also in the small growing towns of Western Sahara itself and in such centers as Tindouf (q.v.), Algeria, and Zouerate, Mauritania, in the 1960s. Thus economic, as well as political, factors prompted Saharawis to settle in southern Morocco, southwestern Algeria, and northern Mauritania in this period.

It was toward the end of 1975, after the signing of the Madrid Agreement (q.v.), that large refugee movements resumed. By December 1975, there were c. 20,000 Saharawis living in camps near Tindouf run by the Polisario Front and its relief body, the Saharawi Red Crescent (qq.v.), which was founded in November 1975. They included about 15,000 Saharawis who had arrived from Western Sahara and about 5,000 Reguibat (q.v.) who had settled in the Tindouf region (in Tindouf, Oum el-Assel, and Hassi Abdallah) and around Bechar over the preceding decade as a result of the droughts and who rallied to the Polisario cause at this time. Meanwhile, thousands more refugees fled from Western Saharan towns to water points in the territory's desert hinterland. The most important concentrations were at Oum Dreiga and Guelta Zemmour (q.v.), where there may have been as many as 20,000 refugees by February 1976, when Moroccan air force jets began bombing the encampments at Oum Dreiga, killing several dozen refugees. Guelta Zemmour came under Moroccan attack a little later and was captured by Moroccan forces the following April. Gradually the Polisario Front evacuated all of the refugees to Tindouf, shuttling them across the *hammada* (q.v.), via such water points as Amgala and Mahbes (qq.v.), in convoys of trucks. The Algerian army entered the territory to assist the exodus, bringing in trucks, medicines, and food, leading to a direct clash between Algerian and Moroccan forces at Amgala (q.v.) on January 29. Algerian troops were then withdrawn from Western Sahara.

By June 1976, the number of Saharawi refugees in Algeria had reached 100,000, according to the Saharawi Red Crescent, though the Algerian government put the figure at about 50,000 when it appealed to the UNHCR for aid the following October. After 1976, however, the number of refugees continued to grow. Many arrived from southern Morocco and northern Mauritania, where large numbers of Saharawis had settled in preceding years, as well as from Western Sahara, and by 1981, the Algerian government informed the UNHCR that it had 150,000 Saharawi refugees in Tindouf camps.

Coping with the refugee influx was a major challenge to the Algerian government, especially in the early months of 1976, when the influx was at its height and most of the refugees were arriving exhausted, undernourished, and without belongings after spending several weeks in camps within Western Sahara. Their resistance to disease was low, and about 400 children died during a measles epidemic in the Tindouf camps in 1976. Algerian doctors were rushed to the camps to set up small clinics and organize a major vaccination campaign. The main responsibility for relief work fell on the Algerian Red Crescent, which faced enormous logistical problems. The camps were situated about 2,000 km. from Algiers, and the roads were poor. There were no wells in or near most of the camps, so cisterns had to be installed and supplied. Firewood, too, had to be transported to the camps, sometimes from 300 km. away, and food, blankets, and tents had to be brought all the way from Algiers.

On December 23, 1975, the League of Red Cross Societies launched an international appeal to its affiliated societies to rush aid to the Tindouf refugees. The league's aid program, which officially ended in July 1976, raised 10.9 million Swiss francs from 22 Red Cross societies. The UNHCR was then asked to coordinate a long-term relief program. In October, it launched an international appeal for annual aid of $5.7 million and 10,000 tons of food for 50,000 refugees.

However, during the whole of 1977, the UNHCR distributed only $1.2 million in aid, and by December 1978, the total contributed during the two years since the appeal's launching had reached only $3.1 million and 2,140 tons of food worth $886,111. Very little was raised and distributed by the UNHCR thereafter. As a result, most of the relief burden fell on the Algerian government and the Algerian Red Crescent.

Despite the difficulties, conditions in the Tindouf refugee camps had improved markedly by 1977–78. Administered by the Polisario Front rather than the Algerian authorities, they were acknowledged by international visitors to be superbly organized. Each of the camps (about 22 in all) became a *daira* (q.v.) of the SADR and was administered by an elected daira popular council, which was headed by an administrative official and had five other members, each responsible for one of the five camp committees supervising education, health, justice, food, and crafts. The dairat were initially grouped into three *wilayat* (q.v.), each of which comprised a complex of closely spaced camps. A "national hospital" and an extensive network of regional hospitals and clinics were gradually established, and a few Saharawis were sent abroad for medical training. Several primary and vocational training schools were built, providing education (q.v.) for several thousand children and some adults. By 1987, almost 100 percent of children aged 6–12 years were enrolled in school. Also during the 1980s, sanitation in the camps improved substantially. In spite of the high birth rate, the refugees' tents were moved further from one another, and separate buildings were constructed for kitchens, which also minimized safety problems arising from the use of butane or propane gas. Also, a fourth wilaya, Aoussert (q.v.), was established in December 1985 to handle the added population. As of 1986, there were 25 dairat, each with about 6,000 refugees. Despite the inhabitants' continued substantial reliance on outside assistance, every effort was made to achieve at least a measure of self-sufficiency: by October 1986, a total of 44.5 ha. of land in the desert had been brought under cultivation (no small task in the circumstances) to produce vegetables. There were plans to expand the area under cultivation to 150 ha. Despite this progress, life remained harsh in the 1980s. Due to sandstorms, about 4,000 tents per year needed replacement, and storms in 1984 destroyed many additional tents and mud-brick buildings. Locusts created a scourge in 1989, and the provision of adequate water continued to call for ingenuity (see WATER RE-SOURCES). Although the cost of assistance to the refugee camps is difficult to quantify, it has been estimated that between $35 and $50 million per year is required to provide all the refugees with minimally sufficient food supplies alone.

REGUIBAT (variant: Erguibat). Sing. Reguibi. The largest tribe in Western Sahara, the Reguibat traditionally nomadized over a vast area, extending from the Oued Draa (q.v.) in southern Morocco, through the Saguia el-Hamra and the massif of Zemmour (qq.v.), to southwestern Algeria, northern Mauritania, and the northwestern tip of Mali.

Their ancestral founder was a saintly marabout by the name of Sidi Ahmed Reguibi, who is said to have turned up in the Draa valley from Fez in 1503. Claiming to be a *cherif,* he seems to have attracted numerous disciples during his wanderings between the valley of the Draa, the plain of El-Gaada (q.v.), and the Saguia el-Hamra. Most, it seems, were Sanhaja (q.v.) who were anxious to resist the encroachments of the Europeans on the coast as well as of the Maqil (q.v.).

The Reguibat are believed to be almost entirely of Sanhaja origin, despite the tribe's adoption of the Hassaniya (q.v.) dialect of Arabic and its claim to *cherifian* status through descent from Sidi Ahmed. IIe, the tribe's genealogists say, married a woman of the Sellam (q.v.), Kaouria Mint Mohammed, who bore him three sons, Ali, Amar, and Qacem, who in turn, it is said, engendered the main Reguibat clans or subtribes. These were traditionally grouped into two geographical blocs—the Reguibat es-Sahel (western Reguibat) and the Reguibat ech-Charg (eastern Reguibat), who are also often known as the Reguibat Lgouacem (the Reguibat supposedly descended from Qacem). The camels of the two blocs were traditionally branded with two letters of the Arabic alphabet, *kaf* for the Reguibat es-Sahel and *qaf* for the Reguibat ech-Charg.

Ali and Amar are said to be the ancestors of the main subtribes of the Reguibat es-Sahel. According to the genealogies, Ali's sons, Moussa, Saad, and Daoud, were the founders of the Oulad Moussa, the Souaad, and the Oulad Daoud (q.v.), respectively, while Moueden, the supposed ancestor of the Lemouedenin, was either a fourth son of Ali or a disciple of Sidi Ahmed. Amar's two sons, Cheikh and Taleb, engendered the Oulad Cheikh and the Oulad Taleb (q.v.). Qacem's sons, Daoud, Bouih, and Faqar, are said to be the ancestors of the Ahel Brahim Ou Daoud, the Lebouihat and the Foqra (qq.v.).

However, the Reguibat are not pure. As a result of intermarriage, numerous groups have been aggregated, starting with the Sellam, who became blood allies by virtue of Sidi Ahmed Reguibi's marriage with Kaouria Mint Mohammed. Another group in the Reguibat ech-Charg that is known to have been aggregated is the Laiaicha. The same was true for the Thaalat (q.v.) among the Réguibat es-Sahel.

It was not until the 19th century that the Reguibat were to acquire their warlike reputation. Until then, they had been a small, peaceable tribe that raised goats, traded with the Oued Noun and Souss regions of southern Morocco, and were respected for their learning.

Gradually, however, they are thought to have specialized in raising camels and extended their nomadic migrations farther south toward the pastures of the Zemmour massif. As their camel herds grew, they acquired the resources for demographic expansion and the mobility needed to assert their military strength.

In c. 1820, a long war began with the Tadjakant (q.v.), a people who controlled much of the caravan traffic in this part of the Sahara in the 19th century and founded the city of Tindouf (q.v.) as a trading center in 1852. *Ghazzi* (q.v.) followed ghazzi until almost the end of the century, when, in 1895, an assembly of all the Reguibat, both ech-Charg and es-Sahel, decided upon a full-scale mobilization of all able-bodied men, under a unified command, with a warrior of the

Oulad Moussa as *dahman* (q.v.). A force of 1,000 Reguibat then attacked Tindouf. After an 11-day siege, the town fell and its inhabitants were massacred. So complete was the Reguibat victory that Tindouf remained virtually deserted until the French arrived there almost 40 years later, in 1934.

Meanwhile, the Reguibat had assisted the Oulad Bou Sbaa (q.v.) in resisting a force from Adrar and the Hodh (Mauritania) led by a fanatical marabout (q.v.), Sidi Ahmed el-Kounti, who was killed by a Reguibi in c. 1866. In 1880, there were conflicts with the Oulad el-Lab from which the Reguibat emerged victorious; then, in 1888, the Reguibat allied with the Oulad Tidrarin (q.v.) in their war of emancipation from the *horma* (q.v.) against the Oulad Delim (q.v.). Ghazzis and counterghazzis continued, punctuated by short periods of peace, until 1892, when the Reguibat made a unilateral peace with the Oulad Delim, selling out the Oulad Tidrarin. In 1897, they began another long struggle, this time with the Oulad Jerir, upon whom they finally inflicted a severe defeat in 1909. A simultaneous war had been fought for much of this time with the Oulad Bou Sbaa. This began in 1905 and climaxed in 1907, when a force of 1,000 Reguibat wiped out their Oulad Bou Sbaa adversaries at Foucht, in Adrar (Mauritania), though intermittent fighting continued until another Reguibat victory at Lemden el-Hauat in 1910. Another war, fought between 1899 and 1904, pitted the Reguibat against the Oulad Ghailan of Adrar.

Though violence and conflict marked the rise of the Reguibat in the 19th and early 20th centuries, they often allied with other tribes to defend or extend their interests. In the north, for example, conflicts alternated with peaceful cooperation in their relations with the Tekna (q.v.), across whose territory they needed to travel to reach the markets of the Draa and the Noun, notably Goulimine, where the Reguibat sold their camels until the 1950s. It was by means of a customary sacrifice, known as the *debiha,* that the Reguibat were accorded protection by the Tekna tribes in these zones.

In its advisory opinion on Western Sahara in 1975 (page 48), the International Court of Justice (q.v.) noted that it "could clearly not be sustained" that the sultans of Morocco had, in precolonial times, displayed authority over the Reguibat. Indeed, as a purely nomadic tribe, without oases or settlements of any kind, they were proudly and assertively independent, regulating their affairs through assemblies of nota- bles, the *djemaas* (q.v.), and, in time of war, through an *ait arbain* (q.v.). Their spirit of independence is reflected in one of their legends that Sidi Ahmed Reguibi "bought" their territory from a Moroccan sultan known as El-Kahal.

The Reguibat were at the height of their expansion just as France was attempting to bring the desert regions of northern Mauritania, southern Morocco, and southwestern Algeria under its control. They were bound to clash. Tribes fearful of the Reguibat, such as the Oulad Ghailan and the Ait Oussa (q.v.), made alliances with the French, from whom they received encouragement in staging punitive ghazzis, sometimes into "Spanish" territory, to bring the Reguibat to heel. Typical was the participation of the Oulad Ghailan in the expedition led by Col. Mouret against the forces of Mohammed Laghdaf, in which the Reguibat were prominent. The expedition, which was marked by the sacking of Smara (q.v.), followed a ghazzi by the Reguibat and the Oulad Delim, which had wiped out a French garrison at El-Boirat.

The Reguibat played a prominent part in the anti-French resistance until 1934, when the French finally completed their "pacification," after occupying Tindouf in March of that year.

During the colonial period, the Reguibat came under the loose administrative surveillance of the French authorities in Algeria, Mauritania, and Morocco and of the Spanish in Western Sahara, though as nomads they continued to cross the artificial frontiers more or less at will. The end of the ghazzis, however, brought changes in the forms of nomadism: security allowed nomadism in smaller groups, that is, a reduction in the size of the average *friq* (q.v.) and a decline in the importance of the *fakhd* (q.v.), or fraction, as a social unit.

Droughts and the growing opportunities to find relief or employment in the little towns springing up in the Sahara gradually encouraged the Reguibat, like other Saharawis, to become sedentary in the 1960s and early 1970s. A small minority were still nomadic at the time of Spain's departure from Western Sahara in 1975–76. In the 1974 Spanish census, which generally underestimated the Western Saharan population, some 38,000 Reguibat, more or less evenly divided between es-Sahel and ech-Charg, were counted. However, there were many more Reguibat living in the neighboring territories. There were an estimated 17,900 Reguibat living in Algeria, primarily in the Tindouf region, in 1975, before the refugee influx there from Western Sahara. There were also substantial numbers living in the Tarfaya (q.v.) province of southern Morocco (9,562 in 1966, according to the Moroccan ministry of the interior) and in northern Mauritania. Some were living even further afield, for example, in Mali. Though it is hard to give an accurate estimate of the total number of Reguibat and the figure of 200,000–300,000 given by Hart (1962, page 515) seems too high, there could be as many as 100,000.

What is striking is their numerical preponderance over the other Saharawi tribes. They made up 52 percent of those counted in the 1974 Spanish census. The vast majority of those Reguibat who had been living in "Spanish" Sahara joined the refugee exodus to Algeria in 1975–76, and they were joined there by pro-Polisario Reguibat coming from southern Morocco, northern Mauritania, and Algeria itself. Though all Saharawi tribes are represented in the Polisario Front, the Reguibat are predominant, by sheer weight of numbers, in the movement, its guerrilla army, and refugee camps.

REGUIBAT ECH-CHARG. The eastern Reguibat (q.v.).

REGUIBAT ES-SAHEL. The Reguibat (q.v.) of the coast, i.e., the western Reguibat.

REGUIBAT LGOUACEM. The Reguibat (q.v.) descended from Qacem Sidi Ahmed Reguibi; they are also known as the Reguibat ech-Charg, or eastern Reguibat.

REGUIBI. Sing. of Reguibat (q.v.).

REVOLUTIONARY COMMAND COUNCIL see COUNCIL FOR THE COMMAND OF THE REVOLUTION

RIO DE ORO. The River of Gold was originally the name given to the inlet running about 38 km. south-southwest to north-northeast between the mainland and the Dakhla (q.v.) peninsula. The name was coined by 15th-century European seamen because of the gold dust that was traded there. It is the only real bay along Western Sahara's 875-km. coastline. It is not surprising perhaps that it was therefore the first place where the Spanish were to establish a settlement at the end of the 19th century during the European "scramble for Africa." In September 1881, the Sociedad de Pesquerías Canario-Africanas (q.v.) established a pontoon in the bay. In 1884, the Compañía Comercial Hispano-Africana arrived and founded the settlement of Villa Cisneros on the Dakhla peninsula. Soon, however, the term "Río de Oro" came to be used for the whole of the Spanish colony ("protectorate" at first) declared along the coast between Cape Blanc and Boujdour (qq.v.) by royal decrees on December 26, 1884, July 10, 1885, and April 6, 1887. The latter, which extended Spanish territory up to 150 miles into the interior, placed its administration in the hands of a "politico-military subgovernor of Río de Oro." The territory's southern and southeastern borders with Mauritania were defined in the Franco-Spanish Convention of June 27, 1900 (q.v.). The term "Río de Oro" became yet more ambiguous when, under the Franco-Spanish Conventions of October 3, 1904, and November 14, 1912 (qq.v.), Spain's Saharan territory was extended far to the north of Boujdour. Sometimes, even in diplomatic agreements and other official documents, "Río de Oro" referred to the whole of Spain's Saharan territory. However, by 1934, it usually meant specifically the territory south of parallel 26° (near Boujdour), whereas that to the north, between parallels 26° and 27°40', came to be known as Saguia el-Hamra (q.v.). Thus defined, the land area of Río de Oro was 184,000 sq. km. However, until 1916, the only Spanish settlement was Villa Cisneros. In 1916, La Guera (q.v.), on Cape Blanc, was occupied. By the 1940s, military garrisons had been established also at Bir Gandous, Tichla, and

Zug. Administration was centered at Villa Cisneros. When Western Sahara was partitioned under the Moroccan-Mauritanian Agreement of April 14, 1976 (q.v.), the southern part of Río de Oro was annexed by Mauritania and was thereafter known as Tiris el-Gharbia (q.v.). The northern part, along with Saguia el-Hamra, was annexed by Morocco. Tiris el-Gharbia was annexed in turn by Morocco on August 12, 1979, and renamed Oued ed-Dahab (Arabic for Río de Oro), after the Algiers Agreement (q.v.) between Mauritania and the Polisario Front (q.v.).

RIVERS. The principal river is the Saguia el-Hamra (q.v.), which is 620 km. long and flows east to west, reaching the Atlantic near El-Ayoun (q.v.). The river bed is dry during the summer, until the autumn rains. Other rivers, which are also dry most of the year, are the Oued Atui, Oued Tenuair, Oued Feida, Oued Sbaira, and Oued Inineguent.

ROADS. Considering the overall size of Western Sahara, there are very few tarmac roads. The main tarmac roads link El-Ayoun (q.v.) with the Moroccan border near Tah, with the phosphate mines at Bou-Craa (qq.v.), with the town of Boujdour (q.v.), with the port at El-Ayoun *Playa* (q.v.), and with Smara (q.v.). The Smara road continues eastward to Haousa and Jdiriya. There are also tarmac roads on the Dakhla (q.v.) peninsula and between La Guera (q.v.) and Bir Gandous in the extreme south of the territory. Between Boujdour and Dakhla, there is a marked road of uncertain reliability, and the rest of Western Sahara has only unmarked tracks.

RODRIGUEZ DE VIGURI Y GIL, LUIS. A colonel in the Spanish Engineers with a long military career behind him, Rodríguez de Viguri was appointed secretary-general of the Spanish administration in Western Sahara in June 1974. "My primordial mission," he later explained, "was to make possible the territory's independence. To that end, I was handed a draft statute of autonomy, which had merited the personal approval of the head of state, of Franco." The statute was the *estatuto político,* which was approved by the

Djemaa (q.v.) at a session held on July 1–4, shortly after his arrival in El-Ayoun (q.v.) and which proposed a system of internal self-government based on the conversion of the Djemaa from a purely consultative assembly into a legislature and the creation of a partially-Saharawi governing council. Later, in November 1974, Rodríguez de Viguri helped to set up the PUNS (q.v.), which was designed to undermine support for the Polisario Front (q.v.) and help to steer the territory gradually to independence in a way that would protect Spain's important interests in the fishing and phosphate industries (qq.v.). "I am convinced to the bottom of my heart," he said, "that the independence of the Sahara is viable, because this people deserves it and moreover has the foundations needed to live autonomously—a viable economic structure and a sufficient civic spirit." Independence could be granted "conserving a mass of interests and influences" for Spain, he added. He continued to support the plans for independence after the demise of the PUNS in the summer of 1975 and began then to favor direct negotiations with the Polisario Front, which he believed would pragmatically allow Spain to retain its economic interests if it headed an independent government.

However, he submitted his resignation in the summer of 1975 in anger at the Spanish government's failure to implement the estatuto político and its decision in January 1975 to postpone the referendum on independence, which it had promised in August 1974 would be held during the first six months of 1975. The stalling was essentially due to Moroccan pressure. The resignation was not accepted and was eventually withdrawn, but Rodríguez de Viguri's alarm grew once more in the autumn, when Madrid's resolve to proceed toward independence seemed to wilt during the build-up to the Green March (q.v.). On the day of the announcement of the march (October 16), he once again submitted his resignation, but it was again withdrawn after he had been reassured that Spain would not renege on its commitment to self-determination. However, after the signing of the Madrid Agreement (q.v.), he found himself in the invidious position of working in the tripartite administration (q.v.) in which Moroccan and Mauritanian deputy governors worked alongside the Spanish governor-general, Gen. Federico Gómez de Salazar (q.v.), while Spanish troops and civil servants were withdrawn and thousands of Moroccan and Mauritanian troops arrived. Moreover, when Gen. Gómez de Salazar left the territory at the end of December 1975, Rodríguez de Viguri found himself at the head of the tripartite administration. His evident distaste for the job led to his suspension on January 27, 1976, and replacement by Lt. Col. Rafael de Valdés Iglesias (q.v.). Two years later, on March 13, 1978, he bitterly condemned the Madrid Agreement in a hearing held by the foreign relations committee of the Cortes, saying that the 180-degree switch in Spanish policy toward Western Sahara at the time had been due to U.S. and French pressure, fears in Madrid that a Polisario regime would give bases to the Movement for the Self-Determination and Independence of the Canary Archipelago (MPAIAC), and lobbying by groups with special interests in Morocco.

RYDBECK, OLOF. A Swedish diplomat, Olof Rydbeck visited Western Sahara on behalf of UN Secretary-General Kurt Waldheim on February 7–12, 1976, to examine conditions in the territory with a view to implementation of UN (q.v.) General Assembly resolutions 3458A and B of December 10, 1975, both of which called for UN involvement in the holding of an act of self-determination. Rydbeck reported back to New York that conditions in the territory made such a popular consultation virtually impossible. In consequence, Waldheim refused to send a representative to observe the crucial Moroccan-inspired rump meeting of the Djemaa (q.v.) in El-Ayoun (q.v.) on February 26, which voted to approve integration with Morocco and Mauritania. This was a major diplimatic rebuff for Morocco, which then refused to receive Rydbeck when he was sent on a second mission by Waldheim at the end of March. This time, his brief was to consult the governments of Spain, Algeria, Morocco, and Mauritania on the implementation of the UN resolutions, but on April 4, the Moroccan government said it would not receive him because he had met leaders of the Polisario Front (q.v.) during a visit to the Saharawi refugee camps at Tindouf (qq.v.) on March 31 and April 1.

- S -

SAGUIA. Arabic term for river (q.v.).

SAGUIA EL-HAMRA (1) The ''Red River,'' so called because of the russet color of both its bed (when the river runs dry during the hot, arid summer) and its waters (after the autumn rains), is the longest river in Western Sahara. Running for some 650 km. from east to west, it is fed by several tributaries and after passing El-Ayoun (q.v.), where it floods a considerable part of its valley when in full flow, forces its way through the coastal dune belt to the Atlantic in a number of channels. The river is usually at its height in November–February.

(2) An administrative division of Western Sahara in the Spanish colonial period, named after the river. After the cession of the Tekna Zone (q.v.) to Morocco in 1958, it was the northern sector of Spain's Saharan territory, covering 82,000 sq. km., compared to 184,000 sq. km. for the southern sector, Río de Oro (q.v.). Its borders were set by the secret Franco-Spanish convention of October 3, 1904 (q.v.), which stated (article 6), ''The government of the French Republic acknowledges that the Spanish government has hencefor-ward full liberty of action in the territory comprised between 26° and 27°40′ north latitude and the 11th meridian west of Paris, which are outside the limits of Morocco.'' This article was confirmed by article 2 of the Franco-Spanish convention of November 27, 1912 (q.v.). But despite France's recognition of full Spanish sovereignty over Saguia el-Hamra, Spain did not establish any permanent settlement there until as late as 1934, when, under French prompting, the Spanish moved out of their coastal enclaves in Río de Oro, at Villa Cisneros (Dakhla) and La Guera (q.v.), and in the Tekna Zone, at Tarfaya (q.v.), to occupy a number of points in the interior, including Smara (q.v.) in Saguia el-Hamra (May 1934). However, it was not until 1940 that a capital was established at El-Ayoun (q.v.). A *delegado gubernativo* (q.v.) was based there, responsible to the governor-general of Ifni and the Sahara, who, until 1946, was the Spanish *alto comisario* (q.v.) in Morocco, based at Tetuan. After the creation of

Africa Occidental Española (q.v.) in 1946, with a governor-general in Ifni, a *subgobernador* was based in El-Ayoun for the administration of both Saguia el-Hamra and Río de Oro. When, finally, in 1958, the administration of Ifni and Spanish Sahara was separated and a "province" (q.v.) established, with its own governor-general, in the Sahara, a delegado gubernativo was responsible for the north, i.e., Saguia el-Hamra. He was based in El-Ayoun and had two outlying administrative centers in Smara and Daora (q.v.). Economic development proceeded more rapidly thereafter in Saguia el-Hamra than in the south, especially after investment began in the phosphate industry set up at Bou-Craa (q.v.) in the late sixties.

After the Spanish withdrawal in 1975–76, all of Saguia el-Hamra (as well as part of Río de Oro) was annexed by Morocco, under the Moroccan-Mauritanian partition agreement of April 14, 1976 (q.v.). However, Moroccan control was restricted in fact to the main towns and a few bases, the guerrillas of the Polisario Front (q.v.) holding the initiative over most of the desert. This began to change in the early 1980s, when Morocco started to construct a series of "defensive walls" (q.v.) in the territory, beginning in Saguia el-Hamra, to push Polisario as far away as possible from Western Sahara's main population centers. By 1985, over 80 percent of Saguia el-Hamra had been "walled off."

SAHARA. A weekly published in El-Ayoun (q.v.) from 1963, it was the country's only newspaper until the appearance of *La Realidad* (q.v.), a daily, in 1975. Its editor was a Spanish officer, Comandante Alonso Allustante.

SAHARAN/SAHARAWI ARAB DEMOCRATIC REPUBLIC. The SADR was proclaimed on February 27, 1976, by the pro-Polisario Provisional Saharawi National Council (qq.v.) at a ceremony near Bir Lehlou, about 125 km. west of the Algerian border, before a crowd of Saharawi guerrillas and a party of 30 foreign journalists. Intended to prevent a juridical fait accompli being created by the Madrid Agreement (q.v.), the creation of the state was timed to coincide with Spain's formal withdrawal from the country the day before. The legitimacy of the SADR's creation hinged, according to the Polisario Front, on the fact that the UN Visiting Mission (q.v.) to the territory in 1975 had already confirmed the overwhelming desire for independence on the part of the Saharawi people and that the Provisional Saharawi National Council, which proclaimed the state's creation, was itself set up by the Djemaa (q.v.), the Spanish-created territorial assembly whose will the Madrid Agreement had pledged to respect. The council announced the composition of the SADR's first council of ministers (q.v.) on March 4, 1976.

The first foreign state to recognize the SADR was Madagascar (February 28, 1976), followed by Burundi (March 1, 1976) and then Algeria (March 6, 1976). Morocco and Mauritania promptly broke off diplomatic relations with Algeria in retaliation. By the end of 1990, 74 states had recognized the SADR. Almost all were from the Third World, though they represented a wide political spectrum. There were 31 from Africa, 25 from Latin America and the Caribbean, 9 from Asia, 7 from the Pacific Ocean region, and 2 from Europe (Albania and Yugoslavia). The full list, with dates of recognition, is as follows:

Madagascar (February 28, 1976), Burundi (March 1, 1976), Algeria (March 6, 1976), Benin (March 11, 1976), Angola (March 11, 1976), Mozambique (March 13, 1976), Guinea-Bissau (March 15, 1976), North Korea (March 16, 1976), Togo (March 17, 1976), Rwanda (April 1, 1976), South Yemen (February 2, 1977), Seychelles (October 25, 1977), Congo (June 3, 1978), Sao Tomé and Príncipe (June 22, 1978), Panama (June 23, 1978), Tanzania (November 9, 1978), Ethiopia (February 24, 1979), Vietnam (March 2, 1979), Cambodia (April 10, 1979), Laos (May 9, 1979), Afghanistan (May 23, 1979), Cape Verde (July 4, 1979), Grenada (August 20, 1979), Ghana (August 24, 1979), Guyana (September 1, 1979), Dominica (September 1, 1979), Saint Lucia (September 1, 1979), Jamaica (September 4, 1979), Uganda (September 6, 1979), Nicaragua (September 6, 1979), Mexico (September 8, 1979), Lesotho (October 9, 1979), Zambia (October 12, 1979), Cuba (January 20, 1980), Iran (February 27, 1980), Sierra Leone (March 27,

1980), Syria (April 15, 1980), Libya (April 15, 1980), Swaziland (April 28, 1980), Botswana (May 14, 1980), Zimbabwe (July 3, 1980), Chad (July 4, 1980), Mali (July 4, 1980), Costa Rica (October 30, 1980), Vanuatu (November 27, 1980), Papua New Guinea (August 12, 1981), Tuvalu (August 12, 1981), Kiribati (August 12, 1981), Nauru (August 12, 1981), Solomon Islands (August 12, 1981), Mauritius (July 1, 1982), Venezuela (August 3, 1982), Surinam (August 11, 1982), Bolivia (December 14, 1982), Ecuador (November 14, 1983), Mauritania (February 27, 1984), Burkina Faso (March 4, 1984), Peru (August 16, 1984), Nigeria (November 12, 1984), Yugoslavia (November 28, 1984), Colombia (February 27, 1985), Liberia (July 31, 1985), India (October 1, 1985), Guatemala (April 10, 1986), Dominican Republic (June 24, 1986), Trinidad and Tobago (November 1, 1986), Belize (November 18, 1986), St. Kitts and Nevis (February 25, 1987), Antigua (February 27, 1987), Albania (December 29, 1987), Barbados (February 27, 1988), El Salvador (July 31, 1989), Honduras (November 8, 1989), Namibia (June 11, 1990).

A constitution for the new state was adopted at the Polisario Front's 3rd general popular congress (q.v.), held on August 26–30, 1976. After undergoing minor amendments twice since that time, it was entirely replaced by a new constitution, provisionally adopted by the front's 8th congress (June 18–20, 1991). The following is its full text:

CONSTITUTION OF THE SAHARAWI ARAB DEMOCRATIC REPUBLIC
Adopted by the VIII Congress of the Polisario Front
June 19, 1991

INTRODUCTION

The Saharawi Arab Democratic Republic (SADR) is the historic fruit of the struggle of the Saharawi people for the recovery of their national independence and the safeguard of their national unity. It is the consecration of their desire to live as a free people, in conformity with their inalienable right to self-determination.

The Saharawi people, aware of the imperative need to bring about gradual economic growth and social development and strengthen their national unity and enforce the law, decided to adopt the following constitution.

CHAPTER I

Article 1.

The Saharawi Arab Democratic Republic—Saguia el-Hamra and Rio de Oro—in her internationally recognized borders— is a democratic and social Republic. It is one and indivisible. No portion of its territory can be the subject of secession.

The national emblem and the national anthem are determined by law.

The capital of the Republic is El-Ayoun.

Article 2.

The national territory is divided geographically and administratively into Wilayas and Dairas.

The political and administrative competence of the Wilayas and Dairas is defined by law.

Article 3.

Sovereignty belongs to the people and is exercised in conformity with the Constitution.

Article 4.

Islam is the state religion.

Article 5.

Arabic is the official national language.

Article 6.

The family is the nucleus of society, based upon religion and morality.

Article 7.

All citizens are equal before the law.

Article 8.

The Saharawi Armed Forces guarantee sovereignty, national independence, and territorial integrity of the Republic. They are the guarantors of respect of the Constitution.

Article 9.

The right to create unions and political associations in accordance with the respect of the Constitution and laws once the liberation of the country has been achieved and after the transitional period, is recognized.

Article 10.

Freedom of the person is inviolable. No citizen shall be denied freedom, unless justice commands otherwise.

Article 11.

All citizens have the right to choose their residence and to move freely within the national territory.

Article 12.

No citizen shall remain in custody for more than 72 hours. After this time, the citizen shall be set free, or in the alternative, transferred to the custody of the juridical authority.

In all cases, a person is presumed innocent until proven guilty.

Article 13.

The death penalty is banned.

Article 14.

No citizen shall be subjected to torture or to inhuman practices degrading to his or her dignity as a person.

Article 15.

Citizens must be able to defend their rights before the competent juridical authority.

Article 16.

The home of the citizen is inviolable. Its trespassing requires at all times a written warrant from the competent juridical authority.

Article 17.

All citizens have the right of access of public functions in conformity with criteria and prerequisites required by law.

Article 18.

The right to private property is a recognized right of all citizens. The law shall establish procedures to enforce this fundamental right.

Article 19.

The defense of the territory is a right and a sacred duty for all citizens.

Article 20.

Work is a right and a duty that honors a citizen. The right to holidays is warranted by law, as is the same reward for equal work.

Article 21.

The right to secrecy in communication and private mail is guaranteed in conformity with the law.

Article 22.

All citizens have the duty to:

—respect the Constitution, in conformity with the laws of the Republic, and to respect the institutions of the State;

—respect public property and the rights of others;

—work for national unity, public order, and stability.

Article 23.

The state enforces the protection of the rights and goods of foreign citizens who are legally in the national territory.

CHAPTER II
Social and Economic Rights

Article 24.

All citizens have the right to education and health care.

Article 25.

The state provides protection for mothers and the elderly and must create institutions to that end.

Article 26.

The state shall work to ensure welfare for all citizens.

Article 27.

The state shall guarantee to fathers, mothers, and the sons of young age of martyrs, as well as to the wounded and victims of the war of liberation, all their social and economic rights in legislation.

Article 28.

The state shall promote through legislation social and economic rights for the Saharawi prisoners of war and for victims of the war of occupation.

Article 29.

The state shall work for the protection of political, economic, social, and cultural rights of Saharawi women and ensure their participation in the building of the society and development in the country.

Article 30.

The state shall adopt a policy of social well-being aimed at protecting elders and the handicapped, and laws must be enacted to that end.

Article 31.

The market economy and free enterprise are recognized.

The public sector shall take charge of the exploitation of national resources of vital importance, to ensure the economic development of the country.

Article 32.

Foreign investments in the country shall be regularized by law.

CHAPTER III
The Parliament

Article 33.

The Parliament is the source of legislative power in the Republic.

The Parliament regulates the actions of the national government.

Article 34.

The members of the Parliament are elected for a term of three years.

Article 35.

The members of the Parliament are elected through direct universal suffrage, in conformity with electoral law and the criterion of parliamentary representation based on the number of inhabitants in electoral districts and on a balance between the regions and Wilayas of the country.

Article 36.

The Parliament shall institute necessary commissions for the follow-up and monitoring of the business of the national government.

Article 37.

The Parliament elects a chairman, its bureau among its members, and sets its internal rules of procedure.

Article 38.

The chairmen of the various commissions are elected on the recommendation of the Chairman of the Parliament.

Article 39.

The various commissions can include nonmembers as aides and technical advisers.

Article 40.

Between the regular sessions of the Parliament, the commissions work continuously.

Article 41.

Commissions shall hold regular meetings with the members of the Government in order to monitor and be informed of the business of the national Executive.

Article 42.

All commissions can convene Ministers as well as request explanations, clarifications, or necessary information.

Article 43.

The chairmen of the Parliamentary commissions shall receive from the Ministers a document summarizing the annual plan to be presented to the Parliament for approval, at the latest one week after its elaboration by the Executive.

Article 44.

Commissions shall seek explanations and hold hearings once the Government has submitted its annual plan for approval.

Article 45.

The Parliament approves or rejects the plan.

Article 46.

In case of approval, the President of the Parliament shall close the meeting.

Article 47.

In this case, the Parliamentary commissions shall continue to work in regular session until the end of the Parliamentary session and maintain necessary contacts with the members of the Government in preparation for the next Parliamentary session.

Article 48.

In case the Parliament rejects by two thirds the plan of action of the Government, the President shall call on the Executive for its revised plan.

Article 49.

In this case, the Ministers and the Presidents of the various commissions shall work to reconcile and harmonize their views in order to arrive at a final agreement.

Article 50.

The national Government presents its revised plan to the Parliament for approval.

Article 51.

In case the revised plan is rejected by a majority of two-thirds of the Parliament, the President of the Republic shall proceed to the nomination of a new Government or for the dissolution of the Parliament.

Article 52.

In case of the dissolution of the Parliament in conformity with Article 51, the President of the Republic shall call for its reelection within one month.

Article 53.

The national Executive can, until the elections of the new Parliament, and if need be, enact decrees.

Article 54.

In case the President of the Republic cannot assume official duties and the office remains vacant for inaptitude or poor health, the President of the Parliament shall assume temporarily the functions of the President of the Republic.

Article 55.

The provisional President shall convene an extraordinary congress of the Polisario Front within forty days.

Article 56.

The Head of the State ad interim shall assume charge of the Executive until the election of the new Secretary-General by the extraordinary congress.

Article 57.

The provisional President shall reassume the functions of the President of the Parliament.

Article 58.

The elections to the new Parliament shall be held within thirty to sixty days from the end of the Parliament as defined in Article 33.

Article 59.

During the time of their Parliamentary tenure, members of Parliament enjoy Parliamentary immunity and cannot be detained except in flagrante delicto and cannot be judged except by the

Supreme Court, once the President has been deprived of Parliamentary immunity.

Article 60.

The Parliament holds two regular Parliamentary sessions: the first in the fall, from September to December, and the second in spring, from February to June.

Article 61.

The Parliament can hold special sessions at the request of two thirds of its members or at the request of the President of the Republic.

Article 62.

The voting of members of the Parliament is individual and non-transferable.

CHAPTER IV
The Juridical Power

Article 63.

Justice in the Republic is independent, and the juridical power is based on the separation of powers within the State.

Justice is made in the name of the people.

Article 64.

Judges must not be detained or be substituted or adjudicate more than what is required by law.

Article 65.

The organization and competence of the juridical instances are established by law.

Article 66.

The courts are divided into tribunals of first instance, the Court of Appeal, and the Supreme Court.

Article 67.

The Supreme Court is the supreme organ of the juridical system. Its President is appointed by the Head of State on the proposal of the Supreme Council of the Juridical Power.

Article 68.

The Supreme Council of the Juridical Power comprises:

—the President of the Supreme Court;

—six other members: two appointed by the Head of State, two elected by the Parliament, and two appointed by the Supreme Court;

—the mandate of the members of the Supreme Council is five years, renewable.

Article 69.

The Attorney General is appointed by the President of the Republic on the proposal of the Supreme Council of the Juridical Power. His mission is to promote justice and enforce the law.

CHAPTER V
The President

Article 70.

The President of the Republic is the Head of the State. He shall work for the implementation of the Constitution and embodies the national unity.

Article 71.

The President of the Republic appoints the members of the Government and calls for their resignations.

Article 72.

He presides over the national Government.

Article 73.

He enacts laws within fifteen days of their approval by the Government.

Article 74.

During the transitional period, the President of the Republic is the Secretary-General of the Polisario Front, elected by the General Popular Congress of the Front.

Article 75.

The term of the President of the Republic is three years, and the President can be reelected for two additional terms.

Article 76.

The President of the Republic is in charge of the general policy of the State.

Article 77.

The President of the Republic takes the Constitutional oath before the Parliament in the following terms:

> I swear by the name of God the Mighty and His sacred book, to respect the Constitution of the Republic, which will guide me, and to be its guarantor, and I will work with all my ability to respond to the will and the aspirations of our people in freedom and justice; to protect the rights and liberties of all citizens, that I will work for the preservation and integrity of the territory; that I will work for the progress and happiness of the people and to be the incarnation of the noble values and traditions of the people; and God is witness to what I have affirmed.

Article 78.

The President of the Republic is the Commander in Chief of the Armed Forces.

Article 79.

The President of the Republic makes appointments to high civilian and military posts.

Article 80.

The President of the Republic appoints ambassadors and receives credentials of the ambassadors of foreign countries.

Article 81.

The President of the Republic can grant pardons and leniency.

Article 82.

The President of the Republic can declare war and sign treaties of peace.

Article 83.

The President of the Republic concludes and revokes treaties.

Article 84.

The President of the Republic awards medals and grants honorific titles.

Article 85.

The mandate of the President of the Republic is not compatible with other activities distinct from official functions.

Article 86.

The President of the Republic is empowered to declare a State of Exception in consultation with the Government, with the President of the Parliament, and of the Constitutional Council, in case of a serious threat to the security and stability of the country.

Article 87.

The State of Exception must not exceed four months. In case of prolongation of this time, the accord of the Parliament is required.

CHAPTER VI
The Government

Article 88.

The President of the Republic supervises the performance of the Government.

Article 89.

The Council of Ministers is an executive organ, comprising the Government and responsible before the President of the Republic.

Article 90.

The Government establishes the General Budget of the State and the plan of national action to be submitted to the Parliament for approval.

Article 91.

The members of the national Government cannot exercise any other enterprise while performing official functions.

Article 92.

The Government cannot promulgate decrees without the concordance of the Parliament, except for the provision provided for in Article 53.

CHAPTER VII
The Constitutional Council

Article 93.

The Constitutional Council is the organ which shall work:

—for the constitutionality of the laws before their promulgation;

—to monitor the regularity of the Parliamentary elections.

Article 94.

The Constitutional Council comprises seven members, designated for a term of four years.

It elects its President and elaborates its internal rules.

Article 95.

The Constitutional Council comprises:

—two members appointed by the President of the Republic;

—three members elected by the Parliament;

—two members elected by the Supreme Council of the Juridical Power.

The members of the Constitutional Council must be either magistrates or distinguished lawyers.

Article 96.

The members of the Constitutional Council cannot exercise any other activity, either political, parliamentary, or union.

All other inconsistencies must be established by law.

SPECIAL CLAUSES

First:

The Saharawi political leadership will elaborate at its eighth congress the draft of the Constitution, to be amended and ameliorated by the citizens, then submitted to the Polisario Front congress to be approved in a popular referendum and adopted as the final version of the Constitution of the SADR.

Second:

The Constitution approved by the eighth congress shall be the fundamental basis for the Constitution of the SADR.

Third:

The duration of the transitional period shall be determined by the congress of the Polisario Front to be held following independence.

Fourth:

The Saharawi National Council shall continue to exercise its functions until the election of the first Saharawi Parliament envisaged following the liberation of the country from foreign occupation.

Fifth:

The Popular Councils shall continue to exercise their normal activities at the local and Wilaya levels as well as at the Popular Base Congress level until the liberation of the country.

Sixth:

The Parliamentary elections as well as the number of members of the Parliament shall be determined after the liberation of the country and the establishment of the necessary conditions for such an objective.

The new SADR constitution expands considerably upon the former document (which contained less than half as many articles), and is clearly designed not for immediate implementation in all essentials but for possible modification in an interim period followed by the application of all of its provisions in an independent SADR. As will be apparent, the new constitution contains many provisions safeguarding the civil liberties of citizens and describing a variety of measures for the social and economic welfare of the Saharawi people. At the same time, it allows a free-market system and the protection of private enterprise. As for the actual governing mechanisms of the state, they include a parliament elected by universal suffrage and which possesses considerable policy-review prerogatives through its standing commissions. Provisions are also in place for handling a deadlock between parliament and the president of the Saharawi Republic. Immunity for members of parliament is also provided (article 59). However, the constitution is somewhat in the French tradition of reserving considerable powers to the president, including the power to declare war and make peace (article 82), conclude and revoke treaties (article 83), dismiss parliament in the event of a deadlock and rule by decree until new elections are held (articles 51–53), and declare a "state of exception" for up to four months (articles 86 and 87). The judicial branch is composed of trial courts, an appeals court, and a Supreme Court, with their jurisdiction established by law. The president of the SADR has overall supervisory powers over the government, which consists, inter alia, of the council of ministers. The new constitution continues the division of Western Sahara into *dairat* and *wilayat* (qq.v.) for local government purposes, except that after independence these bodies would have an actual territorial basis and not be merely descriptive of a group of refugee (q.v.) settlements. Six special clauses round out the 1991 constitution; most pertain to the transition to an independent SADR in the future, although allowance is made for amendments to the constitution before its final ratification after the liberation of Western Sahara.

SAHARAWI. The Saharawis are the Ahel es-Sahel (q.v.), the inhabitants of the Atlantic coastal belt of the desert roughly encompassed by the borders of what is now known as Western Sahara. The term has thus come to be synonymous with "Western Saharan," though the tribes that composed the Ahel es-Sahel nomadized over a wide area, crossing the "frontiers" imposed by the colonial powers in the 20th century. Moreover, during the process of sedentation in the second half of the 20th century, many Saharawis settled in the neighboring territories.

SAHARAWI NATIONAL COUNCIL. A legislative and consultative assembly of the SADR (q.v.). A Provisional Saharawi National Council was set up in November 1975 as a result of the proclamation of Guelta Zemmour (q.v.) dissolving the Djemaa (q.v.). Then, after the founding of the SADR by this provisional council on February 26, 1976, a 41-member Saharawi National Council was elected at the 3rd general popular congress on August 26–30, 1976, which adopted the new republic's constitution. The latter stated that ''the Saharawi National Council has legislative and consultative power.'' Since the 4th congress (September 25–28, 1978), the remaining members have been elected by the popular base congresses in the *dairat* (qq.v.). Although the council has commissions dealing with political and social affairs, foreign relations, and military matters, it meets rarely and has little real power, serving as a rubber stamp for the decisions of the Council for the Command of the Revolution (q.v.) until the abolition of that body at the 8th congress held on June 18–20, 1991. Even so, the council has been viewed as a kind of symbolic revived *ait arbain* (q.v.), the old tribal council of 40, which met in time of war in precolonial days. The council was not abolished at the 8th congress but will remain in operation only until after independence, when its place will be taken by a parliament, elected by universal suffrage.

SAHARAWI POPULAR LIBERATION ARMY. The armed wing of the Polisario Front and the SADR (qq.v.). A very small and poorly equipped force during the front's war with Spain (1973–75), it expanded rapidly after the Madrid Agreement (q.v.) in November 1975 and received training, bases, and large quantities of modern weaponry from Algeria. Most of the c. 1,300 Saharawi members of the Spanish *Tropas Nómadas* and *Policía Territorial* (qq.v.) joined the SPLA, providing a well-trained core of soldiers, after their demobilization by the Spanish authorities, which began at the end of October 1975. Since then, up to 20,000 of the Saharawi men who trekked to the Polisario camps near Tindouf (q.v.), Algeria (mainly between November 1975 and May 1976), have been enrolled in the guerrilla army and trained.

The SPLA's troops were divided into units known as *katibas* (q.v.), which came together to stage large attacks, occasionally involving several thousand men at a time by 1978–79. They had effective control over the desert hinterland of Western Sahara by this time, as they did over much of northern Mauritania until the Algiers Agreement (q.v.) of

August 5, 1979, and over parts of southern Morocco. The Moroccan army was forced to abandon many small, isolated posts by 1979, falling back on the main strategic centers, in particular a "useful triangle" in the northwest, which included El-Ayoun, the Bou-Craa phosphate mines, and Smara (qq.v.). Meanwhile, from 1977, the SPLA also staged numerous attacks on fishing (q.v.) boats and other ships off the Western Saharan coast.

Ibrahim Ghali (q.v.), who became the SADR's defense minister in March 1976, retained overall command of the SPLA, along with a number of regional commanders, until May 1989, when he was replaced by Mohammed Lamine Ould Bouhali (q.v.). Though enjoying logistical support from rear bases in Algeria, the SPLA guerrillas had small, hidden camps, many of them underground, throughout Western Sahara (and at times also in northern Mauritania and southern Morocco), where arms, fuel, and food were stored and from where the regional commanders coordinated military operations. The guerrillas had the advantage of an acute knowledge of the terrain in which they were fighting, a knowledge passed down from generation to generation in the Saharawis' traditionally nomadic society, and they had higher motivation than their opponents. While most of the Moroccan forces were in static positions, guarding the few towns and bases under their control, the guerrillas also had the advantage of much greater flexibility and maneuverability. The Moroccans had little success in detecting and neutralizing their bases and camps, which were small, spread out, often on the move, and usually sited in areas with plenty of cover such as the valley of the Saguia el-Hamra and the massif of Guelta Zemmour (qq.v.). These attributes continued to serve the guerrillas well until the Moroccan Forces Armées Royales (q.v.) constructed an extensive series of "defensive walls" (q.v.) in 1980–87, replacing its isolated and vulnerable garrisons with a continuous, heavily defended line that by 1987 shut the SPLA out of 80 percent of the territory and blocked access to the Atlantic coast of Western Sahara. This was a serious setback to the SPLA, but the guerrillas continued to stage numerous harassment raids against the Moroccan troops dug in along the walls and at times attacked in force, temporarily overrunning sections of the defense lines. In the second half of the 1980s, the SPLA was essentially fighting a war of attrition, forcing Morocco to keep 120,000 troops in Western Sahara to man its static defense lines. And throughout the entire period, moreover, Polisario's motivation, mobility, and superior knowledge of the terrain continued to be as advantageous as before.

What was the strength of the SPLA in the 1980s? It had the reputation of being one of the largest, best-equipped, and most sophisticated insurgent armies in the world, but many details of its equipment and troop strength were not widely known. According to the International Institute of Strategic Studies in London, the armed wing of the Polisario Front consisted of approximately 15,000 fighting men, of whom about 4,000 were in the field at any given time, the rest being rotated out of the field for spells of a few weeks or months. As part of its planning for the implementation of a peace plan, the United Nations (q.v.) estimated at the end of the 1980s that there were between 6,000 and 8,000 guerrillas. As for their equipment, some has been captured from the Moroccan forces, but most has been supplied by Algeria (and Libya until 1983). Much was of Soviet manufacture. By the mid-1980s, Polisario had T-55 and T-62 tanks, SAM-7 ground-to-air missiles (which were a real threat to the Moroccan air force), and multiple rocket launchers. Also of note in the SPLA inventory were captured Franco-Austrian SK-105 tanks and Eland armored cars supplied to the Moroccans by South Africa, as well as two dozen or so Brazilian-built EE-9 Cascavel armored personnel carriers given by Libya. The captured arms and other equipment displayed to foreign journalists in the Tindouf region, all told, represented a cross section of the production of many countries. In keeping with the SPLA's role as part of a "liberation front" organization, no salaries were paid to its men, and no formal rank system existed. Instead, the command hierarchy was based on a more informal system of assigned responsibilities.

SAHARAWI RED CRESCENT. The Saharawi Red Crescent was set up by the Polisario Front (q.v.) on November 26, 1975, and played a key role in assisting the tens of thousands of refugees (q.v.) who made their way to the Tindouf (q.v.) region of southwestern Algeria in 1975–76. It is responsible for the distribution of aid to the Saharawi refugees in the Tindouf camps and works closely with the Algerian Red Crescent.

SAHEL. The littoral, this was the name given by the Saharawis to the western stretch of the Sahara bordering the Atlantic. Much of this region was encompassed by the present territory of Western Sahara, and the *ahel es-sahel* were the inhabitants of this part of the desert.

SALEK OULD BOUBEH. A leader of the Polisario Front (q.v.), he entered the SADR's council of ministers following the front's 3rd congress, in August 1976, as secretary-general of the ministry of health and education, replacing Bouela Ould Ahmed Zine (q.v.), who had died the previous April. After the 4th congress, in September 1978, the education and health portfolios were separated, and he became secretary-general of the ministry of health. The title was later changed to minister of health. He was replaced in that position at Polisario's 5th congress, in October 1982, later serving as ambassador of the SADR (q.v.) to Mexico and then as the front's chief of diplomatic protocol.

SANHAJA. A Berber people, the Sanhaja are, along with the Maqil (q.v.) Arabs, the main ancestors of the Saharawis and Moors of Western Sahara and Mauritania. They are also the ancestors of the Tuareg of southern Algeria and northern Mali and Niger and of the Kabyles of Algeria and, in Morocco, the Rifians and the Berbers of the Middle Atlas. Their migrations into the western stretches of the Saharan desert probably began about 1000 B.C. Rock engravings from this period, when the process of desertification was far less advanced than it is today, reveal that carts or chariots, pulled by horses, were common in this part of the Sahara then, and associated inscriptions in the old Berber script, Tifinagh, suggest that these were ridden by Berbers. The Berbers' use of the horse and of iron appears to have gradually given them the upper hand over the previous inhabitants, an apparently Negroid people who are thought to have taken refuge in the oases and migrated to the south as the desert advanced. Berber penetration of the Sahara may have extended over more than a millennium, and it was not until the arrival of the camel from the east that the Berbers gained the means to ensure their dominance in the desert. The camel was not widespread in this part of the Sahara until between the 1st and 4th centuries A.D.

The Saharan Sanhaja were gradually, though superficially, converted to Islam from about the mid-8th century. Their main subgroups were the Lemtouna, the Gadala, and the Massoufa. The Lemtouna were the most powerful. A Lemtouna chief, Tiloutan, defeated the Soninke and other black peoples in the early 9th century, capturing Aoudaghost, which became an important staging post in the trans-Saharan caravan trade at this time. However, the Sanhaja came under increasing challenge over the following two centuries from both the blacks in the south and a rival Berber people, the Zenata, in the north. Toward 990, the Soninke kingdom of Ghana seized Aoudaghost, and between the 8th and 10th centuries, the Zenata took control of the oases of Tafilalet and the Oued Draa (q.v.), and from their city of Sijilmassa, in Tafilalet, they dominated the northern end of the trans-Saharan trade routes. They also blocked the Sanhaja from their traditional seasonal migration routes between the desert and the Atlas mountains.

It was under a religious banner, that of the Almoravids (q.v.), that the Sanhaja managed in the 11th century to reassert themselves at the expense of these rivals and then, under the leadership of men like Abdallah Ibn Yacin, Yahya Ibn Omar, Abu Bakr Ibn Omar, and Yusuf Ibn Tashfin, destroy the kingdom of Ghana, conquer Morocco and much of western Algeria, and reunify Muslim Spain against the challenge of the *reconquista*. However, only some of the Saharan Sanhaja followed the Almoravids into Morocco and beyond. Those who remained in the Sahara maintained their independent ways. The Gadala and the Massoufa at times fought against the Lemtouna, who had assumed the leadership of the Almoravids, and Abu Bakr Ibn Omar had to descend from Morocco to the desert to quell their rebellions in 1061. From this date, moreover, the Sanhaja forces in the Sahara under Abu Bakr, who commanded the successful campaign against Ghana (1062–76), were completely independent of the Almoravid state, which had been established in Morocco under Abu Bakr's cousin, Yusuf Ibn Tashfin.

While the Sanhaja-based Almoravid state in Morocco collapsed under the onslaught of the Masmouda Berbers of the High Atlas in 1125–50, giving rise to a new dynasty, the Almohads, the Saharan Sanhaja faced invasions by the Maqil Arabs, who migrated westward along the northern fringe of the desert into the Tafilalet and Oued Draa regions early in the 13th century, once again driving a wedge between the Sanhaja of the Sahara and those of the Atlas. Meanwhile, internal divisions among the Sanhaja weakened their resistance in the face of another enemy, the black peoples to their south. The Soninke were once again on the offensive in the 12th and 13th centuries. In the 14th century, the rising empire of Mali was the main threat, taking Timbuctoo from the Sanhaja and extending its domination over the steppelands of southern Mauritania as far as the Atlantic. Another threat was presented by the 15th century from the sea in the form of Portuguese and Spanish slave-raiding expeditions. Most important of all, however, was the southward expansion of the Maqil into what are now Western Sahara and Mauritania from the end of the 13th century in the wake of their failure to break into the fertile Atlantic plains of Morocco and the dispatch of punitive expeditions against them by the post-Almohad dynasty in Morocco, the Merinids. For two centuries, the Beni Hassan, a major wing of the Maqil, slowly migrated south into the Sahara, submerging and vassalizing many of the Sanhaja tribes.

In what is now Mauritania, Sanhaja resistance to the Beni Hassan culminated in a 30-year war, *Char Bouba,* in 1644–74. Led by Nacer ed-Din, a marabout (q.v.) of the Lemtouna, a large number of Sanhaja tribes, from Tiris to the River Senegal, fought against the Arabs, until, weakened by internal divisions, they submitted in 1674 by the peace agreement of Tin Yedfad. This has often been said to have consecrated the caste system that became a major characteristic of Mauritanian society. The victorious Beni Hassan tribes, known as *arab* or *hassan*, formed the caste of "warriors." Many of the defeated Sanhaja became tributaries, known as *znaga*, a corruption of Sanhaja. Other Sanhaja, however, recuperated their social position by "giving up the sword for the book" and becoming *zawiya* tribes, dedicated to religious study and teaching. In fact, the process of interaction between the indigenous Sanhaja and the invading Beni Hassan was uneven and complex. There were considerable regional variations. In Adrar, for example, it was not until the 1740s that the Beni Hassan ensured their supremacy over the Sanhaja, who, at the end of the 19th century, rose against their Maqil emir and murdered him. In this they were aided by the Idou Aich, a tribe of Sanhaja origin that had thrown off Maqil domination in Tagant at the end of the 18th century.

In Western Sahara, a Beni Hassan tribe, the Oulad Delim (q.v.), became dominant in the south of the future Spanish colony. In the Oued Noun and the Oued Draa regions just to the north of Western Sahara, the Sanhaja and the Beni Hassan gradually merged to form the Tekna (q.v.). However, tribes of Sanhaja origin began to assert themselves over much of what became Western Sahara under the leadership of such marabouts as Sidi Ahmed Reguibi and Sidi Ahmed el-Arosi in the 16th century. In c. 1696–97, a force of Beni Hassan suffered a grave defeat at the hands of Sanhaja warriors at the battle of Oum Abana, and, though the Arab Oulad Delim were to reach the height of their power at the end of the 18th century, it was the rise of the Reguibat (q.v.), people of decidedly Sanhaja stock, that marked the 19th century and early 20th century in this part of the Sahara. However, the Reguibat, like all the peoples of Sanhaja or predominantly Sanhaja descent in Western Sahara, had by then adopted the language of the Beni Hassan, the Hassaniya (q.v.) dialect of Arabic. Almost all these peoples considered themselves to be Arabs, having in many cases—such as the Reguibat and the Arosien (q.v.)—given themselves carefully contrived *cherifian* genealogies, tracing descent from the prophet Mohammed. Hence the irony that most of the tribes of essentially Sanhaja origin in Western Sahara have given themselves the caste status of *chorfa*.

SANTA CRUZ DE MAR PEQUENA. Spain's first fortified enclave on the Saharan coast, Santa Cruz de Mar Pequeña was built by a Castilian knight, Diego García de Herrera, in 1476. Master of the Canary Islands, he had been given a private concession over the coast opposite the archipelago by Enrique IV of Castile in April 1468. Spanish interest in the Saharan coast was a by-product of the conquest of the Canaries: Once established in the archipelago, the Spaniards wanted to tap the trans-Saharan trade, fish along the Saharan coast, and raid for slaves to fill the acute labor shortage facing the new plantations in the Canaries, especially in Fuerteventura and Lanzarote, as a result of the extermination of most of their indigenous inhabitants. Santa Cruz was to become a trading post, a fishing station, and a base for slave raids. Its exact location is not known, though most historians have concluded that it was probably at Puerto Cansado, which is about 70 km. northeast of Tarfaya (q.v.). After Herrera's death in 1485, the fort was abandoned, but Spanish interest revived after the Treaty of Tordesillas in June 1494, by which Portugal recognized the 650 km. stretch of coast from Cape Boujdour (q.v.) to Massat, near Agadir, as a Spanish zone of operations. In 1495, Herrera's widow, Inés Peraza, hoped to rebuild Santa Cruz de Mar Pequeña, but she found the Catholic Kings, Fernando II and Isabel I, taking over directly, sending instructions to their governor in the Canaries, Alonso Fajardo, to rebuild the fort as a royal rather than private venture. Fajardo rebuilt Santa Cruz in 1496, but in 1498, his successor in the Canaries, Alonso Fernández de Lugo, suddenly faced a new threat when the fort was sacked by a Portuguese force, which arrived in eight ships, commanded by a relative of Inéz Peraza, Diego da Silva. Despite this setback, the fort was the center of a thriving royal business. In 1497, slave raiding in the region around the fort had been banned by the Crown, in order to encourage trade, much of which was subject to royal monopolies, Santa Cruz being linked to the Casa de Contratación in Seville, the focus of both the African and American trades. Between 1498 and 1505, licensed traders had to hand over 50 percent of their profits to the Crown. After 1505, the ban on slave raiding was lifted, following protests in the Canaries that it was ruining the local economy, and thereafter raiding became one of the Spaniards' principal activities along the coast, stimulated by de Lugo, who received half of the Crown's one-fifth share in the profits from slaving. An attempt by de Lugo to set up three new forts in the region in 1499 ended in disaster at the mouth of the Assaka River, and, as the 16th century opened, Spain's imperial interests started to shift to the Americas. When Santa Cruz was sacked by a large Muslim army, aided by the Saadian chief Mohammed ech-Cheikh in 1524, the Spaniards made no attempt to return . . . until the end of the 19th century.

SEBKHA. An Arabic term for a salt-pan. Formed in depressions, these salt-pans were important economic assets in precolonial times, the salt being exported to both the black peoples in the south and the trading centers of the Maghreb.

SEDENTATION. Most of the Saharawi population abandoned the traditional nomadic way of life and settled in the new growing towns and villages during the 1960s and early 1970s. There were two main reasons for this. First, nomadism became increasingly hazardous during the mid-20th century, because demographic growth outstripped the growth of the livestock herds on which the nomads depended. This was due partly to serious droughts, especially in 1959–63, when about 60 percent of livestock was wiped out, and partly to the disruption caused to traditional patterns of pastoral nomadism by war and refugee movements, notably during and after the uprising led by the Army of Liberation (q.v.) in 1957–58. Demographic growth accelerated during the mid-20th century as a result of falling mortality—due to the end of the *ghazzis* (q.v.) and an improvement in health. Second, the opportunity arose to receive drought relief, education, and, above all, paid employment in the little towns springing up in both Western

Sahara and the surrounding countries. There was a rapid increase in employment in Western Sahara in the 1960s and early 1970s as a result of the expansion of economic and administrative infrastructure made necessary by the plans to explore for and exploit the country's minerals, notably phosphates (q.v.). The growing urban market, which was due partly to the influx of Europeans at this time, as well as the Spanish authorities' "free-zone" policy and the opportunities for cross-border smuggling, encouraged some Saharawis to settle in the towns as traders. Many settled in such southern Moroccan towns as Tan-Tan, Zaag, and Tarfaya (q.v.) following the insurrection of 1957–58, the ensuing cession of the Tekna Zone (q.v.) to Morocco by Spain in April 1958, and the devastating 1959–63 drought. In Algeria, several thousand Reguibat (q.v.) began to settle in the Tindouf-Bechar region in the 1960s. The Algerian government launched a sedentation program in 1966 and established agricultural villages for drought-stricken Reguibat at Abadia (southwest of Bechar), and at Oum el-Assel (1971), Ain Naga, and Hassi Abdallah near Tindouf. In Mauritania, there were growing employment opportunities for Saharawis in the iron-mining city of Zouerate and the port of Nouadhibou. By 1974, most Saharawis had probably abandoned nomadism. The Spanish census in Western Sahara that year recorded 55 percent of Saharawis as living in the territory's three main towns—El-Ayoun, Smara, and Dakhla (qq.v.)—though it should be noted that the nomadic element in the population was certainly underestimated in the census. The war since 1975 between the Polisario Front (q.v.) and Morocco (and briefly Mauritania too) has ended nomadism completely. Saharawis are now totally sedentary—living either in the towns or in Algerian refugee camps (q.v.).

SENGHOR, LEOPOLD SEDAR. Born in 1906 and president of Senegal from 1960 to 1980, he was one of Morocco's few African allies during its war with the Polisario Front (q.v.). At the behest of King Hassan II (q.v.), he helped to persuade Mauritania's President Mokhtar Ould Daddah (q.v.) to drop his claim to the whole of Mauritania in 1974 in favor of a deal with Morocco based on a joint approach to the International Court of Justice (q.v.) and eventual partition. In November 1975, he supported the Madrid Agreement (q.v.). Thereafter, he viewed with alarm the growing military success of the Polisario guerrillas, especially in Mauritania, which borders Senegal. He saw the Polisario Front as an example of the radical movements "destabilizing" pro-Western African regimes and feared that, if the guerrillas were allowed to continue their audacious military thrusts into Mauritania virtually unchecked, a "progressive" regime might come to power there, with Algerian support, on Senegal's borders. In 1976 and 1977, he tried to act as a mediator, but his evident bias toward Morocco and the Mauritanian regime of Mokhtar Ould Daddah—highlighted by his refusal to consider the option of full independence or to include the Polisario Front in negotiations—led to outright rejection of his initiatives by Algeria. In the UN, the OAU (qq.v.) and the Socialist International, representatives of his government or ruling Socialist Party, were forthright supporters of the partition of Western Sahara. On several occasions, he tried to arouse domestic support for his Saharan policy by accusing the Polisario guerrillas of being antiblack racists who murdered their black Mauritanian prisoners, and he threatened to put forward a claim to southern Mauritania if a radical regime came to power in Nouakchott as a result of the war. "If the status of Mauritania, its people, its regime were modified as a result of neoimperialism, Senegal would demand at the UN that the 500,000 Mauritanians who are ethnically and culturally Senegalese be allowed to exercise their right to self-determination," he said in December 1977. That month, French Jaguar bombers began flying missions against the Polisario guerrillas in Mauritania from the Ouakam air force base near Dakar. The French garrison stationed there under the March 29, 1974, Franco-Senegalese defense agreement had been reinforced a month earlier to service the French military personnel sent in to Mauritania to help coordinate the resistance to the guerrillas. Senghor's virulently anti-Polisario policy and his willingness to allow the French to intervene against the guerrillas, which fitted into his broader policy of support for French military intervention in Africa (notably in Chad in 1978 and Zaire in 1977 and 1978) was condemned by the main Senegalese opposition parties. In 1980, Senghor retired as president and was succeeded by Abdou Diouf, who showed more flexibility on the Western Sahara problem than his predecessor had.

SERVICIO DE INFORMACION Y SEGURIDAD. The Information and Security Service was the intelligence arm of the Spanish colonial regime and was responsible for detecting political activity carried out by opponents of the Spanish presence.

SHARIA (variant: *charia*). The Islamic judicial code, based in part on the Koran (the scriptures believed by Muslims to be Allah's revelations to the prophet Mohammed), the *Hadith* (tradition drawn from the words and deeds of the prophet), the *ijma* (the current consensus of Islamic belief), and *qiyas* (elaboration on the law's intent). The *sharia* provided the basis for civil jurisdiction in traditional Saharawi society, civil cases being judged by a *qadi* (q.v.). By contrast, the *orf* (q.v.), or customary law, which was of pre-Islamic, Berber origin and was enforced by the *djemaa* (q.v.), regulated criminal matters. By an ordinance of March 21, 1956, the Spanish authorities, after consulting Muslim experts, tried to streamline and modernize the traditional *sharia*-based system of civil justice by establishing local *qodat* to hear civil cases, as well as an appeal court, comprising a qadi, two *adel,* and a secretary, in El-Ayoun, and a higher review court, the *mejeles.*

SHAYKH see CHEIKH

SHEEP see LIVESTOCK

SIBA see BILAD ES-SIBA

SIDI. A title of respect, meaning, roughly, "sir." (Note: Names in this dictionary of persons usually bearing this title are listed under their actual name, rather than the title, e.g., Ahmed Mohammed Mahmoud, Sidi.)

SKARNA. A small tribe, living traditionally in the north.

SLAVERY. Though slavery was not widespread in Saharawi society, it has died out only gradually during the 20th century, and remnants of the practice may still exist today. The slaves, *abid* (sing. *abd*), are of black African origin, or sometimes mixed race. It is widely held that when the Berbers arrived in what is now Western Sahara and Mauritania, in the 1st millennium B.C., they enslaved some of the remaining black Bafour, who had taken refuge in the oases as a result of the long, gradual process of the Sahara's turning to desert. This is thought to have provided an original source of black slaves, to which were added the slaves procured later, through war and trade, from the south. Within Saharawi society, a slave could be acquired either by way of looting in a *ghazzi* (q.v.) or purchase, or through birth to slave parents. The latter, known as *nama,* were usually employed as domestics and even treated as part of the family. Slaves who were captured or purchased, known as *terbia,* were generally treated much worse and used for heavy labor, including agricultural work, which was generally despised as "slaves' work" by Saharawis. Slavery was far less widespread in Western Sahara than it was in southern Morocco and parts of Mauritania, where slaves were required to work in the palm oases, of which there were virtually none in Western Sahara. The economy of the Western Saharan tribes was essentially based on livestock herding, for which slaves were of little value, and was too poor to allow more than a handful of the wealthiest men to acquire them. Caro Baroja (1955) noted that out of a sample of 578 Lebouihat men and 462 Lebouihat women, there were only 6 black male slaves and 8 black female slaves. He found 12 black male slaves and 15 black female slaves out of 383 male and 323 female Arosien (q.v.). The proportions were similar in other tribes. The Koran described the liberation of slaves as laudable but not obligatory. Slaves were sometimes freed in traditional Saharawi society, but they invariably remained attached to their former masters. Such freed slaves were known as *haratin* (sing. *hartani*).

Slave raiding was one of the principal preoccupations, along with trade, of the first European expeditions to the Western Saharan coast, in the 15th century. The pioneers were the Portuguese seamen sent off on voyages of exploration by Henry the Navigator from 1421. By 1446, a total of 927 slaves had been taken, along the entire Saharan coast, down to the Senegal River. The next to raid the coast for slaves were the Spaniards, who needed slaves for the plantations in the Canary Islands after the extermination of most of the islands' indigenous inhabitants. It was in 1476 that the Spaniards first set up a fort on the Saharan coast opposite the Canaries, at Santa Cruz de Mar Pequeña (q.v.), which alternated as a trade center and a base for slave raiding. The slave trade was one of its principal activities until its abandonment sometime between 1485 and 1495, but after being rebuilt under direct royal ownership in 1496–97, the fort and the neighboring coastal regions were declared no-slaving zones so that other forms of commerce, most of which were under royal monopoly, could proceed in peace. However, the slaving ban was lifted in 1505 as a result of the economic decline the ban had brought in the Canaries. From then on, Fernando II and Isabel I, the Catholic kings, and their successor, Carlos V, stimulated the raids, known as the *entradas* and *cabalgadas,* the crown receiving a fifth of the profits. Carlos V waived his share in 1525, thus encouraging the raiding even more, though, after Moroccan pirates began raiding the Canaries in 1569, the Spanish crown banned the slave raids on the African coast in 1572, to avoid provoking further attacks on the islands. However, illegal raids continued.

During the Spanish colonial period, little was done to end slavery within Saharawi society, though the trade in slaves was formally abolished. The Spanish administration wanted to maintain a modus vivendi with the Saharawis and had no interest per se in reforming Saharawi society. However, as sedentation proceeded, the chances of emancipation improved: Jobs could be found in the new towns, and a runaway could appeal to the Spanish for protection. Legal records show the Spanish authorities intervening occasionally to prevent a slave's being sold or, if on the run, being returned to a former owner. Nonetheless, as late as May 1975, a United Nations Visiting Mission (q.v.) reported meeting slaves and hearing of their occasional sale and suggested that "this problem should be brought to the attention of the United Nations Commission on Human Rights." The mission's report noted that it was usually the *chioukh,* and among them some members of the Djemaa (q.v.), who owned slaves. The eradication of slavery has been a key policy plank of the Polisario Front (q.v.).

SMARA. Western Sahara's only precolonial city, Smara is about 160 km. east of the capital, El-Ayoun (q.v.). Its construction was begun in 1898 by Cheikh Ma el-Ainin (q.v.), the foremost leader of the anticolonial resistance in the first decade of the 20th century. The site chosen for the settlement was a patch of rushes on the Ouain Selouan, a tributary of the Saguia el-Hamra, which is 8 km. to the north. There was plenty of water there, about 50 wells were sunk, and palm trees imported from Adrar and the Draa were planted. The site also seemed likely to be profitable commercially, for it lay along the caravan routes from the Oued Noun to Adrar, and it was near abundant pastureland. Several thousand nomads took part in Smara's construction, aided by craftsmen from Morocco, Adrar, and even the Canaries. Building materials arrived at Tarfaya (q.v.) by sea from Morocco and the Canaries and were then transported overland by camel. By 1902, the main part of the city had been built, and Ma el-Ainin lived there until his move to Tiznit in southern Morocco in 1909 after the defeat of his forces by Gen. Gouraud in Adrar. The settlement was deserted when, in February 1913, it was seized and partially destroyed by a French force under Lt. Col. Mouret that had crossed into Spain's zone of the Sahara in reprisal for a devastating Saharawi *ghazzi* against French troops at El-Boirat in January 1913. The dome of Ma el-Ainin's old council hall was blown up and much of the library destroyed. This act of wanton vandalism by the French troops was viewed as sacrilege by the Saharawis, and a large force was assembled under one of the *cheikh*'s sons, Mohammed Laghdaf, to drive Mouret back to Adrar. Smara remained deserted until it was finally occupied by Spanish troops in 1934, after they had moved into the hinterland of the colony from its coastal enclaves for the first time. A military base and administrative center were established there. However, a little over 20 years later, in August 1957, Spain had to abandon Smara on account of the growing threat from the guerrillas of the Army of Liberation (q.v.). It was eventually reoccupied by a joint Franco-Spanish force during Operation Ouragan (q.v.), in February 1958. After the Madrid Agreement (q.v.), Moroccan troops arrived in Smara on November 27, 1975. After the Moroccan-Mauritanian Agreement of April 14, 1976, by which Western Sahara was partitioned, Smara became the capital of one of three Moroccan provinces (q.v.) in the territory. The city has remained under Moroccan control during the war with the Polisario Front (q.v.), though most of its population (7,295 in 1974) fled to Algeria in 1975–76, and the guerrillas succeeded in breaking briefly into the city after one of the fiercest battles of the war in October 1979 (see SMARA, BATTLE OF). The city has been beyond Polisario's reach since the completion of the first of Morocco's "defensive walls" (q.v.) in 1981. The city was described by some visitors in the 1980s as a virtual garrison town because of the large Moroccan troop presence. An airfield with a runway 3 km. long was built nearby, but it is used almost entirely for military purposes.

SMARA, BATTLE OF. In one of the most daring engagements of its war with Morocco, the Polisario Front (q.v.) attacked the city of Smara (q.v.) on October 6, 1979, briefly breaking through the Moroccan defense lines and evacuating several hundred of its Saharawi residents to the refugee camps (q.v.) near Tindouf (q.v.). According to the defense ministry of the SADR (q.v.) (October 9), the guerrillas burst their way into the city, killing 1,269 Moroccan soldiers, capturing 65, and destroying 19 tanks, 83 trucks, and 114 Land Rovers. The Moroccan ministry of information claimed (October 8) that the attack had failed. It said that 5,000 guerrillas attacked the city from three sides but were beaten back after losing 375 dead and that, the next day, as they retreated, 735 more guerrillas lost their lives when strafed by Mirage F-1 and

Northrop F-5 jets. However, a number of facts suggested that the Moroccan army had suffered a humiliating reverse: The very fact that the guerrillas had decided to attack Smara at all indicated high guerrilla confidence and morale; the commander of the Moroccan forces in Smara, Col. Driss Harti, was killed in the fighting; the Moroccans (unlike the guerrillas) failed to capture any prisoners; and the guerrillas did bring back to Tindouf some 700 city residents, among them a Saharawi deputy in the Moroccan Chamber of Representatives, Mohammed Ali Ould el-Bachir.

SOLB. A plain to the west of Zemmour (q.v.), it divides two hydrographic systems, those of the Khat and Zemmour.

SOLIS RUIZ, JOSE. Born in 1913, José Solís Ruíz was a longtime Francoist, serving as minister and secretary-general of the Falange in 1957–75 and minister of labor in 1975–76. During the period of Spanish-Moroccan crisis in the weeks preceding the Madrid Agreement (q.v.), he was instrumental in defusing the tension created by the announcement of the Green March (q.v.) and was influential in convincing the Spanish government to settle the Western Saharan dispute on terms acceptable to Morocco. It was on October 20, 1975, after a cabinet meeting had discussed the crisis sparked off by the announcement of the march four days earlier by King Hassan II (q.v.), that the Spanish prime minister, Carlos Arias Navarro (q.v.), asked Solís to meet the king. He arrived in Marrakesh the next day and held two meetings with him before returning to Madrid in the evening. Hassan refused to call off the march but agreed to postpone it to allow further negotiations. The broad outlines of a compromise over the Green March also seem to have been worked out, the details probably being settled in ensuing talks in Madrid, involving the Moroccan foreign minister, Ahmed Laraki (q.v.), on October 24–25 and 28–30. By the time that the Green March entered Western Sahara on November 6, it had been agreed that Spain would allow the marchers to cross the frontier as long as they kept their distance from a "dissuasion line," 14 km. from the frontier, to which Spanish troops had been withdrawn.

SOUAAD. The Souaad, one of the principal subtribes of the Reguibat es-Sahel (q.v.), numbered about 3,800 in Western Sahara, according to the census held by the Spanish authorities in 1974, about two thirds of them settled in the cities of El-Ayoun and Smara (qq.v.). However, this was almost certainly an underestimate of the Souaad still engaged in a nomadic way of life. Nomadic Souaad were spread at that time over a wide geographical area, from Jdiriya in the north to the extreme southeast border with Mauritania, where there is also a large Souaad population. Their principal fractions are the Ahel Brahim Ben Abdallah, Ahel Ba Brahim, El-Gherraba, Oulad Bou Said, and Ahel Khali Yahya. The Souaad trace their ancestry to Saad, a son of Ali Ould Sidi Ahmed Reguibi.

SOUILEM OULD ABDELLAHI. A Saharawi politician with a checkered career, he was one of the most forthright supporters of the Spanish colonial authorities in the last decade of Spanish colonial rule. Born in Zug in the extreme southeast of the country in 1913, he became a *cheikh* of the Oulad Delim (qq.v.). In May 1963, after the first municipal elections, he became mayor of Villa Cisneros (q.v.). That year, he took a seat in the Spanish Cortes, of which he remained a member until 1975. In December 1966, he was a member of a pro-Spanish Saharawi delegation that lobbied the UN (q.v.), and in 1967, he was elected to the Djemaa (q.v.), the consultative assembly of conservative tribal *chioukh*. A strong opponent of the Moroccan claim to Western Sahara, he flirted briefly with the Polisario Front (q.v.) when Spanish policy toward the territory underwent a volte-face under Moroccan pressure in October–November 1975. He attended the meeting of the Djemaa held under Polisario auspices on November 28, 1975, which issued the Proclamation of Guelta Zemmour (q.v.), and he then briefly visited Algeria. However, he returned to Western Sahara, where he joined the Front de Libération et du Rattachement du Sahara à la Mauritanie (q.v.), which had been created by the Nouakchott regime on November 16, 1975. He was then elected a PPM (q.v.) deputy for Dakhla (q.v.) in the one-party elections to the Mauritanian parliament held on August 8, 1976. However, after the overthrow of the regime of Mokhtar Ould

Daddah (q.v.) by the Mauritanian armed forces on July 10, 1978, he fled Mauritania to join the Polisario Front in February 1979. He has since lived in the Polisario refugee camps in Tindouf (q.v.), and in 1990 was a member of the legislative and consultative assembly of the SADR, the Saharawi National Council (qq.v.). In May and June 1990, he led a delegation of tribal elders from the Polisario camps in Tindouf to a UN-sponsored meeting in Geneva, attended also by a similar delegation from the Moroccan-controlled portions of Western Sahara, in order to discuss how to identify Saharawis eligible to vote in a referendum of self-determination.

SPANISH CIVIL WAR. The Spanish *delegado gubernativo* (q.v.) in Western Sahara, Lt. Col. del Oro Pulido, joined the fascist uprising of July 17, 1936, immediately after receiving instructions from Tetuan, in northern Morocco, the base of the Francoist movement. During the ensuing civil war, which ended in 1939, Western Sahara became a place of detention for Republican political prisoners. A few Saharawis joined the Francoist army, which first established a recruiting office in Tarfaya in 1937.

SPANISH FOREIGN LEGION. Founded in 1920, the Spanish Foreign Legion was an elite force, composed of volunteers of both Spanish and other nationalities. Modeled largely on the French Foreign Legion, it was created to strengthen Spain's military capabilities in northern Morocco, where regular Spanish conscript regiments and the *regulares* (Moroccan units of the Spanish army) had failed dismally to "pacify" Spain's northern protectorate zone. Most of the legion was transferred gradually to Western Sahara and Ifni after Morocco's independence in 1956. Steeped in colonialist tradition, many legionnaires had been shocked by Morocco's independence, and the Spanish government's decision at this time to hang on to both Western Sahara and Ifni may have been influenced partly by a need to placate the legion and find for it a new African base of operations. In fact, it soon found itself under fire, during the guerrilla war led by the Army of Liberation (q.v.) in Western Sahara and Ifni in

1957–58. The legion was humiliated, however, by the initial successes of the insurgents and its need to rely on French troops to stamp out the guerrillas in Operation Ouragan (q.v.), in February 1958. The legion became the main interlocutor with the Saharawis for much of the later colonial period, playing a major part in civil administration. It was supplemented militarily by several thousand conscript troops from regular Spanish regiments and by the predominantly Saharawi Tropas Nómadas and paramilitary Policía Territorial (qq.v.). The legion had two *tercios,* or regiments, stationed permanently in Western Sahara in the 1960s and early 1970s: the Tercio Alejandro Farnesio, based in the south, and the Tercio Don Juan de Austria in the north. They were gradually withdrawn after the Madrid Agreement (q.v.) between November 1975 and January 1976.

SPANISH WEST AFRICA see AFRICA OCCIDENTAL ESPANOLA

STATE SECURITY COURT. Formerly a special tribunal, set up under the first constitution of the Saharan Arab Democratic Republic (q.v.). Intended to counter dissident movements that might threaten the Polisario Front (q.v.) and the SADR's government, it was abolished by the new constitution provisionally adopted at the front's 8th general popular congress (q.v.) held on June 18–20, 1991.

STEADFASTNESS FRONT. The alliance of Arab states (Algeria, Libya, South Yemen, and Syria) and the Palestine Liberation Organization, which most strongly opposed the détente between Egypt and Israel symbolized by the September 1978 Camp David Accords. The Steadfastness Front decided at a summit meeting in Tripoli on April 12–15, 1980, to back the Polisario Front (q.v.) and give recognition to the SADR (q.v.). Algeria had already recognized the SADR in March 1976, and South Yemen had followed suit in February 1978, but Libya and Syria recognized the republic for the first time as a result of the Tripoli decision. The PLO denied that it was a party to the decision.

SUAAD see SOUAAD

SUAREZ GONZALEZ, ADOLFO. Born in Avila, Spain, in 1932
and secretary-general of the Falange in 1975–76, Adolfo
Suárez was prime minister of Spain from July 1976 until
February 1981 and leader of the Unión de Centro Democrático (UCD) from 1977. Though Spain had already
withdrawn from Western Sahara by the time of his appointment as premier, the continuing conflict in the territory
continued to be a major foreign policy problem for his
government. Officially, he claimed that Spain was neutral in
the war (though Spanish arms shipments to Morocco and
Mauritania continued until 1977), and, while rejecting calls
from the opposition PSOE and PCE for the annulling of the
Madrid Agreement (q.v.), he claimed that Spain had merely
transferred its administrative powers—and not sovereignty—to Morocco and Mauritania. "In particular," he said
in Paris on November 11, 1979, "we are supporters of the
self-determination of the Saharawi people." On April 30,
1979, he broke new ground by meeting the secretary-general
of the Polisario Front, Mohammed Abdelaziz (qq.v.), in
Algiers. The ambiguity and ambivalence of his policy reflected the multiple pressures bearing down on his government—from the pro-Polisario Spanish socialists and communists, from the Polisario Front, and from both the
Algerian and Moroccan governments. The Polisario guerrillas could exert direct influence by capturing Spanish fishermen off the Western Saharan coast, the favored fishing
waters of the Canary Islanders since the 15th century. The
release of eight fishermen, the crew of *Las Palomas,* captured on April 20, 1978, was only secured after Suárez's
UCD had issued a joint statement with the Polisario Front on
October 12 recognizing the guerrilla movement as sole
representative of the Saharawi people. The Algerian government, for its part, put pressure on Suárez by giving considerable support to the Movement for the Self-Determination
and Independence of the Canary Archipelago (MPAIAC),
particularly in the OAU (q.v.), and reminding Suárez of
Spain's important economic interests in Algeria, its main

trading partner in Africa. However, the Suárez government did not itself adopt the UCD policy of recognition of the Polisario Front, refused to recognize the SADR (q.v.), and rebuffed demands to tear up the Madrid Agreement. Countervailing pressures from Morocco were influential in checking the pressures from Algeria, the Polisario Front, and the Spanish opposition. In particular, Suárez was anxious not to jeopardize Spain's important fishing interests off the Moroccan and Western Saharan coasts and wanted to avoid giving a pretext to Morocco for the resurrection of its historic claims to Ceuta and Melilla, the Spanish enclaves on Morocco's Mediterranean coast. Suárez served as the leader of the UCD until 1981, resigned from the party in July 1982, and went on the become founder and leader of the Centro Democrático y Social.

SUBGOBERNADOR. A subgovernor was based in El-Ayoun (q.v.) and responsible for the administration of Western Sahara following the establishment of Africa Occidental Española (AOE) (q.v.) in 1946. He was subordinate to the governor-general of AOE, who was based in Sidi Ifni. In Dakhla (q.v.), a *delegado gubernativo* (q.v.) was responsible to the subgovernor for the administration of the south of the territory. In January 1958, AOE was abolished, and the subgovernor was replaced by a full governor-general (q.v.).

SUILEM ULD ABDELLAHE see SOUILEM OULD ABDEL-LAHI

SUPERCAID. The head of a Moroccan *cercle* (q.v.). *Supercaids* were appointed to administer the cercles established in the Moroccan-annexed sector of Western Sahara in 1976. Additional supercaids were appointed after the Moroccan annexation of Tiris el-Gharbia (q.v.), the onetime Mauritanian sector, in August 1979. Subordinate to the governor of the province (qq.v.) to which their cercle belongs, they are appointed by the ministry of the interior, to which they are ultimately responsible. Beneath the supercaid are the *caids* of the *caidats* (qq.v.), which make up his cercle.

- T -

TAHALAT see THAALAT

TAN-TAN, BATTLES OF. On January 28, 1979, the Polisario Front (q.v.) carried out one of the most daring attacks of its war with Morocco by battling its way into Tan-Tan (q.v.), a heavily defended provincial capital in southern Morocco. After traveling north from Western Sahara by way of a pass through the Zini mountains, a large guerrilla force dislodged Moroccan troops on the city's defense perimeter and broke into the city center, where prisoners were freed from the local jail. After about four hours in the city, which was the site of a Moroccan airforce base and lay astride the strategic coastal highway from Agadir to the Western Saharan capital of El-Ayoun (q.v.), the guerrillas left, returning to their bases. The raid caused a sensation in Morocco, where an official blackout of news on the war had previously lulled the population into a state of complacency. The government immediately faced a barrage of protests from the ultranationalist opposition parties. King Hassan II (q.v.) responded by announcing on March 8 that he would set up a Conseil National de Securité (q.v.), including representatives of the legal opposition parties. At an extraordinary session of the Moroccan Chamber of Representatives on March 9, a resolution was passed unanimously to urge the government to "exercise the right of pursuit and launch retaliation operations each time that national territory is subjected to foreign military aggression." On March 12, Col. Abdelaziz Bennani (q.v.), chief of staff of the Moroccan forces in the Sahara, was replaced by a new commander, Col. Mohammed Abrouq (q.v.), but Polisario guerrillas attacked Tan-Tan twice again, on June 13 and June 27, 1979.

TAN-TAN DEMONSTRATIONS. A series of anti-Spanish demonstrations held in the southern Moroccan town of Tan-Tan by the "embryonic movement for the liberation of the Sahara" (q.v.), a Saharawi student group in Morocco, in March and May 1972. The demonstrations, which were suppressed by the Moroccan authorities and led to several of the embryonic movement's militants' being briefly jailed, were a turning point in the group's evolution, convincing many of its leaders, including El-Ouali Mustapha Sayed (q.v.), that King Hassan II (q.v.) would not allow a Saharawi liberation organization to be established on Moroccan territory and that the movement would have to rely fundamentally on the Saharawis themselves for support and turn to other foreign governments for external aid. The demonstrations themselves were indicative of the group's decision at the end of 1971 to try to stir up support from the Saharawi population of southern Morocco, much of which is concentrated in Tan-Tan. In the first demonstration, early in March, several students, among them El-Ouali, his brother Bachir Mustapha Sayed, and Mohammed Ould Sidati (qq.v.), were arrested. In a larger demonstration at the end of the month, no arrests were made, but more than 30 were arrested when another demonstration was held on May 26 during the town's *moussem* (fair). Though they were released after two or three days, one of the group's leaders, Mohammed Lamine Ould Ahmed (q.v.), was rearrested two months later and detained for a week in Agadir. The suppression of the demonstrations reflected the Moroccan government's desire at the time to maintain good relations with Spain and its fear of allowing an autonomous Saharawi movement to organize in Morocco at a time when the king's regime was particularly unstable. The main lesson learned from the Tan-Tan experience by the El-Ouali group was that it could expect to receive harassment rather than support from the Moroccan government, a factor that influenced its evolution in an increasingly Saharawi nationalist direction. The matter played a major part in founding the Polisario Front (q.v.), a year later.

TAOUBALT. A very small tribe of *chorfa* who were traditionally associated closely with the Izarguien (q.v.) and who lived in the region between the Oued Noun and the Saguia el-Hamra (q.v.). Their two fractions are the Oulad Sidi Djemaa and the Oulad Khelaif.

TARFAYA. Tarfaya lies on the Atlantic coast at Cape Juby, about

35 km. north of the post-1958 border of Western Sahara. It was at Tarfaya that the British trader Donald Mackenzie established a trading post, Port Victoria, in 1879 to do business with local Tekna (q.v.) and Saharan caravans. Mackenzie's activities at Tarfaya elicited protests from the sultan of Morocco, Moulay Hassan (q.v.), and, in 1895, his successor, Moulay Abdelaziz, bought Port Victoria for £50,000. Thereafter, a Moroccan *caid* (q.v.) was based at Tarfaya. Under the Franco-Spanish Convention of November 14, 1912 (q.v.), Tarfaya fell within the southern zone of Spain's protectorate in Morocco, known sometimes as the Tekna Zone (q.v.). However, it was not until June 29, 1916, that Francisco Bens (q.v.), Spain's politicomilitary governor in the Sahara, occupied Tarfaya. It then became a small administrative center with a permanent military garrison. After Bens's death in 1949, Tarfaya was renamed Villa Bens by a Spanish decree on July 26 of that year. It reverted to its traditional name when, under the Agreement of Cintra (q.v.) of April 1, 1958, the Tekna Zone was handed over to Morocco on April 10, 1958. In April 1976, Tarfaya was attached to the new Moroccan province of El-Ayoun (q.v.).

TAYA, MAAOUIYA OULD SID 'AHMED see MAAOUIYA OULD SID 'AHMED TAYA

TEIDE, OPERATION see OURAGAN, OPERATION

TEKNA. The Tekna people, who now live primarily in southern Morocco, extend traditionally from the southern foothills of the Anti-Atlas to the Saguia el-Hamra (q.v.). They are thought to have their origins in a fusion between Lamta Berbers and the Maqil (q.v.) Arab Bedouins. The Lamta had lived in the Oued Noun region, the center of what was to become Tekna territory, for many centuries before the arrival of the first groups of Maqil in 1218. According to de la Chapelle (1934, page 33), "the two fractions of the Lamta, who were called the Zogguen and the Lakhs, incorporated themselves into a group of the Maqil tribe of the Beni Hassan [q.v.], and it is perhaps then, or rather one or two centuries later, that the whole group took the name of Tekna."

The Tekna were partly sedentary, partly nomadic. From the southern fringes of the Anti-Atlas to the lower Draa (q.v.) valley there were Tekna villages. There, agriculture and a sedentary way of life were, and are, possible. Farther south, in the desert, no agriculture is possible, and Tekna tribes engaged in a pastoral nomadic economy, migrating as far south as the Saguia el-Hamra. The whole Tekna region thus had balanced complementary resources. The sedentary and nomadic Tekna depended on each other, the nomads visiting the markets and *moussems* (religious fairs) of the Oued Noun and the Oued Draa to exchange their animals for cereals and other imported commodities, like cloth and tea. As one of the main "gates" of Morocco, the Tekna region was, moreover, a center of the trans-Saharan trade. Many Tekna became traders, traveling north to the cities of Morocco and south to Mauritania and beyond. The Ait Moussa Ou Ali, a sedentary Tekna tribe, who controlled Goulimine and its famous market, were the foremost traders of the region in the 18th and 19th centuries.

There has never, it seems, been a unified Tekna confederation. The Tekna tribes were politically independent of one another, being governed by councils of notables, the *djemaas* (q.v.), or leading noble families. Moreover, they were often at war with each other, as well as with other non-Tekna tribes. In fact, the Tekna were traditionally divided into two unstable rival alliances, the Ait Atman (sometimes also known as the Ait Bella) and the Ait Jmel. Though it appears that the Ait Jmel were originally nomadic and the Ait Atman the settled or seminomadic, by the 19th century each bloc combined both nomads and villagers, partly as a result of the desertion of the largely nomadic Ait Oussa (q.v.) from the Ait Jmel to the Ait Atman. The division ended up having a geographic character, the Ait Jmel representing the western Tekna, the Ait Atman those farther to the east. At the start of the colonial period, the Ait Jmel included the Izarguien (q.v.), a fully nomadic people who traditionally migrated deep into what is now Western Sahara, as far as Boujdour (q.v.), and the Ait Lahsen (q.v.), a partly sedentary and partly nomadic tribe that also had migratory traditions in the region of the Saguia el-Hamra. A smaller nomadic group in the Ait

Jmel was the Yagout. The most important sedentary element in the bloc was provided by the Ait Moussa ou Ali, whose principal center was the town of Goulimine. The rival Ait Atman bloc included the primarily sedentary Azouafid and Ait Yasin and the mainly nomadic Ait Oussa and Id Brahim. Relations between the two blocs were characterized by an almost endless round of *ghazzis* (q.v.) and counterghazzis up until the final colonial "pacification" in 1934. Typical of these conflicts was a war in 1907, sparked off by an Azouafid ghazzi against an Izarguien *friq* (q.v.), which ended up with both the Ait Jmel and Ait Atman tribes broadening their alliances to include tribes from Ifni, some of them Tachelhit-speaking Berbers. The last ghazzi occurred in 1934 when a force of Ait Oussa and their allies attacked a large concentration of Ait Lahsen, Izarguien, and other coastal people outside the little Spanish fort at Tarfaya (q.v.), the Spanish soldiers there looking on bewildered but guarding a strict neutrality.

From the 19th century, the Tekna's most powerful neighbors to the south were the Reguibat (q.v.). Relations constantly shifted, as changing circumstances demanded cooperation or conflict. Livestock raiding could spark off sharp conflicts, especially if human life was lost and the aggrieved party demanded payment of the blood debt, the *diya*. On the other hand, the Reguibat and the Tekna were mutually dependent, much as were the nomadic and the sedentary Tekna. In particular, the Reguibat needed the cooperation and protection of the Tekna to frequent the markets and moussems of the Oued Draa and the Oued Noun, protection they acquired by making a sacrifice known as the *debiha*.

In the 16th century, the Tekna seem to have been closely allied to the Saadians, the dynasty that came to power in Morocco in the middle of that century after spearheading popular resistance to Christian European encroachments along the coast of the Souss, the Oued Noun, and the Oued Draa regions. During the reign of the powerful Saadian sultan Ahmed el-Mansour (1578–1603), the Tekna appear to have played a role as *guish* tribes—that is, they were furnished with land and dispensed from taxation in return for providing military contingents for the defense of the dynasty and its government, the *makhzen*. They were able thus to install a colony in the Haouz of Marrakesh, where some still live today, between the Oued Nfis and Chichaoua. A further group, taken from this initial colony by Sultan Moulay Abderrahman (1822–59) following a revolt by the Cherarda, are still settled near the River Sebou.

At the end of Ahmed el-Mansour's reign, however, as the power of the makhzen declined, an independent statelet was established in the Anti-Atlas at Tazeroualt. The Oued Noun region was its gate to the Sahara and the caravan trade, and Massa acted as its maritime port. It was a period of prosperity for the Tekna, but Tazeroualt's independence was short-lived. The first Alawite (q.v.) sultan, Moulay Rachid (1666–72), took control of its capital and thereafter, until the middle of the following century, most of the Tekna accepted the sovereignty of the makhzen. The most powerful Alawite sultan, Moulay Ismail (1672–1727), once again used the Tekna as guish tribes, sending the Izarguien, under Hammou Said el-Azergui, to what is now southern Mauritania to help the emir of Trarza, Ali Chandora (1703–27), to reestablish his authority.

However, Morocco was plunged into anarchy after Moulay Ismail's death in 1727. For more than 150 years thereafter, the makhzen's writ barely extended to the Souss, let alone the regions farther south. Moreover, Tekna interests were affected when Sultan Mohammed Ben Abdallah (1757–90) established a new port at Mogador, not far from Marrakesh, to attract the Saharan caravans, and so, in the 1760s, the state of Tazeroualt was reborn, and further south, a Tekna chief, Ali el-Hadj, became an independent ruler in the city of Goulimine. The sultan's loss of power in these regions was noted in 1767 in the Spanish-Moroccan Treaty of Marrakesh. The two little states of Tazeroualt and Goulimine virtually monopolized the trans-Saharan trade between the Tekna regions and black Africa. Cheikh Beyrouk, the Ait Moussa Ou Ali chief who was ruling in Goulimine by the end of the 1810s, established agents in all the important trading towns along the caravan routes to the south. Meanwhile, both Beyrouk and Sidi Hashem, the ruler of Tazeroualt, carried on a lucrative trade in the ransoming of shipwrecked European sailors captured along the notoriously dangerous coast. This in turn alerted Beyrouk to the idea of establishing direct relations with European governments and traders in the hope of setting up a port that would allow both European ships and the Saharan caravans to bypass the Moroccan ports to the north. In 1835, Beyrouk tried to interest the British government in his plans, but a British naval vessel, the *Scorpion,* sent to bring gifts to the *cheikh,* failed to negotiate a landing on the coast. Five years later, a French vessel, *La Malouine,* did succeed in landing at the mouth of the Draa, and its commander, Lt. Bouet, agreed with Beyrouk that a port might be built at the mouth of the Assaka River, the French holding a monopoly on the trading to be carried on there. These negotiations were followed by further French missions in 1841 (*L'Alouette*) and 1843 (*La Vigie*) and then by a visit to France by Beyrouk's minister, Bou Azza, in 1845. However, nothing came of the plans. The dangerous coastline, renowned for its shipwrecks, was not encouraging, and the Moroccan makhzen began to be alarmed by Beyrouk's relations with the Europeans. Moulay Abderrahman (1822–59), who was coming under severe pressure from France by the 1840s (notably in 1844 when a Moroccan army was defeated at Isly by the French), decided to placate Beyrouk, granting him a kind of consulate in Mogador and the right to two thirds of the customs revenue from goods coming from the Oued Noun.

Upon his death, Beyrouk was succeeded by an oligarchy of his eleven sons, the most important of whom were El-Habib, Mohammed, and Dahman, who carried on the policy charted by their father. In 1850, they received a Frenchman, Panet, coming from Senegal, who, it seems, interested Napoleon III in the idea of trading with the Oued Noun, but French contacts with the Beyrouk family ended in 1853 when emissaries of the sultan prevented a French ship from making contact with the coast. In 1860, however, El-Habib sent an envoy to Tetuan, which had been occupied by Spanish troops in February, offering to aid the Spanish by attacking the sultan from the south, and, though the brief Spanish-Moroccan war had ended by the time of the envoy's arrival, the Spanish took care to insert a clause in the ensuing peace treaty with Morocco (May 1860) recognizing their rights to establish a base for "fisheries" on the old site of Santa Cruz de Mar Pequeña (q.v.). In consequence, three Spanish explorers (Butler, Puyana, and Silva) landed on the Oued Noun coast in 1867, brought El-Habib to Lanzarote in the Canary Islands, and signed a commercial treaty with him. However, on their return to the mainland, El-Habib changed his tune and imprisoned the three Spaniards until 1874.

Nonetheless, in 1876, another European trader, Donald Mackenzie, arrived in the Tekna country and, after talks with the Beyrouks, returned to London to found the North-West Africa Company, which then set up a trading post at Tarfaya (q.v.). However, by then, a more dynamic and effective sultan, Moulay Hassan (1873–94), determined to put an end to the independence of the Souss and the Oued Noun and to halt the Teknas' trade with the Europeans, which he saw as both a challenge to his port at Mogador and a strategic danger to his realm. In 1882, Moulay Hassan led an expedition in person to Tiznit, and the Beyrouks were sufficiently prudent to decide to make amends with the sultan, who nominated Dahman as *caid* (q.v.) of the Ait Moussa Ou Ali of Goulimine. In 1886, he led a second expedition, this time reaching Goulimine, from which he sent off a force to attack Mackenzie's installations at Tarfaya. But, though the Beyrouks and some other Tekna, notably the Ait Oussa, accepted Alawite suzerainty, some of the Tekna tribes did not. This was especially true of the Izarguien, the Ait Lahsen, and the Yagout, nomadic tribes of the Ait Jmel bloc, who had enjoyed close relations with Mackenzie. In 1888, a Moroccan force, sent to punish these tribes for their relations with the Europeans, was defeated by a force of nomads at the mouth of the Saguia el-Hamra. Again, in 1899, a force of Moroccan and Ait Moussa Ou Ali soldiers, sent out from Goulimine by Dahman to chastise the Izarguien, was routed at Daora (q.v.).

Relations between Mackenzie and Tekna at Tarfaya had, meanwhile, created frictions between the Ait Jmel, in particular the Beyrouks, and Cheikh Ma el-Ainin (q.v.), the leader of the Saharawi struggle against the Europeans at this time, though as Ma el-Ainin's prestige grew and the Beyrouks' declined, some Tekna joined his cause, and in 1912, some 200 Tekna joined the expedition to Marrakesh led by his son, Ahmed el-Hiba (q.v.). They were, however, mainly Ait Atman, and they ended up conflicting with the rest of his army.

Thereafter, while intertribal wars continued, until 1934, the Tekna tribes generally established friendly relations with the French or the Spanish. The Ait Moussa Ou Ali and the Ait Oussa turned mainly to the French, the Ait Oussa becoming auxiliaries of the French army in the closing stages of the French campaign to extend their control of Morocco to the valley of the Draa (1934). The Izarguien and the Ait Lahsen established close relations with the Spanish fort set up at Tarfaya in 1916.

Most of the Tekna ended up under French and then Moroccan rule. After the southward shift in Spain's Saharan border from the Draa to parallel 27° 40' by virtue of the Agreement of Cintra (q.v.) in April 1958, only the Izarguien and the Ait Lahsen remained in appreciable numbers in the Spanish zone. Most of the nomadic Tekna gradually became sedentary in southern Morocco and Western Sahara in the following years, but Tekna can be found much further afield, in northern Morocco and in Mauritania, as a result of their trading history and migrations prompted by droughts. As early as 1930, small groups of Ait Moussa Ou Ali, Id Ahmed, and Ait Oussa were reported to have settled in the region of Rabat.

TEKNA ZONE. A name sometimes given to the northernmost strip (25,600 sq. km.) of Spain's Saharan territory, between the Oued Draa (q.v.) and parallel 27°40', which was defined as part of Morocco in the Franco-Spanish Convention of November 12, 1912 (q.v.), and thus handed over by Spain to Morocco under the Agreement of Cintra (q.v.) in April 1958, two years after the termination of Spain's "protectorate" in northern Morocco. It was also known sometimes as the Tarfaya Zone, after its principal settlement, Tarfaya (q.v.), or as Spanish Southern Morocco. The name Tekna Zone derived from the predominantly Tekna composition of its population.

TERMINOS MUNICIPALES. The *términos municipales,* or municipalities, were the urban areas large enough to be administered by city councils, the *ayuntamientos* (q.v.), under the system of local government established after the conversion of Western Sahara into a Spanish "province" (q.v.) in 1958. Previously, main urban settlements had been deemed too small to be granted the status of municipalities and had been administered by *juntas locales* (q.v.). By a law of April 19, 1961, on the organization of the new province, a distinction was drawn between términos municipales, for the larger towns, and *entidades locales menores* (q.v.) for the smaller settlements. A decree of November 29, 1962, created two municipalities, for El-Ayoun and Dakhla (qq.v.). They remained the only two municipalities in the country until the Spanish withdrawal in 1976.

TERRITORIAL POLICE see POLICIA TERRITORIAL

THAALAT (variant: Tahalat). A subtribe of the Reguibat es-Sahel (q.v.). The Thaalat are said not to be pure descendants of Sidi Ahmed Reguibi, the Reguibat founder, but to have joined the confederation through a process of *asaba,* or solidarity pact. Their fractions are the Ahel Dekhil, the Ahel Meiara, and the Ahel Rachid. One of the most illustrious of the Thaalat in modern times was El-Ouali Mustapha Sayed (q.v.), founder of the Polisario Front (q.v.). According to the 1974 Spanish-held census, which underestimated the nomadic section of the population, there were around 650 Thaalat in Western Sahara then, about a third of them living in El-Ayoun (q.v.).

TINDOUF. Situated on the *hammada* (q.v.), about 50 km. to the east of the Western Saharan border in Algerian territory, Tindouf has played an important historical role in this part of the desert since its founding in 1852 by the Tadjakant, one of the most important trading peoples of the 19th century Sahara. As a halting point on the main caravan routes between Morocco and the trading centers to the south of the Sahara, it was renowned for its prosperity in the late 19th century. It also became well-known as a center of Islamic learning. However, in 1895, it was seized and sacked by the Reguibat (q.v.) at the end of a long intertribal war. Hundreds of its Tadjakant residents were massacred, and the city remained virtually deserted until its occupation by the French army on March 31, 1934. Some Tadjakant then returned. Chaamba soldiers and their families also began to settle in the city, which became France's main base from which to patrol the hammada. The city became part of French Algeria, but after Morocco's independence in 1956, Moroccan nationalists claimed that the city had been historically Moroccan, and, when Algeria gained independence in turn in 1962, the Moroccan army tried unsuccessfully to seize Tindouf in the short and inconclusive Moroccan-Algerian border war of October 1963. The Moroccan claim to Tindouf and much of the rest of southwestern Algeria was part of the "Greater Morocco" vision of Moroccan nationalists like Allal el-Fassi (qq.v.) and was based on premises similar to the claim to Western Sahara. On June 15, 1972, King Hassan II and President Houari Boumedienne (qq.v.) signed a border convention by which Morocco recognized Algerian sovereignty over Tindouf, but the convention was not ratified by Morocco until May 14, 1989, which may have encouraged the Algerian government to throw its support behind the Polisario Front (q.v.) in its war against Moroccan occupation of Western Sahara in 1975. During the 1960s and early 1970s, several thousand Reguibat settled in and around Tindouf as a result of the repeated droughts, the growth of employment and education opportunities there, and the Algerian government's sedentation policy, under which agricultural villages were established in the region. After the Moroccan-Mauritanian intervention in Western Sahara at the end of 1975, about 100,000 Saharawi refugees settled in Polisario camps near Tindouf. The guerrilla movement had its main rear bases there, too.

TIRIS. A desert tableland, about 1,000 feet above sea level, in the extreme southeast of the territory, extending into Mauritania. It is bordered to the southwest by the more mountainous Adrar Soutouf (q.v.) and is one of the most arid zones of the country.

TIRIS EL-GHARBIA. Tiris el-Gharbia, or Western Tiris, was the name given to the sector of Western Sahara annexed by Mauritania in 1975–76. La Guera (q.v.) in the extreme south, which had been abandoned by the Spanish in November, was seized by Mauritanian troops from the Polisario Front (q.v.) on December 20, 1975. Tichla, in the southeast, was taken the same day. The region's main city, Dakhla (q.v.), was entered by Moroccan troops on January 9, 1976, and Mauritanian troops did not arrive there until January 12, the date of departure of the remaining Spanish garrison there. The same day, there was a major battle to dislodge the Polisario Front from Argoub across the Río de Oro (q.v.) Bay. On January 23, 1976, Mauritanian troops captured Aoussert (q.v.), but it was rapidly captured again by Polisario guerrillas and did not fall definitively to Mauritanian troops until February 8. By then, a Mauritanian governor, Hamoud Ould Abdel Wedoub (q.v.), had been appointed (January 15) to administer Tiris el-Gharbia. It was not, however, until the signing of the Moroccan-Mauritanian Convention of April 14, 1976 (q.v.), formally partitioning Western Sahara, that the borders of the Mauritanian sector were set. This gave Mauritania a virtually resourceless slab of desert in the far south, totaling 96,000 sq. km. out of the territory's total land area of 266,000 sq. km. The phosphate mines and the capital, El-Ayoun (q.v.), were taken by Morocco. Besides the fish resources off Tiris el-Gharbia's 460-km. coastline and the tiny fishing industry at La Guera, Mauritania only added to its already vast expanses of sand and rocks. By contrast, Tiris el-Gharbia became a tremendous drain on resources for the Nouakchott government. Not only did the war with the Polisario Front virtually ruin the economy, but recurrent civil expenses in Tiris el-Gharbia itself totaled 162 million ougiyas in 1977 while total tax revenues there were a mere 9 million ougiyas. Investment spending there was about 600 million ougiyas in 1976–77. Moreover, to placate local Saharawi traders, a "free zone" was maintained, allowing a huge flow of duty-free luxury consumer goods to the rest of Mauritania, usually in military vehicles. Most of the civilian population fled, meanwhile, to Algeria, while attacks by the Polisario guerrillas obliged Mauritania to let Moroccan troops remain in the Mauritanian sector. The annexation of the 96,000 sq. km. given to Mauritania under the April 14, 1976, convention with Morocco was formally approved by the Mauritanian National Assembly on April 19. However, a constitutional requirement that a change in Mauritanian's borders required approval in a referendum was simply ignored. No referendum was held. Administratively, the Region of Tiris el-Gharbia was subdivided into four departments—Dakhla (the site of the capital), Aoussert, Tichla, and Argoub. However, La Guera and Bir Gandous, in the extreme southwest, were administratively separated from the rest of the Mauritanian sector of Western Sahara, being made a department of region number 8 (Nouadhibou). Elections held in the Mauritanian sector on August 8, 1976, were said by the Nouakchott regime to indicate popular support there for integration with Mauritania. However, few independent observers believed that the elections, in which seven candidates of the ruling Parti du Peuple Mauritanien (q.v.) were elected to the Mauritanian National Assembly, were genuinely democratic. They were held under Mauritania's one-party electoral system, with no choice of candidates, 96.07 percent of the 10,000-strong electorate allegedly voting and 96.4 percent of them approving the PPM candidates according to the official returns. After two and a half years of war, the Mauritanian army deposed President Mokhtar Ould Daddah (q.v.) on July 10, 1978, and dissolved the PPM. declaring that it wanted to extricate Mauritania from the conflict. A year later, on August 5, 1979, Mauritania and the Polisario Front signed the Algiers Agreement (q.v.) by which Mauritania renounced its claim to Western Saharan territory. On August 14, 1979, Morocco unilaterally declared that it was annexing the Mauritanian zone, which it renamed Oued ed-Dahab (q.v.). Moroccan troops took control of Dakhla and other strategic points in the zone, with the exception of La Guera, which Mauritanian troops refused to evacuate and continued to occupy in 1993.

TRIBES. (See also the breakdown of tribes and fractions in the charts on pages 561–564) Until the early 20th century, Saharawi history consisted primarily of the relations be-

tween autonomous tribes (*qabael,* sing. *qabila*). Until the
13th century, the tribes were essentially of Sanhaja (q.v.)
Berber stock, with an admixture of black African blood in
the lower castes. Then, from the end of the 13th century,
Maqil (q.v.) Arab tribes began migrating into Western
Sahara. By the 18th century, the basic physiognomy of
Western Sahara had been set: After centuries of wars,
alliances, tribal fusions, and migrations, all the qabael of this
part of the Sahara had adopted the Hassaniya (q.v.) dialect of
Arabic and were, to a greater or lesser degree, of mixed Arab,
Berber, and black African descent. As a result of wars and
migrations, there were frequent shifts in the tribes' relative
fortunes. A succession of tribes each achieved temporary
dominance, and many, defeated by rivals, disintegrated or
migrated elsewhere. The Oulad Delim (q.v.), for example,
rose from relative obscurity and poverty to become one of
the strongest tribes in the 18th century; the Reguibat (q.v.)
did much the same in the 19th century. By the 20th century,
the Reguibat were by far the largest qabila in Western Sahara
and were also numerous in what is now northern Mauritania,
southern Morocco, southwestern Algeria, and northwestern
Mali. The other main tribes in 20th-century Western Sahara
have been the Ait Lahsen and the Izarguien, both Tekna
tribes (q.v.), who have lived traditionally in the north of the
territory and in southern Morocco, the Oulad Delim, the
south and across the border in Mauritania, and the Arosien
and the Oulad Tidrarin (qq.v.), concentrated primarily in the
central coastal region. As a result of sedentation and refugee
movements, however, nomadism had ended completely by
the late 1970s, and all Western Saharans had settled either in
the territory's few towns or in neighboring countries.

Every Saharawi qabila claimed to have a founder, an
apical ancestor from whom all or the most important parts of
the tribe were said to be descended. The qabila was seg-
mented into fractions, or *afkhad* (q.v.), each normally
founded by a close descendant of the founder of the qabila,
and into subfractions, *afra* (q.v.). The system of descent was
patrilineal. However, the tribes were not as "pure" as their
genealogies often claimed. Immigrant groups were often
adopted into the tribe as a result of an alliance or pact known

as *asaba.* Tribes had a caste status—*arab,* or warrior; *chorfa,* or religious; and *znaga,* or tributary. The first two were free castes, the last a subservient, exploited one. The arab, who claimed Maqil ancestry and were also known as the *ahel mdafa* (people of the gun), included the Oulad Delim, who are certainly the purest Arabs in the territory, and the Tekna tribes, who have a mixed Sanhaja-Maqil ancestry. The chorfa are of primarily Sanhaja descent, despite their claim to descent from the prophet Mohammed. The most important of the supposedly *cherifian* tribes are the Reguibat, the Arosien, the Taoubalt, the Ahel Cheikh Ma el-Ainin, the Oulad Bou Sbaa, and the Filala (qq.v.). Another category of qabael with a traditionally religious vocation but without the claim to cherifian ancestry is that of the *zawiya.* Zawiya tribes were common in Mauritania but relatively rare in Western Sahara, with the exception of the Oulad Tidrarin (q.v.), who lost their status when reduced to znaga by the Oulad Delim at the end of the 18th century. Besides the Oulad Tidrarin, only the small coastal fishing tribes shared the ignominy of paying tribute to the powerful free tribes. Among them were the Fouikat, the Imeraguen, the Mejat, and the Menasir. Tribal caste status was often neither clear—the Reguibat were, by virtue of their warlike traditions, "people of the gun" as much as chorfa—nor stable, with shifts in status, as in the case of the Oulad Tidrarin, accompanying changes in the politico-military fortunes of the qabael.

TRIPARTITE ADMINISTRATION. The transitional Spanish-Moroccan-Mauritanian government established in Western Sahara as a consequence of the Madrid Agreement (q.v.) of November 14, 1975, it was headed by the Spanish governor-general (q.v.) and two deputy governors, one Moroccan, the other Mauritanian, and administered the territory until the ending of the Spanish presence on February 26, 1976. The Moroccan deputy governor, Ahmed Bensouda (q.v.), arrived in El-Ayoun (q.v.) on November 25 and the Mauritanian deputy governor, Abdellahi Ould Cheikh (q.v.), two days later. The first meeting of the tripartite administration, presided by the Spanish governor-general Gen. Federico Gómez de Salazar (q.v.), was held on November 27; two days later, the two deputy governors were introduced to the Djemaa (q.v.), though they suffered the embarrassment of finding only 32 of its 102 members present, since most of its members were far away in Guelta Zemmour (q.v.), where, under the auspices of the Polisario Front (q.v.), the majority of Djemaa members declared the assembly dissolved on November 28. On December 3, eight Moroccan ministers inaugurated Royal Air Maroc's service from Rabat to El-Ayoun. Meanwhile, most of the Saharawi population fled the cities to join the Polisario Front (q.v.) in the desert and, later, move onto its military bases and refugee (q.v.) camps in Algeria. By the end of December 1975, Spanish journalists in El-Ayoun estimated that there were only 6,000 Saharawis still in the city (compared to over 28,000 previously).

During the three-month transitional period, the territory's Spanish civil servants were gradually evacuated, and Moroccan and Mauritanian administrators arrived to replace them. Up to 20,000 Moroccan troops and about 1,000 Mauritanian troops arrived as the Spanish forces were gradually withdrawn to the Canary Islands. Spanish forces had actually withdrawn from most isolated points in the interior during October, falling back to the main cities, and the first Moroccan units to enter Western Sahara crossed the border on October 31, more than a fortnight before the signing of the Madrid Agreement, moving into areas already vacated by the Spanish and clashing with Polisario guerrillas, most notably at Haousa, Jdiriya, and Farsia. These Moroccan forces finally reached Smara (q.v.) on November 27. Though a small military escort arrived in El-Ayoun with Bensouda on November 25, the first substantial Moroccan force to reach the capital was a 4,000-strong column, which arrived on December 11. The same day, Polisario guerrillas attacked the city's main barracks. Meanwhile, Mauritanian troops started moving into the territory from the south, capturing La Guera (q.v.) on December 19 and Tichla on December 20. However, they did not reach Dakhla (q.v.) until January 12, three days after a Moroccan column had arrived there from the north. The withdrawal of Spanish troops from El-Ayoun was completed on January 9 and from Dakhla on January 12. About 150 Spanish civil servants remained in the territory until the end of February.

As the Moroccan and Mauritanian troops consolidated their hold over the main towns (though some smaller centers were not to be occupied by them until after the final Spanish withdrawal), fighting flared with the Polisario guerrillas in many parts of the country. The long war was starting. The Moroccan and Mauritanian authorities organized a rump meeting of the Djemaa on February 26 to get a resolution of support for the Moroccan-Mauritanian annexation adopted. The Spanish governor-general, by then Col. Rafael de Valdés Iglesias, attended the meeting to announce that Spain was terminating its involvement in the territory's administration from that date. However, his presence at the Djemaa meeting did not imply Spanish recognition of its vote as a genuine consultation of Saharawi opinion. "The decolonization of Western Sahara will reach its climax when the views of the Saharan population have been validly expressed," the Spanish government stated the same day.

TRIPARTITE AGREEMENT see MADRID AGREEMENT (NOVEMBER 14, 1975)

TROPAS NOMADAS. The Nomad Troops were mixed military units of Saharawi and Spanish troops. Most of the officers were Spanish; the rest of the force was Saharawi. The first such unit, a mounted corps of cameleers, was organized in 1926. It was still the only unit as late as 1934, when Spanish troops occupied points in the interior for the first time. Thereafter, it was gradually expanded. In 1974, there were 1,341 Saharawis in the Spanish army, most of them in the Nomad Troops. On October 26, 1975, the colonial authorities began demobilizing the Saharawi troops as Spanish-Moroccan-Mauritanian talks on the territory's future began. At least 90 percent of them then joined the Polisario Front (q.v.), providing the guerrilla movement with a core of well-trained and experienced soldiers.

- U -

UGESARIO see UNION GENERAL DE LOS ESTUDIANTES DE SAGUIA EL-HAMRA Y RIO DE ORO

ULAD see OULAD

UMM see OUM

UNION GENERAL DE LOS ESTUDIANTES DE SAGUIA EL-HAMRA Y RIO DE ORO. The General Union of Students of Saguia el-Hamra and Río de Oro originated as a grouping of student supporters of the Polisario Front (q.v.) in Spain in 1974–75. It developed into a wing of the front from 1976, its secretary-general becoming an ex officio member of the front's political bureau (q.v.).

UNION GENERAL DE TRABAJADORES DE SAGUIA EL-HAMRA Y RIO DE ORO. The General Union of Workers of Saguia el-Hamra and Río de Oro is the labor wing of the Polisario Front (q.v.), its secretary-general being an ex officio member of the front's political bureau (q.v.). Though there was considerable Polisario-led militancy on the part of the small urban work force in 1974–75, this union has carried out little, if any, real labor activity since the exodus of refugees to Algeria in 1975–76.

UNION MAROCAINE DU TRAVAIL. A trade union federation founded in March 1955, the Moroccan Union of Labor (UMT) was the only mass organization on the Moroccan left to give practical support in 1972 to the group of anti-colonial Saharawi students in Morocco, led by El-Ouali Mustapha Sayed (q.v.), who were to play a major part in creating the Polisario Front (q.v.) in 1973. The UMT, which was led by Mahjoub Ben Seddik, held a series of public meetings in Moroccan cities in support of the Saharawi liberation struggle, beginning in March 1972. The union continued to express its support after the founding of the Polisario Front. A statement issued in May 1974 by the UMT-affiliated unions of Rabat and Salé, for example, noted that ''the Saharawi masses have been waging heroic struggles against fascist colonialism for a year under the leadership of the Polisario Front'' and called on workers to attend a solidarity meeting in the UMT club in Rabat on May 18 to mark the first anniversary of the front's first guerrilla raid (May 20, 1973). However, the UMT stopped supporting the Polisario Front later, in 1974, when the Moroccan nationalist parties joined King Hassan's crusade for Moroccan annexation of Western Sahara and denounced the front as ''separatists.'' In Moroccan parliamentary elections in September–October 1984, the UMT won 1.65 percent of the votes, getting five seats in the Chamber of Representatives.

UNION NACIONAL DE MUJERES SAHARAUIS. The National Union of Saharawi Women (UNMS) is a wing of the Polisario Front (q.v.) responsible for the political organization of women (q.v.) behind the front's objectives. It has played an important role in the organization of the refugee (q.v.) camps in southwestern Algeria since 1976 because of the predominantly female composition of these camps (most able-bodied adult men being enrolled in the guerrilla army). The UNMS has participated in literacy campaigns in the camps, which have taught most of the female refugees how to read and write. The movement has opposed polygamy, arranged marriages, and child marriages. It has also generally tried to improve the social status of women. With respect to the dowry, an institution that had become virtually untenable as a result of the general destitution of the refugees, the movement has supported its conversion into a symbolic communal gift, usually a goat, given to a newly-wed couple by the *daira* (q.v.) in which they live. The prolonged absence of most adult men from their families in the refugee camps has sometimes created family strains, which the movement has sought to reduce through counseling. Although divorce is technically legal, the UNMS is strongly opposed to it except as a last resort, because the organization advocates the reinforcement of the family as the basic social unit of Saharawi society. It also encourages women to give birth to as many children as possible, in support of the Polisario Front's campaign to increase the Saharawi population.

UNION NATIONALE DES FORCES POPULAIRES. The main opposition party in Morocco after its founding in 1959 by Medhi Ben Barka and other radicals, the National Union of Popular Forces strongly criticized the royal government for its close relations with Spain and failure to aid nationalists in Western Sahara in the 1960s. However, it did not generally endorse the chauvinist brand of nationalism characteristic of the Istiqlal Party (q.v.) and later, in the 1970s, of the UNFP's successor, the Union Socialiste des Forces Populaires (q.v.). It did not support the "Greater Morocco" (q.v.) idea. From 1962, it supported Mauritania's right to self-determination, and in October 1963, Ben Barka, then in exile in Cairo, issued an appeal condemning the border war with Algeria, earning himself a death sentence in absentia. He was murdered by Moroccan government agents in Paris in 1965. However, the repression suffered by the party and the elimination of some of its most radical and internationalist leaders brought to the fore leaders with a more narrow outlook, notably Abderrahim Bouabid (q.v.). After a party split in 1972, Bouabid formed the Union Socialiste des Forces Populaires (q.v.) in 1974. The rump of the UNFP, under Abdallah Ibrahim, supported the Moroccan annexation of Western Sahara in 1975 but was by then in steep decline as a political force. This trend has continued in subsequent years, with the party boycotting the parliamentary elections held in 1977 and 1984.

UNION SOCIALISTE DES FORCES POPULAIRES. Led by Abderrahim Bouabid, the Socialist Union of Popular Forces has given strong support to the Moroccan war effort in Western Sahara despite its opposition to many of the Moroccan government's domestic policies. It has been the main opposition party in Morocco since it emerged in 1974 following a split in the Union Nationale des Forces Populaires (q.v.) in 1972. Bouabid himself acted as a special diplomatic envoy of King Hassan II (q.v.) in July 1974 during a tour of Asian capitals designed to win support for

Morocco's claim to Western Sahara, and in September 1974, he was sent by the king to the UN (q.v.) to argue Morocco's case. The party gave enthusiastic backing to the Green March (q.v.) of November 1975 and saw the de facto alliance with the monarachy over Western Sahara at this time as a means by which to acquire greater freedom of action for the opposition after years of repression. As Morocco got dragged into a long, drawn-out war with the Polisario Front (q.v.), the USFP tried to differentiate itself from the Moroccan government by urging tougher war measures, notably the staging of cross-border raids into Algeria and the arming of a militia of irregulars. The party crossed the line beyond what King Hassan believed to be permissible discourse on the issue, however, when it reacted to the king's conciliatory overtures toward the OAU (q.v.) in 1981 by publicly attacking his policy. Following the king's acceptance of a referendum, the party issued a communiqué on September 8, 1981, saying that the government's policies ''can only suggest a predisposition to resignation, indeed, the eventual abandonment of Moroccan sovereignty over the provinces of Western Sahara.'' It also opposed any return by Polisario's representatives to the territory; it characterized this prospect as raising the possibility of ''a downright invasion of tens of thousands of elements having full latitude to proclaim their hostility to our country during the electoral campaign.'' The same day, Bouabid was arrested and detained along with several other prominent USFP members, and on September 21, he and two others were given one-year jail sentences. Possibly under pressure from France's new socialist government, however, they were released in late February 1982. In 1983, the USFP joined the interim Moroccan government in the run-up to the September 1984 general elections. According to the official election results, the party won 12.39 percent of the votes cast, obtaining 35 assembly seats.

UNITED NATIONS. Following the creation of the UN's Special Committee on Decolonization, Western Sahara was included in 1963 on the list of non-self-governing territories to which the Declaration on the Granting of Independence to Colonial Countries and Peoples applies. Thereafter, the Western

Saharan question was regularly considered by the Special Committee and in the UN General Assembly—until 1969 in conjunction with the question of Ifni. The Special Committee adopted its first resolution on the two territories in October 1964, and a year later, the General Assembly, in its first resolution on the territories, requested that Spain liberate Ifni and Western Sahara and "enter into negotiations on the problems relating to sovereignty presented by these two territories." In 1966, an important distinction was drawn between the processes for decolonization to be followed in the two territories. While requesting Spain to enter direct negotiations with Morocco over procedures for the transfer of powers in Ifni, the resolution adopted by the General Assembly urged a quite different course for Western Sahara. The resolution, which was adopted by 105 votes to 2 (Spain and Portugal), with 8 abstentions, invited "the administering power to determine at the earliest possible date, in conformity with the aspirations of the indigenous people of Spanish Sahara and in consultation with the governments of Mauritania and Morocco and any other interested party, the procedures for the holding of a referendum under United Nations auspices with a view to enabling the indigenous population of the territory to exercise freely its right to self-determination." The resolution also called for the appointment of a special UN mission to visit the territory. Spain refused to allow a UN mission to visit the territory until 1975 and never allowed a referendum to be held under UN auspices.

The resolutions adopted by the General Assembly in 1967 and 1968 contained almost the same provisions regarding Western Sahara as the 1966 resolution. The retrocession of Ifni to Morocco on June 30, 1969, however, meant that subsequent resolutions concerned only the question of Western Sahara. The General Assembly's 1970 resolution went further than previously by inviting all states to refrain from investing in the territory and by declaring support for the anticolonial struggle. In 1971, there was no General Assembly resolution, but that adopted the following year, by 84 votes (including Algeria and Mauritania) to 10 (including Spain) with 26 abstentions (including Morocco), for the first time explicitly affirmed the right of the people of Western Sahara to independence in addition to (as previously) self-determination. The 1973 resolution was broadly similar. Adopted by 91 votes (including Algeria, Morocco, and Mauritania) to none, with 24 abstentions (Spain and most of the Western countries), it repeated ''its invitation to the administering power to determine, in consultation with the governments of Mauritania and Morocco and any other interested party, the procedures for the holding of a referendum under United Nations auspices to enable the indigenous population of the Sahara to exercise freely its right to self-determination and independence.''

This then was the UN's formula for the territory's decolonization when, on August 22, 1974, Spain finally announced that it would, at last, hold a referendum under UN auspices during the first six months of 1975. It was never held because of protests from Morocco, which, fearing that the Saharawis would opt for independence, renounced its former support for UN calls for a referendum. In a speech to the General Assembly in September 1974, the Moroccan foreign minister, Ahmed Laraki (q.v.), repeated a proposal made a fortnight earlier by King Hassan II (q.v.) that Spain and Morocco should submit their dispute over Western Sahara to the International Court of Justice (ICJ) (q.v.) and that, if Spain should refuse to accept a contentious recourse to the court (which it did), the General Assembly should request the court to give an advisory opinion. By 87 votes to none with 43 abstentions, the General Assembly did adopt a resolution, on December 13, 1974, which, noting that there was ''a legal difficulty'' over the status of Western Sahara at the time of its colonization, requested the ICJ to ''give an advisory opinion at an early date on the following questions:

I. Was Western Sahara (Río de Oro and Saguia el-Hamra) at the time of colonization by Spain a territory belonging to no one (*terra nullius*)?

If the answer to the first question is in the negative,

II. What were the legal ties between this territory and the Kingdom of Morocco and the Mauritanian entity?

In the meantime, the resolution, to Morocco's satisfaction, urged Spain to postpone the referendum until after the General Assembly had been able to assess the ICJ's advisory opinion. The resolution did, however, repeat the traditional call for the dispatch of a UN Visiting Mission (q.v.), which this time Spain allowed to visit the country (May 1975) and which reported in October that the overwhelming majority of the population wanted independence and that the Polisario Front (q.v.) "appeared as a dominant political force in the territory." The ICJ, which accepted the request to give an advisory opinion, published its opinion on October 16, 1975, concluding that it had not found legal ties between Western Sahara and either Morocco or Mauritania at the time of their colonization that might affect the application of "the principle of self-determination through the free and genuine expression of the will of the peoples of the territory."

The same day, however, Morocco announced a 350,000-strong "Green March" (q.v.) into the territory, prompting Spain to request an urgent meeting of the UN Security Council "so that the Moroccan government may be dissuaded from carrying out the announced invasion." A draft resolution, which was introduced by Costa Rica and requested that Morocco desist from the march, was withdrawn under Western pressure when the Security Council met on October 20 and 22, and instead, the council adopted a weak resolution, requesting the secretary-general, Kurt Waldheim, to enter into immediate consultations with Spain, Morocco, Mauritania, and Algeria. Waldheim immediately left New York to visit all four countries, sounding out their views on the possibility of establishing a temporary UN administration in Western Sahara. Spain was favorable to the idea, which came to be known as the Waldheim Plan (q.v.), but Morocco and Mauritania told Waldheim that they believed a solution to the Saharan problem could be achieved through trilateral talks with Spain. Soon after Waldheim's return to New York, the Security Council met again, on November 2, at Spain's request, and adopted a second resolution urging "all the parties concerned and interested to avoid any unilateral or other action which might further escalate the tension in the area" and requesting Waldheim to continue his consultations. However, on November 6, the Green March crossed the border into Western Sahara. During the night of November 5–6, the Security Council decided to send an "urgent request" to King Hassan "to put an end forthwith to the declared march into Western Sahara," and, the following evening, the council "deplored" the holding of the march and called on Morocco "immediately to withdraw" all the marchers from Western Sahara. The marchers were withdrawn, following a speech by King Hassan on November 9, but not because of the action of the Security Council. Spain had decided to settle the dispute on terms acceptable to Morocco and Mauritania, and on November 14, the three governments signed the Madrid Agreement (q.v.).

On December 10, the General Assembly confusingly adopted two resolutions on Western Sahara. The first (3458A), adopted by 88 votes (including Algeria) to none, with 41 abstentions (including Spain) and Morocco and Mauritania not voting, requested "the government of Spain, as the administering power, in accordance with the observations and conclusions of the Visiting Mission and in accordance with the advisory opinion of the International Court of Justice, to take immediately all necessary measures, in consultation with all the parties concerned and interested, so that all Saharans originating in the territory may exercise fully and freely, under United Nations supervision, their inalienable right to self-determination." The second resolution (3458B), which received 56 votes in favor (including Spain, Morocco, and Mauritania), 42 against (including Algeria), and 34 abstentions, took note of the Madrid Agreement, but, like resolution 3458A, also reaffirmed the Saharawi people's "inalienable right to self-determination" and requested the tripartite administration (q.v.) to "ensure that all the Saharan populations originating in the territory will be able to exercise their inalienable right to self-determination through free consultations organized with the assistance of a representative of the United Nations appointed by the secretary-general." Following the adoption of these two resolutions, Waldheim appointed Olof Rydbeck (q.v.), a Swedish diplomat, to assess the situation in the territory with a view to carrying out the mandate entrusted to him by resolutions 3458A and B. Upon his return to New York from the territory early in February 1976, Rydbeck reported that the military situation in Western Sahara made a genuine consultation of the Saharan population difficult, if not impossible. Moreover, when, on February 24 and 25, the Moroccan and Mauritanian governments, respectively, invited Waldheim to send a representative to observe a meeting of the Djemaa scheduled for February 26 (at which a rump of 57 of the assembly's 102 members voted in favor of integration with Morocco and Mauritania), he refused "because it would not have been in line with the existing resolutions," which had stipulated that the UN supervise (3458A) or assist in the organization of (3458B) an act of self-determination.

Western Sahara thus remained on the list of non-self governing territories. In 1976 and 1977, however, the General Assembly shelved substantive consideration of the question, pending action by the OAU (q.v.). In 1978, after the coup in Mauritania and the subsequent Polisario cease-fire there, the General Assembly again tackled the Western Saharan question and, as in 1975, adopted two resolutions, one supported by Algeria, the other by Morocco and Mauritania. They were contradictory in thrust, though some states managed to vote in favor of both. The first (33/31A), adopted by 90 votes (including Algeria and Spain) to 10 (including Morocco and Mauritania) with 39 abstentions, welcomed the Polisario Front's unilateral cease-fire in Mauritania and reaffirmed the right of the Western Saharan people to self-determination and independence. The other (33/31B), adopted by 66 votes (including Spain, Morocco, and Mauritania) to 30 (including Algeria) with 40 abstentions, invited the OAU to find a solution to the problem and appealed to states to refrain from any action that might impede the OAU's efforts.

After the Algiers Agreement (q.v.), the Polisario-Mauritanian peace agreement signed on August 5, 1979, Morocco's international isolation was reflected in the UN by the General Assembly's adoption of a single and forthright resolution (34/37) on November 21, 1979, by 85 votes (including Algeria and Mauritania) to 6 (including Morocco) with 41 abstentions. This welcomed the Polisario-Mauritanian peace agreement, deplored "the aggravation of the situation resulting from the continued occupation of Western Sahara by Morocco and the extension of that occupation to the territory recently evacuated by Mauritania," urged "Morocco to join in the peace process and to terminate the occupation of the territory of Western Sahara," and recommended that the Polisario Front, "the representative of the people of Western Sahara," should take part in the search for a "just, lasting and definitive political solution of the question of Western Sahara." A broadly similar resolution was adopted in the General Assembly on November 11, 1980, by 88 votes to 8 (including Morocco) with 43 abstentions. It urged Morocco to "terminate the occupation of the territory of Western Sahara" and urged Morocco and the Polisario Front to "enter into direct negotiations with a view to arriving at a definitive settlement of the question of Western Sahara." Similar resolutions, with essentially the same language and voting pattern, were passed by the General Assembly in 1981, 1982, and 1983 (the 1983 resolution was approved without a vote). Despite such expressions of broad-based support for Polisario's cause, this was a period when UN activity on Western Sahara was minimal compared to the mid-1970s. Diplomatic attention was focused mainly on the OAU, which in 1983 adopted its important resolution 104 (XIX), calling for direct negotiations between Morocco and Polisario and urging the holding of a referendum. But due to both Morocco's refusal to talk with Polisario and the (eventual) admission of the SADR to the OAU as a member, no appreciable amount of diplomatic activity took place within the framework of the OAU during the second half of the 1980s.

Diplomatic activity began to revive at the United Nations toward the end of 1985, apparently at the initiative of Morocco, which had withdrawn from the OAU in 1984 to protest the OAU's admission of the SADR. Morocco may have approached the UN to try to deflect the diplomatic focus away from the provisions of OAU resolution 104 and thus avoid direct negotiations with Polisario. But King Hassan's hopes were dashed fairly quickly. On December 2, 1985, the General Assembly overwhelmingly passed a resolution (40/50) that not only reaffirmed the right of the Western Saharans to self-determination but also named Morocco and Polisario explicitly as the only parties to the conflict and endorsed OAU resolution 104. The measure also urged that a referendum in the territory take place "without any administrative or military constraints," which implied that Rabat would have to withdraw some or all of its troops and administration from Western Sahara in advance of the plebiscite. Facing an even greater degree of congruence between the UN's positions and those of the OAU, therefore, Morocco withdrew from the UN's fourth (decolonization) committee. For a brief time, it looked as if the UN effort would terminate in a manner similar to the OAU's. But sentiment in the world body was simply too strong to allow the matter to lapse. In late 1985 and early 1986, the UN secretary-general, Javier Pérez de Cuéllar (q.v.), began a long attempt to reconcile the parties. In April 1986, he began hosting indirect contacts between Morocco and the Polisario Front in New York. These "proximity talks" consisted of separate meetings between the secretary-general and the Moroccan and Saharawi delegations. Pérez de Cuéllar transmitted each delegation's views to the other, in this way sparing them the necessity of meeting face-to-face. The secretary-general may have hoped that the meetings would evolve into direct and substantive negotiations between the parties, but this did not happen. Morocco continued to refuse to meet the Polisario directly. In an attempt to maintain at least some momentum, Pérez de Cuéllar visited Rabat in July 1986 to meet with King Hassan, but the meeting produced no tangible progress to speak of. For its part, the General Assembly adopted a resolution (41/16) on October 31, 1986, that asked the secretary-general to continue his efforts.

Pérez de Cuéllar then decided to formulate a comprehensive cease-fire and referendum plan, with the objective that both Morocco and Polisario would accept it and work together toward its realization in practice. As mandated by resolution 41/16, therefore, he undertook an extensive series of consultations with Morocco, Polisario, Algeria, and the OAU. On March 17, 1987, he first broached the idea of sending a United Nations technical mission (q.v.) to the area to gather data preparatory to a new round of conciliation efforts. After receiving the assent and cooperation of the OAU, he sent representatives to both Rabat and Polisario's headquarters and obtained the cooperation of both King Hassan and the secretary-general of Polisario, Mohammed Abdelaziz (q.v.). In fact, the front proclaimed a unilateral cease-fire in the territory for the duration of the mission's work. Between November 21 and December 9, 1987, the mission toured the area, traveling to Mauritania, Morocco, and regions of Western Sahara occupied by both Morocco and Polisario. Led by UN Under Secretary-General for Special Political Questions Abderrahim Farah (q.v.) and accompanied by military personnel from various countries seconded to the United Nations, the mission gathered much information that would help the secretary-general and his staff to refine proposals for a comprehensive peace settlement. The mission's report was not made public and was circulated to only a small number of UN and OAU officials.

Facilitated by the overall improvement in interstate North African relations culminating in the resumption of diplomatic relations between Morocco and Algeria on May 16, 1988, Pérez de Cuéllar completed work on his peace proposal. On August 11, he presented the text of the plan to delegations from both Morocco and Polisario in New York and requested a response within two weeks. On August 30, the Moroccans, represented by foreign minister Abdellatif Filali (q.v.), and Polisario, represented by Bachir Mustapha Sayed (q.v.), gave their assent in principle to the proposal, which was hailed in the international community as a major breakthrough in efforts to settle the Western Sahara question peacefully, although both Morocco and the Polisario Front attached varying interpretations to certain aspects of the plan. The text of the plan was not made public until 1990, but its main points became known fairly soon afterward. They included:

1. The appointment, by the UN secretary-general, of a special representative, charged with preparing the way for

the dispatch of neutral administrators and peacekeeping troops.

2. A cease-fire between the Polisario Front and Morocco, coupled with an "appropriate, substantial, and phased reduction" of Moroccan soldiers in the territory, the confinement of the remaining troops of both parties to specified, supervised areas, and the exchange of prisoners of war.

3. A census of the population of Western Sahara conducted with the assistance of the United Nations high commissioner for refugees, using as a basis a census taken in 1974 by the Spanish colonial authorities and an estimate of the rate of growth and movement of the Saharawi population since that time.

4. A referendum of self-determination in Western Sahara after a campaigning period lasting several weeks, in which voters would choose between independence and integration with Morocco.

Both parties, by accepting the plan, also agreed to abide by the results of the plebiscite and to cooperate fully with the UN task force charged with supervising the voting and the cease-fire. There were no specific numbers of troops or other personnel written into the plan, and there was no definite timetable for implementation. And Morocco still refused to meet directly with Polisario during this period. However, a degree of momentum was generated by the promulgation and acceptance of this plan, and the UN Security Council passed resolution 621 on September 20, 1988, authorizing Pérez de Cuéllar to appoint the special representative and to prepare a more detailed report on the implementation of the peace plan. Also, an Identification Commission was established by the UN, which would work with the high commissioner for refugees to ascertain the location of the Saharawis counted in the 1974 Spanish census. The secretary-general, in late 1988 and early 1989, therefore, began work on his implementation report and appointed Hector Gros Espiell (q.v.) as special representative, who was succeeded in January 1990 by Johannes Manz (q.v.). Meanwhile, in January 1989, King Hassan and three high-ranking Polisario officials met directly in Marrakesh for the first time. After this, a few sources were even predicting that the referendum could take place in 1990.

But there were no further talks between Morocco and Polisario. King Hassan denied that he had ever intended to hold formal negotiations with the Saharawi nationalists, claiming he had merely met with the three Polisario members as Moroccan subjects who had gone astray. This Moroccan policy stance pointed up a weakness in any effort by the UN to hold a referendum: that a presence by the United Nations in the disputed territory could only be established with the assent of the parties actually in physical control. Frustrated, Polisario abrogated its unilateral cessation of hostilities in March 1989 and engaged in military attacks in October of the same year. In an effort to move the peace process forward again, Pérez de Cuéllar himself visited the region on June 17–24, 1989, presaging what was to become a time of intense personal involvement by the secretary-general in an attempt to settle the dispute. Also in this period, the UN Identification Commission began its work in earnest, and the new special representative, Manz, visited the region in the spring of 1990.

The latest and so far most significant round of activity by the United Nations began on June 18, 1990, when Pérez de Cuéllar submitted to the Security Council the implementation plan that had been requested by resolution 621 of 1988. Although still containing no explicit schedule for the conduct of the referendum and remaining silent on the numbers of troops to be retained by each side in the territory, the document fleshed out the skeletal form of the initial peace proposals. Among the provisions were the following:

1. The emplacement in Western Sahara, after a cease-fire between Morocco and Polisario, of UN civilian, military, and security units under the authority of the special representative, to be known as MINURSO, the French acronym for the United Nations Mission for the Referendum in Western Sahara (q.v.).
2. An exchange of prisoners of war and a substantial reduc-

tion in the number of Moroccan and Polisario troops in the territory, coupled with the proclamation of a general amnesty, the abolition of all repressive laws and regulations, and the return of all refugees to Western Sahara after they have established their right to vote.

3. The confinement and supervision, by the military mission of MINURSO, of all the remaining armed units of both disputants, with that part of the Moroccan army still in Western Sahara being left mainly in their positions along the "defensive walls" (q.v.) constructed in the territory.

4. Completion of the work of the Identification Commission, followed by finalization of the voters' roll and a campaign period in which the parties would be free to espouse their respective positions to the Saharawi populace.

5. The referendum, in which it was confirmed that the choice offered the voters would be between independence and integration with Morocco.

The results of the referendum, if all goes as planned, would be announced within 72 hours. Depending on the results of the plebiscite, the units of the Polisario Front would be disbanded or the remaining Moroccan troops in the territory would be withdrawn in a process commencing 24 hours later and extending over a period of several weeks. In both these eventualities, the demobilization and withdrawal process would be supervised by MINURSO. All of the above tasks were expected to take the UN up to 35 weeks from the date of a cease-fire. In his summing up, Pérez de Cuéllar cautioned that "the United Nations operation in Western Sahara will be large and complicated."

Several days later, on the evening of June 27, 1990, the UN Security Council unanimously adopted resolution 658, which approved the secretary-general's report, supported his mission of "good offices," and approved his proposal to send a second technical mission (q.v.) to the region. Significantly, resolution 658 put all members of the Security Council on record as recognizing that the only parties to the conflict were Morocco and the Polisario Front, ending all controversy on that score.

Armed with this mandate, Pérez de Cuéllar put his efforts into higher gear but soon ran into difficulties. For example, in a meeting in Geneva soon afterward, he failed to induce Morocco and Polisario to meet and negotiate directly, and certain modalities for the referendum remained undetermined. On the positive side, a meeting of Saharawi tribal elders from both Moroccan- and Polisario-controlled areas of Western Sahara went forward as scheduled, the Identification Commission made some progress, and the visit to Western Sahara by the second technical mission commenced. But realizing that core issues such as voter identification, schedules, troop withdrawal, and funding were still unsettled, the secretary-general made plans to step up his efforts in the fall of 1990, but such plans had to be postponed for the rest of the year due to Iraq's invasion of Kuwait and subsequent massive demands placed upon Pérez de Cuéllar and the UN. After the conclusion of the Gulf war in February 1991, he restarted his endeavors but soon encountered similar problems with their implementation.

Although Pérez de Cuéllar issued a comprehensive report on the Western Sahara situation on April 19, 1991, urging the establishment of MINURSO and its deployment, and the Security Council, in resolution 690 a week later, approved his efforts without demur, the United Nations still faced formidable obstacles, with the real test still to come: whether the UN could actually deploy its troops and civilians in the territory, receive the cooperation of both parties, resolve the problems still outstanding, muster the relevant data and political will, and carry out the actual plebiscite. The rest of 1991 saw the institution of a fairly durable cease-fire (after some heavy fighting in July and August) on September 6, 1991, and a few hundred UN troops were deployed at various locations in Western Sahara. But Morocco began to raise obstacles to holding the referendum, as planned, in January 1992. It allegedly began moving thousands of people from southern Morocco into the territory, stating they were qualified to vote in the referendum; conducted nearly constant overflights by its aircraft over UN troop positions; and refused to withdraw any of its massive troop presence in Western Sahara until voter qualification matters were resolved. Since Morocco had entered the names of 120,000 or more persons as potential voters, this seemed a long way off. The MINURSO force thus did not grow above 375 mostly military personnel, a level that remained almost constant right up to the end of 1993.

Internally, the United Nations was also having its difficulties relative to MINURSO. Reports soon began to filter out of the territory that the UN peacekeepers faced primitive conditions, disease, and a lack of concern by UN headquarters about their plight. They also faced a lack of cooperation from Morocco (and after a time from Polisario as well), inadequate instructions on dealing with frequent cease-fire violations, and logistical nightmares caused by financial irregularities in New York. These stories were given added credence by a U.S. Senate Foreign Relations Committee report in January 1992, describing these misfortunes in added detail. And it was also rumored that various member states of the UN were considering withdrawing their contingents of "blue helmet" soldiers. In addition, it was charged in November 1991 that UN personnel had improperly given to Morocco some computer disks containing census information that had been entrusted to the world body in confidence by the Polisario Front. Although the person suspected of the deed denied any wrongdoing, it tarnished the UN's carefully cultivated image of probity and impartiality. Reportedly frustrated with these and other problems with MINURSO, Johannes Manz resigned as UN special representative for Western Sahara at the end of December, leaving the post vacant until March 1992.

In his final months in office until his replacement as secretary-general by Boutros Boutros Ghali (q.v.) of Egypt, Pérez de Cuéllar attempted to break the impasse on population and voting qualification disputes by setting forth new criteria for the Identification Commission. Although sincere, he made a clouded situation worse by considerably widening the standards to be applied to Saharawis wishing to vote. By proposing that any Saharawi wishing to vote need prove only residence in Western Sahara for 6 years continuously or 12 years intermittently prior to the 1974 Spanish census, Pérez de Cuéllar seemed, in the eyes of Polisario, to give Morocco a large advantage in the referendum by potentially including many of the persons Morocco had ''imported'' into the territory since the beginning of the conflict nearly two decades before. The Saharawi organization condemned the move and apparently was able to persuade the Security Council to give only qualified approval to the secretary-general's new proposals, expressed in resolution 725 of December 31, 1991. The following day, Boutros Ghali took office, inheriting the Western Sahara problem along with several other unresolved situations around the world. Although he named a new special representative, Sahabzada Yaqub Khan (q.v.), on March 23, 1992, it was unclear by the end of 1993 what new initiatives he would take to attempt to bring to a satisfactory conclusion the long-running Western Saharan conflict.

UNITED NATIONS MISSION FOR THE REFERENDUM IN WESTERN SAHARA (MINURSO). This United Nations (q.v.) interim administration and peacekeeping force was first publicly proposed in detail by UN secretary-general Javier Pérez de Cuéllar (q.v.) in June 1990. MINURSO is the mission's French acronym. In line with prior UN practice in similar circumstances (such as Namibia), MINURSO would serve to create a climate of peace and security in Western Sahara so that a free and fair referendum could be held under United Nations auspices. MINURSO's task would be to monitor a cease-fire between Morocco and the Polisario Front (q.v.), supervise the withdrawal of troops from the territory and the confinement of those remaining to base areas, ascertain voting eligiblity, oversee the return of the Saharawi refugees, and conduct and announce the results of the referendum. The choice offered to the Saharawi voters would be between independence and integration with Morocco. To carry out the many tasks required of the interim regime, MINURSO would have the following elements:

1. A Civilian Unit, composed mainly of officials of the United Nations, who would be responsible for legal, legislative, and administrative matters during the transi-

tion period. The unit would be headed directly by the UN special representative, who would exercise "sole and exclusive responsibility over all matters relating to the referendum, including its organization and conduct."

2. A Military Unit, to consist of military personnel seconded by various member states of the United Nations; to be led by a force commander subordinate to the secretary-general's special representative for Western Sahara; and to be composed of logistical, infantry, air, observer, and administrative units, that would carry light arms.

3. A Security Unit, to be made up of civil police from various member states of the United Nations. This unit would be responsible for both the maintenance of law and order and the absence of intimidation of the Saharawi voters and would closely supervise existing police forces (belonging to Morocco or Polisario) to ensure that a referendum is held under fair conditions. In case of cease-fire violations or threats to order generally, it is envisaged that the Security Unit would call upon the Military Unit for assistance.

As was the case with other United Nations endeavors of this sort, an operation such as MINURSO's could not commence without the approval of all parties to the conflict. This, in turn, was not possible in 1990 due to disagreements over the size of MINURSO and the question of the number of Moroccan troops to be withdrawn during the UN transition period. While these problems were still awaiting solution, UN Security Council resolution 658, passed unanimously on June 27, 1990, requested that the secretary-general make a further and more detailed report on the modalities and cost of the mission, so that he could return to the council and ask it to formally authorize the establishment of MINURSO. Iraq's invasion of Kuwait in August 1990 and the subsequent Gulf war, however, put such a strain on the resources of the United Nations that Pérez de Cuéllar was not able to submit his report until April 19, 1991 (see Bibliography), finalizing the time schedule and other procedures for the referendum. The Security Council, in another unanimous resolution (690 of April 29, 1991), approved the report so that MINURSO could finally be established. After this point, things started going steadily downhill.

In the spring of 1991, Pérez de Cuéllar fixed September 6 as the date for the formal cease-fire between Morocco and the Polisario Front. But in July and August, Morocco launched a series of punishing military strikes against Polisario, apparently causing significant loss of life. The atmosphere in the territory thus poisoned, Pérez de Cuéllar had to use all his diplomatic skill to ensure that the cease-fire went into effect as planned. MINURSO troops and administrators were able to deploy at various locations throughout Western Sahara, but only to monitor the cease-fire—it was understood by this time that the referendum would probably not take place in January 1992, if for no other reason than the fact that population-related disputes were very far from being settled. And Morocco declined to begin pulling out any of its tens of thousands of troops from Western Sahara until all voter eligibility problems were resolved. Under these conditions, the size of the MINURSO force did not grow beyond 375, a figure that had not significantly increased at the time of writing (December 1993). Also, by the end of 1991, reports had begun to filter out of the territory concerning the primitive conditions faced by the UN peacekeepers, the lack of cooperation (and occasional hostility) shown by Morocco, and an alleged lack of support from UN headquarters in the face of Morocco's cease-fire violations. Pérez de Cuéllar's successor as secretary-general, Boutros Boutros Ghali (q.v.), was able to take a fresh look at the situation in the first part of 1992, but implementation of the rest of the UN peace plan, along with the whole MINURSO enterprise, looked very much in doubt.

UNITED NATIONS TECHNICAL MISSION (1987). Conceived as a joint venture of the United Nations and the Organization of African Unity (qq.v.), the UN technical mission toured Western Sahara and the surrounding region in late 1987 in order to gather information as a preliminary step to the holding of a referendum in the territory. The origins of the mission can be found in General Assembly resolution 41/16, passed on October 31, 1986, which, aside from reendorsing the referendum concept and urging direct negotiations between Morocco and the Polisario Front (q.v.), urged Secretary-General Javier Pérez de Cuéllar (q.v.) to pursue efforts to find a peaceful settlement of the Western Saharan conflict. The mission was to gather information about both the territory and the refugee camps in the Tindouf (qq.v.) region of Algeria run by Polisario. It was also to visit Morocco and Mauritania. King Hassan II (q.v.) gave his assent to the mission after being assured that its purpose was purely technical and that the information it gained would remain confidential. The secretary-general of the Polisario Front, Mohammed Abdelaziz (q.v.), was considerably more skeptical. He felt that the UN's overall efforts might be diverted by the sending of the technical mission and that it would be more appropriate first to have an agreement between Morocco and Polisario on outstanding issues before the mission began its work. He also reiterated Polisario's insistence on the removal of the Moroccan military and administrative presence in Western Sahara in advance of any plebiscite. The Polisario Front appeared to be tiring of the seemingly endless rounds of diplomatic activity over the previous few years, which had produced no substantive results for the Saharawis. However, when it was pointed out to Mohammed Abdelaziz that the information gathered by the technical mission would assist the UN in drafting a comprehensive cease-fire and referendum plan, Polisario gave its full cooperation to the endeavor, going so far as to proclaim a unilateral cessation of military activity in Western Sahara for the duration of the mission's work. After making its preparations in New York and Geneva, the mission traveled to the region on November 21, 1987, to begin its task. The mission, headed by Abderrahim Farah (q.v.), UN under secretary-general for special political questions, was divided into civil and military sections. Upon arrival in El-Ayoun (q.v.), the civil section studied material relating to life in the Saharan towns controlled by Morocco, and it conducted a series of interviews. It then visited other areas in Western Sahara, including Dakhla, Boujdour, and Smara (qq.v.). The military section, led by General Terence Liston (q.v.) of Canada, visited the main towns and the series of "defensive walls" (q.v.) constructed by Morocco. On November 29, the mission flew to Zouerate, Mauritania, from which it visited parts of Western Sahara controlled by the Polisario Front. The civil section focused on life in the "liberated" regions, and the military section traveled to various parts of the south of the territory, meeting with personnel of the Saharawi Popular Liberation Army (q.v.). The mission then went to the Tindouf region, visiting the refugee camps before making a final visit to Western Sahara, to Polisario-controlled parts of Saguia el-Hamra (q.v.). The mission completed its work on December 9, 1987. Shortly thereafter, it presented its findings to Secretary-General Pérez de Cuéllar and to the OAU. The data were not made public but served as a foundation upon which the secretary-general formally developed a UN peace plan, including a cease-fire and a referendum. This was presented to Morocco and Polisario in New York on August 11, 1988, and accepted in broad outline by both parties at the end of the month. The only discordant note that was struck during the mission was the discovery that, before the mission's arrival, the Moroccan authorities in Western Sahara had either imprisoned or relocated to Morocco some Saharawis whom it considered suspect in their loyalties.

By UN Security Council resolution 658, adopted on June 27, 1990, the world body approved the dispatch of a second UN technical mission (q.v.) to further refine the secretary-general's comprehensive peace plan.

UNITED NATIONS TECHNICAL MISSION (1990). This was the second of two technical missions to visit Western Sahara as part of the UN's (q.v.) extensive preparations for a referendum of self-determination in the territory. The first such mission had visited the region in November–December 1987 (see UNITED NATIONS TECHNICAL MISSION [1987]), providing the data for the drafting of the UN peace plan, which was accepted in principle by Morocco and the Polisario Front (q.v.) in August 1988. UN Security Council resolution 658, adopted unanimously on June 27, 1990, authorized the secretary-general, Javier Pérez de Cuéllar (q.v.), to send a second such mission to gather information for a more detailed report on the implementation of the plan and its cost. The mission left for northwest Africa on July 29, 1990, and performed its work over the following two weeks. The mission was led by Issa Diallo, the UN secretary-general's special adviser.

UNITED NATIONS VISITING MISSION. An important mission of inquiry sent by the UN secretary-general, Kurt Waldheim (q.v.), to Western Sahara, Spain, Morocco, Mauritania, and Algeria in May–June 1975, it produced an exceptionally well-documented report that concluded that the overwhelming majority of Western Saharans wanted full independence. Its three members were Simeon Aké (chairman), Marta Jiménez Martínez, and Manouchehr Pishva, diplomats from Ivory Coast, Cuba, and Iran, respectively. Their brief was to examine conditions in the territory and the views of its inhabitants and of the governments of Spain and the neighboring countries in accordance with UN General Assembly resolution 3292 of December 13, 1974.

After talks in Madrid with Spanish officials on May 8–12, the mission members spent one week in Western Sahara (May 12–19), visiting all the main towns and holding talks with Spanish officials, leaders of the Partido de la Unión Nacional Saharaui (q.v.), members of the Djemaa (q.v.), and supporters of the Polisario Front (q.v.). They arrived at a time of acute tension in the country. Members of the Front de Libération et de l'Unité (q.v.), who had infiltrated from across the Moroccan border, had been responsible for bomb blasts in the capital, El-Ayoun (q.v.), on May 5 and staged further attacks on May 15. The Polisario Front welcomed the mission members with large demonstrations wherever they went, outpacing the Spanish-supported PUNS, which was able to display significant popular support only in the south. This outflanking of the PUNS by the guerrilla movement prompted the party's secretary-general, Khalihenna Ould Rachid (q.v.), to flee to Morocco right in the middle of the mission's tour of the country. Meanwhile, on May 10 and 11, the Saharawi soldiers in two patrols of the Spanish Tropas Nómadas (q.v.) mutinied, killed one of their Spanish officers and captured 14 other Spanish soldiers (four of them officers), and joined the Polisario guerrillas.

The mission members toured Morocco on May 22–28, meeting King Hassan in Fez, witnessing pro-Moroccan demonstrations by Saharawis living in the extreme south of Morocco, and holding talks with Moroccan political leaders and representatives of the FLU and MOREHOB (q.v.) as well as Khalihenna Ould Rachid. In a subsequent trip to Algeria (May 28–June 1), they talked with President Houari Boumedienne (q.v.) and visited Saharawi refugee camps near Tindouf (q.v.), where they interviewed leaders of the Polisario Front and met the Spanish prisoners captured on May 10–11. After Algeria, the mission members went to Mauritania (June 4–9), where they held talks with President Mokhtar Ould Daddah (q.v.) and toured the north of the country, witnessing demonstrations supporting both the Polisario Front and the Mauritanian claim to Western Sahara.

The mission's conclusions about the wishes of the Western Saharan population were unambiguous:

> Owing to the large measure of cooperation which it received from the Spanish authorities, the mission was able, despite the shortness of its stay in the territory, to visit virtually all the main population centers and to ascertain the views of the overwhelming majority of their inhabitants. At every place visited, the mission was met by mass political demonstrations and had numerous private meetings with representatives of every section of the Saharan community. From all these, it became evident to the mission that there was an overwhelming consensus among Saharans within the territory in favor of independence and opposing integration with any neighboring country.
>
> The mission believes, in the light of what it witnessed in the territory, especially the mass demonstrations of support for one movement, the Frente Polisario . . ., that its visit served as a catalyst to bring into the open political forces and pressures which had previously been largely submerged. It was all the more significant to the mission that this came as a surprise to the Spanish authorities who, until then, had been only partly aware of the profound political awakening of the population.

URANIUM. Though the presence of uranium has not been officially confirmed, the existence of radioactive materials was announced in 1965. Uranium oxides are normally associated with phosphates (q.v.), of which Western Sahara has extensive deposits, and in recent years several commercial plants for the extraction of uranium from phosphate ore have been built in the United States.

- V -

VEINTE DE MAYO. A monthly newspaper of the Polisario Front (q.v.), it has been published since November 1973, usually in Arabic, Spanish, and French editions. The French edition is titled *20 Mai*, the Spanish edition *20 de Mayo*. May 20 is the anniversary of the front's first guerrilla raid, in 1973, against a Spanish post at El-Khanga (q.v.).

VIAH OULD MAYOUF. A colonel in the Mauritanian army, he led the forces that occupied the main towns and settlements in Tiris el-Gharbia (q.v.) between December 1975 and February 1976. He continued to play a major part in the war against the Polisario Front (q.v.), notably in June 1976, when a force under his command rushed from Tiris el-Gharbia to help intercept the guerrilla force led by El-Ouali Mustapha Sayed (q.v.), which made a 1,500-km. raid that month on the Mauritanian capital, Nouakchott. Unlike many of Mauritania's battle-hardened officers, he did not take part in the coup that deposed President Mokhtar Ould Daddah (q.v.) on July 10, 1978, though he served briefly as minister of transport, communications, traditional industries, and tourism in the military-led government in January–March 1979.

VILLA BENS. The name given to Tarfaya in 1946 after the death of Francisco Bens Argandoña (qq.v.). The settlement reverted to its old name of Tarfaya after its cession to Morocco in April 1958.

VILLA CISNEROS. The name given to the town founded by the Spanish at Dakhla (q.v.) in 1884. The town was named Dakhla by the Polisario Front (q.v.) and by both Morocco and Mauritania after Spain's withdrawal from the territory in 1975–76.

VINGT MAI. Title of the French edition of *Veinte de Mayo* (q.v.).

- W -

WALDHEIM PLAN, THE. A plan for a temporary, transitional administration of Western Sahara by the UN (q.v.), which was proposed to the Spanish, Moroccan, Mauritanian, and Algerian governments by Kurt Waldheim, UN secretary-general, in October–November 1975 on the eve of the Madrid Agreement (q.v.). As tension mounted following the announcement of the Green March by King Hassan II (qq.v.), the UN Security Council met on October 20 and 22 and adopted a resolution requesting Waldheim enter into immediate negotiations with the "parties concerned and interested"; so, on October 25–28, he visited Morocco, Mauritania, Algeria, and Spain in turn. Upon his return to New York, he reported (October 31) that the UN "could be called upon to play an appropriate role that might include temporary administration of the territory by the United Nations until such time as the wishes of the population could be ascertained." At a second UN Security Council meeting, held at Spanish request on November 2, Waldheim was once again asked to "continue and intensify his consultations with the parties concerned and interested." This time, he sent a special envoy, André Lewin, to Morocco, Mauritania, Algeria, and Spain (November 4–6). On November 8, Waldheim reported that King Hassan had told Lewin on November 4 that he rejected the idea of a temporary UN administration and opposed the holding of a referendum. In Madrid, on November 6, the Spanish prime minister, Carlos Arias Navarro (q.v.), told Lewin that Spain was "prepared immediately to transfer sovereignty of the territory to the United Nations and leave the Spanish forces, under a United Nations statute, at the disposal of the temporary administration to assist in maintaining order in the territory," but also "expressed the view that a trilateral agreement also could provide an alternative formula if the United Nations were prepared to agree to it." In fact, the Spanish government had little faith by then in the ability of the UN to get Moroccan acceptance of the Waldheim Plan and was virtually resigned to negotiating a tripartite agreement with Morocco and Mauritania. According to Waldheim, King Hassan told Lewin on November 6 that "the main provisions of such an agreement had already been determined and stipulated a transfer of sovereignty from the administering power to Morocco and Mauritania." A final round of tripartite negotiations opened in Madrid on November 12, culminating in the Madrid Agreement (q.v.) two days later. The Waldheim Plan was dead.

WALI. The *wali* is the governor of a wilaya (q.v.), or province, of the Saharan Arab Democratic Republic (q.v.). For further information, see WILAYA.

WATER RESOURCES. Traditionally, the Saharawi nomads drank little water. They needed it mainly for their livestock, though their camels could go for days without drinking. The nomads needed water for their tea, a central part of their diet, but they subsisted mainly on camel's milk. River water was seldom used, being generally considered unhealthy. In the winter months, the nomads usually took advantage of deposits of rainwater collected in the *gueltas* (q.v.), natural cisterns formed from rock, and other cavities. The concentration of water in depressions, known as *daias,* allowed occasional agriculture. In the summer months, when rainfall is very rare and water evaporates rapidly, the Saharawis tended to concentrate around wells, of which there were four main categories—the *tilensi* (up to 1 meter deep) and the *agla* (1–5 meters deep), both in the bed of a river, and, deeper, the *hassi* (up to 12 meters deep) and the *bir* (deeper than 12 meters).

In the early days of the Spanish colony at Dakhla (q.v.), freshwater supplies had to be brought by ship from the Canary Islands to the Spanish settlement there. As late as 1960, there were no more than 130 water sources in the entire country, of which only 100 were of potable water. The total capacity was 1,130 cubic meters of water a day, of which 200 cubic meters were for El-Ayoun (q.v.). After expenditure of P170 million, water supply capacity had been raised to 54,330 cubic meters a day, including 3,000 cubic meters for

El-Ayoun, by 1970. During this decade, one of the world's largest underground freshwater lakes was discovered in 1963–64 near Dakhla. It extends over 60,000 sq. km. and, if significantly exploited, could allow agriculture on a scale hitherto unknown in the country. A well drilled there in the 1960s produced 5,000 cubic meters a day, and the Spanish set up three experimental farms there. Another development during the Spanish period was the provision of water desalination facilities, with a capacity of 3,500 cubic meters a day, at El-Ayoun Playa, for the phosphate-mining company Fosbucraa (qq.v.), in 1972. The water is used to wash the ore in the company's treatment plant.

The search for and exploitation of new water resources continued to be an infrastructural development priority when the Moroccan government took control of the main towns in 1976. Dh1.7 billion was allocated to the Office National de l'Eau Potable (ONEP—National Office of Potable Water) for investment in Western Sahara under the 1976–78 emergency development plan (q.v.). A desalination plant was built in Boujdour in 1976 at a cost of Dh10 million. It has a capacity of 250 cubic meters a day. After prospecting at Foum el-Oued, 16 km. from El-Ayoun, wells were drilled there to supply 3,600 cubic meters a day to El-Ayoun, and at Smara (q.v.), there were plans to exploit water sources 36 km. west of the city, to provide up to 2,000 cubic meters a day.

Although located outside Western Sahara itself, the water situation in the refugee camps in the Tindouf (qq.v.) region of Algeria has always been critical. In some locations, underground sources were found and exploited, the water then being chlorinated by the *daira* (q.v.) health committee. Much additional water, however, had to be trucked in from elsewhere in Algeria, and in the *wilaya* (q.v.) of Smara, the underground water was so saline that imported water (stored in tanks and reservoirs) continued to supply almost all the needs of the inhabitants there.

WILAYA. The *wilaya* is a province of the Saharan Arab Democratic Republic (q.v.). Though intended by the leaders of the Polisario Front (q.v.) to become eventually the regional administrative units of a genuinely independent country, the three wilayat established in 1976 in fact became administrative subdivisions of the refugee (q.v.) population in southwestern Algeria. Each *wilaya* is headed by a governor, known as a *wali* (q.v.), and is divided into about six or seven refugee camps, known as *dairat* (q.v.) for administrative purposes. Since their creation in the spring of 1976, the wilayat have been administered by wilaya popular councils, elected by mass assemblies, known as popular base congresses, which have been held periodically in the refugee camps. The wilaya popular council is headed by the wali and has a number of specialized committees responsible for such matters as food distribution, health, and education.

Political orientation of the wilaya's refugee population was entrusted to a political officer, who was a member of the political bureau (q.v.) of the Polisario Front. Appointed by the political bureau, he headed the wilaya's Department of Training and Orientation. Since 1977, however, the wali has combined both administrative and political roles, being head of the Department of Training and Orientation as well as head of the wilaya popular council. He must be a member of the political bureau. While the wilaya popular council's specialized committees coordinate and give guidance to specialized committees operating at *daira* level, the Department of Training and Orientation supervises the political work of the *arifat* (q.v.), the heads of the cells into which the adult members of each daira are divided. The three wilayat established in 1976 take the names of the three main cities, El-Ayoun, Dakhla, and Smara (qq.v.), indicating their intended future role as real provinces. In November 1985, a fourth *wilaya* was set up, named after Aoussert (q.v.).

WOMEN. The Saharawi woman had a more powerful and respected place in traditional society than her counterpart in sedentary Arab societies. Her important domestic status was due largely to the prolonged absence of menfolk, who were responsible both for herding the livestock and engaging in *ghazzis* (q.v.). Saharawi women have always been unveiled—covering their faces, like the men, only for protection against the harsh climate. Moreover, girls generally had the right to refuse a proposed fiancé, and polygamy was extremely rare. There was, however, a clearly defined sexual division of labor. The women did not take part in political decision making or in such assemblies as the *djemaa* or the *ait arbain* (qq.v), and they did not participate in military or herding activities. Their role was fundamentally domestic. They were responsible for child-rearing, the preparation of food, the erection and dismantling of tents, the making of leather cushions, sandals, and belts, and the stitching of tents and saddlebags. The sewing of tents from the hair of goats and camels was usually a collective affair, known as the *touiza,* in which women from several families all lent a hand. Very few girls or women were taught to read and write in traditional society, and few went to school during the Spanish colonial period. In 1974, there were only 919 Saharawi girls in primary schools (compared to 5,150 boys) and just 3 in secondary schools (compared to 108 boys). The Polisario Front (q.v.), from its early days, officially advocated both an improvement in the status of women and their participation in the national liberation struggle, though the movement was ambiguous about the extent of female liberation it envisaged. The "national general program" of the front, adopted at its 4th congress, in September 1978, advocated, for example, "the achievement of women's political and social rights and the favoring of her access to all domains so that she assumes her responsibilities in national construction, this in accordance with our national realities and our religion."

The front has a women's movement, known as the Unión Nacional de Mujeres Saharauis (q.v.), and in the refugee camps (q.v.) set up in southwestern Algeria in 1975–76, carried out a massive literacy drive, which particularly benefited women. Women also played a major part in the administration of these well-organized camps, making up most of the membership of the committees established in each *daira* (q.v.) for such matters as the distribution of food, education, health, crafts, and justice. However, the traditional sexual division of labor was not altered: the men went off to fight and the women took responsibility for the *friq* (q.v.), albeit a friq transformed into a large, well-administered refugee camp. Since practically all able-bodied men who joined the Polisario Front became guerrillas, the refugee camps consisted almost entirely of women, children, and the elderly. The women received military training, but they were not enrolled in the SPLA (q.v.) and so did not take part directly in the guerrilla war. Moreover, their role in political decision making remained very limited. Despite their great importance in the day-to-day administration of the refugee camps, they rarely held the senior administrative posts there: The *walis,* for example, were generally men, and there were no women to be found on the front's executive committee. On the other hand, three women were elected to the subordinate political bureau at Polisario's 6th congress, held in December 1985. The daira justice committees played an especially influential role in the refugee camps regarding such matters as marriage and divorce. According to the Polisario Front, they sought to change backward ideas by way of persuasion and were successful in suppressing polygamy, arranged marriages, and child marriages. They transformed the traditional dowry, which had become untenable in a refugee context, into a symbolic communal gift, usually a goat, given by the daira as a whole to the newlywed couple. The committees regarded divorce as undesirable, though not illegal, and tried to prevent it by means of marital counseling. This was apparently intended to maintain social cohesion in the difficult conditions of the war and to consolidate the family, as opposed to the tribe (condemned in Polisario writings as a source of division), as the fundamental social unit. Demographic considerations, meanwhile, prompted the Polisario Front to encourage women to bear as many children as possible. Reproduction became a patriotic duty.

WORLD COURT see INTERNATIONAL COURT OF JUSTICE

- Y -

YATA, ALI. Leader of the pro-Moscow communists in Morocco since the 1940s, he was a vocal supporter of Morocco's annexation of Western Sahara. Secretary-general of the PCM (q.v.) from 1945 until its banning by the Rabat regime in 1960 and then secretary-general of its successive reincarnations, the PLS (founded in 1968 and banned in 1969) and the PPS (founded in 1974), he has spent 12 years of his political career in prison or exile. After Morocco's independence in 1956, he became a supporter of the Greater Morocco (q.v.) cause and wrote often in communist journals in favor of Morocco's claim to Western Sahara, often accusing the government of collaborating with Spain in the sixties and early seventies. In 1973, his articles were republished as a book, *Le Sahara Occidental Marocain* (see Bibliography), which was banned by the Rabat government, then still taking a low-key stance on the Saharan issue. However, in 1974, Yata suddenly found himself in virtual alliance with King Hassan II (q.v.) over Western Sahara. In July–August 1974, he carried out an 18-day tour of Eastern Europe as a special envoy of the king in an unsuccessful attempt to win Soviet bloc support for the Moroccan claim. Yata enthusiastically supported the Green March (q.v.) in November 1975 and since then has consistently backed the Moroccan occupation of Western Sahara, though at times he has criticized the Moroccan government for failing to prosecute the war against the Polisario Front (q.v.) with sufficient drive.

YEMAA see DJEMAA

- Z -

ZELLAGHA FORCE. A large, well-equipped force, assembled by the Moroccan army at the end of 1979 and early in 1980, the Zellagha Force was sent, under the command of Col. Mohammed Abrouq (q.v.), to southern Morocco to join part of the Ohoud Force (q.v.) in an attempt, launched on February 27, 1981, to clear a way through the Ouarkziz mountains to the town of Zaag, which had been besieged for months by the Polisario Front (q.v.). This operation, code-named Iman (q.v.), turned out a disaster when guerrillas fought running battles with the Zellagha and Ohoud forces on March 1–11, finally forcing them to give up their attempt to break through to Zaag. The Zellagha Force was named after a great Muslim victory near Badajoz, Spain, in 1086, when the Almoravid (q.v.) leader, Yusuf Ibn Tashfin, defeated the army of Castile.

ZEMLA, MASSACRE OF. On June 17, 1970, troops of the Spanish Foreign Legion (q.v.) opened fire on a crowd of demonstrating Saharawis in Zemla, a suburb of El-Ayoun (q.v.), killing an unknown number of demonstrators. The events became a watershed in the evolution of the Saharawi liberation movement, convincing many Saharawi militants that the Spanish could be forced out of the country only by waging an armed struggle. The organization behind the Zemla demonstration was the Harakat Tahrir Saguia el-Hamra wa Oued ed-Dahab (q.v.), or MLS, a movement founded by Mohammed Sidi Ibrahim Bassiri (q.v.) at the end of 1967, which had gradually won support from young Saharawis in the towns. Previously a clandestine movement, the MLS decided in the spring of 1967 to present its demands openly to the colonial authorities—choosing June 17 because it was the day scheduled for an official rally of loyalty to Spain in the Plaza de Africa in the center of El-Ayoun at which the governor-general, Gen. José María Pérez de Lema y Tejero, was to be the star speaker. The MLS decided that it would draw up a petition, moderate in tone, calling for internal autonomy rather than independence, and then hold a rival rally in Zemla. A large crowd gathered there early on the morning of June 17 while a much smaller turnout was on hand for Gen. Pérez de Lema in the Plaza de Africa. The Zemla demonstrators let it be known that they would not disperse until the governor-general had come to meet them, taken the petition, and responded to its demands. At the end of the morning, he did eventually arrive in Zemla, where the petition was read out in Arabic and translated for the general's benefit into Spanish. He then addressed the demonstrators in an inappropriately paternalistic manner, declaring that Spanish rule was for the Saharawis' own good and that "I am here in the Sahara, like Franco with the Spaniards, the captain of a ship, to steer it to the best harbor." He then gave a warning to disperse and departed, bearing the petition with him. At 5 in the afternoon, the *delegado gubernativo* (q.v.) of the northern region, López Huertas, returned to Zemla, accompanied by a 60-strong squad from the Policía Territorial (q.v.). Hoping that López Huertas was bringing the governor-general's response to the petition, three youths moved out of the crowd to greet the *delegado gubernativo,* but they were promptly arrested. To this the crowd responded by pelting the police with stones, one of which hit López Huertas, who rushed back to the governor-general. In a confidential report after the events a captain in the Policía Territorial gave this account of what then happened.

> At 7:30 p.m. a company of the Tercio [regiment], commanded by Capt. Arocha, made its appearance. Asked about his presence in the aforementioned place, he replied to me that he had orders to dissolve the gathering. He ordered the deployment of his forces, going past our police line. . ... The company of the Tercio continued its slow advance. Already quite near [the demonstrators] and under attack from stones and sticks, like the police beforehand, they opened fire into the air, at which moment some natives fell to the ground giving flight to all the demonstrators, who were pursued by the company of the Tercio.

The government said afterward that 2 demonstrators were killed and 20 wounded. However, the Mauritanian ministry of information claimed on June 20, after receiving eyewitness accounts from travelers who had arrived in Bir Moghrein, that 12 were killed; the Moroccan government, which lodged an official protest with the Spanish foreign minister, Gregorio López Bravo, claimed that 10 were killed; and 2 exiled leaders of the MLS, interviewed in the Algerian newspaper, *La République* (January 21, 1971), put the death toll at 11. The Zemla shootings shattered the MLS. Several hundred Saharawis were detained for a few days, and several MLS leaders were jailed in the Canaries and Dakhla until early in 1971. Bassiri was arrested at 3 a.m. on June 18, and, though the Spanish authorities later claimed that he was deported to Morocco on June 26, he has never been heard of since.

ZEMMOUR. A mountainous region that straddles the border with Mauritania and includes one of the territory's most important *gueltas* (q.v.).

ZOUERATE RAID. On May 1, 1977, in one of its most dramatic attacks against Mauritania, the Polisario Front (q.v.) raided the city of Zouerate, the center of the vital iron ore industry on which Mauritania depends for 80–90 percent of its export earnings. Though the city's defenses had been substantially improved since a mortar attack on December 30, 1975, the Polisario attackers met no resistance from the 1,500 Mauritanian troops there. A 60-km.-long trench, 3.5 meters deep, which had been built all round the city, proved a minor obstacle. The guerrillas, whose main targets were the airport, the power station, and the installations of the Zouerate-Nouadhibou railway (q.v.), remained almost unchallenged in the city for over two hours. During this time, two Frenchmen were killed and another six French nationals captured by the guerrillas and driven off into the desert. The French foreign minister, Louis de Guiringaud, pointed an accusing finger at Algeria, when he addressed the French National Assembly on May 3: "It is a case of an aggressive action staged by forces coming from abroad, and we know very well from where they come. They come from a neighbouring country, and the Polisario bases are in this neighbouring country. It is from there that this column came to commit aggression against Mauritania, against a territory where it is perfectly normal that there reside Frenchmen who are employees of a mining company." All but 60 of the 719 French nationals living in the city at the time of the attack had been evacuated within a few days, disrupting production in the iron ore industry, which depended heavily on French technicians. Moreover, Zouerate was attacked on three further occasions in 1977, on July 4 and 16 and August 19. To boost Mauritania's defenses, 600 Moroccan troops were flown into Zouerate in mid-July, under a Morrocan-Mauritanian defense pact signed a fortnight after the May Day raid, on May 13. When two more Frenchmen were captured by the guerrillas, on October 25, 1977, during an attack on the

Zouerate-Nouadhibou railway, French air force Jaguars started bombing raids against the guerrillas the following December, finally prompting the Polisario Front to release all eight French captives on December 23.

ZOUERATE-NOUADHIBOU RAILWAY ATTACKS. One of the principal targets of the Polisario Front (q.v.) during its war with Mauritania was the 657–km. railway from the iron ore mines of Zouerate to the Atlantic port of Nouadhibou, on which Mauritania depended for the evacuation of the ore. In the mid- to late 1970s, the iron ore from Zouerate accounted for about 80 percent of the country's total export revenue. Skirting around the Western Saharan frontier, the railway was as easy to attack as it was strategic: The small Mauritanian army could not police the whole length of the track, and the trains themselves were very vulnerable, normally consisting of some 200 wagons, pulled by about four locomotives, carrying 14,500 tons of ore. The guerrillas sabotaged the railway three times in 1976 by ripping up stretches of track but began serious attacks in 1977, the first being on February 20, 100 km. south of Zouerate, when a guerrilla group destroyed three locomotives with rocket fire. The front's objective was not only to destroy rolling stock and track. It also wanted to create a general state of insecurity that would force the French government to evacuate the French technicians on whom the whole iron ore industry, including the railway, acutely depended. To this end, the front captured six Frenchmen during a spectacular raid on Zouerate itself on May 1, 1977 (see ZOUERATE RAID), and then, on October 25 kidnapped two more Frenchmen, in an attack on the railway, about 60 km. south of Zouerate. The two new prisoners were among some 86 employees of Sofrerail, a subsidiary of the French state railway company, SNCF, who were working in Mauritania on secondment to the Comptoir Minier du Nord, which owned both the iron mines and the railway to Nouadhibou. For more than a month after the October 25 attack, the railway remained at a complete standstill. However, the French government did not bow to Polisario attempts to exchange the release of its eight French prisoners for a French evacuation of its nationals from Mauritania. Instead, on October 27, at a special meeting at the Elysée, President Valéry Giscard d'Estaing (q.v.), the foreign minister, Louis de Guiringaud; the defense minister, Yves Bourges; and the army chief of staff, General Guy Méry, decided to use the hostage-taking as a pretext to step up military aid to the small, overstretched Mauritanian armed forces. After 200 French reinforcements had been flown out to the French base at Cap Vert, near Dakar in Senegal, on the night of November 1–2, about 50 French military experts arrived in Mauritania during the following week, under the command of Gen. Forget. Another 25, mainly communications experts, arrived later in the month. Meanwhile a squadron of French airforce Jaguar jets arrived at Cap Vert, ready to intervene against the Polisario guerrillas in Mauritania. The first strike took place on December 2, after a guerrilla attack on Boulanour, a railway station 75 km. northeast of Nouadhibou. After another Polisario raid against the railway, between Touajil and Choum, on December 12, French Jaguars intervened again, on December 14 and 15, killing several dozen guerrillas, along with 51 of the 60 Mauritanian soldiers whom the guerrillas had taken prisoner in the initial attack. A third battle took place on December 18, when the Jaguars strafed and bombed a guerrilla force that had raided Tmeimichatt, a hamlet midway down the railway from Zouerate to Nouadhibou.

Meanwhile, Moroccan troops were stationed along the railway to boost its defenses. Six hundred Moroccan troops had been airlifted into Zouerate in July 1977, under the May 13, 1977, Moroccan-Mauritanian defense pact, and by early November there were another 100 in Nouadhibou. By December, however, there were up to 5,000 Moroccan troops in Mauritania, most of them in Zouerate, Nouadhibou, and the small settlements along the railway (Boulanour, Tmeimichatt, and Choum).

The Polisario Front finally released its eight French prisoners on December 23. Their release was unconditional, the guerrillas having failed in their bid to get vital French technicians repatriated and by then anxious to avert a major escalation of French military aid for the Mauritanian regime. However, their attacks on the Zouerate-Nouadhibou railway had done considerable economic damage. According to the Comptoir Minier du Nord, 9 of its 26 locomotives had been severely damaged by the end of the year and needed several months' repair work. One hundred and fifty ore trains had been canceled during the year, holding up the delivery of 1.6 million tons worth $22 million, equivalent to 18 percent of the year's total iron ore exports. After the devastating French air raids in December, the guerrillas switched their tactics: They stopped sending large, vulnerable columns to attack the railway and reverted to smaller-scale sabotage attacks, laying mines on the track to derail rolling stock. There were no less than three such attacks in the three weeks immediately preceding the July 10, 1978, military coup in Nouakchott, which, by helping to undermine the Mauritanian economy, the guerrillas' attacks on the railway had done much to encourage.

had a section on Western Sahara every year since 1964 and which contains all UN resolutions on the subject. Concerning the current UN peace efforts, the UN document *The Situation Concerning Western Sahara: Report of the Secretary-General* (June 18, 1990) is of prime importance. Also of value is a report by the secretary-general dated October 1, 1987, which concerns the background to, and the preparations for, the dispatch of the first UN technical mission to Western Sahara later that year.

Other publications with continuing coverage of Western Sahara are *Africa Contemporary Record: Annual Survey and Documents,* edited by Colin Legum, and *Africa Research Bulletin.* Although newspaper coverage of the conflict in the United States and Great Britain has been minimal, many articles have been published in specialized English-language publications, such as *Africa Confidential, Africa News, Africa Report, The Middle East, Middle East International, New African,* and *West Africa.*

The Bibliography has been divided into subject categories. Consult the Table of Contents below.

BIBLIOGRAPHY: CONTENTS

1. GENERAL

Bibliographies and Dictionaries

Blaudin de Thé, B., Commandant. *Essai de bibliographie du Sahara français et des régions avoisinantes* Paris: Arts et Métiers Graphiques, 1960.

Carnero Ruíz, Ismael. *Vocabulario geográfico-sahárico.* Madrid: Consejo Superior de Investigaciones Científicas, Instituto de Estudios Africanos, 1955.

Funck-Brentano, C. "Bibliographie du Sahara occidental," *Hespéris* (Rabat), Vol. XI, 1930.

Hodges, Tony. *Historical Dictionary of Western Sahara.* Metuchen, N.J.: The Scarecrow Press, 1982.

Rishworth, Susan Knoke. *Spanish-speaking Africa: A Guide to Official Publications.* Washington, D.C.: Library of Congress, 1973.

Sipe, Lynn F. *Western Sahara: A Comprehensive Bibliography.* New York: Garland Publishing (Garland Reference Library of Social Science, Vol. 178), 1984.

United States Government. Army Topographic Command. Geographic Names Division. *Spanish Sahara: Official Standard Names Approved by the U.S. Board on Geographic Names.* Washington, D.C.: 1979.

General Information and Interdisciplinary Studies

Ben Madani, Mohamed. "The Western Sahara: An Historical Survey," *The Maghreb Review,* No. 1, June–July 1976, pp. 13–15.

Criado, Ramón. *Sahara, pasión y muerte de un sueño colonial.* Paris: Ruedo Ibérico, 1977.

Gaudio, Attilio. "Notes sur le Sahara espagnol," *Journal de la Société des Africanistes* (Paris), Vol. XXII, 1952.

———. "Le Sahara occidental espagnol," *Notes et Etudes Documentaires* (Paris: La Documentation Française), No. 2570, September 1959.

———. "Le Sahara occidental espagnol," *Recontres Méditerranéennes* (Paris), October 1962, pp. 368ff.

———. *"Sahara espagnol, fin d'un mythe colonial."* Rabat: Assissala, 1975.

———. *Le dossier du Sahara occidental.* Paris: Nouvelles Editions Latines, 1978.

Hernández-Pacheco, Francisco, and José María Cordero Torres. *El Sahara español.* Madrid: Instituto de Estudios Políticos, 1962.

Hodges, Tony. *The Western Saharans.* London: Minority Rights Group (Report No. 40), 1984.

———. *Western Sahara: The Roots of a Desert War*. Westport, Connecticut, and London: Lawrence Hill, 1983.

Mercer, John. *Spanish Sahara*. London: George Allen and Unwin Ltd., 1976.

———. *The Sahrawis of Western Sahara*. London: Minority Rights Group (Report No. 40), 1979.

Rozpide, R. "El Sahara español y la Guinea española," *Revista de Geografía Colonial y Mercantil* (Madrid), Vol. I, 1903, No. 29.

———. "Las posesiones españolas del Africa occidental," *Revista de Geografía Colonial y Mercantil* (Madrid), July–August 1924, pp. 232–236; published in French in *L'Afrique Française, Renseignements Coloniaux* (Paris), December 1924, pp. 387–389.

Sahara occidental: un peuple et ses droits, Colloque de Massy, 1 et 2 avril 1978. Paris: Editions l'Harmattan, 1979.

"Le Sahara occidental espagnol," *Notes et Etudes Documentaires* (Paris: La Documentation Française), No. 2570, September 15th, 1959.

"Les territoires espagnols d'Afrique," *Notes et Etudes Documentaires* (Paris: La Documentation Française), No. 2951, January 3rd, 1963.

Thompson, Virginia, and Richard Adloff. *The Western Saharans*. Totowa, N.J.: Barnes and Noble, 1980; and London: Croom Helm, 1980.

United Nations. "Report of the United Nations Visiting Mission to Spanish Sahara, 1975," in *Report of the Special Committee on the Situation with Regard to the Implementation of the Declaration on the Granting of Independence to Colonial Countries and Peoples,* Vol. III, General Assembly, Official

Records, 30th Session, Supplement No. 23, UN Document A/10023/Rev. 1 (New York: 1977), pp. 12–128.

United States Government. Department of State. *Spanish Sahara. Background Notes.* Washington, D.C.: May 1974.

———. *Morocco. Background Notes.* Washington, D.C.: April 1982.

Guides and Yearbooks

L'Annuaire de l'Afrique du Nord. Paris: Centre National de la Recherche Scientifique. Published annually.

Legum, Colin (ed.). *Africa Contemporary Record: Annual Survey and Documents.* Chapters on "Spanish Sahara" in Vols. 1 (1968–69), 2 (1969–70), 3 (1970–71), 4 (1971–72), 5 (1972–73), 6 (1973–74), and 7 (1974–75) and on "Western Sahara" in Vols. 8 (1975–76), 9 (1976–77), 10 (1977–78), 11 (1978–79), 12 (1979–80), 13 (1980–81), 14 (1981–82), 15 (1982–83), 16 (1983–84), 17 (1984–85), 18 (1985–86), 19 (1986–87), 20 (1987–88), and 21 (1988–89). New York: Africana Publishing Co.

Statistical Abstracts

Instituto de Estudios Africanos. *Resumen estadístico del Africa española (1963–1964).* Madrid: 1965.

———. *Resumen estadístico del Sahara español (Año 1969).* Madrid: 1970.

Travel and Description

Alvárez Pérez, José. "En el Saguia el-Hamra," *Revista de Geografía Comerical* (Madrid), Vol. II, July–September 1886, pp. 6–8.

Barbier, Maurice. *Trois français au Sahara 1784–1786*. Paris: L'Harmattan, 1984.

―――. *Voyages et explorations du Sahara occidental au XIXe siècle*. Paris: L'Harmattan, 1985.

Benítez, Cristobal. "Notas tomadas por . . . en su viaje por Marruecos, el desierto de Sahara y Sudán y Senegal," *Boletín de la Sociedad de Geografía de Madrid,* June 1886, pp. 337–362, July–August 1886, pp. 7–24, and September–October 1886, pp. 176–199.

Bonelli, Emilio. *El Sahara. Descripción geográfica, comercial y agrícola desde Cabo Bojador a Cabo Blanco. Viajes al interior, habitantes del desierto y consideraciones generales*. Madrid: Peant, 1887.

Ca da Mosto, Alvise da. *The Voyage of Cadamosto, and Other Documents on Western Africa in the Second Half of the Fifteenth Century*. Translated and edited by G. R. Crone. London: The Hakluyt Society, 1937.

Caro Baroja, Julio. "La exploración del Africa occidental española," *Africa* (Madrid), Vol. XI, Nos. 152–153, August–September 1954, pp. 23–25.

Cervera Baviera, Julio. "Expedición al Sahara, de Río de Oro a Iyil," *Revista de Geografía Comercial* (Madrid), Vol. II, Nos. 25–30, July–September 1886, pp. 1–6.

―――. "Conferencia acerca de su viaje de exploración por el Sahara español," *Boletín de la Sociedad de Geografía de Madrid,* January–February 1887, pp. 7–20.

Coello, Francisco. "Nota sobre los resultados geográficos de la exploración de la costa noroeste de Africa por Don Cesáreo Fernández Duro," *Boletín de la Real Sociedad de Geografía de Madrid,* Vol. IV, 1878, pp. 242–247.

Conrotte, Manuel. "Les explorations espagnoles en Afrique," *Afrique Française, Renseignements Coloniaux*, 1913, pp. 370–371.

Cournault, C. "Itinéraire de Tlemsen á Timbouctou, donné par Abd'Allah Ben Cassem de Tlemsen et suivi par lui jusqu'á Saglia Hamra," *Revue de L'Orient* (Paris), Vol. III, No. 3, 1856, pp. 331–332.

Douis, Camille. "Expedición en el Sahara occidental," *Boletín de la Real Sociedad de Geografía de Madrid,* Vol. XXIII, 1887, pp. 145–157.

———. *Voyage d'exploration à travers le Sahara occidental et le Sud marocain.* Rouen: Cagniard, 1888.

———. "Le Sahara occidental entre le Tropique et le Ouad-Draa," *Revue de Géographie* (Paris), Vol. XI, 1888, pp. 255–267.

Eannes de Azurara, Gomes. *The Chronicle of the Discovery and Conquest of Guinea.* Translated and edited by C. R. Beazley and E. Prestage. London: 1896.

Fernández, Valentín. *Description de la côte occidentale d'Afrique de Ceuta au Sénégal, 1506–1507.* Translated by T. Monod and P. de Cenival. Paris: 1938.

Gutiérrez Sobral, José. "El Sahara occidental y la Guinea española," *Revista de Geografía Colonial y Mercantil* (Madrid), Vol. I, 1903, p. 547.

"Itinéraires de Ben Ali et d'Abderrahmane en Seguiet El Hamra," *Bulletin de la Société de Géographie de Paris,* October 1849.

Lhote, Henri. "A propos de l'exploration de Michel Vieuchange à Smara," *Acta Geologica,* No. 6, January–July 1951.

Mármol y Carvajal, Luis de. *Descripción general de Africa.* Granada: 1573.

Quiroga, Francisco. "Apuntes de un viaje por el Sahara occidental," *Anales de la Sociedad Española de Historia Natural* (Madrid), Vol. XV, 1886, pp. 495–523.

———. "La exploración del Sahara occidental," *Boletín de la Institución Libre de Enseñanza* (Madrid), Vol. X, 1887.

Roman, Rainero. *La scoperta della vosta occidentale d'Africanelle relazioni di Gomez Eanes de Zurara, Diogo Gomes, Eustache de la Fosse, Valentin Fernandes e Duarte Pacheco Pereira.* Milan: Ed. Marzorati, 1970.

Rozpide, R. "Expediciones en el Sahara español," *Revista de Geografía Colonial y Mercantil* (Madrid), Vol. V, 1908, No. 1.

Santarem, Viscount. *Recherches sur la priorité de la découverte des pays situés sur la côte occidentale d'Afrique au-delà du Cap Bojador et sur les progrès de la science géographique après les navigations des Portugais au XVème siecle.* Paris: Doney-Dupré, 1842.

Soleillet, Paul. "Territorios adquiridos para España por la Sociedad española de Africanistas y Colonistas en la costa occidental de Africa," *Boletín de la Sociedad de Geografía de Madrid,* May–June 1885, pp. 355–399, and August 1885, pp. 120–128.

Thierry-Maulnier. "Michel Vieuchange," *Revue Universelle,* March 1, 1933, pp. 615–618.

Vieuchange, Michel. *Smara: The Forbidden City, Being the Journal of Michel Vieuchange While Travelling Among the Independent Tribes of South Morocco and Río de Oro.* New York: Ecco Press, 1987.

2. CULTURAL

Archaeology and Prehistory

Almagro Basch, Martín. "El arte prehistórico del Sahara español," *Ampurias* (Barcelona), Vol. VI, 1944, pp. 273–284.

———. "Un yacimiento de tradición Capsiense del Sahara español: Las sebjas de Taruna (Seguia el Hamra)," *Ampurias* (Barcelona), Vols. VII–VIII, 1945–46, pp. 69–81.

———. *Prehistoria del norte de Africa y del Sahara español.* Madrid: Consejo Superior de Investigaciones Científicas, Instituto de Estudios Africanos, 1946.

———. *El estado actual de la investigación de la prehistoria del norte de Africa y del Sahara.* Madrid: Consejo Superior de Investigaciones Científicas, Instituto de Estudios Africanos, 1968.

———. "El arte rupestre del norte de Africa en relación con la rama norteafricana de Cromagnón," *Anuario de Estudios Atlánticos* (Madrid), Vol. XV, 1969.

———. "Las representaciones de carros en el arte rupestre del Sahara español," *Trabajos de Prehistoria* (Madrid), Vol. XXVIII, 1971.

———. "Unos objetos hachiformes representados en el arte rupestre del Sahara occidental," *Muñibe,* 23, 1971.

Balbín Behrmann, R. de. "Excavación de un túmulo preislámico, en la zona de Guelta Zemmur, Sahara español," *Trabajos de Prehistoria* (Madrid), Vol. XXX, 1973.

Biedermann, H., and H. Nowak. "Altkanarische Kultur, Nordwestafrika und Feismalerein der Spanischen Sahara," *Mannus,* 1974.

García Guinea, M. A. "Grabados rupestres inéditos de Smara," *Zephyrus,* 17, 1966.

Gaudio, Attilio. "A propos de deux inscriptions tifinag signalées dans le Sahara espagnol," *Bulletin de la Société des Africanistes* (Paris), 1952, pp. 24–25.

Jordá Cerdá, F. "Los problemas de la investigación prehistórica en el Sahara español," *Archivos del Instituto de Estudios Africanos* (Madrid), Vol. VIII, No. 33, June 1955, pp. 81–97.

————. "Notas sobre el Levaillois-Musteriense del Yebel Zini (Sahara español)," *Archivos del Instituto de Estudios Africanos* (Madrid), Vol. VIII, No. 35, December 1955, pp. 81–97.

Martínez Santa-Olalla, Julio. "Las primeras pinturas rupestres del Marruecos español," *Actas y Memorias de la Sociedad Española de Antropología, Etnología y Prehistoria* (Madrid), Vol. XVI, 1941.

————. *El Sahara español anteislámico.* Madrid: Ministerio de Educación Nacional, Comisaría General de Excavaciones Arqueológicas, 1944.

Mateu Sangre, J. "Nuevas Aportaciones al conocimiento del arte rupestre del Sahara español," *Ampurias* (Barcelona), Vol. VII-VIII, 1945–46, pp. 49–67.

————. "Grabados rupestres de los alrededores de Smara (Sahara español)," *Ampurias* (Barcelona), Vol. IX–X, 1947–48, pp. 301–317.

Morales Agacino, E. "Sobre algunos grabados, dibujos e inscripciones rupestres del Sahara español," *Mauritania* (Tetuan), December 1942.

————. "Grabados e inscripciones rupestres de la Alta Seguia el Hamra en el Sahara español," *Actas y Memorias de la*

Sociedad Española de Antropología, Etnografía y Prehistoria (Madrid), Vol. XIX, 1946, pp. 131–141.

Nowak, Herbert, Sigrid Ortner, and Dieter Ortner. *Felsbilder der Spanischen Sahara.* Graz: Akademische Druck u. Verlagsanstalt, 1975.

Pericot García, Luis. "Los trabajos de los últimos quince años sobre la prehistoria del Africa española," *Third Pan-African Congress on Prehistory, Livingstone, 1955* (London: Chatto and Windus, 1957).

Sáez Martín, Bernardo. *La primera expedición paleontológica el Sahara español.* Madrid: Instituto de Estudios Africanos, 1944.

————. "Sobre la supuesta existencia de una edad de bronce en el Sahara occidental y Africa minor," *Cuadernos de Historia Primitiva,* Vol. V, No. 2, 1949, pp. 111–118.

————. "Carros prehistóricos en el extremo occidental del Sahara," *Comptes Rendus de la 3ème Conférence Internationale des Africanistes, Ibadan, 1949.*

————. "Sobre una supuesta edad de bronce en Africa Minor y Sahara," *Actes du Congrès Panafricaniste de la Préhistoire d'Alger, 1952,* 1955, pp. 659–662.

Vidal y López, M. "Materiales Saharianos en Valencia," *Prehistoria Levantina,* 2, 1945.

Linguistics and Literature

Larrea Palacín, Arcadio. "Canciones del Africa occidental española," *Archivos del Instituto de Estudios Africanos* (Madrid), Vol. X, 1958, No. 44, pp. 20–47.

Massignon, L. "Elements arabes et foyers d'arabisation; leur rôle dans le monde musulman actuel (Mauritanie et Río de

Oro)," *Revue du Monde Musulman,* Vol. LVII, 1924, pp. 45–48.

Monteil, Vincent. "Dictons sur les Reguibat Lgwacem," *Hespéris* (Rabat), Vol. XXXIV, 3rd–4th quarters, 1950, pp. 443–444.

Norris, H. T. *Shinqiti Folk Literature and Song.* Oxford: Clarendon Press, 1968.

Oro Oulido, A. *Algo sobre el hasanía o dialecto árabe que se habla en el Sahara atlántico.* Tangiers: P. Enola, 1940.

Santamaría, Ramiro. "Poesía, cantos y danzas en el desierto," *Africa* (Madrid), Vol. XXV, No. 380, August 1973, pp. 23–24.

―――. "Los poetas del desierto," *Africa* (Madrid), Vol. XXV, No. 382, October 1973, p. 28.

3. ECONOMIC

General

Assidon, Elsa. "Inventaire et exploitation des richesses économiques," in *Sahara occidental, un peuple et ses droits, Colloque de Massy, 1 et 2 avril 1978* (Paris: Editions L'Harmattan, 1978).

"Economie des territoires espagnois d'Afrique," *Marchés Tropicaux et Méditerranéens* (Paris), December 22, 1966, p. 3261.

Gaudio, Attilio. "Le développement économique du Sahara occidental," *Marchés Tropicaux et Méditerranéens* (Paris), July 2, 1976.

Intégration économique des provinces sahariennes et développement économique. Colloque international organisé par l'Association des économistes marocains, Rabat, le 9–10 janvier 1984. Casablanca: Editions Maghrébines, 1985.

La Riva, Manuel. "La provincia de Sahara y su proceso de desarrollo económico," *Africa* (Madrid), Vol. XXII, January 1965, pp. 10–12.

Melis Clavería, Manuel. "La provincia de Sahara ante el Plan de Desarrollo Económico y Social," *Africa* (Madrid), Vol. XXIII, No. 295, July 1966, pp. 4–6.

"La mise en valeur du Tiris El Gharbia," *Europe-Outremer,* 55th year, No. 574, November 1977.

Moroccan Government. *Morocco's Saharan Provinces and Regional Developement.* Rabat: Al Anbaa, 1976.

————. *Programme de 1er urgence pour l'équipement des provinces sahariennes.* Rabat: Ministry of Interior, September 1976.

————. *Les provinces marocaines du sud.* Rabat: Ministry of Information, 1978.

"Morocco Hoists a Development Plan for Western Sahara," *Middle East Economic Digest* (London), April 16th, 1976.

Murillo Goñi, Alejandro. "Desarrollo de la provincia del Sahara," *Africa* (Madrid), Vol. XVII, No. 227, November 1960, pp. 9–12.

Nande. *Las provincias del Sahara, un año después.* El-Ayoun: 1977.

"Nouvelles réalisations dans les provinces sahariennes," *Maroc Magazine,* October 15th–21st, 1978.

Agriculture and Pastoral Nomadism

Bataillon, C. (ed.). *Nomades et nomadisme au Sahara.* Paris: UNESCO (Arid Zone Research Series, No. 19), 1963.

Bisson, J. "Le nomadisme des Reguibat L'Gouacem," *Travaux de l'Institut de Recherches Sahariennes* (Algiers), Vol. XX, 1961.

―――. "Nomadisation chez les Reguibat," in *Nomades et nomadisme au Sahara,* edited by C. Bataillon, Paris (UNESCO), 1963.

Capot-Rey, Robert. "Etat actuel du nomadisme au Sahara," in *Les problèmes de la zone aride,* Paris (UNESCO), 1962.

―――. "Les problèmes du nomadisme au Sahara," *Revue Internationale du Travail,* Vol. XV, No. 5, November 1964.

Cola Alberich, Julio. "El nomadismo sahariano," *Africa* (Madrid), 1953, No. 143, pp. 25–27.

"L'économie pastorale saharienne," *Notes et Etudes Documentaires* (Paris: La Documentation Française), No. 1730, April 21, 1953.

García Calbezón, Andrés. "Posibilidades agrícolas en la provincia de Sahara," *Africa* (Madrid), Vol. XXIII, No. 294, June 1966, pp. 31–33.

―――. *Establecimiento de la agricultura en el Sahara.* Madrid: Consejo Superior de Investigaciones Científicas, Instituto de Estudios Africanos, 1967.

Instituto de Estudios Africanos and Dirección General de Promoción de Sahara. *Agricultura y ganadería en el Sahara español.* Madrid: 1970.

Lemoyne, R. *La transformation moderne de l'économie des nomades au Sahara occidental.* Paris: Centre de Hautes Etudes Administratives sur l'Afrique et l'Asie Moderne, Mémoire No. 1089, May 18, 1946.

Communications

Caffarena Aceña, Vicente. "Realizaciones portuarias en las provincias de Ifni y Sahara," *Africa* (Madrid), Vol. XXI, April 1964, No. 268, pp. 57–63.

———. "Estado actual de los puertos de las provincias de Ifni y Sahara," *Africa* (Madrid), Vol. XXIII, No. 294, June 1966, pp. 34–37.

———. "Las obras portuarias en el Sahara español," *Africa* (Madrid), Vol. XXIII, No. 353, May 1971, pp. 13–17.

Gómez Moreno, P. *Rutas del Sahara*. Madrid: Consejo Superior de Investigaciones Científicas, Instituto de Estudios Africanos, 1958.

Instituto de Estudios Africanos and Dirección General de Promoción del Sahara. *Las telecommunicaciones en Sahara*. Madrid: 1970.

Sabau, Jaime. "Las telecomnicaciones en las provincias africanas," *Africa* (Madrid), Vol. XXI, No. 268, April 1964, pp. 64–66.

———. "Las telecomunicaciones en las provincias españolas de Africa occidental," *Africa* (Madrid), Vol. XXIII, No. 294, June 1966, pp. 41–43.

Santamaría, Ramiro. "Las telecommunicaciones en pleno desarrollo," *Africa* (Madrid), Vol. XXV, No. 373, January 1973, pp. 57–58.

Fisheries

García Cabrera, C. "El banco pesquero canario-sahariano," *Archivos del Instituto de Estudios Africanos* (Madrid), Vol. XVIII, 1964.

Navarro, Francisco de P., and Fernando Lozano Cobo. *Carta de pesca de la costa del Sahara, desde el Cabo Bojador al Cabo Blanco*. Madrid: Ministerio de Marina, Instituto Español de Oceanografía, 1953.

Organización Sindical de Las Palmas. Secretariado de Asuntos Económicos. *La importancia del sector pesquero en la provincia de Las Palmas*. Las Palmas de Gran Canaria: 1975.

Mining and Minerals

Alia Medina, Manuel. "El descubrimiento de los fosfatos del Sahara español," *Africa* (Madrid), Vol. VII, No. 97, January 1950, pp. 8–10.

Comba Ezquerra, Juan A. "Posibilidades mineras del Sahara español," *Africa* (Madrid), Vol. XVII, No. 220, April 1960, p. 160.

————. "Investigación minera en el Sahara occidental," *Africa* (Madrid), Vol. XVII, No. 227, November 1960, pp. 16–20.

————. "La investigación minera en la provincia del Sahara," *Archivos del Instituto de Estudios Africanos* (Madrid), 1961, pp. 7–24.

————. "25 años de investigación geológica y minera de las provincias africanas," *Archivos del Instituto de Estudios Africanos* (Madrid), 1965.

————. "Trabajos y planes de desarrollo de las investigaciones mineras y geológicas en la provincia de Sahara," *Africa* (Madrid), Vol. XIII, No. 294, June 1966, pp. 38–40.

Instituto Nacional de Industria. *Fosfatos de Bu-Craa, S.A.* (Madrid), 1972.

BIBLIOGRAPHY

INTRODUCTION

Since the publication of the first edition of this dictionary, in 1982, a considerable number of English-language books and articles on Western Sahara have appeared, supplementing the earlier literature, which was mostly in French and Spanish. As many English-language sources as possible have been included in this bibliography, but for a more exhaustive treatment, the reader should refer to Lynn F. Sipe, *Western Sahara: A Comprehensive Bibliography*, which was published in 1984.

A detailed study of the origins and nature of the Western Saharan war can be found in *Western Sahara: The Roots of a Desert War*, by Tony Hodges (1983). Another useful work on this subject is *Conflict in Northwest Africa: The Western Sahara Dispute*, by John Damis (1983). A good collection of essays is to be found in a book edited by Richard Lawless and Laila Monahan, *War and Refugees: The Western Sahara Conflict* (1987). I. William Zartman's *Ripe for Resolution: Conflict and Intervention in Africa* (1989) contains a chapter on the Saharan war that provides a valuable perspective. John Mercer's *Spanish Sahara* (1976), although written before the outbreak of the war, is recommended for historical background.

As to the international legal and diplomatic dimensions of the conflict, the opinion of the International Court of Justice (ICJ) on the Moroccan and Mauritanian claims to the territory, entitled *Western Sahara, Advisory Opinion of 16 October 1975*, is still of great value, as is the *Report of the United Nations Visiting Mission to Spanish Sahara, 1975*, which provides a wealth of historical, political, and other information. Articles by Thomas Franck, Malcolm Shaw, and Maurice Barbier on the ICJ advisory opinion are also highly recommended. Another excellent United Nations source is the *Yearbook of the United Nations*, which has

Kolela, Jonathan. "Sahara occidental: l'enjeu d'une guerre," *L'Economiste du Tiers Monde* (Paris), No. 22, January–February 1978.

La Vina Villa, J. "La investigación de fosfatos en el Sahara," *Archivos del Instituto de Estudios Africanos* (Madrid), 1961.

Murge, Bernard. "Les phosphates du Sahara occidental," *Europe-Outremer* (Paris), No. 551.

"Le problème des phosphates au coeur de la souveraineté du Sahara espagnol," *Marchés Tropicaux et Méditerranéens* (Paris), June 13, 1970.

"Les recherches minières au Sahara espagnol," *Industries et Travaux d'Outremer* (Paris), June 1961, pp. 467–468.

Smith, Pamela. "Imbroglio in the Sahara," *Arabia and the Gulf* (London), November 21, 1977.

Petroleum

Andrés Andrés, C. "Características económicas y legales de las concesiones petrolíferas en las provincias africanas," *Archivos del Instituto de Estudios Africanos* (Madrid), 1961.

García-Fuente, S. "La investigación petrolífera en el Sahara," *Archivos del Instituto de Estudios Africanos* (Madrid), 1961.

Hodges, Tony, and James Ball. "Is There Oil in Western Sahara?" *African Business* (London), August 1982, pp. 14–16.

Serfaty, Abraham. "Le pétrole du Sahara occidental derrière les appétits impérialistes," *Souffles* (Paris), nouvelle série, No. 2, October 1973.

Spanish Government. *Decreto por el que se aprueban las normas reglamentarias especiales sobre la aplicación de la ley de hidrocarburos en las provincias españolas en Africa.* Madrid: Presidencia del Gobierno, June 25th, 1959.

Water

Alia Medina, Manuel. "Las aguas superficiales y subterráneas en el Sahara español," *Africa* (Madrid), Vol. II, No. 24, December 1943, pp. 16–21.

Gómez Moreno, Pedro. *Pozos del Sahara.* Madrid: Consejo Superior de Investigaciones Científicas, Instituto de Estudios Africanos, 1959.

Instituto de Estudios Africanos and Dirección General de Promoción de Sahara. *Aguas subterráneas del Sahara español.* Madrid: 1970.

4. HISTORIC

Precolonial

Abun-Nasr, Jamil M. *A History of the Maghrib.* Cambridge: Cambridge University Press, 1971.

Amilhat, P. "Les Almoravides au Sahara," *Revue Militaire de l'Afrique Occidentale Française,* No. 34, July 15, 1937, pp. 1–31.

Bosch-Vilá, Jacinto. *Los Almorávides.* Tetuan: Editora Marroquí, 1956.

Caro Baroja, Julio. "La historia entre los nómadas saharianos," *Archivos del Instituto de Estudios Africanos* (Madrid), Vol. VIII, 1955, No. 35, pp. 57–67.

Díaz del Ribero, Francisco-Lorenzo. *El Sahara occidental: Pasado y presente.* Madrid: Gisa Ediciones, 1975.

Dupas, Capt. "Le commerce transaharien entre le sud du Maroc et le Sahara occidental et la Mauritanie," *France Méditerranéenne,* 1938.

Julien, Charles-André. *History of North Africa.* Translated by John Petrie and C. C. Stewart. London: Routledge and Kegan Paul, 1970.

Mercer, John. "The Cycle of Invasion and Unification in the Western Sahara," *African Affairs* (London: The Royal African Society), Vol. 75, No. 301, October 1976, pp. 498–510.

Norris, H. T. "New Evidence on the Life of 'Abdullah b. Yasin and the Origins of the Almoravid Movement," *Journal of African History* (London), Vol. XII, No. 2, 1971, pp. 255–268.

Portillo, Joaquín. "El Sahara occidental era independiente de Marruecos," *El Pais* (Madrid), November 11, 1978, and November 12, 1978.

Europeans on the Western Saharan Coast, Pre-19th Century

Cenival, P. de, and F. de la Chapelle. "Possessions espagnoles sur la côte occidentale d'Afrique aux XVe et XVIe siècles," *Hespéris* (Rabat), Vol. XXXi, 1935, fasc. 1–2.

Mauny, Raymond. *Les navigations médiévales sur les côtes sahariennes antérieures à la découverte portugaise (1434).* Lisbon: Centro de Estudos Históricos Ultramarinos, 1960.

Pinto de la Rosa, J. M. *Canarias prehispánicas y Africa occidental española.* Madrid: Consejo Superior de Investigaciones Científicas, Instituto de Estudios Africanos, 1954.

Robin, J. "Moors and Canary Islanders on the Coast of the Western Sahara," *The Geographical Journal* (London), No. 121, 1955.

Rumeu de Armas. "Antecedentes históricos del Sahara español," *Africa* (Madrid), Vol. XXII, No. 346, October 1970, pp. 4–10.

Colonial Penetration and Occupation

General

Arrojas García, Enrique. "El Coronel Bens," *Africa* (Madrid), Vol. V, No. 51, March 1946, pp. 22–26.

Bens Argandoña, Franciso. *Mis memorias: Veintidós años en el desierto*. Madrid: Ediciones del Africa Occidental Española, 1947.

Bentzmann, P. de. "La pacification du Sahara occidental," *Revue d'Histoire des Colonies,* 4th Quarter, 1935, pp. 249–284.

Breveté, Col., and Gen. Jean Charbonneau. *Sur les traces du Pacha de Tombouctou; la pacification du Sud marocain et du Sahara occidental*. Paris: Charles Lavauzelle et Cie., 1936.

British Government. Foreign Office. *Spanish Sahara (Río de Oro)*. Handbooks Prepared under the Direction of the Historical Section of the Foreign Office, No. 131, May 1919.

Charbonneau, Jean. "Les problèmes de la liaison Maroc-Mauritanie et les enclaves espagnoles," *Revue des Territoires Coloniaux* (Paris), November–December 1933, pp. 343–370.

Dinaux, General. "Une solution à la question du Río de Oro," *L'Afrique Française,* April 1929, pp. 178–183.

Héraute, S. "La pacification du Sahara occidental et ses conséquences," *L'Afrique Française* (Paris), April 1935, pp. 225–229.

Lebrun, Albert. "La question du Río de Oro," *L'Afrique Française* (Paris), 1929, pp. 13–20.

MacKenzie, Donald. *The Flooding of the Sahara: An Account of the Proposed Plan for Opening Central Africa to Commerce and Civilisation from the North-West Coast, with a Description of Soudan and Western Sahara and Notes on Ancient Manuscripts*. London: Sampson Low, Marston, Searle and Rivington, 1877.

———. "The British Settlement at Cape Juby, North West Africa," *Blackwoods Edinburgh Magazine*, DCCCLXXXVII, September 1889, pp. 412–421.

Marty, Paul. "Le Sahara espagnol," *Revue du Monde Musulman* (Paris), Vol. XLVI, August 1921, pp. 161–213.

Miège, J. L. "Les origines de la colonie espagnole du Río de Oro," in *Le Sahara: Rapports et contacts humains, 7ème colloque d'histoire organisé par la faculté des lettres d'Aix-en-Provence*. Aix-en-Provence: Publications des Annales de la Faculté des Lettres (Série: Travaux et Mémoires, No. XLIII), 1967.

Pastor y Santos, Emilio. "Gestiones que precedieron a la ocupación de Río de Oro," *Africa* (Madrid), Vol. VI, No. 86, February 1949, pp. 22–24.

Ressot, Captain. "La zone dissidente du Sahara occidental," *L'Afrique Française, Renseignements Coloniaux* (Paris), No. 17, July 1926, pp. 322–332.

Yanguas Miravete, José. "La provincia española del Sahara," *Africa* (Madrid), Vol. XIX, No. 251, November 1962, pp. 33–36.

Border Demarcations

Armatte. "La délimitation franco-espagnole au Maroc et ses conséquences," *Questions Diplomatiques et Coloniales*, November 16, 1912, pp. 611–621.

————. "Le traité franco-espagnol," *Questions Diplomatiques et Coloniales,* December 16, 1912, pp. 734–744.

Basdevant. "Le traité franco-espagnol du 27 novembre 1912," *Revue Generale de Droit International Public,* 1915, p. 433ff.

Caix, Robert de. "Le traité du 27 novembre 1912," *Bulletin du Comité d'Afrique Française* (Paris), 1913, p. 12.

Deasy, G. F. "Spanish Territorial Boundary Changes in N.W. Africa," *The Geographical Review,* 32, 1942.

Demay, C. "Partage politique de la côte du Sahara," *Revue Encyclopédique,* 1895, pp. 440–441.

Flores, Angel. "El erréneo artículo 3° del proyecto de tratado de 1902," *Africa* (Madrid), Vol. IX, No. 127, July 1952, pp. 17–19.

Gary, G. "Les accords franco-espagnols de 1902 à 1912," *Revue des Sciences Politiques,* January–February 1913, p. 90ff.

Las Cagigas, Isidro de. *Tratados y convenios referentes a Marruecos.* Madrid: Consejo Superior de Investigaciones Científicas, Instituto de Estudios Africanos, 1952.

Tardieu, A. "France et Espagne 1902–1912," *Revue des Deux Mondes* (Paris), December 1, 1912.

Thomasson, Commandant de. "Le compromis franco-allemand et les négotiations franco-espagnoles," *Questions Diplomatiques et Coloniales,* November 16, 1911, pp. 577–591.

Saharawi Resistance

Albert, P. "Chikh Ma el Ainine de Seguiat el Hamra," *Bulletin de la Société de Géographie d'Alger,* 4th Quarter, 1906, pp. 401–405.

Al-Moutabassir. "Ma el Aïnin ech Changuity," *Revue du Monde Musulman* (Paris), Vol. I, 1907, pp. 343–351.

Ba, Mahmadou Ahmadou. "A propos de Smara," *L'Afrique Française* (Paris), February 1934, pp. 95–97.

Desiré-Vuillemin, Geneviève-M. "Cheikh Ma El Ainin et le Maroc, ou l'echec d'un moderne Almoravide," *Revue d'Histoire des Colonies,* November 1958, pp. 29–60.

Doménech Lafuente, Angel. "Ma el Ainin, Señor de Smara," *Africa* (Madrid), Vol. V, No. 55, July 1946, pp. 9–12, and Nos. 59–60, November–December 1946, pp. 14–17, and Vol. VI, No. 65, May 1947, pp. 22–25.

———. "Ma el Ainin frente a Gouraud," *Africa* (Madrid), Vol. V, Nos. 83–84, November–December 1948, pp. 21–24.

Lévi-Provençal, E. "Ma el Aïn," *Encyclopédie de l'Islam,* Vol. 3, Book 37, 1928, pp. 58–59.

Martinet, Guy. "Ma El Ainin et la Sakiet El Hamra," *Lamalif* (Rabat), No. 41, August-September 1970.

Segonzac, R. de. "El Hiba, fils de Ma el Ainin," *L'Afrique Française, Renseignements Coloniaux* (Paris), March–April 1917, pp. 62–69 and 90–94.

Period of Spanish Rule

General

Areilza, José María de, and Fernando María Castiella. *Reivindicaciones de España.* Madrid: 1941.

Badday, M. S. "Río de Oro: Madrid se dérobe," *Revue Française d'Etudes Politiques Africaines* (Paris), October 1970.

Baker, R. "Breath of Change in Spanish Africa," *Africa Quarterly,* January–March 1968, pp. 343ff.

Bazarov, Konstantin. "Spanish Africa," *Venture,* March 1970.

Bernero Chacobo, H. *Africa occidental española en la actualidad.* Madrid: Instituto de Estudios Africanos, 1961.

Bernoville, Gaetan. "L'odysée des évadés de Villa Cisneros," *L'Illustration,* February 11, 1933, pp. 164–165.

Borras, T. "Los Saharauis son Españoles," *Africa* (Madrid), Vol. XXIV, No. 306, June 1967, pp. 4–7.

Carrington, Stephen. "La lutte pour l'indépendance du Sahara espagnol," *Le Monde Diplomatique* (Paris), August 1974.

Cordero Torres, José María. *Tratado elemental de derecho colonial español.* Madrid: Editora Nacional, 1941.

———. *Aspectos de la misión universal de España.* Madrid: Ediciones de la Vicesecretaría de Educación Popular, 1942.

Devereux. "Spain's Role in North Africa," *World Affairs Quarterly,* July 1958, pp. 152ff.

Díaz de Villegas, José. *Plazas y provincias africanas espanolas.* Madrid: Instituto de Estudios Africanos, 1962.

———. *Africa Española en la geopolítica y geoestrategia nacionales.* Madrid: Instituto de Estudios Africanos, 1967.

"L'Espagne et l'Afrique," *Marchés Tropicaux et Méditerranéens* (Paris), December 22, 1966.

García Figueras, Tomás. *Santa Cruz de Mar Pequeña, Ifni, Sahara.* La acción de España en la costa occidental de Africa. Madrid: Ediciones Fe, 1941.

García Peñalver, Santiago. "La obra de España en el Sahara," *Africa* (Madrid), Vol. XVIII, No. 228, December 1960, pp. 7–12.

———. "Realidades del Sahara," *Africa* (Madrid), Nos. 236–237, September 1961, pp. 15–17.

Gomes Tello. "Verdad española sobre Ifni y Sahara," *Africa* (Madrid), No. 289, January 1953, pp. 12ff.

Instituto de Estudios Africanos. *Sahara, provincia española.* In French as *Sahara, province espagnole.* Madrid: 1966.

———. *La acción de España en Sahara.* Madrid: 1977.

Juárez, C. "Les restes de l'empire d'Espagne," *Démocratie Nouvelle,* April 4, 1964, p. 38.

La Chapelle, F. de. "Les possessions espagnoles au sud du Maroc," *Revue Militaire Française,* November 1934.

———. *Problèmes actuels du Sahara, Río de Oro et territoire d'Ifni.* Paris: Centre de Hautes Etudes Administratives sur l'Afrique et l'Asie Moderne, Mémoire No. 179, 1937.

Menéndez del Valle, Emilio. *Sahara español: una descolonización tardía.* Madrid: Editorial Cuadernos para el Diálogo, 1975.

Moria, Vial de. "España y el Sahara," *Africa* (Madrid), Vol. XVII, No. 227, November 1960, pp. 2–4.

———. "Río de Oro, Sahara (1884 a nuestros dias)," *Africa* (Madrid), Vol. XXIII, No. 355, July 1971, pp. 12–16.

Muñoz, Ary. "L'Afrique et l'Espagne," *L'Afrique Française* (Paris), June 1935, pp. 368–377.

Ortega Cañadell, R. *Provincias africanas españolas.* Barcelona: Teide, 1962.

Pautard, André. "Madrid tente de créer un état sous tutelle face aux revendications des trois pays voisins," *Le Monde Diplomatique* (Paris), No. 197, August 1970.

Pelissier, René. "Spain Changes Course in Africa," *Africa Report* (New York), Vol. 2, No. 8, December 1963.

————. *Los territorios españoles de Africa*. Madrid: Consejo Superior de Investigaciones Científicas, 1964.

————. "Spain's Discreet Decolonization," *Foreign Affairs* (New York), Vol. 43, No. 3, April 1965.

————. "Spain's African Sandboxes," *Africa Report* (New York), February 1966.

————. "D'Afrique et d'Espagne," *Preuves*, No. 188, October 1966.

————. "Sahara espagnol: la ronde des chacals," *Revue Française d'Etudes Politiques Africaines,* April 1967.

————. "Sahara espagnol: l'escalade," *Revue Française d'Etudes Politiques Africaines,* September 1974.

"Les questions des territoires espagnols en Afrique," *Maghreb* (Paris), 1966, No. 18.

Rumeu de Armas, Antonio. *España en el Africa atlántica*. Madrid: 1956.

Sáez de Govantes, Luis. *El africanismo español*. Madrid: Consejo Superior de Investigaciones Científicas, Instituto de Estudios Africanos, 1971.

"Le Sahara espagnol," *Maghreb* (Paris), No. 22, July–August 1967, pp. 35–41.

Santamaría, Ramiro. "Paz, trabajo y progreso en la provincia sahariana," *Africa* (Madrid), Vol. XVII, No. 227, November 1960, pp. 13–15.

————. "La obra de España en el Sahara," *Africa* (Madrid), Vol. XXVII, Nos. 337, January 1970, 338, February 1970, and 339, March 1970.

Spanish Government. Servicio Informativo Español. *España en el Sahara.* Madrid: 1968.

————. Dirección General de Promoción de Sahara. La acción de España en Africa. Madrid: 1971.

Tabernero Chacobo, Hermenegildo. "Nuestra provincia africana del Sahara," *Africa* (Madrid), Vol. XVII, No. 227, November 1960, pp. 5–8.

United Nations. *Ifni and Spanish Sahara: Working Paper Prepared by the Secretariat.* New York: UN Document A/AC. 109/L. 553, 1969.

————. *Spanish Sahara: Working Paper Prepared by the Secretariat.* New York: UN Document A/AC. 109/L. 634, 1970.

————. *Spanish Sahara: Working Paper Prepared by the Secretariat.* New York: UN Document A/AC. 109/L. 728, 1971.

————. *Spanish Sahara: Working Paper Prepared by the Secretariat.* New York: UN Document A/AC. 109/L. 822, 1972.

————. *Spanish Sahara: Working Paper Prepared by the Secretariat.* New York: UN Document A/AC. 109/L. 956, 1974.

Woldbert. "Spain as African Power," *Foreign Affairs* (New York), July 1946.

Administration

Arrojas, E. "Africa occidental española: 50 años de labor administrativa," *Africa* (Madrid), Vol. VIII, No. 117, September 1951, pp. 20–22.

Ballarín Marcial, Alberto. "Organización del régimen de propiedad en Africa occidental española," *Anuario de Derecho Civil* (Madrid), 1950, Vol. III.

Castilla, Ortega. "Se constituye la Asamblea General de Sahara," *Africa* (Madrid), Vol. XXIV, No. 310, October 1967, pp. 6–10.

Miguel, H. L. *Legislación de Sahara, años 1965 a 1973.* Madrid: Minerva, 1974.

Santamaría, Ramiro. "La Yemaa o Asamblea General de Sahara en marcha," *Africa* (Madrid), Vol. XXIII, No. 353, May 1971, pp. 23–26.

Spanish Government. Presidencia del Gobierno. "Decreto por el que se reorganiza el Gobierno General del Africa occidental española," *Boletín Oficial del Estado,* January 14th, 1958.

————. Presidencia del Gobierno. "Ley 8/1961, de 19 de abril, sobre organización y régimen jurídico de la Provincia de Sahara," *Boletín Oficial del Estado,* April 21, 1961.

————. Presidencia del Gobierno. "Decreto de 29 noviembre de 1962 por el que se aprueba el Ordenamiento de la Administración Local para la Provincia de Sahara," *Boletín Oficial de Estado,* December 12, 1962.

Tabernero Chacobo, Hermenegildo. "Organización y régimen jurídico de la Provincia de Sahara," *Africa* (Madrid), Vol. XVIII, No. 234, June 1961, pp. 2–5.

Yanguas Miravete, J. *Antecedentes históricos, organización político-administrativa y legislación de las provincias de Ifni y Sahara.* Madrid: 1961.

————. "El nuevo régimen de administración local de la provincia de Sahara," *Africa* (Madrid), Vol. XX, No. 253, January 1963, pp. 2–4.

"La Yemaa o Asamblea General del Sahara," *Africa* (Madrid), Vol. XXIV, No. 309, October 1967, pp. 17–19.

Liberation Movements: General

Hodges, Tony. "The Origins of Saharawi Nationalism," in *Third World Quarterly* (London), Vol. 5, No. 1, January 1983, pp. 28–57. Published in Dutch as *De Oorsprong van het Nationalisme van het Saharaanse Volk.* Nijmegen: Stichting Gastarbeidwinkel, 1985.

Liberation Movements: Harakat Tahrir Saguia el-Hamra wa Oued ed-Dahab

Abascal, Federico, Sol Gallego and Enrique Bustamante. "Sahara: Documentos secretos," *Cuadernos para el Diálogo* (Madrid), January 21, 1978.

Liberation Movements: The 1957–58 Rising

Boisboissel, H. de. *Situation au Sahara occidental à la veille de l'indépendance mauritanienne.* Paris: Centre de Hautes Etudes Administratives sur l'Afrique et l'Asie Moderne, Mémoire No. 3787, January 1963.

Chaffard, Georges. *Les carnets secrets de la décolonisation.* Vol. I. Paris: Calmann-Levy, 1965.

Cros, Lieut. *Les relations franco-espagnoles au Sahara occidental.* Paris: Centre de Hautes Etudes Administratives sur l'Afrique et l'Asie Moderne, Mémoire No. 3651, January 8, 1962.

Garnier, Christine. "Opération Ecouvillon," *La Revue des Deux Mondes* (Paris), November 1960, pp. 93–102.

Juega Boudon, J. "La aviación española en las operaciones en el Africa occidental," *Africa* (Madrid), 1958.

Pelissier, René. "Le mouvement nationaliste en Afrique espagnole," *Mois en Afrique,* July 1966, p. 72.

Liberation Movements: The Polisario Front

Balaguer, Soledad, and Rafael Wirth. *Frente Polisario: la última guerrilla.* Barcelona: Editorial Laia, 1976.

El-Ouali Mustapha Sayed. "Muthakkarat Mustapha el-Ouali Haoul al-Sahra," *Alikhtiar Athaouri* (Paris), No. 19, October 1977; No. 20, November 1977; No. 21, December 1977; No. 22, January 1978; No. 23, February 1978; and No. 25, April 1978.

Hacene-Djaballah, Belkacem. "Conflict in Western Sahara: A Study of Polisario as an Insurgency Movement," Ph.D. dissertation, Catholic University of America (Washington, D.C.), 1985, 260 pp.

Itani, Leila Badia. *El-Polisario: qaid wa thawra.* Beirut: Dar al-Masirah, 1978.

Polisario Front. *Notre peuple face aux tous derniers crimes de fascisme impuni.* 1974.

———. *El Pueblo Saharaui en lucha: documentos del Frente Popular para le Liberación de Saguia el Hamra y Río de Oro.* 1975.

———. "La situation dans la Saguiat el Hamra et Río de Oro," *20 Mai,* No. 17, supplement, March 1975, pp. 1–6.

———. *Le peuple sahraoui en lutte: documents du Front Polisario.* May 1975.

———. "Bilan de deux années de lutte de notre peuple," *20 Mai,* Year II, No. 21, July 1975, pp. 12–21.

———. "Manifeste politique du 10 mai 1973," *Sahara Libre,* May 20th, 1976; reprinted in *L'Annuaire de l'Afrique du*

Nord 1975 (Paris: CNRS, 1976). p. 985.

———. ''Memorandum adressé au Comité de Décolonisation de l'ONU'' (May 2nd, 1975), *L'Annuaire de l'Afrique du Nord 1975* (Paris: CNRS, 1976), pp. 985–994.

''Western Sahara: Who Is Polisario?'' *Africa Confidential* (London), Vol. 22, No. 2, January 14, 1981.

Moroccan and Mauritanian Policies

Balta, Paul. ''Le Sahara occidental suscite les convoitises de ses voisins,'' *Le Monde Diplomatique* (Paris), August 1975.

Bardos. ''Les relations hispano-marocains,'' *Confluent,* May 1956.

Carr, Richard Comyns. ''Spain and Morocco: A New Phase,'' *Contemporary Review,* Vol. 205, No. 1183, August 1964, pp. 409–412.

Daoud, Zakya. ''Le Maroc et les territoires frontaliers,'' *Lamalif* (Rabat), April 11, 1967.

———. ''Sahara: le prix du sang,'' *Lamalif* (Rabat), No. 41, August–September 1970.

El-Fassi, Allal. ''Livre blanc'' sur les questions mauritaniennes et sahariennes pour le Ministre cs Affaircs Etrangèrcs pour qu'il serve e document de base à la delégation marocaine à l'ONU chargée de débattre le contentieux territorial saharien. Rabat: 1960.

———. *Livre rouge avec documentaires.* Tangiers: Editions Peretti, 1961.

———. *La vérité sur les frontières marocaines.* Tangiers: Editions Peretti, 1961.

———. "Les revendications marocaines sur les territoires," *Le Monde Diplomatique* (Paris), January 1967, pp. 4–5.

———. *Pour la défense de l'unité du pays.* Rabat: 1972.

Gallagher, Charles F. *Morocco and Its Neighbours: Morocco and Spain.* New York: American Universities Field Staff (Field Staff Reports, North Africa Series, XIII, No. 2), March 1967.

Gaudio, Attilio. *Allal El Fassi, ou l'histoire de l'Istiqlal.* Paris: Alain Moreau, 1976.

Hassan II, King. *Discours de S. M. Hassan II, 3 mars 1974–3 mars 1975.* Rabat: Ministère d'Etat Chargè d'Information, 1975.

Husson, Philippe. *La question des frontières terrestres du Maroc.* Paris: Secrétariat Général du Gouvernement, Direction de la Documentation (Monograph No. 35 bis), 1960.

Ilal Amam. "Pour une véritable libération du Sahara occidental," *Maghreb An-Nidal* (Paris), No. 1, June 1975.

Istiqlal Party. "Mémoire du Parti de l'Istiqlal à la mission des Nations Unies (Mai 1975)," *L'Annuaire de l'Afrique du Nord 1975* (Paris: CNRS, 1976), pp. 977–979.

———, and Union Socialiste des Forces Populaires (USFP). "Déclaration du Parti de l'Istiqlal et de l'USFP," *L'Annuaire de L'Afrique du Nord 1975* (Paris: CNRS, 1976), pp. 979–980.

Lacouture, Jean. "Les revendications sahariennes du Maroc," *Le Monde Diplomatique* (Paris), May 1958, p. 5.

Lazrak, Rachid. *Le contentieux territorial entre le Maroc et l'Espagne.* Casablanca: Dar el Kitab, 1974.

Maestre, J. *El Sahara en la crisis de Marruecos y España.* Madrid: Akal, 1975.

Marchat, H. "Les frontières sahariennes du Maroc," *Politique Etrangère* (Paris), 1957, pp. 637ff.

―――. "Les frontières internationales du Maroc," *Le Monde Diplomatique* (Paris), September 1959.

Mokhtar Ould Daddah. *1957–1976: la réunification de la patrie: un objectif sacré pour le peuple mauritanien.* Nouakchott: Ministère d'Etat à l'Orientation Nationale, 1976.

Parti de Libération et du Socialisme. *Waqi iqlimuna al-sahrawi almughtaseb.* Casablanca: 1972.

Parti du Progrès et du Socialisme. "Résolution sur les territoires marocains occupés par l'Espagne (Congrès du PPS du 21–23/2/75)," *L'Annuaire de l'Afrique du Nord 1975* (Paris: CNRS, 1976), pp. 976–977.

Recoules, J. "Les frontières de l'état marocain," *L'Afrique et l'Asie*, 1960, No. 52.

―――. "Notes sur la frontière méridionale du Maroc," *L'Afrique et l'Asie,* 1963, No. 64.

"Les relations hispano-marocaines," *Maghreb* (Paris), No. 3, May–June 1964, pp. 10–12.

"La rétrocession d'Ifni et les relations hispano-marocaines," *Maghreb,* No. 33, May–June 1969, pp. 35–37.

Reyner, Anthony S. "Morocco's International Boundaries: A Factual Background," *The Journal of Modern African Studies,* Vol. I, 1963, No. 3, pp. 313–326.

Rézette, Robert. *The Western Sahara and the Frontiers of Morocco.* Paris: Nouvelles Editions Latines, 1975.

"Sahara espagnol: l'impatience du Maroc," *Revue Française d'Etudes Politiques Africaines* (Paris), August 1974.

"Sahara: les raisons d'une offensive," *Lamalif* (Rabat), No. 40, June–July 1970.

Tabernero Chacobo, Hermenegildo. "Libro blanco y libro verde," *Africa* (Madrid), 1961.

Trout, Frank E. *Morocco's Saharan Frontiers.* Geneva: Droz Publishers, 1969.

Union Socialiste des Forces Populaires (USFP). "Congrès de l'USFP du 10–12/1/75, extrait du rapport politique: le Sahara marocain," *L'Annuaire de l'Afrique du Nord 1975* (Paris: CNRS, 1976), pp. 975–976.

Yata, Ali. "La question des territoires marocains occupés par l'Espagne," *Vie Internationale,* January 13, 1962, p. 80.

———. *Le Sahara occidental marocain.* Casablanca: Al-Bayane, 1973.

Policies of the OAU and the UN

Menéndez del Valle, Emilio. "El Sahara en la OAU o la ceremonia de la confusión," *Cuadernos para el diálogo* (Madrid), No. 134, November 1974.

Organization of African Unity. *Resolution on the Territories under Spanish Domination.* OAU Council of Ministers, Addis Ababa, 1966. OAU Document CM/Res.82 (VII).

———. *Resolution on the Sahara under Spanish Domination.* OAU Council of Ministers, Addis Ababa, 1973. OAU Document CM/Res. 301 (XXI).

———. *Resolution on the Territory of the Sahara under Spanish Domination.* OAU Council of Ministers, Mogadiscio, 1974. Published in *U.S. Policy and the Conflict in Western Sahara,* U.S. Government Printing Office, Washington, D.C., 1979.

————. *Resolution on the So-Called Spanish Sahara.* OAU Assembly of Heads of State and Government, Kampala, 1975. OAU Document AHG/Res. 75 (XII). Also published in UN document A/10297, October 16, 1975.

United Nations. "Question of Ifni and Spanish Sahara" (UN General Assembly resolution 2072, December 16, 1965), in *General Assembly, Official Records: 20th Session,* Supplement 14, UN Document A/6014, pp. 59–60.

————. "Fernando Poo, Río Muni, Ifni and Spanish Sahara," *Yearbook of the United Nations 1964,* Vol. 18 (UN: New York, 1966), pp. 421–422.

————. "Question of Ifni and Spanish Sahara" (UN General Assembly resolution 2229, December 20, 1966), in *General Assembly, Official Records: 21st Session,* Supplement 16, UN Document A/6700/Rev. 1, pp. 72–73.

————. "Ifni and Spanish Sahara," *Yearbook of the United Nations 1965,* Vol. 19 (New York: UN, 1967), pp. 584–585.

————. "Question of Ifni and Spanish Sahara" (UN General Assembly resolution 2354, December 19, 1967), in *General Assembly, Official Records: 22nd Session,* Supplement 16, UN Document A/6716, pp. 53–54.

————. "Ifni and Spanish Sahara," *Yearbook of the United Nations 1966,* Vol. 20 (New York: UN, 1968), pp. 588–592.

————. "Question of Ifni and Spanish Sahara" (UN General Assembly resolution 2428, December 18, 1968), in *General Assembly, Official Records,* Supplement 18, UN Document A/7218, pp. 63–64.

————. "Ifni and Spanish Sahara," *Yearbook of the United Nations 1967,* Vol. 21 (New York: UN, 1969), pp. 676–680.

————. "Question of Spanish Sahara" (UN General Assembly resolution 2591, December 16, 1969), in *General Assembly,*

Official Records: 24th Session, Supplement 30, UN Document A/7630, pp. 73–74.

———. "Ifni and Spanish Sahara," *Yearbook of the United Nations 1968,* Vol. 22 (New York: UN, 1971), pp. 750–755.

———. "Ifni and Spanish Sahara," *Yearbook of the United Nations 1969,* Vol. 23 (New York: UN, 1972), pp. 661–666.

———. "Question of Spanish Sahara," (UN General Assembly resolution 2711, December 14, 1970), in *Yearbook of the United Nations 1970,* Vol. 24 (New York: UN, 1972), pp. 723–724.

———. "Spanish Sahara," *Yearbook of the United Nations 1970,* Vol. 24 (New York: UN, 1972), pp. 720–724.

———. "Spanish Sahara," *Yearbook of the United Nations 1971,* Vol. 25 (New York: UN, 1974), p. 537.

———. "Spanish Sahara," *Yearbook of the United Nations 1972,* Vol. 26 (New York: UN, 1975), pp. 569–570.

———. "Question of Spanish Sahara" (UN General Assembly resolution 2983, December 14, 1972), in *Yearbook of the United Nations 1972,* Vol. 26 (New York: UN, 1975), pp. 579–580.

———. "Spanish Sahara," *Yearbook of the United Nations 1973,* Vol. 27 (New York: UN, 1976), pp. 702–704.

———. "Question of Spanish Sahara" (UN General Assembly resolution 3162, December 14, 1973), in *Yearbook of the United Nations 1973,* Vol. 27 (New York: UN, 1976), pp. 716–717.

———. "Spanish Sahara," *Yearbook of the United Nations 1974,* Vol. 28 (New York: UN, 1977), pp. 794–796.

————. "Question of Spanish Sahara" (UN General Assembly resolution 3292, December 13, 1974), in *Yearbook of the United Nations 1974,* Vol. 28 (New York: UN, 1977), pp. 805–806.

5. JURIDICAL

Barbier, Maurice. "L'avis consultatif de la Cour de la Haye sur le Sahara occidental," *Revue Juridique et Politique, Indépendance et Coopération,* 1976, No. 1, pp. 67–103.

————. "Le Sahara occidental et le droit international," in *Sahara occidental, un peuple et ses droits, Colloque de Massy, 1 et 2 avril 1978,* Paris: L'Harmattan, 1978.

Bennoune, Mohamed. "L'affaire du 'Sahara occidental' devant la Cour Internationale de Justice," *Revue Juridique, Politique et Economique du Maroc* (Rabat), December 1976, pp. 81–106.

Byman, Abigail. "The March on the Spanish Sahara:; A Test of International Law," *Denver Journal of International Law and Politics,* 6, Spring 1976, pp. 95–121.

Carrillo Salcedo, Juan Antonio. "Libre determinación de los pueblos e integridad territorial de los estados en el dictamen del Tribunal Internacional de Justicia sobre el Sahara occidental," *Revista Española de Derecho Internacional* (Madrid), Vol. XXIX, 1976, No. 1, pp. 33–49.

Chappez, Jean. "L'avis consultatif de la Cour Internationale de Justice du 16 octobre 1975 dans l'affaire du Sahara occidental," *Revue Générale de Droit International Public* (Paris), Vol. 80, No. 4, October–December 1976, pp. 1133–1185.

Flory, Maurice. "L'avis de la Cour Internationale de Justice sur le Sahara occidental," *Annuaire Français de Droit International* (Paris), Vol. XXI, 1975, pp. 253–277.

Les fondements juridiques et institutionels de la République arabe sahraouie démocratique. Actes du colloque international de juristes tenu à l'Assemblée Nationale, Paris, les 20 et 21 octobre 1984. Paris: L'Harmattan, 1984.

Franck, Thomas M. "The Stealing of the Sahara," *American Journal of International Law,* Vol. 70, No. 4, October 1976, pp. 694–721.

————, and Paul Hoffman. "The Right of Self-Determination in Very Small Places," *New York University Journal of International Law and Politics,* Vol. 8, No. 4, Winter 1976.

International Court of Justice. *Western Sahara, Advisory Opinion of 16 October 1975.* The Hague: 1975.

"International Court of Justice Does Not Find 'Legal Ties' of Such a Nature to Affect Self-Determination in the Decolonization Process of Western Sahara," *Texas International Law Journal,* Vol. 11 (1976).

Janis, Mark W. "The International Court of Justice: Advisory Opinion on the Western Sahara," *Harvard International Law Journal,* 17, Summer 1976, pp. 609–621.

"The March on the Spanish Sahara—A Test of International Law," *Journal of International Law and Politics,* Vol. 6 (1976).

Moroccan Government. *Le Sahara occidental devant la Cour Internationale de Justice. Mémoire présenté par le Royaume du Maroc.* Rabat: 1975.

Mouvement de Résistance pour la libération des Territoires sous Domination Espagnole (MOREHOB). *Mémoire adressé á l'attention de la Cour Internationale de Justice.* MOREHOB, January 1975.

Naldi, J. "The Organization of African Unity and the Saharan Arab Democratic Republic," *Journal of African Law,* Vol. 26, No. 2 (1982), pp. 152–162.

Pazzanita, Anthony G. "Legal Aspects of Membership in the Organization of African Unity: The Case of the Western Sahara," *Case Western Reserve Journal of International Law,* Vol. 17, No. 1, Winter 1985, pp. 123–158.

————. "Western Sahara: Legal Aspects of the Dispute," *Bulletin* (Association of Concerned Africa Scholars, Los Angeles), No. 23, Spring 1988, pp. 4–5.

Polisario Front. "La Cour Internationale de Justice et les ambiguités sur la question du Sahara," *20 Mai,* No. 18, April 1975, pp. 7–11.

Schulman, Jeffrey. "The Legal Issues of the War in Western Sahara," in *US Policy and the Conflict in the Western Sahara,* Washington, D.C.: U.S. Government Printing Office, 1979.

Shaw, Malcolm. "The *Western Sahara* Case," in *British Year Book of International Law,* 1978, pp. 119–153.

Smith, Mark A. Jr. "Sovereignty over Unoccupied Territories—The Western Sahara Decision," *Case Western Reserve Journal of International Law,* Vol. 9 (1977), pp. 135–159.

Vallée, Charles. "L'affaire du Sahara occidental devant la Cour de La Haye," *Maghreb-Machrek* (Paris), No. 71, January–March 1976, pp. 47–55.

Vance, Robert T. Jr. "Recognition as an Affirmative Step in the Decolonization Process: The Case of Western Sahara," *Yale Journal of World Public Order,* Vol. 7, No. 45 (1980), pp. 45–87.

6. POLITICAL

From Spanish to Moroccan-Mauritanian Rule and Partition

Aherdan. *Le masse . . . ira, ou le journal d'un marcheur.* Casablanca: Editions Gabriel Gauthey, 1976.

Cola Alberich, Julio. "España y el Sahara occidental. Antecedentes de una descolonización," *Revista de Política Internacional* (Madrid), Vol. 154, No. 77, pp. 9–52.

Daoud, Zakya. "Notre marche et leurs démarches," *Lamalif* (Rabat), No. 74, November 1975.

"Declaration of Principles on Western Sahara by Spain, Morocco and Mauritania" (The Madrid Agreement of November 14, 1975). Published as Annex III to UN Document S/11880, November 19th, 1975, in *Security Council, Official Records, 30th Year, Supplement for October–December* (New York: UN, 1976), p. 41.

Dessens, Paul. "Le litige du Sahara occidental," *Maghreb–Machrek* (Paris), No. 71, January–March 1976, pp. 29–46.

Hassan II, King. *Discours de S. M. Hassan II. La lutte pour la parachèvement de l'intégrité territoriale.* Rabat: Ministère d'Etat Chargé de l'Information, 1975.

———. *Conférence de presse de S. M. Hassan II sur la marche verte et le Sahara, 25 novembre 1975.* Rabat: Ministère d'Etat Chargé de l'Information, 1975.

———. *Le Défi.* Paris: Albin Michel, 1976.

———. *The Memoirs of King Hassan II of Morocco.* London: Macmillan, 1978.

Ilal-Amam. "La marche et les manoeuvres de Hassan II," *Maghreb An-Nidal* (Paris), No. 2, November 1975.

———. "Néo-colonialisme, phosphates et Sahara," *Maghreb An-Nidal* (Paris), No. 3, January 1976.

Laroui, Abdallah. *La Marche Verte.* Paris: Editions SEFA, 1976.

Lopezarias, Germán, and César de la Lama. *Morir en el Sahara.* Bilbao: Ediciones AQ, 1975.

Manfredi Cano, Domingos. "El Sahara desde tres miradores," *Africa* (Madrid), Vol. XXVII, No. 407, November 1975, pp. 19–22.

———. "El Sahara en noviembre," *Africa* (Madrid), Vol. XXVII, No. 408, December 1975, pp. 48–54.

———. "Deciembre en el Sahara," *Africa* (Madrid), Vol. XXVIII, No. 409, January 1976, pp. 21–23.

———. "Sahara: Enero," *Africa* (Madrid), Vol. XXVIII, No. 410, February 1976, pp. 18–23.

———. "Sahara: Febrero," *Africa* (Madrid), Vol. XXVIII, No. 411, March 1976, pp. 18–26.

Moroccan Government. "Dahir No. 1–76–380 du 14 rebia 1396 (16 avril 1976) portant ratification et publication de la convention relative au trace de la frontière d'Etat établie entre la République Islamique de Mauritanie et le Royaume du Maroc, faite à Rabat, le 12 rebia 1396 (14 avril 1976)," *Bulletin Officiel du Royaume du Maroc,* No. 3311 bis, April 16, 1976, p. 500. Also in *L'Annuaire de l'Afrique du Nord 1976* (Paris: CNRS, 1977).

Organisation 23 Mars. "La marche verte," *23 Mars* (Paris), April 1976.

Romero, Gerardo Mariñas. *El Sahara y la legión.* Madrid: San Martin, 1988.

Sahara, 14 nov., 1975: la traición. Madrid: Asociación de Amigos del Sahara, 1980.

Salim, Salim Ahmed. "The Question of Spanish Sahara," *Objective-Justice* (New York, UN), Vol. VII, No. 4, October–December 1975, pp. 2–7.

Segura Palomares, Juan. *El Sahara, razón de una sinrazón.* Barcelona: Ediciones Acervo, 1976.

United Nations. Security Council resolutions 377 (October 22, 1975), 379 (November 2, 1975) and 380 (November 6, 1975) on the Green March, in *Yearbook of the United Nations 1975* (New York: UN, 1977). Vol. XXVIII, p. 187.

―――. "Question of Spanish Sahara" (General Assembly resolutions 3458A and B, December 10, 1975), in *Yearbook of the United Nations 1975* (New York: UN, 1977), Vol. XXVIII, pp. 188–190.

Waldheim, Kurt. "Report of the Secretary-General in Pursuance of Security Council Resolution 377 (1975)," UN Document S/11863, October 31, 1975, in *Security Council, Official Records,* 30th Year, Supplement for October–December 1975 (New York: UN, 1976), pp. 27–28.

―――. "Report of the Secretary-General in Pursuance of Security Council Resolution 379 (1975)," UN Document S/11874, November 8, 1975, in *Security Council, Official Records,* 30th Year, Supplement for October–December 1975 (New York: UN, 1976), pp. 33–35.

―――. "Third Report of the Secretary-General in Pursuance of Security Council Resolution 379 (1975)," UN Document S/11880, November 19, 1975, in *Security Council, Official Records,* 30th Year, Supplement for October–December 1975 (New York: UN, 1976), pp. 40–41.

Weiner, Jerome B. "The Green March in Historical Perspective," *The Middle East Journal* (Washington, D.C.), Vol. 33, No. 1, Winter 1979, pp. 20–33.

White, C. C. "The Green March," *Army Quarterly and Defense Journal* (Tavistock, Devon), 106, July 1976, pp. 351–358.

The War Between Polisario, Morocco, and Mauritania

General

Abramson, Gary. "Saharan Statesmanship," *Africa Report* (New York), Vol. XXXIV, No. 2, March–April, 1989.

Aguirre, José Ramón Diego. *Historia del Sahara español: la verdad de una traición*. Madrid: Kaydeda, 1988.

Assidon, Elsa. *Sahara occidental, un enjeu pour le nord-ouest africain*. Paris: François Maspéro, 1978.

Association des Amis de la République Arabe Sahraouie Démocratique. *Le dossier du Sahara occidental*. Paris: 1976.

Barbier, Maurice. "L'avenir du Sahara espagnol," *Politique Etrangère* (Paris), 1975, No. 4, pp. 353–380.

————. *Le conflit du Sahara occidental*. Paris: Editions L'Harmattan, 1982.

Bayart, J. F. "Le conflit du Sahara occidental," *Revue Française d'Etudes Politiques Africaines* (Paris), No. 158, February 1979.

Beam, Alex. "Polisario War in the Sahara," *The Nation,* January 21, 1978.

Benabdellah, Abdelaziz. *Vérité sur le Sahara*. Roanne, France: Horvath, 1977.

Bontems, Claude. *La guerre du Sahara occidental*. Paris: Presses Universitaires de France, 1984.

Bookmiller, Robert J. "The Western Sahara: Future Prospects," *American-Arab Affairs,* No. 37 (Summer 1991), pp. 64–76.

Chenillier-Gendreau, Monique. "La question du Sahara occidental," *Annuaire du Tiers Monde,* Vol. II, 1976, pp. 270–280.

Colin, Jean-Pierre. "Réflexions sur l'avenir du Sahara occidental," *Revue Française d'Etudes Politiques Africaines* (Paris), Nos. 152–153, August–September 1978.

Costa Morata, Pedro. "Reivindicación de la causa saharaui," series of five articles, *El País* (Madrid), August 29, 30, and 31, and September 1 and 2, 1978.

Crozier, Brian. "Spanish Sahara," *Annual of Power and Conflict 1975–76,* London, Institute for the Study of Conflict, 1976.

Damis, John. "The Moroccan-Algerian Conflict over the Western Sahara," *The Maghreb Review* (London), Vol. IV, No. 2, March–April 1979, pp. 49–57.

———. *Conflict in Northwest Africa: The Western Sahara Dispute.* Stanford, Calif.: Hoover Institution Press, 1983.

———. "The Western Sahara Conflict: Myths and Realities," *The Middle East Journal* (Washington, D.C.), Vol. 37, No. 2 (1983), pp. 169–179.

———. "The O.A.U. and Western Sahara," in Yassin El-Ayouty and I. William Zartman, (eds.), *The O.A.U. After Twenty Years.* New York: Praeger Publishers, 1985, pp. 273–296.

———. "The Western Sahara Dispute as a Source of Regional Conflict in North Africa," in Halim Barakat (ed.), *Contemporary North Africa: Issues of Development and Integration.* Center for Contemporary Arab Studies, Washington, D.C., and Croom Helm, London, 1985, pp. 138–153.

———. "Morocco and the Western Sahara," *Current History,* Vol. 89, No. 546, April 1990, pp. 165–168, 184–186.

———. "The U.N. Settlement Plan for the Western Sahara: Problems and Prospects," *Middle East Policy,* Vol. 1, No. 2 (1992), pp. 36–46.

Daure-Jouvin, Christine. "Le Sahara occidental: un procesus révolutionnaire dans l'occident arabe," *Les Temps Modernes* (Paris), July 1977.

De Piniés, Jaime. *La descolonización del Sahara: un tema sin concluir.* Madrid: Espasa-Calpe, 1990.

Dessens, Paul. "Le problème du Sahara occidental trois ans après le dèpart des espagnols," *Maghreb-Machrek* (Paris), No. 83, January–March 1979, pp. 73–86.

Fédération Internationale des Droits de l'Homme. *Sahara occidental: mission d'observation de la FIDH effectuée du 26 au 31 octobre 1976.* Paris: FIDH, 1976.

Fessard de Foucault, Bertrand. "La question du Sahara espagnol," *Revue Française d'Etudes Politiques Africaines* (Paris), 10th Year, No. 119, November 1975, and No. 120, December 1975.

Goytisolo, Juan. *An Eloquent Testimony: Atlantic Sahara, Two Years Later.* Rabat: Ministry of Information, 1978.

Gretton, John. *Western Sahara, the Fight for Self-Determination.* London: Anti-Slavery Society, 1976.

Grimaud, Nicole. "Sahara occidental: une issue possible?" *Maghreb/Machrek* (Paris), No. 121, July–September 1988, pp. 89–98.

Guillerez, Bernard. "L'Afrique en crise de la Corne orientale au Sahara occidental," *Défense Nationale* (Paris), Vol. XXXIII, November 1977, pp. 160–164.

Harrell-Bond, Barbara. *The Struggle for the Western Sahara: Part I: Prelude.* Hanover, N.H.: American Universities Field Staff (Field Staff Reports, No. 37), 1981.

———. *The Struggle for the Western Sahara: Part II: Contemporary Politics.* Hanover, N.H.: American Universities Field Staff (Field Staff Reports, No. 38), 1981.

———. *The Struggle for the Western Sahara: Part III: The Sahrawi People.* Hanover, N.H.: American Universities Field Staff (Field Staff Reports, No. 39), 1981.

Hinz, Manfred O. "The Right to Self-Determination of Western Sahara: The Difficult Road of the Sahraoui People," in *Western Sahara and the Struggle of the Sahraoui People*, Rome, International League for the Rights and Liberation of Peoples, 1978.

———— (ed). *Le droit à l'autodétermination du Sahara occidental*. Bonn: Progress Dritte Welt Verlag, 1978.

Hodges, Tony. "Western Sahara: French Prisoners Released," *Africa Research Bulletin* (Exeter), Political Series, Vol. 14, No. 12, January 15, 1978, pp. 4688–4693.

————. "Western Sahara, the Escalating Confrontation," *Africa Report* (New York), Vol. XIII, No. 2, March–April 1978, pp. 4–9.

———— "Western Sahara: Fighting Escalates as Repercussions Grow," *Africa Research Bulletin* (Exeter), Political Series, Vol. 16, No. 1, February 15, 1979, pp. 5140–5145.

———— "Western Sahara: War's Changing Fortunes," *Africa Research Bulletin* (Exeter), Political Series, Vol. 16, No. 11, December 15, 1979, pp. 5477–5483.

————. "Western Sahara: War Enters Sixth Year," *Africa Research Bulletin* (Exeter), Political Series, Vol. 17, No. 11, December 15, 1980, pp. 5869–5875.

————. "Western Sahara: The Sixth Year of War," in Colin Legum (ed.), *Africa Contemporary Record,* 1980–81, New York: Africana Publishing Company, 1981, pp. A80–A93.

————. "Whither Western Sahara?" *Africa Research Bulletin* (Exeter), Political Series, Vol. 19, No. 2, February 1–28, 1982, pp. 6353–6362.

————. "The Endless War," *Africa Report* (New York), Vol. XXVII, No. 4, July–August 1982, pp. 4–11.

————. "The Western Sahara File," *Third World Quarterly,* Vol. 6, No. 1, January 1984, pp. 74–116.

————. "The Second Decade of War," *Africa Report* (New York), Vol. XXXI, No. 2, March–April 1986.

Hottinger, Arnold. "La lutte pour le Sahara occidental," *Politique Etrangère* (Paris), Vol. 45, No. 1, March 1980, pp. 167–180.

Houser, George M. *No One Can Stop the Rain.* New York: The Pilgrim Press, 1989.

Hultman, Tami. "The Struggle for Western Sahara," *Issue,* Vol. III, No. 1, Spring 1977, pp. 27–31.

International Institute for Strategic Studies. "The Spanish Sahara," *Strategic Survey 1975* (London: 1976).

―――. "The Maghreb: Implications of the Sahara War," *Strategic Survey 1979* (London: 1980).

Iseman, Frederick. "The War in the Sahara," *Harper's* (New York), September 1980, pp. 41–56.

Jacquier, Bernard. "L'autodétermination du Sahara espagnol," *Revue Générale de Droit International Public* (Paris), Vol. 78, No. 3, July–September 1974, pp. 683–728.

Jallaud, Thomas. "Western Saharan Conflict," *New African Yearbook 1980,* edited by Richard Synge (London: International Communications, 1980).

"The King's Arms," *Africa News,* Vol. 28, No. 4, November 2, 1987, pp. 1–3.

Kühlein, Conrad. *Der Westsahara-konflikt: Vorgeschichte, Entkolonisierung, Regionalkonflict und Lösungsvorstellungen.* Ebenhausen, West Germany: Stiftung Wissenschaft und Politik, 1979.

Laipson, Ellen. "Heating Up the Sahara War," *The Washington Quarterly* (Winter 1982), pp. 199–202.

Lalutte, Pauline. "Spanish Sahara: Notes Towards an Analysis," *MERIP Reports* (Washington, D.C.), No. 45, March 1976.

Lawless, Richard, and Laila Monahan (eds.). *War and Refugees: The Western Sahara Conflict*. London and New York: Pinter Publishers, 1987.

Lewis, William H. "War in the Western Sahara," in Stephanie G. Neumann and Robert E. Harkavy (eds.), *The Lesson of Recent Wars in the Third World, Vol. I: Approaches and Case Studies*. Lexington, Mass.: Lexington Books, 1985.

————. "Morocco and the Western Sahara," *Current History*, Vol. 84, No. 502, May 1985, pp. 213–216.

Lippert, Anne. "The Human Costs of War in Western Sahara," *Africa Today*, Vol. 34, No. 3, Fall 1987, pp. 47–60.

————. "Western Sahara: An Introduction to the Struggle," in *Bulletin* (Association of Concerned Africa Scholars, Los Angeles), No. 23, Spring 1988, pp. 2–3.

Maddy-Weitzman, Bruce. "Conflict and Conflict Management in the Western Sahara: Is the Endgame Near?" *Middle East Journal* (Washington, D.C.), Vol. 45, No. 4 (Autumn 1991), pp. 594–607.

Markham, James M. "King Hassan's Quagmire," *New York Times Magazine*, April 27, 1980, pp. 116, 118, 120–125.

Marks, Jon. "Africa's Forgotten War," *Africa Report* (New York), Vol. XXXII, No. 5, September–October 1987.

Marks, Thomas A. "Spanish Sahara: Background to Conflict," *African Affairs* (London), Vol. 75, No. 298, January 1976, pp. 3–13.

Mercer, John. "Confrontation in the Western Sahara," *The World Today* (London: Royal Institute of International Affairs), Vol. XXXII, No. 6, June 1976, pp. 230–239.

Moroccan Government. "Western Sahara: The Challenge of Peace," *Time*, North American Edition, December 4, 1989,

8-page Special Advertising Section; includes interview with Omar Hadrami.

Mortimer, Robert A. "Western Sahara: The Diplomatic Perspectives," *Africa Report,* Vol. XXIII, No. 2, March–April 1978.

Moulahid, Jamil. "Les Sahraouis et le phosphate," *Esprit* (Paris), No. 4, April 1976, pp. 779–803.

Nande (D. Shain). *Sahara vencerá!* Las Palmas de Gran Canaria: Edican, 1977.

Neuberger, Benyamin. *National Self-Determination in Postcolonial Africa.* Boulder, Colo.: Lynne Rienner Publishers, 1986.

Parker, Richard B. *North Africa: Regional Tensions and Strategic Concerns.* New York: Praeger Publishers, 1987.

Pazzanita, Anthony G. "A Plebiscite in Western Sahara?" in *Bulletin* (Association of Concerned Africa Scholars, Los Angeles), No. 24, Summer 1988, pp. 27–30.

Price, David Lynn. "Morocco and the Sahara: Conflict and Development," *Conflict Studies* (London), No. 88, October 1977.

———. *The Western Sahara.* Washington, D.C.: The Washington Papers, No. 63, Center for Strategic and International Studies, Georgetown University, 1979.

Ramchadani, R. R. "Conflict in the Horn of Africa and Western Sahara," *IDSA Journal,* Vol. IX, No. 4, April–June 1977, pp. 449–473.

Reis, Pierre, and Hugues Vega. "Struggle of the Saharan People," *Imprecor* (Paris), October 13, 1977.

Répression dans les zones occupées du Sahara occidental. Geneva: Comité Suisse de Soutien au Peuple Sahraoui, 1980.

Le Sahara occidental et la révolution dans l'occident arabe. Paris: Ligue Communiste Révolutionnaire, 1977.

Saxena, Suresh Chandra. *The Liberation War in Western Sahara.* New Delhi: Vidya Publishers, 1981.

————. *Self-Determination in Western Sahara: Last Chance for Morocco.* New Delhi: Vidya Publishers, 1982.

Schissel, Howard. "Saharan Sandstorm Blows On," *Africa Report* (New York), Vol. XXVIII, No. 3, May–June 1983.

Sélection d'articles parus dans la presse concernant le Sahara occidental. 4 volumes. Paris: Polisario Front, Vol. I, 1976; Vol. II, 1976; Vol. III, 1977; Vol. IV, 1978.

Sidler, Peter. "Trouble in the Sahara," *Swiss Review of World Affairs* (Zurich), Vol. XXVII, No. 9, December 1977, pp. 9–11.

Smith de Cherif, Teresa K. "Peace in Western Sahara?" *Africa Today,* Vol. 38, No. 4 (4th Quarter, 1991), pp. 49–58.

United Nations. *Western Sahara: Working Paper Prepared by the Secretariat.* New York: UN document A/AC.109/L.1185, July 22, 1977.

————. *Western Sahara: Working Paper Prepared by the Secretariat.* New York: UN document A/AC.109/L.1266, 1978.

Urrutia, Leonardo. *Sahara: diez años de guerra.* Zaragoza: Trazo Editorial, 1983.

Villar, Francisco. *El proceso de autodeterminación del Sahara.* Vanencia: Torres, 1982.

Weexsteen, Raoul. "La question du Sahara occidental," *L'annuaire de l'Afrique du Nord 1976* (Paris: CNRS, 1977), pp. 256–275.

Western Sahara and the Struggle of the Sahraoui People for Self-Determination. Rome: International League for the Rights and Liberation of Peoples, 1978.

"Western Sahara: Background to the Conflict," *Africa Currents* (London), No. 10, Winter 1977–78, pp. 15–18.

"Western Sahara: Inching Towards Peace," *Africa News,* Vol. 31, No. 11, May 29, 1989, pp. 2–3.

"Western Sahara: Desert Warriors," *Africa Events,* Vol. 6, No. 5, May 1990, pp. 21–31.

"Western Sahara: Outside the Wall," *Africa News,* Vol. 28, No. 5, November 16, 1987, p. 5.

"Year Ends with Renewed War in Western Sahara," *Africa News,* Vol. 32, Nos. 7 and 8, December 4, 1989, pp. 1–3.

Zartman, I. William. *Conflict in the Sahara.* Washington, D.C., Middle East Institute, Middle East Problem Paper No. 19, 1979.

———. "Foreign Relations of North Africa," in Gerald J. Bender (ed.), *Annals of the American Academy of Political and Social Science* (Newbury Park, Calif.: Sage Publications), No. 489, January 1987.

———. *Ripe for Resolution: Conflict and Intervention in Africa.* Oxford and New York: Oxford University Press, 1989.

Zoubir, Yahia. "The Western Sahara Conflict: Regional and International Dimensions," *Journal of Modern African Studies* (Chagford, Devon), Vol. 28, No. 2 (June 1990), pp. 225–243.

Zoubir, Yahia, and Daniel Volman (eds.), *International Dimensions of the Western Sahara Conflict.* Westport, Conn.: Praeger Publishers, 1993.

Spanish Policy

Goytisolo, Juan. "El Sahara y la izquierda española," *Triunfo* (Madrid), July 10, 1976.

Massip Hidalgo, Antonio. "L'Espagne et le Sahara occidental," in *Sahara occidental, un peuple et ses droits, Colloque de Massy, 1 et 2 avril 1978,* Paris: L'Harmattan, 1978.

Míguez, Alberto. "Le Sahara occidental et la politique maghrébine de l'Espagne," *Politique Etrangère* (Paris), Vol. 43, 1978, No. 2, pp. 173–180.

Naylor, Phillip C. "Spain and France and the Decolonization of Western Sahara: Parity and Paradox 1975–1987," *Africa Today,* Vol. 34, No. 3, Fall 1987, pp. 7–16.

Partido Socialista Obrero Español and Polisario Front. "Communiqué commun du Front Polisario et du Parti Socialiste Ouvrier Espagnol, Madrid, 8 septembre 1977 (extraits)," *L'Annuaire de l'Afrique du Nord 1977* (Paris: CNRS, 1978), pp. 909–910.

Saharawi National Council. "Lettre du Conseil National Sahraoui au Président du Congrès des Deputés espagnols, relative à la libération des pêcheurs espagnols, le 26 novembre 1977," *L'Annuaire de l'Afrique du Nord 1977* (Paris: CNRS, 1978), p. 910.

Algerian Policy

Algerian Government. "Position of the Algerian Government," Annex to UN Document S/11881, November 20, 1975, in *Security Council, Official Records,* 30th Year, Supplement for October–December 1975 (New York: UN, 1977), p. 42.

———. "Memorandum from the Algerian Government of the Question of Western Sahara," *Security Council, Official Records,* 31st Year, Supplement for January–March 1976 (New York: UN, 1977), pp. 87–88.

Ben Hamouda, Boualem. *La question du Sahara occidental et le droit international.* Algiers: 1976.

Grimaud, Nicole. *La politique extérieure de l'Algérie.* Paris: Karthala, 1984.

Laroui, Abdallah. *L'Algérie et le Sahara marocain.* Casablanca: Editions Serar, 1976.

Nelson, Harold D. (ed.). *Algeria: A Country Study.* Foreign Area Studies, American University. Washington, D.C.: U.S. Government Printing Office, 1985.

"Sahara occidental: se conformer au droit," *Révolution Africaine* (Algiers), No. 810, November 6, 1975.

Mauritanian Policy

Ahmed-Baba Miské. "Lettre adréssée au peuple mauritanien en août 1975 par A.B. Miské situant le rôle que celui-ci devrait jouer dans la question sahraouie," in *Dossier du Sahara occidental,* Paris; Association des Amis de la République Arabe Sahraouie Démocratique, 1976.

Doyle, Mark. "Nouakchott's New Nationalism," *Africa Report* (New York), Vol. XXXIV, No. 5, September–October 1989.

Handloff, Robert E. (ed.). *Mauritania: A Country Study.* Federal Research Division, Library of Congress. Washington, D.C.: U.S. Government Printing Office, 1990.

Hodges, Tony. "Mauritania After the Coup," *Africa Report* (New York), November–December 1978, pp. 13–18.

Mauritanian Government, and Polisario Front. "Accord de paix sahraoui-mauritanien" (August 5, 1979), in *La République Arabe Sahraouie Démocratique,* SADR Department of Information, 1980.

Mohamed Abdelaziz. "Lettre ouverte adressée aux frères mauritaniens par le secrétaire général du Front Polisario, Mohamed Abdelaziz, le 9 juin 1977," *L'Annuaire de l'Afrique du Nord 1977* (Paris: CNRS, 1978), pp. 901–903.

Pazzanita, Anthony G. "Mauritania's Foreign Policy: The Search for Protection," *Journal of Modern African Studies* (Chagford, Devon), Vol. 30, No. 2 (1992).

Schissel, Howard. "Taya at the Helm," *Africa Report* (New York), Vol. XXXI, No. 4, July–August 1986.

Taton, Robert. "Le Sahara occidental vu du coté mauritanien," *Europe-Outremer* (Paris), 53rd Year, No. 549, October 1975.

———. "Le Sahara occidental vu du côté mauritanien," *Europe-Outremer* (Paris), 55th Year, No. 574, November 1977.

Moroccan Policy

Abbas, Tariq. "Maroc: Crise de l'Etat compradore, Sahara, et issue révolutionnaire," in *Les Etats du Maghreb et le Sahara occidental,* Dossier la Brèche, Geneva, 1978.

Alikhtiar Athaouri. "Sahara marocain: Visées impérialistes et libération authentique," *Option Révolutionnaire* (Paris), February 1976.

———. *Hiwar min ajil ijad badeel taqadummi lilwadi al-rahin fil maghreb al-arabi.* Paris: 1977.

Amnesty International. *Morocco: "Disappearances" of People of Western Saharan Origin.* London: Amnesty International, November 1990.

Baroudi, Abdallah. "Le complot 'saharien' contre le peuple marocain et son armée," *Les Temps Modernes* (Paris), Vol. XXXIV, No. 394, May 1979, pp. 1805–1842.

Ben Abdellah, Abdellatif. "Laroui et la question du Sahara occidental," *Maghreb An-Nidal* (Paris), No. 6, December 1977, pp. 19–29.

Boucetta, M'Hamed. "M'Hamed Boucetta, Minister of State for Foreign Affairs of Morocco, Interviewed by Anthony J. Hughes," *Africa Report* (New York), Vol. XXVII, No. 4, July–August 1982, pp. 12–14.

Chaoui, Mohamed. "Sahara: poursuivre l'offensive," *Lamalif* (Rabat), No. 110, November 1979.

Daoud, Zakya. "Sahara: après l'automne, l'hiver," *Lamalif* (Rabat), No. 100, September–October 1978.

———. "Sahara: o temps, étends ton vol," *Lamalif* (Rabat), No. 101, October–November 1978.

Fairmont, Robert. "Western Sahara: Morocco's Troubled Monarch," *Africa Report* (New York), Vol. XXIII, No. 2, March–April 1978, pp. 15–20.

Henderson, George. "Oujda on the Rocks," *Africa Report* (New York), Vol. XXXI, No. 6, November–December 1986.

Hodges, Tony. "After the Treaty of Oujda," *Africa Report* (New York), Vol. XXIX, No. 6, November–December 1984.

Ilal-Amam. "A propos des 'spécificités' *Maghreb An-Nidal* (Paris), No. 4, April–May 1976.

———. "Déclaration de la délégation de l'organisation Marxiste-Léniniste Ilal-Amam au troisième congrés (du Front Polisario)," *Maghreb An-Nidal* (Paris), No. 5, October–November 1976.

Maren, Michael. "From the Moroccan-Controlled Western Sahara," *Africa Report* (New York), Vol. XXIX, No. 6, November–December 1984.

Moroccan Government. *The Moroccan Sahara and the Reality Behind Algeria's Attitude*. Rabat: October 1976.

————. Ministry of State for Foreign Affairs. *The Legitimate Decolonization of Atlantic Western Sahara and the Plots of Algerian Rulers Aiming at Hegemony in North-Western Africa*. Rabat: 1977. Also published in UN Document E/CN.4/Sub.2/391, June 15, 1977.

Morrison, Godfrey. "The King's Gambit," *Africa Report* (New York), Vol. XXIX, No. 6, November–December 1984.

Nelson, Harold D. (ed.). *Morocco: A Country Study*. Foreign Area Studies, American University. Washington, D.C.: U.S. Government Printing Office, 1985.

"Sahara: la guerre pour avoir la paix," *Lamalif* (Rabat), No. 92, November 1977.

"Sahara: les anomalies du conflit," *Lamalif* (Rabat), No. 109, October 1979.

Tessler, Mark. "Politics in Morocco: The Monarch, the War, and the Opposition. Hanover, N.H.: American Universities Field Staff (Field Staff Reports, No. 47), 1981.

————. *Continuity and Change in Moroccan Politics*. Hanover, N.H.: American Universities Field Staff (Field Staff Reports, Nos. 1 and 2), 1984.

————. *Explaining the "Surprises" of King Hassan II*. Hanover, N.H.: American Universities Field Staff (Field Staff Reports, Nos. 38–40), 1986.

Union Socialiste des Forces Populaires (USFP). *For a Just and Durable Peace in Maghreb*. Casablanca: Editions Maghrébines, undated.

Vellas, Pierre. "La diplomatie marocaine dans l'affaire du Sahara occidental," *Politique Etrangère* (Paris), Vol. 43, 1978, No. 4, pp. 417–428.

Yata, Ali. "The Moroccan CP and Sahara" (interview), *MERIP Reports* (Washington, D.C.), No. 56, April 1977.

Zartman, I. William (ed). *The Political Economy of Morocco.* London and New York: Praeger Publishers, 1987.

Polisario and the Saharan Arab Democratic Republic (SADR)

Ahmed-Baba Miské. *Front Polisario: l'âme d'un peuple.* Paris: Editions Rupture, 1978.

Argullol, Rafael, and Xavier Berenguer. "Entrevista con el ministro de defensa de la República Arabe Saharaui Democrática, Brahim Ghali Ould Mustafa," *Materiales* (Madrid), No. 6, November–December 1977.

Bachir Mustapha Sayed. "Bachir Mustapha Sayed: Polisario's Policies for Peace," interviewed by Margaret Novicki, *Africa Report* (New York), Vol. XXXIV, No. 3, May–June 1989.

Benigno da Cruz, Carlos. *Guerra do povo no Sahara occidental. A Frente Polisaro.* Coimbra: Centelha, 1977.

Bontems, Claude. "The Government of the Saharawi Arab Democratic Republic," *Third World Quarterly,* Vol. 9, No. 1 (January 1987), pp. 168–186.

Canoura, Cristina. "Frente Polisario, los señores del desierto," *Cuadernos del Tercer Mundo* (Mexico City), No. 18, January 1978.

Caudron, J. P. "Huit jours avec le Front Polisario," *Croissance des Jeunes Nations,* February 1976.

Djemaa. "The Guelta Proclamation (28 November 1975)," in *Western Sahara and the Struggle of the Sahraoui People for Self-Determination.* Rome: International League for the Rights and Liberation of Peoples, 1978.

El-Ouali Mustapha Sayed. "Lettre au président de Mauritanie d'El Ouali es Sayed, le 6 mars 1976," *L'Annuaire de l'Afrique du Nord 1976* (Paris: CNRS, 1977), pp. 918–919.

———. "Lettre au roi du Maroc, d'El Ouali es Sayed, le 6 mars 1976," *L'Annuaire de l'Afrique du Nord 1976* (Paris: CNRS, 1977), pp. 919–920.

Hultman, Tami. *Democratic Arab Republic of the Sahara.* Dobbs Ferry, N.Y.: Constitutions of Dependencies and Special Sovereignties (eds. Albert P. Blaustein and Eric B. Blaustein), Oceana Publishers, 1978.

Mahmoud Abdelfettah. "Mahmoud Abdelfettah of Polisario Political Bureau, Interviewed by Tony Hodges," *Africa Report* (New York), Vol. XXV, No. 3, May–June 1980, pp. 48–49.

Mohamed Abdelaziz. "4ème anniversaire de la révolution sahraouie: discours de M. Mohamed Abdelaziz, secrétaire général du Front Polisario, le 20/5/1977 (extraits)," in *L'Annuaire de l'Afrique du Nord 1977* (Paris: CNRS, 1978), pp. 892–893.

———. "Lettre du secrétaire général du Front Polisario adressée le 1/7/1977 à la XIVème conférence au sommet de l'OAU (Libreville: 2 au 5/7/1977)," in *L'Annuaire de l'Afrique du Nord 1977* (Paris: CNRS, 1978), pp. 894–895.

———. "Mohammed Abdelaziz, Secretary-General, the Polisario Front, Interviewed by Tony Hodges," *Africa Report* (New York), Vol. XXVII, No. 4, July–August 1982, pp. 15–18.

Omar Hadrami. "Omar Hadrami, Polisario Representative, Interviewed by Tony Hodges," *Africa Report* (New York), Vol. XXIII, No. 2, March–April 1978.

Polisario Front. *Memorandum Concerning the Proclamation of the Arab Saharan Democratic Republic and the Constitution of its Government.* Polisario Front, May 25, 1976.

———. *Troisième congrès du Front Polisario, 26 au 30 août 1976.* Polisario Front, 1976.

———. *Memorandum Dated 5 October 1977 from the Frente Popular para la Liberación de Saguia el Hamra y Río de Oro (Frente Polisario) addressed to the Chairman of the Special Committee of 24 on the Occasion of the 32nd Session of the General Assembly of the United Nations.* In UN Document A/32/303, October 26, 1977.

———. *Statement to the Fourth Committee, 32nd Session of the UN, New York, 1 November 1977.* Polisario Front, 1977.

———. "The Political Manifesto Issued by the Third General Congress of Polisario (26–30 August 1976)," in *Western Sahara and the Struggle of the Sahraoui People for Self-Determination.* Rome: International League for the Rights and Liberation of Peoples, 1978.

———. "The National Programme, Issued by the Third General Congress of Polisario (26–30 August 1976)," in *Western Sahara and the Struggle of the Sahraoui People for Self-Determination.* Rome: International League for the Rights and Liberation of Peoples, 1978.

———. "Le manifeste politique" (4th Congress of the Polisario Front, September 1978), *20 Mai* (Algiers), No. 51, November 1978, pp. 10–17.

———. "Programme national général du Front Polisario" (4th Congress of the Polisario Front, September 1978), *20 Mai* (Algiers), No. 51, November 1978, pp. 18–22.

———. *Répression contre le peuple sahraoui.* Polisario Front, 1978.

———. *Sixth Congress of the Polisario Front, 7–10 December 1985.* Polisario Front, 1985.

Pouchin, Dominique. "Polisario and Western Sahara: A State in Search of a Territory," *Guardian Weekly*, June 12, 1977.

Provisional Saharawi National Council. "Acte constitutionel provisoire du 26 fevrier 1976," in *L'Annuaire de l'Afrique du Nord 1976* (Paris: CNRS, 1977), pp. 916–917.

———. "Proclamation of the First Government of Democratic Sahraoui Arab Republic (27 February 1976)," in *Western Sahara and the Struggle of the Sahraoui People for Self-Determination*. Rome: International League for the Rights and Liberation of Peoples, 1978.

République Arabe Sahraouie Démocratique. *La République Arabe Sahraouie Démocratique, passé et présent*. Ministére de l'Information et de la Culture, 1985.

Saharan Arab Democratic Republic (SADR). *Images of the Resistance of a People Fighting for Its Independence*. 1980.

———. *The Collusion of Rabat and Pretoria or the Denial of Africa*. 1980.

"The Saharan Republic," *IDOC Bulletin* (Rome: International Documentation Centre), No. 44, June 1976.

Spillman, G. "La situation au Sahara occidental: le Polisario," *Comptes Rendus Trimestriels des Séances de l'Académie des Sciences d'Outremer*, February 17, 1978.

Weexsteen, Raoul. "Fighters in the Desert," *MERIP Reports* (Washington, D.C.), No. 45, March 1976.

"With the Polisario Front of Sahara," *MERIP Reports* (Washington, D.C.), No. 53, December 1976.

Zunes, Stephen. "Nationalism and Non-Alignment: The Non-Ideology of the Polisario," *Africa Today*, Vol. 34, No. 3, Fall 1987, pp. 33–46.

The World Powers

Clément, Jean-François. *Le conflit saharien.* Paris: Colloque transferts d'armements et conflits locaux, Institut Français de Polémologie, Centre Droit et Défense, Université de Paris V, March 21–22, 1985.

Damis, John. "United States Relations with North Africa" *Current History,* Vol. 84, No. 502, May 1985, pp. 193–196, 232–234.

Dean, Lt. Col. David J. *The Air Force Role in Low-Intensity Conflict.* Airpower Research Institute, Air University, United States Air Force. Air University Press, Maxwell Air Force Base, Alabama, October 1986.

Flaten, Robert. "Robert Flaten, Director, North Africa, U.S. Department of State, Interviewed by Tony Hodges," *Africa Report* (New York), Vol. XXVII, No. 4, July–August 1982, pp. 19–21.

Friedman, Robert O. *Soviet Foreign Policy Towards the Middle East Since 1970,* 3rd ed. New York: Praeger Publishers, 1982.

Gauthier, Gilles. "Le Sahara et la politique impérialiste dans l'occident arabe," *Communisme* (Paris), Vol. VII, Nos. 31–32, November 1977–February 1978, pp. 54–61.

Gretton, John. "Western Sahara: International Implications," *New African Yearbook 1979,* edited by Richard Synge (London: International Communications, 1979).

———. "The Western Sahara in the International Arena," *The World Today* (London), Vol. 36, No. 9, September 1980, pp. 343–350.

Gupte, Pranay. "Morocco: A Friend in Need," *Atlantic Monthly,* Vol. 250 (December 1982), pp. 21–28.

Hearings on United States Policy Toward the Conflict in the Western Sahara, Subcommittees on Africa and on International Organizations and Scientific Affairs, 98th Congress, 1st Session, House of Representatives, March 15, 1983. Washington, D.C.: U.S. Government Printing Office, 1983.

Hodges, Tony. "La stratégie americaine et le conflit du Sahara occidental," *Le Monde Diplomatique* (Paris), January 1980.

———. "Western Sahara: US Arms and the Desert War," *Africa Report* (New York), Vol. XXV, No. 3, May–June 1980, pp. 42–47.

———. "Le nouvel axe stratégique entre Washington et Rabat," *Le Monde Diplomatique* (Paris), July 1982.

———. "François Mitterrand: Master Strategist in the Maghreb," *Africa Report* (New York), Vol. XXVIII, No. 3, May–June 1983.

———. "At Odds with Self-Determination: The United States and Western Sahara," in Gerald J. Bender, James S. Coleman, and Richard L. Sklar (eds.), *African Crisis Areas and U.S. Foreign Policy*. Berkeley and Los Angeles, Calif.: University of California Press, 1985.

Impact of United States Foreign Policy in Seven African Countries, Report, Hearings Before the Committee on Foreign Affairs, House of Representatives, 98th Congress, 1st Session, August 1983. Washington, D.C.: U.S. Government Printing Office, 1984.

Jallaud, Thomas. "Le Sahara occidental dans le monde," in *Sahara occidental, un peuple et ses droits, Colloque de Massy, 1 et 2 avril 1978,* Paris, L'Harmattan, 1978.

Kamil, Leo. *Fueling the Fire: U.S. Policy and the Western Sahara Conflict.* Trenton, N.J.: The Red Sea Press, 1987.

Kazadi, F. S. B. "Carter's Saharan Foray," *Africa Report* (New York), Vol. XXIII, No. 2, March–April 1978.

Laipson, Ellen B. *Conflict and Change in North Africa: Emerging Challenges for U.S. Policy.* Washington, D.C.: Library of Congress, 1980.

———. *War in the Western Sahara: Issues for U.S. Policy.* Washington, D.C.: Library of Congress, 1981.

Layachi, Azzedine. *The United States and North Africa: A Cognitive Approach to Foreign Policy.* New York: Praeger Publishers, 1990.

Manning, Robert A., and Jennifer Noyon. "Maghreb Policy in Disarray," *Africa Report* (New York), Vol. XXIX, No. 6, November–December 1984.

Mohamed Lamine Ould Ahmed. "Affaire de Zouérate: extraits de la conférence de presse du premier ministre du gouvernement de la RASD, Mohamed Lamine, le 21 mai 1977," in *L'Annuaire de l'Afrique du Nord 1977* (Paris: CNRS, 1978).

Mortimer, Robert A. "The Internationalization of the Conflict in Western Sahara," *The Middle East Annual, Issues and Events,* Vol. 2, 1982, pp. 129–149.

———. "Maghreb Matters," *Foreign Policy* (Washington, D.C.), No. 76, Fall 1989, pp. 160–175.

Parker, Richard B. "Appointment in Oujda," *Foreign Affairs* (New York), Vol. 63, No. 5, Summer 1985, pp. 1095–1110.

Porter, Bruce. *The U.S.S.R. and Third World Conflicts.* New York: Cambridge University Press, 1984.

Proposed Arms Sale to Morocco. Hearings Before the Subcommittees on International Security and Scientific Affairs and on Africa of the Committee on Foreign Affairs, House of Representatives, 96th Congress, 2nd Session, January 24 and 29, 1980. Washington, D.C.: U.S. Government Printing Office, 1980.

Regional Stability in North Africa, Report, Hearings Before the Committee on Foreign Affairs, House of Representatives, 96th Congress, 2nd Session, July 8, 1980. Washington, D.C.: U.S. Government Printing Office, 1980.

Rubinstein, Alvin Z. *Moscow's Third World Strategy.* Princeton, N.J.: Princeton University Press, 1988.

Saharan Arab Democratic Republic. "Communiqué du ministère sahraoui de la défense, le 14/12/1977, annonçant la libération des huit otages françaises" in *L'Annuaire de l'Afrique du Nord 1977* (Paris: CNRS, 1978), p. 908.

Solarz, Stephen J. "Arms for Morocco?" *Foreign Affairs* (New York), Vol. 58, No. 2, Winter 1979–80, pp. 278–299.

United States Department of Defense. *Struggle and Stalemate in the Western Sahara.* Defense Intelligence Agency. Washington, D.C.: U.S. Government Printing Office, 1979.

United States Policy Toward the Conflict in the Western Sahara, Report, Hearings Before the Committee on Foreign Affairs, House of Representatives, 98th Congress, 1st Session, August 25–September 6, 1983. Washington, D.C.: U.S. Government Printing office, 1983.

United States Senate, Committee on Foreign Relations Staff Report, *The Western Sahara: The Referendum Process in Danger,* January 1992, 16 pp.

U.S. Policy and the Conflict in the Western Sahara. Hearings Before the Subcommittees on Africa and on International Organizations of the Committee on Foreign Affairs, House of Representatives, 96th Congress, 1st Session, July 23–24, 1979. Washington, D.C.: U.S. Government Printing Office, 1979.

U.S. Policy Toward the Conflict in the Western Sahara. Report of a Staff Study Mission to Morocco, Algeria, the Western Sahara, and France, August 25–September 6, 1982, to the Committee on Foreign Affairs, House of Representatives. Washington, D.C.: U.S. Government Printing Office, 1983.

Volman, Daniel. *A Continent Besieged: Foreign Military Activities in Africa Since 1975.* Washington, D.C.: Institute for Policy Studies, 1980.

Ware, Lewis B. *Decolonization and the Global Alliance in the Arab Maghrib: The Case of Spanish Sahara.* Directorate of Documentary Research, Air University Institute for Professional Development, Maxwell Air Force Base, Alabama, 1975.

Waring, Mowton L. *Spanish Sahara, Focus of Contention.* Professional Study No. 6099, Air War College, Air University, United States Air Force, Maxwell Air Force Base, Alabama, 1976.

Wenger, Martha. "Reagan Stakes Morocco in Sahara Struggle," *MERIP Reports* (Washington, D.C.), No. 150, May 1982.

Wilson, Carlos, and Yahia Zoubir. "Western Sahara: A Foreign Policy Success Waiting to Happen," *TransAfrica Forum* (Washington, D.C.), Vol. 6, Nos. 3 and 4, Spring–Summer 1989, pp. 27–39.

Wilson, Carlos. "America's Secret African War." *On the Issues,* Women's Medical Center, Inc., Queens, New York, Vol. 11, 1989, pp. 12–17.

Wright, Claudia. "Journey to Marrakesh: U.S.-Moroccan Security Relations." *International Security,* Vol. 7, No. 4, Spring 1983, pp. 163–179.

Zoubir, Yahia. "Soviet Policy Toward the Western Sahara Conflict," *Africa Today,* Vol. 34, No. 3, Fall 1987, pp. 17–32.

————. "Soviet Policy Toward the Maghreb," *Arab Studies Quarterly,* Vol. 9, No. 4, Fall 1987, pp. 399–421.

————. "The Soviet Union and the Conflict in the Western Sahara," in *Bulletin* (Association of Concerned Africa Scholars, Los Angeles), No. 23, Spring 1988, pp. 8–9.

————. "L'URSS dans le Grand Maghreb: une stratégie équilibrée et une approche pragmatique," in Bassma Kodami-Darwish, and May Chartouni-Dubarry (eds.), *Maghreb: les années de transition.* Paris: Institut Française des Relations Internationales/Masson, 1990.

Zunes, Stephen. "The United States and Morocco: The Sahara War and Regional Interests," *Arab Studies Quarterly,* Vol. 9, No. 4, Fall 1987, pp. 422–441.

————. "U.S. Support for Morocco and Its Implications for African Unity," in *Bulletin* (Association of Concerned Africa Scholars, Los Angeles), No. 23, Spring 1988, pp. 6–8.

The UN and the OAU

Non-Aligned Countries. "Résolution sur le Sahara occidental de la 6ème conférence des pays non-alignés" (Havana, August 3–8, 1980), in *La République Arabe Sahraouie Démocratique* (Saharan Arab Democratic Republic, Department of Information, 1980).

Organization of African Unity. "Consensus sur le Sahara occidental presenté par le président du Conseil des Ministres, 26ème session du Conseil des Ministres de l'OAU" (Addis Ababa, February 23–March 1, 1976), in *Le droit à l'autodetermination du Sahara occidental,* edited by Manfred O. Hinz, Progress Dritte Welt Verlag, Bonn, 1978.

————. "Résolution relative à la question du Sahara occidental adoptée par le 13ème sommet de l'OAU, tenu à Port Louis (Ile Maurice)" (July 1976), in *Le droit à l'autodétermination du Sahara occidental,* edited by Manfred O. Hinz, Progress Dritte Welt Verlag, Bonn, 1978.

————. *Resolution on Western Sahara* (OAU Council of Ministers, Port Louis, 1976), Addis Ababa. OAU Document CM/Doc. 36 (XVII), 1976.

————. *Resolution of the 15th OAU Summit, Khartoum, 18–22 July 1978, on Western Sahara.* New York: UN Document A/33/337, October 31, 1978.

————. *Question of Western Sahara* (Resolution of OAU Summit, Monrovia, July 17–20, 1979). Addis Ababa: OAU Document AHG/DOC. 114 (XVI), 1979.

————. "Sahara: le verdict des sages" (text of OAU ad-hoc committee report on Western Sahara) in *Jeune Afrique* (Paris), August 8, 1979.

————. "Résolution du Comité Ad-Hoc de l'OAU sur le Sahara occidental" (December 5, 1979), in *La République Arabe Sahraouie Démocratique* (Saharan Arab Democratic Republic, Department of Information, 1980).

————. "Memorandum sur l'admission de la République Arabe Sahraouie Démocratique à l'OUA." (Opinion of Edem Kodjo relative to the admission to the OAU of the Saharan Arab Democratic Republic.) Addis Ababa: Organization of African Unity, 1982.

Polisario Front. "Monrovia, réunion du comité ad-hoc sur le Sahara occidental: le Maroc face au jugement implacable de l'histoire," *Sahara Libre* (Algiers), supplement, February 1980.

United Nations. "Western Sahara," *Yearbook of the United Nations 1976* (New York: UN, 1979), Vol. XXX, pp. 737–740.

————. ''Question of Western Sahara'' (General Assembly resolution 31/45, December 1, 1976), in *Yearbook of the United Nations 1976* (New York: UN, 1979), Vol. XXX, pp. 756–757.

————. *Resolution Adopted by the General Assembly. Question of Western Sahara* (Resolution 32/22, November 28, 1977). New York: UN Document A/RES/32/22, December 9, 1977.

————. *Resolutions Adopted by the General Assembly. Question of Western Sahara* (Resolutions 33/31A and 33/31B, December 13, 1978). New York: UN Document A/RES/33/31, December 21, 1978.

————. *Resolution Adopted by the General Assembly. Question of Western Sahara* (Resolution 34/37, November 21, 1979). New York: UN Document A/RES/34/37, December 4, 1979.

————. ''The Question of Western Sahara at the United Nations,'' *Decolonization* (New York: UN), No. 17, October 1980.

————. ''Western Sahara Question,'' (General Assembly Resolution 36/46, November 24, 1981), in *Yearbook of the United Nations 1981* (New York: UN, 1985), pp. 1193–1197.

————. ''Western Sahara Question,'' (General Assembly Resolution 37/28, November 23, 1982), in *Yearbook of the United Nations 1982* (New York: UN, 1986), pp. 1349–1353.

————. ''Western Sahara Question,'' (General Assembly Resolution 38/40, December 7, 1983), in *Yearbook of the United Nations 1983* (New York UN, 1987), pp. 1087–1088.

————. ''Western Sahara,'' (General Assembly Resolution 39/40, December 5, 1984), in *Yearbook of the United Nations 1984* (New York: UN, 1988), pp. 1066–1068.

————. ''Western Sahara,'' (General Assembly Resolution 40/50, December 2, 1985), in *Yearbook of the United Nations 1985* (New York: UN, 1989), pp. 1137–1141.

———. "Western Sahara," (General Assembly Resolution 41/16, October 31, 1986), in *Yearbook of the United Nations 1986* (New York: UN, 1990), pp. 964–966.

———. *Question of Western Sahara: Report of the Secretary-General* (United Nations General Assembly, 42nd Session, October 1, 1987). New York: UN Document A/42/601, 1987.

———. *The Situation Concerning Western Sahara: Report of the Secretary-General* (United Nations Security Council, June 18, 1990). New York: UN Document S/21360, 1990.

———. *Resolution Adopted by the Security Council* (Resolution 658, June 27, 1990, United Nations Security Council, 2929th Meeting). New York: UN Document S/RES/658 (1990), 1990.

———. *The Situation Concerning Western Sahara: Report by the Secretary-General* (United Nations Security Council, April 19, 1991). New York: UN document S/22464, 1991.

———. *Resolution Adopted by the Security Council* (Resolution 690, April 29, 1991, 2984th Meeting). New York: UN document S/RES/690 (1991), 1991.

———. *Western Sahara: Working Paper Prepared by the Secretariat* (United Nations General Assembly, 46th Session, August 7, 1991). New York UN Document A/AC.109/1082, 1991.

———. *Question of Western Sahara: Report of the Secretary-General* (United Nations General Assembly, 46th Session, October 23, 1991). New York: UN Document A/46/589, 1991.

———. *Report of the Secretary-General on the Situation Concerning Western Sahara* (United Nations Security Council, December 19, 1991). New York: UN Document S/23299, 1991.

―――. *Resolution Adopted by the Security Council* (Resolution 725, December 31, 1991, United Nations Security Council, 3025th Meeting). New York: UN Document S/RES/725, 1991.

―――. *Report of the Secretary-General on the United Nations Mission for the Referendum in Western Sahara* (United Nations Security Council, February 28, 1992). New York: UN Document S/23662, 1992.

7. SCIENTIFIC

General

Hernández-Pacheco, Eduardo, and Francisco Hernández-Pacheco. *El Sahara español, expedición científica de 1941.* Madrid: Universidad de Madrid, 1942.

―――, Francisco Hernández-Pacheco, Manuel Alia Medina, Carlos Vidal Box, and Emilio Guinea López. *El Sahara español. Estudio geológico, geográfico y botánico.* Madrid: Consejo Superior de Investigaciones Científicas, Instituto de Estudios Africanos, 1949.

Lozano y Rey, L. "Una excursión científicas a la costa del Sahara español," *Boletín de la Sociedad de Geografía Nacional* (Madrid), 75, 1935.

Geography

Alfaro y Zarabozo, Sabas de. *Geografía de Marruecos y posesiones españoles de Africa.* Toledo Colegio de María Cristina, 1925.

Almonte, E. d'. "Ensayo de una breve descriptión del Sahara español," *Boletín de la Real Sociedad de Geografía* (Madrid), 1914, 56, pp. 129–347.

Arlett, W. "Survey of Some of the Canary Islands and of Part of the Western Coast of Africa," *The Geographical Journal* (London), 1936, pp. 6–8.

———. "Description de la côte d'Afrique depuis le Cap Spartel jusqu'au Cap Bojador," *Bulletin de la Société de Géographie* (Paris), January 1837, pp. 12–48.

Bonelli, Emilio. *Nuevos territorios españoles de la costa del Sahara*. Madrid: Fortanet, 1885.

———. "El Sahara occidental y la Guinea española," *Revista de Geografía Comercial y Mercantil* (Madrid), Vol. I, 1903, p. 277.

———. "Los posesiones españolas en el Africa occidental," *Revista de Geografía Comercial y Mercantil* (Madrid), Vol. XIII, 1916, p. 122.

"Boundaries of the Spanish Sahara and the Ifni Enclave," *The Geographical Review* (New York), October 1922, pp. 651–652.

Bullón Díaz, G. *Notas sobre geografía humana de los territorios de Ifni y del Sahara*. Madrid: Dirección General de Marruecos y Colonias, 1944–45.

Flores Morales, Angel. *El Sahara español: ensayo de geografía física, humana y económica*. Madrid: Ediciones de la Alta Comisaría de España en Marruecos, 1946.

———. "Ensayo geográfico sobre el Sahara español," *Africa* (Madrid), 1950.

Francisco y Díaz, Francisco de. "El Sahara occidental y la Guinea española," *Revista de Geografía Colonial y Mercantil* (Madrid), Vol. I, p. 561.

Guillermo, R., and J. Sánchez. *El Sahara occidental*. Madrid: Hernando, 1932.

Hernández-Pacheco, Francisco. "Los manantiales de El Aïun y causas de su origen, Sahara español," *Boletín de la Sociedad de Geografía Nacional* (Madrid), Vol. LXXV, 1935, pp. 99–104.

————. "Características fisiográficas del litoral y costas del Sahara español," *Archivos del Instituto de Estudios Africanos* (Madrid), 1961.

Instituto de Estudios Africanos. *Atlas histórico y geográfico de Africa española.* Madrid: 1955.

Lahure, Baron, and Foucault. "Le pays des Tekna (nord-ouest du Sahara)," *Mouvement Géographique,* 1889, pp. 73–74.

Mauny, Raymond. "Tableau géographique de l'ouest africain au moyen ége (d'après les sources écrites, la tradition, et l'archéologie)," *Mémoires de l'Institut Français d'Afrique Noire* (Dakar), No. 61, 1961.

Montagne, Robert. "La limite du Maroc et du Sahara atlantique," 7ème Congrès de l'Institut de Hautes Etudes Marocaines, Rabat, 1930, *Hespéris* (Rabat), Vol. XI, pp. 111–118.

Montaner, Fernando Gil. "Notas sobre el Sahara español," *Boletín de la Sociedad de Geografía Nacional* (Madrid), Vol. LXXI, Nos. 5–6, May–June 1931, pp. 242–245.

Munilla Gómez, Eduardo. "Los caprichos de la arena," *Africa* (Madrid), Vol. XXVII, No. 397, January 1975, pp. 10–14.

Pérez del Toro, Felipe. *España en el noroeste de Africa.* Madrid: Imprenta de Fortanet, 1892.

Peyronnet, Commandant. "Sud-ouest marocain, Río de Oro, Sahara occidental," *Bulletin de la Société de Géologie d'Alger,* Vol. XLIX, 1928, pp. 687–707.

Wilcox, H.–Case. "Exploration of the Río de Oro," *The Geographical Review* (New York), 1921, pp. 372–383.

Geology

Alia Medina, Manuel. "Notas de una expedición geológica a los territorios del Sahara español," *Investigaciones y Progreso* (Madrid), Vol. XIV, Nos. 1–2, January–February 1943, pp. 34–43.

———. "Notas de una segunda expedición geológica por el Sahara español," *Boletín de la Real Sociedad Española de Historia Natural* (Madrid), Vol. XLI, 1943, pp. 291–316.

———. "Notas de una tercera expedición al Sahara español," *Boletín de la Real Sociedad Española de Historia Natural* (Madrid), Vol. XLIII, 1945, pp. 499–513.

———. "El Cuaternario en el Sahara español," *Boletín de la Real Sociedad Española de Historia Natural* (Madrid), Vol. XLIII, 1945, pp. 149–163.

———. *Características morfográficas geológicas de la zona septentrional del Sahara español.* Madrid: 1945.

———. *Enriquecimiento ferruginoso en el Devónico del Sahara español,"* *Estudios Geológicos* (Instituto de Investigaciones Geológicas 'Lucas Mallada'), No. 6, 1946, pp. 101–105.

———. "Resultados de una expedición geológica al Sahara español," *Africa* (Madrid), Vol. V, No. 54, June 1946, pp. 7–11.

———. "Observaciones geológicas cn cl ángulo S.E. del Sahara español," *Boletín de la Real Sociedad Española de Historia Natural* (Madrid), Vol. XLV, 1947, pp. 517–522.

———. "Primeros resultados de dos expediciones geológicas al Sahara español," *Boletín de la Real Sociedad Española de Historia Naturàl* (Madrid), Vol. XLVI, 1948, pp. 725–735.

———. "La tectónica de arcos en el Sahara español," *Las Ciencias* (Madrid), Vol. XIII, 1948, No. 2, pp. 335–352.

———. ''Los perfiles longitudinales de terrazamiento del uad de la Seguiet el Hamra (Sahara español),'' *Boletín de la Real Sociedad Española de Historia Natural* (Madrid), Vol. XLVII, 1949, Nos. 1–2.

———. *Contribución al conocimiento geomorfológico de las zonas centrales del Sahara español.* Madrid: Instituto de Estudios Africanos, 1949.

———. ''Sobre el Paleozoico del Tiris (Sahara español),'' *Notas y Comunicaciones del Instituto Geológico Minero Español* (Madrid), 1950, No. 220, pp. 93–98.

———. ''Estudio mineralógico de algunas muestras de arena del Sahara meridional español,'' *Archivos del Instituto de Estudios Africanos* (Madrid), 1950.

———. ''Le Précambrien du Sahara méridional espagnol,'' *XIXe Congrès Géologique International, Alger, 1952,* Résumé des Communications, p. 1.

———. *Bosquejo geológico del sahara español.* Madrid: Dirección General de Marruecos y Colonias, 1952.

———. ''Interpretación de algunas estructuras petrográficas del Sahara meridional español,'' *Archivos del Instituto de Estudios Africanos* (Madrid), Vol. VI, 1953, No. 20.

———. ''La arquitectura geológica del Sahara meridional español,'' *Archivos del Instituto de Estudios Africanos* (Madrid), Vol. VI, 1953, No. 21, pp. 26–39.

———. ''Sobre la existencia de formaciones de hamada neógena en el Sahara meridional español,'' *Archivos del Instituto de Estudios Africanos* (Madrid), No. 29, June 1954, pp. 49–54.

———. ''El Sahara español. Datos geográficos e investigaciones geológicos recientes,'' *Arbor* (Madrid), No. 100, 1954.

————. "Sobre las variaciones climáticas durante el Cuarternario en el Sahara español," *Africa* (Madrid), December 1955, pp. 544–546.

————. "El origen tectónico de las sebjas del Sahara occidental," *Congrès Géologique International, Mexico, 1956,* No. 20, pp. 393–394.

————, and T. Alvira. "Estudios geológicos-edáficos de unas muestras suelo-salino de la Sebja de Ougranat (Sahara español)," *Anales del Instituto Española de Edafología* (Madrid), Vol. VII, 1948.

————, and A. Arribas. "Formaciones ferruginosas en el Sahara meridional español," *Congrès Géologique International, Alger, 1952,* Résumé des Communications, p. 68.

Célérier, J. "Le Sahara occidental: problème de structure et de morphologie," VIIe Congrès de Hautes Etudes Marocaines, Rabat, May 1930, *Hespéris* (Rabat), Vol. XI, fasc. 1–8, pp. 153–172.

Cervera Baviera, Julio. "Sahara occidental: geología y geografía," *Revista de Geografía Comercial* (Madrid), 2nd half 1886, pp. 63–66.

Depéret, C. "Sur l'âge des couches du Río de Oro," *Comptes Rendus de la Société Géologique de France* (Paris), 1912, pp. 123–124.

Dollfus, G.–F. "Etudes des fossiles recueillies par N. Font y Sagué au Río de Oro," *Bulletin de la Société Géologique de France* (Paris), Vol. XI, 1911, No. 4, pp. 218–238.

Fernández Casado, J.–L. "Notas sobre la morfología de la zona costera en el sur del Sahara occidental," *Boletín de la Real Sociedad Española de Historia Natural* (Madrid), 1949, pp. 103–109.

Font y Sagué, Norberto. "Les formations géologiques du Río de Oro," *Bulletin de la Société Géologique de France* (Paris), 1911, pp. 212–217.

Hernández-Pacheco, Eduardo. "Relieve y geología del norte del Sahara español," *Revista Geológica Española* (Madrid), 1941, No. 10, pp. 17–23.

Hernández-Pacheco, Francisco. "Un período de intensas precipitaciones en el Sahara español," *Boletín de la Sociedad de Geografía Nacional* (Madrid), Vol. LXXV, 1935, pp. 93–98.

————. *Rasgos fisiográficos y geológicos del territorio de Ifni y rasgos fisiográficos y geológicos del Sahara.* Madrid: Dirección General de Marruecos y Colonias, 1944–45.

————. "Las sebjas del Sahara occidental," *Comptes Rendus de la 2ème Conférence Internationale des Africanistes Occidentales, Bissau, 1947* (Lisbon, 1950), pp. 105–113.

————. "Ensayo sobre los diferentes ciclos eroivos normales en el Sahara español," *Comptes Rendus de la 2ème Conférence Internationale des Africanistes Occidentales, Bissau, 1947* (Lisbon, 1950), pp. 123–136.

————. "Morfológico y evolución de las zonas litorales de Ifni y del Sahara español," *Comptes Rendus du Congrès International de Géologie, Lisbonne, 1949,* Vol. II, 1950, pp. 487–505.

————. "Características del localo continental del Africa occidental española," *Boletín del Instituto Española de Oceanografía,* 1955, No. 70, pp. 3–20.

————, and Manuel Alia Medina. "Nota preliminar de una expedición reciente a los territorios del Sahara español," *Boletín de la Real Sociedad Española de Historia Natural* (Madrid), Vol. XL, 1942, pp. 507–512.

Hernández Sampelayo, P. "Carolarios devolonianos del Sahara español," *Boletín del Instituto Geológico y Minero de España* (Madrid), Vol. LXI, 1948, pp. 3–45.

Pérez Mateos, Josefina. "Estudio mineralógico de algunas muestras de arena del Sahara meridional español," *Archivos del Instituto de Estudios Africanos* (Madrid), No. 14, October 1950.

Rodríguez-Mellado, M–T. "El Devónico en el Sahara español," *Boletín de la Real Sociedad Española de Historia Natural* (Madrid), Vol. XLVI, 1948, No. 162.

Vidal Box, C. "Significación geológica de los territorios centrales de Río de Oro," *Africa* (Madrid), Vol. V, Nos. 56–57, August–September 1946, pp. 40–42.

―――. "Las rocas eruptivas del Sahara español," *Boletín de la Real Sociedad de Historia Natural* (Madrid), Vol. XLVII, 1949, pp. 405–449.

Meteorology

Font-Tulot, I. "El régimen de lluvias del Sahara español," *Revista de Geofísica* (Madrid), No. 28, 1948.

―――. *El clima del Africa occidental española.* Madrid: Servicio Meteorológico Nacional, 1949.

―――. *El clima del Sahara, con especial referencia a la zona española.* Madrid Consejo Superior de Investigaciones Científicas, Instituto de Estudios Africanos, 1955.

Zoology

Bauthier-Pilters, H. "Quelques observations sur l'écologie du dromadaire dans le Sahara occidental," *Bulletin de Liaison Saharienne* (Algiers), No. 45, March 1962, pp. 55–69.

Español, F. "Tenebrionidae," in "Misión científica E. Morales Agacino, Ch. Rungs y B. Zolotarevsky a Ifni y Sahara español," *Eos* (Madrid), Vol. XIX, 1943, pp. 119–148.

————. "Nuevos datos para el conocimiento de los Tenebriónidos (col.) del Sahara español," *Eos* (Madrid), Vol. XX, July 10, 1944, pp. 7–30.

————. "Nuevos comentarios sistemáticos sobre la subfamilia *Opatrinae Reitt.* con la descripción de un nuevo representante del Sahara español," *Eos* (Madrid), Vol. XXI, February 2, 1945, pp. 216–232.

Franklin, Pierre. *Ecologie et peuplement entomologique des sables vifs du Sahara nord-occidental.* Publications du Centre de Recherches Sahariennes, Série Biologique, No. 3. Paris: Centre National de la Recherche Scientifique, 1958.

Mateu Sampere, J. "Escarabeidos de Ifni y del Sahara español," *Eos* (Madrid), Vol. XXVI, 1950, pp. 271–297.

Monteil, Vincent. *Contribution à l'étude de la faune du Sahara occidental.* Paris: Larose, 1951.

————. *Essai sur le chameau au Sahara occidental.* Saint-Louis: Centre IFAN-Mauritanie, Etudes Mauritaniennes, No. 2, 1952.

Morales Agacino, E. "Estado actual del problema de la langosta del desierto (Schistocerca Gregaria Forsk) en el Sahara occidental," *Botanía y Patalogía Vegetal y Entomología Agrícola,* Vol. XII, 1943, pp. 100–106.

————. "Las gacelas de Río de Oro: algo sobre ellas y su cacería," *Africa* (Madrid), Vol. IV, Nos. 42–43, June–July 1945, pp. 5–8.

————. "La langosta del desierto," *Agricultura,* Vol. XIV, 1945, No. 154, pp. 64–69.

————. "Algunos datos sobre Ortopteroides del Sahara occidental," *Eos* (Madrid), Vol. XX, February 20, 1945, pp. 310–399.

————. "Datos y observaciones sobre ciertos mamíferos del Sahara occidental y Ifni," *Boletín de la Real Sociedad Española de Historia Natural* (Madrid), 1949, pp. 13–14.

Thomas, O. "On a Small Collection of Mammals from the Río de Oro, Western Sahara," *Novitates Zoologicae*, Vol. X, 1903, pp. 300–302.

Válverde, J.–Antonio. "Aves Paleárcticas en el Sahara español," *Africa* (Madrid), Vol. XII, No. 166, October 1955, pp. 12–14.

————. "Aves del Sahara español," *Archivos del Instituto de Estudios Africanos* (Madrid), Vol. VIII, No. 36, February 1956, pp. 67–82.

————. "Charcas y patos del Sahara español," *Africa* (Madrid), Vol. XIII, No. 173, May 1956, pp. 15–18.

————. *Aves del Sahara español.* Madrid: Consejo Superior de Investigaciones Científicas, Instituto de Estudios Africanos, 1957.

————. "Expedición zoológica en la Provincia del Sahara," *Archivos del Instituto de Estudios Africanos* (Madrid), Vol. XIX, 1965, No. 74, pp. 71–78.

8. SOCIAL

Anthropology and Ethnology

General

Albert, P. "Les tribus du Sahel atlantique: Souss, Tazeroualt, Dra, Oued Noune, Seguiet el Hamra," *Bulletin de la Société de*

Géographie et Archéologie d'Oran, April–June 1906, pp. 116–132.

Alcobé, S. "Grupos sanguinos en nómadas del Sahara occidental," *Trabajos del Instituto Bernardino de Sahagún,* Vol. I, 1945, pp. 23–37.

————. "The Physical Anthropology of the Western Saharan Nomads," *Man* (London), Vol. XLVII, 1947, pp. 141–143.

Benéitez Cantero, V. "Algunos usos y costumbres de nuestro Sahara," *Africa* (Madrid), Vol. XXIII, No. 351, March 1971, pp. 14–20.

Bonte, Pierre. "La guerre dans les sociétés d'éleveurs nomades," *Cahiers du Centre d'Etudes et de Recherches Marxistes* (Paris), No. 133, 1977, pp. 42–67.

Briggs, Lloyd Cabot. *Tribes of the Sahara.* Cambridge, Mass.: Harvard University Press, and London: Oxford Universitiy Press, 1960.

Caro Baroja, Julio. *Estudios Saharianos.* Madrid: Consejo Superior de Investigaciones Científicas, Instituto de Estudios Africanos, 1955.

————. "Una visión etnológica del Sahara español," *Archivos del Instituto de Estudios Africanos* (Madrid), Vol. VII, 1955, No. 28, pp. 67–80.

Doménech-Lafuente, A. "Sahara español: del vivir nómada de las tribus," *Cuadernos de Estudios Africanos,* Vol. XXI, 1953, No. 1, pp. 31–34.

Flores Morales, Angel. "Razas del Sahara español," *Africa* (Madrid), Vol. V, 1948, Nos. 83–84, pp. 441–443.

————. "Tipos y costumbres del Sahara español," *Africa* (Madrid), Vol. VI, 1949, No. 95, pp. 407–410.

Gaudio, Attilio. "Apuntes para un estudio sobre los aspectos etnológicos del Sahara occidental. Su constitución básica," *Cuadernos de Estudios Africanos,* 1952, 3rd Quarter, No. 19, pp. 31–34.

————. *Le Sahara des africains.* Paris: Julliard, 1960.

————. *Les civilisations du Sahara.* Paris: Collection Marabout-Université, No. 141, 1967.

Martin, Henri. *Les tribus nomades de l'ouest et du nord mauritanien, du Sahara espagnol et du sud morocain.* Paris: Centre de Hautes Etudes Administratives sur l'Afrique et l'Asie Moderne, Mémoire No. 300–328, 1939.

Martinet, G. "Les tribus de la Sakiet El Hamra," *Lamalif* (Rabat), October 1970.

Marty, P. "Les tribus de la Haute Mauritanie: Ouled Delim, Reguibat et Tekna du Noun," *L'Afrique Francaise, Renseignements Coloniaux* (Paris), 1915, pp. 73–82, 118–126, and 136–145.

Mulero Clemente, M. *Los territorios españoles del Sahara y sus grupos nómadas.* Las Palmas de Gran Canaria: El Siglo, 1945.

Polisario Front. "L'organisation socio-politique précoloniale dans la Saguiet el Hamra et Río de Oro," *20 Mai,* No. 18, April 1975, pp. 13–14.

Quiroga, Francisco. "El Sahara occidental y sus moradores," *Revista de Geografía Comercial* (Madrid), 1886.

Santamaría, Ramiro. "Algo sobre costumbres del desierto," *Africa* (Madrid), Vol. XXV, No. 384, December 1973, pp. 19–20.

Vilar Ramírez, Juan Bautista. *El Sahara y el hamatismo norteafricano. Estudios antropo-históricos sahárico-magrebíes.*

Madrid Consejo Superior de Investigaciones Científicas, Instituto de Estudios Africanos, 1969.

The Oulad Delim

Aceytuño Gavarrón, Mariano F. "Una tribu del Sahara: Ulad Delim," *Africa* (Madrid), Vol. XVIII, No. 233, May 1961, pp. 13–17.

The Reguibat

Anonymous. *Chroniques des Reguibat, descendants de Sidi Mohamed R'guibi.* Two manuscripts (Arabic), Archives de l'Assemblée Nationale du Niger, Niamey.

Ba, Mahmadou Ahmadou. "Reguibat," *Bulletin d'Etudes Historiques et Scientifiques,* July–September 1933.

———. "Contribution à l'histoire des Reguibat," *L'Afrique Française, Renseignements Coloniaux* (Paris), December 1933, pp. 273–278, and April 1934, pp. 90–92.

Borricand, Lieut.–Col. "Contribution à la connaissance des coutumes regueibat," *Notes Africaines* (Dakar), No. 61, January 1954, pp. 7–9.

Cauneille, A. "Les nomades regueibat," *Travaux de l'Institut de Recherches Sahariennes* (Algiers), Vol. VI, 1950, pp. 83–100.

———, and J. Dubief. "Les Reguibat Lgouacem," *Bulletin de l'Institut Français d'Afrique Noire* (Dakar), Série B, Vol. VII, No. 3–4, July–October 155, pp. 528–550.

Charre, J. P. "Les Reguibat L'Gouacem, système juridique et social," *Revue de Géographie Alpine* (Grenoble), 1966, pp. 343–350.

Dupas, Capt. *Notes sur la confédération des Reguibat L'gouacem, 1937.* Paris: Centre de Hautes Etudes Administratives sur l'Afrique et l'Asie Moderne, Mémoire No. 770, February 20, 1937.

Hart, D. M. "The Social Structure of the Rgibat Bedouins of the Western Sahara," *The Middle East Journal* (Washington, D.C.), Vol. XVI, No. 4, Autumn 1962, pp. 515–527.

Martin, A. G. P. "Contribution à l'histoire des Reguibat," *L'Afrique Francaise, Renseignements Coloniaux* (Paris), April 1927, pp. 137–141.

Toupet, C. "Reguibat L'Gouacem," in *Nomades et nomadisme au Sahara* (Paris: UNESCO, 1963).

The Tekna

La Chapelle, F. de. *Les Tekna du sud marocain.* Paris: Comité de l'Afrique Française, 1934.

Monteil, Vincent. *Notes pour servir à un essai de monographie des Tekna du sud-ouest marocain et du Sahara nord-occidental.* Paris: Centre de Hautes Etudes Administratives sur l'Afrique et l'Asie Moderne, Mémoire No. 1232, September 1945.

———. *Notes sur les Tekna.* Paris: Editions Larose, 1948.

Demography

Lessourd, M. *Le nomadisme en voie de sédentarisation: Sahara atlantique: Les Reguibat.* Paris: Centre de Hautes Etudes Administratives sur l'Afrique et l'Asie Moderne, Mémoire No. 3868, December 1963.

Molina-Campuzano, Miguel. *Contribución al estudio del censo de población del Sahara español.* Madrid: Consejo Superior de Investigaciones Científicas, Instituto de Estudios Africanos, 1954.

Monteil, Vincent. "L'évolution et la sédentarisation des nomades sahariens," *Revue Internationale des Sciences Sociales* (Paris: UNESCO), Vol. II, 1959, No. 4, pp. 599–612.

Pérez Díaz, Víctor. "La sedentarización en una población nómada: observaciones sobre el Sahara occidental," in *Pueblos y clases sociales en el campo español.* Madrid: Siglo XXI, 1974.

Servicio de Registro de Población, Censo y Estadística. *Censo-74.* El Aaiun: Gobierno General del Sahara, 1975.

Education

"El enseñanza media en el Sahara," *Africa* (Madrid), Vol. XXIV, No. 310, October 1967, pp. 11–12.

Martín Morillo, Diego. "La enseñanza primaria y profesional en Sahara," *Africa* (Madrid), Vol. XXIV, No. 310, October 1967, pp. 13–16.

Santamaría, Ramiro. "La cultura, arma de paz en el Sahara español," *Africa* (Madrid), Vol. XXIV, No. 363, March 1972, pp. 6–8.

Health

Conejo García, Alfredo. "La sanidad en los territorios del Africa occidental española," *Africa* (Madrid), Vol. VI, Nos. 92–93, August–September 1949, pp. 31–33.

Servicio Provincial de Sanidad. *La sanidad en la provincia de Sahara. Informe sobre la situación de la salud durante el cuatrenio 1965–1968 en la provincia de Sahara.* Madrid: Consejo Superior de Investigaciones Científicas, Instituto de Estudios Africanos, and Dirección General de Plazas y Provincias Africanas, 1969.

Refugees

El-Chichini, Malak. "Taming the Desert," *Refugees* (United Nations, New York), February 1985, pp. 13–15.

Firebrace, James, and Jeremy Harding. *Exiles of the Sahara: The Sahrawi Refugees Shape Their Future*. London: War on Want, 1987.

Gussing, Nils. *Educational Assistance to Saharan Refugees*. Geneva: International University Exchange Fund, 1976.

Horler, Elisibeth, and Nadia Bindella. "Forgotten War in the West Sahara," *Swiss Review of World Affairs* (Zurich), Vol. 41, No. 1 (April 1991), pp. 15–19.

Lippert, Anne. *The Saharawi Refugees: Origins and Organization 1975–1985*. Ada, Ohio: Saharawi People's Support Committee Letter, Occasional Paper No. 3, June 1985.

Saharawi Red Crescent. *A People Accuses*. Saharawi Red Crescent, 1976.

United Nations High Commission for Refugees. *Aide-Mémoire: UNHCR Programme of Humanitarian Assistance in the Tindouf Region*. Geneva: UNHCR Document HCR/155/42/76–GE. 76–10559, 1976.

Religion

Cola Alberich, Julio. "Magia y superstición en el Sahara español," *Africa* (Madrid), Vol. X, No. 135, March 1953, pp. 21–23.

———. "El 'aaïn' en el Sahara," *Africa* (Madrid), Vol. XII, No. 158, February 1955, pp. 14–16.

Flores, Angel. "La religión en el desierto," *Africa* (Madrid), Vol. VII, No. 119, November 1951, pp. 13–17.

Santamaría, Ramiro. "Antiguas tradiciones del desierto: la 'baraka'," *Africa* (Madrid), Vol. XXV, No. 383, November 1973, pp. 25–26.

Sociology

Caro Baroja, Julio. "Los nomadas y su porvenir," *Archivos del Instituto de Estudios Africanos* (Madrid), Vol. XX, 1965, No. 74, pp. 71–78.

Chassey, Francis de. "Des ethnies et de l'impérialisme dans la génèse des nations, des classes et des états en Afrique: le cas du Sahara occidental," *L'Homme et la Société,* Nos. 45–46, July–September and October–December 1977, pp. 113–125.

———. "Données historiques et sociologiques sur la formation du peuple sahraoui," in *Sahara occidental, un peuple et ses droits, Colloque de Massy, 1 et 2 avril 1978.* Paris: L'Harmattan, 1978.

Guera, Nicole. "Femmes Sahraouies," *Aujourd'hui l'Afrique* (Paris), 1978, No. 13.

Komorowski, Zygmunt. "Formation de la conscience sociale supratribale en partant des conditions ethniques du Sahara occidental," *Africana Bulletin* (Warsaw: University of Warsaw, Center of African Studies), 1975, No. 23, pp. 95–123.

Watson, A. D. "Women of the Western Sahara," *The Moslem World,* Vol. XXXIX, 1949, pp. 6–10.

TRIBES OF WESTERN SAHARA

TRIBES	SUBTRIBES	FRACTIONS
Reguibat ech-Charg or Lgouacem	Ahel Brahim Ou Daoud	Ahel Sidi Allal Ahel Belqacem Ou Brahim Sellam Selalka Ahel Lahsen Ou Hamad Lehmeidenet Oulad Sidi Hamad Jenha
	Lebouihat	Ahel Daddah Ahel Qadi Ahel Haioun Ahel Sidi Ahmed Ben Yahya Lemrasguia Ahel Sidi Abdallah Ben Moussa
	Laiaicha	Ahel Belal Ahel Beilal
	Foqra	Ahel Ahmed Ben Lahsen Ahel Lemjed Ahel Taleb Hamad Rema Lemnasra Seddadgha Oulad Sidi M'hamed

TRIBES	SUBTRIBES	FRACTIONS
Reguibat es-Sahel	Oulad Moussa	Oulad el-Qadi Ahel Bellao Oulad Moueya Oulad Lahsen Oulad Hossein
	Souaad	Ahel Brahim Ben Abdallah Ahel Ba Brahim El-Gherraba Oulad Bou Said Ahel Khali Yahya
	Lemouedenin	Ahel Ahmadi Sereirat
	Oulad Daoud	Ahel Salem Ahel Tenakha Ahel Baba Ammi
	Oulad Borhim	
	Oulad Cheikh	Ahel Delimi Ahel Baba Ali Lemouissat Lahouareth Lahseinat Ahel el-Hadj
	Thaalat	Ahel Dekhil Ahel Meiara Ahel Rachid
	Oulad Taleb	Oulad Ben Hossein Oulad Ba Brahim Oulad Ba Aaissa Oulad Ba Moussa Ahel Dera

TRIBES	FRACTIONS
Arosien	Oulad Khalifa Oulad Sidi Bou Mehdi Ahel Sidi Brahim
Oulad Tidrarin	Ahel Taleb Ali Oulad Moussa Oulad Ali Laboubat El-Faaris Lahseinat Oulad Souleiman Ahel Esteila Ahel Hadj Lidadsa
Filala	Oulad Sidi Ahmed Filali Ahel Ben Mehdi Ahel Faki Ben Salah
Fouikat	Ahel Cheheb Ahel Lagoueyed Ahel Abdahou Aila Ould Said
Ait Lahsen (Tekna)	Id Daoud Ou Abdallah Injouren Ait Bou Meghout Ait Yahya Rouimiat Ait Bou Guezzaten Ait Hassein Ait Saad
Izarguien (Tekna)	Echtouka El-Guerah Ait Said

TRIBES OF WESTERN SAHARA (cont.)

TRIBES	FRACTIONS
Oulad Delim	Oulad Tegueddi Loudeikat Oulad Khaliga Serahenna Oulad Ba Amar
Oulad Bou Sbaa	Oulad el-Hadj Ben Demouiss Oulad Sidi Mohammed Ben Demouiss Oulad Brahim
Skarna	Ahel Bakar Adhahla Oulad Moumen
Tao ›alt	Oulad Sidi Djemaa Oulad Khelaif
Lemiar	Ahel Sidi Amar Ahel Brahim Ahel Ahmed
Mejat	El-Grona El-Beyed Ahel Mohammed Ben Brahim Ahel Ali Ben Salem
Imeraguen	
Menasir	Oulad Ali Serg Oulad Mohammed Aidi
Chenagla	
Ahel Cheikh Ma el-Ainin	
Ahel Berikallah	

ABOUT THE AUTHORS

ANTHONY G. PAZZANITA is a graduate of Franklin and Marshall College and then earned a J.D. at Case Western Reserve University and an M.A. at the University of Pennsylvania. He is a researcher and writer whose interests center mainly on North Africa and sub-Saharan Africa. During the past few years, Mr. Pazzanita has attended several professional conferences on the Western Sahara conflict, has visited the Western Sahara region, and has published several articles on North African and other topics in the *Journal of Modern African Studies,* the *Journal of South Asian and Middle Eastern Studies,* and the *Case Western Reserve Journal of International Law,* and contributed a chapter to the book *International Dimensions of the Western Sahara Conflict,* edited by Yahia Zoubir and Daniel Volman.

TONY HODGES is a graduate of Oxford University. He was Africa editor at the Economist Intelligence Unit, a part of *The Economist* group, in 1983–87 and editor of the United Nations magazine *Africa Recovery* in 1987–88. He subsequently lived in Dakar, Senegal, where he was a program officer in the West Africa office of the Ford Foundation in 1988–91, and he is now based in Nairobi, Kenya, as training coordinator of the African Economic Research Consortium. Mr. Hodges has conducted research in several parts of Africa, particularly Angola and the Maghreb. Following research funded by the Ford Foundation in 1978–82, he wrote two books on Western Sahara: the first edition of *The Historical Dictionary of Western Sahara* (Scarecrow, 1982) and *Western Sahara: The Roots of a Desert War* (Lawrence Hill and Croom Helm, 1983).